A History of Japan, 1582–1941
Internal and External Worlds

This book offers a distinctive overview of the internal and external pressures responsible for the making of modern Japan. L. M. Cullen argues that Japanese policies and fears have often been caricatured in western accounts which have viewed the expansion of the west in an unduly positive light. He shows that Japan before 1854, far from being in progressive economic and social decay or political crisis, was on balance a successful society led by rational policymakers. He also shows how when an external threat emerged after 1793 the country became on balance more open rather than more oppressive and that Japan displayed remarkable success in negotiation with the western powers in 1853–68. In the twentieth century, however, with the 1889 constitution failing to control the armed forces and western and American interests encroaching in Asia and the Pacific, Japan abandoned realism and met her nemesis in China and the Pacific.

L. M. CULLEN is Professor of Modern Irish History at Trinity College, Dublin and Visiting Research Scholar at the International Research Center for Japanese Studies, Kyoto. He is a leading historian of early modern trade.

A History of Japan, 1582–1941

Internal and External Worlds

L. M. Cullen

Trinity College, Dublin

CAMBRIDGE
UNIVERSITY PRESS

PUBLISHED BY THE PRESS SYNDICATE OF THE UNIVERSITY OF CAMBRIDGE
The Pitt Building, Trumpington Street, Cambridge CB2 1RP, United Kingdom

CAMBRIDGE UNIVERSITY PRESS
The Edinburgh Building, Cambridge, CB2 2RU, UK
40 West 20th Street, New York, NY 10011-4211, USA
477 Williamstown Road, Port Melbourne, VIC 3207, Australia
Ruiz de Alarcón 13, 28014 Madrid, Spain
Dock House, The Waterfront, Cape Town 8001, South Africa

http://www.cambridge.org

First published 2003

Printed in the United Kingdom at the University Press, Cambridge

Typeface Plantin 10/12 pt   *System* LaTeX 2$_\varepsilon$ [TB]

A catalogue record for this book is available from the British Library

ISBN 0 521 82155 X hardback
ISBN 0 521 52918 2 paperback

To the memory of Matsuo Taro, friend and *sensei*

Contents

Maps

Preface

This book is intended for undergraduates studying Japanese history, and for the serious reader wishing to read an account of Japan's past. Its purpose is to take a broad view, chronologically and thematically, of trends in Japanese history, and to integrate into a single interconnected narrative many themes from economics, politics and administration, some of which, like linguistic communication, vital for Japan's understanding of the outside world in the period of its isolation, tend to be studied only in specialised works. It also gives prominence to the period before 1868, because all too often accounts of Japan concentrate on the later years.

In the interest of making the narrative accessible to the reader with no specialist knowledge, the book presents a minimum of technical detail, and is sparing in its use of names of individuals and regions. As a history book should be, it is necessarily chronological, though chapters do not hesitate in the interest of analysis of major themes to look backwards and forwards, as chapter 3 does in exploring the context of the remarkably stable eighteenth century, or chapter 6 in discussing the existing levy on rice as a basis of taxation when new demands arose in post-1868 Japan.

The terminal dates of 1582 and 1941 in particular need comment. By 1582 Oda Nobunaga's unification of central Japan had laid the basis on which, by a varied process of combat, moderation and compromise, a unity of sorts for all of Japan was fashioned over the final twenty years of the century and early decades of the following one. In the wake of failure in the 1590s to create a buffer zone in Korea, the fear of outside contacts undermining a precarious harmony led to the progressive introduction of seclusion (sakoku) by the 1630s, destined to last until western pressure in the 1850s and 1860s forced its abandonment. The years from 1868 to 1941 were then to become a period in which Japan could, and increasingly did, exercise its own initiative in dealing with problems in Korea and in China and finally, and more dramatically, in challenging the United States for supremacy in the Pacific. That brought on defeat in 1945 and occupation under an American umbrella, with Japan becoming something of a dependent state (the largest United States military bases in Asia are still in Okinawa): though Japan is the second economic power of the world, it remains a political pigmy. The years 1868–1941 are the only period in four or more centuries when, along with its war years 1941–5, Japan played a prominent role on the world stage.

The story of Japan is of an interplay between unity (informal, or since 1868 formal) and foreign complexities, which were first avoided by the introduction of sakoku, and then after 1868 became the siren song which lured Japan, the initially reluctant participant in the outside world, fatally on to the rocks of Asia and into the storms of the Pacific. Japan's relations with its neighbours and with the United States are still remarkably unsettled. A peace treaty has still not been signed with Russia, whose move south in the 1780s and 1790s in the cold regions to the north of Honshu triggered Japan's serious political study of the west. Its relations with the United States remain a curious combination of dependency and resentment, though, faced with a choice, a large majority of Japanese would opt for the present situation rather than for the unknown.

This book is concerned centrally with the shaping of Japanese unity, and with the interaction between that process and the outside world: successively sakoku, the opening of the country in 1868, and the dilemmas of resisting forceful intrusion, in the age of imperialism, by western countries into Asia, culminating in 1941 in conflict with the United States. Its main emphasis is on the state (both government and administration), the patterns of foreign trade, menace from the outside world and the shaping of policy under sakoku. It was never an enclosed country to the extent of ignoring the outside world, either intellectually or politically. In turn study of the west and some administrative steps taken over decades made it possible for Japan to negotiate with success first with Russia and then more dramatically with the United States in the 1850s.

The problems of Japan are also seen as political, not economic. The absence of a foreign trade had not been economically harmful. The trade before sakoku was a small one in bulk and shipping alike, though one in an exchange of two high-value commodities, silver and silk. Smuggling – which, if it existed on a large scale, would contradict a benign assessment of Japan's restricted trade regime under sakoku and would support assertions that sakoku was damaging – is a mirage (though contemporary shogunal officials, haunted by security, had an obsession with it). Currency problems likewise have been allowed to take too large a part in the story: the debasements in 1695–1711 or after 1818 mirrored simply the straitened financial state of the shogunate, and the economy itself was an orderly one. Sakoku has had many and varied interpretations, reaching even as far as denial of its existence or at least to the claim that in its full sense it was introduced only in 1793 or 1804. There has been less attention to *uchi harai* (driving off foreign vessels): internal debate from 1793 to 1848 reflected a policy more pragmatic and sensitive than the caricature in textbooks.

Japan faced two real challenges, one fiscal, an inelastic revenue system which put limits both to government income and to that of its direct employees, the other external: in the face of new challenges from the 1840s Japan would have to form either a unitary state or a confederacy of units. The country's policies at the highest level were handled by remarkably few men and were never set out on paper to the degree they were within western countries. Interpretation, open for this reason, has also been bedevilled by debates, between Marxists and non-Marxists, but sometimes even among non-Marxists, on whether pre-1868 society fared well economically or not. Modern efforts to read history backwards and to find in social and philosophic thought an explanation of how Japan developed have further added to distortion. Ironically, two very different groups, Marxists and the intellectual supporters of the Allied Occupation of 1945, both had a vested interest in emphasising divides, the Marxists because of their theory of class war, a new generation of Allied (and largely American) historians, closely identified with the Occupation administration, because they wanted to find traditions of dissent as an indigenous basis for the creation of an open society.

What originality this book has rests on its study of the structure of foreign trade (and the role of sakoku within it), the importance of the perimeter of Japan (especial the north and the Ryukyus) in the story and the coherence of change in the country's administrative processes, limited but purposeful especially from the 1840s. The story also embraces the competence of the interpreters at Nagasaki, and the eclectic, flexible and competitive nature of Japanese thought. In contrast to frequent emphasis on control of thought, or on conformity, this book sees Japanese thought as open or eclectic, a strength in many ways, though equally in others a limitation. As the older fashion of emphasis on economic decline recedes in current historiography, incipient political collapse has tended to be stressed. This book discounts the existence of a political crisis in Japanese society in the mid-nineteenth century. Divides in Japan sprang either from factionalism among officials in the 1820s or late 1830s or in the 1850s and 1860s from a more serious substantive divide, one at first over the consequences if Japan refused to make concessions and then over the fiscal distribution within Japan of the benefits of change, if change was inevitable.

Other topics are outlined to ensure that the reader has some overall view of Japan. However, some readers may wish to have more information, on artistic life, the structure of agricultural society, urban society, high and low. For those who wish to read further, the bibliographical note and comment in the footnotes will, it is hoped, furnish guidance. For the twentieth century, there are many books, especially on economic changes. Relatively few books cover the earlier periods, or often do superficially and sometimes with sweeping and simplistic assumptions. Though they may be detailed for some readers the two best books are unquestionably Marius B. Jansen, *The making of modern Japan* (Harvard University Press, Cambridge, Mass., 2000) and Conrad Totman, *A history of Japan* (Blackwell, Oxford, 2000). They cover both pre- and post-1868 years, as does the fresh and vigorous treatment in James L. McClain's recent *A modern history of Japan* (New York, 2002). Of shorter books the one which best complements the present book in its coverage of agriculture, urban development and the great business conglomerates is *Tokugawa Japan: the social and economic antecedents of modern Japan* (University of Tokyo Press, 1990, paperback 1991) edited by Chie Nakane and Shinzaburō Ōishi. The introductory and concluding chapters by the editors are short but effective surveys, all the more welcome as they are written from a Japanese perspective, and hence devoid of the patronising tone that so often creeps into western accounts. For an introductory text with a strong flavour of Japan, Charles J. Dunn, *Everyday life in traditional Japan*, though first published in 1969 (first Tuttle edition, Tokyo, 1972), remains, after three decades, a remarkably fresh and readable introduction to Tokugawa times. In a more political framework, E. O. Reischauer and A. M. Craig, *Japan: tradition and transformation* (1973, later reprints by Tuttle, Tokyo), a generous and insightful book by two of the pioneers of post-1945 Japanese studies in the United States, remains perhaps the most rounded introduction.

Although some awareness of Japan was prompted in the mid-1960s by teaching a course on economic development, a serious interest only followed the stay in Ireland of Matsuo Taro (a former student of the great Otsuka Hisao), who interrupted his teaching career in Hosei University in 1972 to come to Dublin to spend two years as a student. The dedication of this book to him is both in very inadequate repayment of many debts of friendship and in recollection of many hours spent in both Japan and Ireland talking on the byways of the two countries, and in the intervals, a long correspondence over twenty-four years. He would disagree with much that is in this book, but without argument with him, advice from him and contacts established by him it would not exist at all. His invitations to teach at Hosei in 1985, 1993 and 1997 played a large role in widening my knowledge. There are advantages as well as real handicaps in coming late, from a long apprenticeship in Irish, British and French archival sources, to Japanese history. This book is not an exercise in comparative history, though contrasts between administrations and archival sources in Japan and Europe prompted a growing interest in administration and especially in identifying the ways in which the loose administration of the 1780s was gradually strengthened to the point that the Japanese could negotiate on something akin to equal terms in the 1850s and 1860s.

Of other longstanding debts, my greatest ones are to Professor Kawakatsu Heita (International Research Center for Japanese Studies, Kyoto) for encouragement and for support in innumerable ways and to Professor Saitō Osamu (Hitotsubashi University) for advice and comments over many years. I am grateful also to Professor Mitani Hiroshi (University of Tokyo), Professor Miyachi Masato (at the time director of the Shiryo Hensanjo), to both Professors Iguchi Takeo (Tokai University) and Kondō Kazuhiko (University of Tokyo) and to Dr Clare Pollard, Chester Beatty Library, Dublin, for advice and comments. Other accumulated debts are to Professors Ueno Itaru (Seijō University, Tokyo), Matsuoka Toshi (Hosei University, Tokyo), Honda Saburo (Osaka Keizai University), Shimizu Yoshifumi (Momoyama University, Osaka), and to my former students Drs Takagami Shinichi (Osaka Sangyō University) and Goto Hiroko (Hosei University, Tokyo). My debts are large to the libraries of Waseda and Hosei Universities, Watanabe Tsuyoshi and Tsukamoto Akira of the Shizuoka Chuo Kenritsu Toshokan, Dr Honma of Nagasaki chuo kenritsu toshokan, and Tokunaga Hiroshi of the Shiiboruto Kinenkan, Nagasaki. Many of the issues have been worked out in classes in Dublin or in seminars in Japan, and a debt remains to those who participated. I am grateful also to Professor Jean Parmentier of Ghent who gave me a copy of his edition of the diary of a deserter from service in the Dutch East India Company army. A large debt must be recorded to Mathew Stout of St Patrick's College, Drumcondra, Dublin, who drew the maps.

The final revision of the book has taken place in the congenial atmosphere of the International Research Center for Japanese Studies, Kyoto, and of its splendid library, to whose staff I am greatly indebted. Two large debts have accumulated in this period, one to Professor Kozo Yamamura of the University of Washington in Seattle who has painstakingly made comments and criticisms on the text, the other to Dr Katsuta Shunsuke, a former student, now of Gifu University, who after pursuing many bibliographical enquiries in my absences from Japan, then kindly read all the Japanese in the text. Neither is responsible for errors that remain. Without their generous assistance they would have been much more numerous.

There are two special debts outside the academic world. The first is to Eileen Kato of Tokyo who has provided many books and newspaper cuttings which kept me in touch in long intervals between visits, and who has commented on the text; the second to Tsukahara Sueko *sensei*, Professor Matsuo's kanbun teacher many years ago in Nagasaki, whose help ensured that all doors in Nagasaki were opened to me.

Finally, an author's appreciation has to be expressed to many in Cambridge University Press, especially Richard Fisher who in 1991 suggested the idea of the book and later encouraged its progress, Michael Watson, history editor, supportive during a large revision, and Rose Bell, who as copy editor banished many errors and inconsistencies.

The research for this book was aided by a fellowship from the Japan Foundation for three months in 1995, and by grants from the Arts and Social Sciences Fund, and from the Provost's and Incentives Funds of Trinity College, Dublin, towards the cost of short visits.

L. M. C.
Kyoto

Conventions

Macrons are used in the text to indicate long vowels in Japanese. Very frequently used words in the English text (e.g. han, bugyo, daimyo, shogun, sakoku, Tokaido, bushido) and place names (e.g. Tokyo, Hyogo, Choshu, Hokkaido) are not italicised in the text, and the macron where there is one is not indicated. The policy is not followed rigidly: to make it easier for the reader to read the text, both less frequently used words (e.g. *sankin kōtai*, *kan*) and words implying a distinction (e.g. *tozama*, *fudai*), are given in italics, and the macron, where there is one, retained. In the case of the Ryukyu (or Ryūkyū) islands, in which English-language practice varies widely, the usage in the text is that the islands are described as the 'Ryukyus', and 'Ryukyu' is used as an adjective (thus, Ryukyu islanders). Macrons are retained for proper names. The softening of consonants in Japanese in certain contexts is followed in the Japanese in the book (thus, '*kaibō gakari*' and not '*kaibō kakari*') but not in the English if other usages are more common (thus 'Tempō' for 'Tenpō' and 'Deshima' for 'Dejima'). The chronological term *kinsei* covering seventeenth, eighteenth and part of the nineteenth centuries is translated as 'early modern'.

Japanese names are indicated in the Japanese fashion: surname first and given name following. The names of Japanese and Japanese-Americans writing in English are given in the English word order. For Japanese authors, cited for works in Japanese who also appear in the footnotes as authors of texts in English, the author's name for the English-language book is given in the English style (given name followed by surname). In the bibliography, surnames precede in all cases. To avoid confusion in footnotes, for authors who are cited for both languages (or are translated), for English texts the given name is abbreviated to the first letter of the name. Thus in the footnotes Shinbō Hiroshi, elsewhere the author of texts in Japanese, appears as H. Shinbō when his name appears before an English-language text. In a very small number of cases, where confusion could arise and where given name and surname are both cited the surname has been put in capitals. In Japanese the given name is often widely used in place of the surname: thus Ienari in place of Tokugawa Ienari and Sorai in place of Ogyū Sorai.

The identification of territorial divisions can cause confusion to the uninitiated as they are frequently identified by the name of the han, ruling family, castle town, and even, where boundaries do not greatly differ, by the name of the historical province. As far as possible the descriptions in the text are standardised on the han name, and where provinces are distinguished in text or maps this is indicated. There is also (with some slight variations in boundaries in different works) a modern usage to distinguish eight geographical regions (see map no. 1). See also the glossary under Kansai, Kanto and Kuni.

Japan followed a lunar calendar, which had a twelve-month year of 353 to 355 days, and which had to be adjusted by the addition periodically of an intercalary month to bring it abreast of the solar seasons. Dates in the book are usually given in the western calendar: where the month is described as first month, second month etc., the dates are in the lunar calendar.

Abbreviations

CHJ	*Cambridge history of Japan*, general eds. J. W. Hall, M. B. Jansen, Madoka Kanai and Dennis Twitchett, 6 vols. (Cambridge, 1988–99)
Kaempfer	*Kaempfer's Japan: Tokugawa culture observed*, ed., B. M. Bodart-Bailey (Honolulu, 1999)
PP Japan	*Area studies. Parliamentary papers, Japan* ed. W. G. Beasley, 10 vols. (Irish University Press, Shannon, 1971–2)
PRO	Public Record Office, London

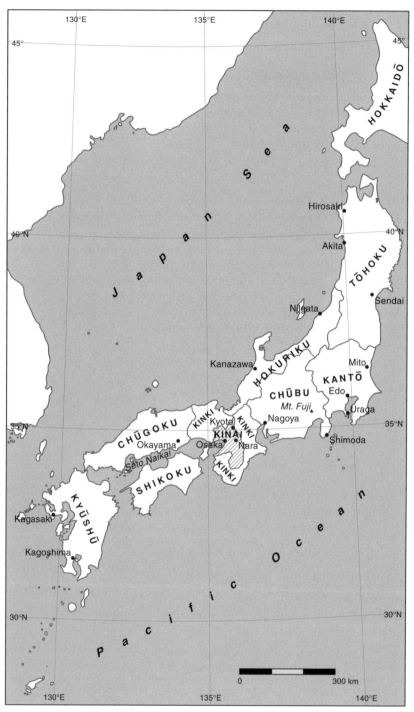

1. Geographical regions of Japan (the shaded Kinai is a subregion of Kinki)

1 Introduction: Japan's internal and external worlds, 1582–1941

The two most widely held historical images of Japan are its self-imposed isolation (sakoku) from the outside world for almost two and a half centuries, and admiral Perry's challenge to it in 1853. Japan is equally known for its rapid economic growth after 1868 and, already famous for its cars, electronics and pioneering high-speed trains, for becoming in the 1980s the world's second economic superpower. Two questions stand out. Why did Japan pursue from the 1630s a policy of isolation; and why abandoning it in modern times did it succeed so well economically? Between the sakoku period ending in 1853–9 and its post-1960 economic triumphs stand its years of wars and conflicts, culminating in its challenge to the United States in the Pacific war. These events raise their own questions. Were they in some way a consequence of aggression latent in Japanese history, or were they simply part of a complex and mainly post-1840 story embracing the western rape of China, a failed effort by Japan to fashion a successful security policy in a changing Asia, and America's aggressive exercise of its new imperial mantle in the Pacific?

Westerners had long seen a policy of exclusion as either irrational or unnatural (though this was qualified in the accounts by four keen-sighted contemporaries, the well-known Kaempfer and the much less well-known Thunberg, Titsingh and Golownin (Golovnin), all of whom spent time in Japan). Modern writing has often made a distinction between Japanese who favoured exclusion and those who wanted to end it. In other words, writers in recent times, Japanese as well as western, sought to find a tradition which it was hoped would underpin the struggling democracy of the 1930s or the Occupation-imposed one after 1945. There has even been more recently a popularisation inside and outside Japan of a view that a full-blown sakoku policy dates only from 1793 or 1804. Likewise, Japanese trade before the 1630s is sometimes presented in Japanese accounts as large and innovative, and as trade contracted, a traffic between Japan and Korea conducted through the island of Tsushima (in the strait separating Japan and Korea) has been seen rather loosely as much larger and more central to the Japanese economy than it was. Sakoku also has been represented as an intended mercantilist or development policy. In all these interpretations lies a reaction, in itself intelligent, against older and more simplistic views which saw sakoku as a blindly repressive policy. A reluctance has long existed in western economic thought to conceive of a comparatively closed economic system as workable or prosperous. The western urge to open Japan (in essence aggression), for justification rested on a belief that sakoku (seclusion) both deprived the country of a foreign trade necessary for Japan's own good and could only have been imposed by internal despotism. The growth of foreign trade, when sakoku was removed in mid-1859, might be seen as a measure of Japan's loss in earlier times.[1] Had sakoku not existed, gains in foreign trade, perhaps as large as those of the 1870s and later, could have been reaped earlier. Yet that overlooks the experience under sakoku. Europeans in the seventeenth century had found few Japanese goods, silver and copper apart, that they wanted, and on the other hand there were, with the exception of silk, few goods from the outside that the Japanese needed in quantity. Japan was self-sufficient in food, and there was no international trade in food in east Asia and no ready supply to turn to in the event of need. The trade arguments, whether special pleading in the nineteenth century to justify western intervention or academic ones in more recent times influenced by the assumed benefits of foreign trade, did – and do – not take account of the fact that an absence of foreign trade outside relative luxuries justified sakoku, or at least made it workable. Agricultural productivity rose sharply in the seventeenth century, and there was also a wide range of technological innovation.[2]

In economic terms the Japan of Tokugawa times was in its way a success tale. It was also at peace with itself (not riven by internal dissent, or by a clamour for the figurehead emperor to replace the shogun as the administrative ruler of Japan). Peace together with the political compromise in the shogunate of Tokugawa Ieyasu (1543–1616) from 1603 meant that institutional changes were taken no further. In a sense Ieyasu did not seek to profit from his victory at Sekigahara in 1600 by an attempt to turn Japan into a more unitary state, and resistance ended on the basis that his victory would be pressed no further. The permanence of this outcome depended on external menace losing pace and on the

---

[1] The assumption that foreign trade altered things is evident in the statement by the justifiably highly respected T. C. Smith that 'in fact when foreign trade commenced in the 1850s, both national and town population *began* to grow rapidly, after more than a century of stagnation' (T. C. Smith, *Native sources of Japanese industrialization, 1750–1920* (Berkeley, 1988), p.36; italics mine.

[2] See K. Nagahara and K. Yamamura, 'Shaping the process of unification: technological progress in sixteenth- and seventeenth-century Japan', *Journal of Japanese studies*, vol. 14, no. 1 (Winter 1988), pp.77–109.

advance of Christianity (i.e. the values of western powers) ceasing: an alliance between foreigners and trade-enriched or disaffected han would have threatened the delicate internal compromise and led to a resumption of conflict. The 1630s, the decade in which sakoku was introduced, were years of crisis, but sakoku thereafter worked for two centuries. A fear that the protracted process of transition from Ming to Ching dynasty in China might threaten stability had haunted the Japanese from the 1620s. But after the 1690s, with no Chinese threat eventuating, the eighteenth century became a remarkable, even unique, century of external security. Western ships (the handful of vessels at Nagasaki apart) were recorded only in 1771 and 1778 and again in 1792. The six western castaways who in 1704 arrived in Satsuma for long remained unique.

The question arises why, when Japan finally had to admit a foreign presence, it chose to create western-style institutions of government and more remarkably of justice. Japan's fears in the 1860s (allowance made for changed external circumstances) were similar to those which in the 1630s had justified the introduction of sakoku. Japanese views of the outside world were realistic. In the early seventeenth century, foreigners were weak and divided even if their warships were large and bristled with cannon (Portuguese, Dutch, English and Spanish all engaged in wars with one another at one time or other); commercial interest also shifted south to India and the equatorial region; Japanese silver ceased to be abundant after mid-century. Two centuries later, when the focus of western attention had shifted northwards from India to China, the maritime powers, though rivals, were not at war with one another. France and England were allied in war against China in the late 1850s and they worked together in 1864 when the ships of four western countries in concert pounded the batteries on the Choshu shores of the strait of Shimonoseki. In other words the price of attempting to preserve sakoku, as the many warships in the north Pacific and the example of China showed, was a war which Japan could not win.

Through the limited channels left open by sakoku, Japan had never disregarded the west. Conversancy with Portuguese and then with Dutch as the successive lingua franca of Europeans in Asia existed among a small corps of linguistically competent officials. When Hirado was closed in 1641 and the Dutch transferred to Deshima, the artificial island in Nagasaki bay, the interpreters not only moved but, from the status of private employees of the Dutch, became direct employees of the shogunate. While the famous *fūsetsugaki* – reports which from 1644 on the arrival of vessels the Dutch were required to make on events in the outside world and which were translated into Japanese by the interpreters for transmission to the shogunate in Edo – were political, modest steps in privately translating medical and technical texts began a decade later. Gradually awareness of the west spread from the indispensable interpreters in Nagasaki into professional circles (medical doctors and astronomers) around the shogunal court in Edo. From the 1780s, when fear of the western threat for the first time since the 1640s recurred, Japan began wide-ranging though limited political study of the west. The famous *uchi harai* policy (firing on and expelling foreign vessels), though formulated as a concept in 1793, became applicable by decree only in 1807 and was at that stage confined to Russian vessels. It was extended to all European vessels from 1825, and when it was seen that it could prove provocative, it was amended in 1842 to admit of succour to the crews of vessels in distress, and a proposal in 1848 to restore it was rejected. After 1780, isolated country though Japan was, there was an evolution of study of the outside world and a constantly changing framework for foreign policy. This awareness of the outside world was accompanied by a gradual creation, starting when Matsudaira Sadanobu (1758–1829) was senior councillor or prime minister (1787–93), of an administrative competence to cope with foreign challenges. *Rangaku* (Dutch or western studies) also had to be reorganised, to become not a somewhat maverick form of knowledge or indulgence pursued by the interpreters after hours, so to speak, and by a few highly opinionated individuals, but a continuous process serving administrative purposes. The result was that Japan had some elements of strengthened administration for foreign affairs by the 1850s, a highly competent knowledge of Dutch (and even some knowledge of other languages), and a practical if incomplete understanding of the west.

When the real challenge came in 1853 and 1854 from the largest groups of warships ever seen off its coasts, Japan was surprisingly capable of dealing with it. In 1853–4 concessions were kept to a minimum and from 1857–8 Japan not only in realistic mode made concessions but in tortuous negotiations succeeded in dragging out over a period of ten years their full application. If concessions became an issue in 1857–8, opinion divided on the extent of concession necessary, and, if concession seemed too much, on the ability of Japan to resist. While no one wanted outsiders, a degree of consensus was established by acceptance of the argument that the unwanted treaties would buy time and, when renegotiation became possible under treaty terms in 1872, it would take place from a position of strength: foreigners could then be confined to a few Nagasaki-style enclaves in isolated centres. Remarkably, from the outset individuals from different generations, whether Yoshida Shōin (1830–59), a young and relatively lowly samurai in Choshu, or Tokugawa Nariaki (1800–60), a powerful daimyo from a collateral branch of the shogunal family, had an urge to study the foreigner on his own ground. The systematisation of this urge was a series of missions to the west from 1860 to 1871: they gradually made the Japanese aware that the west was too powerful to admit of the radical renegotiation that in 1858 or in the early 1860s had seemed attainable, and for some optimists or bold spirits sooner rather than later. Hence the concept of radical undoing of the treaties was replaced by a limited and realistic one of bringing to an end the humiliating concession of extraterritorial sovereignty wrung from a defenceless Japan in 1858. The prospect of achieving this lay in creating new institutions reassuringly like western ones and under which westerner residents would feel safe rather than in diplomatic negotiation itself.

Concern with economic development has dominated western writing on Japan. Many, perhaps most, undergraduate courses and many textbooks concentrate on the century after 1868 and primarily on reasons for Japan's industrialisation. Early post-1945 study of Japan rested on the assumption that Japan's development after 1868 could be explained by a modernisation process, an approach made fashionable in the 1950s by new theories of development intended to make impossible a recurrence of the depression of the 1930s and to quicken diffusion of the benefits of growth to less developed countries. Walt Rostow's *Stages of economic growth* picked Japan out as the sole case of an allegedly less developed country which had attained take-off. The interest in Japan's success was in no small measure inspired by the Cold War, and by the fact that India had modelled its development plans on the Soviet and centrally planned model. Hence as a model based on private enterprise principles or at least on politically more orthodox principles and of proven success, Japan was seen as an alternative to the new and ideologically suspect Indian model.

If democracy was to be successful in the defeated and occupied Japan of 1945, indigenous traditions which would suggest that democracy rested not simply on values imposed by an occupation power but on domestic traditions of dissent had to be discovered, even manufactured (ironically Marxist and non-Marxist historians agreed on this). John Hall, doyen of post-war American historians of Japan, chose to make Tanuma Okitsugu (1719–88), prime minister 1772–86, the subject of his first monograph, and to cast him in the role of moderniser. Tanuma fell in 1786, and the *uchi harai* policy, at least in its first and mitigated form, was broached or threatened in a document handed to the Russians in 1793. Hence, quite apart from the urge that also existed to find dissident individuals in Japanese history and to turn *ikki* (outbursts of unrest) into a form of political protest, this interpretation of Tanuma as a modernising politician displaying readiness to modify sakoku and sympathy for the opening of trade, offered the basis of an indigenous tradition even at a political level which could be appealed to. More than forty years after the appearance of Hall's book a re-echo of the same outlook recurs in the final work by Marius Jansen, a close collaborator of Hall and a man deeply sympathetic to modern Japan.[3]

In holding out Japan as a persuasive model for less developed countries queuing up in the 1950s like aircraft on tarmac for take-off, the assumption was that Japan itself had been a backward country. Yet Japan was not backward in the 1850s. Its food output was very high not only by Asian standards of the 1850s but of the 1950s, and on orthodox principles of political economy, it already had the food surplus necessary in theoretical terms to finance economic development, an elaborate trade network and strong industrial and craft traditions. In any event, industrialisation itself was not a central feature of early policy after 1868. Exports were desirable more as a means of paying for imports than as an end in themselves. If unfortunate in having to open its markets from 1859, a crisis in silk in Europe and, fortuitously, the growth of markets in the United States created outlets for tea and silk which a few years previously, even if the will to trade had been there, would not have existed. As a result, the costs of paying for the import content of re-equipping the country on new lines proved much easier than observers, Japanese or foreign in the 1860s, had foreseen. As it was, the process of change proved painful in the 1880s when a policy of deflation had to be pursued and public investment was pruned.

The government, inheriting at the outset the inelastic revenue structure of the shogunate and han (the subordinate political units, some of them semi-independent), lacked the resources to finance widespread change, and infrastructure necessarily took precedence over industrialisation. Given these constraints and competing claims on resources, Japan's army of early Meiji times was a small one, smaller than its population warranted, and defence of the vulnerable northern territories was token. What was significant was simply that the country which in the past had either no army, or, in fragmented fashion, several or many armies, depending on how one counted its slight military strength, now had a sole and national army. Militaristic values did not run deep in early Meiji society. Bushido, the code of the warrior, as it is understood in the twentieth century was an artificial construct first published in Philadelphia in 1899 in very changed circumstances by a pacifist Nitobe Inazō (1862–1933) and, in 1933, by a militarist Hiraizumi Kiyoshi (1895–1984).[4] Its diverse origins and at such key points in Japan's military involvement with

---

[3] M. B. Jansen, *The making of modern Japan* (Cambridge, Mass., 2000), p.244. He had already repeated the view in *CHJ*, vol. 5, M. B. Jansen (ed.), *The nineteenth century* (Cambridge, 1989), pp.6, 8, 51, 60, 87–8.
[4] See chapter 8, pp.265–71.

the outside world as 1899 and 1933 reflected its ersatz qualities. External events, not internal circumstances, shaped Japanese foreign policy, whether sakoku in the 1630s, its forced abandonment in the 1850s, or the vigorous role which Japan took, with Korea the main background factor, in its successive confrontations with China (1894–5) and Russia (1904–5). China and the Pacific were to determine Japan's future. Japan's efforts to establish a foothold, economic and territorial, on mainland Asia, to match both Russian encroachment in Manchuria and the growing western stake in a debilitated China, created new tensions. In particular they aroused the distrust of the United States which had its own ambitions in both Asia and the Pacific. Its sense of insecurity led Japan to assume onerous burdens in both China and the Pacific. Competing for scarce resources, both army and navy were in conflict, and rivalry reflected an unresolved problem of allocating resources to cope with challenges in the world's largest country (China) and largest ocean (the Pacific). Even after Japanese victory over Russia in 1905, the fear of Russia, in the wake of the collapse of czarist Russia in 1917, turning into dread of its Soviet and revolutionary successor, accounted for Japan's policies in Siberia (1918–22) and throughout the inter-war period in Manchuria and China. The interests of the United States were to prove even more deadly for Japan. A race by maritime countries to occupy the scattered islands of the north Pacific, beginning in the 1850s, had already added to Japan's insecurity. With the acquisition by the United States in the 1890s of external territories, the Philippines and Hawaii, the possibility of a future conflict between the two countries began to emerge.

Japan in its post-1600 history had been variously helped and handicapped by its institutions or lack of them. The Japan of 1600, at the end of a long period of civil war, was in essence a political compromise, a balance between on the one hand the authority of the shogun or ruler of Japan in foreign policy and on the other the independence in their territories or han of local rulers (daimyo). This was certainly the case for the *tozama* or han which before 1600 were effectively independent, variously supportive, hostile or neutral, and thus contrasting with *fudai* daimyo, mere camp followers, already holding daimyo status or soon to be rewarded with it. Above all there was no central taxation. The delicate nature of the compromise has been underestimated in modern terminology: the term feudal, an ambiguous term often applied to the country, has had to be refined to one of centralised feudalism. This, of course, creates a further problem as Japan demonstrably was not centralised. The term *bakuhan taisei* (bakufu-han system) – a modern creation in Japanese historiography – suggests that the government of Japan was more systematic than it was.

In particular the notion of a system of between 260 and 280 han is misleading; many han were not meaningful institutions in any sense, some so small as to be marginal economically, socially and administratively. The power of the shogun rested on the support of one to two dozen small to middle-sized han, and its political limitations were created by the need not to alienate the large *tozama* han of the south and west. The repeated use of the term bakufu in modern historiography, Japanese and foreign alike, to denote the shogun's government or the action by his officials, suggests a greater freedom of action, a larger number of policy-making officials and a greater capacity for decision making than was the case. There is an irony in the use of the term bakufu at all as it was an archaism popularised in the 1860s by its opponents from the *tozama* as a term of abuse of the shogun's government. A small number of decision-making figures (*fudai* daimyo) apart, there were few functionaries or civil servants to define or execute policy. Except in Nagasaki, Japan's centre of foreign contact, there was nothing akin to government ministries, and in Edo, below *ō-metsuke, metsuke, kanjō bugyō* and *daikan*, there were few officials with a training to execute the routine tasks of policy administration.

Three circumstances, sakoku, fiscal weakness and internal political compromise, went together. However, if serious challenges to sakoku, such as the sort of external crisis that threatened in the 1630s, were to persist over the years, internal political compromise in facing them could become unworkable. Would the Japanese response to external events – a foreign threat which became progressively more alarming in the middle decades of the nineteenth century – be determined by the shogun or by the han; would the benefits of trade – and trade became an issue when the opening to foreigners of Osaka, long the centre of domestic trade, was in prospect – go to the shogun or to the han? When the shogunate collapsed in 1867–8 Japan had no constitution (apart from a fiction that the shadowy figure of the emperor conferred legitimacy on the leaders of the revolt as it had on the Tokugawa dynasty itself from 1603). From 1868 to 1889 Japan was governed by the representatives of two to four former han, a situation made possible only by use of imperial authority for the legitimisation of the new regime, moderation in demands by Japan's new ad hoc rulers, and grudging acceptance of others (a situation made easier by the knowledge that Japan faced an external challenge). It was a rerun of some of the circumstances of the early 1600s.

Under a parliamentary system created by the constitution of 1889, insecurity, caused by Russian ambitions on land and growing foreign encroachment in Korea, could be responded to more decisively as a result of the ability to raise money by taxation. The risks, apart from the immediate uncertainty over prospects of victory or defeat in the field, were from a long-term perspective finite as long as the armed forces were small, and the commanders were the first generation of political generals who saw action as subordinated to politics. However, what was to happen when the army became permanently larger and the first generation of generals as they aged or died were replaced by new officers? The risks were compounded by the keenness of the first generation of politicians to minimise outside political interference in administration. In surrendering their authority under the constitution of 1889, they kept as much power as possible in their hands: cabinets were nominated by the emperor, not dependent on approval by the two houses. That ensured at the outset that cabinets consisted of *ex officio* members, and appointment of army and navy officers as heads of the war ministries kept the control of the armed forces safely beyond the control of parliament. Ironically, the constitutional Japan of 1889 was politically weaker than the less legitimate Japan of the preceding two decades. Its army was potentially a semi-independent force; its parliament fractious (predictably hostile to extra taxation) but equally unable to determine policy. Given the vagueness of the constitution, it soon led to the informal emergence of the *genrō*, a small elite of retired senior politicians, who advised the emperor on major issues (notably the nomination of prime ministers) and whom prime ministers in turn were also expected to consult. It was in effect an attempt by the old guard to ensure continuity, one which inevitably broke down in time. Cabinet government, which became true parliamentary government in 1918 (when a majority of cabinet members were parliamentarians), was stable in the 1920s (though ominously the army had sought to plough an independent furrow in Siberia). An unstable China and Soviet strength in Siberia threw things out of balance in the 1930s. Divides between interest groups, divides within factions and even within the foreign ministry itself, traditionally the most open, pointed to an alarming situation. Hence policy drifted dangerously: intervention in China was incoherently planned, the risks were not clearly appreciated. The complacency of politicians, strident militarism in and beyond the armed forces, and ambivalence in public opinion which resented – in the tradition of all that transpired from 1853 – foreign pressure on Japan, can be seen with hindsight to have prepared Japan's nemesis. At the time, foreign diplomats remarked that it was hard or even impossible to meet anyone who really had authority over events.

A question which is unanswerable is the precise assessment of the benefit conferred by sakoku or the price paid for it. Sakoku gave Japan two and a half centuries of peace and a remarkable freedom from external complications. Japan's economic vitality was powerful; intellectually, thought had been free to the point of anarchy (whatever the contrary image painted in much modern literature); expansive internal trade meant that its tea and silk, inadequate in the seventeenth century, were able to command new markets when unexpectedly such markets appeared after 1860. Did sakoku enable Japan to relate better to the outside world after 1868, or had isolation left the country poorly equipped to cope with challenges? Or if put a different way, had Japan engaged more and earlier with the west, would it have lost out as all other Asian countries who had truck with the west did, or would it have become more unitary, and hence have combined preservation of its distinctive character with a not necessarily entirely harmonious but none the less constructive *modus vivendi* with the west? The balance sheet is complex. Japan's policy of sakoku was itself in its time successful. Equally, the realism of its policies in the 1850s and 1860s was striking, and, despite the swirling complexities of China in subsequent decades, abroad Japan retained much respect to the end of the first decade of the new century (Japanese intrusion in Korea as a bulwark against Russian advance was welcomed by the other powers). On the other hand, misjudgements accumulated in the 1910s and more alarmingly in the 1930s. Foreign attitudes to Japan reflected the changes. An admiration, somewhat patronising but also in many ways unqualified for Japan, was replaced by growing dislike and by diplomatic hostility. A final judgement on this equation would also require detailed scrutiny of western intentions and behaviour. Western presence in Asia, its proselytising Christianity, its aggressions, its rampant colonial expansion of the nineteenth century, the rivalries among western powers themselves, these are as much part of the equation as Japan and its policy. They are in a sense the catalyst of all that happened in Japan and in east Asia.

The argument of this book in a nutshell is that the Japanese policy-makers were rational and for its time sakoku policy was equally rational; the economy was highly developed; and the obsession by western writers for explaining why and how Japan could rival the west is not only patronising but, as far as its economic content is concerned, directed to a non-problem created by reluctance to accept that an eastern country, or at least one eastern country, when it willed it, could apparently effortlessly equal the west. The one problem was that at the outset of its opening Japan had no exports and fortuitous circumstances created the outlets for tea and silk. The economic uncertainties of the 1860s are greatly minimised in modern accounts because foreign trade itself is uncritically seen as not simply a long-term aid to development but an immediate and automatic answer to the international payment needs created by the opening of the country.

The economic resilience as well as the rationale of its institutions, both old and new, has to be a central concern of any study of Japan. The question is not why Japan succeeded, but why it followed the western model. If it was imitative (a process which at different times led to both praise and criticism of Japan), the motives for imitation were primarily on the security front: the need to gain a defence strong enough to resist the west, and, in the long interval from 1868 to 1894, the paramount necessity of impressing on the west that Japanese institutions had changed sufficiently for outsiders to have confidence in the protection of their interests, if the unequal clauses of the 1858 treaties were abandoned. Many changes (in themselves superficial, even if their adoption might seem surprising in its rapidity), in the style of dress, in the prohibition of near-nakedness by workmen in torrid weather and of mixed bathing, were intended consciously to avoid Japan appearing barbarous to westerners, and hence to ensure that the country was taken seriously. It was not a country in progressive crisis before 1868 (even if a rigid revenue ensured restricted government). In other words, famine or *ikki* (social unrest) were not central to the story. Nor was the country more oppressive after 1793; if anything it was on balance more open, and only bouts of factionalism, caused by the fewness of officials and the loose administrative structure, contradict that picture. After 1868, while economic aspects are important, they are not the decisive feature. The country was already developed, and the defensive dimension of its new role was central to its westernisation. The slogan *fukoku kyōhei* (rich country, strong defence)[5] summarises its intent. The emphasis on Japan as an imitator not only springs from the premise of seeing Japan at the outset as a backward country but, by its emphasis on imitation across a broad range of activities, it also avoids giving recognition to the central role of western aggression as the motivating force for imitation. What Japan wanted to imitate in the 1850s and 1860s was western technology in armaments in order to defend itself. In the urge to imitate the west, admiration for the west was strong in the 1870s; it was, however, significantly qualified within a decade. Even Fukuzawa Yukichi (1835–1901), who had written so much in favour of lessons from the west, became more muted in his admiration: another slogan, *wakan yosai* (western science and Japanese values), equally summarised the situation.

The critical issues of 1868 were political and constitutional change and the foreign threat. Sakoku itself was a complex response in its time (the fact that there was earlier debate over the external risks of adhering

---

[5] Usually translated as 'rich country, strong army'. The term defence is preferred here, as the early Meiji army was in fact a small one, and the emphasis in the defence debate had been more on artillery and western firearms than on an army as such. The term came from the Chinese classics and acquired currency in debate among highly educated and politically aware Japanese in Japan in the 1850s.

to it unchanged explains why emphasis has been put in some modern historiography on 1804: the modern emphasis, though overdone, is not of itself arbitrary). Japanese awareness of potential outside risks and the debate to which it gave rise for almost a century preceding 1868 is central to appreciating Japanese politics after 1853 and the success of its adjustment from closed country to open one. The country was sensitive to changing circumstances and its immediate responses over many preceding decades to challenges had been informed ones. The role of one or more external languages as a means of communication, the importance attached to language interpretation and a steadily growing accumulation of translation in Dutch as a vehicle for understanding the outside world was a cornerstone in this success. This gets little attention in western monographs, and in Japanese historiography it is examined in specialised monographs rather than in more general works. As a result the motivation behind sakoku and the sensitive shifts of emphasis in the foreign concerns of Japan from 1793 onwards are often not fully appreciated. The return of shipwrecked Japanese and the question of aid for foreign mariners in distress has often led to misunderstanding of what Japanese policy was. This was not an issue for foreigners before 1793 (because they had very rarely approached Japan), nor was it a problem for the Japanese, except when they were faced with the novel crisis situation involving Russia. When shipwrecked Japanese were returned, the requirement was that their return should be effected though Nagasaki, and some regular transfer of seamen occurred through Korea. The few Europeans likewise were sent on to Nagasaki. As for aid to distressed foreign mariners, despite growing concerns it remained the practice, except for Russian vessels from 1807, until 1825. Older practice was restored in 1842. In other words, except between 1825 and 1842 there was help for distressed mariners.

One of the arguments of this book is that there was little if any backing in Japan for the principle of opening up the country. A guarded view is taken of the role of the much-lionised 'Dutch' experts in the rights and wrongs of famous quarrels in Japan: the quarrels are instances of recurrent factionalism in Japanese behaviour, unrelated to philosophic debate (the way the quarrels widened has a striking similarity to the manner in which factionalism in departments – particularly in politically sensitive subjects such as law, economics and history – in state universities in the 1930s acquired national notoriety). The book stresses too the administrative problems, the changes over a half century before 1853, and, a fact that needs to be said, that by any standard and by definition for an isolated country, there was a high degree of both success and realism in Japanese negotiation in the 1850s. In a very real sense realism was one of

Japan's strengths from the 1850s onwards: abandonment of realism was the country's later undoing in the 1930s.

In chapter 2, following this introduction, foreign trade in the seventeenth century is analysed. Trade within east Asia depended entirely on an exchange of high-value goods (silk for silver) effected on a small number of comparatively large ships. There was not a significant exchange in more prosaic or voluminous goods, and for that reason sailings were few compared with the intensive trades in the East Indies and Indian Ocean or in Europe: there were dozens of sailings and, except in the late 1680s for Chinese vessels, never hundreds. Chinese and Japanese traders were viewed with suspicion on one or other or on both coasts, and controls and restrictions affected the conduct of trade. Japanese distrust of the Chinese deepened in the 1620s and 1630s; equally, acts of aggression by Europeans added to doubts about westerners. They were, however, at least on the Japanese side, a welcome supplementary aid to essential exchanges which were constrained by many circumstances when conducted on Chinese or Japanese vessels. In a high-value trade carried out in a small number of vessels, European traders were not at a handicap in actual operations, especially as they were more capitalised than the numerous small traders (running into hundreds) who crowded onto the larger of the Chinese vessels. The offsetting factor was that if financial losses occurred, Europeans were more likely than Chinese to withdraw or run down operations. If trade was to be confined to one or two ports, and if the numerous Chinese and also the Portuguese, who were the Europeans with the most numerous, intimate and diffuse ties in Japan, were constrained to depart within the year as they were in the 1620s, risks were reduced. The five regulations of the 1630s – the core of sakoku policy – were a refinement of controls rather than a novelty. The Portuguese finally fell foul of the shogunate less because of Christianity itself than because, as the sole westerners who were numerous, widespread, sometimes intermarried, and also friendly with daimyo, they were a political risk to a degree that the Dutch were not. With Chinese and Dutch alike finally confined to a single port supervised by officers of the shogun, control for the future preserved the delicate balance between shogun and daimyo, which could be upset if trade enhanced wealth or foreigners were either numerous or scattered across southern Japan and hence uncontrollable. Japan was an example of limited government; no central tax fell on the daimyo or their domains; except in Nagasaki it had no specialised bureaucracy outside accounting offices, and, as peace lasted, the country effectively demilitarised.

Chapter 3 describes the growth of the economy in the seventeenth and eighteenth centuries. If foreign trade contracted in the seventeenth century, the economy itself expanded steadily. The accompanying dynamic of this boom was the growth of Edo as major consumption centre of shogun and daimyo and of Osaka as the marketing centre for the produce of han and as the financial centre to turn products into hard cash. The monetary system was one of two currency zones, with Osaka serving as the exchange market between them. Overland trade was limited, given the mountainous terrain; on the other hand the coastal trade was probably the largest in the world. There was not an economic crisis. What did occur, however, was a persistent fiscal crisis, insoluble given the constraints that the 1600 settlement of Japan imposed on fiscal innovation. If the revenue of the shogun and in the han of daimyo was limited, that meant that the incomes of their servants were also inelastic. Hence, the sense of gloom in writing reflected the unhappiness of a small class, amounting to less than five per cent of the population, but which included the main writers of reform proposals and of complaints alike.

Chapter 4 examines the way a sense of freedom from attack by Europeans (from the 1650s) and from China (after the 1680s) led to a century of unprecedented ease on the security front. Economic conditions were favourable apart from the harvest failures of 1732 and of the 1780s. There was, however, no threat from widespread rural disorder and no political challenge to the shogunate. Nor was there an orthodoxy in belief or in teaching imposed by the state. One result of the situation was that philosophic thought and teaching alike expanded through growing numbers of teachers and schools: schooling was private, eclectic and competitive. In such a framework western studies could find a niche. They began in Nagasaki, as a modest outcrop of scholarly work and teaching by the interpreters. Edo later became the focal point. The need to understand the outside world acquired a new urgency for political reasons in the 1790s.

Chapter 5 argues that the 1780s were doubly a decade of crisis: on the economic front because of harvest failure which reached beyond the north, and on the foreign front because of uncertainty created by Russian expansion in Ezo. However, a long period of prosperity followed to be interrupted only by bad harvests in the 1830s. Political responses to the external crisis were cautious, with definition and redefinition of *uchi harai* reflecting a readiness to comprehend the crisis. Study of the outside world become more systematic and focussed from the first decade of the nineteenth century under government auspices: surveying and mapping teams were created under the technical auspices of the shogunal astronomer, and existing translation work was formalised in a Translations Bureau created in 1811, likewise under his direction. The Hayashi family, already responsible for some of the paperwork of the shogunate, was given what seems an overall role as liaison between this new or intensified activity and the exiguous administration in Edo castle; from 1845 *kaibō gakari* (defence officials) were instituted, in part to co-ordinate defence, in part to free defence from factional disputes. The Edo government resisted pressures to expand vigorously into the Ezo islands: its caution on this front caused controversy when in 1822 it handed back responsibility for security from its own officials to officials of the han of Matsumae in Ezo. Inevitably outbreaks of factionalism occurred as in 1824–5, 1828 and 1839–40, before tighter administration prevented its recurrence.

Chapter 6 examines how, as it became clear by 1845 that a new challenge was looming, government policy sought to achieve national consensus. This, combined with an imperfect but real knowledge of western strength, made it possible to respond to external challenge successfully. Concessions in 1853–5 which permitted vessels to call but did not allow of trade did not encounter deep opposition (they were a logical extension of the flexible approach evident in *uchi harai* itself). The conceding of trade in 1858 (and in ports on the coast of central Japan) was more controversial. A consensus did, however, develop around the fact that the trade treaties would buy time to arm and they could be renegotiated and whittled down from a position of strength. A reluctant emperor himself acceded when the general views of han were clear and a contentious shogunal succession was out of the way. The trade divide might not have proved so deep if Japan's rulers had not faced the most difficult succession in the history of the shogunate, and the resultant bitterness (deepened by the brusque imposition of a controversial successor on the death of the ailing shogun a month after the American treaty was signed) carried on into the 1860s. The 1860s were a complex decade, inevitably so given the compromise nature of Japanese institutions and the delicate balance between them (power divided between han and shogunate, the imperial institution itself a legitimising device to which both sides could appeal). Three things make it easier to explain the sequence of events. First, some were overconfident of the ability to resist militarily. Second, as the opening of Osaka (the original date for which was deferred) loomed into prospect, the question of whether the benefits of trade would accrue to the han or to the shogun became a central one. Third, in reaction to the urge of shogunal officials and of the emperor (who was a strong supporter of the political authority of the shogun) to punish dissentient han, grew the idea that in a time of crisis war among Japanese was intolerable. Hence loyalism to the shogun wavered. Again, as in 1858, deaths triggered development. The shogun, only twenty years old, died on 29 August 1866, and the emperor unexpectedly a bare five months later. The new shogun Yoshinobu was a young and forceful man who unwisely had backed those in the shogunate who favoured a crackdown on dissentient han, and he also pushed strongly for shogunal control of the revenues which would accrue in Osaka. The death of the emperor, who was sensitive to the many preoccupations of han, meant his replacement by a young and in-experienced emperor who would be malleable in the hands of a forceful shogunate. The shogunate fell because of the alliance of Choshu (a dis-sentient han which not only favoured the resumption of *uchi harai* but had put it into practice in 1863–4) and Satsuma (up to this time a loyal supporter of the shogun).

Chapter 7 considers how contact with the outside world through mis-sions sent abroad convinced the Japanese of the strength of the western powers. Undoing of the treaties was soon seen to be unrealistic, and the way of ending the humiliating and unequal conditions, notably extraterri-toriality (which meant that foreigners were tried only in consular courts), was by adopting western-style institutions. After 1868, under the abo-lition of han jurisdictions, termination of the role which Satsuma and Tsushima had held in contacts with the Ryukyus and Korea respectively made urgent a new basis for relations. Korea was particularly worrying be-cause Chinese and Russian encroachment could threaten Japan. Japan's growing stake in Korea in the wake of its wars with China and Russia was acceptable to western powers, but other issues such as trade rivalries among all the countries over China and hostility in the United States to Japanese immigration point to fresh sources of tensions in the first decade of the new century. A Japanese constitution came only in 1889. If the imperial institution had been used to legitimise the pretensions of four han, especially Satsuma and Choshu, the constitution, enshrining the emperor at the centre of the state and very vague as to how cabi-net ministers were appointed, was also calculated to protect the stake of Satsuma and Choshu in government and in control of the armed forces. In practice, the emperor nominated ministers (on advice), and the lack of constitutional clarity about the process also ensured that office-holders and not parliamentarians dominated in the three decades from 1890. Army and naval officers were appointed to the war ministries, thus en-suring that Choshu and Satsuma dominance of the armed forces further secured the interests of leaders from both these han.

Japan was a beneficiary of the First World War in terms of its economic boom, diversification of its industrial base, some territorial acquisition and the status of inclusion among the five major powers at Versailles. However, chapter 8 examines how its interests in China and Manchuria and naval rivalry with the United States led eventually to wars with China from 1937 and with the United States from 1941. Cabinet instability in Japanese constitutional government worsened once external issues be-came central: army and naval ministers were capable of bringing cabinets down. Moderate Japanese and foreigners resident in Japan alike tended to be complacent that a stable political arrangement could be achieved. While Japan never became totalitarian (and the militarism of the attempted coup by young officers in 1936 revealed the limitations as well as the dangers of the situation), cabinet weakness, combined with the perception in public opinion that opposition abroad to Japanese policy was motivated by selfish ambitions, ensured that there was no reassessment of policy and international crisis widened. Despite the rather artificially contrived campaigns mounted by militarists against individuals, the press itself remained independent, as did teaching except during bouts of factionalism among academic rivals in the state universities (though not in the private universities) when militaristic views served as the dividing line between friend and foe. Japanese history poses greater problems of interpretation than the history of other countries both because it was influenced by the political imperatives of legitimacy (in support of orthodox political institutions in the 1890s and of an effort in the 1930s by militarists to 'reform' them), and because both Marxists in the Japanese universities in the 1930s and, in the wake of the Allied Occupation in 1945, western historians, mainly though not exclusively American, were anxious to find historical evidence of dissent from authority, as proof of traditions to support democracy against authoritarian government in the 1930s or to underpin post-1945 Occupation-imposed institutions. Much of the concluding section of the chapter is devoted to these issues, because from both sides of the spectrum, and from without as from within Japan, views on bushido, militaristic traditions, the imperial system and the nature of dissent in Japanese history have distorted history or even manufactured a false continuity.

2   Japan and its Chinese and European worlds, 1582–1689

Japan in the sixteenth century was an archipelago of which the main component was a large island (Honshu) separated from three middle-sized islands (Kyushu, Shikoku and Ezo) by narrow straits. It was already in physical and human terms a remarkably isolated country. To the west, it faced two inward-looking countries, one the great landmass of China, the other the Korean peninsula whose proximity to Japan made it the vehicle of contact with China. To the east lay the enormous north Pacific ocean, little explored until the late eighteenth century. Cultural influences (Confucian philosophy and Japan's writing system, both Chinese in origin, and the Buddhist religion itself) had all been transmitted through Korea more than a thousand years previously, by a small elite body of monks, scholars and noblemen, some of them returning Japanese. Later contact was fitful, and at the end of the sixteenth century, there was little trade and even less cultural movement between Korea and Japan. However, unsettled international conditions would give Korea, in the seminal decade of the 1590s and again after 1868 in the troubled times of renewed western encroachments in Asia, an importance transcending existing isolation. Isolation to the east and west was reinforced by an absence of contacts to the north, accounted for by climatic conditions, and to the south, created by economic circumstances.

To the north of Honshu (and in the adjoining Tohoku, or north-east of Honshu itself) the climate was influenced by the frontier of cold and hot currents and winds on the interface of the world's largest landmass and its largest ocean. Cold currents pushing down along the coast of Siberia in meeting the upward-moving warm currents of the Pacific resulted in both pervasive fog and in sudden winter storms. As the summer monsoon weakened, the winds of the Siberian landmass, pushing out into the Pacific in a great anti-cyclonic sweep, curled in from a north-easterly direction. On their path, they met the moisture-laden air of the Pacific: in summer precipitation was heavy if they pushed out prematurely, and in winter snow lay deep on the ground in both the Ezo islands (of which the principal one, Ezo-ga-shima, was renamed Hokkaido after 1868) and the Tohoku. If autumnal change set in early, the contact with the southerly air currents resulted in cloudiness or even rain as the harvest was still ripening. One of the consequences was that even as low as the latitude of 40 degrees (the same latitude as Washington, D. C.) permanent settlement was relatively unattractive. Although a small number of Japanese had migrated in medieval times, there was in 1600 only a minute colony in the south-west corner of Ezo-ga-shima across the 30-mile Tsugaru strait. Two centuries later the fiction grew that the Ezo islands had been a Japanese possession in past times. That, however, was simply an argument to strengthen the Japanese claim against rivals; the true occupants were the Ainu, rather like the Eskimos of even colder regions, the only permanent inhabitants. The region was only vaguely mapped: Kaempfer, the German doctor at the Dutch factory in Deshima in 1690–1, noted that 'because Japanese maps differ from each other I cannot establish the shape of this island: in some the island is depicted as round with many bays; in others it is broken up ... it is impossible to say whether these are separate islands'.[1] Northern Honshu was in 1600 underdeveloped and underpopulated. Even further south, Edo, the future capital of Tokugawa Japan (the Tokyo of modern Japan), was a creation of the seventeenth century, its region – Kanto – itself a somewhat retarded frontier with the richer and more densely populated south.

To the south of Japan, climate and ease of navigation off the coast of south China and the East Indies archipelago created a region of active exchanges in rice, spices, textiles, sugar (in the seventeenth century) and in gold and silver; from early on economic activity was further diversified by its attracting traders both from China and from the west, first Arabs, and later Europeans. The problem for the more northerly countries of east Asia was how to finance exchanges for the exotic goods of the south. Requiring both silver and spices, China itself had a trade with the south. It was an even more serious problem for Japan than for China, because originally Japan had little to offer. China at least had its prized silks. The poverty of Japanese trade accounts for the existence of the *Wako* (sea pirates described as Japanese, though often Chinese engaged in the Japan trade with the tolerance of Japanese daimyo or lords) who preyed on such trade as existed along the coasts of China, and whose destructiveness led to the prohibition by the Ming government in 1557 of trade with Japan.[2] In China Japanese were excluded, and equally China's traders, if

---

[1] *Kaempfer's Japan: Tokugawa culture observed* (Honolulu, 1999), ed. B. M. Bodart-Bailey, p.44. On Kaempfer, see also *The furthest goal: Engelbert Kaempfer's encounter with Tokugawa Japan*, ed. B. M. Bodart-Bailey and D. M. Massarella (Folkestone, Kent, 1995).

[2] For a short account of the *Wako*, see M. B. Jansen, *China in the Tokugawa world* (Cambridge, Mass., 1992), pp.6–7. The trade ban of 1557 was relaxed within ten years to

they ventured to Japan, were disregarding prohibitions imposed in their homeland. In Japan Chinese were suspect as the hand of Japan's ruler, Hideyoshi, began to fall on domestic rulers and coastal pirates alike in Kyushu in the 1580s: furthermore, acute fears that an alliance between daimyo in Kyushu and outside trading interests might disturb the delicate political balance persisted thereafter.

The payment problems in foreign trade – if not the political complications – were eased by the sudden advent of great quantities of Spanish silver, as silver flowed into the region from the time that the Spaniards made Manila a base of their operations in 1571. Spanish silver was traded in Manila for silks from China, and a Spanish presence in the western Pacific grew after 1580 when Portugal fell under Spanish suzerainty for sixty years. The usefulness of silver as an exchange commodity (in an age of large military expenditure), combined with the Chinese demand for it, led to the introduction from Korea of improved techniques in mining and in refining the metal, and hence to a mining boom in Japan. Possibly as much as one third of the huge outflow of silver onto world markets in this period was Japanese.[3] This outflow helped to trigger the economic boom of China from 1570 to 1620 as silver oiled the wheels both of tax payment and inland exchanges. The coastal regions sold silk and silver to the inland regions and received payment in rice. Disregard or evasion of the prohibition on trade illustrated the growing weakness of the Ming imperial dynasty, one which became dramatically evident when the Manchu challenge to the Ming rulers reached crisis point with the taking of Peking in 1644. As a result of turmoil and warfare, China's trade fluctuated sharply over the years up to the 1680s. The prolongation of momentum in Japan's mining boom to mid-century meant that up to that time Japan's rulers were not concerned over the export of silver. As a result, Japan, once a backwater, had became an economic power house, with an appeal for Europeans as a source of the silver which held the key to participating in the trade currents of east Asia: there was also the opportunity of replacing the Chinese traders, suspect in China and Japan alike, in exchanges between the two countries. The repute of Japan as a mineral-rich country was to haunt the European imagination for decades after Japan had ceased to have a surplus of silver.

admit of trade with the Chinese communities in south-east Asia, but was continued on trade with Japan (Jansen, p.17).
[3] See A. Kobata, 'The production and uses of gold and silver in sixteenth- and seventeenth-century Japan', *Economic history review*, vol. 18, no. 2 (1965), pp.245–66; W. S. Atwell, 'International bullion flows and the Chinese economy, circa 1530–1650', *Past and present*, no. 95 (May 1982), pp.68–90.

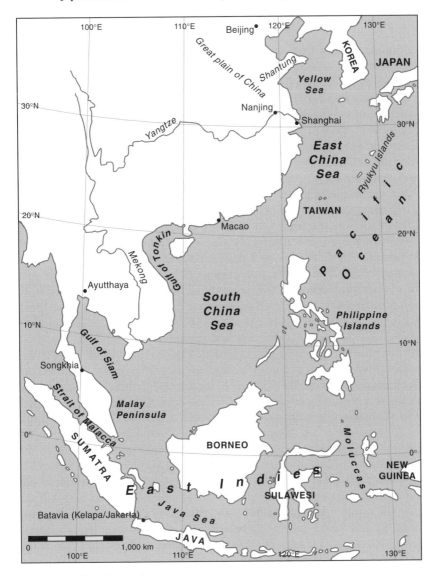

2. South-east Asia

All trade between China and Japan, it must be emphasised, was one
in high-value goods, in essence silk and some gold for silver and copper.
It was, moreover, less a trade with China than a trade with the areas of
Asia frequented by *tōsen* (Chinese vessels): manned by *tōjin* (Chinese)

they sailed directly to Japan from as far afield as Siam, bearing spices, sandalwood and silk. The silver, which oiled the wheels of Chinese commerce, came from two sources: first, from Japan, making possible Japanese purchase of the products of China, Indochina and Siam; second, from Spanish America, arriving via the Philippines into the spice regions and to a very limited extent, by a trade from Manila, into Japan. As the output of silver expanded and military expenditure wound down after 1600, silver in Japan ceased to be a commodity to hoard for either domestic or military purposes, and became one to sell on the open market. The silk, whose import the silver financed, was highly desirable. Raw silk was troublesome to prepare. Separating the silk spun by the silkworms from the cocoons was a difficult task: this raw silk, once reeled, was the basic material of the weaving branch of the textile industry. High-quality silk was the prized dress of the upper classes; it was also an important gift good, and to some degree a store of value. Cloth was woven in Japan, but the fineness of cloth depended more on the raw silk than on weaving skills. The preparation of raw silk involved a complex sequence of mulberry groves, the raising of the silkworms (fed on the leaves of the mulberry trees), care of the cocoons and finally reeling the thread separated from the cocoons. It was labour-intensive and had exacting requirements of space, cleanliness and discipline, at this stage possessed by the inhabitants of few rural regions. The making of raw silk was not widespread even in China, and it took root slowly in Japan. World output itself even as late as the close of the eighteenth century was small, and perhaps not greatly in excess of Chinese output two centuries before.[4] For all these reasons imported raw silk was in demand among the highly skilled weavers of the Kyoto region. Chinese exports were about 6,000 piculs (or 8,000 cwt); of these some 2,500 to 4,000 went to Japan.[5] The scale of the outflow of silver in payment itself emphasises the high price of the raw silk. The figures also point to the negligible demands of silk for space in shipping. A mere 200 tons of shipping would carry all the raw silk brought into Japan in a year (though in the inconceivable event of all the silk being on a single vessel, its loss would occasion a financial disaster in foreign trade). What was in essence an exchange of goods as prized as silk for a precious metal, emphasises the exceptional nature of the region's foreign trade, and how it should not be readily assimilated to concepts derived from bulk trades in low-value goods elsewhere.

---

[4] For an estimate of 44,500 quintals (approx. 36,000 piculs) for the end of the eighteenth century, see G. Federico, *An economic history of the silk industry 1830–1930* (Cambridge, 1997), p.202.

[5] G. B. Souza, *The survival of empire: Portuguese trade and society in China and the South China Sea, 1630–1754* (Cambridge, 1986), p.53.

The number of sailings in the various divisions of foreign trade in east Asia could be counted in dozens rather than in hundreds (though individual vessels were quite large, up to 1,000 tons for the trade from Siam). Rice, sake and other goods of daily use featured in cargoes, if at all, only in minute quantities. Moreover, a trade confined largely to high-value goods was handled by numerous traders, each man with a small consignment. As bulk trade was not significant, a large fleet of smaller and middle-sized ocean-going vessels did not exist, and the high risks from the sea run by a small number of large vessels carrying expensive cargoes, once spread in small consignments over many merchants, acted as a crude form of insurance. The Chinese, with silk to offer and an insatiable demand for silver, had a near monopoly of international trade in east-Asian waters. Once tensions affected trade between east Asia and Japan, adverse political circumstances made it comparatively easy for outsiders to acquire a foothold, whether the Portuguese in Macao and Nagasaki or, at first less securely, the Dutch in Hirado (and they also explain why, for the Dutch who lacked a secure base in China itself, the plundering of a few vessels with rich cargoes was often a decisive event in their early fortunes).

The existing trade lacked a sophisticated merchant network; the many men aboard Chinese vessels meant that the Chinese communities in Nagasaki and elsewhere at any time both had large numbers and a remarkably high turnover of personnel within the year. The Chinese, whose numbers in Japan increased around 1630 when Dutch and Portuguese were for security reasons temporarily excluded, were not permitted a fixed residence, and were required to depart from Japan on their vessels before winter, and to leave their accommodation vacant until the following season.[6] This pattern explains too the appearance of chaos in unloading Chinese vessels at Nagasaki, 'with total want of order, the cargo consisting of small bags and boxes being thrown out of the ship without any regard either for the goods themselves or the boats destined to receive them'.[7]

Diffuse ownership and management of vessels inhibited bold diversification. In any event a common monsoon climate meant that the same commodity, rice, was grown in the southern regions; further north, in northern China, Korea and the Tohoku of Japan, barley rather than rice was the food grain. Moreover, as trade was conducted in a small number of vessels, the flexibility to enlarge trade at short notice scarcely existed.

[6] *Kaempfer*, p.226.
[7] I. F. Krusenstern, *Voyage round the world in the years 1803, 1804, 1805 and 1806*, 2 vols. (London, 1813), vol. 1, pp.276–7.

A region like Siam, usually with a degree of surplus and low prices,[8] was not a regular exporter of rice even to China. Some trade in rice could occur between north and south (as occurred, or at least was intended, in both ways for a mere handful of ships between Siam and Taiwan between 1682 and 1683[9]). However, such trade was rare, and even in the most favourable circumstances of low prices in Siam and high or famine prices in China, nine or ten, though admittedly large, vessels would have sufficed for what purchases were made.[10] Areas of east Asia above 40 degrees latitude, with uncertain ripening seasons and harsh winters and little settlement or trade, contrasted with Europe, where the oceanic drift and mild westerly winds made possible up to a latitude of 60 degrees a dense population and intensive exchange of lumber, grain, iron, flax and fish for the voluminous cargoes of wines as well as the sophisticated manufactures of more southerly regions. The fleets and seamen of many nationalities engaged in bulk traffics; in the east, by contrast, long-distance voyages were few, their commodities high-priced and handled by numerous very small operators. The Arabs had acquired a surprising ascendancy in south Asia by the fifteenth century. In turn the Chinese at first held an almost unchallenged ascendancy in the overseas exchanges of east Asia. The direct Japanese intrusion into the trade in Indochina, prompted by the silver boom, was late and small.

As trade between Japan and China was overshadowed by the diplomatic and political issues of the period, western vessels were an accepted and at times essential ingredient in the conduct of the exchanges of silver for silk. Foreign trade for the Japanese was particularly sensitive, as its location in Kyushu raised the spectre of outside support for local independence, the more so as its expansion coincided with order being restored in Japan in the wake of the century-long Sengoku period (literally 'Warring States' period, meaning a period of hegemonic struggle). New or unimpeded foreign relations could destabilise the emerging order.

[8] Yoneo Ishii, *The junk trade from south-east Asia: translations from the tōsen fūsetsugaki 1674–1723* (Singapore, 1998), pp.55–6. The main market for the surplus was within the densely populated regions of Malaya and the islands of Indonesia. On the later pattern of the trade, see A. J. H. Latham, 'The dynamics of intra-Asian trade: the great entrepots of Singapore and Hong Kong', in A. J. H. Latham and H. Kawakatsu (eds.), *Japanese industrialization and the Asian economy* (London, 1994), pp.145–6.

[9] Ishii, *Junk trade*, pp.28, 35.

[10] Ishii's translation gives 300,000 koku as 4,200 tons (*Junk trade*, p.101). However, a figure of 300,000 koku would be approximately 42,850 tons. The figure seems to be an erroneous reading either in the text or in the original for 30,000 koku which would give a figure of 4,285 tons. That there is a misreading seems to be confirmed by the further statement that three ships 'of larger burden' were ready to carry 100,000 koku of the total. A figure of 100,000 koku would be an impossible scale for three vessels of the period combined. A figure of 10,000 koku – 1,425 tons, or an average of 475 tons per vessel – is, on the other hand, perfectly credible.

The story of trade relations on either side of 1600 has to be related to the recent growth – or, more accurately, restoration – of central authority in Japan. Order had been restored in central Honshu between 1567 and 1582 by Oda Nobunaga (1534–82),[11] and after 1582 among the daimyo in the south of Honshu and in Kyushu by his former lieutenant and successor Toyotomi Hideyoshi (1537–98).[12] To the north of his own power centre in Osaka, Hideyoshi as regent entrusted land and authority to his own foremost lieutenant, Tokugawa Ieyasu, who in turn took over the reins of authority on Toyotomi's death in 1598. The daimyo or lords whom Nobunaga and Hideyoshi successively ruled were variously of noble origin (e.g. the Mori of Choshu were descended from court nobles), families with centuries of local domination behind them (the Shimazu of Satsuma), or mere military upstarts from the Sengoku period. The *fudai* were lords who were in effect retainers of Japan's rulers, the *tozama* were lords of dominions of independent and usually earlier origin. Lords were formidable only in proportion to the number of samurai (fighters who had become a hereditary military caste) and armed peasants in their han or principality. The bigger and distant lords, either remaining neutral in 1598 or defeated at the battle of Sekigahara in central Japan in 1600, conceded allegiance; in the central regions of Japan daimyo were either already followers of Hideyoshi or of Tokugawa Ieyasu or were replaced by proven supporters at various stages on either side of 1600. Though Tokugawa Ieyasu confirmed his military authority at the battle of Sekigahara, the victory was not of itself a final crushing defeat for the forces of particularism in Kyushu, far to the south.

The restoration of order had been facilitated by the fact that amid the military anarchy of the Sengoku period, a sophisticated thread of constitutional legitimacy had never been lost. Though the emperor in Kyoto was a figurehead, and even the shoguns, the military rulers of Japan, to whom the emperor had in the distant past devolved administration, had, amid the anarchy of the Sengoku period, become powerless figures, both Nobunaga and Hideyoshi derived such moral authority as they had from a status of regent, conferred, or at least recognised, by the emperor. Ieyasu's standing derived initially merely from his status as guardian of Hideyoshi's son and intended successor, Hideyori. However, in 1603

[11] Hisashi Fujiki and G. Elison, 'The political position of Oda Nobunaga', in J. W. Hall, K. Nagahara and K. Yamamura (eds.), *Japan before Tokugawa: political consolidation and economic growth 1500 to 1650* (Princeton, 1981), pp.149–93.
[12] The precise status of both Oda Nobunaga and Toyotomi Hideyoshi, neither of whom was shogun, but both of whom nominally acted for the shogun and held honorific offices from the emperor, is hard to define in western terms. On Oda's status, see H. Ooms, *Tokugawa ideology: early constructs 1570–1680* (Ann Arbor, 1998), pp.28–9.

Ieyasu had himself invested as shogun by the emperor, and three years later nominally retired and had his son invested as shogun to ensure a Tokugawa succession. Inherent in these transactions was an implicit constitution: a shogun was not an absolute ruler, his power was a trust given to him by higher authority, and failure to discharge it could call his authority into question. Moreover, the emperor was in some sense a symbol of unity: hence in the midst of natural disasters in the 1780s, or fear of foreign threat in and after the first decade of the nineteenth century, the symbolism of the institution was enhanced.[13] In the wake of the downfall of the Tokugawa dynasty in 1868, it was greatly added to by the new power brokers of Japan to legitimise their own authority. By putting some limit to the powers of a ruler, the shadowy but real implication of a constitution made it somewhat easier for Tokugawa to command allegiance and for others to concede it. While over time many of the smaller *tozama* daimyo were ruthlessly dispossessed, an implicit understanding existed with the powerful lords of western Japan. Tokugawa Japan began and ended with events there: in 1600, acceptance by Choshu and Satsuma of a Tokugawa dynasty after Ieyasu's incomplete military victory; in 1867, alliance between the two han bringing the 265 years of the Tokugawa dynasty to an end.

The Japanese invasions of Korea in the 1590s are a major event in Japanese history, standing between the preceding isolation and, immediately afterwards, the resumption of relative seclusion. A huge Japanese invading force landed near Pusan in 1592 and, fanning out in eight columns, reached Seoul quickly. Eventually, driven back, it continued to hold the region around Pusan, which became the bridgehead for another thrust by an almost equally large army in 1596. The Japanese armies usually prevailed on land; the weakness on both occasions was Japan's poor resources at sea, with Korean ships cutting off the lines of communication. They had to contend further with the forces of the Chinese Ming dynasty intervening in support of the Korean king, with a hostile Korean population and the insufficiency of rice in economically poor Korea to sustain the armies. Inevitably, the two invasions were followed by bouts of negotiation; the death of Hideyoshi in 1598 finally provided the excuse for ending an invasion whose successful outcome had already proved beyond Japanese resources.[14] Indeed, if it were to continue, by increasing reliance on *tozama* manpower, it would have had repercussions on central authority.

---

[13] See chapter 4, pp.117–18.
[14] Kitajima Manji, *Toyotomi Hideyoshi no chōsen shinryaku* [Hideyoshi's invasion of Korea] (Tokyo, 1995). In English, there is is a clear account in *CHJ*, vol. 4, J. W. Hall and J. L. McClain (eds.), *Early Modern Japan* (Cambridge, 1991), pp.265–93.

The Japanese armies in Korea had consisted mainly of forces from the south, the region imperfectly crushed in 1587 by Hideyoshi. Though both Kaga, the powerful uncommitted han (the word han signifying a daimyo principality)[15] on the west coast, and Tokugawa Ieyasu, Hideyoshi's most powerful lieutenant, sent forces to Kyushu, they did not cross to Korea. Why did the southern han participate (apart from the obvious reluctance to offend their recent conqueror)? One reason may have been the hope of territorial acquisition, wealth and occupation in Korea. The southern han had larger samurai forces than the weaker han of the central regions of Honshu, and defeat in 1587 had created problems of livelihood for their samurai. The eclipse of Satsuma, which had at one stage conquered half of Kyushu, was as much made possible by resentment both in Kyushu and on the southern shores of Honshu of its expansionism as by the force of Hideyoshi's own forces. After the loss of its former conquests, Satsuma's swollen samurai force of 30,000, easily the largest in Japan, was confined in reduced circumstances to its old heartland. When Hideyoshi's forces occupied Seoul, one of his first steps was to appoint a bugyo or governor, which suggests that he envisaged a permanent administration in Korea. However, with virtually no forces of his own in the invasion force, Korea offered a vista of compensatory expansion of territory for powerful Kyushu han like Satsuma and Saga. For Hideyoshi, a successful bridgehead under the control of a bugyo nominated by him would have warded off any prospects of disaffected han finding succour abroad, using foreign trade to acquire muskets, or even creating a satellite territory of their own across the waters. The concept of bridgeheads was central to Hideyoshi's foreign preoccupations: at the outset of the 1590s, after the subjugation of the two most northerly han in Honshu, he extended to the Matsumae family recognition of their minuscule stake in Ezo-ga-shima (the future Hokkaido), and in the south in the 1590s he indicated his approval to Satsuma for a project of invading the Ryukyus (his approval itself being a recognition of the need to placate Satsuma ambitions). It is sometimes suggested that the aim of Hideyoshi's invasion was the hope of advancing the legitimacy of his rule by securing recognition by China, or creating an empire which would embrace China itself. However, even if his language sounded exalted, his underlying aims had been much less ambitious.[16]

The increased use of cash and centralisation of resources made necessary by the campaigns over decades of Nobunaga and Hideyoshi turned

---

[15] The term han for the territory ruled by a daimyo or 'prince' is of very late origin. The term in the sixteenth century – and much later – was *ryōgoku*.

[16] M. E. Berry, *Hideyoshi* (Cambridge, Mass., 1989), pp.216, 234.

Osaka (close to Kyoto and to the home regions of both Nobunaga and Hideyoshi), as centre of the rice trade, into the economic base of the new power in central Japan. By the 1590s it was already drawing in rice from the south of Honshu and from Kyushu.[17] That meant more cash in the south, which also benefited from the boom. A surplus of silver and a demand for luxury goods led in turn to a boom in foreign trade, even if one, because of its high value in proportion to bulk, conducted in a small number of vessels. Moreover, prospects of foreign trade led to a Spanish interest in Japan in the 1590s and soon afterwards to a Dutch and English interest. The southern han stood to be the most immediate beneficiaries because they guarded the trade routes. Trade could create wealth for *tozama* daimyo, among the most independent of daimyo, and could also give them access to firearms (which had proved their worth at Sekigahara). Japan's output of silver was already increasing; it was making Japan into both magnet and lynchpin of trade in the region; and Hideyoshi's fear of Christianity (reflected in a ban on Christianity in 1587, and in 1597 in the execution of twenty-six Christians, Spanish Franciscans and others in Nagasaki) can be seen more as a crude expression of a strategic concern than of a religious one.

Thus, in the Japan of the early seventeenth century, there were three interrelated features: economic boom, a strengthening of its constitutionally precarious central authority, and novel foreign contacts. Hence trade had to be controlled. Even before 1598 Hideyoshi had made systematic a use, known to his predecessors, of red-seal permits (*shūinjo*) for Japanese ships; under the new regime, well in place by 1604, red seals were granted to 150 named parties for 350 ships up to the end of the system in 1633, or an average of almost 12 a year.[18] The red-seal system reflected the weakness as much as the strength of the shogunate (administration of the shogun). Red seals to Kyushu daimyo, including Satsuma, meant that, in contrast to the successful Tokugawa effort for revenue reasons to control mining (mostly in Honshu), it proved impossible to turn foreign trade, conducted from Kyushu, into a Tokugawa monopoly. Nine or ten Kyushu daimyo received red seals, and the main beneficiaries among

---

[17] *Osaka fu-shi* [History of Osaka administrative district], 7 vols. plus supplementary vol. (Osaka, 1978–91), *kinsei* [Early modern period], pt. 1, vol. 5 (Osaka, 1985), p.525.

[18] Hamashita Takeshi and Kawakatsu Heita, *Ajia kōeki ken to Nihon kōgyōka 1500–1900* [The Asian trading region and Japanese industrialisation 1500–1900] (Tokyo, 1991), p.105. In the peak period from 1606 to 1617 red seals were granted to 80 named parties in respect of 178 vessels (*Osaka shi-shi* [History of Osaka city], 10 vols. (Osaka, 1988–96), vol. 4 (Osaka, 1990), p.143). On the passport system at large, see also *Osaka shi-shi*, vol. 4, pp.139–64.

them were the daimyo families of Shimazu and Matsuura (Satsuma and Hirado respectively).[19]

Peace, an expanded area of cultivation and increased productivity, growth in domestic trade and a mining boom, all in combination laid the basis of the vibrant society and economy which Meiji Japan would inherit much later in 1868. The long period from the beginning to the end of the Tokugawa era was of course punctuated by both booms and depressions. The expansion of early Tokugawa times was followed by a heady boom in the Genroku period (1688–1704), and by the perhaps even greater, because widely diffused, prosperity of the Bunka and Bunsei periods from 1804 to 1830. Food shortages recurred frequently in the north-east or Tohoku region, but shortages which affected the whole nation to the point of famine were less common: in the seventeenth and eighteenth centuries, they occurred only in the early 1640s, 1732 and 1786–7. Later the Bunka–Bunsei prosperity itself was to be followed by the Tempō famines of the 1830s, with famine in one year, between 1836 and 1837, reaching far south. Despite vagaries of climate and food production, the longer-term economic trend was favourable. Equally, political circumstances followed a cycle of their own of alternating foreign menace and domestic security. The sense of external crisis in Hideyoshi's time was revived in 1614–15 by the rebellion of varied dissident forces which gathered about Hideyori (Hideyoshi's son, whom Tokugawa Ieyasu had done out of his political inheritance). Two later occasions, the Shimabara rising in 1637–8 which attracted a wide range of dissidents (including Christians) in Kyushu, and the final victory in China of Manchu forces over the Ming dynasty in the 1680s, prompted rekindled fear of outside intrusion. However, a near-century of ease followed from the 1690s until the 1780s, when a small Russian movement southwards in the Kurils created uncertainty and fear over the northern frontier.

If there was a long-term internal crisis, it was one of public revenue, and of inability to solve a fiscal problem. From the rice-producing land they held as their directly managed demesnes, daimyo and shogunate alike received a revenue of some forty to fifty per cent of the nominal output; from the remainder of the land within their territory they received no benefit, and its output provided an income shared between samurai and occupying peasants. In other words, in the case of a han, the bulk of the land provided its ruler with no revenue: it provided variously the

---

[19] *Nagasaki ken-shi* [History of Nagasaki prefecture] (Tokyo, 1973–85), *Taigai kōshō* vol. [External relations] (Tokyo, 1985), p.162.

income of collateral branches of the ruling family and of the samurai and in every case of the occupying peasants. The shogun was no different from a daimyo. Of his lands, some sixty per cent directly held in his possession (*tenryō*) provided the income of the shogunate and of the peasants who worked them; the remaining forty per cent, either occupied by, or its income earmarked for, his hatamoto (the term which denoted the senior samurai of the shogun), provided neither the shogun nor his family with an income. In the case of Yoshimune (1684–1751), he struggled throughout his period of rule (1716–45) with the problem of the rice income of the shogunate. In 1724 the levy was imposed on a permanent agreed assessment instead of being settled annually by haggling between shogunal officials and peasants. This could be more advantageous than the existing system for the shogunate (with its possibilities of either oppression or connivance or corruption), and it was not unfair to occupiers as built into it was a principle of rebate in the case of disastrous harvests. However, it also broke down. The variation in returns to the shogunate in various periods in the reign, while it has been seen as a result of success or failure in shifting practices in policy, reflected more the fluctuating harvest outcomes themselves. As time went by, increasingly in the governance of Japan, whether in the shogunate based on Edo or in the han, the phenomenon of poor government and poor samurai or officials in an increasingly rich country emerged.

The key problems of Japan were fiscal and defence ones. The fiscal challenge was to find a way to increase the income of government; the defence one was not simply of how to resist the danger of foreign invasion, but of how to finance resistance, a task all the more intimidating as there was no central revenue to enlarge military expenditure. The foreign threat created *gaiatsu*, or foreign pressure; and foreign pressure in turn played a central role in forcing Edo governments to resort to either innovation or desperate expedients, neither of which enjoyed consensus. Thus, in politically secure times in the 1720s, the highly experienced and greatest of the shoguns, Yoshimune, toyed with new methods of taxation and then abandoned them; in 1822 Ienari (1773–1841), with the longest period of reign of any shogun, abandoned, once the foreign – or Russian – crisis seemed to be over, the novel administrative responsibilities from 1799 assumed for Ezo. On the other hand, Tanuma Okitsugu, prime minister in the 1770s and 1780s, and Mizuno Tadakuni (1794–1851), a successor at the end of the 1830s, in the wake of foreign threat and famine, resorted to harsh methods of income generation. These did not command ready consent, were quickly abandoned, and their controversial approach enshrined both men in history as tyrants. The same fate befell Ii Naosuke (1815–60) in 1858 who, faced with the demand of western powers to turn a new and limited presence established in 1854 into a wide-ranging trade, resorted to quick action and draconian methods to enforce compliance from his subjects. His assassination in 1860 has been seen as the loss of the strong man who could have led Japan into an open world. More accurately, he deprived the regime of the moral authority that might have secured its survival. More recent historiography has sometimes done the same thing for Tokugawa Yoshinobu (1837–1913), the fifteenth and last of the shoguns. Ignored in much writing, he has been turned into the man who might have saved Tokugawa Japan.[20]

In 1600 Ieyasu faced two challenges, one internal, establishing the legitimacy of his own authority, the other external, that of relations with both Korea and western traders, an issue itself relevant to the pursuit of internal peace. At the outset, he inherited failure in Korea, and his military victory at Sekigahara had not really crushed the southern han who had fought against him. If he were to force himself on the south, he would face the armies which had constituted the backbone of the Korean invasion forces and who would outnumber his army. Rice represented the ability to keep an army in the field; even a century later, his successors' territories (*tenryō* and hatamoto lands combined), most of them far from the south, represented only a quarter of the rice output of Japan. These circumstances explain why the control of mining wealth in the boom of the early seventeenth century had been vital to Tokugawa solvency. Even including the *sanke* (the three domains created by Tokugawa Ieyasu's land grants to the three brothers of his heir), other houses with a blood or honorific relationship to the Tokugawa dynasty and the *fudai*, the shogunate accounted for only two thirds of the output of Japan. In the south of Honshu and in Kyushu, *tenryō* lands were minute. War, far from the economic base of Tokugawa financial strength and against large and samurai-rich han, could be a daunting prospect. The consequence of Ieyasu's moderation was both the acceptance by the han of his dominance and his legacy to later times, and to modern textbooks, of the image of the founder of order, stability and prosperity.[21]

Korea itself was a vital link in the chain of securing order both on the external front and in Kyushu. Ieyasu made peace in protracted negotiations with Korea, and the large Korean embassy of 1609 was a prelude to a later series of diplomatic missions from Korea, usually after the accession of

---

[20] A recent NHK drama series revived interest, and there had been an outpouring of books on the subject of the last shogun. The historical novelist Ryōtarō SHIBA was, however, well ahead of the fashion with his book, *Saigo no shōgun* [The last shogun] (Tokyo, 1967).

[21] There is a short and readable biography by Conrad Totman, *Tokugawa Ieyasu* (San Francisco, 1983).

a new shogun.[22] Relations with Korea were the centrepiece of Japanese diplomacy. Almost a third of the pre-1825 section of the great collection of diplomatic precedents compiled in 1849–52, when the Japanese were preparing to meet a new challenge, concerned Korea.[23] The somewhat unequal diplomacy of Korean missions unreciprocated by Japanese ones satisfied Japanese concerns more than Korean ones. While the missions offered the Koreans some reassurance of Japanese goodwill and hence Japanese overtures were responded to, the underlying theme on the part of the Koreans was to keep actual contact to a minimum. Korea, invaded by Japan in the 1590s and vulnerable on its land frontiers as incursions by Manchu forces in the 1620s and 1630s showed, became an even more hermetically sealed country, far more isolated than Japan. Japanese traders (and only from Tsushima) were confined to the port of Pusan and the number of vessels not only limited but confined to vessels sailing to and from the small island han of Tsushima in the strait separating Japan and Korea. In other words, trade was an exchange between an isolated country and an even more closed country. Confinement of trade to this channel, with a good deal of superintendence from Edo, answered the security purposes, domestic and external, of the shogunate.

Foreign trade as a source of direct profit was not central to the policy of Tokugawa Ieyasu. His revenues were already expansive both because he and his successors secured control of the mines in Japan, and rice cultivation, as it spread northwards, enlarged the output of shogunal demesnes. Output on *tenryō* lands was further enhanced in the seventeenth century by massive investment in irrigation and flood control. The control of trade rather than the profits of trade was the central feature of policy. The failed attempt at establishing a Korean bridgehead had already reflected a security concern. The transfer of Nagasaki, the port which the Jesuits had founded in 1570, from Portuguese or Jesuit ownership into direct management by Hideyoshi in 1587 arose from political concern over Kyushu.[24] Moreover, when the policy of granting permits to Japanese vessels was resorted to, they were granted primarily for trade to distant regions and, Taiwan apart, not to China. As far as silk is concerned, Macao, base for the Portuguese stake in east Asia, remained

---

[22] For a discussion of this diplomacy, see Nakao Hiroshi, *Chōsen tsūshin shi to Tokugawa bakufu* [History of diplomatic ties with Korea under the Edo bakufu] (Tokyo, 1997). There is a very solid analysis in English by R. P. Toby, *State and diplomacy in early modern Japan: Asia in the development of the Tokugawa bakufu* (Stanford, 1991).

[23] Naikaku bunko, Tokyo, Tsūkō ichiran. It was published in 1913, and reprinted in more recent times.

[24] On the origins of Nagasaki, see Diego Pacheco, 'The founding of the port of Nagasaki and its cession to the Society of Jesus', *Monumenta nipponica*, vol. 25, nos. 3–4 (1970), pp.303–23.

the main centre of the silk trade, and the Portuguese usually provided more silk than Chinese traders and red-seal ships combined. There has been an overemphasis on the significance of Will Adams (1564–1620), the Englishman who had been second in command of the Dutch fleet which arrived in 1600, and who is sometimes presented as Ieyasu's man of business. Adams spent much of his time near Sunpu, Tokugawa's main residence, but more because he was useful as a foreigner in liaising with Dutch-speaking and English-speaking outsiders than as a lieutenant in building up a direct Tokugawa stake in foreign trade.[25]

Trade presented many problems. From one point of view, the foreigners were essential as a source of supply of silk, and as an outlet for silver; not only the Portuguese, the real beneficiaries of the China–Japan standoff, but the Dutch and English who in 1609 and 1613 also opened up trade.[26] The small Japanese communities abroad were to be found only in far-afield areas such as Siam. In the Siamese capital of Ayutthaya, at a peak there were 1,500 Japanese.[27] In all there were some 3,000 Japanese abroad in the 1630s.[28] This was far short of the size of Chinese communities in Japan or elsewhere. All foreigners raised security issues, none, however, as acutely as the Spanish. While the allocation by the papacy of separate zones of influence for the Portuguese and Spaniards in the Pacific had left Japan within the Portuguese ambit, the conquest of Portugal by Spain which lasted from 1580 to 1640 whetted Spanish ambitions of spreading its influence beyond the Philippines, and the presence of Spanish missionaries in Japan in the mid-1590s was followed by efforts to open up trade. Japanese suspicions are sometimes said to have been aroused by careless or arrogant remarks by Franciscans or by Spanish officials in the mid-1590s. The Japanese did not depend, however, on overheard comments to come to their own conclusions. Spain's dominant position in the Philippines, acquired in 1571, was potentially much more dangerous than Portugal's small trading colony in Macao, hemmed

---

[25] Adams and his contemporaries Cocks and Saris are by the standards of the time unusually well represented in surviving correspondence, giving intimate detail lacking in all other accounts of the period, Japanese and Dutch alike. For a modern telling of the story, see R. Tames, *Servant of the shogun* (Tenterden, 1981). Derek Massarella's *A world elsewhere: Europe's encounter with Japan in the sixteenth and seventeenth centuries* (New Haven, 1990) also uses much of the evidence.

[26] The first Dutch vessels arrived in 1600, but the first effective commercial fleet reached Japan only in 1609.

[27] Ishii, *Junk trade*, p.2.

[28] Ichimura Yūichi and Ōishi Shinzaburō, *Sakoku: yuruyaka-na jōhō kakumei* [Sakoku: a gradual information revolution] (Tokyo, 1995). Marius Jansen has somewhat colourfully referred to 'a tide of Japanese adventurers', providing 'some idea of a trend, that, had it been permitted to continue, might have been very significant for later Japanese and world history' (Jansen, *China in the Tokugawa world*, p.19).

around by Chinese. On the commercial front, Spain was a rival of Japan in exporting silver in east Asia, and more importantly a rival in seeking silk (the basis of the trade from central America to the Philippines was silk purchased by means of silver). In other words, the Spanish interest in Japan did not have a powerful trading rationale (and the small amount of trade was in Japanese red-seal vessels to Manila). Spain represented a political or strategic danger and, in contrast to the English who simply abandoned their trade as unprofitable in 1623, the Spaniards were the first people to have a formal overture for trade rejected in 1624.

The Portuguese played a central role in foreign trade: through their presence in Macao, the only territorial base of Europeans in China, they were relatively immune to local obstacles to trade encountered by Europeans, Japanese and Chinese alike. The Dutch lacked a Chinese base until they acquired by force an incomplete one at the outset of the 1620s in the underdeveloped island of Taiwan.[29] Nor did that base prove at first a challenge to the Portuguese hold on the silk trade. The danger of a semi-monopoly by the Portuguese was of course adverted to early in the day. In 1604, the purchase of raw silk was regulated by the Itowappu, a form of regulation of buyers intended to ensure that purchasing was monopsonistic. To combat the fear of a Portuguese monopoly, Chinese traders, some bringing silk from China, some from ports in the Chinese outreaches of south-east Asia, had not only to be tolerated but, despite misgivings, even encouraged.

Foreigners presented a military challenge because of the size of their vessels, their gun power and their sheer aggression towards Asians and one another. While Christianity with its missionary drive added to trading and military impetus, the Japanese did not clearly distinguish Christianity from other motives: it served as a sort of shorthand for all the aggression latent in the western presence in east Asia. The Portuguese stood out as the longest established outsiders, unique in their pattern of some intermarriage with Japanese, of a sequence of conversions to Christianity of daimyo and of the creation by their missionaries of a not insignificant native Christian population in northern and western Kyushu.[30] The *shūmon aratame chō* held in temples and intended to identify Christians,

---

[29] On Taiwan and the fall of the Dutch stake in 1662, see Yamawaki Teijirō, 'The great trading merchants, Cocksinja and his son', *Acta asiatica*, no. 30 (1976), pp.106–16.

[30] On the Portuguese in Japan, see Manuela and Jose Alvares, *Porutogaru nihon kōryū shi* [Intercourse between Portugal and Japan] (Tokyo, 1992); *Via orientalis: porutogaru to nanban bunka ten: mesase tōhō no kuniguni* [Via orientalis: Portugal and Nanban culture exhibition: voyages to eastern countries] (Tokyo, 1993). The latter volume has a translation in English of the text on pp.225–48. C. R. Boxer, *The Christian century in Japan 1549–1650* (Manchester, 1951) and *Portuguese merchants and missionaries in feudal Japan 1540–1640* (London, 1986); M. Cooper, *They came to Japan: an anthology of European reports on Japan 1543–1640* (London, 1965, new edn 1981) are important sources.

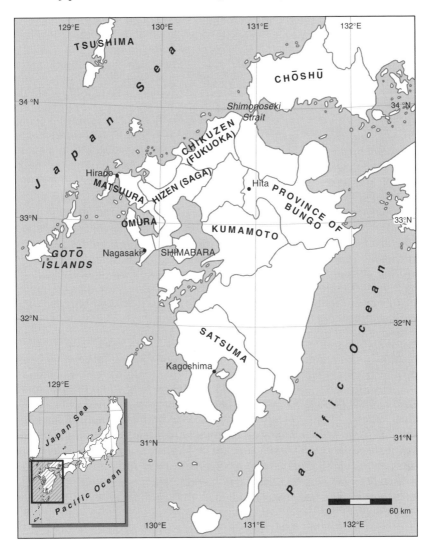

3. Han and towns of Kyushu mentioned in the text

often said to have started in post-1640 decades, began in the 1620s (the
second instance of such registers occurring from 1627 in Ōmura han in
Kyushu).[31] By contrast, the Dutch and English were late arrivals, and

---

[31] Ohashi Yukihiro, 'Kirishitan kinsei to shūmon aratame seido' [Christians in the early
modern period and the system of religious registration], in Fujita Satoru (ed.), *Jūnana
seiki no nihon to higashi ajia* [Seventeenth-century Japan and east Asia] (Tokyo, 2000),
p.71; Fujita, 'Mondai teiki' [Posing the problem], in Fujita, *Jūnana seiki*, p.8.

the beginning of their trade coincided with Japanese policy moving in 1614 into a markedly more restrictive mode. It is not clear that the Portuguese were excluded by virtue of a clear Japanese distinction between Portuguese Christianity and that of other European countries. Up to the end of the 1630s, an effort was made to draw a line between trade and religion in the case of policy.[32] Christianity itself had attracted prohibition in 1587 from Hideyoshi in his campaign in Kyushu and again in 1596–7, during the time of the second invasion of Korea, when the presence of Spanish Franciscans in Kyoto and indiscreet words by a Spanish sea captain led to the first executions in Nagasaki in 1597. Finally, under Tokugawa Ieyasu, the suppression of Christianity became a sustained policy from 1614 when a determined challenge by Hideyori and his followers in Osaka was taking shape. In the wake of an attack in 1628 off the coast of Siam on a Japanese red-seal ship by a Spanish galleon, the Portuguese trade (as the Portuguese were at the time under the suzerainty of Spain) was halted, and was not permitted to resume until 1630. A second *jiken* or incident – the Taiwan *jiken* of 1628, conflict between the Dutch and Japanese on the island – resulted in the halting of Dutch traffic from 1628 until 1632. In these years, encouragement of Chinese vessels had perforce to be positive.

When Portuguese ships reappeared in 1630 the trade at first soared to unprecedented levels. However, misgivings were such that as early as 1634 the decision was taken to confine the Portuguese to an artificial island (Deshima) in Nagasaki harbour. Before they could become prisoners of the island they were excluded entirely from Japan, less because they were Christians per se than because in a turbulent decade in Kyushu, their multiple ties over many decades with daimyo and subjects alike made them suspect. The Shimabara rising of 1637–8, occurring in a territory contiguous to Nagasaki itself, added to fears of their disloyalty. If the presence of the Dutch, themselves suspect, was to be tolerated, it could only be by their becoming in turn in 1641 the prisoners of Deshima. The bugyo of Nagasaki had visited Hirado the preceding year; the solid buildings of the Dutch alarmed him, and he ordered them to be pulled down. Both the prohibition of Dutch womenfolk and the admission of no women other than prostitutes to Deshima reflected the fear that, if not policed, the little community too could become the fifth column that the Portuguese were, or were imagined to have been. It was itself a continuation of policy applied in 1625 which aimed at preventing Portuguese

---

[32] This is one of the arguments of Nagazumi Yōko, *Kinsei shoki no gaikō* [External relations in the early years of the modern period] (Tokyo, 1990). For a summary of Nagazumi's views on this point in English, see Nagazumi, 'Japan's isolationist policy as seen through Dutch source materials', *Acta asiatica*, no. 22 (1972), pp.33–5.

from residing more than a year, and at breaking up family units.[33] It differed only in allowing the Dutch to stay beyond the year, but at the price of confining their numbers to a round dozen. However, residence by the head of the Dutch factory was limited by decree to a year (a requirement which was relaxed in much later times).

The security concern, moreover, was not confined to control of westerners. In 1609, when the Dutch trade was limited to Hirado, an order was made to confine the Chinese who arrived at many locations in Kyushu to Nagasaki. It was revoked two months later.[34] However, as dependence on the Chinese increased during the period of Portuguese and Dutch exclusion from traffic in 1628 to 1630 and 1632 respectively, the policy would inevitably be revived to end the menace of a diffuse Chinese presence along the coasts. By a decision in 1631, Itowappu buying was applied to Chinese ships, a step which reflected not only the urge to control the buying but the wish to confine trade to Nagasaki.[35] The policy finally became explicit in 1634 when dealings outside Nagasaki with Chinese ships were prohibited. The daimyo of Satsuma where, Nagasaki apart, the Chinese presence was most numerous, on his return from Edo gave orders for Chinese ships on their arrival off the coast to be escorted to Nagasaki.[36] A corollary of the policy at large was of course that Chinese residence outside Nagasaki was no longer permissible; it was to be also a strictly trade presence, and the Chinese were expected to return home before the winter. Chinese in 1639 were also ordered not to come accompanied by wives.[37]

The change was intimately linked to changes in the governance of Kyushu. None of Hideyoshi's bugyo actually resided in Nagasaki; one of them was even a Kyushu daimyo. From 1605 to 1625, members of the Hasegawa family, engaging in trade as well as looking after the trading interests of the first two Tokugawa shoguns, served as bugyo. A constant problem was a conflict of interest through local entanglements. Real change in the office began in 1626, and from 1633 the office was filled at any time by at least two bugyo, all hatamoto or shogunal officials from Edo or Osaka. Staying for relatively short periods, purely as administrators and during their service taking turns in a rotation between Edo and Nagasaki, they never became part of a local set-up. The bugyo, responsible for both the internal and external affairs of Kyushu, employed 1,041

[33] Nagazumi, 'Japan's isolationist policy', p.21.   [34] *Nagasaki ken-shi, Taigai kōshō*, p.139.
[35] *Nagasaki ken-shi, Taigai kōshō*, pp.177, 181–2.
[36] Yamamoto Hirofumi, *Kanei jidai* (Tokyo, 1989), p.52. For a succinct account in English of the Chinese trade in Nagasaki, see Jansen, *China in the Tokugawa world*, pp.9–34, 41.
[37] Hayashi Rokurō, *Nagasaki tōtsūji: dai tsūji Hayashi Dōei to sono shūhen* [Chinese interpreters in Nagasaki: chief interpreter Hayashi and his environment] (Tokyo, 2000), p.2.

clerks by 1681, almost double that figure by 1724.[38] Their administration was thus to become the largest office in Japan, larger even than the *Kanjōsho* in Edo which was simply an accounting office – on a huge scale – for the income and expenditure of the directly held territories of the shogun. In 1633, suspected of disloyalty, the daimyo family of Kumamoto *han* was deprived of its possessions – the only radical move, post-1603, by the Tokugawa regime against a major *tozama* house. However, under its new daimyo family it remained a *tozama han*. Despite the sensitivity of Kyushu, the shogunate was careful not to upset the balance of forces by adding to its *tenryō* or by creating *fudai han*. Its only large holding was a block of land, held from Hideyoshi's time, around the strategically located little castle town of Hita. It was itself one of the largest single *tenryō* administrations in Japan (rated at 124,000 koku in the 1830s), which gave it and its *daikan* (or intendant) a significance in Tokugawa housekeeping terms. However, it accounted c.1700 for an insignificant five per cent of the valuation of Kyushu.[39] Hita itself derived its significance from the road which ran along the southern frontier of the fertile flat lands of the north of Kyushu and which at Hita intersected with the roads which, along precipitate river valleys, penetrated the central mountain fastnesses. Its site led to its becoming the location of one of the largest and most important schools of early nineteenth-century Japan.

Just as steps in 1609, 1614 and 1616[40] foreshadowed the sakoku policy of the 1630s, the presence of hatamoto bugyo signalled the new vigour in dealing with the security problems of Kyushu which would culminate in a more clear-cut policy in that decade. Japanese contact with the outside world, a source of both entanglements (well illustrated in the two *jiken* of 1628) and a possible conduit of disaffection into Japan, was brought to an end by the famous series of five ordinances from 1633 to 1639, which are broadly the sakoku policy as described in modern texts, when westerners and Chinese alike were restricted to dealings in Nagasaki. The

---

[38] Toyama Mikio, *Nagasaki bugyō: Edo bakufu no mimi to me* [The Nagasaki bugyo: the eyes and ears of the Edo bakufu] (Tokyo, 1988), pp.68–9. There is little detailed knowledge on the staffing of the bugyo office in Nagasaki, and for the fullest account available, see the account of numbers and structures in *Nagasaki ken-shi, Taigai kōshō*, pp.394–404. For a detailed list giving 1,754 names which survives for 1855, and has been recently published, see *Yorozu ticho* (Nagasaki kenritsu toshokan, 2001, pp.730–65). Recently Nakamura Tadashi in 'Nagasaki bugyōsho kankei monjo ni tsuite' [On the subject of the Nagasaki bugyo office documentation], in *Nagasaki bugyōsho kankei monjo chōsa hokoku sho, Nagasaki ken bunkazai hōkoku, dai 131 shū* (Nagasaki-ken Kyoiku iinkai, 1998), pp.1–21, has illustrated the changes at the end of the Bakumatsu period (p.9).

[39] Fujino Tamotsu, *Kyūshū to tenryō* [Shogunal domains and Kyushu] (Tokyo, 1984), pp.21–3.

[40] In 1609 an abortive effort was made to confine the Chinese to Nagasaki, in 1614 the ban on Christianity was renewed, and in 1616 European ships were formally confined to the two ports of Hirado and Nagasaki.

Dutch trade in Hirado had been a self-regulating activity: the interpreters essential to the conduct of operations were hired by the Dutch and were in effect Dutch employees. At least eleven of the interpreters in Hirado were transferred to Nagasaki, and provided the nucleus of a corps of interpreters who were shogunal officials.[41] From 80 private employees in Hirado the number grew to 150 officials in Nagasaki. A still larger corps – larger because the number of Chinese was greater – was built up to handle relations with the Chinese as they also finally came to be restricted to a single centre. The Japanese word – *tsūji* – is wider in its implication than the Dutch word *tolk* (interpreter): they were in effect a corps combining the roles of interpreters, customs officials, clerks specialised in foreign business, and security officers.

Precisely because both Dutch and Portuguese were objects of fear, orders were given at the time to increase exchanges through the relative safety of Tsushima, an island halfway between Kyushu and Korea. Distrust of the Dutch was scarcely less than of the Portuguese. Almost immediately after their return to trade in 1632, they had made a *hofreis* (visit to the capital) in 1633, and it became an annual requirement from 1636. The requirement, in effect a form of *sankin kōtai*, was also far more draconic than that imposed on daimyo. It limited scope for mischief by requiring the *oranda kapitan* to spend three months each year on the road or in Edo. The fears were hardly allayed in 1643 by a voyage northwards by two Dutch vessels along the east coasts of Japan for the purpose of exploring the coast of Tartary: one of the vessels put some of its crew ashore and they were made prisoner.[42] Fears were heightened by two Portuguese warships sailing in 1647 into Nagasaki bay to test the determination of the Japanese.[43] Forces were brought from other han from as far afield as Shikoku. Some 48,000 men manned the shores, and from a fleet of 898 vessels a barrier of boats was drawn across the bay. Defence arrangements in Nagasaki were increased. Saga from 1644 was required to provide men for the defence of Nagasaki, and Fukuoka was soon required to do so also, each han in rotation providing 600 to 900 men: their *sankin kōtai* was reduced to 100 days in recognition of the burden. Orders were also given for permanent stations or lookouts at twenty-one points around Kyushu.[44] A key location in this chain of defences was

---

[41] *Nagasaki ken-shi, Taigai kōshō*, p.689.
[42] Yamamoto, *Kanei jidai*, pp.220–3. On the negotiations which followed the arrest of the Dutch, see R. H. Hesselink, *Prisoners from Nambu: reality and make-believe in seventeenth-century Japanese diplomacy* (Honolulu, 2002). The episode illustrated Japanese unease about the Dutch, and led to an effort by the Japanese to get an embassy from Europe, not simply one from Batavia. Hesselink's account is an interesting one of this obscure episode, though his tale depends on a good deal of supposition.
[43] Yamamoto, *Kanei jidai*, pp.213–18.   [44] Yamamoto, *Kane jidai*, pp.107–8.

Satsuma, as currents often carried vessels to its coast as the first sighting of Japan. Satsuma's observance of the duty remained part of the implicit compact between Satsuma and the shogunate for the next 220 years. Chinese shipping, carried by wind or currents to Satsuma on its way to Nagasaki, was accosted by patrol boats and accompanied or towed to Nagasaki.[45] The Ryukyus trade itself, conducted on either Ryukyu or Satsuma vessels, would not be regulated, and in return Satsuma played its part in the commonly shared interest in protecting the country against outside intrusion.

If the western threat receded after 1647, the challenge to the existing Ming dynasty by the advance in China of the Manchu (Ching) invaders, who had intruded into Korea in the 1620s and again in the 1630s, added to Japanese fears: the breakdown of Ming order could lead to invasion of Japan. While it has been claimed that the Japanese policy directed against Europeans was a purely practical one of excluding individual countries from trade but not decreeing a blanket exclusion, the reality was that it was part of a broad defence policy increasingly dictated by fears over China. The concern lasted into the 1680s and beyond. The struggle between Ming and Manchu worsened in the 1660s in coastal China, with both Ming loyalists driving the Dutch out of Taiwan in 1662, and the Manchu ordering the inhabitants to vacate the coasts of China. In these years, Chinese trade overseas inevitably contracted quite sharply from the high level to which it had recovered in the 1650s. As the prospect of a final Manchu victory in 1684 approached, the spectre of a Manchu invasion of Japan took shape. The book *Daigaku wakumon* (A discussion of public questions in the light of the great learning) by Kumazawa Banzan (1619–91), one of the most admired texts of Tokugawa Japan, is shot through with expressions of such a fear, further fed, once peace set in, by the arrival of an unprecedented number of Chinese vessels and the spectre of a fifth column. The Chinese visiting Nagasaki rose to 10,000 a year, some of those aboard the arriving vessels being an early breed of tourist.[46] The Chinese colony which hitherto could live freely within the city of Nagasaki was in 1689 confined to a large walled enclosure of about 230 by 130 metres. The famous account by Engelbert Kaempfer (1651–1716),

---

[45] Ishii, *Junk trade*, pp.57, 151, 141–2. On patrol boats from Hirado, see Ishii, *Junk trade*, pp.147, 253. An interesting perspective on the operation of the system is provided in the account of a Dutch soldier from the East India Company army who with five companions in a small boat reached land at an island off Satsuma in 1704. *De avonturen van een VOC-soldaat: het dagboek van Carolus Van der Haeghe 1699–1705*, ed. Jan Parmentier and Ruurdje Laarhoven (Zutphen, 1994).

[46] *Kaempfer*, p.224.

the doctor in the Dutch settlement, of the zeal of the inspection of the vessel on which he arrived in 1690, related to a period of high tensions. As the control of Chinese vessels and of their cargoes tightened, an obsession with smuggling emerged. Kaempfer noted in 1691 that more than 300 people had lost their lives within the last six or seven years, and in his two years of residence (1690–1) more than fifty had been executed.[47] The harshness of the anti-smuggling regime represented a heightened alarm. For the same reason, new vigour had been given in 1685 to the policy of examining books written in Chinese for fear of their containing any reference to Christianity.[48]

Security apart, Japanese doubts about the China trade and indeed about the unattractiveness of all foreign trade grew from mid-century, when declining mining output and growing domestic demand for currency combined to make the export of silver undesirable. The export of silver, it has been suggested, could have been on the highest estimates as much as 35,000 to 50,000 *kan* a year.[49] Such figures are doubtful. Raw silk (which accounted for sixty to seventy per cent of imports) amounted at most to 400,000 *kin* weight. If valued at 3 *kan* of silver per 100 *kin*, the total value would have been some 12,000 *kan*.[50] Even generously assuming that the total value of imports was double that figure, the outflow of silver by way of payment for imports should have been no more than 24,000 *kan*. For that reason, the highest figures suggested for the outflow of silver have to be regarded as suspect. Of course, both the commodity trade and the metal outflow were sizeable. Converted into sterling at £23.37 per *kan*, 24,000 *kan* of silver would have been £560,880. This is a substantial figure. However, to put it in perspective, English exports averaged £3.2 million in the 1660s.[51] The year-to-year trends in early Japanese trade are not clear, in part because while there are statistics

47 *Kaempfer*, pp.221–3. For further details, see *Kaempfer*, pp.227, 259, 391, 393–5, 397, 435, 437.
48 ITŌ Tasaburō, 'The book banning policy of the Tokugawa shogunate', *Acta asiatica*, no. 22 (1972), p.39. See also *Kaempfer*, pp.225, 226–7.
49 Souza, *The survival of empire*, pp.57–8. The total given in the text above is converted on the basis of a *tael* weighing 0.0375 kilogrammes (Souza, p.xvii), into *kan*.
50 Tashiro Kazui, 'Tsushima han's Korean trade, 1684–1710', *Acta asiatica*, no. 30 (1976), p.100. The figure of 3 *kan* may be a high price for the early seventeenth century. The price of silk before the restraints on its purchase in 1685 sent prices up was 2.3 *kan*.
51 The mint price per pound of pure silver was 67 shillings at the end of the seventeenth century (see T. S. Ashton, *An economic history of England in the eighteenth century* (London, 1954), p.168n). As Japanese silver, outside the periods of debasement, was eighty per cent pure, the price in effect was 53.6 shillings per pound or £23.37 per *kan* weight. The export figures are from Ralph Davis in Walter Minchinton, 'The Canaries in the British trade world of the eighteenth cenury', in Francisco Morales Padron (ed.), *IX Coloquio de historia Canario-Americana* (Las Palmas, 1990), p.678.

from Dutch sources,[52] there are fewer data for red-seal, Chinese and Portuguese vessels, and generalisation is complicated by the fortunes of individual branches varying widely in the short term. The number of Chinese vessels in the first three decades was about thirty a year until, favoured by the circumstances of the 1630s, they began to increase rapidly to a peak of ninety-seven vessels in 1639, and the outflow of silver reached 17,000 *kan* in 1640.[53] Shipments grew rapidly again from a reduced level of 10,000 *kan* in the late 1640s to a new peak in 1661 when 25,000 *kan* of silver were exported by the Chinese alone. A shortage of silver did not really exist before mid-century. The first shortage experienced had been of copper, and its export was for a while banned in the late 1630s and 1640s. Trade fell sharply in the immediate wake of the 1661 peak figure.[54] Moreover, war in China and Japan's own security preference ensured that from the 1660s a high proportion of the diminished number of vessels came from Chinese communities overseas and not from China proper.[55] A flurry of regulations in the 1660s and early 1670s regarding shipment of gold, silver and copper reflected official unease and uncertainty. The prohibition on exports of silver in 1668 was prompted by diminishing returns in mining and growing need of silver in Japan itself as both population and domestic trade expanded. For the Dutch, gold became their staple export in the short term and in the long term copper. After the initial prohibition, silver at a reduced volume was allowed to the Chinese vessels. Their exports averaged a low 5,952 *kan* in 1672–4.[56] Except to Tsushima, silver exports halted after 1685.[57]

[52] See KATŌ Eiichi, 'The Japanese-Dutch trade in the formative period of the seclusion policy: particularly on the raw silk trade by the Dutch factory at Hirado, 1620–40', *Acta asiatica*, no. 30 (1976), pp.34–84; *Tokyo daigaku shiryō hensanjo ho* [Reports of the University of Tokyo Historiographical Institute] (Tokyo, Shiryō hensanjo), vol. 3 (1968), pp.24–63, vol. 5 (1970), pp.76–9, vol. 6 (1971), pp.58–79; Yamawaki Teijirō, *Nagasaki no oranda shōkan sekai no naka no sakoku nihon* [The Dutch factory in Nagasaki, sakoku Japan and the outside world] (Tokyo, 1980), passim, especially pp.203–12.

[53] IWAO Seiichi, 'Japanese foreign trade in the 16th and 17th centuries', *Acta asiatica*, no. 30 (1976), p.11; Nagazumi Yōko, *Tōsen yūshutsu-nyūnyu-hin sūryō ichiran 1637–1833 nen: fukugen tōsen-kamotsu aratame-chō, kihan-nimotsu kaiwatashi-chō* [Survey of the volume of exports and imports on Chinese vessels] (Tokyo, 1987), p.8. For a table of ships, 1623–51, see Yamamoto, *Kanei jidai*, p.225.

[54] See also a graph of shipments of silver by the Chinese and Dutch in moving five-year averages, 1648–70, on p.146 in Hayami Akira and Miyamoto Matao (eds.), *Nihon keizai-shi* [Economic history of Japan], vol. 1, *Keizai shakai no seiritsu: 17–18 seiki* [The establishment of economic society, 17th–18th centuries] (Tokyo, 1988).

[55] Iwao, 'Japanese foreign trade', p.12; Ishii, *Junk trade*, p.10.

[56] Tashiro, 'Tsushima han's Korean trade', p.95. For details of the disposal of goods 1673–84 see *Nagasaki ken-shi, Taigai kōshō*, vol. 4, p.304.

[57] The downward path in exports of silver was clear even before 1685. From an average of 10,129 *kan* in 1648–55 and 12,626 *kan* in 1656–72, total exports averaged 6,183 *kan* over 1672–84. Thereafter they ceased (*Nagasaki ken-shi, Taigai kōshō*, p.307). Nevertheless

In addition to the prohibition of silver, other restrictions were imposed on the Chinese and their trade. In the immediate aftermath of peace in China in 1684, the number of Chinese vessels reached an unprecedented total of 199 in 1688.[58] While the rise itself merely represented the fact that Chinese vessels, resuming a long-interrupted foreign trade, threw everything on the nearest market and their activity was likely to lose momentum, the Japanese response was swift. Faced with the arrival of a soaring number of vessels, outward shipments were limited to a commodity value equivalent to 6,000 *kan* of silver (though the export of silver itself was not permitted); once that amount was reached, ships were sent away without being allowed to sell their incoming cargoes. As the mere presence of vessels created an opportunity for smuggling in or out (quite apart from adding to the menace of thousands of Chinese ashore), the strategy was further refined in 1688 to limit the number of vessels: the figure, at first fixed at seventy, was progressively reduced in subsequent decades. A requirement was later introduced of vessels not being permitted to arrive without securing a permit in advance. By these means the rise in the Chinese trade was reversed. The changes did not of themselves adversely affect the trade with Chinese communities outside China: in 1689 fourteen or fifteen vessels arrived from Siam; in 1696 the total from Siam (including the independent territory of Songkla) and Cambodia was twenty-five or twenty-six.[59] For the Dutch the limit to their trade was fixed at 3,000 *kan* (or more precisely its equivalent in other commodities, mainly gold or copper). Thus, assuming that the actual commodity outflow corresponded to the fixed limit on its size, the combined value of exports would have been a mere 9,000 *kan* of silver. The Tsushima trade, attractive to the Japanese because it involved dealing with the Chinese at third hand with traffic filtered through the intervening staging posts of Tsushima and Korea, had been favoured from the 1630s: approval of the trade was signalled also in the dispatch in 1635 of monks from the Gozan group of Zen monasteries in Kyoto (whose members had been known for centuries for their skill in reading and drafting documents in Chinese) to play a supervisory role.[60] While the peak year in the trade was 1694, it remained healthy, bringing in most of the reduced supply of silk purchased by Japan. Average total exports in 1684–1710 were valued at

small quantities of silver wrought in artifacts were tolerated in the China trade for several years after 1685.
[58] Nagazumi, *Tōsen yushutsu-nyū-hin sūryō ichiran*, p.19.
[59] Ishii, *Junk trade*, pp.53, 75, 150, 180.
[60] Ichimura and Ōishii, *Sakoku*, p.50. On the Gozan monks, see Martin Collcutt, 'Zen and the Gozan', in *CHJ*, vol. 3, Kozo Yamamura (ed.), *Medieval Japan* (Cambridge, 1990), p.598.

2,977 *kan*, of which silver itself amounted to 1,791 *kan*.[61] This exceeded an officially sanctioned level of 1,000 *kan* of silver (an export privilege withdrawn from the Chinese in 1685), and may have reflected less violation of policy than official tolerance for the trade which best satisfied security considerations. The Tsushima trade is said in much of the modern literature to have been large. However, it was large only in the sense that it had a silver trade when none was permitted from Nagasaki, and that in a greatly reduced intake, silk imports through Tsushima quickly came to exceed those arriving in Nagasaki on Chinese vessels.

An officially sanctioned export of 1,000 *kan* of silver to Korea, added to the notional value of non-silver exports worth 9,000 *kan* in the Chinese and Dutch trades, gave a nominal export commodity total of 10,000 *kan*. The Ryukyus trade would add somewhat to the total of trade. Officially, it was at the outset limited to about 1,242 *kan*.[62] Its actual scale was unknown to the shogun's officials (as to attempt to regulate it directly would call in question the Tokugawa political settlement with the south). While those who worried in Nagasaki or in Edo about trade saw in it a source of abuse, in the last analysis the concern was less the volume of trade than the fact that it was de facto to a unique degree free from regulation. An export ceiling measured notionally as worth 10,000 *kan* of silver implied imports to the same value. An export trade – or an import trade – worth crudely 10,000 *kan* would have approximated to £233,700 sterling. As English exports in 1700 were £6 million, Japan's trade was by international standards minute. Even for a small country like Ireland for which good statistics also exist, exports in the same year were £800,000. Of course some trade was permitted in goods beyond the decreed upper limits, if it did not draw out of Japan goods which the Japanese wanted to retain. There was, however, a clear limit to it, as few Japanese goods were in demand overseas. This dilemma is reflected in the soaring exports of copper, the one Japanese commodity in universal demand. The Chinese took a staggering figure of 7,477,502 *kin* (74,213 piculs of 133 lb) by 1696.[63] Japanese copper went throughout Asia, and by the hands of the Dutch also reached Europe. Japanese output must have been the largest – and the highest quality metal – in the world, and the comparatively (i.e. in Japanese terms) small imports to Europe by the Dutch were a significant supplement to Spanish copper on the Amsterdam market.

[61] Tashiro, 'Tsushima han's Korean trade', pp.90, 95–6.
[62] Kaempfer noted that the trade was limited to 125,000 *tael* per annum. *Kaempfer*, p.228. The 1,242 *kan* in the text is a conversion of that figure.
[63] Yamawaki Teijirō, *Kinsei nichū bōeki-shi no kenkyū* [Studies in trade between China and Japan in the early modern period] (Tokyo, 1961), p.67, has a table of exports on Chinese vessels, 1684–97. A table in his *Nagasaki no tōjin bōeki* [Chinese trade in Nagasaki] (Tokyo, 1964), p.219, gives a breakdown of both Dutch and Chinese exports of copper.

The import trade in value (i.e. in terms of items significant to the balance of trade) consisted of silk and, in the eighteenth century, increasingly of sugar from China. Other items were not important in commercial terms, though often assuming an importance transcending their aggregate turnover. The most significant, for their medical value, not for their balance of payments importance, were medical and pharmaceutical products, Chinese but also Dutch. While data on quantities ceased from 1735, the shogunal authorities in 1820 ordered their recording. At that date no less than 400 distinct items were noted. Before 1820 details on imported items and on their prices can be studied from account books of various traders in Osaka.[64] If not in quantities significant for the balance of trade, a wide range of non-pharmaceutical items from Holland came in, imported either formally as merchandise or more privately by crew members of the Dutch vessels. Books, some paintings, but also, especially late in the eighteenth century, copper-plated engravings, glass, mirrors, eye glasses, mechanical gadgets, microscopes and magic lanterns all featured, quite apart from the sometimes very exotic items brought in as intended presents for the shogun. These items were widely diffused among a restricted group in Nagasaki but more especially within a well-placed Edo circle, either collectors of the exotic or alive to their artistic or scientific import. The flavour of the trade is captured fleetingly in 1799 in a reference to a consignment of 'several hundred Dutch copper plates [i.e. engravings]' which were returned to Europe as not pleasing the market.[65]

The coastal traffic of Osaka, if shipments inwards and outwards are aggregated, was worth on the evidence of figures for 1714 and 1766 about 300,000 *kan*.[66] The total foreign trade of Japan, inward and outward, even at its higher level of an earlier date, would have been a mere 22,484 *kan*.[67] The prohibition of silver and progressively tighter control of copper ensured that trade continued to fall. The number of Chinese vessels declined steadily over the eighteenth century, and the value of trade, as fixed in officially decreed quantities in *kan*, was further reduced. In 1719 the amount of Chinese trade was limited to 4,000 *kan*, and after many minor variations was fixed at 2,740 *kan* in 1791. Chinese vessels

---

[64] See chapter 14, 'Yakushu bōeki monjo' [Texts regarding trade in pharmaceuticals], in Miyashita Saburō, *Nagasaki bōeki to Osaka yunyū kara sōyaku e* [Nagasaki trade and Osaka: pharmaceutical products from import to warehouse] (Osaka, 1997), pp.250–67.

[65] T. Screech, *The western scientific gaze and popular imagery in later Edo Japan: the lens with the heart* (Cambridge, 1996), p.94.

[66] See chapter 4.

[67] Calculated from the regulation of trade in 1685 as 6,000 *kan* for China, 3,000 *kan* for Holland, 1,000 for Korea, and 1,242 for Satsuma, all multiplied by two on the assumption that imports matched in value the authorised level of exports.

were cut back to twenty in 1740, and to ten by 1791. By the late 1840s the actual number of Chinese vessels arriving was as few as four or five a year.[68] However, subject to strict scrutiny of cargoes inwards and outwards, the practice remained that the ceiling could be breached, subject to the exports being permissible.[69] The extra imports and exports were varied, and imports on occasion from as early as the second half of the eighteenth century included some silver on official account. The Dutch were limited to two vessels and from 1791 to one. The value of the Dutch trade permitted was officially stabilised in the range of 700–800 *kan* from the mid-1740s. For the Dutch, as for the Chinese, the supply of copper was the mainstay of business.[70] While a deaf ear was turned to Dutch requests for more copper, the Dutch trade in copper was quite large, amounting to 10,000 piculs a year (half the level of their exports of the late seventeenth century).[71]

The Dutch factory was losing money from mid-century though this may be mitigated if the profits on the sale of copper in Asia or Europe are taken into account. The Tsushima trade virtually folded up after midcentury, and Tsushima han became dependent on an annual subsidy from the shogunate. There were frequent attempts at regulation of the Ryukyus trade even from early times. A characteristic of later times was the effort to limit the range of items imported (more precisely the number of items sold in Nagasaki, as all Satsuma sales outside the han had to be channelled through Nagasaki). The idea was that if the range of goods was restricted, illegal silver exports would be contained. The permitted figure of 1,720 *kan* annually from 1818 to 1844 for the total trade[72] was not ungenerous given the small figure for the Chinese trade, and significantly had increased from the permitted level of the 1680s.[73] Exports from

[68] *Nagasaki ken-shi, Taigai kōshō,* pp.789–90.
[69] The permitted volume of exports was exceeded by 4,605 *kan* in 1804 and 6,477 *kan* in 1839. See Yamawaki Teijirō, *Nagasaki no tōjin bōeki,* pp.106, 199–209. For a brief account of the trade from the Chinese side, c.1834 see Takeshi Hamashita, 'The tribute trade system and modern Asia', in Latham and H. Kawakatsu (eds.), *Japanese industrialization,* pp.99, 102.
[70] For the Dutch and Chinese trade see the table in Nakamura Tadashi, *Kinsei Nagasaki bōeki-shi no kenkyū* [Studies in the history of early modern Japanese trade] (Tokyo, 1988), pp.372–3. There are differences with the figures given in Hayami and Miyamoto, *Nihon keizai-shi,* vol. 1, pp.149–50. For an account of the Dutch trade in a European language, see J. Feenstra Kuiper, *Japan in de buitenvereld in de achtiende eeuw* (The Hague, 1921).
[71] This of course greatly understates the contraction of the Dutch trade, as when silver was refused to them in 1668, they exported considerable quantites of gold in the 1670s and early 1680s. See the table in Yamawaki Teijirō, *Nagasaki no tōjin bōeki,* p.58, and for 1664–1762 Hayami and Miyamoto, *Nihon keizai-shi,* vol. 1, p.147.
[72] Nakamura Tadashi, *Kinsei taigai kōshō shi ron* [Study of the history of negotiations in the early modern period] (Tokyo, 2000), p.503.
[73] Kaempfer quoted the figure as 125,000 *tael* (*Kaempfer,* p.228) which would be the equivalent of 1,242 *kan.*

Japan, including shipments to Tsushima and the Ryukyus, as measured in the notional valuations in *kan* of silver of permitted trade, fell sharply from the 11,242 *kan* of 1685 to a mere 5,260 *kan* in the nineteenth century.[74] On this basis the Satsuma trade with the Ryukyus had gained greatly in relative importance; it was also the only branch of external trade which was expansive. Its Edo-sanctioned outlay at 1,720 *kan* was a third of the total permitted outlay on foreign trade. The English naval officer Broughton in July 1796 saw in the harbour of Naha in the Ryukyus 'twenty large junks at anchor, chiefly Japanese, from 200 to 300 tons burden'.[75] The trade can hardly have contracted in later decades, since in the 1860s British consular officials, at a time when the trade had been upset by political events, reported that the trade had formerly occupied around twenty vessels, fifteen or so from Satsuma sailing in the spring to the Ryukyus, and some four or five vessels belonging to the Ryukyu islanders.[76] Given Satsuma's effective immunity from interference by Edo officials in Nagasaki, the ships had a capacity to carry goods in excess of the decreed level of 1,720 *kan*.

A belief in a large smuggling trade, either through Kagoshima or by goods from Chinese vessels being unloaded into small boats off the coast of Kyushu, remained a persistent feature of official concern. A distinction has also to be made between the Satsuma trade – conducted exclusively on vessels from the Ryukyu islands and Satsuma – and the supposed smuggling from Chinese vessels about which officialdom was paranoid. However, given how few Chinese vessels were engaged in the Japan trade (except during the influx of Chinese vessels in the 1680s) and the fact that executions even for minute amounts of goods reflected the strictness of justice more than the scale of activity, such smuggling was probably not of great economic consequence.

A renewed drive against the trade in the 1830s, based both on existing and new intelligence, provides a rather good idea of its scale. The alarm was heightened by evidence that the Chinese had built warehouses and

---

[74] Earlier figures are for actual exports of silver. Figures for 1685 and later years are of notional maximum limits for export values, expressed in silver currency. The figures are, however, minimum estimates for exports and imports. Provided goods exported were not regarded by the Japanese authorities as of vital importance, an exchange of commodities beyond the notional ceiling to exports and imports could take place. In the case of the China trade, as the exchange of copper for silk contracted, the relative importance of the comparatively small trade in other goods, especially dyestuffs and medicines, increased, and notional figures understate by a significant margin the total volume of what remained a modest trade.

[75] W. R. Broughton, *A voyage of discovery to the north Pacific Ocean*, 2 vols. in 1 (London, 1804), vol. 1, p.239. He also saw there English broadcloth imported from China.

[76] *PP Japan*, vol. 5, p.681. When Kagoshima was shelled by the British in 1863, five junks from the Ryukyus were destroyed (*PP Japan*, vol. 2, p.109).

residences at a named location on the Satsuma coast. Powerless to act against activities within Satsuma, officials in Nagasaki, because the comparatively few Chinese vessels involved in the Japan trade typically combined legal and illegal activity, were able to act vigorously when owners and seamen appeared in Nagasaki itself. The *metsuke* Togawa, already at work in Nagasaki, was in unprecedented fashion given the acting rank of bugyo in 1836.[77] The number of vessels arriving in Satsuma rarely exceeded ten in a year, and estimates of precious metals taken away by them only once exceeded 500 silver *kan*, and usually fell well short of that figure. In other words, the value of this contraband trade paled beside both the legitimate Nagasaki trade and Satsuma's own trade with the Ryukyus. The activity represented a small but streamlined enterprise.

Restrictions such as those pursued by the Japanese were by no means unique. In the years immediately before 1722, a renewed ban on western trade was imposed in China.[78] This ban was prompted by fresh western efforts to trade. Limited concessions for trade at Canton were thereafter accompanied by rigid controls, contact was confined to dealings with Chinese official merchants, and tea constituted the main item.[79] The traffic never expanded beyond twenty to thirty European vessels a year, as fear of glut in Europe overhung the business.

Sakoku (national seclusion) is the term used in modern times to denote the policy introduced in the 1630s and applied until the 1850s. The term itself came into existence as a translation of the word *besluiting* in an appendix to Kaempfer's book which was translated from Dutch into Japanese by the Nagasaki interpreter Shizuki Tadao in 1801.[80] The appeal of the appendix lay in Kaempfer's favourable words on the policy of closing Japan:[81] the question as to whether concession to foreigners

---

[77] The drive against the trade in 1835–7 takes up a huge 25 *kan* or volumes of the published *Tsūkū ichiran zokushū* [*Tsūkū ichiran*, continuation], 5 vols. (Osaka, 1968–73), vol.1, pp.130–535. Togawa greatly upgraded the intelligence already available from 1825. The account by the Hayashi in the *Tsūkū ichiran zokushū* relies heavily on diaries or compilations by Togawa, and his importance is reflected in the fact that compilations by him survive in two locations in Nagasaki itself. The absence of comparable or indeed any concern about other locations suggests that officials saw the entire focus of the contraband trade at this time as centred on Satsuma. Of course, Chinese residence outside Nagasaki of itself warranted security as well as economic concerns.

[78] Ishii, *Junk trade*, p.99.

[79] L. Dermigny, *La Chine et l'occident, le commerce a Canton au xviii^e siecle*, 4 vols. (Paris, 1964).

[80] Ichimura Yūichi and Ōishi Shinzaburō, *Sakoku*, p.128; KATŌ Eiichi, 'Development of Japanese studies on sakoku (closing the country): a survey', *Acta asiatica*, no. 22 (1972), p.84. The translation was republished under a different title in 1850.

[81] The view expressed in the appendix is, it should be noted, much more favourable than that in the main text of Kaempfer's book. The main text appears to have followed closely diaries he kept at the time; the appendix was written many years later and more reflectively in Europe.

was unavoidable was under vigorous discussion around 1800. The term did not enter into current use in Japanese until the 1850s. The modern interpretation of sakoku has swung between a caricature of a repressive policy and a more benign perception. In particular, because the parameters of the policy were not set out or defined in the 1630s other than through the detail contained in five orders, recent writing has suggested that Japanese policy was neither one of a wholly closed economy nor even one of excluding foreigners. It was, it has been argued, dictated by a fear of Christianity, and if foreign countries which were not tainted by a Christianising policy had sought permission to trade, they could have been granted permission. In other words, in telling the Russian negotiators who had arrived in Nagasaki in 1804 seeking trade that Japanese law excluded foreigners totally (excepting, on restricted terms, the Chinese and Dutch), the Japanese were not stating the policy but reinterpreting it to introduce a new exclusion.[82] The problem with this line of argument is that it underestimates the scale of Japanese fears in the seventeenth century and their doubts even about the Dutch; it also sees sakoku in terms of trade policy rather than of overall policy, and ignores the fact that fear of Christianity was a form of shorthand for an omnibus fear about western intentions. The repeated statement in modern times that the English were turned down when they sought readmission to trade in 1673 because King Charles II was married to a Portuguese princess, is based on a mere assumption: because the *opperhoofd* or head of the Dutch trading post in Deshima was instructed in 1663 to stress the adverse implications of the royal alliance, this determined Japanese policy a decade later.[83] The Japanese raised the question of the princess in their negotiations with the English, but it was simply one of several issues on their mind. The pattern of the negotiations in their evasions and procrastination was remarkably similar to that of those with Laxman in 1792–3 or Rezanov in 1804, and included, in response to an English suggestion of opening negotiations again when the princess died, a firm statement that 'the emperor's commands admitted of no alteration'.[84] Likewise, the restoration

---

[82] Toby, *State and diplomacy*, pp.10–14, 241–2.

[83] IWAO Seiichi, 'Japanese foreign trade', p.16. A similar and even more forced view is evident in his earlier article in regard to the effect of representations by the Dutch on the decline of the Siam trade from the late 1680s ('Reopening of the diplomatic and commercial relations between Japan and Siam during the Tokugawa period', *Acta asiatica*, no. 4 (1963), pp.30–1).

[84] See *A copy of the Japan diary received on a Danish ship 18 July 1674 and given to Sir Robert Southwell by Sir Nathaniel Hearne*, p.10 (in Engelbert Kaempfer, *The history of Japan giving an account of the ancient and present state of that empire . . . to which is added, part of the journal of a voyage to Japan, made by the English in the year 1673*, 2 vols. (London, 1728), second appendix, separately paginated). The British trade request was noted summarily in the *Tsūkū ichiran*, vol. 6, p.353.

of diplomatic ties with Siam is not as open as it seems. As far as trade was concerned, the ships, both private and those on the account of the king of Siam, were fitted out and manned almost exclusively by Chinese.[85] Siam was a part of the 'Chinese' world with which Japan dealt, and the diplomacy represented a pattern of restoring relations at the outset of the 1660s with a region which supplied silk, at a time of progressively more difficult relations with China proper.

The China trade, supplemented by Satsuma's commerce with the Ryukyus and, before the 1750s, Tsushima's links with Korea, provided all the goods that Japan needed. Ezo at this time was unimportant, and did not figure in Japanese preoccupations until the 1780s. If trade links running from Nagasaki to Satsuma and Tsushima, for Ryukyu and Korean commodities respectively, created the framework for handling foreign exchanges, surveillance of them was central to political security. Tsushima held a monopoly of contact with a Korea which on the maritime front was otherwise hermetically sealed. The Ryukyus had a complex constitutional position: as in the case of Korea, occasional embassies, in all eighteen over two centuries, were sent to Edo. The status of the islands combined four elements: they had their own king, tribute paid to China denoted allegiance to the Chinese emperor, Satsuma had some degree of sovereignty over them by the conquest of 1609 (which however did not challenge the tributary status with China), and the missions to Edo denoted a diplomatic relationship with the shogun. The Ryukyus did not fit comfortably into sakoku; they traded with China, and Satsuma's trade with them was beyond effective shogunal regulation. A decade before Perry arrived in Japan the presence of some foreigners in the Ryukyus elicited uneasy acceptance by both Satsuma and Edo. The Ezo islands presented an even less defined position. The islands were almost unknown to seventeenth-century contemporaries, and outside the small enclave of Matsumae han inhabited by *Wajin* (Japanese) in the south-west of Ezoga-shima (i.e. the future Hokkaido), there were no defined frontiers, and no surveying had been undertaken before the 1780s. Of course, in 1604 Ieyasu had confirmed the position of Matsumae han in a charter. The Matsumae family were given the monopoly of contact with the Ainu. But the Ainu, their emerging contacts with Japanese apart, inhabited a vast

[85] See the detail in Chinese *fūsetsu* of vessels arriving from Siam in Ishii, *Junk trade*, pp.18–102. See also IWAO Seiichi, 'Reopening of the diplomatic and commercial relations', p.2. The only singularity of the trade is that a few Siamese, hardly ever more than two or three, were often included in the crews, and that this was accepted by the Nagasaki authorities. A report of a vessel in 1693 which included the uncommonly large number of four Siamese in a complement of 106, plus nineteen people from south-west Asia rescued at sea, observed that 'you might be suspicious of us for carrying foreigners on board this time in addition to tojin and Siamese' (Ishii, *Junk trade*, p.69).

and almost empty chain of islands. What were their contacts with foreigners, once a handful of Russians began to traverse the region? What was the status of this trade in Japanese jurisprudence as it lay beyond defined frontiers, and, if security required a frontier to be defined, where did it lie? Thus at both geographical extremities of the Japanese archipelago, sakoku, if for other purposes clearly defined by the five decrees of 1633–9 (unless modern interpretations which read ambiguities into them are accepted), dissolved into the complexity of multiple jurisdiction in the Ryukyus or into the sheer absence of geographical knowledge and known frontiers in Ezo. In the case of Ezo, it was this dilemma, not a rethinking of sakoku, which posed the practical problem that had to be faced around 1800.

Internal and external policy under Toyotomi Hideyoshi and again under the Tokugawa dynasty went together. Hideyoshi laid the basis of a policy which was completed by the Tokugawa regime. On the internal front, policy had three central features. The first was for military reasons the disarming of peasants (first evident in the so-called sword hunt of 1588); the second was defining social order in terms of well-defined social groups of samurai, peasants, craftsmen and merchants. In effect both these policies reflected a single concern: the reduction in the size of potential armies. This was reinforced post-1600 by a requirement of samurai living in the castle towns that prevented them from becoming leaders of peasant bands, and as a consequence armies would be confined to the relatively small samurai populations isolated from the countryside by urban residence. With some inevitable pragmatic acceptance of variations, daimyo were also limited to a single castle. The third feature was the execution of a national land valuation: land was graded into three qualities, and payment of levies by peasants to lord or samurai was made on the basis of this valuation. The conduct of a national valuation was in itself an enormous task (conscientiously, the regulations even required the surveyors to abstain from drinking sake in the course of their work). Its object can only have been fiscal: to ascertain the wealth of the component parts as the basis for levying tax in the future on the daimyo or han. Attempts at using the valuation for such purposes did not occur until the 1720s in the time of Yoshimune.

The incomplete victories by Toyotomi Hideyoshi and Tokugawa Ieyasu and the consequent delicate balance of power in Japan made it impossible to increase demands on the han. Yoshimune's attempt was explained by both the prestige of a politically powerful and secure shogun, and acute fiscal embarrassment. The weakness of central government was reflected in the original execution of the valuation: the surveying of the han, *fudai* and *tozama* alike, was conducted by daimyo officers and not by central officers, and local variations were so many that they make generalisation somewhat simplistic. The movement of samurai into castle towns was itself realistic only where the number of samurai was small. In Satsuma, the great bulk of the samurai continued to reside, under the name of *gōshi*, in the countryside. A somewhat similar pattern existed in Tosa, isolated, mountainous and poor. As in all regulation by the shogunate, variation was widespread, indicating either the inability of government to impose uniform regulation, or the sheer necessity of accepting local conditions. The weakness was most evident in fiscal incapacity: the shogunate dared not proceed beyond occasional arbitrary demands for stated great purposes. The demands were mitigated by their infrequency, and were compensated for by shogunal grants to han when they in turn were in distress.

Hostages had always been required as a basis of allegiance, and family members were demanded by both Hideyoshi and Ieyasu in the wake of their victories. At the time of the Osaka rebellion in 1614–15, a law settling han–shogunate relations was issued; and in the uneasy 1630s, when both the foreign threat and insubordinacy in Kyushu were feared, the celebrated *sankin kōtai* (attendance in Edo by rota) was introduced. In itself, the principle of giving hostages or of paying court was not novel. Only its systematic nature was an innovation. It entailed the permanent residence of daimyo wives and children in Edo, and the presence of the daimyo himself each second year. A complex rota was set out for the daimyo sojourns, and an even more elaborate timetable for the dates of travel of daimyo retinues across Japan. The results of the *sankin kōtai* have been seen as negative. It has been suggested that its purpose was to cause the wasteful expenditure of han resources (it absorbed as much as half of han official income). There is no evidence of this. Temporary dispensations were often granted in the wake of local distress. The daimyo of Matsumae, a very poor han, was required to make an infrequent *sankin kōtai*, and han like Saga and Fukuoka, which assumed in rotation the duty of providing a garrison to protect Nagasaki from invasion, were granted permanently a greatly reduced duration for their *sankin kōtai* sojourn. It had positive elements. In political terms, it was the price for the independency of the *tozama* in the crisis-ridden 1630s. More dynamically, it created daimyo with a metropolitan culture, just as the presence of daimyo gradually turned Edo from a cultural backwater into the intellectual centre of Japan. Educated in Edo when they were young, they became more attached to Edo life than castle-town life. If the *sankin kōtai* was in a way a burden on han, it was also an effort to limit the number of retainers which daimyo brought to Edo (this requirement was one of the few regular uses made of the arithmetic of the

Hideyoshi valuation). Emulation rather than frugality was the daimyo way of life. The presence also of samurai in Edo, meeting more freely than the daimyo, created an interchange of views, and provided a basis for interacting consensus and divides, often including contacts by ambitious or intellectual young men with shogunal retainers on policy matters. It played a vital role in establishing the intellectual and cultural homogeneity of the upper classes of Japan. Moreover, the traffic made necessary improved maintenance of roads, and a dense chain of inns and post-houses promoted not only local commerce which profited from passing traffic, but greatly facilitated the general movement of men, goods and knowledge.

Japan is usually described as divided into between 260 and 280 han (the precise number is impossible to enumerate because the shogun liquidated individual han, either absorbing them into his dominions or, from his fluctuating land bank, variously adding to the size of existing han or, by grants, creating new han). A picture of Japan in political terms as an amalgam of 260 han makes authority more diffuse than it was. Most of the han were small; they had few retainers and even fewer ones of intelligence; the rulers of small han carried little weight, either political or intellectual. In many instances, the han consisted of several isolated pieces of territory; residence in the han in a meaningful sense could not arise – there was not even a castle – and perforce life remained focussed more on Edo than on the countryside. The real political force of Japan resided in some three dozen large or middle-sized han, both *fudai* and *tozama*. The *fudai* han originated in supporters of Hideyoshi and Ieyasu. As such they owed fealty to the patron or his descendants, and they identified with the regime. The *tozama* were han whose origins were entirely independent of these bonds. Hence they were outside the household, so to speak, and never acceded to office in Edo government. It was this independence of origin, and separate existence, which distinguished them from the *fudai*. They were not necessarily hostile to the regime. In 1600 they had variously fought for or against Ieyasu or, like Kaga, remained neutral. Nor were they necessarily large; many of them were in fact small. Neither were they necessarily distant from Edo (the kanji, or character, for *to* in the word *tozama* is ambiguous, meaning 'outside' rather than 'distant'). Very naturally, changes were more likely in the number of the *tozama* than of the *fudai*, who were the most loyal of shogunal supporters: the number of small *tozama* fell in the seventeenth century. A consequence of the award of *fudai* status to followers meant that *fudai* were numerous in a protective circle around the land held directly by the shogun or by the collateral branches of the Tokugawa family: the great han, either in the south or north of Japan or, like Kaga, on the far side of the central mountain spine of Japan, seemed peripheral in a geographical sense. Excluding the *sanke* houses (the three han of Kii, Owari and Mito held by the collateral branches created by grants by Tokugawa Ieyasu to three younger sons),[86] the five largest han were all *tozama*. The greatest was Kaga, rated at over 1 million koku; Satsuma was third at 700,000 koku. The *sanke* were rated at 619,000 koku (Owari or Nagoya), 550,000 koku (Kii) and 350,000 koku (Mito). Of the related han, Fukui was largest at 320,000 koku. Among the *fudai*, sixteen were in excess of 100,000 koku, mostly by a small margin, and only one, Hikone (350,000 koku), could bear any comparison with *tozama* or *sanke*. Even a change in *tozama* daimyo did not necessarily alter things. The dramatic case is Tosa. Its daimyo family had been removed because of the military opposition of the family to central government, and a local retainer, rewarded with the han, created a new ruling dynasty. Yet, with a large warrior population, cut off by almost impenetrable mountain and forest fastnesses, Tosa retained a strong sense of its own identity, and in time the Tosa daimyo and his retainers because part of the opposition to shogunal government in the 1860s. Largest of the han was Kaga on the west coast; its large lowland plain and the protection that the central mountain spine of Japan gave it from autumn and winter winds from the north-east meant that it was also a rich han. Its army had not fought at Sekigahara, and it retained a neutrality (though also a lively sense of opposition to burdens imposed by the shogun).

Japan, the territories directly administered by the shogun apart, consisted of a large number of *fudai* and *tozama* han plus the *sanke* han. The shogun's own territories (combining both *tenryō* and hatamoto lands, sixty and forty per cent respectively of the total) amounted to about a quarter of the notional value of Japanese agricultural output. The hatamoto, or senior samurai of the shogun, some 5,000 men, were rewarded either directly with lands from which they collected their income or more indirectly with lands which they held in name only and for which the income came from the shogun's coffers. This land provided no effective income for the shogun, as the income either went directly to hatamoto and peasant occupiers or, if the levy on output was gathered into the shogun's warehouses, was in effect earmarked as the stipend of the hatamoto concerned. The shogun's basic income for his household and government together had to be gathered from the remaining sixty per cent of the territory he held (with a nominal valuation of 4.2 million koku), deriving from a levy of about thirty-three per cent on the notional output. It

---

[86] Literally, three families or households.

represented an income of about 1.5 million koku; if valued in sterling it was about £1.5 million.[87] This had to pay for the costs of maintaining the shogun's court, his castles, his administration, including the cost of 17,000 lesser samurai or *gokenin* (though some at least were maintained out of hatamoto income), and extra payments to hatamoto who took on higher duties beyond their hereditary ones. In other words, it was a rather small income. It paled beside the income of France or England. It covered needs only because in effect there was no standing army.[88]

In strategic terms, only two to three dozen han carried any weight. Foremost among these were the large *tozama*, and the *sanke* or three houses (Kii, Owari and Mito). Because *sanke* and *tozama* alike stood outside the ranks of retainers, they were excluded from any role in direct administration. The *fudai* han of consequence were a handful of large and middle-sized han. Some of the daimyo were descended from Tokugawa ancestors, in other words were *shinpan* or related households and carried a Tokugawa name such as Matsudaira; others were made honorary members of the family, and had the right to bear the Matsudaira name. From about two dozen *fudai* han, either large or related to the family, were drawn the active functionaries, especially the *rōjū*, or ministers, of the shogunate. The great majority of *fudai*, small and with few retainers, played no part whatever in the administration of Japan, and even less in its politics. Politics revolved around a handful of powerful *fudai* han. The *sanke* and *tozama* did not have a formal place in the public sphere of the shogunate. More informally they did have a place. In particular, in the absence of a male heir, a successor would come from the *sanke*. The *tozama* too carried weight, a fact reflected in marriages between shogunal daughters and *tozama* daimyo. If playing no part in the daily politics of Edo, they had a vital role when foreign security was the issue, and were also enlisted as allies by one side in the debate over the succession in the late 1850s when, in the absence of a close relative to provide an heir, and amid external crisis, the resolution of the succession problem had an

---

[87] Calculated on the basis of 1.5 million koku as the equivalent of 1,000,000 quarters of wheat valued at 30 shillings per quarter, a common price in England for the early decades of the eighteenth century. The price should be roughly doubled for the final decades of the eighteenth century. If one opted for a different approach and took Conrad Totman's value of a koku of rice at 1 *ryō* (*Early modern Japan* (Berkeley, 1993), p.148n), and converted at an exchange of 16 *ryō* to 1 *kan*, the value in silver would be 93,759 *kan* which at £23.37 sterling per *kan* would be £2,191,148. Though higher, this figure does not alter the basic proposition of low public revenue. These comparisons are crude. Technical problems and refinements have been ignored, and any comparison remains valid for only very broad orders of magnitude.

[88] For the demilitarisation of Japan, see Noel Perrin, *Giving up the gun: Japan's reversion to the sword, 1543–1879* (Boulder, Colo., 1979).

unprecedented complexity.[89] Some 144 years previously, when the ruling house failed to provide an heir in the direct line, accord had centred readily on Yoshimune, daimyo of the collateral Tokugawa branch of Kii and a close cousin, as the favoured candidate. In 1858, for the first time, there was no near relative of a ruling shogun. There were only two distant cousins, a candidate (Yoshinobu) from the Mito *sanke*, strongly backed not only by his father, but by a powerful coalition embracing Satsuma, the large *fudai* han of Fukui and even the Owari branch of the *sanke*, and another, equally a distant cousin, young and sickly from the Kii branch of the Tokugawa family. One consequence was that Japan entered the decade of growing crisis in the 1860s in an exacerbated state of factionalism. In 1866 (or in a formal sense in January 1867) Yoshinobu himself, passed over in 1860, became shogun; as it proved, he was the last shogun.

The high tensions of the 1630s and 1640s (associated with fear of the Portuguese and the Dutch) gradually eased off, and the massing of forces in Nagasaki in 1647 to overawe two Portuguese vessels had no sequel. As a result, with a decline in military preparedness, the transformation of samurai from warriors into clerks progressed apace. Fiscal constraints had already meant that the shogun's retainers were proportionately much fewer than those of other han. The number of samurai shogunal retainers, including the hatamoto, was about 22,000. Including *fudai* retainers, the total came to a mere 80,000. There were, however, perhaps 400,000 samurai in all Japan. In other words, shogunal retainers and those of the *fudai* han fell short of the forces of the other han. Satsuma alone, with the largest number of samurai of any han, accounted for 30,000, Choshu for 15,000. The *sankin kōtai* ensured that there were probably about 100,000 samurai in Edo at any point of time either in attendance on their lord or, in the year of his absence, attending to his family, in what was for all practical purposes a permanent embassy staffed with samurai. Shogunal retainers were a mere fraction of the total number of samurai. That gave its point to the famous barrier on the southern approach to Edo on the Tokaido road at the mountain pass of Hakone: officials searched travellers on the way out from Edo to ensure that hostages did not depart in disguise, and inward travellers to ensure that they did not carry weapons. In typical Japanese fashion, even when security considerations lessened, bureaucratic procedures were still followed faithfully. Military training had, however, become a mere token element in the instruction of samurai: sword play or fencing were simply the hallmarks of gentlemanly status.

---

[89] There is an illuminating discussion of this in Shimomura Fujio, 'Disintegration of the political principles of the Edo regime and the formation of the han clique', *Acta asiatica*, no. 9 (1965), pp.1–30.

Muskets disappeared; the ceremonial armour was still that of the seventeenth century; cannon aged and were not replaced: when the Russian naval officer Golownin (Golovnin) was a prisoner of the Japanese in 1811–13 in the Japanese region in which military preparedness was at its highest, he commented that 'in the art of war they are still children'.[90] Attendance at the kabuki theatre, a commoner activity, was prohibited to samurai as unseemly. However, they attended, disguised as *chōnin* or townsmen. Quite apart from the general disarming of Japan, Edo residence contributed to the loss of warriorhood in more subtle ways. When in Mito in the 1830s plans were made to transfer samurai from the castle town both into the countryside and to the coast for defence against invasion, the measure proved highly unpopular. The heavy emphasis by defence experts from the 1840s onwards on muskets and drill reflected the fact that, in so far as a Japanese army existed at all, it was far more behind European armies than it had been two centuries previously. Confrontation among military advisors and would-be advisors of the shogun was stark because at issue was not simply the provision of state-of-the-art weapons, but also the underlying need for a roots-and-branch reorganisation.

The effective absence of an army was one aspect of the general want of what we would now understand as infrastructure. The Japanese were well aware of the structural contrasts between their own society and others. In an imprecise way, this is implicit in the comparison writers made from the end of the eighteenth century between the bigness and scale of objects and buildings in Europe and in Japan. The sense was more precise by the 1850s, and Yoshida Shōin, saturated in all the Japanese writing of the preceding century, wrote in 1853 that 'Concern for the four hardships is an important aspect of royal government. I favour the establishment of good institutions to take care of them. Even western barbarians have poorhouses, hospitals, orphanages, and practice the way of charity to the lower classes. Is it not a serious defect that we lack such institutions in this auspicious land of Yamato?'[91] Most striking of all was of course the absence of central institutions of government. The Edo bureaucracy itself was large. However, the four main administrative offices which employed about 1,477 clerks were concerned narrowly with relations with daimyo, ceremonial, judicial proceeding and, in the *Kanjōsho*, the management of the directly held lands of the shogunate. The largest of these offices, the *Kanjōsho* itself with its 618 clerks, was far

---

[90] W. M. Golownin, *Recollections of Japan* (London, 1819), p.32.
[91] M. Maruyama, *Studies in the intellectual history of Tokugawa Japan* (Princeton, 1975; reprint 1989), p.309.

bigger than any European government ministry.[92] However, its purpose was mere estate management: this involved the collection of the rice income from what in itself could be described as the world's largest estate, the directly held lands of the shogun, and the conversion of the income into cash and control of its expenditure. If its field staff of *daikan* and subordinates who had field duties (but spent much of their time in Edo) is included, a further 800 were added to its total. The *Hyōjōsho*, which dealt with legal disputes, was simply a specialised administrative department. There were no courts of law in the sense of institutions independent of the executive, and no lawyers. This issue was to become a central one in the 1870s and later, when the provision of institutions recognised as legal ones in a western sense became an essential step in seeking to undo the extraterritorial jurisdiction that the 'unequal treaties' in 1858 had compelled Japan to concede to foreigners. The want of a judicial system and, *a fortiori*, of such institutions in a central role, is but one aspect of the general absence of organs of central administration dealing with broad administrative matters: in the 1870s Japan had to set about creating what we might describe as a western-style infrastructure of justice.

Government matters were handled by the *rōjū*, a senior or leading councillor, and four or five other councillors who were in effect a prime minister and cabinet, drawn from the *fudai*. In contrast to the west they did not preside over well-defined departments of state (defence, marine, justice, police, foreign affairs). The higher the matter the more informal the administration. Ogyū Sorai (1666–1728), so admired in the eighteenth century for his commentaries on public life, observed that 'No Office should fail to keep records of business. At present it is the general practice to deal with business on the base of precedents and established procedures committed to memory. It is entirely due to the lack of records of business that the officials are vague and ignorant of the duties of their offices.'[93] The defect was due less to deficiencies in attention than to the mere fewness of high officials, though Sorai did not venture into argument on that score. The absence of well-defined administrative structures explains why monks or 'clerics', less distracted by public duties, were originally so important for bureaucratic processes: they could provide well-defined

---

[92] The other three were the *Kinjū* (shogunal chamber) dealing with daimyo affairs, *Denshū shō eki* (office of ceremonial) and the *Hyōjōsho* (office of justice) dealing with disputes and litigation. These figures exclude offices which were concerned with purely Edo matters, the offices of the city magistrates, the army garrison and and the keepers of Edo castle (the latter of which included the city fire brigade of 370). For details, see Kozo Yamamura, *A study of samurai income and entrepreneurship: quantitative analyses of economic and social aspects of the samurai in Tokugawa and Meiji Japan* (Cambridge, Mass., 1974), pp.19–25.

[93] J. R. McEwan, *The political writings of Ogyū Sorai* (Cambridge, 1962), pp.94–5.

administrative services for a shogunate itself bereft of them. Buddhist priests (as also the less influential Shinto priests) were part of a decentralised religious structure, and certainly from the time of the crushing by Oda Nobunaga of the huge armed Buddhist monastic network at Mount Hiei overhanging Kyoto, they did not represent a threat to the state. Clergy were at first almost the only corpus of men well-versed in the arcane science of writing documents, keeping archives and coping with the intricacies of Chinese, the international language of east Asia. Frois, a Jesuit priest in Japan, had noted as early as 1585 their use for administrative purposes.[94] Several monks were employed by Ieyasu. So closely identified were monks with paperwork that Hayashi Razan (1582–1657), one of the chief advisors of Ieyasu, though not a monk, shaved his head and dressed like one (i.e. he was performing 'clerical' services). The second shogun, Hidetada (1579–1632), also employed for his most delicate missions Ishin Suden, a Zen monk. Monks from the Gozan monastery in Kyoto were formally located in 1635 in Tsushima as shogunal observers. The *rōjū* were of course the centre of this administration. As ministers, their role was not well defined at the outset. The term itself only gradually came into use. As the institution developed into a form of cabinet, its importance increased steadily as shoguns personally handling the detail of government came to an end with Tsunayoshi and Yoshimune. That meant also that the advancing from lowly rank of the personal favourites of shoguns ceased: Yoshimune, also the last shogun to occupy himself in detailed management, in effect ended it (the widespread hatred for a later prime minister, Tanuma, was in part because he represented a departure from the new practice). However, even *rōjū* dominance itself raised questions of political management: whether it should be by collective decision or exercised, with the acquiescence of the others, by a forceful member among them.

Urban government in the sense of independent local municipalities did not exist. The more important cities were administered by bugyo, appointed by the shogun (the number of such cities rose from three to eleven over the Tokugawa period). This was the case for Edo, whose administration absorbed many samurai and much of shogunal funds. It was, of course, the case also for Osaka. The city of Osaka was dominated by merchants. The purpose of the bugyo was not only to control the administration of the town to which he was appointed but to keep an eye on its trade. Hence the functions of the bugyo extended beyond urban administration, especially in Nagasaki and Osaka, into economic matters.

---

[94] *Traité de Luis Frois, S. J. (1585) sur les contradictions des moeurs entre Européens et Japanais*, translated from the Portuguese by Xavier de Castro (Paris, 1993), p.64.

Trade administration in Osaka, moreover, was of itself limited, though the bugyo advised Edo on economic matters, and in years of crisis they were commissioned to buy grain for the Edo market. The functioning of the Osaka bugyo office is rather shadowy, because scarcely any of its records survive. Many of the records of the Nagasaki bugyo survive. If shogunal administration lacked a national administrative focus, Nagasaki was the exception: it was unique in Japan by becoming in the seventeenth century a city dominated by its administrative functions. The services of the bugyo employed 2,000 employees. With dependants they would have made up 10,000 of the city's 60,000 or so inhabitants. The largest bureaucratic element in the administration was the interpreters or *tsūji*, *oranda tsūji* (interpreters of Dutch) and *tō-tsūji* (interpreters of Chinese). Interpreters they were, but their functions were also much wider. They recorded cargoes (and sent copies of their records to Edo); also kept a record of passengers arriving (important because of the danger of Christians coming in either from Batavia or from China); inspected the vessels and literature carried on them (a task which combined security concerns at large and the fear of subversive Christian literature in Chinese, a language theoretically accessible to Japanese because the Japanese writing system employed Chinese symbols); and supervised the conduct of trade. At Hirado, the interpreters had been employees of the Dutch; reflecting enhanced shogunal control at Nagasaki they had become employees of the shogun. From the days of the great insecurity of the 1640s, the role of the interpreters expanded enormously. From this decade, foreign vessels were required to file reports on their voyages and on their experiences in the outside world. These are the *fūsetsugaki*, compiled from 1644 both from *tōsen* (Chinese ships) and from Dutch ships. From 1644 to 1724, 2,000 Chinese reports were made.[95] There was a corresponding stream of Dutch reports.[96] Given the enormous linguistic problems, these were very considerable tasks. In all there were 150 Dutch interpreters and some 200 Chinese interpreters, about a fifth of the total clerical force in Nagasaki.

In the seventeenth century Portuguese and Chinese each served as a lingua franca of international contact in the east, and for western traders

---

[95] For a very good introduction and for translations of many of the reports, see Ishii, *Junk trade*. One of the major collections of these reports is covered by Ōba Osamu (ed.), *Tōsen shinkō kaitō roku, Shimabara bon tōjin fūsetsugaki, Wappu tomechō* [Record of Chinese ship movements, the Shimabara volume of Fūsetsu reports, and the Wappu tomechō] (Kyoto, 1974). In the Shiiboruto Kinenkan in Nagasaki, there is a large collection of almost 500 pages of reports from 1667 to 1763 in the Nakamura papers (14–2–93). They are in different hands, and suggest a process of updating over time.

[96] Itazawa Takeo, *Oranda fūsetsu-sho no kenkyū* [Studies in the *oranda fūsetsu* documents] (Tokyo, 1938). See also IWAO Seiichi, *Oranda fūsetsugaki shūsei: a collection of the 'world news' presented annually by the Dutch factory*, 2 vols. (Tokyo, 1979).

Portuguese exclusively was the language of communication with eastern businessmen and officials. The interpreters employed by the Dutch in Hirado, recruited from 1640 for shogunal employment in Nagasaki, spoke and wrote Portuguese. This helps to explain why up to the 1670s Portuguese remained the language used in external contacts. As the use of Portuguese decayed as Portuguese power receded, the older Dutchmen in eastern service were by this time being replaced by a new generation with no knowledge of Portuguese. The consequence was that the interpreters in the 1670s faced the problem of having to master what was for most of them an entirely new language. There were, of course, no Dutch–Japanese grammars or dictionaries (they had existed in Portuguese, compiled by the Jesuit missionaries). In 1673, at the bugyo's orders, a number of ten to twelve year olds went each day to Deshima to learn to read and write Dutch.[97] Kaempfer spoke somewhat dismissively of the competence of the interpreters. However, it was an early stage in the enormous task of learning an entirely new language from the other side of the globe, and in any event it is clear from his own evidence that he found one very proficient interpreter and another enthusiastic learner.[98] Examination of the historical and empirical lore Kaempfer recorded shows that a lot of highly abstract information had changed hands during his two short years in Japan. Dutch was the language of a very advanced and rich people (with many translations also of books from other languages): hence it opened up much wider and more empirical worlds than books in Portuguese had. Nor were the interpreters necessarily dull and incompetent. Even when Portuguese was still predominant, there was an interest in the Dutch doctors' knowledge as early as the 1640s.[99] One of the interpreters translated a Dutch anatomical text in 1682 and another translated a book on surgery in 1706.[100] Dutch became the foreign language of the interpreters at large in the 1680s (though a knowledge of Portuguese seems to have lingered on beyond the final decade of the century). The spread of knowledge of Dutch among the interpreters thus occurred during a period in which the distrust of outsiders was at its highest pitch for years. Through the interpreters, the Dutch had obtained details of the cargoes on Chinese vessels (and Japanese historical knowledge today of the cargoes is heavily reliant on the Dutch records). This relay broke down after

---

[97] *Nagasaki ken-shi, Taigai kōshō*, p.691.

[98] From recent research the names of five interpreters have been clearly identified as having had contact with Kaempfer, plus more fleetingly several others. See Detlef Haberland, Wolfgang Michel and Elizabeth Gossmann (eds.), *Heutiges Japan. Engelbert Kaempfer, werke, kritische ausgabe in einzelbanden*, 2 vols. (Munich, 2001), vol. 1, pp.76–90.

[99] *Nagasaki ken-shi, Taigai kōshō*, p.693.

[100] Motoki Ryoi (1628–97) and Narabayashi Tinzan (1648–1711). See Sugimoto Tsutomu, *Edo no oranda ryū i shi* [Dutch-style doctors of the Edo period] (Tokyo, 2002) for an authoritative analysis of the literary evidence.

1682 and was not to be restored until the 1710s. While the reason for the breakdown is not perfectly clear, it may have been because of the growing tensions of the 1680s (when Manchu invasion was feared).[101]

The great fear of the seventeenth century – invasion inextricably linked to Christianity either as a direct threat or, more insidiously, as one that might be introduced from China, where Christianity had had much success and produced a literature of books in Chinese – gradually lifted,[102] and Japan was to enter on a long period marked by security on the external front and an absence of need to innovate on the internal front. While smuggling continued to be punished on the evidence of the *Hankachō*, or records of the judicial department of the Nagasaki bugyo, there was in the future, excepting the 1820s, nothing on the scale of the frenzy witnessed by Kaempfer. The seventeenth century had been a period of administrative innovation: the replacement of suspect daimyo by shogunal supporters, the creation from the 1630s in Nagasaki of what was in real terms a bugyo bureaucracy and a rigidly controlled foreign trade. A secularisation of higher administration also occurred. Buddhist monks had played, like the clergy of medieval Europe, a vital role in public life; from a vivid memory of their might in the sixteenth century, their power was viewed with less than equanimity. A more confident shogunate from the 1630s replaced them by scholars whose training came from entirely secular Confucian teachers, and whose politically weaker place in society accounted for the tone of hostility to Buddhism which permeated their thought. Administrative innovation was required again from 1799 onwards (to secure territory in Ezo from Russian occupation). In the interval, however, for over a century, there was a Japan relaxed on the external front and at grips with problems which were essentially domestic. The *gaiatsu* of the seventeenth century had vanished; that of the nineteenth century lay in the future.

[101] Nagazumi, *Tōsen yūshutsu-nyūnyū-hin sūryō ichiran*, p.6.
[102] On the issue of the survival of Christian communities, see Miyazaki Kentarō, *Kakure Kirishitan no shinkō sekai* [The religious world of the hidden Christians] (Tokyo, 1996), and in English, Stephen Turnbull, *The Kakure Kirishitan of Japan: a study of their development, beliefs and rituals to the present day* (Japan Library, Richmond, Surrey, 1998).

3   The Japanese economy, 1688–1789

The seventeenth and eighteenth centuries offered sharp contrasts: rapid economic growth in the seventeenth century, slower growth in the eighteenth century; at the same time the eighteenth century was free from the recurrent fears in the past of invasion. Yet if there was no serious external threat on the horizon, a sense of crisis, social or economic, permeated contemporary accounts. Are the *ikki* (or unrest) and the famines so prominent in many modern accounts of Japan an embodiment of real crisis, or is their extent and significance exaggerated? Is the sense of crisis more an expression of the pessimism of samurai, victims, through the fiscal constraints on han rulers, of falling incomes? And are the contemporary population estimates which seem to support a picture of stagnation seriously flawed? In this chapter the evolution of the economy is studied together with the urban society and industrial sector which Japan's advanced agriculture of the eighteenth century sustained. Osaka's importance in trade and banking, and the existence of separate Osaka and Edo currency zones are likewise examined. Osaka was at the zenith of its business in the eighteenth century: hence a look backwards to its rise and forwards to later change is relevant. In the following chapter (chapter 4), economic crisis, famine and unrest are examined. Amid general economic expansion, fixed public income entailed constraints, even crisis, in shogunal and daimyo expenditure, and hence also in the incomes of their direct employees or samurai. As the concept of crisis raises political and intellectual issues as well as economic ones, the political and intellectual discourse of the century is central to understanding Japan aright.

Military campaigns and later mining boom had started the process of rapid change on both sides of 1600. A growth of both foreign and inland trade and the economic role acquired by Osaka are some of the obvious results. Over the century, Osaka's role as a commodity market and as a source of loans to daimyo steadily became more dominant. The combination of a large daimyo trade in rice, daimyo need for funds, and their ever more straitened fiscal circumstances determined the pattern. In the early decades of the century in distant Kyushu there had even been some daimyo dealings in rice with the Dutch to help to balance their accounts.[1]

The population has been estimated at 10 to 12 million in 1600, and 30 million by 1700. More certain than these unreliable figures of a rising population was growth in rice output as measured by the land valuations (expressed in koku of rice). The valuations themselves understated real output; the valuation data as originally communicated to the shogun, and which remained the public or external measure of the wealth and status of han, were usually less than later figures within han; internal figures themselves remained understatements, as resurveying occurred, if at all, with long lags and hence actual output was even larger.[2] A koku of rice (5 bushels) was notionally the amount of rice which would keep an adult alive for a year. With the passage of time arable cultivation intensified, and within cultivation a high-yielding crop – rice – was substituted for low-yielding barley. Rice was a crop of monsoon regions: it required abundant moisture around its roots and a temperature of 20 degrees or above for its ripening. Irrigation, necessary to direct water by channels into the paddy-fields, required communal regulation of its storage and use. Rice was a highly productive crop: a given area fed a far larger number of families than the same acreage planted with other cereals. Perceived also as more palatable than barley or beans, it was consumed by the upper classes, and at the outset much less so by the lower classes.

In contrast to south-east Asia where rice output centred on the great river deltas, in Japan rice production was first concentrated in the upper reaches of rivers. This was because, as the short rivers rushing from the mountains could rise abruptly in monsoon rains and cover the rich alluvial soil with gravel and sand, it was easier to manage water resources in the upper course of rivers than in the flat lands where they approached the sea. In Shikoku and in Kyushu, the typhoon season of early autumn was a further and unpredictable hazard. However, the diffusion of 'red' rice

---

[1] Osaka's dynamic market offered a much more attractive outlet than sales forced by debts to the Dutch. Before 1639, Matsuura, the daimyo of isolated Hirado, and, on their transfer to Nagasaki, some other Kyushu daimyo, sold rice to the Dutch. The quantities were not large. Hirado usually sold below 4,000 koku to the Dutch, a trade reflecting Matsuura's difficult circumstances in getting enough silver more than real marketing skill. The amounts by daimyo averaged a mere 1,450 koku from 1648 to 1661, and had ceased well before exports were prohibited in 1668. For the Dutch, their only regular market was in Taiwan where they finally lost their precarious foothold in 1662. For details of this small but little studied trade, see Yao Keisuke, *Kinsei oranda bōeki to sakoku* [The Dutch trade in early modern times and sakoku] (Tokyo, 1998), pp.12–30, 48–66.

[2] On the valuations see T. C. Smith, 'The land tax in the Tokugawa period', in T. C. Smith, *Native sources of Japanese industrialization*, pp. 50–70. See also P. C. Brown, 'The mismeasure of land: land surveying in the Tokugawa period', *Monumenta nipponica*, vol. 42, no. 2 (Summer 1987), pp.115–55.

(a strain from Champa in Vietnam which was already in Japan) for its early ripening qualities reduced the hazard. In the west of Japan it replaced the native or Japonica rice: early ripening meant that the harvest often avoided the typhoon season of western Japan. It in turn went hand in hand with flood prevention works, largely embankments which prevented flooding. These works in the alluvial soil of estuaries and in low-lying marshy areas, starting in the Sengoku period and sustained through the early Tokugawa decades, together with the adoption of red rice, made possible a dramatic increase in food output.[3] Inland output also increased as deforestation in the valleys expanded the area of cultivated land; irrigation works, variously storing rainfall in reservoirs and controlling and channelling water into paddy-fields, some of them terraced, were sustained through the century. The terraces, however, were very different from those in European terrace agriculture. In the Mediterranean, a region with a sparse rainfall, terraces often ran in narrow strips in successive banks up the sides of hills. In Japan such terraces would be washed away in landslides. As a rule, paddy-fields rose in stairs only at the back of valleys where the pitch was less steep and the irrigation works could be devised to guide water away from the terraces as well as to admit it in controlled fashion into the fields.[4]

The expansion in rice output made possible the substitution of rice for beans and barley. Barley was not very palatable as a bread or gruel. In Europe, once there was choice, preference shifted to wheat and even the potato. Rice, where it could be grown, had a similar appeal, both intrinsically and socially, because it was already perceived as a food of the upper classes. Within the seventeenth century, even in the north of Honshu, it had replaced barley and beans for the samurai class, although not for others. Of course, in the northern regions, if cloudy conditions lasted beyond the normal monsoon season, reduced temperature slowed ripening and led at best to a poor harvest. 'Red' rice was no help, requiring heat and therefore not ripening in cooler districts. Hence, its cultivation did not reach beyond Echigo on the Japan Sea coast or Iwaki on the east coast.[5] There was thus a contrast between two Japans. One was a

---

[3] For a good background account, see Kozo Yamamura, 'Returns on unification: economic growth in Japan, 1550–1650', in Hall, Nagahara and Yamamura, *Japan before Tokugawa*, pp.327–72. K. Nagahara and Kozo Yamamura, 'Shaping the process of unification', pp.83–8, has a very good account of capital investment and engineering advances in water control.

[4] The British naval officer Broughton had noticed this, referring to 'the lands ... cultivated in the Japanese manner, rising in ridges above each other *between the hills*, which gave them an opportunity of easily conducting water to the rice grounds'. Broughton, *A voyage of discovery*, p.343 (italics mine).

[5] Hayami and Miyamoto, *Nihon keizai-shi*, vol. 1, p.183.

southern – or western – region, with a reliable food supply, with rice becoming progressively the main food; the other, the Tohoku (north-east),
with a precarious food supply, and low-yielding barley – and beans – the
basis of the popular diet. It was in other words a poor region; it remained
less densely populated than the south of Honshu; and the spectre of
intermittent food shortage persisted.

If population grew, so did towns. Osaka and Kyoto and later Edo were
easily the largest cities. The castle towns grew over the seventeenth century. Kanazawa, capital of the han of Kaga on the Japan Sea coast, with
an extensive rice-growing hinterland and with the highest rated rice valuation of all the han, had become by the 1670s the largest castle town
in Japan. It tapped the rice surplus of the Hokuriku, and shipped rice
northwards to rice-deficit regions of the Tohoku. It also developed a
large rice trade southwards for Osaka through the Shimonoseki strait.[6] By
Genroku times, the Hokuriku (Kaga and Echigo were its great granaries)
was, next to Kyushu and the Chugoku (a region of Japan bordering the
Inland Sea), the main supplier of rice to Osaka, accounting for about one
fifth of total supply.[7] A traffic northwards supplemented locally cultivated
rice in the Tohoku. However, as barley and beans remained the staple of
the ordinary people there, the rice they grew was more for shipment to
Edo than for local consumption. It provided the income of daimyo and
samurai: what they did not consume was exported. As early as 1614
Tsugaru was exporting; other han followed in a traffic nourished by 'tax'
rice.

New tastes and new production went hand in hand in the changing
Japan of the seventeenth century. Most dramatic of all was of course the
manner in which rice had replaced coarser grains to become the staple
food of all who could afford it. Kumazawa Banzan's *Daigaku wakumon*,
written between 1686 and 1691, recorded the changes. Cotton cloth was
appearing in the dress of ordinary people as well as of samurai. Tobacco
was widely smoked, and some in modern fashion advocated its prohibition. Tea plantations had become, in Banzan's view, a hundred times
more numerous, a change attributed, rather implausibly, to 'gloom of
spirit [which] has marked men and women alike, and consequently they
have taken to drinking more tea'.[8] In contrast to the past when sake was

[6] *Osaka fu-shi, kinsei*, pt. 1, vol. 5, p.494–9. Its trade to Osaka was more important than a
trade to the northern regions, which it also supplied. See Takase Tamotsu, 'Kaga han no
Kyōhō-ki no Tsugaru, Nanbu, Matsumae bōeki' [The trade of Kaga han with Tsugaru,
Nanpu and Matsumae in Kyōhō times], *Kaiji-shi kenkyū*, no. 17 (Oct. 1991), pp.1–12.
[7] *Osaka fu-shi, kinsei*, pt. 2, vol. 6 (Tokyo, 1987), p.58.
[8] G. M. Fisher, 'Kumazawa Banzan, his life and ideas', *Transactions of the Asiatic society of
Japan*, 2nd series, vol. 16 (1938), p.309.

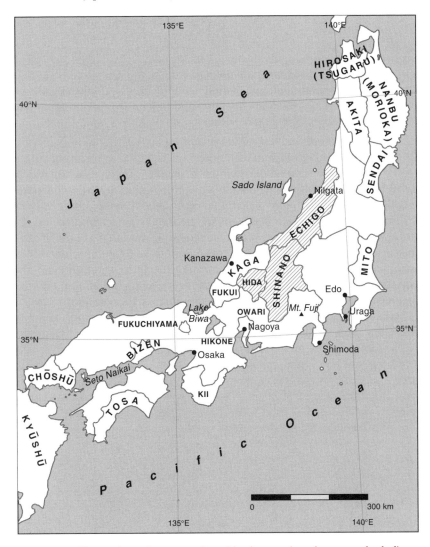

4. Han and provinces mentioned in the text (provinces are shaded)

largely confined to samurai who invited guests twice or three times a year
to consume the brew they made, it was now retailed for cash and traded
over long distances.[9] Ogyū Sorai noted, very sweepingly, that

[9] Fisher, 'Kumazawa Banzan', pp.297–8.

An example of what I mean when I speak of articles of high quality being consumed even by those of inferior status may be seen in the fact that the common people in Edo, who originally lived in the country and ate inferior grains such as barley, millet, and barnyard grass, drank inferior sake, ate no miso, used brush wood for fire, wore clothes made of hempen or cotton cloth of their own weaving, having been allowed to come and live in Edo, now eat miso, drink fine sake and equip their houses with shoji, karakami partitions, tatami mats and mosquito nets which they did not have in the country.[10]

Such reliance on varied and regular purchases would not have been possible without the use of money. In other words, in the more advanced regions money had replaced barter in exchanges. Moreover, already widely used in the commodity exchanges of the more backward han with other regions, it gradually found a place in retail trade in those han.

The Genroku period (1688–1704) marked the apotheosis of the seventeenth-century boom. If seen as a crisis, it was largely because of its novelty. As expenditure outran income, a moralistic tone crept into contemporary writing. Kumazawa Banzan lamented over and over again the substitution of money for rice: 'we must first make it unnecessary for the people to sell all their rice in exchange for money to support themselves'.[11] The lamentation was still there a generation later in the writing of Sorai, like Banzan an intellectual who wrote on economic issues. The celebrated statement that even great lords lived in an inn, i.e. had to pay cash for everything, was his. There was not in fact an economic crisis. The long-term trend was still one of economic growth, and Osaka flourished as artistic and economic centre of Japan. The port's wealth was to lead to claims, already well defined by the 1720s, that merchants in communication with one another across Japan were responsible for high prices inimical to the state and to samurai.[12] An official hostility to the city's wealth was to survive for the long term, and culminate much later in tension between the shogunate and the rice-selling *tozama* who saw interference with Osaka's wealth by the shogunal authorities as detrimental to their interests.

The eighteenth century itself is often seen today, and more widely still was so seen by contemporaries, as a period of crisis. The first twenty years of Yoshimune's shogunal administration from 1716, the years of the so-called Kyōhō reform, were dominated by such a sense. The state's expenditure outran its income; for the same reason, the incomes of samurai, the employees of fiscally 'poor' daimyo and shogunate, no longer matched their outgoings. There is a danger of projecting their personal gloom, prompted by their own poor economic circumstances, into an interpretation of wider society and the real issues in it. In other words, as a

---

[10] McEwan, *Ogyū Sorai*, p.44.

[11] Fisher, 'Kumazawa Banzan', p.282.   [12] McEwan, *Ogyū Sorai*, p.45.

persistent phenomenon the crisis was fiscal. Monetisation of the economy had affected adversely the incomes of rulers (shogun and daimyo alike) and of retainers whose incomes likewise were fixed amounts of rice. The wealth of shogun and daimyo lay in the rice from their own domains. The rice from other lands in a han or, in the case of the shogunate, from lands held by its hatamoto, yielded no return to the daimyo or shogun respectively: these lands provided income for the occupying peasants and for the samurai/hatamoto alone. Higher samurai had originally held fiefs, but increasingly higher samurai themselves ceased to collect rents from peasants, and like lower samurai received salaries or stipends. In other words the rice was gathered directly into the storehouses of the shogunate and han. The change conferred no benefit on the daimyo or shogunate, as any new inflow from non-demesne lands which followed management changes in collection of the rice levy was matched by an equivalent outlay on stipends. Indeed, stipends often had to be supplemented for samurai who took on extra responsibilities. Increasingly the rice was converted by its recipients into cash before other consumer goods were purchased. In the eighteenth century, part of the stipends themselves was paid in cash, and public income itself was received in both cash and rice.

As long as the margin of cultivation was extending, the income of shogun and daimyo expanded as some of the new paddy-fields were on directly held or demesne land. Inevitably, as the opening of new fields slowed, income grew more slowly. Other factors also reduced income. One was the infrequency and even absence of revaluation. Another was that on dry land (producing barley, beans and so on) there was either a lighter levy or none at all. Ogyū Sorai, for instance, noted c.1720 that land in the Musashi region close to Edo which switched from rice paid no levy. Even more serious as a long-term factor, the price of rice, despite a growing population, began to fall. Conversion into cash then meant an immediate reduction in purchasing power. For the shogunate the income problem was worsened by the fact that mining output began to fall from the 1650s, depriving it of a large windfall income. With falling real incomes, debts, once contracted, became all too quickly onerous for public administrations and samurai alike; some daimyo in mid-century had already reduced the number of retainers, so that rōnin became more numerous, and with no stipend lived in misery even though rice was becoming cheaper. The plight of shogun, daimyo and samurai alike explains why wealth centred on Osaka rather than Edo, the national centre of samurai and daimyo life, and why chōnin or townsmen, benefiting from trade in rice and from interest on loans, were rich enough to be the patrons of the Genroku cultural flowering.

From the 1680s the emerging fiscal problem prompted across Japan a novel practice of withholding some of the stipends of high and middle-income samurai. Intended as a temporary expedient – the fiction was that it was a short-term loan by samurai to their lord – it became an integral part of finances. The deduction explains why throughout the eighteenth century, the condition of their own class was a central obsession of writings by samurai, and why a hankering after a return to a pristine state of affairs occurred in so much writing. If incomes were depressed by public action, a corollary also was advocacy of reducing sumptuary expenditure and of keeping living costs down. The idea of returning samurai to the countryside, where moral values would be restored and living costs were lower, was a constant theme at least of those who advocated reform, although not necessarily of other samurai. When for the first time a daimyo – Tokugawa Nariaki of Mito – put into effect in the 1830s a policy, in part prompted by defence needs, of returning samurai both to the country-side and to the coast, it encountered resistance. Samurai were only about 400,000 heads of family in a population of perhaps 30 million in 1700. In other words, including their dependants, their numbers were too small to drag down the economy at large, even if their plight served to depress Edo relative to Osaka.

By the end of the seventeenth century the entire country was linked together by a complex pattern of coastal traffic involving on the west coast flows northwards and southwards from Kaga and Echigo, and on the east from the north to Edo (and to a lesser extent Osaka), from the south to Osaka and from Osaka to Edo. An economically unified econ-omy favoured the expansion of industry. While raw silk supplied through Nagasaki sustained the weaving industry of Kyoto, the progressive re-placement of raw silk from China from early in the eighteenth century triggered an expansion of feeding silkworms and reeling raw silk which boosted the incomes of the mountain valleys of central Japan.[13] The com-bination of increased population and the spread of industry meant that the districts bordering the Tokaido, the road north from Kyoto to Edo, were by the 1690s highly developed; between its castle towns, the road be-came a chain of informal townships living off intensive economic activity more than off the passing traffic itself. Advanced though the region ap-peared to Kaempfer in 1690, it became even more so in the eighteenth century. Commercial crops – cotton, tea, tobacco – assumed a new

---

[13] The best account in English is of the spread of silk in the Ina valley in Shinano province in the southern Japanese Alps in K. Wigen, *The making of a Japanese periphery 1750–1820* (Berkeley, 1995).

importance, and industrial activity had become more diffuse. If in the eighteenth century castle-town population was still growing in the south and west of the country,[14] in the highly developed east of Japan, especially in the Kinki towns, population fell. Osaka itself began to lose numbers from the 1740s onwards. As had happened already in Europe, business-men appeared in the countryside, either putting out raw materials to workers or directly conducting manufacturing enterprises. As far afield as Mito, a han behind the more southerly ones in economic development, a list of 197 wealthy men in 1804 showed that less than a quarter were to be found in the castle town.[15]

There was therefore no long-term economic crisis. Nor arguably was there a monetary one: the spread of copper money, much more suit-able than gold and silver coins for lesser purchases, released the precious metals for other tasks, monetary, decorative or simply as a store of value against a rainy day. The debasement of the gold and silver currency in ma-jor currency operations (four affecting silver, three gold) between 1695 and 1711 took place less because of a currency crisis than because in a fiscal crisis such operations provided windfall profits. Currency was called in and was reissued in the case of gold in lighter coin, and in the case of silver in an alloy with inferior metals. Of course this operation provided extra income only for the short term, and hence, if income was to be maintained, the operation had to be repeated. By 1711 silver, eighty per cent pure in 1695, had been debased to a mere twenty per cent.[16] Even the short-term benefits became doubtful, because people quickly realised the smaller intrinsic worth of the coins, and began to demand larger amounts of coin in exchange for their commodities. As the policy hurt the real incomes of public employees, i.e. samurai, the resistance to devaluation grew, and coin of a pristine standard was put into circula-tion from 1714. The solution to the problem created its own difficulties, because if at a stroke of a pen a better currency was introduced and the new coin itself appeared slowly, by definition the supply at first was in-sufficient: prices fell sharply and abruptly. In other words, there was a short-term monetary deflation, and it in turn created a real short-term downturn in economic activity.

Japan was in essence a classic example of a poor state in a rich country. The pattern in France at much the same time was of a similar tinkering

---

[14] T. C. Smith, 'Pre-modern economic growth: Japan and the west', in T. C. Smith, *Native sources of Japanese industrialization*, pp.15–49.
[15] T. C. Smith, 'Pre-modern economic growth', p.27.
[16] The clearest summary of Japanese coinage operations is in the table in Kawakatsu Heita, *Atarashii ajia no dorama* [The drama of new Asia] (Tokyo, 1994), p.262.

with the currency followed, as public resistance stiffened, by a long period of sound currency management from 1726. While debasements occurred in later Japanese history, the flagrant experiments of 1695–1711, intended for shogunal profit, were not repeated for a very long time, and objectively currency management of the shogunate for the next century was responsible. This in turn was reflected in a stable price level.[17] The sharp price rise of 1695–1713 was not to be experienced again until successively the early 1840s and the 1860s when the combination of external crisis and rigid income forced the shogunate into expedients in somewhat more justifiable circumstances.

The overriding public problem was, to express it in modern terms, the fixed income of the state and hence of its direct employees. This, especially because it was accompanied by an absence of taxation on the wider community, was beneficial to others: by the 1720s it was clear that Osaka was not carrying its fair share of the public burden, and supporters of the shogunate argued that this preferential treatment should end.[18] The currency itself was abundant (a situation contributed to by the combination of a prohibition from 1685 of the export of silver, regulation of exports of gold and copper, and less hoarding, i.e. a rise in velocity of circulation). If copper was becoming scarcer, it was because, as it reached the countryside, it was retained there to underpin the growing retail payments of a population which over much of Japan was moving from barter to cash transactions. The currency needs explain a whole range of restrictions, such as regulation of exports of metals or of their sale outside the mints, or on occasion on the movement of coin from Edo. Because copper was in greater demand than silver, the amount of silver paid for a *kan* weight of copper rose.[19] However, the change occurred mainly in the 1770s, and a relatively stable exchange between silver and copper thereafter suggested an ordered market for copper money.[20] Silver and gold were too large for retail purchases and the premium on copper reflected the price paid for convenience. Moreover, the fact that copper as a currency rose in value in proportion to its relative value as a metal meant that there was no reason to withdraw it from circulation. Its relative scarcity also led to the emergence and acceptance of iron and brass coin as a token money, and to a limited but significant circulation of paper or IOUs as a form

---

[17] See the detail and graphs in Miyamoto Matao, 'Bukka to maguro Keizai no dōkō' [Trends in prices and the macro economy], in Shinbō Hiroshi and Saitō Osamu (eds.), *Nihon keizai-shi* [Economic history of Japan], vol. 2, *Kindai seichō no taidō* [The beginnings of modern growth] (Tokyo, 1989), pp. 68–126.

[18] McEwan, *Ogyū Sorai*, p.100.

[19] Takizawa Takeo, *Nihon no kahei no rekishi* [History of Japanese coinage] (Tokyo, 1996), pp.130–5.

[20] See graph in *Osaka fu-shi, kinsei*, pt. 2, vol. 6, p.370.

of money by han administrations. While contemporaries feared that the precious metals had drained away,[21] and that post-1713 they continued to do so on a smaller scale (unverifiable statements were made about the extent of smuggling), it is far from clear that there was a debilitating shortage of currency. The exchange rate between silver and gold was not distorted by violent fluctuations except in the wake of the debasement of gold in 1710.[22] This stability was helped by the fact that Japan was de facto divided into two currency zones, one, Edo, where wholesale trade was conducted in gold, and the other, Nagoya, Osaka and the entire west – as a region, the more developed part of seventeenth-century Japan – where wholesale trade was based exclusively on silver.

Thus the pattern was one of copper coins circulating in massive quantities across all of Japan (supplemented later by iron, brass and paper), largely in retail payment; and at wholesale level, of two currency regions, a silver zone and a gold zone. The currency situation was superficially complex because the gold coins were denominated by their value measured in the *ryō*, the money of account for gold;[23] and silver consisted of small bars officially stamped and passing in payments at the fluctuating price of the metal. In other words, silver was not rated by value but circulated on the basis of its value as a metal measured in *kan* weight (a unit of 1,000 *momme* or 3.75 kilos). There was a fluctuating exchange between the *ryō* (the money of account for gold) and the *kan* (the measure of weight of silver). The shogunate, with a keen interest in controlling the exchange, because some of its debts had to be paid outside the gold or Edo zone and hence it was intermittently a purchaser of silver (the precious metal which tended to appreciate), had often sought to create a fixed rate for the exchange of gold for silver. Although it had decreed at first a rate of 50 *momme*, later 60 *momme* to the *ryō* (or approximately 16 *ryō* per *kan* of silver), exchanges were in practice effected at fluctuating market rates. In 1777–9, for instance, in Edo the rate fluctuated between 58 and 60.25 *momme* to the *ryō* and was down to 54 in the Tenmei years (1780s).[24] The exchange operated smoothly, and the shift against gold in the 1780s reflected the Tenmei crisis, the impact of which was harshest in northern Japan. The central role of Osaka as trade and banking centre minimised the amount of cash in actual circulation. Instead of transfers

---

[21] Arai Hakuseki dwelt on this issue, with calculations which are often quoted. See Joyce Ackroyd, *Told around the brushwood fire: the autobiography of Arai Hakuseki* (Tokyo, 1979), pp.246–8.

[22] Takizawa, *Nihon no kahei*, p.213.

[23] In the seventeenth century the *koban*, the smallest of the gold coins, was rated as a *ryō*. In later times, with debasement, the *ryō* became a pure money of account, i.e. not necessarily embodied in a single coin whose value corresponded to its metal content.

[24] Takizawa, *Nihon no kahei*, pp.212, 231.

of coin, sterilised by their slow passage along the trade routes, the Osaka houses provided credit instruments and bookkeeping entries. Only small amounts of cash had to be moved physically to settle the general balance of accounts between the two regions.

The financial structure of Tokugawa Japan was based in essence on the fact that the western daimyo, lords of the regions with the real food surplus of Japan, sold their rice in Osaka. In all some ninety-five han from the west opened houses there.[25] The northern han traded with Osaka mainly in goods other than rice, and possessing their own agencies there, borrowed money from the trading houses. Daimyo income in Osaka (either the proceeds of sales of rice or of other goods, or cash advanced on the security of future shipments) was earmarked primarily to acquire gold to cover the cost of residence of their households and samurai in Edo. In effect, through commodity sales in Osaka, daimyo obtained drafts on the Edo correspondents of Osaka houses. The nature of the operation survives in the modern word for exchanging currencies, ryōgae. The system was fully in place by 1670.[26] A system of two exchange zones was in no sense peculiar. Many western countries also attempted to keep two metals in circulation. However, because the relationship between gold and silver fluctuated constantly, and new and hence realistically denominated issues of coin were rare, the coin whose relative worth in metal increased relative to its face or nominal value was either hoarded or exported. The result was that in Britain and Ireland there was a chronic shortage of silver in the eighteenth century, and effectively a gold standard came into existence. In France, on the other hand, gold tended to circulate in the north, and the south of France, which had intensive and favourable exchanges with Cadiz and experienced an inflow of silver from Spain, in effect was on a silver standard. The floating exchange rates between Osaka and Edo were essential to the working of this system, otherwise one metal – in practice silver – might become more valuable as metal than as currency and through hoarding or speculation disappear from circulation. The Japanese system was de facto a highly sophisticated way of rationalising a near-closed monetary system and maximising the money supply by ensuring that both currencies remained in circulation. It has been argued that the shogunate wished to introduce a ryō or gold standard system.[27]

---

[25] Osaka fu-shi, kinsei, pt 1, vol. 5, pp.536, 545, 548–52.

[26] Osaka fu-shi, kinsei, pt 1, vol. 5, p.560.

[27] Takizawa, Nihon no kahei, p.229; H. Shinbō and O. Saitō, 'The economy on the eve of industrialisation', chapter 10, p.241, a revised and expanded chapter to appear in an English-language edition of Hayami Akira and Miyamoto Matao (eds.), Nihon keizai-shi, vol. 1. See also Takehiko Ohkura and H. Shinbō, 'The Tokugawa monetary policy in the eighteenth and nineteenth centuries', Explorations in economic history, vol. 15 (1978), pp.102, 112–14.

The issue from 1818 onwards of silver coin denominated as a fraction of the *ryō* (and hence not circulating by weight) might suggest so. The coins were at an artificially high face value in relation to their metallic content, itself increasingly debased over time. Inevitably under Gresham's law (that bad money drives out good) they circulated rather than being hoarded, becoming a token currency and hence usefully circulating in Osaka as well as in Edo. The net effect of an increase in the token currency was the opposite to establishing a new standard: by minimising the amount of silver passing by weight in small wholesale transactions (to the shogunate's own advantage as it was a purchaser of silver), it prevented a demand for silver for currency purposes from driving the bullion price of silver even higher. Since a metal serving as a currency standard needed to be scarce but not too scarce, the measures effectively helped to preserve a two-zone currency system. The amount of silver in circulation in Bunsei and Tempō times seems to have been 300,000 to 400,000 *kan*.[28] This would have been roughly the equivalent of a year's import/export trade in Osaka or, using another comparative measure, three to four times the value of rice shipments to Osaka. Most of Osaka's external outlay on current account was in *ryō* in Edo, in the form of foreign exchange for western daimyo and loans to northern daimyo. Loans to the latter were discharged from the sale of northern rice in Edo. Osaka's transfers between the silver and gold zones were increasingly dominated by capital movements and service payments. A relatively small amount of silver was necessary to underpin such an operation.

In technical terms, there was a difference between the market rates for gold (*ryō*) and silver between Edo and Osaka of about ten per cent.[29] In other words, using their monopoly position in the exchange market in both centres, Osaka houses widened the spread in the exchanges, demanding in Osaka a high rate in silver for *ryō* to be made available in Edo, and in Edo offering only a low rate in silver in Osaka for *ryō*. The spread was high by European standards, as in theory the gap should not much exceed the direct costs of carriage and insurance of coin overland. There were too few houses – sellers and buyers alike – in the Japanese exchange market: this reflected the concentration of the rice market on *kura* (daimyo warehouse) rice, in which a relatively small number of daimyo

---

[28] Taking the figures for recoining in Genroku times (400,000 *kan*) and Bunsei times (300,000 *kan*). Figures two years into the Meiji era probably reflect the state of the currency before the fall of the Tokugawa dynasty: gold accounted for forty-seven per cent of the money supply, silver for thirty-seven per cent. Takizawa, *Nihon no kahei*, p.260. *Zeni*, or token money, accounted for three per cent and *hansatsu*, or paper money, for thirteen per cent.

[29] For some of the rates see Takizawa, *Nihon no kahei*, pp.213, 231.

houses did business with a likewise restricted range of wholesale rice-buying houses. There were far fewer (but much larger) buyers and sellers of exchange in Osaka than in Europe.

The exchange between silver and gold fluctuated in a fairly narrow band: in Osaka it reached a high of 65 *momme* to the *ryō* in the early 1770s (and a still higher rate of 70 in the late 1770s), and a low of 54 in the late 1780s. Thereafter, gold recovered ground in the 1790s. However, in the late 1810s and again in the late 1830s a *ryō* purchased less than 60 *momme*, and its value fell again in the early 1850s.[30] The fluctuations reflected several circumstances. The short-term factor in the late 1780s and late 1830s was the northern harvest crises; Edo dependence on Osaka for loans and some rice meant hard bargains struck in Osaka for the amount of credit or rice that a *ryō* would purchase. The abrupt dip at the end of the 1820s, or in the early 1850s, reflected the financial penury of the shogun's administration and the enhanced value of silver metal in a renewed round of currency debasement. The massive debasements of the Ansei period (from 1854) corresponded to an acute crisis (and a very sharp dip in the number of *momme* of silver that a *ryō* would purchase on the exchange).

Nevertheless, looking at the long-term rather than the short-term movements in Edo's finances and its exchange market with Osaka, several factors – a deepening of the Edo currency zone and the political strength of Edo authorities – led to the silver zone losing some of the dominance which it held in the seventeenth century. This shift, too, corresponded to the fact that the interests of the western han (and of their partners the Osaka trading houses) and of Edo did not converge, something first evident in the forced levies on Osaka houses in 1761 and their repetition in all later crises. The consequences were stark once Japan in 1859 moved from a closed monetary system to an open one. At this stage, in the wake of the sharp currency debasements of the 1850s, silver as a metal had acquired an even higher purchasing power. Relative to gold, it was now dramatically more valuable than in the outside world. Hence in 1859–60 under a semi-open system, an outflow of gold occurred to China (gold was cheap relative to silver in Japan; in China, dear relative to silver) and the proceeds of its sale were returned in silver at a large profit. The solution to these movements, which if unhalted would be destabilising politically and economically, was a revaluation of gold (i.e. offering more silver for gold) in 1860 which created a parity ratio between gold and silver in Japan which matched the ratio abroad.[31] Internally, however,

---

[30] See table in *Osaka fu-shi, kinsei*, pt 2, vol. 6 (1988), p.370.

[31] There is a résumé of the currency problem in W. G. Beasley, 'The foreign threat and the opening of the ports', in *CHJ*, vol. 5 (1989), pp.285–7, and in E. S. Crawfour, 'Economic change in the nineteenth century', *CHJ*, vol. 5 (1989), pp.601–2.

that meant a dramatic loss in the purchasing power of silver relative to gold, and hence considerable cost to trading houses in Osaka. It added to the conflict of interest between Osaka (both its trading houses and the western *han* which relied on Osaka as a market) and Edo.[32]

The currency changes corresponded to a growing shift in the relative fortunes of Osaka and Edo. Only the partial cancellation of the *sankin kōtai* by the shogunate in 1862 with its adverse consequences for the prosperity of Edo concealed for the time being the extent of the change. With Edo's deeper *ryō* zone (evident for instance in the spread of the silk industry in the highland areas to the north-west of Edo), the dependence of Osaka's financial fortunes on the single region, western Japan, became starker. By the end of the 1860s the new statistics of trade, documenting the rise in Yokohama's fortunes relative to Osaka, brought to light the economic strength that its hinterland had conferred on Edo. It was the counterpart to the cumulative decline, which had begun earlier and was still evident in the 1830s, in Osaka's commodity business: traffics from very far afield were moving more frequently direct to Edo rather than through Osaka as an intermediary. Demographic decline continued: the city was down to 280,000 by Meiji times.[33] While shipments of rice to Osaka were high in the abundant harvests of Bunka and Bunsei times (1804–29), marketing at low prices reflected the growing indebtedness of daimyo. In other words, Osaka had become ever more central to the solvency of the western daimyo. The conflict of interest between shogun and daimyo was to become an open one when the prospect in 1865–6 of opening Osaka to foreign trade raised the issue of taxing Osaka's prospective new wealth. It was highlighted by the rise in prices in Osaka and western Japan as, with some time lag, gold replaced silver in Osaka and the west of Japan: the result was that, in what was already for other reasons an economically difficult year, prices rose much more quickly than in Edo and the north of Japan. While prices fell back sharply in the wake of the transition, Osaka was permanently damaged as a commodity market.

---

[32] The same outcome could have been achieved, in a technical sense, by raising the price of gold. It has been suggested that this was not done because of the interest of foreign powers who operated on a gold standard, and because the Japanese, despite the shogunate's interest in the *ryō*, regarded silver as the basis of their currency. The outcome in either case would have been the same for Osaka: in both cases revaluation by depressing the relative value of silver would have benefited the shogunate in whose territories the *ryō* was the standard of value. Under the Meiji regime, despite Japan's new place in a world system, relative currency valuations became seriously out of step again; gold values were not raised in line with its rising value on world bullion markets, and it disappeared from circulation. On the rise in value of gold, see also T. Tsuchiya, 'An economic history of Japan', in *Transactions of the Asiatic Society of Japan*, 2nd series, vol. 15 (Dec. 1937), pp.212–13. A *ryō* commanded 89 *momme* of silver by the end of the Tokugawa period.

[33] Wakita Osamu, *Kinsei Osaka no keizai to bunka* [The economy and culture of early modern Osaka] (Kyoto, 1994), p.39.

Comparisons of averages of rice prices between 1855–9 and 1871–5 when the price level had stabilised show that prices had risen more steeply in Osaka than in Kyoto, Nagoya or Edo.[34]

Crisis in the 1860s highlighted the cumulative effect of changes in Osaka's place in the economy. Its role had emerged originally in its replacement of Kyoto by the 1650s as the financial market of Japan. By the 1670s it was also the national rice market. From early on rice moved to it from the surplus regions of the west. More slowly, a movement of commodities from poorer and initially more backward districts in the north of Japan to Osaka also emerged, mainly bulky or low-value cargoes of timber and especially fish. Its trade from Ezo rose rapidly in the second half of the eighteenth century. The trade in metals, copper – especially to Nagasaki – and raw silk from Nagasaki, both large in the seventeenth century though smaller in later times, were important traffics. Copper was, in value, Osaka's principal export until it fell very sharply over the first half of the eighteenth century.[35] Sakai, the centre of copper smelting, had been variously an independent bugyo office or had been administered by the bugyo of Osaka, and again became a separate bugyo office in 1702.[36]

Rice itself was the key commodity in the trade of sakoku times. Two circumstances determined the rise of Osaka as a rice market. One was the fact that it had two large cities to serve: the combined population of Kyoto and Osaka was at first larger than that of Edo, and in the eighteenth century was not much below it (800,000 compared with 1 million in Edo). Moreover, their hinterland was densely populated, and the centre of the textile industry (silk and cotton alike) and of much of the metal crafts. Hence, despite a rich lowland agriculture, it was a food deficit area: in other words, it imported much rice (from western Japan). The region's savage famine of 1836–7 was contributed to by an abrupt fall in imports in what proved a very poor season in western Japan: imports to Osaka, normally above 1 million koku, were a mere 510,000 koku.[37] The second circumstance was of course the needs of daimyo to acquire cash by rice sales or to borrow on the security of future rice shipments. Osaka's *ryōgae* activity, i.e. the provision of *ryō* in Edo for silver in Osaka, secured its hold on the economy of western Japan, just as the resources of its merchants tempted the shogunate to negotiate loans on occasion and from 1761 intermittently to impose forced levies.

The rice output of Japan was perhaps 27 million koku: western Japan probably accounted for at least 10 million koku of that total. Probably

---

[34] Nishikawa Shunsaku, Odaka Kōnosuke and Saitō Osamu (eds.), *Nihon keizai no 200 nen* [Two hundred years of the Japanese economy] (Tokyo, 1996), pp.61–3.
[35] *Osaka fu-shi, kinsei*, pt 1, vol. 5, p.766.   [36] *Osaka fu-shi, kinsei*, pt 1, vol. 5, p.310.
[37] *Osaka fu-shi, kinsei*, pt 3, vol. 7 (Osaka, 1989), pp.28–9.

2 million koku of this output corresponded to the income, public and private combined, of daimyo and their han administrations. The million koku or more of rice sold in Osaka[38] originated principally in rice from daimyo, and secondarily in the sale more speculatively in Osaka of rice which was converted into cash within han by daimyo governments, by retainers who had received their stipends in rice and more marginally by peasants. Daimyo or han rice in Osaka, the more regular traffic, was know as *kura* or warehouse rice, because it was lodged in han warehouses, and then disposed of on the market. Han had need of cash to service borrowings in Osaka and to acquire, by an exchange of silver, the *ryō* to defray the costs of the *sankin kōtai* in Edo. On the other hand, the rice marketed by private traders fluctuated sharply in volume, depending on the state of local markets and the movement of Osaka prices. It was several hundred thousand koku at maximum, less when profits promised to be meagre. A prohibition on business in futures was removed in 1730 in the hope of supporting the price.[39]

The million or more koku of rice disposed of in Osaka in years of good harvests when speculative or private sales were small was a rough estimate of the cost of servicing the indebtedness of the han and the exchange requirements of their *sankin kōtai*. Its costs amounted to a half of the total outlay of han,[40] less because they were high – which they were – than because other han administrative expenses were extremely low. There were no figures kept of Osaka trade before 1714. In that year, in an effort to facilitate intervention in the event of merchants withholding goods from the Edo market, goods entering Osaka and leaving it were recorded, and a further recording was made at Uraga at the entrance to Edo bay.[41] Intended purely as a guide to public intervention, they were very rough and ready statistics; they did not embrace all goods (notably often excluding *kura* rice, of which little was reshipped, as opposed to free rice, i.e. rice purchased speculatively by merchants for sale in distant

---

[38] Documentation on quantities is poor. A figure of 1.4 million koku has been suggested for the traffic in warehouse rice in J. L. McClain, 'Space, power, wealth and status in seventeenth-century Osaka', in J. L. McClain and O. Wakita (eds.), *Osaka: the merchants' capital of early modern Japan* (Ithaca, 1999), p.61.

[39] *Osaka shi-shi*, vol. 4, p.3.

[40] Suzuki Kōzō, *Edo no keizai seisaku to gendai: Edo ga wakareba ima ga mieru* [Edo economic policy and the modern age: the present can be seen in understanding Edo] (Tokyo, 1993) p.15.

[41] On this obscure operation, see Ōishi Shinzaburō, *Shōgun to sobayōnin no seiji* [The politics of the shogun and of his public servants] (Tokyo, 1995), pp.167–71. Its aim was, if rice prices were falling behind other prices, to proceed on the basis of controlling the price level of other commodities. The concept was influenced by the belief that it was relative prices which mattered. If rice prices were falling (to the detriment of samurai), intervention, to ensure that other prices fell, would restore a balance.

Osaka). Though the figures were kept to the end of the Tokugawa regime, the inexperienced Osaka officials made very heavy weather of compiling true trade figures from the late 1860s. At the time such figures as existed were, as the Osaka bugyo told the British in 1867, approximate, and returns did not exist for some of the articles of trade: the guilds, moreover, did not keep books of statistics.[42] In 1868 when its foreign trade began, the compilation of the first figures of the new foreign trade of Osaka presented problems. The difficulties arose not from secrecy, but simply from lack of statistical competence. A British report on the educational system in 1873 noted the 'science of statistics [is] in its infancy; and the difficulty of obtaining information on any special subject'.[43]

Because of the intensely practical purpose behind their collection and the fact that in most years the figures served no immediate purpose, few of the Osaka data survived even at the time, and Uraga material not at all. The most regularly quoted figures are those for 1714, which valued the recorded inward shipments to Osaka at 286,500 *kan*, and outward shipments at 95,800 *kan*, leaving an adverse balance of 190,700 *kan*, which should be even larger as the recording did not include *kura* rice. However, the values in the 1714 figures are quite unrealistic, recorded as they are at the high and distorted prices reached in the wake of the last of the debasements in 1695–1711.[44] The returns for 1766 (which included imports of 1.4 million koku of rice) at uninflated prices are more reliable: imports amounted to 194,927 *kan* and exports to 76,218. This gives a still large but more realistic deficit of 118,709 *kan*.[45] While the figures are themselves of poor quality and too much reliance should not be placed on them, the trade structures they suggest are plausible. A large trade deficit points to the favourable commodity trade balance of the daimyo arising from their debtor status: an export surplus from the han was necessary for them to be able to service their debt.

If Osaka's own commodity trade deficit was so large, how could Osaka houses provide drafts on Edo? No doubt, there is more unrecorded trade for semi-manufactures and manufactures than for the more easily recorded bulk cargoes, and probably there was also an advantageous trade with its own hinterland. However, all that would have made only a modest

[42] *PP Japan*, vol. 4, pp.274, 278, Report on Hyogo, June 1867.
[43] *PP Japan*, vol. 5, p.225, Mr Watson to Sir Harry Parkes, 30 Nov. 1873. See also vol. 6, p.14, Report on the public finances of Japan 1877.
[44] The launch of the operation at a time of high inflation seems to confirm its purpose, and the inflation obsession is reflected in the fact that the figures for 1714 were quite unrealistically valued at high levels, despite the fact that the trend was already downward.
[45] *Osaka shi-shi*, vol. 4, p.16. For a comparison of the prices in 1714 with the prices in an enquiry of 1736, see ibid., p.15. The 1714 figures are widely reproduced. In English, they are given in McClain and O. Wakita, *Osaka: the merchants' capital*, pp.62–3.

difference. The gap between commodity imports and exports was closed by invisible income arising from a surplus on current account. Crude calculations would suggest that interest on the debt of western daimyo and banking charges on transferring money to Edo to defray the costs of the year's *sankin kōtai* could have amounted to 70,000 *kan* of silver. This would still fall short of the deficit incurred in commodity trade. However, to it should be added income from dealings with the daimyo of northern Japan. Advised on their finances by Osaka houses, they also borrowed in Osaka. Most of the surplus rice from the northern han was sold in Edo. However, directly or indirectly, much of the income from northern rice sold in Edo came into the hands of Osaka houses to repay or service daimyo debt, and hence created for the Osaka houses a regular supply of *ryō* in Edo. In brief, the structure of Osaka's global payments must have been a deficit on commodity trade, more than matched by a net surplus on lending and exchange, leaving finally a net surplus which financed further lending.

The Osaka houses originated in the seventeenth or early eighteenth century.[46] While they marketed rice, their real growth came from an ability to lend money to han, and to meet their 'foreign' exchange needs in *ryō* in Edo. In turn, this ability depended on involvement in inward commodity business and in exports of a miscellany of goods from Osaka to generate a 'foreign' income. Thus, they were from very early on conglomerates, which lent money, handled commodities and dealt in the Osaka–Edo exchange. While the western han maintained warehouses in Osaka, managed by a small number of samurai, their commodity dealings were with the big Osaka houses who acted variously as buyers of rice and purveyors of banking and exchange services. A small number of houses managed the commodity business of a number of han, and also advised them financially. Ultimately this led to sophisticated observations by their managers on the nature of the Japanese economic system and of the financial problems of the han. However, that is to look forward as much as a century and a half to the writings of Kusama Naokata (1753–1831) and Yamagata Bantō (1748–1821), managers in two of the great conglomerates, Kōnoike and Masuya respectively.[47] The Osaka houses also dealt in precious metals. The earliest of the houses, Kōnoike, had emerged in copper smelting at Sakai, an outport of Osaka. Copper was in great

---

[46] For details of the three great houses of Kōnoike, Sumitomo and Mitsui, see *Osaka fu-shi, kinsei*, pt 1, vol. 5, pp.566–71, 586–7; Yotaro Sakudō, 'The management practices of family business', in C. Nakane and S. Ōishi, *Tokugawa Japan: the social and economic antecedents of modern Japan* (Tokyo, 1991), pp.147–166.

[47] Tetsuo Najita, *Visions of virtue in Tokugawa Japan: the Kaitokudō merchant academy of Osaka* (Chicago, 1987), pp.225–51, 263–71.

demand both by the Chinese and Dutch and by the currency needs of Japan. A house with a large stake in copper inevitably had a strategic advantage in metamorphosing into one of the two largest conglomerates in Japan.

The complex pattern of Japanese trade – the centralised marketing of rice by western han linked in turn to servicing han demand for *ryō* – had favoured the growth of such conglomerates. In essence, daimyo as a consequence of *kura* rice were both the largest commodity marketeers in Osaka, and at the same time the largest purchasers there of acceptable credit instruments drawn on accounts in Edo. That was a contrast with Europe. In Europe, the big borrowers were not as a rule large-scale commodity dealers. The consequence was that in Europe there was a whole host of borrowers, cumulatively on a large scale but individually small, and at the same time a wide range of commodity dealers and financial houses in major centres. Interest rates in Japan, while not exactly usurious, were high by European standards, running at five to ten per cent or so, and were commonly at or near the upper limit.[48] In other words, interest rates were not altogether competitive. Another consequence of the pyramid concentration of business was that though merchant houses were numerous in Osaka, the turnover of the port was dominated by a small number of houses, of which several were huge (foreshadowing and in some cases providing the origins of the *zaibatsu* of Meiji times). In a shogunal administration made desperate by the straitjacket of its public finances, the diffuse belief that Osaka did not contribute to public costs made it tempting to raid the coffers of less than a hundred great houses for contributions to the public exchequer.

Little of the huge long-distance commercial traffic of Japan went overland. Given the mountainous nature of the terrain and the problem of fording rivers – shallow wisps of water during much of the year and raging torrents in the monsoon season – long-distance wheeled trade was impractical and bridges would have been swept away. The *kaidō*, or great roads, were confined to passenger traffic moving to or from Edo, and to high-value goods being transported by pack-horse. There was also a network of lesser roads, the *shio no michi* or salt roads, so called because they carried essential goods like salt from the coast, running laterally across Honshu.[49] These carried from the coast into the interior vital traffics such

---

[48] Suzuki, *Edo no keizai seisaku*, pp.64, 65, 66, 68, 73, 76, 82, 83, 95, 115, 134, 148. See also R. P. Toby, 'Both a borrower and a lender be: from village moneylender to rural banker in the Tempō era', *Monumenta nipponica*, vol. 46, no. 4 (Winter 1991), pp.500–4, 508.

[49] See in particular maps in Tomioka Gihachi, *Shio no michi o saguru* [In search of the salt roads] (Tokyo, 1983), pp.vi–vii, 143.

as dried fish for manure, salt, tea and cotton. Statistics compiled because of a dispute over carriage rights on the roads into the castle town of Ida, with a population of 6,500 people, in the southern Japanese Alps, showed 73,000 pack-horse loads in the year 1763.[50] The coastal traffic was huge. The carriage of 1 to 1.5 million koku of rice to Osaka required up to 200,000 tons of shipping space. As ships were confined to a maximum size of 500 koku, this implies 3,000 sailings or more to Osaka.[51] In 1866, when a poor rice trade and political uncertainty deflated turnover, 1,967 junks entered Osaka.[52] In that year, the coastal inflow of rice was a mere 311,258 koku: the small intake would imply that in normal years a further 1 million or so koku of rice would add a further 1,000 to 2,000 vessels to the actual 1866 total.[53] Apart from rice, other goods were timber, fish, sake and so forth, and the number of vessels, especially with the bulky though cheap products of Ezo, must have been substantial. High-value traffics like copper from Osaka or silk from Nagasaki raised the value of traffic, but would not have added greatly to the tonnage. Overall, sailings to Osaka must have been at a minimum, in the order of 4,000 to 5,000 a year. Kaempfer reported seeing as many as 100 ships in a day in the Inland Sea. Other centres of coastal traffic were active also. On the western coast of Japan, the Hokuriku was the focal centre of traffic, some of it destined for Osaka, but much for the north of Japan. In Genroku times the han of Kaga was shipping 250,000 koku of rice to Osaka alone.[54] In neighbouring Echigo, in 1870 the number of junks recorded in its principal port, Niigata, was 2,055.[55] There was also a large traffic south from the Tohoku itself, both to Edo and to Osaka. One of the rare figures for the trade of Edo is for the arrival of 7,741 junks in 1871.[56]

The gross tonnage of the coastal fleet of Japan would have fallen far short of the figure, given with statistical insouciance by the governor of Shimoda, of 100,000 vessels of 60 to 200 tons,[57] but the observation by

[50] Wigen, *The making of a Japanese periphery*, p.56.
[51] Wakita suggests a figure of 3,000 sailings for the trade at large (*Kinsei Osaka*, p.112). A figure of 2,500–3,000 vessels from the spring to the ninth month of the year is cited in *Osaka fu-shi, kinsei*, pt. 1, vol. 5, p.499.
[52] *PP Japan*, vol. 2, p.275, Report on ports of Osaka and Hyogo, June 1867.
[53] The consular report somewhat misleadingly referred to imports, but imports in the literal sense were not permitted in Osaka until 1 January 1868.
[54] Takase Tamotsu, 'Kaga han no kaiun seisaku to fukushiki no fune donya: shuto shite tsuru tonya-kabu no hōkai' [Kaga han policy on maritime transport and the submission of the shipping guild], *Kaiji-shi kenkyū* [Research in maritime history], no. 7 (Oct. 1966), p.61.
[55] *PP Japan*, vol. 5, p.101. The report dated 1 Aug. 1872 has a very full account of Niigata trade (vol. 5, pp.76–105).
[56] *PP Japan*, vol. 5, p.62, Report of vice consul at Edo, 15 Feb. 1872.
[57] The restriction on vessels to a size of 500 koku had been repealed by this time.

Harris, the first resident American diplomat, that Japan's tonnage could be the largest fleet in the world, might still be correct.[58] In value the combined inward and outward trade of Osaka in 1766, at 271,145 *kan*, converted to about £6.3 million sterling.[59] In other words, the total trade of Osaka, all of it domestic, would have been worth almost half the exports and re-exports of England and Wales in that year. The total of English shipping in 1766 was 562,000 tons. Japanese tonnage was probably a little below that figure. Certainly in 1872 there were 471,000 tons of *wasen*, meaning Japanese-style vessels, and hence in effect sailing ships, few or any of which were engaged even at that date in foreign trade.[60] In the eighteenth century the total tonnage of Japanese shipping would certainly have made it the largest coastal fleet of the era, not far short of the combined coastal and foreign-going fleet of England and Wales. The coastal traffic to Osaka and the coal trade from Newcastle to London must have been the two largest coastal traffics of the world of their day. Trade to Osaka would have been exceeded in volume by the huge but low-grade coal trade from Newcastle to London (in tonnage, though not in value, the world's largest coastal traffic of the time). On the other hand, in value the Osaka trade would have been by far the more valuable traffic. Moreover, the gap in the tonnage of vessels engaged in the two traffics would have been narrow, as the intensive use for many trips – as many as seven or eight a year – of a specialised fleet of remarkably hardy and efficient Newcastle colliers contrasted with a low turnabout in Japanese vessels (reflecting the agricultural nature of the Japanese traffic, the singular winter weather on the west coast, and the much poorer sailing qualities of the vessels). The maritime traditions of Japan, despite its near absence of a foreign trade, were reinforced by its fisheries. They were everywhere along the coast, and even if Japan lacked transoceanic fisheries such as the cod fleets of England or France, the vitality of its fisheries is seen in its expanding long-distance traffic in fish from Ezo (Hokkaido) to the south, and in its pioneering whale fisheries.

The feeding of Edo was a major challenge in food production. One response was of course food production in its immediate vicinity in the Kanto plain. The Musashi region, for instance, once the most renowned in Japan for breeding horses, switched to food production: the change

---

[58] *The complete journal of Townsend Harris* (Tokyo, 2nd edn, 1959), p.287.

[59] Calculated on the basis of £23.37 sterling to one *kan* of silver. See chapter 2, p.41 and note 51.

[60] From a figure of 3.3 million koku in 1872 in W. D. Wray, 'Shipping: from sail to steam', in M. B. Jansen and G. Rozman (eds.), *Japan in transition, from Tokugawa to Meiji* (Princeton, 1986), p.252. Calculations of tonnage were notoriously imprecise. The suggested conversions in the article are a net 6 koku to a ton or a gross 11 koku to a ton. The calculation in the text is based on 7 koku to the ton.

was lamented by Sorai (though the switch provided new income for the Tohoku as a centre of horse breeding). However, food from further afield also had to be drawn in, and rice cultivation in the north of Japan provided both a means of extending Edo's food supply and the vehicle for acquiring the *ryō* necessary to repay in Edo advances by Osaka houses to finance the costs of the *sankin kōtai* of northern daimyo. The operation depended on peasants in the poor Tohoku forgoing consumption of rice, thus creating the surplus which both fed status-conscious samurai in the north and underpinned daimyo finances. In this way, the growth at an early stage of an economic region binding together the economies of Tohoku and Edo strengthened the *ryō* currency region. Even as Osaka's commodity role began to weaken by the late eighteenth century, its financial role still dominated the financial arrangements of the Tohoku han. In short, Osaka's economic structure was that of a mature economic area, which had advanced progressively from commodity trade into financial services on a grand scale. The sequence of development is fairly clear: population peaked by 1740 (as industry migrated to the countryside), and commodity trade did so probably by 1780: in other words, though its commodity trade remained large, much trade now bypassed it. However, it still handled the banking elements of the traffic and, as indicated above, it did so too for much of the growing traffic between Edo and the Tohoku.

The growth of Osaka and Edo was a key part of the story of the seventeenth century. Osaka was not far short in size of late seventeenth-century London or Paris. Edo was already larger. Its population was soon to reach one million, making it the largest city in the world of its day.[61] Osaka was, at least well into the eighteenth century, the richer of the two cities, and, rather unusually for a commercial city, it was at that stage the centre of luxury and culture. As it was not a capital, that was inherently an unstable situation, and it was later to cede its cultural leadership. Its culture had blossomed in the Genroku period. Painting flourished, and the plays of Chikamatsu Monzaemon (1653–1724) in the early decades of the eighteenth century marked the high point of Japanese non-aristocratic theatre.[62] The theme of wealth came out strongly in its literature. In one of Chikamatsu's plays, a *chōnin* (townsman) exclaimed that 'a customer is a customer, whether he is a samurai or townsman. The only difference is that one wears swords and the other doesn't. But even if he wanted to,

---

[61] A very readable introduction is Hidenobu Jinnai, 'The spacial structure of Edo', in Nakane and Ōishi, *Tokugawa Japan*, pp.124–46. J. L. McClain, J. M. Merriman and Kaoru Ugawa (eds.), *Edo and Paris: Urban life and the state in the early modern era* (Ithaca, 1994) provides a wide-ranging account of aspects of Edo life.

[62] *No* theatre was older and court-centred.

he couldn't wear five or six swords.' In a novel there was even a recipe for 'a millionaire pill' to cure 'a disease called poverty'.[63] Osaka's Yodo river was sluggish. It was impossible for deeply laden vessels to navigate it. Much of the trade was handled in the first instance by outports, both Sakai (centre of copper smelting), and Hyogo (the future Kobe), centre of commodity and passenger traffic, as boats of above 200 koku could not reach Osaka itself and goods were forwarded by barge. There in turn they were moored in channels or canals reaching off the river to serve the vast number of warehouses.[64] In appearance Osaka was an unromantic Venice, and only in the twentieth century, especially after 1945, has the infill of many of the canals obliterated an all-pervading image of water-borne traffic. Even if Osaka's place in the economy in the fulness of time altered, that did not alter the wholesale basis of its economy. In comparison to Edo, the proportion of employees and apprentices to principals in business rose, and was much higher in the 1860s, reflecting the scale of its large business firms.[65] Edo by comparison had many casual workers and one-man stall holders, catering to the needs of what had become a massive centre of consumption.

Few samurai lived in Osaka, other than the small number around the *bugyōsho*, office of the bugyo or intendants who represented shogunal government, and the handful of samurai who were the clerks of the agencies that daimyo maintained there. The contrast with Edo was thus social as well as economic. Edo's commoner population was about 500,000. Its samurai population, permanent and transient, including dependants, was reputedly another 500,000. This would suggest a figure of 80,000–100,000 samurai heads of family. If so, it would suggest that up to one third of the samurai in Japan were resident in Edo. Most of the shogun's 20,000–22,000 samurai were permanently in Edo discharging the ceremonial, clerical and guard-house duties of the court and administration. As hereditary office holders, they were automatically on the payroll: a consequence was that offices were chronically overmanned, and the office-holders agreeably underworked. Most of them however were also badly paid. Many took menial work to supplement their meagre incomes, and the more fortunate married merchants' daughters. Even if in

---

[63] Quoted in Maruyama, *Intellectual history of Tokugawa Japan*, pp.124–5.

[64] For a map and details of the canals, see McClain, 'Space, power, wealth and status', pp.51–2. Aston, one of the early British diplomats in Japan, has left a vivid account of Osaka in *PP Japan*, vol. 4, pp.621–6, Memorandum by Mr Aston on the commercial system of Osaka. See also *PP Japan*, vol. 4, pp.271–84, Report by Mr Lock on ports of Hyogo and Osaka, 10 Jan. 1867.

[65] Saitō Osamu, *Shōka no sekai, uradana no sekai: Edo to Ōsaka no hikaku toshi shi* [World of merchant houses; world of stall holders: a comparative history of two metropolitan centres] (Tokyo, 1987), pp.54–62, 73–7, 127–32.

a crude sense most of the shogunal samurai lived in Edo, their numbers were swamped by the large number of retainers who accompanied their lords to Edo for the *sankin kōtai*. If there were crudely 60,000 *fudai* and 300,000 *tozama* samurai, some 360,000 in Japan, perhaps 60,000 of the total were at any time in Edo. This was all the more likely as included in their number were the *rōnin*, samurai without a charge, who had either lost their position in a han or had thrown it up in search of fame or fortune. Many samurai who retained their charge spent the year in Edo with their lord, some of them remaining in Edo to serve the court constituted by the wife and children who remained in Edo permanently, to maintain an embassy to look after the affairs of the han, and to arrange for the return a year later of the lord and his retinue. The number of retainers that a lord might bring to Edo was set out minutely in regulations. Inevitably, given the fact that they were permanently on the payroll and that retainers also advertised the prestige of lords, daimyo overmanned rather than economised on staffing, both permanent and biennial for the *sankin kōtai* year. The costs of the *sankin kōtai* have been exaggerated, in the sense that the major cost, the salaries or upkeep of samurai, would have been incurred even if the already underworked retainers had remained at home. The real problem was less the costs per se than the fact that they were incurred outside the han, either on the road to or from Edo (the combined journeys took up to two months) or in Edo, and hence made necessary recourse to the 'foreign' exchange houses in Osaka. Even in the case of Kaga, the largest han in Japan, they absorbed from a third to one half of han income.[66]

There was no court life in the western sense in Edo. Ceremonial occasions existed, but there was neither a public nor a private social life in which daimyo freely mingled with shogun and one another. The court struck the Dutchman Henry Heusken in the late 1850s as not conspicuous for its luxury.[67] Among the daimyo, contacts were stiff and formal, and conducted more through their samurai than by personal encounter. Public life itself was officially puritanical. Samurai were expected, on paper at least, to conform to high expectations of rank. The pleasure district, of which the main attractions were prostitution and the theatre, was frowned on, and it was moved by public order on several occasions even farther afield from the centre of an expanding Edo.[68] Nevertheless,

---

[66] J. L. McClain, *Kanazawa: a seventeenth-century Japanese castle town* (New Haven, 1982), pp.70, 106.
[67] *Henry Heusken: Japan journal 1855–61*, ed. J. C. Van der Carput and R. A. Wilson (Rutgers, 1964), p.150.
[68] For the officially frowned-on erotic aspects of Edo life, see T. Screech, *Sex and the floating world: erotic images in Japan 1700–1820* (London, 1999).

samurai moved freely in Edo society. The lower ones often executed menial work. Higher ones, in disguise as *chōnin* or commoners, attended the kabuki theatre and graced the other distractions of the pleasure district: drinking, prostitution and print shops whose big sellers were prints of kabuki actors. The kabuki had originally actresses as well as actors. However, as actresses provided sexual favours, female parts were later required to be performed by males. That did not eliminate problems, and an aura of male prostitution was to hang around the theatre. Edo was also the mecca of *rōnin* as a source of ready, though often disreputable, employment. As intellectual life in Edo grew, it also acquired an appeal for more intellectual samurai. Some *rōnin* were important figures and, in contrast to the stiff and limited court life, a world existed of easy contact between shogunal retainers, han samurai on *sankin kōtai* duties, and *rōnin*, who discussed the intellectual and political issues of the day, and all of whom in their advice and comment were busybodies. In other words, a new form of discourse developed over time among them. Inevitably too through their jockeying for reputation and position, they drew the authorities into their quarrels with ill consequences either for themselves or their rivals.

If long-distance trade was mostly routed by sea, passenger traffic was by land, apart from a large passenger traffic on the Inland Sea with its usually calm waters, and prospects of nights spent ashore. The *sankin kōtai* was the most striking manifestation of all this traffic. As it required the presence of so many in Edo, not only were the stays in Edo determined by decree but so were the routes and times of travel so that congestion on the roads and in the city alike could be avoided. Each daimyo journey was in effect a procession, the daimyo and his senior officials in palanquins, other retainers, samurai and servants, walking, and pack-horses and/or porters carrying the baggage. The Tokaido was the busiest of the roads; by 1822 the schedule for Edo visits envisaged that 146 of the daimyo would travel by it.[69] The Dutch, whose visits to Edo were based on the same model, had to organise and pay for a movement of near 200 people, and unlike daimyo made the trip every year to 1791. Inns existed along the roads, lesser ones for ordinary travellers, more exalted ones for daimyo. Some of the inns used by the Dutch were celebrated, notably the *Nagasaki-ya* in Edo and the *Ebi-ya* in Kyoto.[70] In economic terms, the

---

[69] C. N. Vaporis, *Breaking barriers: travel and the state in early modern Japan* (Cambridge, Mass., 1994), p.275n.

[70] Katagiri Kazuo, *Oranda yado Ebiya no kenkyū* [A study of the Ebiya Dutch inn], 2 vols. (Kyoto, 1998). The same author's very succinct account of the *hofreis* itself, *Edo no orandajin: kapitan no edo sanpu* [Edo's Dutchmen: the opperhoofd's Edo visits] (Tokyo, 2000) is, of many, the most convenient source for a full account of the *hofreis* or, in Japanese, the *sanpu*.

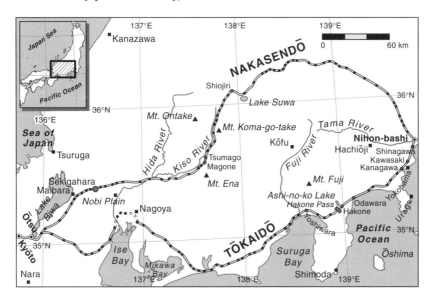

5. The Tokaido and Nakasendo roads and posting stations

cost of accommodation and subsistence on the journey to and from Edo, taking up to a month each way for several hundred retainers (2,000 for the grandest daimyo), was the one real cost which would not have been incurred in the absence of a *sankin kōtai*. From the west, the daimyo travelled on the Inland Sea as far as Osaka. From Osaka and Kyoto, there were two routes to Edo. One was the Tokaido (literally, eastern sea road), which remained close to the sea before winding its way over the mountain barrier by the pass at Hakone at the foot of Mount Fuji; the other the Nakasendo (inland line of road), a precipitate route through the mountains of the centre of Japan. Inns, horses and porters were available at the posting stages on the road (such as the fifty-three stages immortalised in the engravings by Hiroshige c.1830 of the 300 miles of the Tokaido from Kyoto to Edo).[71] Other roads led to Edo from the north of Japan or from the west. The Nakasendo, second to the Tokaido for traffic from the west, also served as the last stage of the travel of many who set out from the Japan Sea coast.

As well as the daimyo traffic, pilgrims, people on private business, officials and merchants crowded the roads. Much of the traffic was

---

[71] A small volume combining the pictures of the fifty-three stages plus the starting point in Edo (Nihonbashi) and ending point at Sanjōbashi in Kyoto with commentary is NARAZAKI Muneshige, *Hiroshige: the 53 stations of the Tokaido* (Kodansha International, 1969, 8th printing, Tokyo, 1982).

commercial and the pack-horse is a familiar image in the many pictures of traffic. Porters for daimyo and for official carriage were provided by a corvée on peasants living near the road. There were fixed rates for their services. However, the burden was heavy, especially because the demands were often at times which competed with work in their own fields. There were also the official messengers on foot carrying government messages and mail, either at normal pace or, at higher rates, at an express pace. The policing of traffic has been exaggerated.[72] At Hakone the scrutiny of traffic was strict (there was no comparable scrutiny on the other roads, a fact which reflected the shogunal belief that trouble came from the west). In theory, also, a peasant leaving his district required a passport. In practice, this was largely disregarded or, given the huge volume of movement, unenforceable.

By the 1860s the level of rice output in Japan was already as high as in the most advanced parts of Asia even a century later.[73] In other words, Japan entered the Meiji era as a food-surplus region. The growth of the cultivated area and the demand for timber had accelerated the pace of deforestation in the seventeenth century. Wood, not stone, was the basic building material. Hence the demands of domestic dwellings and of castles and shrines alike were heavy on the forest resources of Japan. They were further swollen by the proneness of wooden structures to fire: the prodigal use of wood was enlarged by regular replacements as much as by new structures. Thus, there were two underlying problems behind population growth and economic activity. One was to cope with the consequences of a wet climate by flood control and irrigation works (made more acute by the effects of deforestation); the other was the provision of manure for expanding arable cultivation.

Deforestation made water control more pressing. It loosened soil; there were no longer tree roots to hold soil together and to halt, by absorbing water, an excessive run-off. Moreover wherever river flow slowed, as in meanders when the narrow valleys widened momentarily into sheltered plains, or in the lowland estuaries, the gravel and sand from the run-off were deposited on the river bed, raising its level and revealing the inadequacies of the river banks or dikes erected to protect the paddy-fields. Kumazawa Banzan had commented on the need for retaining woodland to prevent soil being washed away, and on the danger of badly constructed dams or reservoirs bursting and filling the fields with gravel. The pace of forest cutting had been particularly heavy in the first half of the

---

[72] Vaporis, *Breaking barriers* is a very readable account of the traffic and its regulation.
[73] Shigeru Ishikawa, *Economic development in Asian perspective* (Tokyo, 1967), pp.94–5, 98–100.

seventeenth century. However, woodland management and reforestation gradually became a practice: the heavily wooded mountain province of Hida had been stripped, but much of its forest was restored over the century from 1760.[74] Deforestation, irrigation and water control presented a complex equation in which all three elements played a role.

Japan, it has also been argued, was a society in which a delicate ecological balance between nature and human endeavour limited both economic and demographic expansion and kept total output and population within a severe ceiling from which it escaped only in a few periods, the decades immediately after the 1642 crisis, and again over the Bunka and Bunsei decades.[75] An argument that harvests worsened in the eighteenth century is a widespread one.[76] The increased incidence of failures in the eighteenth century is in part a mirage created by the poorer documentation for the preceding century (some of the shortages were quite serious especially in the northern regions of Honshu) which served to highlight problems experienced in the better-documented story of the eighteenth century. The argument also gained plausibility from an apparent stagnation of population in the eighteenth century. It may, however, be prudent to lay less emphasis on the ecosystem and more on climatic conditions isolated from a concept of long-term ecological change. If famine occurred more frequently in the Tohoku, the reason was less over-exploitation of forest resources than the region's exposure to a premature climatic cooling in the early autumn. On a rare occasion as in 1755 it could lead to a major famine which had no parallel in western Japan. In the rest of Japan – in western Honshu and in Kyushu – failures were much less frequent.

Moreover, far from the frequency of famine increasing – which would support the case for excessive exploitation of the ecosystem – their occurrence depended on uncommon features. Two of the worst disasters – in 1641–3 (the first well-documented famine) and 1732 – were caused primarily by a locust-like insect. In 1732 a preceding very mild winter followed by heavy rains from early summer which maximised humidity provided perfect conditions for the incubation and diffusion of the

---

[74] Conrad Totman, *The green archipelago: forestry in preindustrial Japan* (Berkeley, 1989), p.167. On forestry see also Totman, *The lumber industry in early modern Japan* (Honolulu, 1995).

[75] The ecological problem is set out in Totman, *Early modern Japan*, pp.xxvii, 34, 224–5, 228, 230–1, 243, 249, 263, 269–70, 315, 466. The emphasis is heightened by the styling of two general chapters on population and resources from 1732 to 1850 as 'Ecological trends: the period of stasis'.

[76] Maruyama wrote that 'famines still went on tormenting the peasants' and they were 'plagued . . . by famines and floods since the Tenmei era' (*Intellectual history of Tokugawa Japan*, pp.152, 345), and Totman that 'the seventeenth century experienced famines, notably of the Kan'ei period, but after 1700 their frequency, severity and geographical scale increased substantially' (*Early modern Japan*, p.236).

insect: crops were ravished from Kyushu to as far north as the Kinki. In the cooler north, the crops fared well (a contrast with the early 1640s when cold seasons had extended famine to Honshu at large); rice shipments from Sendai to Edo were at a high level. Exports from Osaka to Edo (always small in any event) were prohibited, and the shogun sent money and rice to the western han. Edo prices which had at first fallen later rose. That made the year a lucrative one for Sendai shippers, but as a result of a steep rise in the spring, *uchi kowashi* occurred in Edo.[77] Disasters as acute as this had later parallels only in the 1780s and more markedly in the 1830s when wet and cool seasons spread famine from the Tohoku further afield to the Kanto and, especially in 1836–7, to the Kansai. The 1780s were to experience two famine seasons, the first one, 1783–4, not only in the Tohoku but in the Kanto. The second famine was in 1786–7, reaching far south: this, like the famine of 1836–7, was a near-national disaster. In 1783, the volcanic explosion of Mount Asama in June, through the massive release of ash into the atmosphere, led to a cloudy and cool ripening season not only in the Tohoku but in the Kanto. Though the harvest had been good in 1783 in the west, a remarkably heavy typhoon season in the preceding year ensured that rice stocks in granaries were already low before the 1783 harvest.[78] Some exports occurred from Osaka to Edo in 1784.[79] However, their effect was to send up prices further afield and, uniquely, *uchi kowashi* in the cities spread though the west even into Kyushu. The 1786–7 famine, caused by incessant rain and abnormal coolness in the Tohoku and Kanto, was felt further afield because a heavy and uncommonly widespread typhoon season led to a meagre harvest across the entire western half of Japan. However, the effects were most evident in the Tohoku and in Edo in which the scale of the *uchi kowashi* had an unnerving effect on the political world. The spectre of urban unrest and foreign crisis coinciding (for the first time Ezo had become a serious concern) became an abiding one for Japanese statesmen.

It is essential to make a distinction between the Tohoku and the rest of Japan. The Kanto was less vulnerable, the Kansai rarely at risk; and

---

[77] Kikuchi Isao, 'Kyōhō Tenmei no kikin to seiji kaikaku: chūō to chihō, kenryoku to shijō keizai' [The Kyōhō and Tenmei famines and political reform: centre and regions, sovereign power and market economy], in Fujita Satoru (ed.), *Bakuhansei kaikaku no tenkai* [The evolution of Bakuhansei reforms] (Tokyo, 2001), pp.56–64.

[78] For the famine and near-famine years of Japanese history, see Kikuchi Isao, *Kinsei no kikin* [Famines in early modern history] (Tokyo, 1997), pp.1–10; Arakawa Hidetoshi, *Kikin no rekishi* [History of famines] (Tokyo, 1967), pp.4–8. The social and political circumstances of famine are documented in some detail in Kikuchi Isao, *Kikin no shakai-shi* [The social history of famines] (Tokyo, 1994).

[79] Kikuchi, 'Kyōhō Tenmei no kikin', p.71.

in the west, locust damage apart, only a heavy and prolonged typhoon season was a harbinger of trouble. An efficient agriculture in a monsoon society depended on water-control works and, under conditions of intensive cultivation, on manuring also. Without water control the rains would wreak havoc in the upper reaches of river valleys, and in the lower reaches embankments to protect paddy-fields from the sudden intrusion of water and sediment were essential if farming was to become intensive (as it did in the course of the seventeenth century). As much low-lying land, locking water in, became swamp, drainage works, not all of them successful, helped to bring such land into cultivation, and expensive attempts recurred time and time again also to drain the swamps to the north of Edo. The building of reservoirs as part of the water-control works in the upper courses of rivers had reduced the incidence of drought. Kumazawa Banzan noted that through such works, some areas had already had several decades of adequate supply. Of course a heavy or prolonged monsoon would put the physical survival of such works to the test. Monsoon and typhoon rainfall were the reason for the comparative absence of bridges. Thus the Rokugo bridge, just south of Edo and considered one of three great bridges, was swept away six times in the seventeenth century.[80] Nevertheless, investment in building up river banks and in irrigation works tamed the worst effects of the monsoon, and made agricultural life less precarious.

Agriculture also depended of course on manuring. Japanese agriculture, apart from horses (for which the Musashi on the western approaches to Edo and later the Tohoku were famous), was not a livestock one. Hence farmyard manure scarcely existed. Human night-soil was one resource. Along the roads farmers thoughtfully, but with self-interest in mind, provided toilets for passing traffic. The night-soil of cities commanded a price, and it was collected daily and systematically brought into the countryside. For agricultural areas near cities, that reduced or eliminated the manure problem. The swift removal of night-soil, in contrast to the failure to deal with it efficiently in European cities, is regarded as a reason for the remarkable absence of epidemic diseases in Tokugawa towns and cities. Of course, night-soil carried the risks of parasites: this was lessened if it was exposed to the air to decompose before use. Brushwood and vegetation, if rotted, were also useful manures. They still did not satisfy the demand. Hence the use of dried fish as a manure was important, especially for inland districts without nearby large towns. With the growth of Ezo trade in the second half of the eighteenth century, dried fish became ever more important, and the fishery expanded, worked by

---

[80] Vaporis, *Breaking barriers*, p.52.

Ainu and by as many as 60,000 seasonal migrants from the Tohoku.[81] The region, largely unknown in the seventeenth century, was acquiring an economic significance, even before it also acquired its less welcome strategic importance.

The seventeenth century was an era of growth and change culminating in the Genroku period. The novelty of sweeping change inevitably led to an advocacy of the restoration of the past as a panacea for the problems which arose with growth. Yet repeated advocacy by writers reflected their awareness of the scale of the change rather than any capacity to suggest realistic remedies. The classic Genroku period, in the sense of *nengo* or regnal period, was limited to 1688–1704. But in a cultural or economic sense the term is a broader one, reaching further into the eighteenth century. The greatest literary embodiment of this change, the Osaka dramatist Chikamatsu, actually flourished in later years. Kumazawa Banzan, Itō Jinsai and Sorai, the most admired thinkers, were a trio who variously survived into or lived beyond the Genroku period, and whose writing on philosophical and political issues was based on an intensely rational – and secular – view of the world. There was also from the first decade of the eighteenth century an emerging lack of fear of an external threat, and this novel sense was accompanied by a new knowledge of the European world. It is an important feature of eighteenth-century Japan, one that helped to prepare the country to confront a new and more serious external crisis in the nineteenth century.

---

[81] *PP Japan.* The regular consular reports from Hakodate are very useful on the fishery and settlement from the 1860s. See also, for an account of Ezo in later Tokugawa times, David L. Howell, *Capitalism from within: economy, society and the state in a Japanese fishery* (Berkeley, 1995).

4   An age of stability: Japan's internal world, 1709–1783, in perspective

The interrogation in Edo in 1709 (with the aid of a Nagasaki interpreter) of Sidotti, an Italian Jesuit who had entered the country as a missionary, and the calm analysis by Arai Hakuseki of its implications, pointed to a dramatically more relaxed view of external challenge than in the early 1690s. Japan was about to enter on almost a century of remarkable freedom from anxiety on the external front. Only the apparition on its coasts in 1771 from Kamchatka of the Hungarian adventurer Moric Alasdar Benyowsky (1746–86) escaping from detention in Siberia seemed to call this security into question. He addressed two letters to the Dutch which announced the imminence of attack from the north. Many modern writers have argued that the Benyowsky (rendered later in Japanese as *Bengoro* or, in modern Japanese, *Benyofusuki*) affair reinforced an existing state of paranoia. There is no evidence of an immediate reaction to Benyowsky. The text of his letters is known only in the reporting of the Dutch to Batavia which contained translations from German into Dutch, which in turn were translated by the Japanese interpreters in Nagasaki.[1] There are only two – fleeting – mentions of the event in the *Tsūkō ichiran*, the huge compendium of official documents in the 1850s.[2] Only from 1785 when Edo missions of enquiry were sent to Ezo, did the northern frontier acquire a political significance. With the arrest of a Russian naval officer, Golownin (Golovnin), and some of his crew in 1811, it presented Japan with what was arguably its most serious external crisis

---

[1] The German text of the letters, the translations into Dutch, and the letter from the *opperhoofd* to the bugyo of Nagasaki survive only in the Deshima factory records, now in The Hague. For the details, see *Historical documents relating to Japan in foreign countries: an inventory of microfilm acquisitions in the library of the Historiographical Institute (Shiryō Hensanjo)*, 5 vols. (Tokyo, 1963–6), vol. 1 (1963), pp.196–7. The text of one of the letters is in Donald Keene, *The Japanese discovery of Europe: Honda Toshiaki and other discoverers* (Stanford, 1969), p.34. The scant Japanese documentation of the episode is shown in the Japanese translation of the diaries, *Benyofusuki kōkai-ki* [The account of Benyowsky's sea journey], ed. Mizuguchi Shigeo and Numata Jirō (Tokyo, 1971).

[2] *Tsūkō ichiran*, 8 vols. (Tokyo, 1913), vol. 7, p. 88 (*kan* 273), vol. 8, pp.229–32 (*kan* 321), opening and concluding *kan* of the 49 *kan* on Russia, with Japanese translations of the letters appended to the final *kan*. There is no evidence of a large correspondence at the time.

between 1647 when two Portuguese warships had sailed into Nagasaki bay and 1853, the year of arrival of Perry.

In the course of the eighteenth century, foreign trade had steadily lost importance. Foreign trade in neighbouring countries also lacked buoyancy. The traffic between Batavia and China, carried on Portuguese and Chinese vessels, fell. While a direct trade in tea to Europe from Canton began to develop, the European market, small enough to be often glutted, was mainly in Britain and in its American colonies (and even the European companies trading to Canton were in business primarily to smuggle tea into Britain where the monopoly supplier was trying to keep prices up).[3] The trade did not involve more than one or two dozen ships in a traffic in which early arrival in Europe alone guaranteed profit. The centre of economic gravity had shifted much more firmly than in the preceding century to India and to the regions close to it. While the Russians, sharing in Siberia a long frontier with China, had enjoyed relatively easy relations in an exchange of furs and skins for Chinese wares, British efforts to widen contacts beyond the confined European stake at Canton had been rebuffed. Japan itself disappeared entirely from the reckoning. The British East India Company, last concerning itself about Japan in 1673, did not do so again until 1793.[4]

Europeans, however, were to remain obsessed by the idea that China's huge population could provide markets for European wares. Hence interest in China inevitably recovered. Encouraged by a small but functioning trade across land frontiers, Russian interest in a maritime trade between Kamchatka and Canton emerged in the 1790s, and the British sent the famous Macartney diplomatic mission in 1792, which was at least received in Peking, though its entreaties were rejected.[5] The Americans, who famously imported their tea from England (the Boston Tea Party was one of the events preceding their revolution) made their first appearance as traders in Canton in the 1780s. Ironically, the markets for western wares continued to be elusive, a reason for the importance that opium began to assume in European trade even before the end of the eighteenth century.[6] By the 1830s it was a key commodity in redressing an adverse British balance of trade with China.[7]

---

[3] Dermigny, *La Chine et l'occident.*

[4] Massarella, *A world elsewhere*, pp.359–61; W. G. Beasley, *Great Britain and the opening of Japan 1834–1858* (Folkestone, Kent, 1995), pp.xvii–xix, 1–2; *Report on Japan to the secret committee of the English East India Company by Sir Stamford Raffles*, with a preface by M. Paske-Smith (London, 1971).

[5] Robert A. Bicker (ed.), *Ritual and diplomacy: the Macartney mission to China 1792–4* (London, 1993).

[6] Krusenstern, in his observations from 1798, noted that opium 'is imported with impunity in almost every ship'. Krustenstern, *Voyage round the world*, vol. 2, p.338n.

[7] J. Y. Wong, *Deadly dreams: opium and the Arrow War (1856–1860) in China* (Cambridge, 1998), pp.376–433.

Equally significant was exploration, prompted as much or even more by a modish curiosity about the unknown as by immediate commercial concerns. In the 1760s and 1770s, with Cook's and Bougainville's voyages, study of the unknown reaches of the Pacific took centre stage again. La Pérouse's famous voyage in 1785 launched the serious exploration of the coast of Tartary. While books on Japan had been few and slow to move from manuscript to print form, books on exploration now became numerous, and translation from one language into another was speedy. The original edition of La Pérouse's journals in 1797 quickly appeared in a further fourteen editions or translations in all.[8] A Japanese translation of the somewhat fictional journeys of Benyowsky (which had been published in many languages from 1790 onwards) was one of three translations which the Japanese sent to Ezo when officials there were interviewing their Russian prisoner Golownin.[9] Ironically, in the light of the notoriety given to this account in later historiography, the Japanese 'paid but little attention' to their Benyowsky text.[10]

Exploration (accompanied by the more ominous charting of coastal waters) inevitably drew close to the very shores of Japan in the 1780s and 1790s. The Russians under Laxman in 1792–3 and Rezanov in 1804 broached the question of trade relations, the first such request in over a century. It came not only from a western country, but from one with a land base in Siberia which had already made it possible for a few nationals to advance into Kuril islands which were unknown, or almost so, to the Japanese. The contact of the aboriginal inhabitants with the Russians in turn revived the spectre of Christianity: the Ainu might be either politically seduced or converted by Russian policy and religion. The abiding Japanese concern, however, was how to avoid war. The simplest response in face of a request was to procrastinate, a valid tactic in itself as well as a reflection of indecision as to how best to respond. It was not a case of a divide between a group who wanted to open up Japan and others who wanted to maintain sakoku. Broadly speaking all Japanese favoured isolation. Tension was heightened by the rising in 1789 of the oppressed

[8] *The journal of Jean-Francois de Galaup de la Pérouse*, translated by John Dunmore, 2 vols. (London, 1994).
[9] *Memoirs and travels of Mauritius Augustus Comte de Benyowsky* (London, 1790; Glasgow, 1904).
[10] W. M. Golownin, *Narrative of my captivity in Japan in the years 1811, 1812 and 1813*, 2 vols. (London, 1818), vol. 1, p.253–4. There appears to be no extant reference in Japanese to this translation of Benyowsky, which must be either a draft or an incomplete translation that did not proceed further or that has not survived. Although Benyowsky's memoirs were widely translated into European languages, there does not seem to have been a contemporary Dutch translation (see the list of editions in the bibliography and on p.3 in Numata and Mizuguchi, *Benyofusuki*). The interpreters must have translated from a language other than Dutch: in the state of their knowledge at the time, the translation must necessarily have been both incomplete and imperfect.

Ainu in Kunashiri, the more important of the two Kuril islands with Japanese settlement, which raised the spectre of Russian encroachment profiting from Ainu discontent. The *uchi kowashi* or urban riots in Edo in 1787 only added to the alarm: what would be the position if Russian advance coincided with paralysing disturbance in either Edo or Osaka? The wish by Laxman, the Russian who had sought external trade in 1792, to proceed to Edo to pursue his negotiations, had prompted concern about the state of defence of Edo bay itself. At the order of the prime minister, Matsudaira Sadanobu, a Nagasaki interpreter, Ishi Shosuke, made a compilation of information, *Ensei gunki-ko*, from western military books.[11] Matsudaira also drew up proposals for the establishment of bugyo and *kanjō bugyō* posts, and the stationing of men, on the coast line of Edo bay and its approaches.[12] These do not seem to have been acted on, though they provided something of a framework for action over forty years later, when the threat to Edo became more concrete.

If Japanese officials feared a coincidence of unrest and of foreign threat, did this signify a straightforward strategic worry, or did it spring from concerns already long-established about potentially explosive discontent? In other words was there a chronic social or economic crisis? Some have seen an underlying proof of this in the apparent stability of population over the whole period. In 1721, and at six-year intervals from 1726 onwards, the shogunate had required the compilation of population returns by each han, and these in turn were carried into national totals.[13] No evidence survives of how the data were compiled by han samurai or how in turn han figures were aggregated by shogunal officials. Although twenty-five censuses should have been conducted between 1726 and 1864, no data whatever exist for six of these years, for nine other years a mere grand total exists, and for the remaining years alone does a breakdown at provincial level survive.[14] The figures, though they did not circulate publicly, were certainly known to officials, and helped to fuel the pessimism widely felt about long-term trends which samurai writers expressed from time to time. They also help us to understand why official concern with infanticide was so strong and the efforts to outlaw it persistent.

[11] T. Screech, *The shogun's painted culture: fear and creativity in the Japanese states 1760–1829* (London, 2000), pp.34, 269n.
[12] Fujita Satoru, *Matsudaira Sadanobu* (Tokyo, 1993), pp.203–4.
[13] As population totals for some han actually preceded 1721, it seems likely that the shogunal requirement was simply based on a practice which existed already within some han administrations.
[14] Table no. 94 in Minami Kazuo, *Bakumatsu edo shakai no kenkyū* [Studies in Bakumatsu Edo society] (Tokyo, 1978), p.180. The years entirely missing are 1738, 1810, 1816, 1852, 1858 and 1864. No data survive for 1852, 1858 or 1864, nor any evidence of decisions, positive or negative, in regard to a census in those years.

The figures themselves pose real problems. First, apart from little groups of scholar advisors (bookish and Confucian in their intellectual formation) in each han administration and the quite large groups of accounting officials supervising the collection of rice or recording its entry and outflow in han warehouses, public officials were not numerous, and certainly none had a known competence in statistical data. Debate in writing, currency matters apart, was invariably barren of statistical detail. Such statistics as existed certainly circulated, as did, in informal or private fashion, all official information in Tokugawa times. Thus, the writings of Katsu Kaishū, whose father had been a low-ranking samurai, contain a copy of the Tokugawa population figures, and Fukuzawa Yukichi in 1878 quoted the population figures of one han c.1854 in a monetary argument.[15] Such scant traces in Meiji times only confirm the indifference of Tokugawa times, which boded ill even for the survival of data. Within the han themselves han officials discarded the primary returns, sometimes even systematically destroying them or selling them as scrap paper, to the extent that where they survive, it is through duplicates retained by village head men.[16] It is asking much to assume that a society which lacked a group of statistically minded officials could, to start with, compile on a regular basis even crudely reliable demographic data. If so, the long-term stability suggested by the statistical data may be to a large degree fictitious. However, the insensitivity of the data worked two ways. If the national aggregates suggested a spurious stability, they may have equally failed to reflect accurately the severity of intermittent crises. In other words, we may have to see population as rising, and on the other hand, the famines of Tenmei and Tempō times as more unique and more serious than they have been taken to be.[17] This conclusion is consistent with Hayami Akira's observation in his path-breaking work on

---

[15] Nishikawa Shunsaku, *Fukuzawa Yukichi to sannin no kōshin tachi* [Fukuzawa Yukichi and three successors] (Tokyo, 1985), p.52. For the information on Katsu Kaishū I am indebted to Prof. Saitō Osamu.

[16] A. Hayami, *The historical demography of pre-modern Japan* (Tokyo, 1997), pp.79–80.

[17] This runs counter to some conclusions such as the one that 'we are on safe ground in assuming that population losses due to famine were far smaller than the domain of Morioka would have the Bakufu believe' (S. B. Hanley and K. Yamamura, *Economic and demographic change in preindustrial Japan* (Princeton, 1977), p.153). Appraisal of the general pattern would then shift from a picture of chronic crisis to a somewhat more benign trend in which fewer real food shortages occurred but the impact of the major famines is actually understated in the estimates. See O. Saitō, 'The frequency of famines: demographic correctives in the Japanese past', in *The demography of famines: perspectives from the past and the present*, ed. T. Dyson and C. O. Grada (Oxford, 2002), p.224, for a similar conclusion. On the suggestion of the benign trend in economic growth in the Japanese economy from the 1820s, see S. Nishikawa and O. Saitō, 'The economic history of the restoration period', in Michio Nagai and Miguel Urrutia (eds.), *Meiji ishin: restoration and revolution* (Tokyo, 1985), pp.180–2.

the Suwa region that in contrast to the relative stability suggested by population statistics, population fell quite sharply in the Tenmei and Tempō crises.[18]

The second consideration underlining the suspect quality of the demographic data is that the first count approximating to a modern census in 1872 has a higher grand total than the final surviving old-style compilation of 1846. Overall, population appeared to increase by twenty-three per cent from 1846 to 1872, which suggests a substantial underestimate in 1846. While a rise may not be implausible, the scale of the variations at regional level adds to doubts about the figures at large. Moreover the rise in the Tohoku and Kyushu in 1846–72 (thirty-eight and forty-two per cent respectively) contrasts with near-stagnation and rather slow growth respectively in the decades preceding 1846. Likewise the persistent stagnation of the Kanto and Kinki regions, the most marked in Japan, appears suspect. In particular in the Kanto, a fall in 1786 (sharper even than in the Tohoku); persistent stagnation in subsequent returns (even the Tohoku managed modest growth); a further fall in 1834 and an upswing in 1846 (when population actually fell in Kinki), are more easily explained by arbitrary compilation than by what is a very strained effort to relate these figures to actual conditons.[19]

Population counts, based ultimately on figures in the *shūmon aratame chō* (religious registration records) which were revised annually in each temple, and on their subsequent collation in the han administration, would have been a large bureaucratic exercise. Moreover, success would depend on close supervision of the process, and confidence in the exercise is not increased by evidence in some han of the existence of aggregates on an annual basis, unadjusted from year to year. In Morioka han two series of annual population aggregates survive. In the 1780s both sets are characterised by stability, one undisturbed by other than nominal adjustments, the other, equally stable apart from being marked down on one occasion (1784, clearly reflecting the famine in 1783).[20] It has been speculated that the reason for downward adjustments was to exaggerate the losses to the shogunal government.[21] It then remains puzzling why if population was marked down in 1784 the figures remained virtually

---

[18] Hayami Akira, *Kinsei nōson no rekishi jinkōgaku-teki kenkyū: shinshū suwa chihō no shūmon aratame-chō bunseki* [Researches in the demographic history of early modern farming villages: the temple registers of the Suwa district in Shinshu] (Tokyo, 1973), p.38. See also tables of population trends in selected Nobi villages for the Tenmei and Tempō periods in Hayami Akira, *Kinsei nōbi chihō no jinkō, keizai, shakai* [Population, economy and society of the modern Nobi region] (Tokyo, 1992), pp.61–2.

[19] Hanley and Yamamura, *Economic and demographic change*, pp.39–68, 182–3.

[20] Hanley and Yamamura, *Economic and demographic change*, p.149.

[21] Hanley and Yamamura, *Economic and demographic change*, pp.150, 153–4.

unaltered in the wake of the 1786–7 famine. Their common tendency to stability suggests arbitrary manipulations of data, for reasons and by processes of which we know nothing. Instances of what seem arbitrary changes can be found in other *han*. In Mito earlier population counts were sharply reduced in 1774: in the remainder of the Tokugawa era they variously fluctuated or stagnated between a range of 227,000 and 250,000.[22] Other considerations add to doubts about *han* aggregates. For instance, stable sex ratios from one census to the next in Morioka suggest a rule of thumb approach to processing figures.[23] There were also widely differing practices between *han* as to categories of commoner included (samurai and their servants were excluded), and there is some uncertainty as to the extent of the inclusion of people without a fixed domicile and castle-town populations. The basic source – the *shūmon aratame chō* – also revealed differing practices as to the inclusion of children and at what age.[24]

If the population estimates of shogunal times conceal some real rise in numbers, that does not of itself make for an optimistic appraisal of conditions in the worst years. Heavy losses reported in various *han* writings (which may even have influenced the 'adjustment' of population totals), though inevitably subjective as coming from eye-witnesses, should not be disregarded. Inevitably the graphic accounts, 1836 apart, come from the Tohoku. There, the effects of late ripening seasons were sometimes compounded by winters which proved savage beyond the norm (with heavy losses of both wild and farm animals). Harrowing accounts exist for the famine years, not only of loss of lives supposedly running into thousands, but of desperate peasants, who as Buddhists did not usually consume meat, resorting to eating dogs, horses, carrion flesh, and even to cannibalism.[25] Even in the Tohoku, poor though it was, a single bad season was not sufficient to reduce the community to the degree of deprivation experienced in the worst years. Famine in late 1786 into 1787 was made all the more devastating because in the preceding autumn standing rice and dry crops alike had suffered huge losses from remarkably strong winds, and famine conditions were beginning to appear at the very end of 1785.[26] In contrast to Europe, Japan has surprisingly graphic

---

[22] *Mito shi-shi* [History of Mito city], 9 vols. (Mito, 1963–98), middle series, vol. 3 (Mito, 1976), p.523. For village counts see ibid., pp.514, 524–6. An image of demographic decline is heightened by falls suggested by the early figures which are clearly more suspect than later figures.

[23] Hanley and Yamamura, *Economic and demographic change*, p.151.

[24] E. Honjō many years ago set out a very good summary of the inadequacies of the data in *The social and economic history of Japan* (Kyoto, 1935), pp.145–58.

[25] Kikuchi Isao, *Kinsei no kikin*, pp.53, 66–7, 69–70, 158–60.

[26] See the evidence of two travellers in the Tohoku at the end of 1785 and beginning of 1786 in H. Bolitho, 'Travellers' tales: three eighteenth-century travel journals', *Harvard journal of Asiatic studies*, vol. 50, no. 2 (Dec. 1990), pp.502–3.

and realistic pictorial representations of famine itself, a genre almost unknown in Europe: in the really bad years they exist also for districts beyond
the Tohoku.[27] Chronic bad or worsening conditions are hard to recon-
cile with a fall in rice prices over the eighteenth century and the early
decades of the following century. In the Hida village of Miyamura, deep
in the mountains near Takayama, the range of excess mortality was not
wide, and really serious only in 1837 when it was four times the average
for the entire period 1771–1851.[28] Folk wisdom was more optimistic.
As late as 1890, in the wake of the singular autumnal rains and disastrous harvest of 1889, one of the British consuls reported that 'country
folks still believe in an old tradition that every sixty-first year the rice crop
fails and a famine ensues'.[29] The rate of natural increase is likely in any
event to have been low: crude death and birth rates were low by European
standards.[30] Lower death rates suggest that the emphasis on hunger and
disease has been exaggerated (fevers were less common in Japanese cities
than in European, and in rural famine epidemic disease itself wreaked a
lesser toll than in Europe).[31]

Certainly, case studies in the advanced regions of central Japan suggest both a declining birth rate, and marriage ages, lower than in Europe
(and higher than in other parts of Asia), tending to rise. From the evidence of a sample of 43 villages in the Nobi plain (30 kilometres to the
north-west of Nagoya) from 1675 to 1875 the age of marriage of women
rose from 18 to 21,[32] and in 45 to 55 villages in Suwa *gun* or district in
Shinano province, for 150 years from 1670 (and for 25 to 45 villages for
the later years), both death and birth rates fell.[33] Yet as Hayami Akira,

---

[27] The most interesting, perhaps because it relates to Kyoto in 1837, is a scroll by Tanaka
Yubi, *Tenpō hachinen kimin kyūjutsu zukan*, in the Chester Beatty Library, Dublin. See
also *Kikakuten-kikin-shokuryō kiki o norikoeru* [Catalogue of special exhibition. Famine:
living through food crisis] (Nagoya City Museum, 1999).

[28] Ann Bowman Jannetta, *Epidemic and mortality in early modern Japan* (Princeton, 1987),
pp.37, 181.

[29] *PP Japan*, vol. 8, p.596, Report on Hyogo and Osaka for 1890.

[30] Hanley and Yamamura, *Economic and demographic change*, p.211, for rates for a sample
of four villages. For details of rates on the Nobi plain see Hayami, *Kinsei nōson*, p.46.

[31] Infectious diseases were, however, a significant factor in 1837. See A. Hayami,
'Population changes', in Jansen and Rozman, *Japan in transition*, p.295. Cholera epi-
demics – which occurred outside a famine context – were a major health hazard of the
1860s. Cholera first made its appearance in Nagasaki in 1832.

[32] Saitō Osamu, 'Jinkō' [Population], in Nishikawa, Odaka and Saitō, *Nihon keizai no 200
nen*, pp.43–4. For a fuller account see A. Hayami, *Historical demography*. In one of the
Nobi villages, Yokouchi, the marriage age of seventeen in c.1701 had risen to twenty-
one by 1826. A. Hayami, *Historical demography*, pp.106–7. Another case study of three
villages in Okayama and one in Mikawa suggests a female age of marriage of twenty-one
years. Hanley and Yamamura, *Economic and demographic change*, p.246.

[33] A. Hayami, *Historical demography*, pp.87–90. For fuller details see his *Kinsei nōson*, especially pp.16–24, 46. In this region the overall death rate was 20 to 25 per 1,000 at the

the pioneer of Japanese demographic studies, has noted, the overall stability in these cases is deceptive because the aggregates conceal a contrast between old settled lowland villages, where population grew little in the eighteenth century, and other districts, more recently settled, in valleys in which population growth was higher and remained so into the nineteenth century. Moreover, recent work suggests rather persuasively a hypothesis about a contrast between the Tohoku and regions of central Japan. In the Tohoku, marriage ages as low as 13 in the seventeenth century may have remained stubbornly as low at 17 in later centuries. Yet the birth rate equally remained low, in part because after marriage women entered service.[34] In central Japan, on the other hand, marriage ages were higher, in part because, in contrast to the Tohoku, the pattern was of women working away from home before marriage. In the remarkably complete temple records from 1773 to 1869 of Nishijo on the Nobi plain, the average age of female marriage for those who never left the village was 21.5 and for those who had outside work experience (almost two thirds of the women) 25.9.[35]

For very different reasons, both Tohoku and central Japan had low rates of increase. Even in central Japan, while Nishijo women who married at 20 had 5–9 children, those marrying at 25 had an average of 4.3.[36] In other words, circumstances in both Tohoku and central Japan, though different, tended to reinforce the tendency towards a low birth rate. Morever, infant mortality as elsewhere was high (as in Europe around 200 per 1,000); hence, if fertility was already low, household size should be low also. In Suwa *gun* in Shinano province a household size of 6 to 7 in the 1710s and 1720s was down to 5 by the 1780s and thereafter was even lower.[37]A household size of around 5 was below European norms. This raises inevitably the question of whether there was birth control in some form. Contemporaries certainly believed in infanticide, and han authorities, convinced of a static or even falling population, sought to prohibit it.[38] However, the evidence is in many cases not compelling and in the prosperous regions of central Japan, a number of studies failed to find the evidence of selective survival, e.g. sex ratios favouring males, which

---

outset and by the end of the period as low as 15 to 20; the birth rate, as high as 40 to 60 per 1,000 in the seventeenth century, was probably 30 per 1,000 in later times.

[34] A. Hayami and S. Kurosu, 'Regional diversity in demographic and family patterns in pre-industrial Japan', *Journal of Japanese studies*, vol. 27, no. 2 (Summer 2001), pp.290–321.

[35] A. Hayami, *Historical demography*, p.137.

[36] A. Hayami, *Historical demography*, p.135.   [37] A. Hayami, *Kinsei nōson*, pp.147–9.

[38] Hanley and Yamamura, *Economic and demographic change*, p.324; T. C. Smith, *Native sources of Japanese industrialisation*, pp.9, 36, 119, 108–13, 130–2. Smith's conclusions were heavily influenced by the evidence of one village, Nakahara, on the Nobi plain.

would have arisen if infanticide was practised.[39] In the prosperous Bunka period, the Russian captive Golownin was even told by an official that there was no official obsession with enquiring into infanticide.[40] However, recent work suggests that in the Tohoku, where both marriage age and birth rate remained low, a pattern of children surviving birth less well where there were already two or more girls than when there were no children may suggest infanticide.[41] Abortion was of course another resort, though not all abortion may have been intended. Heavy labour by women in the fields, supplemented by their executing a growing number of tasks in a combination of housework and domestic industry, may have led to high rates of spontaneous abortion.[42]

Price data at least were continuous and reliable. The downward trend in rice prices, already noticed as early as the 1680s by Kumazawa Banzan, reasserted itself outside short harvests, and rice prices in the spring of 1729 were the lowest so far recorded. The highest ever recorded occurred in 1786, 1787 and 1788 when they roughly quadrupled.[43] Thereafter the price trend was downwards, culminating in a remarkably long period of low prices, which was reversed only at the end of the 1820s. By the spring of 1837 prices were at levels not reached since the 1780s. A decade of falling or relatively favourable prices then followed.[44]

Practical responses to the fear of harvest failure took several forms. One step by farmers themselves was to put linseed or whale oil in the paddy-fields so that the young plants as they grew had a protective coating to repel locusts. Another was the official urge to encourage the extension of rice cultivation. This of course proved self-defeating. As Kusama Naokata and Yamagata Bantō, two advisors to Osaka houses handling daimyo accounts, later pointed out, it simply reinforced the fall in prices and defeated the aim of expanding income. The best way of coping with the problem, they argued, would be to increase storage (which would halt the price fall) after good harvests and carry the stocks forward to moderate

---

[39] O. Saitō, 'Historical demography: methodology and interpretations', in *Historical studies in Japan (viii) 1988–1992* (National Committee of Japanese Historians, Tokyo, 1995), p.84.

[40] Golownin, *Recollections*, pp.221–2.

[41] A. Hayami and S. Kurosu, 'Regional diversity', pp.290–321.

[42] See also O. Saitō, *Gender, workload and agricultural progress: Japan's historical experience in perspective*, discussion paper series A, no. 268 (Hitotsubashi University, 1993), especially p.24 where it is noted that women usually continued to work right up to the week the baby was due.

[43] See table of retail prices from Moto'ori Norinaga's diary, 1759–99 in Shigeru Matsumoto, *Motoori Norinaga 1730–1801* (Cambridge, Mass., 1970), p.122.

[44] There is a table of market rice prices, 1675–1867, in Yamamura, *A study of samurai income and entrepreneurship*, pp.49–53. For the low rice prices from 1789, see *Osaka shi-shi*, vol. 4, pp.216, 221–2; *Osaka fu-shi, kinsei*, pt 2, vol. 6, pp.589, 604, 611–13.

the price of rice in other years.the shortages of the 1780s were an island of disaster between two periods of low prices and rising prosperity.[45]
In some of the northern han, rice output seems to have fallen in the eighteenth and early nineteenth centuries. In Morioka, for instance, the assessed rice output fell by ten per cent over the century preceding 1837.[46] In Mito, following a new survey in Tempō times, assessment was reduced sharply from 418,394 koku to 317,086.[47] All this might suggest progressive impoverishment. However, as rice was not a food of the common people in the north, and levies were an object of systematic collection (as the source of the income of samurai and daimyo alike), the attractions for peasants of rice growing were not compelling, and every reason, communal and individual, ensured that rice paddy-fields encroached to the minimum on dry fields for barley and beans, hardy crops of cooler latitudes. Demands from the early seventeenth century by daimyo for the payment of the levy in rice (marketable outside the han) in place of other crops or, in poor districts with few desirable commodities, even in cash, created the surplus which daimyo could dispose of on the market. Daimyo and samurai personal consumption excluded, the bulk of rice was exported to discharge bills in Edo and debts in Osaka. Here, the production of rice – not featuring in the diet of the peasants themselves – could be represented as an oppressive requirement,[48] and over time peasants may in fact have converted paddy-fields to dry fields. These developments hardly pointed to a rosy picture: peasants maintained, perhaps even increased, their consumption of inferior foods; and, given modest development of textile and other industries, any surplus rice, after levies had been discharged, must have been sold as a means of getting cash, rather than consumed. The consequences were serious for the han administrations. Rice, through the levy on it, was the basis of the income of daimyo and of samurai. While han administrations sought to expand output, the results were less successful than elsewhere, and a fall in rice output ensured that the crisis in han – and hence samurai – finances persisted, embedded in a straitjacket of rigid income and rising expenditures. Mito han was in receipt of regular assistance from the shogunate in the 1820s and 1830s. The living style of samurai in Mito, even senior ones, as late as the 1840s and 1850s was extremely frugal.[49]

---

[45] Contrary assumptions are widespread. For instance, Maruyama claimed that riots and uprisings increased 'spectacularly' during the Hōreki, Meiwa, An'ei and Tenmei eras (1751–89). Maruyama, *Intellectual history of Tokugawa Japan*, p.275.
[46] Hanley and Yamamura, *Economic and demographic change*, p.133.
[47] *Mito shi-shi*, middle series, vol. 3, p.835.   [48] Kikuchi, *Kinsei no kikin*, pp.79–81.
[49] See Kikue Yamakawa, *Women of the Mito domain: recollections of samurai family life*, translated by Kate Wildman Nakai (Tokyo, 1992).

Whatever the contrast in harvest conditions between the Tohoku and the rest of Japan, a restricted public income was a feature of han finances everywhere. The outlook of officials and samurai writers at large was profoundly coloured by a crisis in income more than by one in the economy. This was all the more serious for samurai and government alike as inelastic incomes did not compensate for high urban living costs. Harvest failures created immediate problems: while prices rose, output was down, and abatements to peasants on the rice levy were usually necessary. However, the fiscal crisis lasted through good years as well as bad. Of the several threads of continuity behind three great bouts of official reforms occurring in 1716–36, 1787–93 and 1841–3, and taking the names of the periods in which they took place – Kyōhō, Kansei and Tempō respectively – the fiscal dimension is central.[50] The Kyōhō reform was triggered by deflation following the replacement in 1714–15 of the debased currency by a sound currency. Of itself the deflation would have been a short though painful experience in which all prices fell sooner or later and at a new and lower price level economic activity recovered its buoyancy. However, remarkably good harvests through the 1720s (with the lowest rice prices of Tokugawa history) kept samurai real incomes depressed. Various proposals floated about on moving people out of Edo, or on transferring samurai from Edo and the castle towns to the countryside (with moral as well as economic benefits). Shogunal decrees actually seeking to enforce a frugality of life style were essentially methods of attacking the expenditure side of the income equation. The rationale was that if costs were reduced, incomes would go further. The attempts were doomed to failure. Society itself had changed, and both proposals and decrees were no more than an aspiration which underlined the political and fiscal impotence of the state.

This failure had led the shogunate, as the extension of paddy land slowed down (bringing to a halt the seventeenth-century rise in public income) and expenditures rose amid the buoyant expectations of the Genroku era, into tinkering with the currency. In the debasements

---

[50] Declared intentions and specific measures, shared by all three reforms, give them a certain uniformity. However the Kyōhō reform, almost coterminous with Yoshimune's long period of rule, is distinct from the others. As Fujita Satoru has noted, its concern was with strengthening the shogunal system on a very broad basis; the timing of the launch of the later reforms was determined by very specific concerns, the Kansei reform with the Ezo problem (and famine), the Tempō reform with the effects of the devastating famine of 1837. See the succinct summary of a large literature and of the issues of interpretation in Fujita Satoru, 'Kinsei seiji shi to san dai kaikaku ron: Kenykū shi no seiri to tenbō' [Debate on politics in the early modern period and the three reforms: analysis and observations on historical research], in Fujita, *Bakuhansei kaikaku no tenkai*, pp.3–14. For a still more recent statement of his views, see his *Kinsei no san daikaikaku* [The three great reforms in the early modern period] (Tokyo, 2002).

between 1695 and 1711 the state succumbed to the temptation of easy and immediate profit by calling in money and turning a given amount of metal into a much larger amount of newly denominated currency. Debasement on this scale led in the short term to soaring prices. In consequence, political pressure made the introduction of good money unavoidable.[51] The abrupt replacement in 1714 of the debased metal by new money of high quality entailed inevitable deflation: rice income converted into cash fell quickly while the burthen of debt remained unchanged, and other prices proved 'sticky'. In other words, for state and for samurai alike the cure was as bad as the disease. The litany of complaints and lamentations remained a persistent one, and it is important to see the pessimism of writers as originating as much – or more – in their own circumstances as in the economy at large. Short-term deflation apart, paradoxically it was exceptionally good times – the 1720s were a near legendary decade in their harvest outcome – that proved disastrous for the solvency of shogunate and samurai alike. As a result, Yoshimune himself debased the currency in 1736: the purity of the silver currency, for instance, was reduced from the eighty per cent content of 1714 to forty per cent. Unlike other major debasements, the benefits of this operation were passed on to holders of the old currency, instead of being pocketed by the shogunate. The operation therefore led to no political storm. Partly for this reason, the later view has been that the operation succeeded in its objective. The fact that very low rice prices did not recur was only partly the consequence of debasement: in the long term, harvests, good but not in the way of the 1730s superabundant, were more decisive. In any event, even higher rice prices could not prevent the public income showing signs of distress again by the 1760s. Such, however, was the ill repute of currency tinkering that, despite ongoing fiscal penury, it did not begin again until 1818. Some of the new coins introduced in the 1780s were actually of higher standard than existing coins.

The state – or more accurately, the han and shogunate alike – was unable to create new fiscal devices for the purpose of widening the sources of income. Bad though this was for the state, it was of course good news for the citizens. Europe's fiscal systems had grown to cater for standing armies and the huge costs – carrying into peace-time – of repeated wars. The sophisticated financial system of a state like England grew around

---

[51] Arai Hakuseki, who was not primarily responsible for the decision on the recoinage, was well aware of the deflationary dangers of a sudden recoinage and opposed the precipitate action which for political reasons was adopted. Ackroyd, *Autobiography of Arai Hakuseki*, pp.5, 166, 214–15. On the currency reform, see the excellent account in Kate Wildman Nakai, *Shogunal politics: Arai Hakuseki and the premises of Tokugawa rule* (Cambridge, Mass., 1988), pp.97–106.

the servicing in peace-time of the large debt, paid out of new taxes voted in war-time. Japan had its financiers, perhaps the largest in the world, in Osaka and from the mid-eighteenth century in Edo as well. Hence, there was an ability to lend, provided that the borrower had the capacity to repay. However, the narrow income of shogunate and han meant that expenditure had to be kept down, and the situation remained manageable only because military expenditure virtually dried up. The effect of sakoku was that Japan in effect demilitarised; its armed forces were puny, decentralised; and even the once promising manufacture of firearms ceased.[52]

In a sense Sorai, in his commentaries on public affairs, grasped the problem perfectly. Writing in the 1720s, when Japan was anew in fiscal crisis, he said that the death of Ieyasu had left the task of creating Japanese institutions unfinished. Peace itself was a great boon to Japan, but in every rose, there is a thorn. Japan had not only a materially poor government but a weak government (in some respects, it did not have national institutions at all). The shogunal administration was able in the seventeenth century to ensure that trading towns passed into its possession (notably Osaka in 1619), it controlled mines, and it held an exclusive control of the currency. *Hansatsu*, or paper money, was introduced over time by many han. Its potential significance can be seen in the fact that the shogunate took note several times of its existence. However, its inelastic amount (until well into the nineteenth century), and the fact that the shogunate itself did not resort to a paper money, reveal that it was a suspect device, resorted to by public debtors.

The question has been posed why the public authorities – shogunate and han – failed to resolve their indebtedness simply by increased demands on peasants. The answer, it has been suggested, lay in political weakness on their part. Their power was not absolute, and the likelihood – indeed the certainty – of resistance had to be borne in mind.[53] This view seems to be confirmed in the pattern of later unrest in han which was often triggered by attempts at fiscal innovation: the new measures were usually abandoned and officials either reprimanded or punished. In the case of the shogunate, it could also in theory seek to add to its income by expanding its *tenryō* or directly managed demesne. Daimyo could be removed from their possessions, and in the seventeenth century a very

[52] See Perrin, *Giving up the gun.*
[53] K. Yamamura, *A study of samurai income and entrepreneurship*, pp.190–2, 204; 'From coins to rice: hypotheses on the *kandaka* and *kokudaka* systems', *Journal of Japanese studies*, vol. 14, no. 2 (Summer 1988), pp.345–6. The assumption of political weakness can be seen carrried to its extreme in the work of James White (*Ikki, social conflict and political protest in early modern Japan* (Ithaca and London, 1995)), who argues, against the drift of emphasis in most work on social crisis, that in its later decades peasants were better off but the political powers of the shogunate and han were collapsing.

large number of the smaller *tozama* han were variously eliminated or transferred from one territory to another.[54] Though lands were usually distributed to existing daimyo or used to create *fudai* han for favourites useful to the shogun, some lands were retained by the shogunate. However, Tsunayoshi was the last shogun to take advantage of circumstances to enlarge shogunal demesnes. The question remains why the shogunate did not add more land to its directly managed territories, and why did it cease doing so almost altogether?[55] The answer is that extra demesne meant little income for the shogunate. Peasants retained their share of output, some sixty per cent or so, and the collection of the balance on small, and often isolated, territories would have been eaten up in stipends of officials sent from Edo to oversee the administration of the area. The real income, in the form of rice or cash, transferred to Edo would have been small. A political philosopher like Sorai, keen to suggest ways of strengthening the shogunate, argued that many han were too large, and that they should be reduced in size. How this could be done politically was not spelled out. It was not attempted, and to have done so would have put the compromise peace in Japan in jeopardy.

Given the small profits to be gained by the shogunate, and also the sense of political security which set in by 1700, the replacement or removal of daimyo, either *fudai* or *tozama*, slowed down dramatically in the eighteenth century. In other words, the smaller daimyo, vulnerable throughout the seventeenth century, especially if *tozama*, acquired a vested interest in the possession of their han. The precise powers of the shogunate remained ill defined: han could be asked to contribute to special tasks such as the building of Edo castle or its reconstruction after fires, and to defence, but, arbitrary though the demands at times were, there was a delicate balance in these relations between shogunate and han. Fresh demands were made infrequently (and only for tasks which were seen as in the public interest), and, in turn, made only for such purposes, they were acceded to. The common interest of shogunate and han is reflected in the policy of reducing *sankin kōtai* in recognition of temporary or longer difficulties of individual han. In addition, the shogunate itself made contributions to han which experienced problems, regularly in some cases, in years of exceptional difficulty in other instances. Thus, simply to take some examples, in the wake of the 1732 famine it dispensed largesse even to great *tozama* of the south; the tiny han of Tsushima was

---

[54] Fujino Tamotsu, *Tokugawa seiken ron* [A study of Tokugawa rule] (Tokyo, 1991), pp.101–20. Removals and transfers of daimyo, both *tozama* and *fudai*, over the Tokugawa period are summarised in a table on p.109.

[55] H. Bolitho, *Treasures among men: the fudai daimyo in Tokugawa Japan* (New Haven, 1974), p.177.

subsidised as its trade contracted, and Mito received support in the 1820s and 1830s.

Even if the balance of distribution of territory between han and shogunate began to stabilise well before the end of the seventeenth century, the question as to how Japan could be governed had to be settled. There were two tendencies. One was to draw the *fudai* more into government. The other was for shoguns to centralise government into their own hands, and rely on political advisors who were not *fudai*, or who from modest backgrounds were turned into daimyo by shogunal grants of lands. The shoguns of the late seventeenth century, including the powerful and capable Tsunayoshi (1646–1709), illustrate the latter tendency. Tsunayoshi, entering into history with the epithet 'Dog-shogun' because as a Buddhist he prohibited the killing of animals, may sound a dilettante: he was, however, a scholarly man and powerful figure concerned to increase the position of the shogunate.[56] The rise of Yanagisawa Yoshiyasu (1658–1714), a patron of Sorai's, as the main advisor of Tsunayoshi is an example of an advisor or courtier accumulating demesnes, and rising ever higher in his new status as daimyo. His political role did not outlive the death of his patron. Arai Hakuseki is a comparable figure. A mere *jusha* or scholar from 1693 to Ienobu, at the time a daimyo, he became the chief advisor of Ienobu when he became shogun in 1709, and of his successor Ietsugu who ruled from 1712 to 1716. Remaining lowly in formal status however, he was quite dismissive of the *rōjū*.

Between the seventeenth and eighteenth centuries, political evolution could have swung either way: towards cabinet government under *rōjū*, and a rise in *fudai* prestige, or towards more centralised decision making by shoguns and immediate advisors drawn both from favourites turned into daimyo and from their own hatamoto (a process which would have to be financed, given straitened income, by perpetuating the acquisition of *fudai* or *tozama* lands). The direct personal stamp of shoguns on decision making continued up to the end of Yoshimune's years as ruler. Yoshimune is, Ieyasu apart, the greatest of the shoguns, partly because he was long-lived and cultivated, but more directly because he maintained the tradition still evident with Tsunayoshi of personal decision making.[57] He was his own man, not overly impressed by individuals: his dismissive view of Arai Hakuseki, who lived well into Yoshimune's years, was

---

[56] *CHJ*, vol. 4 (1991), pp.427–39.
[57] For an account of Yoshimune, see Totman, *Early modern Japan*, pp.281–315. The Yoshimune exhibition in Tokyo in the Suntory *bijutsukan* in 1995 had many of the artifacts and writings of his era, but was disappointing in more intimate evidence of the man or his policies. *Shogun Yoshimune to sono jidai ten* [Shogun Yoshimune and his era exhibition] (Tokyo, 1995).

that he was 'overly concerned with ornament'.[58] As the century wore on, the *rōjū* grew in prestige. They performed as a cabinet, and the consequence was that the period from the 1780s to the 1850s can be seen increasingly in terms of the personality and work of a series of prime ministers: Tanuma Okitsugu, Matsudaira Sadanobu, Mizuno Tadakuni, Abe Masahiro (1819–57), Hotta Masayoshi (1810–64) and Ii Naosuke. After Yoshimune, only Ienari seems to stand out as shogun, though more by the length of his rule than by personal prominence. Apart from Matsudaira Sadanobu, at the outset of Ienari's years, no prime minister really holds the centre of the stage during what was to prove the longest rule (from 1787 to 1837) by any shogun. The question remains whether Ienari was simply fortunate in the circumstances of the intervening half century (good economic circumstances which resumed in 1789, and the easing after 1813 of the foreign threat), or was wise in his management of them. However, the marriage alliances he arranged of members of his family to *tozama* daimyo created a network of support, and his sustained cultivation of good relations with Satsuma was a key prop which, to the cost of the shogunate, both Ii Naosuke and Tokugawa Yoshinobu thoughtlessly sacrificed in later times.

The immediate advisors of the shoguns and the political philosophers like Sorai on their fringe were well aware of the issues and, in reaction to the loose framework of Japanese government, advocated in effect a more centralised administration. This meant both advocating more powers and, as Japan was divided between shogunal and non-shogunal territories, their application to all of Japan. Arai Hakuseki was active in advocating changes to the *buke shohatto* of 1615 in a way which would strengthen the shogun vis-à-vis the han; ahead of the Korean embassy of 1711, he sought to insist on the shogun being described as *kokuo*, king of a country, rather than, as was customary, *taikun* (great ruler); in 1711–12 the styling of lands held by the emperor and the mode of addressing the emperor in messages from the shogun was made less deferential.[59] Arai Hakuseki, unique in his prominence as a powerful personal aide of non-daimyo background to shoguns, anticipates the novel views expressed in the writings of Sorai. The key reforms Sorai advocated were twofold. First, he argued that han should be reduced in size; the thrust of this argument would have been directed towards reducing the size of the powerful *tozama*, as he argued that the distinction between *fudai* and *tozama* should be abolished. Second, he argued for the advancement of hatamoto of ability in the administration. The hatamoto were direct retainers of the shogun, and in

---

[58] Nakai, *Shogunal politics*, p.347.
[59] Nakai, *Shogunal politics*, pp.195–8, 202–8, 313–14.

effect he was arguing for administration under officials of the shogun rather than under *fudai* daimyo, princes in their own right rather than servants. The hatamoto were already the administrative backbone of day-to-day operations; they also provided the inspectors or *metsuke* who exercised high-level and flexible functions of trouble-shooters; and as bugyo, they controlled the cities, the mining centre of Sado island, and the finances. The office of Nagasaki bugyo, concerned with the foreign trade of Nagasaki and the internal and external security of Kyushu, is the best single example of their importance; their Nagasaki administrative office was the largest in Japan; from Genroku times, they ranked in status with the Edo *machi bugyō*.[60]

Sorai also put his finger on two central fiscal features of the shogun's administration. First, *chōnin* did not make a contribution to the costs of government. This in effect was an argument for taxing Osaka and its traders: as it was a shogunal city and its administration in the hands of bugyo, the implication seems clear. Some of the logic of this argument was acted on in the form of arbitrary levies on Osaka from 1761.[61] The second feature was that the han should be taxed to contribute to the general costs.[62] This step Yoshimune actually took in 1722 in the imposition of a levy, calculated in proportion to the *kokudaka* of han, which continued until 1730.[63] Its introduction was balanced by a reduction in *sankin kōtai*. It thus satisfied a double object: it imposed a true tax on han, and at the same time by reducing the length of time spent outside the han it was seen as operating to reduce the costs of living. In a fashion reminiscent of the reform programmes of *ancien régime* France, the measures were abandoned quickly. However, thoughts of strengthening the shogunate lingered on in the minds of advisors. Nakai Chikuzan, as head of the Kaitokudo school in Osaka, who even had the opportunity in Osaka in 1788 of giving a three-hour lecture on the Japanese polity to the prime minister Matsudaira (in the wake of the economic crisis of 1786–7 and great fire in 1788 in Kyoto), advocated actions at an all-Japan level. His writing was greatly admired by contemporaries, almost on a part with Sorai's in its prestige, and this advice was to be re-echoed in the thoughts of advisors in later times, notably Satō Nobuhiro,[64] whose

---

[60] Toyama, *Nagasaki bugyō*, p.20.
[61] *Osaka shi-shi*, vol. 4, pp.42–66; *Osaka fu-shi, kinsei*, pt 2, vol. 6, pp.249–50, 655–8; *Osaka fu-shi, kinsei*, pt 3, vol. 7, pp.175–8.
[62] On the various proposals of Sorai, see McEwan, *Ogyū Sorai*, pp.75–6, 95–6, 100, 138.
[63] Shinbō and Saitō, *Nihon keizai-shi*, vol. 2, p.153.
[64] For brief accounts of his thought, see T. Morris-Suzuki, *A history of Japanese economic thought* (London, 1989), pp.34–8; Maruyama, *Intellectual history of Tokugawa Japan*, pp.289–93, 299–300, 346–50.

thinking pointed to the underlying centralising and resented tendencies in the forceful years of Mizuno's leadership of Japan.

Yoshimune's retreat from sweeping innovation set a pattern for avoiding structural alterations. Yoshimune himself was both a consensus ruler and a man of high moral purpose. His currency debasement was a unique operation in that it was motivated by concern for the public good, and helped to earn his name in history as 'rice shogun'. His most solid claim to fame remains the brilliant cultural life of his era (marking the beginning of the shift of cultural leadership from Osaka to Edo), and his interest in technical reforms and in learning. He reportedly mingled with the Dutch disguised as a monk. In the 1720s, at the shogun's request, European horses were given as a gift to the shogun: a groom accompanied them to Japan, and he was given permission to stay on in Edo in 1729 and, on a second visit to Japan in 1735, enjoyed a similar liberty to give instruction on the care of horses and riding in the European manner.[65]

Government by compromise was the norm. However, later, as problems occurred (and in a more acute form), the challenge as to how to face them became more daunting. As Japan's problems became more evident and the need for a structural solution more pressing, a reciprocating swing between consensus-style action and more heavy-handed measures can be detected in Japanese policy. In general one can draw a distinction between leaders who sought compromise – Yoshimune himself (last of the shoguns who held a high public profile in his actions), Matsudaira Sadanobu (1787–93), Abe Masahiro (1845–55) and Hotta Masayoshi (1855–8) – and others – Tanuma Okitsugu (1772–86), Mizuno Tadakuni (1841–3) and Ii Naosuke (1858–60) – who departed from the more consultative path. Yet harsh or conciliatory, from the time of Tanuma, the prime ministers all stand out because they dealt with real and large-scale problems. Even if the political costs of their periods of management seem high, innovative measures in the time of Tanuma, Mizuno and Ii became part of official policy. The hostility which Tanuma stirred up was unprecedented as much because his central role, good or bad, was novel as because of the actions themselves. It also reflects the fact that Tanuma was a favourite advanced from low status by a shogun, a situation ruled out in future, given the greater weight of office, by political considerations. The question remains whether Tanuma, reputed once as one of the 'three worst men in Japanese history',[66] was simply a corrupt politician or, while

---

[65] Cord Eberspacher, 'Johan Georg Keyserling (1696–1736): a German horseman at Nagasaki and Edo', *Crossroads: a journal of Nagasaki history and culture*, no. 2 (Summer 1994), pp.9–25.

[66] Ōishi Shinzaburō, *Tanuma Okitsugu no jidai* [The age of Tanuma Okitsugu] (Tokyo, 1991; reprint, 1997), p.37.

corrupt, was he also seriously addressing critical issues? He has in fact been variously dismissed and overpraised for his innovative role; given the theme in modern historiography of a divide on opening up Japan he has also rather unconvincingly been presented as an advocate of foreign trade and openness.[67] At heart his dilemmas were fiscal. Tanuma raised money by the sale of monopolies, also made heavy demands on Osaka, and the arbitrary powers of the shogunate, made acceptable in the past by their infrequent employment at han expense, became more controversial. He also confiscated lands which *fudai* held in the immediate vicinity of Edo (a measure which was largely undone after his departure). Tanuma was followed by Matsudaira Sadanobu.[68] Matsudaira, scholar and writer of literary works (including a novel), was arguably the most cultivated prime minister of any eighteenth- or nineteenth-century state. Moderate and cautious in his approach, he represented a re-establishment of political stability by backing away from highhanded demands and by resisting ill-judged exhortations to attempt a daring policy in Ezo.

Tanuma and Matsudaira are the politicians who most stand out in biographical studies, a measure not only of their impact on their times but of their novelty. They had no immediate successor who stood out either to contemporaries or in modern biography. This is in part due to the retreat into caution by the shogunate (notably on Ezo, where Matsudaira set the pattern) and to the better economic conditions of the 1790s and the first twenty-five years of the nineteenth century. Japan was able to keep the peace with its pushy Russian neighbour and, equally important, to maintain harmonious internal relationships. That inevitably brings us back to the problem, already referred to, of appraising Ienari's role or abilities. Coinciding with Ienari's retirement in 1837 (he lived on to 1841), problems fell fast and thick on Japan, internally and externally. The story of Japan over the next twenty years could as easily be woven around the public careers of four prime ministers, two harsh and demanding, Mizuno and Ii, and two, in the intervening years, milder and conciliatory, Abe and Hotta, as around any other theme. The personality of shoguns themselves was no longer central: one, moreover, was sickly and not expected to have a long life in becoming shogun in 1853, and his successor, nominated in 1858 and acceding to office in 1860, was a mere boy. Certainly after 1837, the weight of the shogunal office weakened (a circumstance that may add retrospectively to the elusive stature of Ienari). That made ministers more important. It also meant that when crucial questions of how to balance

---

[67] J. W. Hall, *Tanuma Okitsugu 1719–1788: forerunner of modern Japan* (Cambridge, Mass., 1955; reprint 1982), pp.95–100, 105, 142.
[68] On Sadanobu, there is a stylish account in English. H. Ooms, *Charismatic bureaucrat: a political biography of Matsudaira Sadanobu 1758–1829* (Chicago, 1975).

han rights and the need for a stronger shogunate arose, there was not a wise or moderating central presence and the prestige of the shogunate was damaged by the actions of its chief minister, the harsh Ii Naosuke, and, years earlier, the heavy demands on Osaka by Mizuno. Defence in particular was a divisive subject, not on the principle of resisting foreigners (which indeed was a bond between shogunate and daimyo) but on its costs. Defence requests on fiscally hard-pressed han grew. Such demands were not a solution to the fiscal problem of the shogunate itself; the demands simply ensured that the problems of the han were no less acute. Resentment of levies on Osaka lived on, and the fiscal ghost of Mizuno came to haunt the shogunate. The question of how Osaka's new foreign trade would be taxed and who would benefit from it became the central divisive issue in internal politics in 1865.

The shogunate has often been presented in terms of oppression or tyranny; the *metsuke* (inspectors) as a sort of travelling inquisitor, whereas they were an administrative device, often used for narrowly administrative purposes. Likewise, while Satsuma's relationship with the shogunate has been seen in terms of tensions, the links became closer from the years of Ienari's ascent with the daimyo becoming father-in-law of the shogun, and in the early 1860s Satsuma was seen by both foreign and domestic observers as a firm supporter of the shogun's fortunes. Was the shogunate, or bakufu as it came to be called in its twilight years, a tyranny, and did unrest threaten it? That brings us to two very different questions, the emperor's place in Japanese life and the significance of peasant unrest, but which have often been interlinked. The Tokugawa shogunate is often said to have been resented both for its origins and its actions and hence to have been confronted not only by opposition but by an urge to replace it with an imperial institution restored to political power. There is little evidence of this. When the Tokugawa dynasty came to power, Ieyasu had the problem of making legitimate what was an actual usurpation, though of the rights of the son of Hideyoshi for whom he had been appointed guardian, and not of the powers of the emperor. As in the case of the great regents Nobunaga and Hideyoshi, the shogun's political status was reinforced by his ensuring that the emperor conferred on him honorific offices. In copper-fastening legitimacy, the early Tokugawa shoguns visited Kyoto up to 1634, a marriage was arranged for the future third shogun to a daughter of the emperor, and Ieyasu was 'deified' in the 1630s in the great shrine created at Nikko. The real significance of the imperial link was that the shogun's power was a trust; hence he was answerable for its exercise, and his powers were not absolute. In other words, the emperor acted as an implied constitution. Modern reasoning, both that which from the 1890s conservatively favoured an 'emperor system' (as it came to be called in the twentieth century) and that which from the inter-war years for different reasons rejected it, sought the seeds of rebelliousness in a historical past. However, there was no such discourse, though, in an effort to argue that one existed, much has been made of the writings of the obscure and eccentric samurai doctor Andō Shōeki, who was unknown in his day. The only other possible discourse, the background to the famous Meiwa incident of 1767 involving the execution of Yamagata Daini, likewise lacks the significance given to it. It began in a bout of factionalism among officials; Daini was executed for disrespect to the shogun; intended rebellion on his part, even in the sentence of the court, was ruled out, and he seems not to have enjoyed the sympathy of contemporaries.[69]

The han of Mito has been cast in the role of keeping the ideal of imperial legitimacy alive. Mito han promoted scholarship in the study of the neglected historical classics in the Japanese language, as opposed to other accounts written in classical Chinese which had long enjoyed the admiration of rulers and scholars alike. This study of the Japanese classics came to be known as *kokugaku* – national learning – and also through Mito's support of it as *mitogaku*. The greatest exponent of this learning had been Moto'ori – often less correctly rendered in English as Motoori – Norinaga (1730–1801), who wrote between 1764 and 1798 his famous commentaries on the *Kojiki*. The *Kojiki* had been neglected in favour of the *Nihonki*, the earliest of the Chinese-language chronicles of Japanese history. Norinaga regarded the *Kojiki* as earlier and more accurate. He felt that human nature itself was good, and that its goodness preceded the advice of sages; that there were limits to the powers of human reason, and that men were unable to explore the questions of human or social origins. He criticised the arrogance of commentators, and argued that they required of man things that were beyond him.[70] The main purpose of his work was an examination with great philological skill of the *Kojiki*. Moreover, it was not political. While accepting the myth that the imperial line began with an offspring of the sun goddess Amaterasu, and also seeing the role of the shogun as a trust from the emperor, his views on power, like his views on reason, reflected his underlying humanity. Holding power as a trust from above, both shoguns and at a lower level daimyo had the duty of discharging it faithfully and caring for the people under their charge. Norinaga himself respected the shogunate, and he regarded it as the

---

[69] B. T. Wakabayashi, *Japanese loyalism reconstructed: Yamagata Daini's Ryushi Shinron of 1759* (Honolulu, 1995).
[70] Matsumoto, *Motoori Norinaga*, pp.64, 79, 95, 110, 111.

legitimate government of Japan.[71] In Mito both Tokugawa Nariaki and his scholar advisors, despite their respect for the imperial institution, all upheld the authority of the shogunate. Respect for the emperor had in it the sense of a constitution, and was a key concept in fact in making possible the compromise of the Tokugawa era, in which at one level the han respected the shogun, and at another level, the shogun was cautious in his own actions in regard to them. The concept itself made possible the early acceptance of the Tokugawa regime and in 1868 of the Meiji regime alike. In other words, what had made the legitimacy of the Tokugawa dynasty possible could also undermine it. That did not seem likely at any time up to the end of the 1850s. Only foreign pressure – *gaiatsu* – could set *tozama* and shogunate on a collision course, because to resist the foreigners Japan had to become a more unitary state, either by power being exercised by a more forceful shogun or by the han confederating.

The emperor was a symbol more than a political force.[72] If in normal times a symbol of legitimacy, in crisis he was even more a symbol of the unity of Japan: this sense is brought out quite dramatically in the concept formulated by a *jusha* of the Mito branch of the Tokugawa family, Aizawa Seishisai (1782–1863), in the famous *Shinron* of 1825, of *kokutai* or national unity: the concept (diffuse in a political sense) did not challenge the role of the shogun, and was to be exercised by an implied communal commitment, under the emperor, of shogun and nation. In the quite novel crises which occurred from 1787, emperor and shogun communicated with one another. Thus the emperor conveyed his concern to the shogun in the wake of the 1787 crisis and urban riots, and the shogun communicated to the emperor news of the Russian attacks in Ezo in 1807 in what became a pattern of communications every ten years or so. Hayashi Jussai had already explained to the emperor in 1804 shogunal foreign policy.

---

[71] Matsumoto, in his study of Norinaga, wrote that 'Norinaga's theory deprives the Tokugawa government of its substantive legitimacy' (p.139). It did not; quite the reverse in fact, the trust which Norinaga recognised so clearly was the very basis of its legitimacy. This misunderstanding has been the basis for much modern writing seeking to find a questioning of the Tokugawa dynasty in earlier commentary on the imperial institution. While the modern writing is interesting in itself, its political concerns seem displaced. In the twilight final years of the shogunate, the emperor Kōmei saw emperor and shogun, in the crisis which Japan faced in the 1850s and 1860s, as having a common interest (see chapter 6).

[72] Herbert Ooms in his *Tokugawa ideology* has argued that the relationship of emperor and shogun was less one of delegation of power than a relationship determined by Tokugawa subjection of others to its power (pp.163–5). However, he seems to overstress the power aspect, a fact reflected in choosing the shadowy figure of Andō Shōeki as opposing 'a particular system of domination' and as 'another voice ... [which] unambiguously spoke of ideology and society in an even more radical way ... Shōeki's views are more to the point' (pp.295–6).

The tie became closer in the wake of the 1837 riots in Osaka, the occasion of another shogunal report to the emperor. In 1846, with external crisis even more evident, the imperial court exhorted the shogun in the matter of defence.[73] Urban rioting on an unprecedented scale in major cities in 1787 and 1837 was a spectre which added to the fears from the 1780s of foreign incursions. Alarm was heightened by an awareness of the vulnerability to disruption of the trade route for rice from the north to Edo. The symbolic significance of the emperor grew as foreign crisis became more evident. The nuances of the situation were well reflected in the career of the last emperor of Tokugawa times, Kōmei, who reigned from 1846 to 1866: he was highly sensitive to the divided opinion of daimyo on opening the country; however he also conceded that the shogun had no other choice than the negotiation of the treaties of 1858; and, if never an enthusiast for opening ports close to Kyoto, was nonetheless a firm supporter of Tokugawa rule.

Popular unrest has a large part in the story of Japan, and loosely related to the concept of a doubtful Tokugawa legitimacy, it acquires a wider significance than it merits. In any reappraisal of Japanese history, the question of *ikki* is often a stumbling block. The *ikki* are usually related to a pessimistic appraisal of the Tokugawa economy. Immiseration, it is argued, caused unrest and in turn, if doubt about the evidence of misery is entertained, the existence of the *ikki* dispels it.[74] This picture is often further coloured by the stress on a pattern in highly commercialised regions of larger peasants renting land to tenant farmers. By way of contrast, in less developed areas tenancy was slow to appear and there the *honbyakushō* families, i.e. the families entered on the original valuation registers, mostly farmed on their own account. A highly commercial farming in the Kinki with tenant farming becoming a vital component did not of itself imply exploitation and immiseration (though this was to become a theme of the Marxist writing prominent in later Japanese historiography).[75] *Ikki*, enumerated as an accumulation of individual events, are represented as

---

[73] Fujita Satoru, *Kinsei seiji-shi to tennō* [Early modern political history and emperor] (Tokyo, 1999), pp.65, 84, 106, 131, 313.

[74] On the themes of unrest and rebellion against authority, see especially H. P. Bix, *Peasant protest in Japan 1590–1884* (Newhaven, 1986); S. Vlastos, *Peasant risings in Tokugawa Japan* (Berkeley, 1990); Irwin Scheiner, 'The mindful peasant: sketches for a study of rebellion', *Journal of Asian studies*, vol. 32, no. 4 (Aug. 1973), pp.579–91. See also Anne Walthall (ed.), *Peasant uprisings in Japan* (Chicago, 1991) and *Social protest and popular culture in eighteenth-century Japan* (Tucson, 1986); Tetsuo Najita and J. Victor Koschmann (eds.), *Conflict in modern Japanese history: the neglected tradition* (Princeton, 1982). For a broader theme on the basis of the same premises, see G. M. Wilson, *Patriots and redeemers in Japan* (Chicago, 1992).

[75] For agricultural structure and conditions, the best account in English is T. C. Smith, *The agrarian origins of modern Japan* (Stanford, 1959). Japanese tenant farming should not be

rising exponentially to a culminating high point within the 1860s, and as a proof of a simmering discontent which could topple the shogunate. The concept in modern writing of endemic unrest gained some of its prominence from the assumption that lack of foreign markets compounded the effect of insufficient domestic outlets: on this basis, tenurial relations and monopoly buying for home outlets ensured that the condition of countrymen was of the worst. Ironically, the worst case of exploitation was in the han often most praised for its openness to trade, Satsuma. Its great and long-lived daimyo, Shimazu Shigehide (1745–1833), was an aesthete, also a friend of Isaac Titsingh (1744–1812) – *opperhoofd* in Deshima in 1779–80 and again in 1781–3 and 1784 – and spoke and wrote Dutch. However, under him and his successors, Satsuma's development of commercial crops was conducted on the basis of settling production quotas for peasants for delivery at fixed prices, and of even compelling producers to grow them. This was highly disadvantageous to the peasants, and their economic conditions were among the worst in Japan. The real irony is that the han with the most 'open' daimyo in Japan, Shimazu Shigehide, was, if we judge by an illiteracy rate of eighty-one per cent in a 1884 report, probably the most illiterate han in Japan.[76] The case of Satsuma is a warning against a simple equation of either enlightenment or trade with prosperity. Similar instances of exploitation occurred to a lesser extent in other han, such as Tosa and Yonesawa, where there was an official drive to expand production of commercial crops for export beyond the han.[77] Ironically, with its poor and exploited population, Satsuma has little place in the story of *ikki*.

Unrest is not an easy phenomenon to study. Curiously, it has been studied on the basis of counting the number of incidents of unrest. This has the result, as evidence is more abundant for recent times than for earlier, of adding to the likelihood of an exponential rise: it was more frequent in the eighteenth century, it has been argued, than in the preceding century, and rose to new peaks in the 1780s, 1830s and 1860s.[78] However, this statistical basis is a poor one. Moreover, the events classed

equated with English or Anglo-Irish style landlordism or with latifundia. See chapter 8, note 119.

[76] R. P. Dore, *Education in Tokugawa Japan* (London, 1984), p.322.

[77] L. S. Roberts, *Mercantilism in a Japanese domain: the mercantile origins of nationalism in 18th-century Tosa* (Cambridge, 1988); M. Ravina, *Land and lordship in early modern Japan* (Stanford, 1999), pp.71–114.

[78] Of the large number of accounts, the most widely used is Aoki Koji's work, revised in his *Hyakushō-ikki sogo nenpyō* [Chronological listing of peasant unrest and of riots] (Tokyo, 1971). See also Aoki Michio, 'Bakuhansei-shi kenkyū to hyakushō ikki kenkyū' [Studies in bakuhansei history and in peasant risings] in Minegishi Sumio, Fukaya Katsumi, Satō Kazuhitō and Aoki Michio (eds.), *Ikki-shi nyūmon* [Introduction to the history of unrest], 5 vols. (Tokyo, 1981), vol. 1, pp.219–86. The earliest account in English is

as unrest or *ikki* cover a very broad range of incidents, defined broadly as contention (spread over as many as fifty-two categories), and by no means all fitting easily into the concept of unrest.[79] Peasant representations to the han authorities required prior permission. The incidents included in the statistics of *ikki* ranged from petitions which were not in proper form as lacking formal permission for their presentation, to more violent events, large gatherings in the han and, especially in the towns, riots with property destruction (*uchi kowashi*). Evidence resting on such a broad range of events and on such a flimsy statistical basis is not compelling. The very nature of the rice levy explains why representations, authorised or unauthorised and usually involving no violent action, were numerous. If the harvest was bad, there was a case for adjustments in the levy, and concessions were often made. Moreover, violent protest itself had a high rate of success. In the wake of protest, even if put down with some rigour of judicial process, new impositions were usually cancelled. Ringleaders were punished, perhaps even executed. Officials were also accused of failure by having caused discontent and were removed from office.

It has been argued persuasively that as the prospects of success were high, *ikki* were a rational calculation and not acts of desperation.[80] The argument is more convincing than the alternative one of unrest having roots in chronic and progressive immiseration. It also takes account of the fact that *ikki* were increasingly directed against what were in effect attempts at fiscal innovation by han in the way of taxes on industrial or consumer goods. While *ikki* increased in number, they did so, on this argument, because people were better off; by putting a halt to fiscal demands, the *ikki* played a dynamic role in preventing the state, whether in the form of han or shogunal administrations, from increasing revenue. This rational calculus by countrymen is held to explain both the uncommon height of unrest in the decade of greatest political upheaval, the 1860s when the public institutions were at their weakest, and the ability of the new Meiji government, a more forceful institution than its Tokugawa predecessor, to end it. It has been claimed that 'by the middle of the [eighteenth] century the state had for all purposes capitulated to popular resistance' and that 'in the mid-nineteenth century... respect for the state was at an all time low'.[81] Yet if this interpretation gets away from the simplistic

Hugh Borton's detailed and useful but uncritical account, 'Peasant uprisings in Japan of the Tokugawa era', *Transactions of the Asiatic Society of Japan*, second series, vol. 16 (May 1938), pp.1–219.
[79] White, *Ikki*, pp.xii, 348.   [80] See the argument in White, *Ikki*.
[81] White, *Ikki*, pp.78, 302. White goes as far as saying that 'even a tottering government may remain free from attack if no one thinks it worth knocking over' (p.191).

account of immiseration and identifies the fiscal implications of the story, its argument is too sweeping. The state did not lose its fiscal powers; it did not have them to start with. Nor were the events, fiscal or non-fiscal in their background causation, endemic, widespread or large scale. In the prosperous decade from 1842, the number of *ikki* contracted sharply. In essence, the unrest can be regarded as meaningful only when incidents occurred across a large number of regions at the same time. On this definition, there are really only three periods of serious unrest for whatever reason, the 1780s, 1830s and 1866.[82]

Japan, at peace with itself, was able to develop intellectually with great dynamism in the eighteenth century. It was a century of intellectual debate, of many new strands of thought and their communication across the entire country. At less exalted levels, information was readily available. Guide books for pilgrims were published, a practical necessity, providing information on where the pleasures of the senses could be satisfied as well as details of the shrines and itineraries.[83] What Golownin described as 'a kind of commercial gazette' with prices in different ports was also published.[84] Lacking a civil service in the western sense (which served administrative rather than scholarly functions) and a periodical press (though street-vended broadsheets did exist), Japan might at first sight seem secretive. However, official society was far from hermetically sealed. One illustration of this is how the *fūsetsugaki*, or reports provided by the Dutch, which, though they were confidential documents and were never printed, seem to have circulated widely. The reports have survived in quite different sources, and some individual reports exist in several copies.[85] If administration was secretive (law, even where codified, was never published) and justice was administered by officials (an independent judicial system did not exist), a body of civil case law grew up. At any rate within shogunal territory, law became consistent. Representations were numerous and village, han and shogunal justice was subject to processes both of appeal and scrutiny. As Ooms has observed, 'one cannot avoid the impression that lawyer-less Tokugawa Japan was far more litigious than the Japan of today'.[86] Criminal law progressed much less, if at all: it was characterised by a tendency to punish both sides, and as confessions were the basis of procedure, torture was used to secure

---

[82] James White's argument is a complex one suggesting both that major crises became more widespread and aggressive, and that the magnitude of the average incident was diminishing (*Ikki*, p.138): undue weight was not to be attached to economic causes (p.244).

[83] Vaporis, *Breaking barriers*, pp.233–8.   [84] Golownin, *Recollections*, p.204.

[85] Iwao, 'The development of the study and compilation of *Oranda fūsetsugaki shūsei*', in *Oranda fūsetsugaki shūsei*, vol. 2, pp.1–27. See also Itazawa, *Oranda fūsetsu-sho*.

[86] H. Ooms, *Tokugawa village practice: class, status, power, law* (Berkeley, 1996), p.8.

them: for whatever reason a significant number of those charged died in prison.

Literacy had increased enormously across the seventeenth and eighteenth centuries. Even before 1600 foreign missionaries had been impressed by literacy, and especially by the fact that there were, in comparison to Europe, literate women.[87] Without schools existing in any formal sense at the time, Buddhist monks provided instruction such as it was in Japanese society. In 1585, Frois noted that children learned from monks to read and write.[88] The majority of medical doctors also were monks. A century later Banzan, noting that necessity prompted many to become monks, advocated that they should become school teachers.[89] By 1695, the term *terako* (temple child) had entered the language, and two decades later the term *terakoya* (temple child school) had appeared: both pointed to the role of Buddhist priests and to schools they maintained.[90] This implied less the temple as centre of education, than Buddhist priests as teachers acting on private initiative either in the temple or outside its precincts. There was equally no barrier to teaching by others, notably by *rōnin*, and a consequence was that, as time went by, education became increasingly secularised, imparted by laymen or, if by monks, as a livelihood rather than as a priestly function. In other words a process of secularisation had begun which was to take learning out of the domain of what was originally a Buddhist monopoly. The change was most complete in the case of medicine. Medicine was far more lucrative than teaching, and increasingly fell into the hands of laymen, whether *rōnin* or others, and even more so in hereditary fashion into the hands of sons of existing doctors.

These changes increased the range and variety of individuals involved in education, and in contrast to the role of official – state or church – institutions in western society, higher learning, whether medical or scholarly, was imparted by individuals who set up schools of their own, primarily to add to their own income. In imparting a supposedly higher education, teachers, in acute competition with one another for students, were loudly critical of all rivals, even of those whose views were essentially similar. One thing that all secular purveyors of instruction agreed on, however, was the inadequacies of Buddhism. Abuse of Buddhist thought or denunciation of Buddhist teachers as drunken oafs quite unsuited to become teachers became a much repeated refrain. This animosity conceals the fact that, even if gradually pushed out of higher education which was

---

[87] *Traité de Luis Frois, S.J. (1585) sur les contradictions de moeurs entre Européens et Japonais*, translated by Xavier de Castro (Paris, 1993), p.56.
[88] Frois, *Traité de Luis Frois*, p.60.   [89] Fisher, 'Kumazawa Banzan', p.327.
[90] Dore, *Education in Tokugawa Japan*, pp.252–3, 252n.

increasingly secular, Buddhism remained a real force. Buddhist monks, far from being mere humble primary school teachers, were for instance numerous among the pupils attending the more literary of the famous academies of the day and into the nineteenth century.

Japanese society was shot through with a sense of teaching as a supplementary economic activity. Many of the great figures of the age were to run their own academies. The Hayashi family, which acted as paper keepers to the shogun, ran a private academy. Sorai, himself the son of a *rōnin* who had became a doctor, is a good example. He was from 1696 an advisor or scholar to Yanagisawa, a courtier turned daimyo and government minister. When Yanagisawa's fall left Sorai without a patron or employment, he ran a literary academy. The association with Yanagisawa had helped to make him known and among his students he was to number two future daimyo. He was never an advisor to the shogun, though his work circulated in hand-written copies in high circles, and he met Yoshimune on one occasion.[91] Intellectually Sorai's thought, though that of an establishment figure, was subversive. In essence, he argued that Neo-Confucianism (the Chu Hsi Confucianism developed in eleventh-century commentaries on the writings of Confucius and which was fashionable in Japan) was simply a later interpretation of much older authorities; hence as Chu Hsi and his followers could misunderstand documents, it was necessary to go to the originals and interpret them afresh. From one point of view, that put an emphasis on philological competence in Chinese (Sorai was very proud of his own prose compositions in Chinese); from another perspective, it meant that thought had to be critically appraised, and the canons were scholarly, not based on authority itself.[92] This critical approach passed imperceptibly into wider criticism. Institutions in society were established not by divine authority, but by innovation by man: hence, they were not immutable and could be altered.

The impact of Sorai, one of the great thinkers of the age, on Japanese thought was profound. His approach itself tended to confirm classic scholarship and sources written in Chinese. This itself changed with time. Moto'ori Norinaga studied the old Japanese chronicles, with their details of the origins of Japan. From one point of view, he shifted the emphasis from the Chinese classics to Japanese origin tales; from another from the Chinese language to Japanese. From yet another point of view, while like Sorai and others he wrote on political issues as a private teacher rather than a public figure, he was sympathetic to the welfare of ordinary people:

---

[91] O. G. Lidin, *The life of Ogyū Sorai: a Tokugawa Confucian philosopher* (Lund, 1973); and *Ogyū Sorai's journey to Kai in 1706, with a translation of the Kyochukiko* (London and Malmo, 1983).

[92] Tetsuo Najita, *Tokugawa political writings* (Cambridge, 1998), pp.xxiv–xxv, xlviii.

he was, for instance, critical of the execution of the ringleaders of unrest on the ground that in difficult times they were mere nominal leaders of large numbers of people with real grievances. In 1787, at the peak of the Tenmei crisis, Tokugawa Harusada, the head of the Kii branch of the Tokugawa family, asked for his views on politics and the economy.[93]

These two men are the greatest scholarly names of the eighteenth century, pointing to great philological competence and immense critical faculty. Both were teachers; Moto'ori Norinaga in particular had an enormous following, and in his final years the number of his students was as many as 500. However, powerful though they were, and overwhelming in their prestige, they could not dominate Japanese thought, and Japanese intellectual life remained divided into many currents and cross-currents. Kumazawa Banzan in the 1680s had noted these divides. Though he did not see an intrinsic conflict between the three great currents of thought, Buddhism, Shinto and Confucianism, he noted the emergence of the rivalry between them: in particular, he observed that 'Confucianism is the child of a royal past, but today it is inclined to be self-sufficient, and to look with scorn on others. Ignorant of real values, Confucian scholars are but one sect. Little virtue not fed from the perennial springs of great virtue is like a rivulet.'[94]

Schools of thought, if in competition with one another, also had their own bitter internal rivalries. Less than a generation after Kumazawa, Arai Hakuseki had lamented that Confucian thought itself was divided into competing schools or factions.[95] Japan had no central intellectual or religious institutions, and the prestige of writers depended on the appeal of their thought allied to personal magnetism, and on the desire of students to benefit from instruction by famous *sensei* (teachers) as their first step on the rungs of the ladder of personal advancement. In the absence of universities, a multitude of schools run by individual teachers existed. The Hayashi school, which taught Chu Hsi Confucianism, though keeper of the papers of the shoguns, was not before the 1790s an official academy. It was simply the foremost exponent of Neo-Confucianism, benefiting from the prestige which its access to the shogunate gave it. The Kaitokudo, a merchant academy in Osaka, founded by merchants in 1726 and managed by the Nakai family as its hereditary head, held a charter from the shogun, and its teachers, though *chōnin*, enjoyed the privilege of carrying two swords. In other words, it was in a sense the first school to enjoy formal recognition from the shogunate, and the prime minister attended a lecture by its head in 1788. Its late eighteenth-century appeal depended

[93] Matsumoto, *Motoori Norinaga*, p.126.
[94] Fisher, 'Kumazawa Banzan', pp.332, 334.   [95] Nakai, *Shogunal politics*, pp.83–4.

on the repute of Nakai Chikuzan (1730–1804), as a teacher who, if good enough to attract a prime minister, equally could attract less exalted students. Each teacher or school had to struggle hard to survive. It is very difficult to write of the decline of Neo-Confucianism itself.[96] There were schools of Neo-Confucianism, of *kogaku* (Sorai and his followers), *kokugaku*, even *rangaku*, and so on; these in turn were not well-defined bodies of homogeneous thought, but approaches greatly influenced by the personality and learning of each teacher.[97]

Over time schools increased in number and in the variety of approaches they offered. Denunciations of each other by teachers testified to the ferocity and economic significance of the competition. Andō Shōeki, the obscure medical man and teacher from Akita, turned in some modern accounts into a great thinker of Tokugawa times, was not really interested in political or social issues at all: he was a difficult and eccentric man, who appeared to have fallen out even with those around him. His eccentric writing denounced Buddhism, Shinto, Confucianism of all kinds, the medical knowledge of his day and authority at large: it lacks any coherent purpose.[98] He advocated a crude agrarianism; the arts including poetry, dance and *No* drama were declared frivolous; study was to be prohibited, and scholars were to be set to cultivate land; and 'all of the thousands and thousands of medical books are, each and every one, in error'.[99] At stake in the end was economic success, whether as a teacher or the prospect of being retained as an advisor by a daimyo. Neo-Confucianism was attacked by teachers, who wanted to recruit students or secure employment for their students in place of those of rival teachers. This abuse extended even to criticism of daimyo or of the shogunate itself for supporting or employing people holding a particular philosophy. Within the Hayashi academy, there were variants in philosophy. The

---

[96] P. Nosco, 'Introduction: Neo-Confucianism and Tokugawa discourse', in P. Nosco (ed.), *Confucianism and Tokugawa culture* (Princeton, 1984), pp.21–2.

[97] The comment by a Swedish scholar that 'the whole of the Tokugawa era vibrated with intellectual activity' (Lidin, *Life of Ogyū Sorai*, p.9) is a fair reflection on the situation, and closer to the mark than accounts which stress mainly oppression of thought. Maruyama's dismissal, because of his anxiety to find a central theme in Japanese thought, of many teachers as eclectics, greatly underplays the essentially diffuse character of Japanese thought.

[98] Toshinobu YASUNAGA, *Andō Shōeki: social and ecological philosopher in eighteenth-century Japan* (New York, 1992). The author concedes 'a failure to recognise when reasoning had long departed from the logical structures it was based on ... he was one of the Japanese thinkers who, though susceptible to the dangers of disjunction, superficiality, and one-sidedness, unfailingly strove to overcome those obstacles and reach for the universal' (pp.8–9). From later times the *kokugaku* teacher Hirata Atsutane is a striking example of a scholar who denounced rivals and their branches of learning (H. D. Harootunian, 'Late Tokugawa culture and thought', in *CHJ*, vol. 5 (1989), pp.199–201).

[99] Yasunaga, *Andō Shōeki*, pp.236, 239, 270.

famous order by Matsudaira in 1790 was not one of imposing a form of Neo-Confucian orthodoxy on teaching at large.[100] Its target was simply the Hayashi academy, and an imposition of uniformity on a school which reflected the burgeoning eclecticism of the age. The decree was not particularly repressive. Its immediate consequence was an outcry against the order itself inside and outside the school.[101]

Teaching was eclectic. Medical doctors, whether obscure and cantankerous ones like Shōeki or in the case of Moto'ori Norinaga, the most successful scholar of the age, taught philosophy as well as practising medicine. Linguistically, teaching continued to be dominated by Chinese, starting from the Chinese classics as its basis. This was true not only of the Hayashi academy, but of a merchant one like the Kaitokudo in Osaka, or even of the great school founded by Tokugawa Nariaki in Mito. The Chinese classics enjoyed the same role as the classics of Greek and Roman civilisation in European education in the same period: from them models of behaviour and canons of wisdom were elaborated, which could be applied to public life (think of the models of Roman behaviour by the French revolutionaries). *Kanbun* was the term to denote composition in classical Chinese by Japanese (or by Koreans): some like Ogyū Sorai, for instance, were very proud of their *kanbun* compositions. Reading classical Chinese presented real problems for less exalted scholars. While the Japanese language employed Chinese characters or ideograms for its writing, the two languages were, except for a common writing system, very far apart. Japanese has a different word order and, in contrast to Chinese, it is inflected. Hence to make the texts accessible, a special form of aid known as *kandoku* (the reading of *kanbun*) was used: diacritic marks to the left of the vertical lines of text (Japanese and Chinese were both written in vertical lines) indicated the word order, and inflections and sometimes the pronunciation of words were set out in the Japanese syllabic alphabet on the right-hand side of the lines of text. One of the consequences of the prestige of the Chinese classics was that compound words based on the Chinese pronunciation of the component words were widely used in the language, and in preference to good Japanese ones.[102] A consequence was that right up to the end of Tokugawa times written

---

[100] For the text, see R. Tsunoda, W. Theodore de Bary and Donald Keene, *Sources of Japanese tradition* (New York, 1958), pp.502–3.

[101] Dore, *Education in Tokugawa Japan*, p.28; Ooms, *Charismatic bureaucrat*, pp.141–2.

[102] An example is the word of Japanese origin, *tabi*, for journey, and the more widely used *ryōko*, a compound made up of two Chinese ideograms using a Chinese-style pronunciation. (Imitation of Chinese pronunciation was approximate, as Japanese, like western languages, has a single level of pitch in contrast to the four levels of pitch in Chinese, which in speech gives a single sound several different meanings. Confusion does not arise in written Chinese as these sounds are rendered by different ideograms.)

discourse was expressed in a stiff and formal language, not easy now or then to read by those without a classical education. Learning in such a context necessarily remained abstract and bookish. It led to two obvious weaknesses. One was the absence of empirical scientific teaching. In so far as it existed at all, it was in the hands of medical doctors. Ogata Kōan, who was the first head of the Tekijuku school founded in Osaka in 1838, had among other things studied medicine, and according to Fukuzawa Yukichi, later Japan's most powerful advocate of westernisation, who had been a student there in the 1850s, the students were mostly sons of doctors.[103] The second limitation, not unrelated to the first, was that study of social and political problems was entirely non-statistical. Statistical data rarely if ever appeared in exposition of problems, and han administrations were staffed entirely by literary scholars. There were also no public offices with well-defined statistical responsibilities. Even Nakai Chikuzan, head of the merchant academy in Osaka, close to the bugyo office, has a non-statistical view of problems. This absence, a dramatic one compared with the change that had taken place in European discourse over the preceding hundred years, is evident in the otherwise very sophisticated work of Kusama Naokata and Yamagata Bantō, economic advisors in Osaka to many han, in the early nineteenth century.

Schools varied from tiny academies based on the teaching of one man to larger institutions with several teachers. The Shoheiko, the academy in Edo run by the Hayashi family, who acted as paper keepers and advisors to the shogunate, was of course a highly successful school: however, located in Edo, drawing on shogunal retainers, themselves destined to be drawn into shogunal service, its impact outside Edo was negligible. The schools which had the greatest appeal in numbers and in range of han from which students were drawn were all outside Edo. Their number and their student population far exceeded that of official academies throughout Tokugawa history.[104] These schools attracted students from all of Japan. Moto'ori Norinaga's success is a case in point. Perhaps more striking, because it was so far from the centre of Japan, was the academy run by a private teacher, Hirose Tansō, at Hita in the heart of Kyushu: it had a number of teachers and drew students from virtually every han in Japan. Han official schools were few before 1800, educated small numbers of students, provided only a classical instruction, and by definition taught only students from within the han. The Mito han school or Kodokan (including a medical school in

---

[103] *The autobiography of Fukuzawa Yukichi*, translated by Eiichi KIYOOKA (Tokyo, 1948), p.73.
[104] A useful account in English is R. Rubinger, *Shijuku: private academies of the Tokugawa period* (Princeton, 1979, 1982).

its grounds), founded only in 1841, was larger than the Hayashi school, and was indeed the largest academy in Japan.[105]

From one point of view, in such a varied and competitive field, *rangaku* (Dutch, i.e. western, studies), once their utility was evident, easily found a niche. Despite the abusive tone of scholarly work, even some teachers who had no knowledge of Dutch spoke well of it. The interpreters, like so many Japanese, added a teaching function to their work. Moreover, their sophistication of knowledge was growing, and from 1777–8 arrangements were made with the Dutch for the systematic training in Deshima of apprentice interpreters on perhaps sixty to one hundred occasions in the year.[106] In Edo, early Dutch studies depended on medical doctors and astronomers. For Yoshimune, calendar study was particularly important. The lunar calendar fell short of the solar calendar by a fluctuating number of days, and regular adjustment by an intercalary month was necessary every few years: hence prospects of reforming the calendar were a perennial source of attraction. From very early in his rule – from 1717 – the Dutch found themselves quizzed on astronomy.[107] The shogun's doctors, like his astronomers, gathered around the Dutch doctor on the *hofreis*. As language proficiency in Dutch began to develop, the visits became an ever more exhausting experience for the unfortunate Dutch. The *dagregister* has the *oranda kapitan* in 1763 noting that 'we have been visited by all kinds of people from this day until the 11th [April]'; in 1772 he complained that they 'tired me with their difficult questions'.[108] Even the scholarly Thunberg, who was interested in the contacts, in 1776 found the visits of the doctors somewhat 'inopportune', as they called without ceremony, and stayed till late at night.[109]

The annual visits by the Dutch to Edo, in which they were accompanied by several Nagasaki interpreters, were a short but constant support to Dutch studies in the shogun's capital. After 1790 such studies were strong enough to flourish despite Dutch visits being reduced to one year in four.[110] A key factor in the progress of Dutch studies is that in addition to the interest of the shogun's doctors and of the highly placed

[105] *Mito shi-shi*, middle series, vol. 3, pp.165–99.
[106] P. Van der Velde, 'The Dutch language as a medium of western science', in Ton Vermeulen, P. Van der Velde and Cynthia Viallé, *The Deshima Dagregisters: their original tables of contents*, 10 vols. (Leiden, 1986–97), vol. 8 (1760–80) (Leiden, 1994), pp.iii–v.
[107] G. K. Goodman, *The Dutch impact on Japan (1640–1853)* (Leiden, 1967), pp.66–7.
[108] Van der Velde and Viallé, *The Deshima Dagregisters*, vol. 8, pp.27, 161.
[109] C. P. Thunberg, *Voyages de C. P. Thunberg au Japon*, 2 vols. (Paris, 1796), vol. 2, pp.73–4.
[110] The pattern of visits is often misunderstood or inaccurately stated in textbooks. Some books in English state that the visits were reduced to every second year in 1764. The Dutch had demurred at the 1764 visit, but it and later visits went ahead as normal. The change in 1790 was not dictated by considerations about the Dutch at all: it reflected a cutback in all 'foreign' ceremonial. Post-1790 visits have been variously stated as

astronomers, they enjoyed from the 1760s the support of Konyo, an officer of the supreme court of justice. Out of this circle Maeno Ryōtaku and Sugita Gempaku published their epoch-making *Kaitai shinsho* (New writing on anatomy), a translation from Dutch of an anatomy text in 1774.[111] One of Sugita's students, Ōtsuki Gentaku, keenly interested in *rangaku*, visited Nagasaki and spent some months in the house of one of the interpreters: returning to Edo he founded the first school of *rangaku* in Edo, the Shirando, in 1786. In turn one of his students, Udagawa Yoan (helped by his stepfather Udagawa Gensi), established a school. The numbers actively engaged in Dutch studies, which presented acute linguistic problems and lacked the tools of easy learning, were inevitably small. Ōtsuki's school over its lifetime counted only ninety-four students. The New Year's party of Dutch scholars in 1795, featured in a famous painting, counted a mere twenty-nine people.[112] Dutch studies in Edo were boosted afresh from 1808 when the astronomer's office was made responsible for translating foreign works: a number of interpreters were transferred from Nagasaki and from 1811 the Translations Bureau was formed under its wing.

Given their interest in the natural sciences, medical men were responsible in the long run for diffusing, outside narrow or official circles, an interest in both Dutch medicine and natural sciences. Of fifty-eight students in Von Siebold's school at Narutaki whose professions are known, forty-three were doctors.[113] Some knowledge of, or at least respect for, western medicine, was held in late Tokugawa times by a large number, though still a minority, of doctors.[114] The merits of western medicine, however, while very real were not overwhelming. Some Chinese therapies were very effective, and western medicine as much as Chinese had areas of nonsense. Western leadership in surgery was itself largely negatived by the general absence of antisepsis. What impressed Japanese was western

occurring every fourth or every fifth year, and even every third year. The decree in late 1790 referred to a visit in a fifth year – in other words counting the year 1790 (for which the visit had already taken place), and hence intimating the next visit in four years' time. Divergence from this pattern occurred only after 1844. For a full list of the *hofreis* or *sanpu* since the first one in 1633, see Katagiri Kazuo, *Oranda tsūji no kenkyū* [Studies of the Dutch interpreters] (Tokyo, 1985), pp.208–26. The total number of visits to Edo is 167: slightly different totals are given by other authors, and elsewhere by Katagiri himself. For an accessible and illustrated short account of the *hofreis*, see *Shiiboruto no edo sanpu ten* [Exhibition of Von Siebold's *sanpu*] (Shiiboruto kinenkan, Nagasaki, 2000).

[111] Ishida Sumio, *Edo no oranda i* [Dutch doctors in Edo] (Tokyo, 1988).
[112] R. H. Hesselink, 'A Dutch New Year at the Shirandō Academy: 1 January 1795', *Monumenta nipponica*, vol. 50, no. 2 (Summer 1995), pp.205–23.
[113] Aoki Toshiyuki, *Zaizon rangaku no kenkyū* [Studies in the geographical disribution of rangaku] (Kyoto, 1998), p.19.
[114] In 1876, of 22,428 medical doctors, 5,097 were western style. M. B. Jansen, 'Introduction', in *CHJ*, vol. 5 (1989), p.28.

knowledge of anatomy, its emphasis on scientific observation, and the ability of western medicine to deal with some widespread specific conditions (e.g. treatment of the eye).[115] An impressive number of texts was translated from Dutch into Japanese: in all, 189 works, either medical or containing medical knowledge, were translated from Dutch into some 473 books or manuscripts (the latter sometimes recopied).[116]

Two daimyo knew Dutch. One was the long-lived Shimazu Shigehide, daimyo of Satsuma and father-in-law of the shogun, Ienari: he had been a frequent visitor to Deshima, was a friend of Isaac Titsingh the *opperhoofd*, and after Titsingh's departure from Japan, corresponded with him.[117] As late as 1826 at eighty-four years of age he paid the departing Dutch the ultimate courtesy of seeing them off at Shinagawa, recalling his friendship of many years before with Titsingh.[118] The courtesy of a farewell meeting with the lord of Satsuma on the departure of the Dutch for their return to Nagasaki seems to date from 1767 or perhaps even earlier.[119] The other daimyo was Kuchiki Masatsuna (1750–1802) of Fukuchiyama (also a correspondent of Titsingh's), who many years before in 1776, disguised to conceal his high status, visited the Dutch doctor at an inn as the Dutch on their *hofreis* were on their way to Edo and stayed till late at night.[120] He was later among the participants in the New Year's Day party in 1795. Hendrik Doeff (1777–1835), the longest serving *oranda kapitan* or *opperhoofd*, in the light of the evidence of Titsingh's correspondence, after his departure with daimyo and interpreters, was to exclaim that 'on the basis of my own experience and better knowledge' such correspondence was not possible. However, Doeff exaggerated the importance of his own long stay in Nagasaki, exceeded for length only by Caron's in the seventeenth century (though Caron served as *opperhoofd* for only two years[121]), and

[115] Comparative observations in Akira NAKANISHI, Ryōichi TSUCHIYA, Masahide MIYASAKA and Toshiya ITŌ in *The history of surgery in Nagasaki* (Nagasaki, 1999) are of interest.

[116] Miyashita Saburō, *Waran isho no kenkyū to shoshi* [Researches in Japanese–Dutch medical writings and their history] (Tokyo, 1997). This volume contains a bibliography of writings on pp.69–134. A useful supplement is P. F. Kornicki, 'Japanese medical and other books at the Wellcome Institute', *Bulletin of the School of Oriental and African Studies*, vol. 60, pt 3 (1997), pp.489–510.

[117] C. R. Boxer, 'Isaac Titsingh 1745–1811', in *Jan Compagnie in Japan 1600–1817* (The Hague, 1936), pp.134–81. The status of Titsingh, so often underestimated, will receive a fillip from F. Lequin, *The private correspondence of Isaac Titsingh, 1785–1811*, 2 vols. (Amsterdam, 1990).

[118] P. F. Von Siebold, *Nippon: archiv zur beschreibung von Japan*, 2 vols. (Tokyo, 1965), vol. 1, p.222.

[119] Van der Velde and Viallé, *The Deshima Dagregisters*, vol. 8, p.113.

[120] Thunberg, *Voyages*, vol. 2, p.251.

[121] See Introduction in C. R. Boxer, *A true description of the mighty kingdoms of Japan and Siam by Francis Caron and Joost Schouten: reprinted from the English edition of 1663* (London, 1935).

was to publish a somewhat self-serving, though useful, *Herinneringen uit Japan* in 1833.

Contrary to what has often been said, there was never a ban on western books. From the 1630s however, there was a ban on books in Chinese dealing with Christianity. This had the effect that even books on astronomy and mathematics were often excluded because of minor references. The change in 1720 was not an unbanning of western books (which in fact had never been prohibited), but an easing of an existing restriction, so that books in Chinese would not be excluded simply because of bureaucratic thoroughness in suppressing all reference to Christianity.[122] One of the problems in studying European books was of course the fact that there were no Japanese grammars or dictionaries of Dutch. The Portuguese, or more accurately their clergy, had produced both but with the Portuguese language later forgotten by Dutch and Japanese alike, they were inaccessible and forgotten. Moreover, as the Portuguese dictionaries rendered Japanese in roman script and not in kanji, they were not user-friendly for the interpreters.[123] Maeno Ryōtaku and Sugita Gempaku's *Kaitai shinsho* in 1774 was by no means the first translation from Dutch (manuscript translations of excerpts from medical works can be traced back to the seventeenth century[124]), but it was the first occasion on which a full-blown translation of a technical text appeared in book form and hence publicly.

Yoshimune's personal interest in learning and in Dutch as a source of scientific knowledge led to the compilation of a small dictionary by Aoki in 1745. However, if translation was to cease being heroic and time consuming, a large-scale dictionary was necessary. The small circle of *rangakusha* in Edo did this, producing the first *Edo-Haruma* in 1795. The dictionary was called *Haruma* because it took a Dutch–French dictionary by Halma as a model for its structure. In all it had an impressive 30,000 entries. This competence drew on Edo knowledge, but also to an extent on Nagasaki knowledge as the key collaborator was a Nagasaki interpreter. It was not the only dictionary: under the guidance of Doeff (Doeff claimed credit for proposing the project, but it is more likely to have rested on Japanese initiative) a dictionary was begun under shogunal order with the participation of twelve interpreters in Nagasaki in 1811. Its compilation was not completed till 1833. However, the first draft was

---

[122] There is an excellent short survey of this subject, often misunderstood not only in western but in Japanese books, in English in Itō, 'Book banning policy', pp.36–61.

[123] P. F. Kornicki, 'European Japanology at the end of the seventeenth century', *Bulletin of the School of African and Oriental Studies*, vol. 56, pt 3 (1993), p.505.

[124] For a useful short summary in a western language, see Jacques Proust, *Europe au prisme du Japon: xvie–xviiie siècle* (Paris, 1997), pp.226–8.

in existence by 1816, and a second draft was ready by 1822. Copies of both dictionaries were made (and the copying of the Nagasaki *Haruma* occurred at various stages of its composition and revision), and were available widely across a small but influential circle. In the case of the Nagasaki dictionary a copy of the 1822 version immediately reached Edo Gensin's school where further copies were made of it.[125] Mito han, with an interest in *rangaku* even before the ascent of Nariaki in 1829, had its own copy of the *Haruma*.[126] By the 1850s daimyo were commissioning needy students at the Tekijuku in Osaka to transcribe the copy of the Nagasaki *Haruma* in the academy's possession.[127] *Rangakusha* preferred the Nagasaki *Haruma* as it included sentences illustrating each entry and was easier to use.[128] This reflected the fact that Nagasaki interpreters had conversational knowledge of Japanese, whereas Edo knowledge was more of the written language.[129] If Dutch presented grammatical and syntactical problems for Japanese, its pronunciation, with consonants profusely used and not economically as in Japanese, made conversational knowledge particularly difficult.

The new competence provided two things: a preparation for direct negotiations with unwanted foreigners, and an ability to translate foreign works into Japanese. Scientific, geographical or general works of political or strategic interest and, in 1808, the first treatise on western gunnery appeared in translation. The texts of a hundred or so works survive, and others certainly were attempted. Townsend Harris later mocked the tendency of the interpreters to put Dutch in the Japanese word order.[130] This criticism, making no allowance for men whose knowledge was essentially bookish and who lacked the opportunity of regular verbal intercourse with foreigners, was in effect the comment of a man himself without linguistic competence, hence alive more to defects than to accomplishments.

[125] The key work on the development of Dutch knowledge is Sugimoto Tsutomu's magisterial *Edo jidai ran-gogaku no seiritsu to sono tenkai* [Emergence and evolution of philological knowledge of Dutch in Edo times], 5 vols. (Tokyo, 1976–82). Vol. 5, pp.905–18, has a useful synopsis in English. The second is Uehara Hisashi's *Takahashi Kageyasu no kenkyū* [Studies of Takahashi Kageyasu] (Tokyo, 1977).
[126] *Mito shi-shi*, middle series, vol. 3, pp.1064–5.
[127] According to Fukuzawa, 'The work of the whole dictionary of some 3,000 pages would therefore bring in a substantival sum for a needy student' (*Autobiography of Fukuzawa Yukichi*, p.89).
[128] See Sugimoto, *Edo jidai ran-gogaku*, vol. 5, p.917. For a short and helpful summary of the dictionaries, see *Onko-chishin: Shizuoka kenritsu chūō toshokanzō no kichōsho shōkai* [Drawing lessons from the study of the past: introduction to rare books in the Shizuoka prefectural central library collection] (Shizuoka, 1997). The Shizuoka Library has copies of both the Edo and Nagasaki *Haruma*.
[129] Katagiri Kazuo, *Mikan rangaku shiryō no shoshi-teki kenkyū* [Bibliographical history of unpublished *rangaku* materials] (Tokyo, 1997), p.254.
[130] See *The complete journal of Townsend Harris*, pp.352, 375, 550.

Even the more sympathetic Kaempfer almost 170 years previously seems to have underestimated the painful task for the *oranda tsūji*, without any aids in the way of dictionaries or grammars, of starting from scratch to learn Dutch. A century later, judging by the comments of a successor, Van Rheede, in 1787 to Titsingh, by then in Batavia, the interpreters were a mixed bag, though this was a judgement based on their personal qualities more than on their linguistic ability.[131]

Translation itself was specialised work, and it required few rather than many collaborators. Some came to Edo from the han, and in reverse, especially from the 1830s, scholars were attracted from Edo into han service. Medical studies (including under their umbrella botany, chemistry and the natural sciences at large) were more decisive than political events in accounting for the diffusion of *rangaku* outside Edo and Nagasaki: medical men alone in Japanese society had wide empirical interests, and they were the pioneers of intellectual change. Thus the Von Siebold academy in 1824 immediately attracted students from afar; the Tekijuku, which in 1838 grew out of the Kaitokudo, and of which its prized possession was its Nagasaki *Haruma*, taught medicine and natural sciences, drawing on western knowledge. The career of Ogata Kōan (1810–63), head of the Tekijuku, illustrated the new pattern of Dutch experts. He had been a student in Gensin's rather literary academy in Edo, and later studied under Philip Von Siebold (1796–1866) in Narutaki.[132] For the first time Dutch was becoming easy to learn as grammars, linguistic texts and dictionaries began to appear; the consequence was that the teaching of science through western texts to large numbers was now feasible, and the subject from the 1830s was tacked on even to the curriculum of some of the han academies of western Japan. A total of thirty-four *rangaku* schools have been identified, twenty-eight of which appeared after 1800.[133] The Tekijuku's 600 registered students (there were unregistered students as well) from 1838 to 1862 made it into not only the largest school of *rangaku* but the first stable school of empirical science in Japan.

Teaching was a measure of the changes. Given the prestige attached to Chinese and classical literature, instruction, with its heavy emphasis on philology or on classical texts, was often arid, but, whatever the loyalty of students to *sensei*, it was not conformist to any general body of knowledge,

---

[131] Lequin, *Private correspondence of Isaac Titsingh*, vol. 1, pp.71–2.

[132] For Ogata's career, see Tetsuo Najita, 'Ambiguous encounters: Ogata Kōan and international studies in late Tokugawa Osaka', in McClain and Wakita, *Osaka: the merchants' capital*, pp.213–42.

[133] Aoki, *Zaison rangaku no kenkyū*, pp.70–1. The total of 9,324 students is, however, inflated by the large number of students recorded for some of the schools at the end of the shogunate.

and some or much of it had critical elements. The Sorai and Kaitokudo type of teaching also discussed changes in institutions. A key pattern of the private schools – one which the Shoheiko and han schools did not enjoy – was that the students came not from the shogunal territories or from a single han but from many places. Thus, they were doubly important: not only were they by nature nonconformist, making an independent choice of school, but the schools brought together in a single location students from many parts of Japan and from all walks of life. Lay students dominated, but Buddhist and Shinto priests were numerous. One vital consequence was that despite the abuse of Buddhism by educators (Shinto was less abused as it was less of an educational rival), members of both belief systems continued to hold an effective place in public life. In particular, Buddhism, despite a preference by the new Meiji state after 1868 for Shinto as the weaker belief system (to the point of unsuccessfully attempting to compel people to register at Shinto shrines), survived the Meiji period very well. In the private schools, not in the han schools greatly overrated in modern historiography, lay the intellectual vitality of Japanese education: private, competitive and eclectic. It is impossible to find in education hidden tensions between society and shogunate or an open conflict between the philosophies of their teachers and a state philosophy. More personal rivalries of course remained. It was open to anyone to open a private academy, a reason for the competition for pupils; and, hereditary though official posts were, variously either daimyo recruited new men for tasks, or retainers relinquished a charge in their own han to seek one further afield. The lack of establishment values gave Japanese education a strength – its openness – and at the same time constituted a weakness because, despite many common values in society, a standardisation of basic tenets, imposed as in the west by authority of church or state, was lacking. It left Japanese thought free to go in different ways all at once or to fall an easy prey to fashions, whether in the 1870s the adoption of western ideas, in the early twentieth century the conversion of a number of intellectuals to an enthusiastic Christianity, in the 1920s sympathies for Marxism, or, in the 1930s, ultra-nationalistic ideals.

5   Prosperity amid crises, 1789–1853

The period from 1789 to 1853 was marked at the beginning and towards the end by prolonged external crisis. While its outset followed the severe Tenmei economic crisis of the 1780s, the period, 1830s apart, was free from economic difficulties. After the late 1780s the economy entered a period of great prosperity and low prices. Even the number of *ikki*, that doubtful measure of discontent, fell, and was remarkably low in most years. Low prices of rice, while reducing the purchasing power of samurai, were a positive boon to townsmen. The consequence was that the Edo population, though modestly enough, grew again (while, significantly, the population of Osaka, whose fortunes were linked to rice prices and daimyo finances, did not). There was a boom in consumer expenditure, and the city's social activity and artistic role expanded in an unprecedented fashion. It was a period of abundant cheap reading-matter, and also of a more popular *uki-yo-e* woodblock printing, best known in the west today from the work of Hiroshige and Hokusai, which sold in multiple copies. In contrast to the boom of Genroku times occasioned by the concentrated merchant wealth in Osaka, the flowering was more wide-ranging and popular, reaching further down the social ladder: it centred also on Edo's commoners more than on its disgruntled samurai.

If the Bunka–Bunsei flowering in Edo was less exalted than the brilliant creativity in Genroku Osaka, its economic base was stronger, and that helped to explain its wider social reach. Intellectual life strengthened. Schools flourished and increased in number: they were larger, the students more numerous, the teaching more structured and less dependent on the personality of one individual. The scale and appeal of the Hita academy of Hirose Tansō is an example of this.[1] Scholarship in Mito han on the Japanese classics not only continued, but was beginning to acquire national attention. Japanese thought was not, of course, being even remotely westernised, but Japanese awareness of western civilisation was no

---

[1] Marleen Kassel, *Tokugawa Confucian education: the Kangien academy of Hirose Tanso (1892–1856)* (Albany, N.Y., 1996).

longer confined to a limited group, and to specialised interests in mathematics and medicine. A growing, even if small, number of Japanese were aware of western thought in some form, and had absorbed ideas as diverse as perspective in painting or, in Hirata Atsutane's case, western theological concepts.[2] Some knowledge of western gadgets and mechanical devices existed, and is illustrated in the work of fashionable painters of the period. The daimyo of Akita had a collection of western prints; Tani Bunchō, a painter employed by the prime minister Matsudaira Sadanobu, also had a collection, and the bookseller and artist, Shiba Kōkan, both painted in the realistic western mode and engraved on copper plates in western style.[3] Comments on the west and on its politics, compared with those of the eighteenth century, were also much better informed. They were of course also promoted by the need to know more about countries which rather dimly offered a challenge and whose power, organisation and aggression as evidenced in multiple wars elsewhere were beginning to be appreciated. Knowledge of Dutch by the interpreters had reached a new scale of linguistic sophistication, itself a prelude to the extensive study and translation of western books.[4] Dutch studies, requiring a knowledge of a difficult foreign language, necessarily reached very few individuals directly. However, the findings of the 'Dutch' scholars were widely known, and individuals with no personal competence in Dutch and very different political leanings, ranging from Honda Toshiaki through some of the members of the Hayashi family itself, to Aizawa Seishisai (1782–1863) and Watanabe Kazan (1793–1841), were familiar with their import.

In a Japan richer than ever before, the paradox of poor public administration – in the case of shogunate and han alike – was inevitably ever more of an anomaly. This explains why debasement of the currency was resorted to again in 1818 and 1830. It also accounts for some upswing in unrest in the 1820s: at this time it often stemmed from attempts by han administrations to impose novel imposts on industry or trade. Neither phenomenon – debasement or *ikki* – should be seen as evidence of an underlying economic crisis. Debasement – and debasement had become a dirty word in the canon of Japanese financial practice – hinted, however, at the narrow margin of public solvency, and suggested that if either a new run of harsh harvests or more serious foreign threats occurred, the state of public finances, precarious even in good times, would become even more the central feature of domestic policy.

[2] Keene, *Japanese discovery of Europe*, pp.164–9.
[3] See Screech, *Western scientific gaze*. On Tani Bunchō see Screech, *Shogun's painted culture*.
[4] Sugimoto's massive five volumes (*Edo jidai ran-gogaku*) is the key source of study. It should be supplemented by Katagiri's *Oranda tsūji no kenkyū*.

External crisis was to prove more long-lasting than economic problems. The Ezo crisis dominated official thinking on external relations through the 1790s and the first decade of the nineteenth century. The Russians, pushing further afield in exploration of the Kurils, had even asked for permission to trade with Matsumae in 1778. As the trade from Ezo to Edo was expanding rapidly, the news inevitably filtered back, probably through several channels, to Edo. The Sendai samurai Hayashi Shihei (1739–93), who had visited Nagasaki in 1775, published his first work in 1785 – *Sankoku tsūran zusetsu* (A general survey of three countries) – a geographical work dealing with three regions, Ezo, Chosen and the Ryukyus, on the periphery of Japan. Though he had heard about the 1771 message from Benyowsky from the Dutch *opperhoofd* when he visited Nagasaki,[5] it crops up only in his *Kikoku heidan* (Military talks for a maritime nation) of 1791, at a time when there was now widespread unease in Edo.

The slow-paced and under-resourced Russian colonisation gathered some momentum in the 1780s. With little navigation from Europe and frozen seas in winter, the problems of developing their Asian empire led them inevitably to look eastwards into the Pacific and southwards to the coasts of China. A future for eastern Siberia would depend on south-ward navigation for food, and for commercial success both eastwards to America and southwards to Canton. As there was no carriage road be-yond Irkutsk, heavy equipment like anchors and ship's cables had to be carried in sections and spliced together on arrival at Okhotsk. A company to trade in the north Pacific as far as America, the Russian-American Company, was established in 1789. Two naval officers, Davidoff (Davidov) and Chwostoff (Khostov), seconded to the company, made the first commercially successful voyages from Kodiak in 1802 and 1803.[6] Under the Russian admiral, Ivan Fedorovich Krusenstern (1770–1846), a voyage around the Cape of Good Hope to Canton had already been made in 1798: its basic purpose was to make Canton the centre for the projected Russian long-distance trades, and the prospect of a trade in tea (which might replace spirits) with Russia was a further attraction.[7] Devel-opment would depend on an intimate knowledge of the obscure seas and islands standing between Kamchatka and Canton along which the path of future commercial voyages would have to lie. In 1803 Krusenstern set out on the second of his great voyages from Europe, a three-year voyage, holding the Laxman licence of 1793 (a permit granted in Ezo to Laxman

---

[5] Akizuki Toshiuki, *Nihon hokuhen no tanken to chizu no rekishi* [A history of exploration and cartography of the northern region] (Sapporo, 1999), p.145.

[6] Krusenstern, *Voyage round the world*, vol. 2, pp.108, 114.

[7] Krusenstern, *Voyage round the world*, vol. 2, pp.334–7.

for the Russians to proceed to Nagasaki for negotiations), with two objects: firstly, to carry ambassador Rezanov and to negotiate at Nagasaki for trade with the Japanese; secondly, to explore the lands and channels between the Ezo islands and Tartary.[8]

For the Japanese, the issue was straightforward: less one of opening up Japan, than whether peace would be imperilled if the concessions in trade sought by the Russians were refused. The issue was not about creating a Nagasaki-style trade as existed with the Chinese and Dutch, but about admitting some trade along an uncertain or even non-existing frontier in the waters surrounding the northern isles. In 1793 unintentionally this had been turned into a larger issue by the Japanese referring the Russians to Nagasaki and giving them the licence for such a visit, which Rezanov held in 1804. For the Russians the objective at heart – where Japan was concerned, if not the north Pacific at large – was access to harbours which were unfrozen in winter and to a food supply to supplement the resources of the tiny population of their east Asian empire.[9] Another factor had added to Japanese fears. Outnumbered by the Ainu, the Japanese, in the wake of the Ainu revolt in Kunashiri in 1789 in which seventy-one Japanese had lost their lives,[10] feared a link-up between Russians and Ainu malcontents. Both Honda Toshiaki (1744–1821), an armchair theorist in Edo and author of several tracts on the north which circulated among officials, and Mogami Tokunai (1755–1836), the main figure in the actual exploration of the islands, put a heavy emphasis on the need to conciliate the Ainu.

Ezo as an ongoing defence issue was a more persistent problem than the short-lived necessity in 1792–3 or 1804 of responding to diplomatic démarches. Because of the Russian presence, it had already become incumbent on the Japanese to learn more about Ezo, to map it and define its frontiers. The first surveying Japanese mission had already occurred in 1785.[11] It was prelude to a large amount of writing, and to much

---

[8] *Memoir of... Admiral John de Krusenstern* (London, 1856). For further information, see both Krusenstern, *Voyage round the world*, and the account by G. H. Von Langsdorff, physician and naturalist to the mission, *Voyages and travels in various parts of the world during the years 1803, 1804, 1805, 1806, and 1807*, 2 vols. (London, 1813).

[9] Post-1868, part of the Russian eastern fleet wintered in Nagasaki. This accounts for the presence of a Russian cemetery beside the Dutch one there. The cemetery was damaged by a conventional bomb in 1945, and hence the names and dates of all the 270 graves are not now known. For a brief detail, see L. R. Earns and B. Burke-Gaffney, *Across the gulf of time: the international cemeteries of Nagasaki* (Nagasaki, 1991), pp.6–7.

[10] Akizuki, *Nihon hokuhen no tanken*, p.157. On the story of Ezo, for an Ainu perspective, see Brett L. Walker, *The conquest of Ainu lands: ecology and culture in Japanese expansion, 1590–1800* (Berkeley, 2001).

[11] Kaempfer referred to 'a shogunal junk' sent 'a few years ago' (i.e. before 1691) to between 40 and 50 degrees latitude (*Kaempfer*, p.46). It is the only such reference, and nothing is known of the venture.

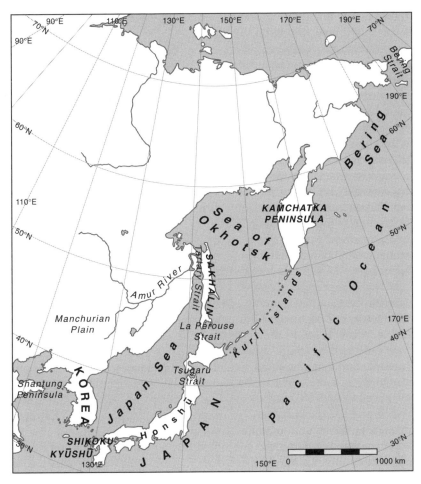

6. North-east Asia

official activity, all concerned with the fundamental question: was there a military threat and how serious was it? As there was not really a divide of opinion about the existence of a problem a second question was how to respond to it. It was on this ground that opinion divided. Some, like Hayashi Shihei, argued that the threat was imminent and that immediate action had to be militaristic, including investment in western-style warships.

The danger of aggressive action, that is, forward movement to stake out a frontier deep into the Ezo region, was of course that it could bring about the military conflict that everyone wanted to avoid. For this reason

Hayashi was arrested in 1793 for his inflammatory writing and exiled to his home han of Sendai. The dangers of loose thought are evident from the writings of the samurai Honda Toshiaki, less highly placed than sometimes suggested (he was a teacher of geography, wide-ranging in his curiosity, highly opinionated in the way of teachers, with no administrative experience and no personal knowledge of the region he wrote about). He merits a place in the story largely because of the rising prominence of one of his pupils, Mogami Tokunai. Honda's writings have been seen in modern times as arguing for the opening of Japan.[12] He argued for trade to foreign countries, but in a highly unrealistic way in which no reciprocity was incumbent on Japan to admit foreigners and in which the trade would take the form of some exchange of commodities for precious metals from abroad. His lack of realism is evident in his argument that, in extending its frontiers, Japan should even transfer the capital from Edo to Kamchatka. Such a step would ensure conflict with Russia: the fact that Kamchatka was a Russian territory was ignored (prior ownership of Kamchatka by Japan in earlier times was assumed by Honda). Honda's case was demonstrably absurd.[13] He saw Ezo as a source of vast wealth, agricultural as well as mineral, and hence Japan should saturate the region with settlers. This would both ease economic problems – his advocacy began in the 1780s – and remove the foreign threat. His assumptions were bolstered by jejune arguments that Ezo was at a lower latitude than London, and that its mineral wealth was large because it was in the same longitude as some of the mines in Japan. He was well placed enough to have contact with a *kanjō bugyō* and two *metsuke* who were involved in Edo policy, and who favoured ambitious steps in Ezo.[14] Matsudaira, however, opted for a more cautious policy. Even after the visits in 1796 and 1797 by a British warship under the command of Captain Broughton prompted emergency direct control of east Ezo in 1799 and its perpetuation by the establishment of a bugyo office in Hakodate four years later, caution

---

[12] Keene, *Japanese discovery of Europe*, pp.v–vi, 108–9, 122. Keene's book was 'inspired' by the lectures of one of his Japanese professors in Columbia University, Tsunoda Ryūsaku, motivated by 'the need to believe that the traditional intellectual life of the Japanese was not monolithic but allowed the possibility of dissent' (Keene, *On familiar terms: a journey across cultures* (New York, 1994), p.12). G. A. Lensen also sees the prospects in 1804 of opening Japan as good (*The Russian push towards Japan: Russian-Japanese relations 1697–1875* (New York, 1971), pp.118–19, 160–1). However, the overriding issue in the Japanese concern was simply how to avoid war. On this subject, the most suggestive work is in Japanese by Mitani Hiroshi, and is best summarised in his *Meiji ishin to nashonarizumu: bakumatsu no gaikō to seiji* [Meiji Restoration and nationalism: bakumatsu diplomacy and politics] (Tokyo, 1997).

[13] Disillusionment set in after he became acquainted with the north on an actual voyage in 1801. See Keene, *Japanese discovery of Europe*, p.93.

[14] Fujita Satoru throws important new light on them in 'Kansei kaikaku to ezo-chi seisaku' [The Kansei reform and Ezo policy], in Fujita (ed.), *Bakuhansei kaikaku no tenkai*, pp.113–39.

dominated policy: expansion beyond areas where there were Japanese was ruled out. Carrying no weight in the definition of policy in the 1790s, Honda and his writings slipped into oblivion until some were printed in 1888–9.[15]

The dilemma in Ezo in the last analysis was less one of intercourse with foreigners than of defining the frontiers. Russians and Japanese in these regions had at times been surprised to meet one another, knowing of each other's existence more by report than by contact. The early Japanese, moreover, were simply traders, operating afar in isolated waters, and it was only from the time of a direct request from a Russian to Matsumae officials in 1778 for trade that it became an issue of substance. Mogami Tokunai, one of the future leaders of exploration, participated in the 1785 mission, and the work became more extensive with the appearance of Murakami Shimanojō in 1788. By 1798 some 180 people were in direct employment in survey work.[16] Mamiya Rinzō (1775–1844), the forceful explorer who was to complete the final survey of Karafuto, first appeared in 1798, working in the Kurils. From 1797, Kondō Jūzō (1771–1829), a Nagasaki official returning to Edo with one of the rotating Nagasaki bugyo and already having an interest in the northern question, was made responsible for defence policy there: Broughton's first visit in 1796 had prompted his appointment. His long stay until 1808 (when he was promoted to bugyo rank) signalled the beginning of an unprecedented direct shogunal involvement in the affairs of the region. Before Broughton's second visit in 1797, two of the han in the north of the Tohoku had already been deputed to station troops in Ezo. The Chief Astronomer's Office in Edo was made responsible for the direction of the technical work of surveying in 1799: the results in turn were fed back to Edo where Takahashi Kageyasu (1785–1829), inheriting his father's post of chief astronomer in 1804, was responsible for producing the first scientific maps of the region.[17]

---

[15] Keene, *Japanese discovery of Europe*, pp.94–5. However, there were copies of Honda's and other writings of the 1780s and 1790s in the Mito han library, and Aizawa, in an early tract he wrote in 1801, quoted Honda. B. T. Wakabayashi, *Anti-foreignism and western learning in early modern Japan: the New Theses of 1825* (Cambridge, Mass., 1986), pp.76–8. They gained little attention even then and their growth in prominence had to await the edition by the economic historian, Honjō Eijirō, in 1936 in *Honda Toshiaki shū* [The collected writings of Honda Toshiaki] (Tokyo, 1936). Following Honjō's editing, the Columbia historian, Tsunoda, gave them attention in his teaching, and his pupil Donald Keene in 1952 made Honda the centrepiece of his readable and influential *Japanese discovery of Europe*.

[16] Uehara Hisashi, *Takahashi Kageyasu no kenkyū*, p.232.

[17] The Ezo problem is the best documented single episode in Japanese policy in these years. It takes up part of two volumes of the *Tsūkō ichiran*, and can be supplemented by several sources of which the surveying work of Kondō Jūzō, recently published in *Dainihon, kinsei shiryō, Kondō Jūzō ezo-chi kankei shiryō* [Japan, sources for early modern history,

The first missions were divided into two work parties, one to the east, one to the west. The eastern surveyors proceeded as far north as Uruppu, and the western ones to the southern parts of Sakhalin (Japanese name, Karafuto), at the time known only to a handful of Japanese, who seasonally and only from very recent times occupied a small number of fishing stations. In 1798 Kondō and Mogami raised pillars in a number of locations, none beyond Etorofu, to indicate Japanese ownership. For defence reasons settlement was reinforced in Etorofu: on the advice of Kondō, fishing stations were increased to seventeen. Karafuto had little settlement. Its name implied a Chinese origin: officials sometimes crossed from the Tartar (or Manchu) mainland,[18] and it was the channel of supply through Ainu hands of a small amount of Chinese goods to the Ezo islands in exchange for prized seal and otter skins. In all, from 1785 four surveying missions visited Karafuto until the final survey of Mamiya together with Matsuda Denjurō in 1808 established conclusively, what some suspected but none knew for sure, that it was a island. While there had already been a few Russians, the first permanent Japanese trading post had been set up only in 1790, and a few watch-houses were set up by officials from Matsumae han.[19] The belief lingered in Japan that there were two islands, one of which they called Karafuto (with its handful of Japanese), and the other 'Tsoka' or 'Sakhalin', regarded as a Tartar possession.[20] Krusenstern, in exploring in 1805 the waters between Karafuto and the Asian mainland, had concluded that the people ashore in the north seemed Tartars. The only Japanese he encountered were in the south: he observed their establishment to be 'quite recent, as both the habitations of the Japanese officers and the warehouses were entirely new, some of them being even still unfinished'.

The geography of Sakhalin or Karafuto had fascinated westerners from the outset of the new vogue in exploration. La Pérouse had set the pattern. He was followed by Broughton who in 1797 surveyed the coast between

---

Kondō Jūzō sources concerning Ezo], 3 vols. (Tokyo, 1984–9), plus supplementary box with maps and pamphlet (Tokyo, 1993), is the most important. Some documents survive in the Hayashi papers in the *Naikaku bunko* (National archives), and a small number of items also survive in the public archives in Hokkaido. See also the very complete recent work on the surveying and mapping by Akizuki, *Nihon hokuhen*. The ten-volume *Hoppō mikōkai komonjo shūsei* [Collection of unpublished or inaccessible private documents for the northern region] (Tokyo, 1959–90), ed. Wada Toshiaki, Kurata Hidetoshi and Terazawa Hajime, is also a useful source.

[18] On the identification and definition of Tartary, see Mark C. Elliott, 'The limits of Tartary: Manchuria in imperial and national geographies', *Journal of Asian studies*, vol. 59, no. 3 (Aug. 2000), pp.603–46.

[19] The most compact account of the Japanese presence in the Kurils and in Karafuto is Hora Tomio, *Mamiya Rinzō* (Tokyo, 1960).

[20] Van Langsdorff, *Voyages and travels*, vol. 2, p.333; Krusenstern, *Voyage round the world*, vol. 2, pp.6, 29, 47.

Sakhalin and the Tartar mainland up to the latitude of 52: however, with the inlet narrowing and winter setting in, he dared go no further.[21] Krusenstern too in 1805 was under a handicap, though in his case it lay in his instructions, which were not to go near the Chinese coast for fear of giving offence to the Chinese (which could damage the hoped-for trade prospects with them): for that reason as the inlet narrowed, he withdrew. Krusenstern, having had reports that there were two islands, had kept an eye out for a strait separating 'Sakhalin' from 'Karafuto' but without finding one. As for the inlet separating the mysterious island or islands from the coast of Tartary on the Asian mainland, he concluded that there was a channel between them, but that it narrowed to the extent that it could be fully explored only by long boat.[22]

If frontiers were defined aggressively in this little-known and thinly populated region, it would actually promote the conflict with Russia that the Japanese wanted to avoid. Hence, if frontiers had to be defined, it was desirable to do so cautiously. This was what was involved in Matsudaira Sadanobu's belief in a buffer zone, in effect a no-man's-land, or at least one to which Japan did not stake a claim and over which it avoided conflict by not entering it.[23] That concept itself was a riposte to those who saw a far-reaching definition of frontier as solving the problem. Wisely, Sadanobu and his successors saw such an attempt as creating a certainty of conflict, and attached urgency simply to strengthening the areas where Japanese were already present. Hence, though the first missions had covered much of the Kurils quickly, surveying was soon confined to the southern parts.[24] In the case of Uruppu, the fitful Russian presence (at one stage they had abandoned residence), reinforced by thirty Russian families in 1795,[25] posed delicate problems. On orders from the *rōjū* a halt was called to the survey of Uruppu at the outset of 1802 (which might have led to conflict with the Russians); later in the year the movement of Ainu between Etorofu and Uruppu was prohibited.[26] In the case of Karafuto on the other hand, separated from Ezo-ga-shima only by a short channel, surveying and settlement alike became more urgent. The Japanese population there grew more rapidly than elsewhere in Ezo.[27]

[21] Broughton, *A voyage of discovery*, p.311.
[22] Krusenstern, *Voyage round the world*, vol. 2, pp.142, 175–82.
[23] This was the view of the powerful figure of Nakai Chikuzan, an advisor of Sadanobu, and a little later, of Yamagata Bantō. See E. Honjō, *Economic theory and history of Japan in the Tokugawa period* (Tokyo, 1943), p.114.
[24] Akizuki, *Nihon hokuhen no tanken*, p.265.
[25] Van Langsdorff, *Voyages and travels*, vol. 1, pp.296–7; Lensen, *The Russian push towards Japan*, pp.121–2.
[26] *Kondō Jūzō ezo-chi kankei shiryō, bessatsu* [separate pamphlet], pp.40, 42, included in *fuzu* [supplementary box with maps] (Tokyo, 1993).
[27] Von Siebold, *Nippon: archiv zur beschreibung von Japan*, vol. 2, p.269.

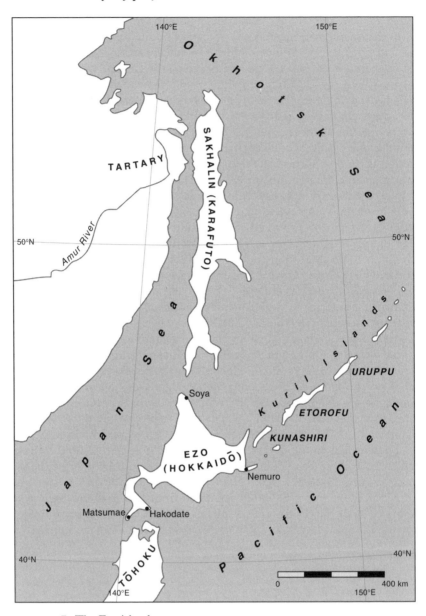

7. The Ezo islands

Modest permanent settlement replaced the largely seasonal pattern of the past. In the follow-up detailed mapping of the region, repeating the pattern in Uruppu, northern Karafuto was left out.[28] Administration and defence of what were now defined as the Japanese territories on the southern fringe of a novel and originally unsought frontier became a priority. Matsumae han itself lacked resources; its small territory was occupied by a minuscule samurai group of 600 men. The 1604 charter by Ieyasu to the Matsumae did not regulate dealings by Ainu with foreigners: in contrast to dilemmas to the south, to its drafters no problem existed. As a defence against Russian encroachment, in 1799 eastern Ezo and the islands were taken under direct shogunal control. When late in 1806 two Russian sea captains, Davidoff and Chwostoff, raided and burned a small Japanese settlement in Sakhalin, the decision was quickly taken to transfer western Ezo to direct Edo control early in 1807 at the time when navigation was due to resume in these cold waters. Before the change could enter into practical effect, the Russians who had wintered in Uruppu attacked the two Japanese settlements in Etorofu (on the second occasion the Japanese garrison abandoning its fort), a settlement in Sakhalin, and ships at a small island near Soya harbour in the north-west of Ezo-ga-shima itself. On the last occasion, the Russians left a message threatening to drive the Japanese out of their northern possessions, if they did not agree to trade.[29] The immediate Japanese response was to increase the number of soldiers from the two Tohoku han to 3,000 in the Ezo islands, and to give added urgency to the central administration of Sakhalin. Its name officially was changed from the commonly used term Karafuto, of Chinese origin, to Northern Ezo Region.[30] Losing control of western Ezo, the Matsumae family gave up their castle as well (they were compensated by territory in the Tohoku) and the bugyo office was transferred from Hakodate to Matsumae castle, symbolising the radical change in government.[31]

The Russian raids, later claimed to be a private initiative, were authorised by Rezanov, the ambassador of 1804, himself chairman of the

---

[28] Uehara, *Takahashi Kageyasu no kenkyū*, pp.418–19.

[29] W. G. Aston, 'Russian descents in Saghalin and Itorup in the years 1806 and 1807', *Transactions of the Asiatic Society of Japan*, vol. 1 (1874), pp.86–95. Golownin noted that the ships had operated without displaying a Russian flag.

[30] Akizuki Toshiyuki, *Nichirō kankei to Saharin-tō: bakumatsu meiji shonen no ryōdo mondai* [Japanese–Russian relations and Sakhalin island: a problem of territorial sovereignty in Bakumatsu and early Meiji times] (Tokyo, 1994), pp.48–49. For an account in English, see John J. Stephan, *Sakhalin: a history* (Oxford, 1971).

[31] The number of bugyo, reflecting the intensification of administration, was increased from two to four. *Hokkaidō-shi* [History of Hokkaido], 7 vols. (Tokyo, 1936–7, reprint Osaka, 1989–90), vol. 2 (Tokyo, 1937, reprint Osaka, 1990), pp.462–3. As in Nagasaki, in subsequent times the number of bugyo varied, but never fell below two.

trading company, in an order allegedly given in a fit of pique at the failure of the embassy, to the two captains who had themselves a past history in commercial voyages.[32] The overlap of public and private interests in the company made it impossible to draw a clear line between them. The only thing that seems to have been beyond all doubt is that a private initiative was responsible for the actual message left at Soya. Like the Benyowsky letter of 1771, the message was imprecise and delivered unconventionally; it was also unsigned, and delivered without seal or clear expression of authority. To add to the complications, while a version in garbled Japanese seems to have been communicated, the formal version was in French. Relayed back to Nagasaki, it was translated with the help of the Dutch, and communicated back to Matsumae.[33] The Japanese, benefiting from the presence of experienced bugyo supported by some able officials, were well-versed in diplomatic niceties: the question was a straightforward, though not an easy one, of deciding between the possibility that the raids were simple acts of piracy (even if their significance was somewhat heightened by the inglorious show by the Japanese forces on the occasion of the second Etorofu raid) or some form of uncouth gunboat diplomacy to give substance to the demands of Rezanov in Nagasaki in 1804. If the former, the consequences were minor; if the latter, they were far more serious. One result, however, was that the Japanese forces were now on the alert, and unlikely to be taken totally by surprise as had occurred on every occasion in 1806–7.

Uchi harai (firing on and driving away foreign vessels) was not in itself a novelty and may well have had its origins in orders from earlier times for driving off Chinese vessels hovering on the coasts with smuggling intent.[34] There was never a formally decreed policy of forcibly repelling foreign vessels. The well-documented experiences of six western seamen

[32] The fullest account in English is in Lensen, *The Russian push towards Japan*, pp.161–9.

[33] In the absence of an actual copy, there has been doubt about its precise wording. See Lensen, *The Russian push towards Japan*, p.172n. However, the French text, with a translation which was forwarded to Matsumae, and some correspondence, are in a small volume of copies of correspondence in the Keizaigakubu toshokan, University of Nagasaki, 511 M186. The firm western hand of the French text (which is described as a copy) suggests one made directly from the original by the Dutch. The sense of the text, moreover, is identical with the version from Russian sources given by Lensen. One of the consequences of the translation dilemma was that the interpreters were instructed to learn French as well as Russian and also English (made topical by the *Phaeton* incident). A further document by a *bugyōsho* official describing, with the aid of sketch maps, the 1806 and 1807 events in Ezo, is in the Nagasaki kenritsu chūō toshokan, 13/4 (Seiyama collection), 1807. Though it does not appear to feature in the Dagregister of the Dutch factory in Nagasaki, the French-language text and its translation are referred to, for 1807, in the *Tsūkō ichiran*, vol. 6, p.250.

[34] Yamamoto Hirofumi, *Sakoku to kaikin no jidai* [The sakoku and maritime-closure period] (Tokyo, 1995), p.159.

(three Dutch and three English) who had escaped from the Philippines and, hoping to reach Canton on a small vessel of 36 feet, arrived at an island off the coast of Satsuma in July 1704, illustrate both the determination to keep foreigners from having any liberty ashore and the readiness to provide succour. Transferred to Kagoshima, they were held for several days in a house specially prepared for them, before being taken by land (with a large military guard) and, for the last stage, by sea to Nagasaki. In Nagasaki the bugyo's suspicions at first were that they had been dispatched by the Spanish or Portuguese either to infiltrate the country as Christians or to disseminate Christian books. Their own explanation of the prayer books and of a set of rosary beads in their possession was plausible enough (the highly embarrassing rosary beads were allegedly to provide spare buttons for garments), and they eventually sailed in November 1704 in a Dutch vessel bound for Batavia.[35]

The official letter to Adam Laxman in the sixth month of 1793 did refer to *uchi harai*.[36] However, the novelty lay not in the statement within it that dealings were confined to countries with which contact already existed (which has in recent times been seized on as a proof of sakoku policy being made comprehensive for the first time), but in the declaration of an unqualified *uchi harai* to Laxman, the terms of which were repeated in 1804 to Rezanov.[37] The intention was to indicate a more clear-cut legal framework than was the case. It was not followed up by a decree with the same import, though several decrees immediately before and after 1793 did reveal real concern about foreign vessels. The reality was simply a reinforced watchfulness. A decree in 1791 had required foreign ships which dallied off the shore to be sent to Nagasaki, and several orders in 1792 and early 1793 enjoined coastal defence obligations on daimyo.[38] A decree in 1797, referring to the order of 1791, stressed that the policy should be a passive one, in which the Japanese were not to take the initiative in resorting to violence, or to do so only if a foreign vessel persisted

[35] Parmentier and Laarhoven (eds.), *De avonturen van een VOC-soldat*, especially pp.132, 133, 142–3, 147, 151, 155, 156–7, 161, 165–9, 190. The text edits the diary of one of the six, Van der Haeghe, a deserter from the Dutch East India Company army; it also includes the relevant extracts from the *dagregister* of the Dutch factory in Deshima. One of the three reputed Englishmen, Robert Jansen, was in fact Irish and had lived in Ireland for his first six years of life.

[36] Fujita Satoru, 'Jūkyū seiki zenhan no nihon: kokumin kokka keisai no zentei' [Japan in the first half of the nineteenth century: prerequisites for the formation of a nation state], in *Nihon tsū-shi* [The course of Japanese history], vol. 15 (Tokyo, 1996), p.16; Fujita Satoru, 'Taigai kankei no dentōka to sakoku sohō-kan no kakuritsu' [Changing practices in foreign relations and the establishment of the sakoku restrictive code], in *Jūnana seiki*, ed. Fujita, pp.199–200.

[37] Fujita, *Kinsei seiji-shi to tennō*, pp.14–15.

[38] Yamashita Takashi, *Sakoku to kaikoku* [Sakoku and the opening of Japan] (Tokyo, 1996), p.55; Fujita, *Kinsei seiji-shi to tennō*, p.1.

in a determination to make a landing.[39] In early 1805, Krusenstern, the captain of the Russian vessel, when leaving Nagasaki at the end of the Rezanov mission, was assured that orders would be dispatched along the coasts of Japan for him not to be detained if circumstances forced him ashore.[40] A decree in 1806, in its terms for providing supplies to Russian ships in need, was very clearly a follow-up to this favour. It neither created a new policy nor gave a favour to Russians not enjoyed by others: it was simply an exhortation to coast watchers, in the interest of not giving a *casus belli* to the Russians, to use to the full their discretionary powers.[41] In 1807, in the wake of the Russian raids in Ezo, the order was amended for Russian ships to be fired on in all circumstances on their approach. This was the first *uchi harai* order in the sense in which it is understood in modern historiography. Japanese readiness was soon put to the test. In 1811 a Russian naval officer Vasilii Mikhailovich (Wasely Mikhaylowich) Golovnin (Golownin) (1776–1831), was surveying off the coasts of Etorofu and Kunashiri in the *Diana*. Needing water, he and some men went ashore, and, through a ruse, they were made prisoners. The Kunashiri *jiken*, or incident, made it necessary for the Japanese to decide what had been the original purpose of the activity of their prisoners. In other words, had the *Diana*'s voyage been purely a surveying mission, as Golownin claimed, or was the visit prelude to a Russian attack? Cautiously the Japanese did not jump to conclusions and engaged in obsessive but increasingly amicable questioning of Golownin over more than two years. One thing that must have weighed in the decision was that the 1804 request for trade did not have a follow-up: that made the piracy explanation the more credible. For the Japanese the stakes were high: they had to decide what were the Russian intentions and, depending on their decision, either hostilities could break out or the status quo could be perpetuated.

If still not well prepared militarily, the Japanese had already made extensive intellectual changes, and on that front were well prepared by the time the *jiken* occurred. The problems posed by the Rezanov mission (the Japanese knowing no Russian or German; the Russians depending on the Dutch-language knowledge of Langsdorff, their German-speaking physician; and a cumbersome process of translation of Russian into Dutch, and then of Langsdorff's Dutch into Japanese by the Nagasaki

[39] Yamashita, *Sakoku*, pp.55–6. There are few references to the 1797 instruction.
[40] Krusenstern, *Voyage round the world*, vol. 2, p.4.
[41] The text of the 1806 order is in *PP Japan*, vol. 2, p.376, Correspondence respecting affairs in Japan 1865–6. The translation has created the ambiguity that it related to a single ship. The 1825 order, however, made it clear that it had related to Russian ships at large.

interpreters) had already prompted the Japanese to improve their language knowledge. In 1804 the negotiations in Nagasaki on the spot were handled by officials dispatched from Edo who had no language skills, helped by interpreters whose competence in Dutch was in turn nullified by the poor linguistic skills of the Russians. The events made it necessary for some of the interpreters to learn Russian and French, as did the arrival of the English warship *Phaeton* in Nagasaki in 1808, English. In 1811 two major steps were initiated on the language front. The first was that in Nagasaki from 1811, the interpreters started drawing up their famous Dutch–Japanese dictionary: this was in effect a training venture for the corps of interpreters in enhancing their translation competence for much more challenging tasks than the routine ones of trade. Some Nagasaki interpreters were also from 1808 transferred to Edo, a step which anticipated the foundation in 1811 of the *Banshowagegoyō* (Office for translating foreign books). For the first time the small *rangaku* circle in Edo was dominated by officials rather than by scholars. The heads of the new office were Takahashi Kageyasu, already, as head astronomer, one of the most senior Edo technocrats; and Ōtsuki Gentaku (1757–1827), the aged doyen of the private *rangakusha*. Takahashi Kageyasu (1785–1829), inheriting from his father the office of shogunal astronomer, was also in charge of the calendar reform office (responsible for mapping), and acquired his knowledge of Dutch, apparently, though by unknown methods, around 1808.[42] The greatest Dutch expert of the office was Baba Sajūrō (1787–1822), a young interpreter transferred as the brightest star of the Nagasaki interpreter corps to Edo.[43] Like Takahashi in Edo, who had asked the Dutch missions to given him a western name, Baba in Nagasaki had requested Doeff to give him one ('Abraham'), and he had frequented the house of the *opperhoofd* daily. As well as the Dutch of his profession, he had mastered English and French in Nagasaki, and in the autumn of 1811 found himself charged with deciphering the letters in Russian found on the Russian captives, learning Russian from a shipwrecked Japanese who had been returned to his homeland. In Edo, he also conducted – within the Translations Bureau – a language school.[44] The office itself was a classic illustration of Japan's practice of combining officials of heterogeneous background to confront new tasks. It was

---

[42] Uehara, *Takahashi Kageyasuū no kenkyū*, p.247. He was also the foremost expert in Manchu, the language of the Tartars, the race from which the Manchu dynasty had originated. This was a useful knowledge for appraising political and geographical knowledge of the mainland close to Sakhalin.

[43] Sugimoto Tsutomu, *Edo yōgaku jijō* [The state of western studies in Edo] (Tokyo, 1990), pp.148–55.

[44] Katagiri, *Oranda tsūji no kenkyū*, pp.383–4.

headed by Takahashi, a high official, and more nominally by Ōtsuki, a private entrepreneur of Dutch studies; at lower level both in Edo and in the field, officers of different background were brought together, either Nagasaki interpreters or, in Matsumae, the young Murakami Teisuke (1780–1845), a man switched from surveying work for reasons which are not clear, but which may be explained by confidence in his language ability.

In the wake of the *Phaeton*'s presence in 1808, six interpreters were ordered in the following year to learn English, and in the same year similar steps were taken for interpreters to learn Russian.[45] Some of the interpreters had already been sent to Edo in 1807–8, to translate urgently works on Russia and the west from Dutch into Japanese.[46] The staff of the *Banshowagegoyō* was some thirty officials in all.[47] The result was that responsibility for negotiations with foreigners was shifted from the bugyo office in Nagasaki (the reason for the granting to Laxman in 1793 of the licence to go to Nagasaki) to a specialised office in Edo, staffed by men with linguistic competence. Edo was also closer to the districts where problems arose, and officials were sent out as necessary from Edo to face problems of interviewing the captive Russians in Ezo in 1811–13 or, a few years later, distressed whalers off the eastern coasts of Honshu. Takahashi himself visited Ezo as did Baba Sajūrō,[48] who accompanied the new bugyo in March 1813, returning to Edo seven months later. A wide range of aspects of Russia and its policy had interested the Japanese, quite apart from the specific question of what Golownin's intentions had been. The daily liaison fell on Murakami Teisuke, who appeared in Hakodate no more than a month after the Russian prisoners reached it in August 1811. He already had, or quickly developed, considerable ease in the use of Russian.[49] Teisuke was a likeable and intelligent man; by coincidence Golownin was a similar person, and the resolution of the

---

[45] Katagiri, *Oranda tsūji no kenkyū*, pp.82, 84. The *Phaeton* episode is well described by W. G. Aston in 'H.M.S. *Phaeton* at Nagasaki in 1808', in *Collected works of William George Aston*, 6 vols. (Bristol and Tokyo, 1997), vol. 1, pp.107–20.

[46] Katagiri, *Oranda tsūji no kenkyū*, pp.356–7, 359. According to Doeff, Baba, a student of his, was transferred in 1808 (H. Doeff, *Herinneringen uit Japan* (Harlem, 1833), p.146).

[47] None of the administrative records of the office survive, and knowledge of its role is therefore very oblique.

[48] Sugimoto, *Edo yōgaku jyō*, p.148: Katagiri, *Oranda tsūji no kenkyū*, p.363; Doeff, *Herinneringen uit Japan*, pp.146–7, 227. Takahashi Kageyasu is not to be confused with a second official also bearing the name Takahashi who was in Ezo. Takahashi Kageyasu is not mentioned by Golownin.

[49] The main source for much of the episode lies in Golownin's *Narrative of my capitivity*. The only tangible work by Murakami Teisuke (1780–46) is a few papers in the *Naikaku bunko* (National archives) and elsewhere, and references to him in bibliographies are sparse. Japanese accounts themselves rely heavily on Golownin's text. He is infrequently mentioned in modern accounts, though he does appear in Hora, *Mamiya Rinzō* and in

matter was helped by the relationship between two men who shared an intellectual curiosity. The protracted negotiations reflected as much indecision and divides among the Japanese as doubts about Russia's real intentions. Mamiya, a strong partisan of the view of the danger the Russians posed, spent time in Matsumae in the spring of 1812. Teisuke, together with one of the bugyo, departed for Edo in July 1812: he reappeared in the spring of 1813 along with a new bugyo and with Baba Sajūrō (one of the men of learning whom the Russians had been assured at an earlier stage were to come from Edo). The instructions they brought made it possible to resolve the affair later in the year.[50]

Late in 1813 Golownin and the other Russians were released. The Golownin *jiken* has been described as the greatest crisis in Japanese foreign policy between the seventeenth century and the arrival of Perry in 1853.[51] The event had an interesting sequel as Golownin's own account in Russian influenced later happenings. The book appeared in 1816. Because of the quickened awareness in Europe of the north Pacific, it was immediately translated into German and Dutch. Once the Dutch edition came into the hands of the *Banshowagegoyō*, Baba Sajūrō was deputed to translate it. He died in 1822, before he had completed the task. The translation was finished in 1825 by two other interpreters, and the final text also had the personal overview of Takahashi. In taking a decision in 1822 on restoring the han to the Matsumae family, and ending

Akizuki, *Nihon hokuhen no tanken*, pp.292, 301, 302; and *Kondō Jūzō*, p.27. He did not have an interpreter background, and is recorded in 1810 as an assistant said to be aged twenty-four or twenty-five (sic) in the surveying work of Mamiya (Hora, *Mamiya Rinzō*, p.177). He wrote an account of the experiences of the watch-house men in Karafuto after the Russian attack (Hora, *Mamiya Rinzō*, p.177), which might suggest that he was there shortly after the date of the attack (1807). Golownin, impressed by his linguistic aptitude, thought that he had already been learning Russian. While his surveying work may have provided an opportunity, through some contact with multi-lingual Ainu, it has been said also that he was instructed by the bugyo to learn Russian. Hiraoka Masahide, *Nichiro kōshō-shi wa: ishin zengo no nihon to roshia* [An examination of the history of Russo-Japanese negotiations before and after the Restoration] (Tokyo, 1982), p.261.

[50] There was also correspondence in the interval, but the lack of central records for the office or for the *rōjū* means that the decision-making process is obscure. The amount of material in the *Tsūkō ichiran* also reveals the attention the matter got. The few surviving documents from the field survive in what remains of the Hayashi archive, which was broken up in the 1860s. There is only one direct reference to Baba Sajūrō in Golownin's account (though references to the 'Dutch interpreter' are in fact to him). His presence and that of Takahashi was obviously to appraise the wider implications of the event, and daily contact with the Russians was conducted by the interpreters and on formal occasions by the bugyo.

[51] For a very good summary of policy for Ezo, see Mitani Hiroshi, 'Tai-ro kinchō no kōchō to shikan' [Climax and decline of anti-Russian tensions], *Nihon rekishi taikei* [Compendium of Japanese history], vol. 3, *kinsei* [Early modern period] (Tokyo, 1988), pp.903–14; Mitani, 'Tenpō-ka'ei no taigai mondai' [The external problem in Tempō-Kaei times], *Nihon rekishi taikei*, vol. 3, *kinsei*, pp.1127–51.

direct administration, the Japanese may have been influenced by the conclusions that had been reached at the time of the Golownin *jiken*. The
Japanese translation itself was begun too late to be likely to have had a direct influence on the decision. However, a measure of the weight attached
to it is the fact that years later, in the compilation of the Tsukō ichiran, its
text, more or less in its entirety, was reproduced in sections interspersed
amid Japanese records from the period. The survival of at least seven
copies of the original translation is a further testimony to its circulation
among officials.[52] Knowledge of its contents in the 1820s may already
have added to the easing of fears about the challenge from the north,
and have justified the relatively assured attitude of official Edo, against
which Aizawa Seishisai railed vigorously in the *Shinron* of 1825, and in
response to which Nariaki in the 1830s continued to agitate. Golownin's
personal views were pacific; his comments on the Japanese themselves
extremely favourable, and more importantly the book did not hint at any
large Russian purpose in the east. In fact, quite independently Russian
interests in the east lost pace, and did not quicken again until the end of
the 1840s.

Neither Golownin's release in 1813 nor the termination of direct administration of Ezo in 1822[53] ended the debate as to whether it was
in Japan's strategic interest to base its actions on a reasonable, but
not demonstrably established assumption about Russian pacifism. While
Murakami Teisuke, as reported by Golownin, held a relaxed view, his
former employer, Mamiya Rinzō, displayed a very different temper in
his visits: Golownin took an immediate dislike to him. However, in the
bugyōsho and in Edo, the moderate view prevailed. By 1824, in a permission without precedent in the history of sakoku, Von Siebold, the medical
doctor in the Japanese factory, was given permission to set up a school
of medicine and natural sciences, the celebrated Narutaki *juku*, within
earshot of the waterfall on one of the streams rushing down from the hills
ringing Nagasaki. The intellectual worth of Dutch studies was not questioned; some alleged, however, that uncritical passion for Dutch studies
bred complacency about the larger risks posed by the outside world. It
may be assumed that for Mamiya, who had remained in Ezo until the

---

[52] There are five copies in the *Naikaku bunko* (National archives), plus Takahashi's an-
notated copy in the Hakodate library. See Uehara, *Takahashi Kageyasu no Kenkyū*,
pp.648–9. The text edited as *Sōyaku nihon kiji: Gorounin* [Diary of my tribulations in
Japan: Golownin] by Wada Toshiaki is in *Hoppō mikōkai komonjo shūsei*, vol. 6, and is
based on the Hakodate copy. Uehara does not list the copy held in the Shizuoka kenritsu
chūō toshokan, also completed in 1825 (Shizuoka Kenritsu chūō toshokan, AJ 12).

[53] The date is give variously in both Japanese and western books as 1821 or 1822. The
confusion is explained by the fact that the transfer took place at the end of the Japanese
lunar year of 1821 or the beginning of the solar year 1822.

Matsumae family were restored in 1822,[54] the decision was not to his liking, and that rewarded with a relatively high post in Edo, his views carried some weight.

The immediate issue in 1824 concerned the novel problem of foreign whalers: were they innocent fishermen or spies using a cover to reconnoitre the coasts of Japan? American and English whaling, hitherto almost unknown in the north-west Pacific, had increased rapidly in the 1810s and 1820s. No less than ten instances had been noted between 1818 and 1822, and sometimes the crews not only came to get food or water, but allegedly used force to attain their end.[55] To deal with the problem the questions drawn up in Dutch to put to foreign mariners were translated by the versatile Baba Sajūrō into a halting English: in polite terms they set out the prohibition on coming to Japan, offered fuel, water and food, and instructed them to leave without further delay and not to return. The text included a little glossary, besides their Japanese equivalents, of words in English and Dutch both for a rather wide range of foods and for the practical requirements of the anticipated negotiations.[56] When the crew of a British whaler landed on the coast of Mito han in 1824, the members were interviewed by Aizawa Seishisai, a rising *jusha* or scholar of Mito han. They were also interrogated by Takahashi, once more an illustration of the risky practice of combining officials of different background for a task. The fundamental question, not readily answered from individual episodes, was whether such incidents were one-off cases, or instances of spying missions. The presence of Takahashi in a number of these instances – two in Uraga in 1818 and 1822, and the one at Otsuhama in Mito in 1824 – revealed the serious unease in Edo. In 1824 Aizawa and Takahashi came to different conclusions.

Takahashi, back in Edo and with personal experience of at least three of the whaler incidents, drafted a proposal to deal with the problem. It was in effect the first version of the famous *uchi harai* (fire on and expel) decree of 1825. His proposal was that if whalers approached,

---

[54] Akizuki, *Nihon hokuhen no tanken*, p.303.
[55] The occurrence of violence is not well documented: however it was stated as fact in the 1825 order itself, and elsewhere an account refers to food being seized by the foreign mariners. By the nature of the situation, the linguistic problem of itself was likely to occasion difficulties not easy to resolve.
[56] For this remarkable compendium see Katagiri Kazuo, 'Bakumatsu ni okeru ikokusen ōtetsu to oranda-tsūji Baba Sajūrō' [Communication with foreign vessels in the Bakumatsu period and the Dutch-language interpreter Baba Sajūrō], *Kaiji-shi kenkyū*, no. 10 (April 1968), pp.22–36. Baba himself had visited Uraga in the fifth month of 1822 to interpret for an English whaler (*Tsukō ichiran*, vol. 6, p.384). It would have been one of the last months of his existence. The *Tsukō ichiran*, vol. 6, is the fullest source for documenting comparatively obscure visits to Japanese waters by the whalers.

they should be fired on with blank shot to warn them off; if they persisted in landing, and they needed supplies or had sick sailors, they were to be given supplies and a notice to warn them from approaching the shores again. In the subsequent discussion, the response was made more drastic: ships would be fired on with real shot, no distinction was made between whalers and other vessels, and no provision was envisaged for aid.[57] The final decree was thus a more far-reaching order. In referring specifically to the *Phaeton* incident in 1808, when an English warship forced its way into Nagasaki bay,[58] the decree showed that the underlying fear was that English whalers were prelude to a more formidable attack. Takahashi's original draft with its distinctions between different vessels was in any event unrealistic in operational terms. Nevertheless, in eliminating all provision for aid, the decree was itself, as events proved, unrealistic and later had to be modified. Modern commentators have expressed surprise that Takahashi, friend of the Dutch in Edo and formidable scholar in Dutch, was one of its drafters. Scholars like Takahashi took pleasure in intellectual contact with foreigners and in foreign books. They were not xenophobic, minimised the foreign threat (as events in 1813 and 1824 showed), but saw nothing inconsistent in still favouring a closed Japan: that did not preclude foreign books, curiosity about the outside world and free-ranging and open discussion with the handful of foreigners in the Dutch factory. If they were scholars so much the better.

The *uchi harai* decree did not deny a foreign threat: by extending an existing obligation to fire on Russian vessels to all foreign vessels, it increased the emphasis on it. If vessels approached, firing on them would warn them off. Even in its revised form, it was premised on the assumption that the Russian presence in the north was pacific, and that the crisis had wound down (the precedents of the *Phaeton* and English whalers were a more immediate concern). The low-key and cautious response in Edo had already led to the Matsumae family being restored to their han, and the mainland han in the north of Honshu were no longer required expensively to station forces on Ezo. Inevitably, such steps engendered controversy as to whether it was wise to assume that there was no longer a threat. The consequence was that the clash between Aizawa and Takahashi in 1824 and the underlying moderation of the *uchi harai* decree itself in 1825 led to a violent attack later in the year by Aizawa in the *Shinron* on the policy and on Takahashi (though without particularising

[57] Uehara, *Takahashi Kageyasu no kenkyū*, pp.289–302. The text is available in English in *PP Japan*, vol. 2, pp.375–6, Correspondence respecting affairs in Japan 1865–6.
[58] The *Phaeton* was not mentioned by name, but it is clear from the terms of the decree that that was the incident which the Edo drafters of the ruling had in mind.

him by name).[59] The thrust of Aizawa's argument was less foreign contacts per se (in passing, the book conceded merit in foreign knowledge) than the existence of continued dangers and the necessity of measures to combat them. Aizawa concluded, reasonably enough for an intellectual in a country which had isolated itself 200 years previously, that Christianity itself was the motivating force in the western drive for conquest. The concrete threat was in Ezo, and the response he argued was military preparedness and the moving of soldiers from the towns to the coasts, not just in Ezo but elsewhere. The *Shinron*, while written in an exalted language (its tone unavoidably exaggerated by translation), is a rational and intelligent essay. Subsequent history vindicated its concerns.[60]

Whatever the realities of the 1820s, Ezo had been overwhelmingly the central feature of foreign policy for the preceding thirty years. After 1822, the Edo authorities did envisage the possibility that intervention might be necessary anew.[61] Tokugawa Nariaki, daimyo of Mito, made the case for action in Ezo on many occasions to the *rōjū* and in particular to Mizuno during the 1830s and early 1840s.[62] The issue, behind the divides in 1824–5, surfaced anew in the Von Siebold affair in 1828 in which the central issue was the giving of information about Ezo to foreigners. In the course of the 1826 *hofreis*, maps had been given by Takahashi to Von Siebold the doctor on Deshima; others were later dispatched to him through the hands of interpreters. Von Siebold had therefore access to the most up-to-date information on the fruits of Japanese surveying in the northern region. Two years later, in late 1828 when about to leave Japan, apart from maps already sent to Europe, some were in Von Siebold's trunks aboard the vessel, while others were still in his possession ashore.[63] The assumption that maps were not to be shown to foreigners merits

---

59 On Takahashi's role in drafting the decree, see Uehara, *Takahashi Kageyasu no kenkyū*, pp.288–97. The story can be worked out only in outline, as few central documents survive.
60 There is a translation in English with a useful introduction by Bob Tadashi Wakabayashi in *Anti-foreignism*. On Aizawa's significance in Japanese thought, see also Mitani, *Meiji ishin to nashonarizumu*.
61 *Nihon tsū-shi*, vol.14 (*Kinsei*, no. 4) (Tokyo, 1995), p.250. Hirosaki was required from 1822 to maintain one hundred troops ready for dispatch in emergencies (Ravina, *Land and lordship*, p.152). See also *Hirosaki shi-shi* [History of Hirosaki city], 2 vols. (Tokyo, 1973), vol. 1, p.800.
62 The best source for Nariaki's Ezo concerns is in *Mito shi-shi*, middle series, vol.3, pp.76, 111–21.
63 Before surrendering maps in 1829, Von Siebold made copies of them, which he secreted among his effects when he was finally expelled from Japan. The treatment of Von Siebold and maps being taken into possession by formal request show that the Japanese officials recognised and respected a form of diplomatic immunity. His residence was searched, but the diplomatic niceties continued to be observed. He was not interrogated directly: questions were submitted in writing, and he replied in writing to them.

comment, because officials were in fact quite casual with them, as illustrated by the experience of Titsingh in the early 1780s, Laxman in 1792, Langsdorff in 1804, Broughton in Ezo in 1796 and again in 1797, and finally even Golownin amid the diplomatic uncertainties of 1811–13. Kaempfer, widely familiar with the Japanese maps of his day, had also recounted how, when the Dutch deputation on the 1691 *hofreis* were entertained by the Nagasaki bugyo, he showed them two maps of Ezo.[64] The problem on this occasion was less the fact itself than whether doing so created a security threat: that depended in the last analysis either on divides among officials about the scale of the danger or mere factionalism. In the 1820s, the precise geography of Karafuto, despite speculation abroad, was unknown except to the Japanese. Hence the maps had the security rating of, say, drawings during the Cold-War period of highly secret nuclear installations, or at least it could be so claimed at a moment of heightened debate about the external threat. A repeated concern in the episode was that in 1826, through Von Siebold, a map had come into the possession of the preceding *oranda kapitan*, de Sturler, and had already been sent by him to Europe to be engraved in the Netherlands.[65] The only categorical official statement ever made about maps occurred in 1829, and was simply to the effect that Japanese law prohibited maps of Japan being sent abroad.[66]

The assumption that Mamiya was responsible for the proceedings in 1828 against Takahashi, Von Siebold and those interpreters who acted as intermediaries is not itself well-documented.[67] Mamiya, who had not accompanied Mogami in 1826, did not make a secret report at the time. An indiscreet letter in early 1828 by Von Siebold to Mamiya implying an exchange of maps proved the origin of the crisis. Mogami had emphasised discretion: their first meeting is recorded in Latin in Von Siebold's diary. When the vessel which he had yet to board capsized in a typhoon in late 1828, the cargo was unloaded, and his trunks inspected. The matter was referred to Edo; Takahashi was jailed, as were some of the interpreters and some of Von Siebold's students. Today details of the case are few: brief reference in the *Hankachō* (or records of Nagasaki bugyo court), copies from various sources of decisions handed

---

[64] *Kaempfer*, p.414. Maps were also published commercially and were widely available. On Japanese maps and map making, see Marcia Yonemoto, 'The spacial "vernacular" in Tokugawa maps', *Journal of Asian studies*, vol. 59, no. 3 (Aug. 2000), pp.647–8.

[65] Shiiboruto kinenkan, Nagasaki, Nakayama collection, 14–3–5. Various letters, especially bugyo to Meylan, 25 Koeguats (sic) 1829, 2 and 7 zuguats (sic) 1829, 31 October 1829.

[66] Shiiboruto kinenkan, Nagasaki, Nakayama collection, 14–3–5, bugyo to Meylan, 7 zugatsu (sic) 1829.

[67] Akizuki, *Nihon hokuhen no tanken*, p.314.

down in the *Hyōjōshō* in Edo, and copies of some of the correspondence which survived in the family of one of the interpreters.[68] While the *Shinron* was concerned first and foremost with Ezo, it was aware also of the wider menace from western powers, especially from England. Despite having been sometimes seen as the bible for the restoration of the emperor, it was not hostile to the shogun. It was in essence an essay not on government (though the problems of a decentralised country necessarily heightened the rhetoric of the book by its appeal to a sense of unity of purpose, defined by Aizawa as *kokutai*), but on a foreign threat, and was a call for a general response.[69] It was not published at the time, but copies circulated widely, and it was to become for the next thirty years or more, even before its publication in 1857, the textbook of those who were concerned at the foreign threat. It was resurrected by militarist ideologues in the 1930s who wanted a historical context to justify their arguments.

As part of a wider security concern, unease also reached a new pitch in the 1810s and 1820s concerning Satsuma and its largely unregulated trade. The range of permitted imports from the Ryukyus had actually grown.[70] In 1817 the shogunate made clear to Nagasaki an absence of

---

[68] *Hankachō: Nagasaki bugyōshō hanketsu kiroku* [Nagasaki bugyo office: register of Nagasaki bugyo decisions in criminal matters], 11 vols. (Nagasaki kenritsu toshokan, 1959–61), vol. 8, pp.31, 44–5. A very full Japanese account of the events appeared in Kure Shūzō, *Shiiboruto sensei: sono shōgai oyobi kōgyō* [Siebold: his life and achievements] (Tokyo, 1926). This has been translated into German as *Shūzō Kure, Philipp Franz Von Siebold: leben und werk*, 2 vols. (Tokyo, 1996). See also Ōtani Tsunehiko, 'Shiiboruto jiken no haikei to Mamiya Rinzō: shiron "Rinzō wa mikoku shiteinai" ' [The background to the Von Siebold affair and Mamiya Rinzō: the debate about a private purpose: 'Rinzo was not making secret reports'], *Shiiboruto kinenkan Narutaki kiyō*, no. 5 (Shiiboruto kinenkan, Nagasaki 1995), pp.37–72. There is a huge literature in Japanese on the events, but most of it simply repeats what is already known, and points to the dearth of first-hand documents outside what appears in Kure Shūzō's volume. The suggestion that the documents in the Nakayama family, interpreters over five generations, originated as a result of indignation and a wish to keep a record for posterity, may not be well founded: many documents over several generations survive in the Nakamura collection (now in the Shiiboruto kinenkan, Nagasaki).

[69] Professor Mitani Hiroshi has seen Aizawa as marking the first stake in the emergence of a modern nationalism in Japan, in *Meiji ishin to nashonarizumu* .

[70] Yamawaki Teijinō, *Nukeni: sakoku jidai no mitsu bōeki* [Contraband: illegal traffic in the sakoku period] (Tokyo, 1965), pp.21, 97, 98, 99. The amount of products sent on from Satsuma and handled through the Kaishū – the bugyo office which surveyed the Nagasaki trade – remained quite modest. See Nakamura, *Kinsei Nagasaki bōeki-shi no kenkyū*, pp.501–8. This can be taken as either proving that smuggling was rife, or equally that the dynamic of the trade, while by no means insignificant for a single han like Satsuma, was limited. Nagasaki was the main market for 'Chinese' goods, frequented by merchants from all the main ports of Japan, and was a far more effective – and hassle-free – market for purchasers than a market in Satsuma itself. A trade did take place in later times in the early nineteenth century, but it was subordinate to business in Nagasaki,

stomach to interfere.[71] In any event, whatever the wild concerns of officials in Nagasaki, as Satsuma benefited from its own trade with the Ryukyus, neither the han administration nor Satsuma merchants had an interest in tolerating Chinese interlopers unloading freely along its coasts as opposed to conducting a confined trade. In the long term there was not a significant rise in the incidence of judicial cases in Nagasaki concerning smuggling offences. However, the security concerns were reflected in an abrupt rise in court cases to a total of fifty-three in 1825–9 (compared with an average of less than two a year from 1666 to 1718, and one still below three a year from 1718 to 1862).[72] This coincided broadly with the frenzy in 1828–9 which the Von Siebold *jiken*, technically a case involving outward contraband, engendered. Mamiya Rinzō's first visit to Nagasaki was in 1829, which has led to the belief that he was behind the Nagasaki *jiken*. However, his expertise, very real and appreciated, was used in various missions of consequence (one of the last being to help the shogunal official Egawa Hidetatsu in defence preparations in Edo bay in 1842). His missions to Nagasaki seem to have been concerned with illegal trade, much at issue from the mid-1820s and about which concern recurred in 1835.[73] In his stays in Edo he had also repeated contact with Nariaki, daimyo of Mito, and Fujita Tōko (1806–55), his chief *jusha*. Evidence on Mamiya is thin; reporting on secret trade was a pointless duty (as it was either a purely economic – and overrated – matter, or one which in the case of Satsuma the shogunate was powerless to do much about) and his sinister role has been exaggerated. Nor were these men wrong in their fears (and within their argument there was also an accurate sense of the danger that England was likely to present). The external danger from aggressive and ruthless westerners was made only too clear with the Opium War in China in 1840–2. The Japanese knew about its progress both from the Dutch *fūsetsugaki* and more regularly from the reports made by Chinese ships reaching Nagasaki. The risks were already foreshadowed in novel episodes in the 1830s. The vessel *Morrison*, using some shipwrecked mariners as an excuse, attempted to open trade in 1837 by calling at Uraga bay and then at Kagoshima, and was fired on.[74] At Uraga it brought the threat close to the heart of Japan.

was smaller in volume, and was conducted by the same vessels as visited Nagasaki (see chapter 2, p.48).

[71] Matsui Masato, 'Shimazu Shigehide 1745–1833: a case study of daimyo leadership' (Ph.D. thesis, University of Hawaii, 1975), pp.244–5. See also Yamawaki, *Nukeni*, p.104.

[72] Nakamura, *Kinsei taigai kōshō shi ron*, p.142.

[73] Yamawaki, *Nukeni*, pp.99–100, 134–7.

[74] W. G. Beasley, 'Japanese castaways and British interpreters', *Monumenta nipponica*, vol.46, no. 1 (Spring 1991), pp.92–4. The return of castaways to Japan of itself was not a problem in Tokugawa times. For an interesting and informative, though at times inaccurate, account, see Katherine Plummer, *The shogun's reluctant ambassadors: Japanese sea drifters in the north Pacific*, 3rd edn (Portland, Oreg., 1991).

The events of 1837 made defence measures around Edo itself a pressing necessity. A first step was surveying. However, it had to be quite different from the straightforward surveying, a generation earlier, of ill-defined frontiers in Ezo. As Edo bay was well mapped, the issue in surveying was identification of the best defence points, in other words locations for artillery emplacements. This task was now in the hands of individuals with no professional training, and no first-hand technical knowledge of gunnery requirements. There was already in Edo a small circle of individuals who met to discuss defence issues, ranging from a high official, the *daikan* Egawa Hidetatsu, through *jusha* (Confucian scholars) in or on the fringes of the Hayashi school, to Watanabe Kazan (1793–1841), an intellectually versatile and underworked official from the small Tawara han: he had no Dutch and relied for translations on the medical doctor Takano Chōei, who had trained under Von Siebold in Dutch medicine, and on Hatasaki Kanae, an interpreter who had fled Nagasaki in the Von Siebold *jiken* in 1828.[75] In 1839 Egawa and a quite senior official – the *metsuke* or inspector Torii Yōzō, second son of Hayashi Jussai, head of the Hayashi family adopted into the Torii family – were charged with the survey of Edo bay. Egawa drew heavily on the knowledge of his friends Watanabe Kazan and Takano Chōei. The object of the surveying was the selection of gun emplacements, a subject on which no one, officially appointed or self-appointed, knew much apart from a little book knowledge. Watanabe Kazan was an official with responsibility for the coastal defences of his own tiny han Tawara, a light task which left him with rather too much leisure and hence the opportunity to express controversial views in Edo. Together with Chōei, Kazan had some knowledge of the outside world; unfortunately he had acquired in 1838–9 a high profile because of criticism he had made in writings of the topical subjects of *uchi harai* and defence policy. Torii is made the villain of the episode known as the *Bansha no goku* (the jailing of 'foreign' experts). It was, however, a straightforward case of tactless outside interference by Watanabe and Chōei and, what was most serious of all, of some of the work being redone as a result of their criticism.

The reverberations of the dispute reached beyond the overweening individuals concerned to affect others. In other words, if there was a falling out about the gun emplacements, there could equally be a dispute over the type of guns to fill them. Takashima Shūan (1798–1866), seen

---

[75] Satō Shōsuke, *Takano Chōei* (Tokyo, 1997), pp.89–90; M. C. Morland, 'Watanabe Kazan 1793–1841: tradition and innovation in Japanese painting' (Ph.D. thesis, University of Michigan, 1989), pp.134, 185n. There is a useful summary of the case, although open to question in some of its generalisations, in Bonnie Abiko, 'Persecuted patriot: Watanabe Kazan and the Tokugawa Bakufu', *Monumenta nipponica*, vol. 44, no. 2 (Summer 1989), pp.199–219.

as a gunnery expert, advising several Kyushu han, had been made a Nagasaki *toshiyori* or senior administrator in 1840, and was sent the following year to Edo to give a demonstration of western gunnery.[76] Here again, official though he now was, was an example of an outside expert recruited into shogunal service. His main public function in Edo was to display western-style rifle drill. However, on the relative merits of western-style or Japanese artillery, sharp differences between Torii's faction and Takashima ensued. Whether Torii was vindictive or not, the root of the problem was less the personality of Torii or those with whom he fell out than the absence of formal administrative structures and of a corresponding well-defined chain of command for new tasks. A multitude of amateur opinions compounded a lack of structures. The shogunate itself was powerless. Takashima had been invited officially to Edo. Mizuno, who was badgered by Nariaki on the benefits of western guns, decreed that two of the guns should be ordered, and finally in 1843 restrictions on the use of western-style artillery were removed.[77] This decision, as a vindication of the defence approach already adopted by the western *tozama*, conceded a subtle – and constructive – shift in the relationship entertained by Edo with the great daimyo and Nariaki. In the factionalism surrounding these episodes, Chōei and Kazan were punished, and Takashima, though vindicated in 1843 by shogunal authority in his argument for western artillery, had already been escorted back from Nagasaki in early 1843 to be held in confinement. The issue was not, as it is often represented, a confrontation between western knowledge (or *rangaku*) and Confucian training.[78] The conflict was one on highly technical matters in which both sides were amateurs, and the conflict did not halt the remorseless process of facing up to outside realities on which Japan was now launched. The major result was that a tightening up of administration accelerated in the wake of the disputes.

The underlying administrative dilemma was that the *rōjū*, the effective cabinet, had no civil service. Hence the prominence in less secular times of monks, and also of the Hayashi family (at the outset favoured precisely because they were not monks) later becoming in the 1790s a link in the chain of command between *rōjū* and others. However, they were not

[76] Satō, *Takano Chōei*, p.111; Fujita Satoru, *Tenpō no kaikaku* [The Tempō reform] (Tokyo, 1989), pp.198–9; Fujita, *Bakuhansei kokka no seiji shi-teki kenkyū: tenpō-ki no chitsujo, gunji, gaikō* [Studies in the politics of the *Bakuhansei* state . . .] (Tokyo, 1984), pp.266–72.

[77] Fujita, *Bakuhansei kokka no seiji shi-teki kenkyū*, pp.266–7, 271–2. *Bakuhan taisei* or *Bakuhansei* is a modern coinage, to denote a system based on the compromise political structure of Tokugawa Japan. Useful as a form of telegraphese, it has its own limitations.

[78] Fujita puts the responsibility on Torii, not on Hayashi Jussai or the family at large. Fujita, *Tenpō no kaikaku*, pp.108–11.

civil servants, and the *rōjū*, supported by a handful of permanent officials, *kanjō bugyō, metsuke* and *daikan,* had below them no standing professional administration to deploy. As occasion demanded, the response was an ad hoc one. In Europe, from as far back as the sixteenth century, for the definition of policy and for the conduct of business, each minister had a small but permanent, disciplined and well-trained corps of clerks or 'servants' (the civil servants or *fonctionnaires* of modern jargon). That in turn was reflected in the good order of papers, arranged in separate sections, often even further subdivided and in continuous or chronological form, for each area of activity. Administrative matters were handled in a diffuse way, and surviving correspondence reflects the situation. Responsibilities were devolved in crisis on individual senior figures and on the ad hoc redeployment of lesser officials. Some of the formal papers had to be drafted by outsiders, such as the Hayashi or famously in the *uchi harai* decree by Takahashi; papers were often held privately; all too often what survived was a copy written into a compilation (the originals were recycled), or a mere brief reference or summary in the *nikki* or office diaries of officials.

The training of officials was scholarly (classical rather than numerate or empirical), and *rangaku* can be seen in some respects less as foreign knowledge than, one or two centuries behind Europe, the beginning of empirical studies. Given the loose administration, the quantity of surviving scattered information is arguably impressive, though remarkably little of it is statistical. The only effective core of ongoing administrative process under the immediate supervision of senior officers was the offices of the bugyo in Osaka and Nagasaki. Little trace of their role survives centrally in Edo, though there are traces of it in Osaka, and especially in Nagasaki where some 2,500 archival items survive or have been gathered together in the prefectural archives (plus a not insignificant number of documents in other locations in Nagasaki) to give an idea of its not unimpressive administrative functioning.[79] Nagasaki was the largest government office in Japan – and before 1811 arguably the only one – dealing with matters others than accounting and justice. Its bugyo officers were promising hatamoto, with bright careers ahead of them when they had served their term.

In Edo itself, through the press of business and the growing complications of affairs, the need to streamline administration in some form was evident in the 1790s. Matsudaira's famous decree on orthodox teaching in

---

[79] See *Nagasaki bugyōsho kankei monjo chōsa hōkoku sho, Nagasaki ken bunkazai hōkoku, dai 131 shū* [Reports of investigations into the Nagasaki bugyo office, Nagasaki-ken, cultural reports, collection no. 131] (Nagasaki-ken kyoiku iinkai, 1998), pp.41–183.

1790 was first and foremost an effort to contain what might be described either as factionalism or free-ranging intellectual discourse within the Hayashi academy, and by giving the school a tighter agenda, to harness its teaching to the practical requirement of turning out officials trained to some sort of set syllabus rather than scholars luxuriating pedantically in the divisive minutiae of intellectual argument. Exclusion later in the decade of students from outside the shogunal domain provided formal recognition of its role in training shogunal officials. The Hayashi academy now became a twofold operation, a private one indulging in academic thought, and an institute, formally made the *Shōheizakagakumon* or shogunal school in 1797,[80] training in effect future civil servants (it was later the progenitor of the University of Tokyo). On the practical front, the measure was the first stage in a modest though real reform of shogunal administration. It was soon followed by other steps. The question as to whether Takahashi, head of the *Banshowakegoyō* (Office for translating foreign books), has to be seen just as a technician or as a politician has no answer.[81] He was, given the lack of central administrative groups under the *rōjū*, both: he superintended technical services and, in making the first draft of the *uchi harai* decree, was drawn into a major policy matter. In his dual role, however, he lacked powers to direct policy, and ultimately, like all Japanese officials, even the highest, lacked effective protection from opponents, as the Von Siebold incident with Takahashi's arrest and subsequent death in prison showed dramatically.

In the absence of an overall administrative framework, some effort seems to have been made to give a co-ordinating role to the Hayashi family.[82] From 1804, this role can be dimly traced. Some of the operational instructions for mapping in the sensitive north were conveyed to Takahashi through them,[83] and surveying both in Edo bay and in the Ezo region was itself part of a wider mapping of all Japan which went on for decades, and in which the Hayashi had an ongoing role.[84] They had some part in the framing of policy for negotiations with the Russians. Scattered working papers of Edo officials during the Russian crisis and even some

---

[80] Kizaki Hiromi, 'Shozōshō yori mitaru shōheizaka gakumonjo no tokushitsu – ikokusen uchi hari rei to taigai jōhō' [Features in the Shoheizaka gakumonjo collection of books: the foreign ship uchi harai order and external information], *Tochigi-shigaku*, no. 8 (March 1994), pp.9.

[81] Sugimoto, *Edo jidai ran-gogaku*, vol. 4, p.556.

[82] See Fujita, 'Jūkyū seiki zenhan no nihon', pp.7–8, for some perceptive comments on this little-studied subject of the changing Hayashi role.

[83] Akizuki, *Nihon hokuhen no tanken*, p.277.

[84] Shirai Tetsuya, 'Chiri-tadashi to Kansei kaikaku: kanjōshō no katsudō o chūshin ni' [Geographical investigation and the Kansei reform: its central place in the activity of the *kanjōshō*], in Fujita, *Bakuhansei kaikaku no tenkai*, pp.87, 108–9.

working documents of interpreters as well as of others in the field survive in the Hayashi archives.[85] Whatever the attitudes of some Confucian scholars and officials (including, under the adoptive name Torii, Hayashi Jussai's second son), the main members of the family had wide interests. They were, notably its long-lived head of the early decades of the nineteenth century, Hayashi Jussai (1768–1841), and Satō Issai (1772–1859), himself adopted into the family, well disposed to *rangaku*.[86] The Hayashi of course neither made decisions nor executed them; their role was, in modern language, one of scholarly backup.

The *rōjū*, in executing foreign policy, were served by services spread between bugyo en poste in Nagasaki, a colleague or colleagues on *sankin kōtai* in Edo, the Hayashi office and the Astronomer's office (with, under its wing, the *Banshowagegoyō*). The Hayashi were involved at least from 1806 in Ezo matters; and their continued interest is confirmed in their possession of the 1825 translation of the Golownin narrative. In the growing crisis in the late 1840s they were requested to compile the diplomatic precedents of foreign policy. The *Tsūkō ichiran* begun in 1849 was the outcome. The first section running up to 1825 had been edited by the time Perry arrived. Of itself, it was an impressive achievement: in its later printed form it runs to 4,600 pages, and had been the work of a team of up to twelve men. However, with the knowledge in 1853 that Perry's arrival was imminent, work was already under way, before the editing of the first part was finished, on putting together a post-1825 compendium, a task itself completed by 1856. Hayashi Akira, who succeeded in 1853 to the role of *Hayashi daigaku no kami* (head of the Hayashi academy), was more conversant with the detail of foreign policy than any single man in Japan, and he was the obvious figure to front the negotiations in 1854 with the Americans. He created a good impression on them, added to as he remained sober when others let themselves go in partying.[87]

Defence policy had fared worse than foreign policy and surveying: responsibility for it was shared between the han and the shogunate. The shogunate lacked funding to mount defence on a serious scale; and it found itself in the contradictory position of both calling on the han to defend Japan, and being reluctant to give them a free rein in the matter of ships above 500 koku and artillery. On these issues Nariaki was from the outset a persistent critic. Matsudaira's plans for officials, or *kakari*, in 1793 to exercise defence responsibilities for Edo bay (in contrast to

---

[85] Two of the documents relate to the linguistic problems of translation from Russian. Naikaku bunko, *bunka* 7, 185/283: *bunka* 10, 185/281.

[86] Satō, *Takano Chōei*, pp.95–6; Fujita, *Tenpō no kaikaku*, pp.108–11.

[87] *Dai nihon ishin shiryō* [Japan, sources for the Restoration], 2nd series, 5 vols., vol. 5 (Tokyo, 1942, reprint 1985), p.336 (from American dispatch of 27 March 1854).

the surveying work in the bay) seems never to have been put into effect, a good example of what happened when an administrative backup was not created.[88] There is no evidence that the bugyo and *kanjō bugyō* posts proposed were actually allocated. In the case of Ezo at least the steps were more concrete: an active directive role from 1799 was exercised by Kondō Jūzō, a capable official from Nagasaki on whom the day-to-day co-ordinating on the spot and on the wider canvas fell. On the other hand, for the hugely ambitious project of mapping and surveying all of Japan (a project somewhat ahead in time of similar work in much of Europe), responsibilities appear to have been stretched out between on the one hand three *kanjō bugyō*,[89] and on the other the Hayashi and Takahashi as executants. Planning in concrete terms for the defence of Edo bay languished until the *Morrison* episode in 1837 gave urgency to renewed surveying for the purpose of selecting gun emplacements. Destructive though the events in 1839–42 were (of men more than of policy itself), they provided a warning of the consequences of confusion. Defence needs began to be seriously co-ordinated from 1845 under the tutelage of *kakari* answerable directly to the prime minister Abe.

Foreign affairs (and defence policy), a recurrent preoccupation of the shogunate and han from the early decades of the century, were not complicated by domestic factors until the 1830s. The story of that decade has two aspects: one, harvest failure and its grim message for public order, and two, the worsening of the fiscal problems at the very time when foreign crisis added to demands on resources. The crisis is usually referred to as the Tempō crisis, and the measures to deal with fiscal and other reforms as the Tempō reform. The harvest failures of 1833 and 1836 were alarming. These were among the rare occasions in which the spectre of hunger gripped the prosperous Kansai. As in the 1780s, unrest spilled over from the countryside into *uchi kowashi* in the towns. A large part of Osaka was destroyed. Unrest in Osaka, like that in Edo in 1787, alarmed the government; the samurai Ōshio Heihachirō sought to channel unrest in the city and surroundings into a rising, and a large section of the city of Osaka was destroyed as fire spread among the wooden buildings.[90] The

---

[88] Little is known about the surveying work in Edo bay in the early 1790s. Matsudaira accompanied some of the coastal inspectors, and twelve realistic paintings of the coast showing every bluff and scar by the artist Tani Bunchō, who accompanied the team, survive. An image in one of the original paintings of the survey team at work in measuring was not retained in the many reproductions of it made later (Screech, *Shogun's painted culture*, pp.34–6).

[89] Shirai, 'Chiri-tadashi to Kansei kaikaku', p.108.

[90] On Ōshio Heihachirō, see in English Tetsuo Najita's account, 'Ōshio Heihachirō (1793–1837)', in A. Craig and D. H. Shively (eds.), *Personality in Japanese history* (Berkeley, 1970), pp. 155–79.

question remains whether Heihachirō's presence at the head of the urban rioters represented symbolically any deeper alienation, or whether, moved by the philosophic stress on the obligation of government to provide care for the people, he untypically put himself at their head. However, famine, devastating riot, the *Morrison* affair (a foreign ship off the coast at Uraga in 1837) and serious fires (not due to unrest) devastating much of Edo castle in 1839 and 1843 as a grim parallel to the devastating fire in Kyoto in 1788, all seemed to create an ominous state of affairs.

The Tempō crisis was palpable in many directions. At its heart, however, was the fiscal problem. Mizuno Tadakuni, already prominent and the dominant figure by the late 1830s in the councils of the shogunate, launched in 1841 the Tempō reform addressing the fiscal problem, which made his administration, though short-lived, as controversial as Tanuma's much longer one sixty years before. A reform movement had developed in many of the han even sooner than in the shogunate. In the han the reform included efforts to develop or find han monopolies, notably in Satsuma, in which at the expense of the peasants (who suffered by compulsory levies or by fixed prices) commodities were put on the market to the profit of the han administration. The shogunate was incapable – constitutionally even more than fiscally – of organising defence nationally; it was also incapable of contributing on a large scale to defence expenditure by the han. The main burden fell on the han themselves. As one of the vigorous or reform-minded han, Mito in the 1830s set out to redeploy samurai from the castle town to the coasts to ensure adequate coastal defences. Nariaki also agitated for Mito to be given the responsibility of defending Ezo.[91] Equally to the fore were the han in the west. In Choshu, also, a modern-style budget was drawn up for the year 1840. Han schools became larger and embraced practical studies as well as classical learning: inevitably in the climate of the times defence studies were important, and western medicine was also introduced.

The levy on rice, source of the income of shogun and daimyo alike, is usually referred to as taxation. In fact, this poses problems, and it is better to regard the levy as a rent rather than as a tax.[92] If regarded as a tax, the levy paid by the peasants working the lands directly held by the shogun or by a daimyo and going into their coffers is on a par with the

---

[91] This is not as highhanded as it sounds. During the direct administration of Ezo from 1799 to 1822, some of the han in the north of the Tohoku had been directed to provide troops for its defence. In this case, a han, admittedly to the south, was in somewhat unprecedented manner actually volunteering its services.

[92] This is not recognised in the Japanese literature, though one source, while regarding it as a tax, recognised that before Meiji times it had elements of rent as well as tax. Hayami and Miyamoto, *Nihon keizai-shi*, vol. 1, p.39.

levy paid in han and shogunal territories alike by the occupying peasants and going either directly into the pocket of the samurai or more indirectly via the rice store of the authorities. Both types of payment might be equated, it could be argued, in the sense that both the ruler and the samurai performed public duties, and that the rent levy was the payment for them. On the other hand, it was paid exclusively by *honbyakushō* (i.e. those whose rights were recorded in the original valuations, and payment was in a sense a recognition of status). It has to be clearly distinguished from contractual rents paid by a subtenant to a *honbyakushō*, a relationship long known though one which spread rapidly in later times in the more developed areas. It is more akin to a *cens* or feudal rent paid by freeholders or copyholders for land in Europe. In Europe such payments became rigid and unchanging, and in time, with inflation, even came to disappear. In Japan they did not (they were payments emerging out of the crucible of the Sengoku period, whereas in Europe, they were already 400 to 500 years old). However, paid as a proportion of valuations and not on actual output, they were remarkably stable, and given lags in reassessments, and either a lighter levy or no levy on non-rice land, the effective levy was in favoured instances said by observers in the 1850s to be as low as twenty per cent of real output. Thus in essence the rice levy was a fixed payment for the occupation of land, and by far the greater part of this rent – going to samurai and hatamoto, and not to daimyo or shogun – was unrelated to the expenses of government. Even when the levy was collected under the supervision of officials and carried to official storehouses, it conferred no benefit on daimyo or shogun: superficially inflow to a storehouse might suggest a parallel with taxation, but the inflow was matched by a corresponding outflow of rice or cash to the samurai.[93]

It was precisely the fact that the levy was not a tax that made it possible to introduce from the late seventeenth century the concept of a deduction to the benefit of the daimyo or shogun from samurai incomes: this was

---

[93] The calculation of actual production – showing the real weight of rice levies – as opposed to fiscal valuations is fraught with difficulties, as records do not lend themselves to calculation, and case studies which successfully address the problems are necessarily few (see Satō Tsuneo and Ōishi Shinzaburō, *Hin no shikan o minaosu* [A revisionist view of historical views of rural poverty] (Tokyo, 1995), pp.104–19). In the new and realistic land valuation of 1874, the rice levy of late Tokugawa times for four villages in a case study in the Nagano region would have ranged from seventeen to twenty-eight per cent of output. In villages with widespread proto-industrialisation, as in the Kinki, the proportion would have been even lower (Satō and Ōishi, op. cit., pp.117–18). For a study in English which gives some idea of the sources and the complexity of using them, see W. J. Chambliss, *Chiraijima village, land tenure, taxation and local trade 1818–1884* (Tucson, 1965). Chambliss suggests an effective tax rate of 26.9 to 29.39 per cent for the village he studied in late Tokugawa times. He also stresses circumstances in which in villages the effective rate could be lower (pp.6, 127).

made administratively much easier by the extent to which daimyo and shogunate not only supervised collection of the rice levy, but actually conducted it. Such deductions, which did go into the coffers of shogun or daimyo, were imposed on samurai whose incomes in rice koku were above a certain low level. At this point taxation in its strict sense was beginning to emerge: it affected all relevant incomes and the proceeds benefited the central treasury without a matching outgoing. As early as 1744 Dazai Shundai (1680–1747), who at that time regarded the deductions as universal, claimed that they often took up to fifty or sixty per cent of stipends. According to the historian Thomas Smith, the Matsuyama han made deductions every year but one from 1709 to 1869: in eighty-seven per cent of the years the rate was thirty per cent or more. These deductions have often been seen as arbitrary or repressive, but they had a clear fiscal logic. The great problem was of course that as samurai incomes were fixed, once the deductions became regular, there was no scope for expanding this source of revenue further. In other words, once the beneficial effect of introducing the deduction wore off, the shogunate – or the han – then faced once more the problem of static income. The only recourse was then to convert de facto the levy first seen as a loan into an outright payment.

If this interpretation is correct, Japanese peasants were not taxed: the *honbyakushō* occupiers were originally feudal camp followers from whom rice had been levied by their warrior superiors, and whose lot was actually improved where daimyo or shogunal control increased (a situation confirmed by the grim plight of peasants in Satsuma, who were at the mercy of the han's rural-resident samurai). Moreover, the absence of excise taxes, universal and highly developed in Europe, meant that indirect taxation, highly regressive and falling on necessities consumed by lower income social categories, was remarkably undeveloped in Japan. Townsmen in the shogunal trading towns – and manufacturers in the countryside – were not taxed. The absence of any taxation structure systematically and regularly taxing townsmen, and the lack of taxation on goods in transit within or across han boundaries, is the most striking single feature of the Japanese situation: the word 'situation' is chosen advisedly here, because it is not possible to speak of the Japanese 'taxation system': there was not one. Increasingly and successfully, *ikki* were intended to halt fiscal innovation.

Given the absence of precise concepts of taxes in the writing of Tokugawa times, the public debate on policy which in Europe revolved around taxation, either the creation of new taxes or increases in the rate of existing taxation, in Japan revolved around questions of expenditure and income as the primary terms of analysis. In choosing to look at the expenditure side of the equation, the emphasis was on economy and frugality, in other words on 'reform' programmes, as a way out of public problems. As far as the income side of the equation was concerned, trade or larger output would in some ill-defined way increase public income. Taxation itself was never defined.

The absence of a coherent taxing system in Japan is obscured by treating the rice levy as a *rice tax*. If we do treat it as a tax, one of the consequences is that the significance of the 'borrowings' (the political fiction behind the introduction of the deductions) from the samurai as a tax is blurred; they become a tax paid by samurai on a tax paid by occupying peasants, which is by definition either confusing or absurd. Supplementary taxes in the form of *komononari* did exist, consisting of dues on forests, moors, rivers and ponds; taxes on handicrafts and other non-farming occupations; a great number of miscellaneous taxes with little uniformity from place to place. However, they were negligible in all instances, and showed a tendency to stability. Again, as in the case of the rice levy, the *komononari* where they existed were a shogunal source of income only in the shogunate's own dominions.

The reform programmes of periods of fiscal crisis, the Kyōhō programme from 1716, the Kansei one of 1787–93, and the Tempō reform of 1841–3, have been criticised for their lack of originality: the same diagnoses were made, and the same measures were implemented. This oversimplifies the story, as politicians were coping with what was politically possible. Ironically, an inelastic taxing capacity conferred one benefit by placing a real ceiling on public borrowing. In other words, as the ceiling was rigid, the reforms were directed to cutting back expenditure more than designating new taxes to finance fresh borrowings. The consequence was that though finances became disordered, order was always subsequently restored, and the shogunate (and many of the han which tended to have programmes of their own to solve their financial problems) entered the subsequent boom period with finances in comparatively good order. The price paid was of course limited public expenditure, and hence limited infrastructure (though that had its own benefits as the main public infrastructural feature of Europe was its vast and well-equipped armies and fortifications). In contrast to the *ancien régime* of Europe, there was no progressive growth of indebtedness which, for instance in France, made a revolution inevitable in 1789. The ability, however conservative the outlook and static the framework, to institute reform, if defined in this very narrow sense, was impressive, and is an added reason for not lightly using the term feudal in its application to Japanese circumstances. In the han, paper money had emerged before 1700 – *hansatsu* – and its use subsequently widened. However, the quantity in circulation was limited until the exceptional circumstances of the 1860s.[94] It underlines the fact that in the last analysis, despite the unremitting struggle with a narrow revenue basis, Tokugawa finances were well, if conservatively, handled. The shogunate itself never issued paper money, and intermittent shogunal survey of its issue by han reveals some unease about *hansatsu*.

The introduction of samurai contributions had helped to ward off immediate crisis among the han in Genroku times. The political or fiscal weakness of the shogunate explains the attraction of debasements as a response to the fiscal dilemma in Genroku times or again from 1818. However, the profits of debasement were a windfall income, and its benefits shor-lived. On the other hand, levies – *goyōkin* – by the shogunate in the form of demands by the bugyo on a selected number of large merchant houses in Osaka did not have these drawbacks. Introduced in 1761 when the income of the shogunate contracted once more, in time they became more common and more onerous. Good times – adequate harvests but also stable rice prices – deferred systematic resort to them, until the 1780s ushered in a long period of straitened public income. The writings of Kusama Naokata and Yamagata Bantō, though written in a shogunal city, were in effect a political plea against levies by arguing that heavy taxation of merchants reduced their buying of rice when prices were low, and thus the shogunate lost as well as gained by heavy levies.[95] Levies reached a peak with the difficult times of the late 1830s and 1840s. The single house of Sumitomo was subjected to thirteen exactions between 1837 and 1841, and ten between 1841 and 1853.[96] Merchants resented these levies, and Yamagata Bantō in particular made a very effective analysis of the damage they could do. But though he criticised them, the principle of levies was itself accepted.

Good harvests from the 1790s to the 1820s, though the basis of prosperity in the economy, brought the government itself to its knees. With rice prices falling to a nadir point in 1819 and 1820 and fiscal desperation in evidence once more, debasement was resorted to in 1818 and repeated in 1830. From 1838, it was attempted on an unprecedented scale: between the years 1838 and 1843, the shogunate's profits averaged 840,000–850,000 *ryō*.[97] The *goyōkin* brought in a further 1 million *ryō*.[98] It was these measures – debasements unprecedented since Genroku times, and levies on a scale harking back to the grasping demands of Tanuma – not any innovation, which brought about a transformation in finances. Already in 1841 some forty-eight per cent of income came from

---

[94] Nishikawa and Saitō, 'The economic history of the restoration period', pp.183–4.
[95] Tetsuo Najita, *Visions of virtue*, pp.225–51.
[96] Tetsuo Najita, *Visions of virtue*, p.293.
[97] Fujita, *Tenpō no kaikaku*, pp.153–4.   [98] Fujita, *Tenpō no kaikaku*, p.198.

sources other than rice income, in 1844 some fifty-three per cent.[99] The shogunate was thus able to face up to emergency demands such as famine relief and the rebuilding of Chiyoda castle (badly damaged by fire). In 1844 despite large expenditures the shogunate had a surplus of 435,000 ryō.[100] Repeated many times over in the Tempō years, debasement was, as in the notorious Genroku debasements a century and a half previously or later in the crisis-laden years of the 1860s, a mere short-term expedient of desperation. The raiding by means of goyōkin of Osaka's wealth by the shogunate had fewer short-term adverse consequences, though a high long-term cost of growing resentment which burst into the open in the 1860s, crucially deepening in mid-decade the emerging rift between Satsuma and Edo.

The other measures in the reform policy itself were conventional. Among the various steps common to reform programmes were efforts to control prices and expand output. One unusual intervention in the Tempō reform, however, was the abolition of the ten guilds in Edo and twenty-four in Osaka in the belief that they had raised prices. In encouraging greater production, efforts were renewed to drain the great Inbanuma swamp to the north of Edo, and to cut a drainage canal to the sea. The decreeing of the pilgrimage to Nikko in 1843, with its expensive participation of 140,000 persons, reflected the crisis. Faced with foreign threat, internal dissensions on policy, and fears that large-scale riots like the Ōshio Heihachirō one might recur at a moment of foreign menace, it was an effort to mobilise opinion. It was the first such pilgrimage in sixty-seven years, and was, even at the time, curiously anachronistic.

Although a political failure, the Mizuno years were not wholly negative. The uchi harai decree was made more flexible in 1842: aid was to to be given to foreign seamen in distress. Even if the rise in direct shogunal outlay was modest, defence administration of the sensitive Edo bay area was also simplified somewhat: the inner bay was made a shogunal responsibility; the outer bay the responsibility of two han. The office of Shimoda bugyo was revived, and one created at Haneda. Guns were ordered; Takashima had enjoyed Mizuno's support in the dispute with high officials, and an order was placed with the Dutch for a steam ship: it was envisaged that it would be manned by Dutchmen. The disputes in Edo had made the importance of gunnery more central. Even if Takashima's work had been the first book on the subject since a western book had been translated in 1808, nevertheless thirteen translations appeared in 1840–3, twenty-one in 1844–7. Cannon especially required iron of high

---

[99] Conrad Totman, *Politics in the Tokugawa bakufu 1600–1843* (Berkeley, 1988), pp.87–8.
[100] Totman, *Politics in the Tokugawa bakufu*, p.83.

quality in some abundance. The first modern blast furnaces were built in Saga in 1850 and Satsuma in 1854. The driving force in this was Ōshima Takatō. Born in Fukuoka, he had gone to Nagasaki in 1846 to study Dutch medicine. Becoming interested in metallurgy and artillery, with the help of a friend he translated a Dutch work on the subject. Invited to Mito, his supervision set the first reverbatory furnace to work in 1856. In all, ten furnaces were built, producing 70,000 to 80,000 *kan*, or roughly 3,000 tons, of iron.[101] There was a rise in the number of officials with a knowledge of gunnery (in shogunal employment some ten, and in han employment another thirty); and there was no interference with those who went to Nagasaki to learn more on the subject.[102] By 1853, cannon – some 100 guns in all – were located in batteries at several strategic locations around Edo bay.[103] Putting in perspective the pointlessness of the factional disputes among the Japanese 'experts' a decade earlier, the cannon did not much impress the Americans who noted in 1854 the promontories covered with batteries, 'which are more formidable in aspect than in reality, for their guns are but of small calibre, and the defences slight in construction'.[104]

While the Tempō reform has been seen as a response to internal economic crisis, it has also been argued that it was promoted more by insecurity on the external front than by internal problems.[105] Even the expensive attempt to drain the Inbanuma marshes to the north of Edo and to draw the waters off by a canal to the sea (a project which had weighed heavily in the crisis last years of Tanuma's government also) was driven not by the need to expand food supply but by the urge to guarantee a food supply to Edo that could not be cut off by hostile shipping.[106] Mizuno fell from office in 1843 in the course of a power struggle (he even regained office fleetingly later in the year) that ended only when Abe Masahiro became the undisputed head of the *rōjū* in 1845. In those years, when the factions sought to assert themselves, Takashima, something of a protégé of Mizuno, was jailed, and more predictably the dispute with Nariaki worsened. He was removed from daimyo office in favour of his heir; as the heir was a young minor, a shogun-selected regent was appointed, and Nariaki's loyal supporters in the han administration were put under house

---

[101] Nishikawa Shunsaku and Abe Takeshi (eds.), *Nihon keizai-shi* [Economic history of Japan], vol. 4, *Sangyōka no jidai* [Industrialisation era], pt. 1 (Tokyo, 1990), pp.26–8.

[102] Sato, *Takano Chōei*, p.114.

[103] Matsumoto Kenichi, *Nihon no kindai* [Modern Japan], vol. 1, *Kaikoku ishin 1853–1871* [Opening of country and Restoration 1853–1871] (Tokyo, 1998), p.8.

[104] *Dai nihonishin shiryō*, 2nd series, vol. 3, p.908 (reprinted from the American official reports, published in 1856).

[105] This is the central argument of Fujita's *Bakuhansei kokka no seiji shi-teki kenkyū*.

[106] Fujita, *Tenpō no kaikaku*, pp.211–12.

arrest. With the ascent of Abe in 1845, a period of thirteen years began in which despite, and in part because of, external threat, there was an emphasis on consultation.

The appearance of *Morrison* in 1837 off both Uraga and Kagoshima harked back disturbingly to the British warship *Phaeton* in Nagasaki in 1808. More seriously the episode was precursor to an almost regular appearance off the Japanese coast of foreign vessels, mainly warships, some of them surveying or charting the coasts from the mid-1840s.[107] However, if external menace grew more serious, internal conditions improved, a fact which reduced some of the fears uppermost in the late 1830s and early 1840s. The economic conditions of ordinary people were probably much better than they had been a century and a half previously. Sorai, perhaps as an out-and-out urbanite not the best judge, in 1710, travelling to Kofu, had been shocked by the poor condition of the country people.[108] Foreigners who made the acquaintance of Japan from the end of the 1850s noted with surprise, expecting to find the squalor and poverty of the rest of Asia, the satisfactory living conditions. Thus the American consul, Townsend Harris, settling into Shimoda from 1856, among other favourable comments, observed that 'in no other part of the world are the labouring classes better off than in Shimoda', and later noted that 'I have never seen a case of squalid misery since I have been in Japan.'[109] Rutherford Alcock also made similar comments: 'The impression is irresistibly borne in mind that Europe can not show a happier or better-fed peasantry.'[110] Years later, Isabella Bird, travelling in the relatively poor Tohoku in 1878, recalled the comfortable conditions of rural areas in southern Japan.[111] Arguably, however inferior they were, the conditions she found in the Tohoku were less primitive than those of the Scottish highlands or western Ireland.

Fences were gradually mended between Nariaki and the shogunate, and an intense correspondence took place between Nariaki and Abe.[112]

---

[107] For English and French vessels in the Ryukyus, see Fujita, *Bakuhansei kokka no seiji shi-teki kenkyū*, pp.195, 310, 360. On the subject, see also Mitani, *Meiji ishin to nashonar-izumu*, pp.92–3. For an excellent survey of the defence issues, see Tanji Kenzō, 'Ka'ei-ki ni okeru Edo-wan bōbi mondai to ikokusen taisaku: Uraga bugyō mochiba o chūshin to shite' [Defence problems and policy against foreign ships in Edo bay in the Kaei period . . .], *Kaiji-shi kenkyū*, no. 20 (April 1973), pp.98–112.

[108] Lidin, *Ogyū Sorai's journey to Kai in 1706*, p.76.

[109] *The complete journal of Townsend Harris*, pp.258, 441. There is an even more remarkable tribute on pp.428–9.

[110] Sir Rutherford Alcock, *The capital of the tycoon: a narrative of three years residence in Japan*, 2 vols. (London, 1863), vol. 1, p.432.

[111] Isabella Bird, *Unbeaten tracks in Japan* (London 1880; reprint, Tokyo, 1984).

[112] Conrad Totman, 'Political reconciliation in the Tokugawa Bakufu: Abe Masahiro and Tokugawa Nariaki', in Craig and Shively, *Personality in Japanese history*, pp.180–208.

A national policy and the consensus to give effect to it began to develop from 1845. In that year the office of *kaibō gakari* (coastal defence officer) was established, designating officials with a responsibility to co-ordinate defence measures. The term itself had often appeared in shogunal or even han use, as *kaibō gakari* simply means to be in charge of a designated task; now, the purpose of a well-defined office was to avoid the type of fracas that had notoriously occurred in the work on protective measures around Edo bay from 1839 to 1842. The erection of gun emplacements on the approaches to Edo bay got a fresh impetus, proceeding in a routine way rather than amid high contention. The post of Uraga bugyo, at the southern approach to Edo bay, acquired a new importance: the correspondence between the bugyo and the *rōjū* is a measure of how vital his role had become.

In 1848, despite debate about restoring *uchi harai* in its 1825 form, policy remained unchanged.[113] For the time being, given the inactivity of the Russians, the Ezo problem had retreated to the background. The major threat was western – non-Russian – warships appearing off Uraga. The second problem lay in the Ryukyus, well to the south and hence close to the path of foreign vessels. The rapport between Satsuma and Edo did not end with the death of Shimazu Shigehide, its titular daimyo, in 1833, and of Ienari in 1841. With the increase in British and French activity, the Ryukyus were vulnerable in the 1840s, and their complex suzerainty shared between four poles – China, its own monarch, the daimyo of Satsuma and, through its Satsuma ties, a vague vassalage to the shogun – meant that responses to foreigners were more nuanced than elsewhere in Japan or in its islands. To put it more plainly, the writ of *uchi harai* did not run in the Ryukyus. As is clear from the correspondence between Abe and Satsuma's Shimazu Narioki, foreigners who came to the Ryukyus had to be handled carefully: if they were not military men (and even then policy had to be a guarded one), they could neither be ejected, which could become a *casus belli*, nor, on the other hand, ignored.[114] It was, however, only too clear that so many isolated appearances off the coasts of Japan and the toleration of a few foreigners in the Ryukyus would soon lead to something greater on the diplomatic or security front. Debate in 1848 over *uchi harai* showed that realism prevailed. Moreover, anticipating the challenges ahead which might impel a change of policy, a

---

[113] Fujita, *Tenpō no kaikaku*, pp.208–10. See also Fujita, *Bakuhansei kokka no seiji shi-teki kenkyū*, pp.353–5; Mitani, 'Tenpō-ka'ei no taigai mondai', pp.1144–5.

[114] Naruiwa Sōzō, *Bakumatsu nihon to furansu gaikō: reon rosshu no sentaku* [Relations between France and Japan: the conduct of Léon Roches] (Tokyo, 1997), p.15. For a useful short summary in English, see M. Medzini, *French policy in Japan during the closing years of the Tokugawa regime* (Cambridge, Mass., 1971), pp.5–8.

year later an order followed to compile, as a guide to policy, the diplomatic precedents of two and a half centuries of Tokugawa rule: this resulted in the *Tsūkō ichiran* (Survey of intercourse), edited by the time Perry arrived in 1853.[115] Isolated though Japan was, it had prepared for its new encounter with the west, and Hayashi Akira (1800–59), the main compiler of the *Tsūkō ichiran* and from 1853 *Hayashi daigaku no kami*, became chief Japanese negotiator.

[115] For the history and background of the *Tsūkō ichiran*, see Kizaki Hiromi, 'Tsūkō ichiran no hensan to denrai ni kansuru kōsatsu' [The compilation and use of the *Tsūkō ichiran* considered], *Kaiji-shi kenkyū*, no. 47 (March 1990), pp.54–70; Kizaki, 'Tsūkō ichiran no shoshigaku-teki kōsatsu' [Bibliographical view of the *Tsūkō ichiran*], *Kaiji-shi kenkyū*, no. 49 (April 1992), pp.66–77. See also *Tsūkō ichiran zokushū* (see below), vol. 5, pp.454–69. The remainder of the work for the *Tsūkō ichiran*, dealing with the decades subsequent to the *uchi harai* decree of 1825, was completed in 1856. Much less well known than the *Tsūkō ichiran* of 1852, its 152 *kan* have been edited in *Tsūkō ichiran zokushū* [*Tsūkō ichiran*, continuation] in 5 vols. (Osaka, 1968–73). For further details on the background to the *Tsūkō ichiran*, see also Kizaki, 'Shozōshō yori mitaru shōheizaka gakumonjo no tokushitsu', pp.109–42.

6   Sakoku under pressure: the *gaiatsu* of the 1850s and 1860s

Threats to sakoku had in the past been posed by individual ships. Perry in 1853 bore the first communication from a western government in forty-nine years; more disturbingly it was delivered by a fleet of four warships, and an even larger American fleet came a year later. What the Japanese feared (and expected, as the Dutch had kept them informed of American plans) had occurred. Emphasis on consultation in Edo policy was reinforced. In the wake of Perry's first visit, Abe Masahiro (1819–57) wrote to the daimyo, inviting them 'to express your opinions freely without reservation, for even if they are disagreeable, no offence will be taken'.[1] This reflected less weakness than an underlying strength of Japanese society. With defence a collective responsibility, consultation was central to facing the challenge. An illustration of this is a long and frank correspondence by both Abe and his successor Hotta from 1855 as prime minister with the powerful daimyo of Mito and of Satsuma. These two men were all the more important because by precedent, unlike *fudai*, the daimyo of both han as members of the *sanke* and *tozama* respectively were excluded from government office. Satsuma, the han best informed on encroachments from the south, represented the maritime aspect; Mito, preoccupied by the need to strengthen the Japanese presence in Ezo, argued for far-reaching reorganisation on land. Both han offered a contrast with Choshu, no less forthright in the 1850s in preparing for the future contest with foreigners, but lacking the close personal ties with the Edo shogunate which the daimyo of Satsuma and Mito enjoyed. Choshu scarcely figured in correspondence, a circumstance which marked the gulf between Choshu and the shogunate and which was to widen alarmingly from 1858.

Narioki's successor from 1851 as daimyo of Satsuma, Nariakira (1809–58), already experienced in han policy, regarded defence as his main priority and pursued a vigorous policy of putting his heavily taxed han in military readiness. His correspondence with the *rōjū* was a lynchpin

---

[1] Maruyama, *Intellectual history of Tokugawa Japan*, p.364.

in the security policy of the shogunate as it faced into its years of foreign crisis.[2] His contacts also reached beyond the shogunate itself. Saigō Takamori, one of his officials, moved between the Satsuma, Mito and Fukui residences in Edo in the 1850s: he met Fujita Tōko, the main Mito advisor in 1854 and 1855, and was impressed with his ideas.[3]

The unwelcome suggestions of Tokugawa Nariaki of Mito over a decade for expensive reinvolvement in Ezo were in a sense vindicated by the evidence of the Opium War in China in 1840–2 and its naked English aggression.[4] He was at his most unpopular in 1843–5, when factionalism ran riot. The head of Mito had enjoyed a right of regular residence in Edo, a circumstance which itself reflects the scale of the slight he suffered in 1844 in being confined to Mito. Mito was important, in part because it represented a northerly link in the coastal defences of the capital, but primarily because of the vigour of its ruler. He had recruited experts from all over Japan. Mamiya, the explorer of the north, knew Nariaki and his advisors in Edo and on one occasion visited Mito; and Aoki Rinzō, one of the translators of Golownin (Golovnin), later in his role as a medical doctor became one of the *rangakusha* recruited by Nariaki.[5] Tokugawa Nariaki was highly critical of existing defence methods, and wanted root and branch reorganisation.[6] The Heihachirō rising in 1837 added to his alarm. His fear was that foreigners might take advantage of unrest in Japan.

Once the gravity of the crisis began to sink in in earnest in Edo, Nariaki had to be brought in from the cold: between 1845 and 1849 one of the

---

[2] The most convenient survey of Nariakira's role is Kanbashi Norimasa, *Shimazu Nariakira* (Tokyo, 1993). A readable and useful account in English is R. K. Sakai, 'Shimazu Nariakira and the emergence of national leadership in Satsuma', in Craig and Shively, *Personality in Japanese history*, pp.209–33.

[3] Charles L. Yates, *Saigo Takamori: the man behind the myth* (London, 1995), pp.32–3. Fujita was killed in the Edo earthquake of 1855; the Satsuma residence itself was destroyed.

[4] On the Chinese events of 1840–2 and the later French and English attacks of 1856–60, see especially Wong, *Deadly dreams*.

[5] Ogata Tomio (ed.), *Edo jidai no yōgakusha-tachi* [Western scholars of the Edo period] (Tokyo, 1972), pp.150–3. Nariaki's interest in medicine and in spreading its benefits to the populace was far ahead of its time.

[6] For a succinct account in English of the reorganisation of society in Mito, see J. Victor Koschmann, *The Mito ideology: discourse, reform, and insurrection in Tokugawa Japan* (Berkeley, 1987), pp.103, 109–12. Tokugawa Nariaki, whose adoption as a hero by the militarists of the 1930s seems to have turned him into an unfashionable subject for later study, is still neglected. The only major contribution has been a collection of many of his letters and writings with commentaries: Kawauchi Hachirō, *Tokugawa Nariaki Date Munenari ōfuku shokanshū* [The collected correspondence between Tokugawa Nariaki and Date] (Tokyo, 1993). There is also some of Nariaki's own writing in *Zoku shintō taikei: hachishū bunsō Tokugawa Nariaki* [A sequel to the Shinto Compendium: Tokugawa's hachisu writings] (Tokyo, 1999). For his administration and the Mito background, the best source remains the very full account in *Mito shi-shi*, middle series, vol. 3.

tasks of Abe as new prime minister was to rehabilitate Nariaki. Finally he was put in charge of defence in 1853, a somewhat honorific post, as unified defences did not exist, but symbolically important as a public expression of a common interest (it is also the first instance of a *sanke* or *tozama* lord retained formally in the service of a ruling shogun). Nariaki has been little studied. He has been seen as ineffective or as a windbag. However, his image to many at the time was positive. Satow, the interpreter to the British mission in the 1860s, recorded his impact on the young Choshu men, who praised him for a youth spent 'in wandering about the country and acquainting himself with its actual condition... habits of simplicity and frugality which distinguished him in after life' and for three decades of dedication, practical as well as theoretical, to defence matters.[7]

The correspondence with Shimazu Nariakira and Tokugawa Nariaki is the most significant element in the compilations from various sources of what might be regarded for want of a better term as the public records of Bakumatsu Japan. The irony is that Nariaki and Nariakira, important to the shogunate because they both supported it and were avant-garde in defence policy, died in 1860 and 1858 respectively. That means we can only speculate on the role they would have played as the twilight crisis of 1858–60 became the more ominous one of later years. Mito dissolved in internal conflict and ultimately civil war in 1864. As Mito was swallowed up in its own problems, Satsuma, the most cohesive of the large han, became an ever more vital element, and a necessary counterbalance to the menace of Choshu. Ultimately it was the attempt by the shogunate to discipline dissentient han (in particular the two bouts of war with Choshu), in effect war by Japanese on Japanese, which led Satsuma, reluctantly but decisively, to become an opponent of the shogunate.[8] That sealed the fate of the Tokugawa house.

Scarcely a single Japanese, it could be said with little if any exaggeration, was in favour of opening up Japan in 1853. The dilemma remained, as half a century previously, as to how to avoid foreign war, and how to

---

[7] Ernest Mason Satow, *A diplomat in Japan* (London, 1921), pp.382–4.
[8] Yoshinobu, the last shogun, retained throughout his later life a resentment of what he regarded as the betrayal by Satsuma, which had been an ally, and especially at the role of Saigō and Ōkubo of Satsuma (Ryōtarō SHIBA, *Le dernier shogun*, translation of *Saigō no shōgun* by Corinne Atlan (Arles, 1992), p.234). The repayment of Satsuma loyalty by shogunal loyalty in the reverse direction had been displayed in the aftermath of the Richardson episode (the murder by some of the samurai of Satsuma of the English merchant who had been discourteous to the procession accompanying the retired daimyo of Satsuma in 1862). The reluctance of the shogun to interfere to punish the guilty or to get compensation has been seen as a sign of the weakness of the shogun. An underlying feature also was the existing good relationship with Satsuma and the importance for the shogunate of its continuance.

define the minimum concession consistent with that end. Should there be outright resistance to foreign encroachment, or agreement struck with foreigners, with concessions kept to the bare minimum? If treaties were signed, they could, if Japan modernised its armaments in the interval, be later renegotiated or even ended from a position of strength.[9] This was the policy of the shogunate itself, and in 1858 the provision in the treaties that they would be renegotiated in fourteen years was central: it was of course also the basis of the later understanding between the emperor Kōmei and the shogunate. Even for someone like Hotta accepting that ports had to be opened, the premise was that it was 'one scheme very eminently fitted to increasing wealth and armaments on the profits of the foreign trade in the prevailing circumstances'.[10] In other words, the justification for the treaties was that they provided the only means by which Japan could equip itself to resist foreign intrusion and to undo concession. It was not wholly removed from the policy of Nariaki, the man who for thirty years had argued for a forceful policy and who, despite his opposition to treaties, supported the shogunate in the crisis that their signature created. The slogan *fukoku kyōhei* (rich country, strong defence), which was to ring though the following decades, grew out of this dilemma. There was no broad divide in the 1850s on fundamental principles.

All had changed however with the arrival off Uraga of Perry's four black ships (two steam vessels, two sailing vessels) in 1853 bearing a letter from the American president seeking the opening of Japan's ports. Perry's fleet was intended to overawe the Japanese. He announced that he would return the next year for a reply. The immediate response was to put Nariaki in titular charge of defence. The other was to consult widely. Perry returned in the spring with nine vessels, a quarter of the entire American navy, in what was intended to impress the Japanese even more than had the guns of his first squadron. The firing power of the guns of his ships, even on the first visit, was several times that of the batteries around Edo bay. The Japanese negotiating team, led by the head of the Hayashi family, *Daigaku no kami* Hayashi Akira, negotiated very well, keeping concessions to a minimum, and the original American reports – far more electrifying in interest than modern retelling of the story – convey a sense of respect for the chief Japanese negotiator.[11] The purport of the treaty – or of the

---

[9] There is a succinct summary of this attitude in W. G. Beasley, *Japan encounters the barbarian: Japanese travellers in America and Europe* (Newhaven, 1995), pp.43–7.

[10] *The complete journal of Townsend Harris*, p.382.

[11] The American official account, Francis L. Hawks's *Narrative of the expedition of an American squadron . . . in the years 1852, 1853 and 1854*, which was published in Washington in 1856, has been reprinted in chronological stages in the Shiryō hensanjo, *Dai nihon ishin shiryō*, second series, vols. 2–5.

broadly identical treaties signed subsequently with other western countries – was limited. They provided only for supplies being made available to ships, and for the appointment of consuls. Foreign trade as such remained as theretofore limited to the Chinese and Dutch, and Nagasaki was still the only port in which the trade could be conducted, and by the old trading partners alone. In a sense, the treaties themselves did not advance greatly in principle beyond the succour concept in the *uchi harai* decrees. For that reason, though a growing apprehension existed about the future, Japanese did not divide fundamentally.

For the same reason shogunal defence expenditure did not rise sharply, though this was less true of the forward han. However, the appointment of Tokugawa Nariaki signified an unqualified approval for han initiative in defence measures. The prohibition of vessels of above 500 koku burden was removed, and the han were encouraged to build up their defences. Saga, Choshu and Satsuma, and far to the north Mito, already forceful han, were within the limit of their finances to the fore. In particular, under Nariakira, Satsuma added to its naval and coastal defences. Negotiations with Putiatin, a Russian admiral, dragged out over 1853–5, meant that Russian access to Hakodate was in prospect. Matsumae was swiftly and without fuss taken into Edo administration in 1854, and a bugyo office restored; han in the north of Honshu were once more required to station troops in Ezo.[12] Thus, a confrontation between defence needs and Japanese political structures (or their lack) did not arise. However, calm in internal events depended on the absence of further western demands.

The emphasis by the Americans in 1853 and 1854 on succour to distressed mariners and on the law of nations was no more than an excuse to justify blatant intrusion into a foreign country which for two and a half centuries had troubled no neighbours. If a country did not harm its neighbours, it was not under an obvious obligation, under international law such as it was, to open its frontiers, and particularly not so when the 1825 *uchi harai* decree was modified in 1842. Given the moral dilemma of forcing access on another country, the Russians in 1792 and in 1804 and the *Morrison* in 1837 dressed out their démarche with an effort to return Japanese castaways. The public professions of American motives in 1853 were not to be taken at face value. They were already the second largest purchasers of tea at Canton,[13] and there was a consuming interest in commercial expansion in the Pacific. The American consul,

---

[12] The story of the re-established office is partly told in Taguchi Eiji, *Saigo no Hakodate bugyō no nikki* [The diary of the last Hakodate bugyo] (Tokyo, 1995).
[13] Wong, *Deadly dreams*, p.11.

Townsend Harris (1804–78), taking up residence in Shimoda in 1856, lost no time in demanding an effective commercial treaty. Using the example of British and French armed intrusion in China, he argued the benefits of alliance with the United States. By the early spring of 1858 the American demands were clear and uncompromising. The Japanese were divided. How should the Americans be negotiated with? Should a treaty be signed? Also, what alternative to a treaty was there? Harris's proposals raised the stakes. It was now not a question of admitting foreign ships for non-trading purposes (in itself simply an elaboration of the principle which had existed in the 1806 and 1842 orders), or of opening ports other than Nagasaki (long the specialist centre of foreign trade), Hakodate (a key interest of the Russians, and a remote centre) and Shimoda (consular post of the Americans, at the tip of a peninsula, itself not a port of commercial importance), but of going much further in concession. The detailed proposals provided for the opening of Osaka and of Kanagawa (close to Edo) in 1859, to be followed in 1860 by the opening of Niigata on the west coast, and of Hyogo (the outport of Osaka) in 1862, with general residence in Osaka and Edo allowed from 1863. Effectively this would mean the end of sakoku, and the presence of foreigners, a security risk, in or close to the heart of governmental Japan in Edo and in imperial Kyoto.

If the opening of the ports raised difficult issues, the events of the 1850s also brought to a head once more the Ezo problem and fear of the Russians. Russian policy in the east, dormant after the 1810s – and thus lending credibility to the 1822 return of Ezo to the Matsumae family – had become expansive in the late 1840s.[14] A small but interesting pointer to the direction of the wind was the Russian reprinting of Golownin's book in 1851. The frontier problem in Ezo emerged even in the first treaty with Russia in 1855.[15] While the treaty drew a line in the Kurils between the possessions of the two countries, with Kunashiri and Etorofu being recognised as Japanese, Sakhalin proved a stumbling block. Given the incompatibility of the views of the two sides, with Russia laying claim to the entire island, the only basis for an accord was to leave the frontier matter unsettled.[16] The Russians' stake in the region also gave them a leverage in negotiation which the Americans and British did not enjoy: their treaty conceded a right in Nagasaki, Shimoda and Hakodate to pay

---

[14] Lensen, *The Russian push towards Japan*, pp.262–5.

[15] For an account in English of frontier issues both before and after 1855, see John J. Stephan, *The Kuril Islands: Russian-Japanese frontier in the Pacific* (Oxford, 1974).

[16] Akizuki Toshiyuki, *Nichirō kankei to saharin tō: bakumatsu meiji shonen no ryōdo mondai* [Russo-Japanese relations and Sakhalin island: problems of sovereignty in late Tokugawa and early Meiji times] (Tokyo, 1994), p.117.

for goods not only in cash, but in commodities they had brought with them, and personal freedom in the ports. In the autumn of 1857 these advantages were widened to a right of making purchases (though still intended for ship's use only) direct from merchants and not, as in the past, through officials. When the Russians sought to reopen negotiations about Sakhalin in 1859, they did so with the supporting argument of a fleet moored off shore.[17] For British diplomats unease about Russian designs on Sakhalin was a recurrent theme.[18] In 1861 the Russians occupied Tsushima, and were forced to withdraw only by the British.

Difficult as the opening of the ports issue was on its own, Japan's misfortune in the late 1850s was that the shogunal succession was simultaneously a major internal issue. Iesada was sickly, without male heir, and not likely to live long. For the first time in the history of the Tokugawa line, there was no son, brother or close cousin of a ruling shogun. Of the two distant cousins in contention, one, Yoshitomi (as Iemochi, the future fourteenth shogun), was from the Kii branch of the Tokugawa, the house which had provided shoguns from the time of Yoshimune, and was a mere child. The other was Yoshinobu, a son of Nariaki (his claim strengthened further by adoption as heir into the Tokugawa-related house of Hitotsubashi), and he was personally capable. Abe favoured Yoshinobu, as finally did his successor Hotta. Yoshinobu's claim was backed by powerful daimyo; Nariaki obviously, but also by Matsudaira Shungaku, daimyo of the major *fudai* han of Fukui (whose diplomatic agent was Hashimoto Sanai (1834–59), who proved central to the contacts between the large han of independent disposition in the 1850s[19]), Shimazu Nariakira of Satsuma, and the alcohol-addicted but shrewd daimyo of Tosa, Yamauchi Yōdō. In other words, Yoshinobu was the candidate of a powerful lobby which not only favoured a vigorous defence policy, but had clear views on the role of the han. As the Mito house had never provided a shogun, a Mito succession would imply (quite apart from Nariaki's views about the need for sweeping changes) both the replacement of the Kii dynasty which had provided all the shogun since 1716 and the divorce of its *fudai* supporters from power. Ii Naosuke, daimyo of Hikone, a *fudai* han whose head over a long interval had often borne the rather honorific title of *tairo* though not the duties of office,[20] was the implicit or informal

[17] The negotiations aborted. See Alcock, *The capital of the tycoon*, vol. 1, pp.234–43.

[18] Iida Kanae, *Eikoku gaikōkan no mita bakumatsu nihon* [Bakumatsu Japan as seen from the English mission] (Tokyo, 1995), pp.281–2; G. Daniels, *Sir Harry Parkes: British representative in Japan 1865–83* (Richmond, Surrey, 1996), pp.59, 75, 80, 89, 101–2.

[19] G. M. Wilson, 'The Bakumatsu intellectual in action: Hashimoto Sanai in the political crisis of 1858', in Craig and Shively, *Personality in Japanese history*, pp.234–63.

[20] On the status of the Ii family, daimyo of Hikone, see Totman, *Politics in the Tokugawa bakufu*, pp.164–5.

spokesman of the many *fudai*, who saw their interests as linked to the existing shogunal family. The confrontation was thus between on the one hand a group with whom Abe had cultivated ties, a broad-based clique combining powerful interests ranging through two branches of the Tokugawa family (Mito and Owari), a powerful *fudai* han (Fukui) on the west coast, and the most forceful *tozama* (Satsuma), and, on the other hand, an interest narrowly identified in status and geographical location with the ruling branch of the Tokugawa family and even more with its *fudai* supporters.

Thus there were simultaneously two controversial issues, the opening of the ports and the shogunal succession. As far as the ports (with Ezo a further complication in the background) were concerned, the formal advice of the daimyo was sought once more. In introducing a principle of extraterritoriality, meaning that foreigners would be tried in their own consular courts and not by Japanese jurisprudence, the proposals were a radical challenge to Japanese sovereignty and political caution warranted their referral to the emperor for approval as part of a line of defence against opposition. That itself bore risks. The real question was less whether Japan should accede to concessions than what precisely they should be – daimyo replies, while hostile to concession, put an emphasis on avoiding a conflict for which they felt Japan was poorly prepared, and thus in effect shared the views of both Hotta and his successor Ii that there was no alternative. The only solace on offer was that the accommodation with the foreigner might be temporary. On this issue at least realism was widespread. As Townsend Harris's informant described the situation, 'taking 10 persons in authority, three would be in favour of opening the country at once, two would be in favour but with delay, three would refuse, so long as force is not used, but would yield to such a demonstration without fighting, and two would fight to the last'. It is in fact a remarkably good summary of what we know from the surviving daimyo replies was the Japanese outlook.[21]

But for the accidents of history, Hotta or his successor Ii Naosuke could probably have ridden out the storms. The death in 1857 of Abe (still a powerful member of the *rōjū* at Hotta's accession in 1855 to the position of leading member) and the unexpected death from cholera, a month after the American treaty was signed, of Nariakira, deprived the shogunate of support which might have made it possible to work out an internal *modus vivendi*. If what was in legal terms the most complex

---

[21] Mitani Hiroshi, 'Kaikoku, kaikō o meguru shodaimyō no taigai iken' [The views of daimyo about opening the ports and the country], in *Jūkyū seiki no Yokohama* [Nineteenth-century Yokohama] (Yokohama kinsei-shi kenkyū-kai and Yokohama kaiko-shiryokan, 1993), pp.3–24.

succession in Tokugawa history had not been in the air with the factionalism that it unavoidably generated, it would have been still easier to
reach compromise. With Abe's death, the division among the *rōjū* over
the anticipated succession, given the circumstances of a sickly and men-
tally feeble shogun, made possible the rise of Ii. His strength was that of
defender of the narrow interests of the *fudai* who, in the best factional
fashion, put the interest of the existing dynasty above keeping the most
vigorous han aboard the ship of state, difficult of course though the concept of polity was to grasp in a society as decentralised as Japan. When
the emperor, asked for his approval of the draft treaty, referred the matter
back to Hotta in May 1858 for further consultation with the daimyo and
the *sanke*, Hotta fell. He was replaced by Ii Naosuke, assuming the rank
of *tairo*, this time held by a member of the family at a time of real crisis
and on the only occasion in which a member of the family was also a *rōjū*.

If factionalism was a problem, so also in a novel fashion was the position of the imperial court. As daimyo were consulted on the broad treaty
issue, recourse to the the emperor was no less unavoidable: the changes
engendered in the prospective treaty with the Americans were the most
revolutionary ones in Japan for 250 years. The symbolism of the imperial institution was enhanced by the fact that those who opposed change
appealed in effect to a higher court as a form of restraint on shogunal
action. In suggesting reference back to the han and *sanke*, the emperor
both avoided committing himself to acceptance and at the same time
cautiously took account of the divide among the han and an uncertain
outcome to the shogunal succession (which found a *fudai* faction which
benefited from the present regime and a much broader alliance of *tozama*
and of *fudai* and *sanke* elements on different sides). As Townsend Harris
had recognised, he was likely to go with the majority.[22] Kōmei (1831–67)
himself was no cypher as he grew to manhood (he was only fifteen years
of age when he succeeded in 1846), seeking to balance, amid divides in
the country and in the court alike, a firm opposition to the principle of
concession to foreigners and unwavering support of the shogunate. Twice
he was talked by courtiers out of a threat of abdication.[23] The deepest
concern was the prospective residence of foreigners some thirty miles
from the imperial city, and the fear that treaties might prove permanent
rather than temporary concessions to the foreigner. Ii Naosuke, in the difficult situation where imperial approval was not forthcoming and under
pressure from the Americans, opted for action as his only recourse: the

---

[22] *The complete journal of Townsend Harris*, p.560.
[23] Donald Keene, *Emperor of Japan: Meiji and his world, 1852–1912* (New York, 2002)
pp.39–41, 42.

treaty was signed in July 1858, its terms quickly extended to other countries, and a month later, the sickly shogun dying, the succession was
settled on *fudai* terms. The emperor's ultimate outlook, like that of many
of the daimyo, was of opposition followed by reluctant acceptance of a
fait accompli on the basis that it was a temporary measure wrung from
him under duress and hence to be undone on another day. Hayashi Akira
along with a *metsuke* was sent to Kyoto in October for the purpose of
explaining the treaties. In the wake of clarifications the emperor accepted
that the shogun had no option but to concede them (in itself a signal of
acceptance of the primacy of the shogun's role in foreign relations), and
in February 1859 he formally acquiesced on the basis that the shogun
would seek to alter the terms.

Ii's own weak political standing led him to attempt to consolidate his
position by a purge of opponents and by a number of executions and
punishments, which have become known in Japanese history as the Ansei
Purge. In all, seventy-nine persons were detained, seven of whom were
executed. More important than the numbers was of course the status of
some of those punished. Nariaki was for a second time in his life put under house arrest, as were nine other daimyo.[24] Shimazu Nariakira might
have become a victim had he lived.[25] Han were also required variously
to surrender politically obnoxious individuals to the shogunate, or to exile them. Yoshida Shōin of Choshu, important as a teacher of political
ideas whose thought was already having repercussions outside Choshu itself, was surrendered to the shogunate and executed in 1859. Hashimoto
Sanai of Fukui, the forceful figure in Fukui's diplomatic contacts in the
1850s with Satsuma and Mito, was likewise executed. Saigō Takamori
(1827–77) of Satsuma, Nariakira's man of business with other han, was
exiled to a remote island off the coast of Satsuma. No comparable trail of
political blood and punishment had marked the harsh administrations of
Ii's strong-arm predecessors, Tanuma and Mizuno. The events surrounding Chōei and Kazan in 1839 had involved a mere half dozen individuals,
and were a case of faction among officials (though with a small and sad
tale not of executions but of imprisonment, exile or suicide), not an off-
shoot of *rōjū* high policy. The internal political crisis of Japan really dates
from Ii's actions on his advent to power. He was assassinated in 1860,
and an attempt was made on the life of his immediate successor.

Ii Naosuke has been represented as both a capable man and the last
hope for the shogunate. While the latter claim is doubtful, at one level

---

[24] Matsumoto, *Kaikoku-ishin*, pp.154–65. For a fuller account, see Yoshida Tsunekichi,
Ansei no taigoku [The Ansei repression] (Tokyo, 1991).
[25] Shiba, *Le dernier shogun*, p.66.

his legacy was far from negative. The development of a more professional administration was taken a further and decisive step forward during his administration. Just ahead of negotiating the 1858 treaties, he created the five *gaikoku bugyō*, or commissioners of foreign affairs, to handle, under the general guidance of one of the *rōjū*, the conduct of foreign policy.[26] What that meant was the professionalisation of foreign negotiations. A systematic administrative process emerged with its papers surviving in chronological sequence, western-style, in the originals (the main corpus kept together in what later became the Foreign Ministry) and with each *gaikoku bugyō* responsible for a well-defined area of policy.[27] It pointed to the emergence of a central negotiation machinery in foreign policy. While the importance of this is considerable, it should be recognised that it had antecedents, which can be traced from the evidence in the surviving correspondence, in Abe's *kaibō gakari* (coastal defence officers), and especially from 1855 in the increased direct administrative role of Hotta (itself a reminder of the need to see change as a process and not to overstress the role of individuals).[28] The internal conflicts among officials, such as in the 1820s or in the Kazan and Takashima incidents at the outset of the 1840s, too expensive to afford at a time of crisis, had already sidelined the *rangakusha*. In other words, with Abe's *kaibō gakari* and Hayashi Akira given well-defined tasks – all for non-ideological reasons – an administration like the one Matsudaira Sadanobu must have envisaged in the 1790s was beginning to emerge. The Hayashi family disappears from the *komonjo* or public records of Japanese diplomacy (Akira himself died in 1859).[29] The administrative role of the Hayashi family quickly vanished as the *gaikoku bugyō* took over, and over the next decade their more sensitive papers were broken up at various points.

Rangaku itself played its role in this outcome, but no longer as the voice of at times opinionated and interfering outsiders. It was finally integrated into what Matsudaira Sadanobu had desired, a more streamlined public service. The translation of foreign books had become more routine.

[26] See Doi Ryōzō, *Bakumatsu gonin no gaikoku bugyō: kaikoku o jitsugen saseta bushi* [The Bakumatsu five commissioners for foreign relations: samurai who made the opening of the country a reality] (Tokyo, 1997)

[27] The series of Shiryō hensanjo *Dai nihon komonjo, bakumatsu gaikoku kankei monjo* [Public records of Japan, records of Bakumatsu foreign relations] (Tokyo, 1910–61) changes dramatically with the advent of the *gaikoku bugyō* in the two years Ansei 5 and 6 (1858 and 1859). Letters for these years are contained in vols. 19–33.

[28] Vols. 1–14 of *Dai nihon komonjo: bakumatsu gaikoku kankei monjo* are a somewhat miscellaneous collection of papers from Kaei 6 to Ansei 3 (1853–6). The Hotta focus is well illustrated in vols. 15–18.

[29] The decline in the Hayashi role can be traced very clearly in the *Dai nihon komonjo* series in the course of the 1850s.

Hence we know less about the the *Banshowagegoyō* and *rangakusha* of the 1840s and 1850s precisely because in a changing world they were increasingly confined to their narrow, though vital, professional role as translators and interpreters.[30] In addition to artillery books, the office was engaged on orders issued by Mizuno Tadakuni on the translating of Dutch legal texts.[31] It was reinvigorated in 1856 as the *Bansho-shirabesho* (Institute for investigating foreign books). The title, however, by its new word *shirabe* (gathering information) as opposed to *wage* or *wakai* (work of understanding in Japanese, i.e. translating) also reflected a new purpose: it had shifted from a role of translating works selected on authority to one of studying western knowledge as such, and it had an explicit teaching function. In other words, sixty-seven years after the appearance of the first private school of *rangaku* in Edo – Ōtsuki's Shirando – an official one appeared. The surviving remnants of the shogunal library also reveal surprisingly wide purchases of foreign works.[32] By western standards, the natural sciences were the weakest link in Japanese scholarship, and their study had been, astronomy and calendar research apart, entirely private, culminating in the foundation of the famous Tekijuku in Osaka in 1838.[33] It studied natural sciences, and was moreover by Japanese standards a large school. The head of the Tekijuku, Ogata Kōan, was in 1862 appointed to a new academy in Edo, and its teachers were drawn widely from across Japan.[34] While foreign policy was tightened up, defence itself remained a weakness. Defence policy was divided between officers immediately under the *rōjū* (several of the *gaikoku bugyō* exercised defence responsibilities), and the *kaibō gakari*. The links between *rōjū*, *gaikoku bugyō* and *kaibō gakari* were the beginning of a chain of command. Defences themselves, however, still remained fragmented.

---

[30] It is expressed differently but to the same effect by NUMATA Jirō: 'The Japanese observations of the Opium war, the visit of Perry's ships, and the various other encounters with foreigners all combined during [the] last days of the Tokugawa Shogunate to force Rangaku into this military and technological mould', 'Dutch learning (Rangaku) in Japan: a response pattern to the foreign impact', *Acta asiatica*, no. 22 (1972), p.65.

[31] F. B. Verwayen, 'Tokugawa translations of Dutch legal texts', *Monumenta nipponica*, vol. 53, no. 3 (1998), pp.335–57.

[32] See *Edo bakufu kyūzō yōsho mokuroku* [Catalogue of the former Edo bakufu collection of western books] (Shizuoka Kenritsu Chūō Toshokan,1971)

[33] On the Tekijuku, see Tetsuo Najita, *Visions of virtue*, pp.300–5.

[34] All interpretation of Japanese history is ambiguous in some ways. The fact that most of the teachers came from outside shogunal territories is emphasised as a proof of the weak state of *rangaku* in Edo. Equally, the recruitment could be seen as an innovation in harnessing resources from across all of Japan. In any event, Ogata's Osaka school, even if a private one, was of course in a shogunal city, and, as both Edo and Osaka were shogunal cities, the distinction made between them in modern accounts is in some respects a false one.

The crisis at least up to 1856, serious though it was, had seemed containable.[35] From one point of view, the increase in expenditure was limited. There was also no inflation. While there had been a bad harvest in 1853, and a devastating earthquake in Edo in 1855, overall the political situation was benign enough for some uncompromising Japanese to contemplate going abroad to study on his home ground the foreigner whom, in some form or other, they would have to confront. Shōin had tried to stow away on one of the American vessels in 1854, and several years later, in even worse circumstances for Japan, Nariaki himself had proposed leading a band of 300 or 400 *rōnin* to the United States.[36] The relative calm had been seriously ruffled in 1856 with the arrival of Harris as the first American consul, and the outbreak in China in the same year of the Arrow War. The treaty and its quick extension to other powers had sprung from Japanese alarm at the French and English aggression, with its quite gratuitous killing and destruction, in China from 1856 to 1860. Put at its simplest, the treaties were the price of avoiding war.

There was an outcry against the treaties from samurai like Shōin enjoying the luxury of having no responsibilities. Opposition itself would not have destabilised Japan, because there was a widespread belief, shared even by the emperor Kōmei, in the inevitability of at least temporary concession. The Ansei executions, intended by Ii to crush dissent, kept opposition alive. They created a ferment among some samurai who, seeing Japan as rudderless, gave up their posts in order to oppose daimyo or shogunate openly. They became known as *shishi* (men of purpose), who, no longer tied by an obligation of loyalty to a lord, expressed their opposition openly, and, themselves powerless, often advocated recourse to violence. Shōin, after his imprisonment in 1859 on the charge of plotting to assassinate one of the *rōjū*, denounced shogunate and daimyo alike, and wrote wildly of 'the complete transformation of the world today' to come.[37] Objectively, the *shishi* were only minor actors in the events of 1860 and the following years, in the first instance made up of *rōnin* from Satsuma and especially Mito (the two han which had lost their great daimyo). They resented the lack of opposition to the Ansei repression, took the model of Shōin to heart, and held Aizawa's *Shinron* (now for the first time available in print) aloft as their bible. A spiral of assassinations and attempted assassinations, on a scale unprecedented in Japanese history, followed. This was Ii's real legacy to history, an ugly pattern which

---

[35] The most succinct account is that by Mitani Hiroshi in *Meiji ishin to nashonarizumu*, pp.327–38.
[36] Masao Miyoshi, *As we saw them: the first embassy to the United States* (New York, 1994), p.187.
[37] Maruyama, *Intellectual history of Tokugawa Japan*, p.362.

was to last through the early and mid-1860s, and to provide the model in the 1930s for young army officers who opposed constitutional politics. Inevitably attacks from 1859 by the *shishi* on foreigners, seamen or diplomats, got attention abroad. However, the attacks were not in essence xenophobic. Japanese themselves were far more at risk in what had become, in the early 1860s, effectively the political centre of Japan, Kyoto.

Foreigners did not appreciate the extent and depth of the opposition to the treaties. For long they had regarded Japan as inherently despotic. Its laws, they felt, were oppressive, and the people, groaning under tyranny, would welcome government by outsiders. Ernest Satow, interpreter to the British mission, noted in his diary in the early 1860s that the Japanese had a great appetite for being governed: owing to the submissive character of the people, it would be easy for foreigners to govern them, once the 'samurai problem' was overcome. Much later he noted wryly that 'looking back now in 1919, it seems perfectly ludicrous that such a notion should have been entertained, even as a joke, for a single moment, by anyone who understood the Japanese spirit'.[38] The British looked at Japan in terms of their Chinese experience, and their early heads of mission had all first served in China. Rutherford Alcock (1809–97) believed that easterners were impressed only by force, and in particular that the capacity of the Japanese for higher moral civilisation was far below that of any other nation including the Chinese.[39] His views contrasted with the perception of Townsend Harris, who more shrewdly saw that the shogun's position reflected less dishonesty than internal political divides. When the new foreign settlement was transferred in 1859 from Kanagawa to Yokohama by the Japanese unilaterally, though for the good practical reason that Kanagawa was on the Tokaido and foreigners would be in collision with large *sankin kōtai* retinues (as the Richardson episode three years later proved only too well), the diplomats saw it as an effort to create a second Deshima. The crisis was defused only by the alacrity with which merchants, totally against the wishes of diplomats, accommodated themselves to the new plans. The highhandedness so often displayed was in evidence once more in 1867 when, in the wake of the murder of two sailors from HMS *Icarus*, the demand was made that all Tosa samurai in Nagasaki at the time should be detained and made to account for their movements:[40] subsequent events proved that Tosa samurai were innocent of the crime. There is through Satow's book a muted and discreet

---

[38] Satow, *A diplomat in Japan*, p.327.
[39] Alcock, *The capital of the tycoon*, vol. 2, p.301. Given such views, perhaps not surprisingly the French saw Harris as much more persona grata with the Japanese (Medzini, *French policy in Japan*, pp.27–8).
[40] Satow, *A diplomat in Japan*, pp.265, 267.

criticism of his boss, Rutherford Alcock's successor from 1864, Sir Harry Parkes (1828–85).[41]

Real gunboat diplomacy was displayed on three occasions, two in 1863. The first involved the silencing by French vessels of Choshu batteries which fired on shipping in the Shimonoseki strait, the second the shelling in the same year by a British fleet of Kagoshima, castle town of Satsuma, and the final time was in 1864 when the Choshu batteries were dismantled by warships from four western powers.[42] At the time of the 1864 Shimonoseki expedition, Rutherford Alcock proposed seizing territory in Choshu and attacking Hagi, the castle town of Choshu han. The admiral in charge of the British naval unit refused to act on this proposal.[43] The British shelling of Kagoshima city did not pass without criticism in England of what was a heavy-handed episode involving unnecessary and extensive loss of civilian lives (perhaps 18,000).

The strength of feeling in Japan increased the problems of the shogunate whether in dealing with the han or with foreign powers, and Japan over several years was characterised by a contradictory pattern of apparent political paralysis and forceful efforts to build up strength. In 1862 the *sankin kōtai* was suspended in an effort to allow han the opportunity of redeploying their resources to defence. Shogunate and han alike, despite a divide on the degree of acceptability of accommodation with foreigners, were at one in taking defence measures. At the outset of 1860 the nervous Rutherford Alcock reported that 'in nothing do they show so much energy as in the erection of forts; two in the bay opposite Edo, and one at Kanagawa, have been solidly built and raised out of the water since I arrived. The commonest sound in Edo is the musket and artillery practice of the soldiery.'[44] By 1863 batteries were being erected on the shores of the Inland Sea as well as in Edo and Uraga.[45] From 1864 under the drive of Tokugawa Yoshinobu (1837–1913), his hand strengthened by becoming regent for the boy shogun, investment became more focussed, directed towards creating effective directly managed shogunal military

---

[41] On Parkes, see also the comments of Satow's friend, the British medical doctor, the Irish-born Willis. H. Cortazzi, 'The pestilentially active minister: Dr Willis's comments on Sir Harry Parkes', *Monumenta nipponica*, vol. 39, no. 2 (Summer 1984), pp.147–61.

[42] For a succinct account of the Shimonoseki events, see H. J. Moeshart, 'The Shimonoseki affair, 1863–64', in Ian Nish (ed.), *Contemporary European writing on Japan* (Ashford, Kent, 1988).

[43] Satow, *A diplomat in Japan*, p.122. On British plans for taking Edo and Osaka by force and opposition to them by navy, foreign office and army, see Kumazawa Tōru, 'Bakumatsu no sakō mondai to eikoku no gunji senryaku: 1864 nen no tai-nichi sensō keikaku ni tsuite' [The problem of Bakumatsu closed ports and British military invasion: 1864 war plans against Japan], *Rekishigaku kenkyū*, no. 700 (1997, pt 8), pp.13–27.

[44] *PP Japan*, vol. 1, p.155.

[45] *PP Japan*, vol. 2, p.119, Col. Neale, 30 Sept. 1863.

and naval forces. By 1866 the shogunate had at least 600 riflemen organised on western principles. The han likewise invested in armaments, and
especially in steam ships purchased with the help of foreign merchants
in Nagasaki. In 1862 a British consular report commented on the reckless purchase of steamers.[46] Military expenditure rose sharply. Moreover,
Japan was quick to realise that it should appear on the diplomatic stage
abroad rather than merely wait at home to face pressures and demands
from foreigners. In 1860 it sent a large mission to the United States to exchange the ratification of the treaties.[47] There was no compelling reason
that the exchange of documents should take place in Washington; it could
just as easily have been done in Japan.[48] It was in its way a resurrection of
Nariaki's idea of some hundreds of *rōnin* going abroad. A further mission
in 1862 to Europe negotiated a deferment of the opening of the ports,
and yet another mission was dispatched in 1864.[49] Diplomatic missions
though they were, they were also occasions for learning about the west,
and for assessing the foes, diplomatic and in the worst scenario military,
that they had to deal with. A large number of young men accompanied
the first mission, to be placed abroad as students. In the following years,
shogunate and han alike sent young men abroad to study, and others
went abroad without any authority.

Rising expenditure on armaments in the early 1860s fed a naive belief
that the country could resist militarily in the immediate future. A number of han, especially southern *tozama*, seemed to have confidence in
Japan's capacity to drive off the foreigners.[50] The view was most strongly
held by Choshu, ahead of most han in defence and proud of its new
batteries which from the heights on its shoreline held a commanding
overview of the narrow strait of Shimonoseki. Choshu's batteries were by
no means ineffective (inflicting substantial damage, the damage and that
at Kagoshima in 1863 being the first by Japanese fire power) as the duels
with the western fleets showed. Some of the expenditure, however, arose
from a new shogunal intent from 1863 to impose itself by force, if necessary, on recalcitrant han. The means of financing this was a combination
of *goyōkin* and currency debasement in operations in four of the years
between 1861 and 1866.[51] In 1863 the profits of debasement were the

---

[46] *PP Japan*, vol. 4, p.61, Report on trade and shipping of Nagasaki for 1862.
[47] Miyoshi, *As we saw them*, is a very readable account of this mission.
[48] Matsumoto, *Nihon no kindai*, vol. 1, p.166.
[49] On Japanese missions abroad at this time, see Beasley, *Japan encounters the barbarian*,
    pp.71–4, 96–8.
[50] *PP Japan*, vol. 2, pp. 60–62, Acting consul Enslie to Lt. Col. Neale, 9 March 1863.
[51] Details of the profits are in a table in Yamamoto Yuzō and Umemura Mataji (eds.),
    Nihon keizai-shi [Economic history of Japan], vol. 3, *Kaikō to ishin* [Opening of the ports
    and Restoration] (Tokyo, 1989), p.122.

largest item in revenue. The largest profits were realised in 1864, the year in which the shogunate faced up to the challenge of assembling an invasion force to enter Choshu. Inevitably the price of rice rose at a rate unparalleled in Tokugawa history: it had trebled by 1865. A bad harvest in 1865, and in the following summer 1866, especially in the Tohoku, a very cool season, gave a new impetus to the price rise.[52] The resulting fall in reserves, combined with daimyo and shogunate buying to meet military contingencies, spilled over into widespread food scarcity which lasted into 1867 or later. Rice shipments into Osaka were even lower than in 1837. Food prices rose at twice the level of the price level at large. The real wages of day labourers in Edo were lower in 1866 and 1867 than in the bruising year of 1837.[53] The devaluation of the silver token coins, widely held in the community, served to add to the loss of popular purchasing power.[54] *Ikki* were numerous and widespread in 1866. Though often dramatised in analysis of unrest as a singular example of millenarian expectations (*yonaoshi*) and, rather imaginatively, as a culmination of two centuries of rising rural unrest, the *ikki* themselves to a surprising degree fail to register in contemporary accounts, Japanese and foreign alike, of political and economic events.

Defence demands on the already straitened finances of the han served to sharpen tensions over the opening of the ports which offered a possible source of new income. The han administrations, in the habit for centuries of marketing *kura* rice in Osaka, were beginning to engage on their own account in commercial transactions in the open ports. They also sent without shogunal authority students of their own abroad, and Satsuma itself, which sent fifteen students to England and France in 1865, in a striking manifestation of its growing ambitions, participated in its own right in the Paris exhibition of 1867.[55] Their rising export income was absorbed in heavy outlay on steamers and rifles, a pattern which continued up to 1867.[56] Foreign trade was not a reason for the rise in prices, except in so far as an import of arms and currency meant at least theoretically that the outflow of goods was not replaced by a matching inflow of consumer commodities to replace them. Ironically, given the han resentment

---

[52] Arakawa, *Kikin no rekishi*, pp.121–3. For general details see C. Totman, *The collapse of the Tokugawa bakufu 1862–1868* (Honolulu, 1980), pp.219–24.

[53] See table in Saitō Osamu, *Chingin to rōdō to seikatsu suijun: Nihon keisai-shi ni okeru 18–20 seiki* [Wages, labour and and living standards in Japanese economic history, 18th–20th century] (Tokyo, 1998).

[54] T. Ohkura and H. Shinbō, 'Tokugawa monetary policy', pp.116–17.

[55] For a useful survey of students abroad, see Beasley, *Japan encounters the barbarian*, pp.119–37.

[56] *PP Japan*, vol. 4, pp.186–7, Nagasaki report for 1865; pp.224, 226, Report from Nagasaki for 1866; pp.372–3, Report from Nagasaki for 1868.

of control of trade by the shogunate, the treaties had been of little direct benefit to the shogun in generating a tax income. Many of the taxes were already fixed at five per cent, and this rate was near universalised in an agreement in 1866. The British cynically and misleadingly had strongly pushed the argument that the resulting increase in trade would augment the shogun's income. Moreover, income from customs duties (based on declared values of goods) was massively diluted by fraudulent under-valuations by foreign merchants to the inexperienced Japanese customs officers.

The most damaging commercial issue followed immediately the entry into effect of the treaties in 1859, and at the time soured Japanese percep-tions of both the benefits of foreign trade and the goodwill of foreigners. Under the 1858 treaties, Japanese currency was to be made available at stated terms of exchange for Mexican dollars. This prompted foreigners not simply to acquire Japanese silver for their own use, but in violation of the spirit, as Harris recognised, though not of the letter of the treaties, to use the access to the silver which the Japanese authorities were obliged by treaty to supply, to engage in currency speculation. Gold, undervalued in Japan relative to silver (as the price of silver in Japan's closed circum-stances had risen well above world levels in the 1850s), was purchased with the silver, and exported in massive quantities to China; there it was converted into silver (cheaper there than in Japan) which on its return financed the export of further gold. The speculation was dealt with, as foreign diplomats had advised, by revaluing Japanese gold. Revaluation, however, by causing the steep rise in the value of Japanese gold had an immediate inflationary effect. In other words, it was indirectly in cur-rency adjustments rather than directly in changes in commodity trade that the opening of Japan affected the price level. At the outset the vol-ume of trade was too small in relation to total domestic output and the commodities involved too few, to have of themselves the effects often at-tributed to commodity trade. Nor was the currency adjustment in 1860 by any means the only factor: repeated debasements were more central to the price spiral of the following years.

Suspending the *sankin kōtai*, while intended to assist defence measures, threw a cloud over the formal ties binding shogunate and han, and cre-ated a constitutional problem the more so as Kyoto simply replaced Edo as the focus of external attention of han. A readiness to oppose the shogu-nate outright was at this stage a feature of only a few han. While Choshu was prepared to do so (though not to demand its toppling), Satsuma still supported the shogunate (to the extent of providing troops which helped to drive the Choshu forces from Kyoto). Choshu itself originally had been prepared to accept the opening of trade as a temporary measure, but switched to opposition as it saw the benefits as likely to be enjoyed exclusively by the shogun. The slogan *Sonnō* (worship the emperor) was less a call for restoration of emperor than a call to curb the powers of the shogunate, and to give the han a greater weight in decision making. A significant straw in the wind too was that the term 'bakufu', not at this stage used of or by Edo government, came into vogue. Satow, interpreter to the British mission, noted that 'This was the term, meaning "military power" by which the adversaries of the Tycoon were in the habit of speaking of his government.'[57] It was essentially a demeaning term denying the shogunate functions other than the narrowest. With the shogun spending his time in Kyoto, samurai and daimyo did likewise. Moreover, han other than Choshu had the motive to send some of their military forces there, illegal though that was, as self-appointed protectors of the emperor variously from the pressures of the shogunate or of one another. The *shishi* from many places also, unsummoned and unwelcome, made an appearance, extending their attacks from foreigners and high officials in Edo to moderate supporters of the shogunate.

External crisis made it urgent to restore a sense of unity such as had existed under Abe and Hotta. In 1862 a reaction within the shogunate itself set in to the policy introduced by the Ansei repression. The reinstatement of former leaders began, and Colonel Neale, a member of the British mission, on 10 February 1863 commented on 'ever recurring dismissals and appointments'.[58] The house arrests of daimyo were terminated, and Yoshinobu's release made possible the beginning of his ascent in the councils of the shogunate. As part of the changing of the guard, Tokugawa Yoshinobu was made guardian of the young shogun, and the daimyo of Fukui was made a senior adviser to the shogun. Together with the daimyo of Uwajima, Tosa, and Aizu – all daimyo who had incurred the wrath of Ii Naosuke – they put a new liberty to good use, aiming at some sort of advisory council of shogun and daimyo. This view was shared also by Saigō of Satsuma.[59] Its aim was echoed in the slogan *kōbugattai* (alliance of emperor and shogun).

These ideas could not, however, solve immediate political problems. While all Japanese officials were prepared to accept some concessions in trade as an interim measure, pending the building of the strength to resist or expel the foreigner (the original meaning of the slogan *fukoku kyōhei*), some officials in han, shogunate and imperial court alike quickly overestimated the fruits of five years of investment in military

---

[57] Satow, *A diplomat in Japan*, p.279. See also p.174.   [58] *PP Japan*, vol. 2, p.37.
[59] See Yates, *Saigo Takamori*, pp.62–3, 92; *PP Japan*, vol. 2, pp.173–4. The British were aware of a proposal in 1864 for a cabinet of daimyo under the emperor (Rutherford Alcock to Russell with enclosure, 31 March 1864).

preparedness. The slogan *Sonnō* now had joined to it in such han and also among the *shishi* at large the slogan of *jō-i* (expel the foreigner). Two young Choshu samurai, Itō Hirobumi (1841–1909) and Inoue Kaoru (1836–1915), who had gone abroad to London in 1863, returned in haste in 1864 in the hope of persuading the han elders of Choshu to abandon such a belief. From a British warship they were put ashore in August 1864 on the Choshu coast in the hope of preventing the han authorities from persisting in their intent to fire on foreign vessels in the Shimonoseki strait, but failed in this effort.[60] Others, the emperor Kōmei in person included, had not dissimilar views, but less confidence in artillery as the solution. While resolutely opposed to concessions on Osaka and Hyogo (which could become the base from which Kyoto could be attacked), Kōmei and shogunal officials had in essence a common outlook. Thus, in 1863, the shogunate despite its public commitments in the treaties, on the prompting of the emperor gave orders in secret for the ejection of foreigners: in essence this order sprang from unreal and overoptimistic assumptions held by many in Japan.[61] However, the emperor no more than the shogunate had welcomed the presence of Choshu troops in Kyoto in 1863, and, after their expulsion the following year, authorised the shogun to invade the defiant han itself.

The common ground between emperor and shogun was evident in a readiness in 1863 to take a similar line in accepting the hotheaded confidence of others on military opposition to foreigners, and on the delicate issue of relations between shogunate and *tozama* (the emperor firmly supported the shogunate on this explosive subject): it all illustrated the fact that neither shogunate nor emperor had a solution to the problems of Japan. The immediate advisors of the emperor were of poor calibre, a view held by people as different as Parkes, the English minister, and Saigō, and the few *kuge* (imperial courtiers) of ability like Iwakura were under house detention. In turn, the shogun's own advisors were deeply divided. For some in the councils of the shogun the support of the emperor promised unity by giving sanction to military measures against dissident han. For others, greater realists, such actions imperilled any prospect of consensus, and added to disunity in the face of foreigners. The gathering together of an army in Kyoto for an attack on Choshu brought to a head the tensions

[60] Satow, *A diplomat in Japan*, pp.96–100.
[61] Beasley has a somewhat more positive view of the shogunate's purpose. His interpretation is that the shogun and his advisors, arriving in Kyoto in April 1863, under presssure to fix a date for the expulsion, 'finally chose June 25 as the date for action, making *the unstated assumption* that because implementation of the decision would be the bakufu's business, "expulsion" could in practice be turned into a series of time-consuming negotiations with the treaty powers' (Beasley, 'The foreign threat and the opening of the ports', p.292 (italics mine)).

in Edo itself and led to a sweeping change of the entire cabinet of *rōjū* in August 1864[62] and to further delays in appointing a commander for the expedition. These tensions within the shogunate were a counterpart to views widely held outside it that, with foreigners on the doorstep, conflict between Japanese was a luxury that the country could not afford. This had become the view of Saigō Takamori, and it was also the view of one of the main advisors of the shogunate, its naval expert Katsu Kaishū (1823–98), who also helped to sharpen Saigō's views on the concept of a daimyo council.[63] Even the eventual leader of the expedition against Choshu, Tokugawa Yoshikatsu, shared this view.[64] At the end of the year, amid so many divides, the attack was called off, the price in a face-saving compromise being an undertaking by the han leaders in Choshu to move against the *kiheitai*, which were strongly anti-bakufu, and which were an unofficial force of samurai and well-off peasants engaged on one side in an internal political conflict within Choshu which finally turned to civil war. Former students of Yoshida Shōin – Yamagata Aritomo (1838–1922), Kido Yakayoshi (1833–77), Maebara Issei (1834–76) and others – were well represented in the leadership of the *kiheitai*. Others associated with the *kiheitai* had likewise come under novel influences: Ito, Inoue and Takasugi Shinsoku (1839–67) had been abroad, and Ōmura Masujirō (1824–69) had studied *rangaku* at Nagasaki. The official han forces were defeated by the *kiheitai*, under the leadership of Ito, Inoue and Yamagata, in a short civil war from December 1864 to January 1865. From the subsequent peace conference within the han, a new administration emerged in which the interest opposed to the former han authorities predominated.[65] The significance of this outcome was that it made possible a rapprochement with other han, especially with Satsuma.

At this stage, two countervailing tendencies existed. One was a movement among some han to favour some form of confederation of han, and an end to dissension and conflict within Japan. In 1864, Satsuma forces in conjunction with *fudai* troops had helped to drive the Choshu forces out of Kyoto. However, as the planning of the emperor–shogun expedition against Choshu came to overshadow all other issues, those who like Saigō believed that some form of han confederacy was desirable became more numerous.[66] Such a development hinged on the prospect of an alliance between Choshu and Satsuma, militarily powerful han, hostile to one another for centuries, and rivals in Kyoto in 1862–4 (Choshu wanting to minimise the role of the shogunate; Satsuma still a supporter of the

[62] *PP Japan*, vol. 2, p.226, Rutherford Alcock to Russell, 23 Aug. 1864.
[63] Yates, *Saigo Takamori*, p.73.   [64] Yates, *Saigo Takamori*, pp.75–6.
[65] A. M. Craig, *Choshu in the Meiji Restoration* (Cambridge, Mass., 1961), p.267.
[66] Yates, *Saigo Takamori*, pp.73–4.

shogunate). Sakamoto Ryōma (1836–67), a samurai from the *tozama* han of Tosa (whose views were in advance of the supportive but more cautious ones of his daimyo), was the key agent in negotiating this union, playing a role akin, though more colourful, to that of Hashimoto of Fukui in the 1850s among the great dissident daimyo of his day.[67] In 1865 Satsuma helped Choshu to acquire firearms and ships through its contacts with the English merchant, Glover, in Nagasaki. Its secret alliance with Choshu in 1866 was in the open by 1867.

If contemplation of confederacy of powerful han was one response to the crisis, a second or countervailing one was for the shogun, or more precisely for shogunal officials, to seek to strengthen his position, for the purpose of undoing such a prospect. The driving of Choshu forces out of Kyoto in 1864 had the immediate result of strengthening the shogunate. It also strengthened the hand of officials in Edo, now isolated from the world of Japanese politics, over those in Kyoto who were more aware of the problems. The pace of the cycle of fluctuation between hard and conciliatory policies quickened. If the fall of Ii Naosuke had finally led with a time lag to a more conciliatory administration in 1862, there was a reversion in 1864, encouraged by success in Kyoto and by imperial alliance, to a hardline approach, this time headed by Tokugawa Yoshinobu, a likely candidate to succeed the young shogun. Rumours reached the British diplomats in early 1864 that with the help of his supporters he might even set aside the shogun.[68] Yoshinobu began building up direct bakufu forces: in this he was helped by Léon Roches (1809–1901), who arrived as French minister in 1864 and was eager for France to supplant England as the best placed foreign power in Japan.[69] With the help of a French military mission a force directly retained by the shogunate, armed with foreign rifles and trained on French principles, was being developed, and in 1866 French workmen, constructing a naval arsenal at Yokosuka, were given an unprecedented permission to live outside the treaty ports.[70] A loan from France to the shogunate was also arranged.[71]

---

[67] M. B. Jansen, *Sakamoto Ryōma and the Meiji Restoration* (Princeton, 1961).

[68] *PP Japan*, vol. 2, pp.172–3, Rutherford Alcock, 31 March 1864. See also Yates, *Saigo Takamori*, p.67.

[69] The dates of publication of books acquired for the *Bansho-shirabesho* show a sharp rise of books in French in 1865–6: *Edo bakufu kyūzō yōsho mokuroku* (Shizuoka kenritsu chūō toshokan, 1971).

[70] Medzini, *French policy in Japan*, p.124. On the French links, see also Shiba, *Le dernier shogun*, pp.167, 176; Miyoshi, *As we saw them*, p.155; Totman, *Collapse of the Tokugawa bakufu*, pp.210–16, 253–4. For an account in English putting the French relations in a wider context, see J.-P. Lehman, *France and Japan 1850–1885* (Oxford, 1975). Ships were also purchased from Holland, and young men sent for naval training there. Matsuura Rei, *Tokugawa Yoshinobu: shōgun-ke no meiji ishin* [Tokugawa Yoshinobu: a shogunal family under the Meiji Restoration] (Tokyo, 1997), p.162. On Yokosuka after 1868, see R. Sims, *French policy towards the bakufu and Meiji Japan* (London, 1998), pp.246–9, 251–2.

[71] Matsuura, *Tokugawa Yoshinobu*, p.166.

Franco–Japanese trade, which had been small, increased.[72] Following the practice since 1860 of sending missions abroad, one was sent expressly to Paris in 1865, and another headed by a young Tokugawa prince (Yoshinobu's brother) left to represent the shogunate at the Paris fair in 1867. Almost symbolically, in the mid-1860s more books in French than in English were purchased, and the edition of the complete works of Charles Dickens in the *Bansho-shirabesho* was in French, not English![73] All this, allied to efforts by the bakufu to create an army and navy, only added to bakufu–*tozama* tensions, holding out a prospect of turning the bakufu, without the consent of the *tozama*, into a politically centralised government, one ultimately likely to be made even stronger by foreign trade. In other words, it was, or threatened to be, the end of the *Pax Tokugawa.*

From one point of view, all shared a common purpose to halt foreign encroachment and, at a later date, from a position of strength, to renegotiate the treaties. Western arguments have often been that at heart Japanese had wanted to open Japan. At the time no less a person than Satow shared this conclusion.[74] However, the shogunate itself was no different from the han: its problem was that it was more directly under pressure from foreign military and naval power and from endless diplomatic representations. The building up of bakufu strength raised questions of balance between shogunate and han. In the course of 1864 shogunal influence began to replace daimyo influence in Kyoto, and late in the year the *sankin kōtai* requirement was restored.[75] Ironically, the more successful the bakufu, the more the internal crisis would deepen. If divergent views on external questions were not fundamentally deep among Japanese (no one welcomed the foreign intrusion), divides on internal political issues would widen in proportion to either a growth in independent shogunal strength or successful arrangements for foreign trade under shogunal auspices. Yoshinobu had pushed ahead in 1864 with the Choshu expedition amid growing doubts even within the bakufu itself, and had 400 of some 700 Mito *rōnin* loyalists who had advanced into central Japan executed in early 1865. This more than any other single episode added to resentment, and Saigō in particular was moved less by the execution of leaders than by the ruthless killing of their lower-rank followers.[76] The effects of Ii's 1859 purge – modest in numbers, especially in executions, and 'excused' by the exalted status of the victims – were now repeated on a far larger scale: the executions were Yoshinobu's greatest error of judgement. To put the

---

[72] Naruiwa, *Bakumatsu Nihon to Furansu gaikō*, p.108; Medzini, *French policy in Japan*, p.69.

[73] *Edo bakufu kyūzō yōsho mokuroku* (Shizuoka kenritsu chūō toshokan,1971).

[74] Satow, *A diplomat in Japan*, p.43.

[75] Totman, *Collapse of the Tokugawa bakufu*, pp.140–6.   [76] Yates, *Saigo Takamori*, p.79.

matter in perspective, there was no parallel in post-1638 Tokugawa history; though highly arbitrary, Japanese repression was always bloodless by western standards.

Propelled by Yoshinobu's new broom of vigorous action, preparations for a second attempt at invading Choshu through 1866 were part of the story of that year. Again this had the support of the emperor, illustrating the common cause of both institutions, and how the emperor no more than the shogun recommended himself as a real political institution to the new men in the southern han who were dictating the pace of events. The spectre of trade and defence as a vehicle for shifting the weight of the constitution from han to shogunate haunted the *tozama*. Shogunal attempts to regulate or control trade left even foreign diplomats, especially British, uneasy. To an even greater degree, they unsettled politically aware Japanese: the prospect in 1866 of the imminent opening of Osaka, the country's largest port, raised the stakes dramatically. In 1862 the shogunate had secured a postponement of the opening of Osaka, due for 1 January 1863, to 1 January 1868, in return for an undertaking to facilitate trade in the ports already open. In November 1865 the emperor's approval of the treaties was secured by the western powers negotiating with the help of a huge fleet in Osaka bay. The emperor's approval was based on a linguistic conceit: as there is no definite article in Japanese, he approved 'treaties' (i.e. the principle of treaties) rather than *the* treaties.[77] This reflected a touching faith in unreal distinctions that the Japanese sometimes displayed, and which contrasted with the more brutal or at least simplistic western approach.[78] Specifically, in the Japanese mind the issue of opening Hyogo had not been settled outright: to them, the opening of Hyogo was to await a referral to a daimyo council.[79] Even in 1867, no less a person that Saigō proceeded under the illusion that the absence of active arrangements for the opening of the port did not put Japan on a collision course with the foreign powers.[80]

As had happened on several occasions in the recent past, deaths, rather than the divides among the Japanese, determined the immediate pace and directions of events. The shogun died in August 1866; some months later, and a mere twenty days after the nomination of Yoshinobu to the office of shogun, in February 1867 the emperor Kōmei died. Even if a very reluctant supporter of the concept of port opening, by his death the shogunate had lost an ally steadfastly opposed to any change in the

---

[77] Satow, *A diplomat in Japan*, p.155.
[78] Many years earlier, a small but illuminating example was furnished by Golownin (*Narrative of my captivity*, vol. 2, p.166).
[79] Yates, *Saigo Takamori*, p.89.   [80] Yates, *Saigo Takamori*, p.94.

constitutional relationship.[81] The accession of a young and inexperienced emperor, easy prey to a forceful shogunate, precipitated the final crisis, as it underlined the need for rapid action by the *tozama*, who now saw themselves as having all to lose or all to gain. Initially Kōmei's death strengthened the hand of Yoshinobu: by making the death of the emperor an excuse to abandon the campaign against Choshu, he put himself in the favourable position of seeming to end the shogunal military menace to the *tozama*, and of becoming the somewhat unconvincing backer of the concept of a confederation. Precisely for these reasons, the *tozama* leaders saw the dangers of a more powerful shogun manipulating a new and puppet emperor. In the absence of any accommodation between the shogunate and the *tozama*, that would mean that Yoshinobu's policies could continue, and through the emperor's dependence on the shogun, legitimacy would be conferred on what would be in effect a new constitution. Moreover, in contrast to the han, the shogunate gained by the fact that it was the sole regular centre of high-level contacts with foreigners. The view in the older historiography that the English at this stage were anti-bakufu, and favoured Satsuma, is now generally considered incorrect. In June 1866 they were to the fore in negotiating a rounding of the duties at large to five per cent and to streamlining customs procedures (arguing that the revenue from trade would strengthen the shogunate). The key concern of Parkes was to ensure that British influence on the shogunate was not replaced by French, and Parkes offered assistance with the development of a navy and with the opening of an educational academy.[82]

The advent of a new emperor, and of a new shogun, Yoshinobu, intent on taking over the wealth of Osaka, meant both that there were no imperial misgivings (such as those held by Kōmei) about the opening of its outport to contend with, and that it was possible to disregard the undertaking months earlier to make the issue await the decision of a meeting of daimyo. In April 1867, the novice emperor, under the rising influence of Yoshinobu, gave his consent for the opening of Hyogo. Saigō, the han activist who most attached importance to the Osaka question, was taken by surprise by the news. With the treaties approved in some form from the end of 1865, and confirmed beyond all doubt in early 1867, the danger of an enriched bakufu gave urgency to defining the relationship between han and shogun. The shogunate, having at last overcome

---

[81] Yates, *Saigo Takamori*, p.93.
[82] On Britain's role in the development of the navy, see Ikeda Kiyoshi, 'The Douglas mission and British influence on the Japanese navy', in S. Henry and J.-P. Lehman (eds.), *Themes and theories in modern Japanese history: essays in memory of Richard Storry* (London, 1988), pp.171–84.

formal opposition to the opening shortly of Hyogo, now planned to put the trade of Osaka and Hyogo (Kobe) in the hands of a guild of twenty merchants,[83] a proposal which alarmed foreigners and *tozama* alike. The opening of the ports became the central shogunate–han divide. It was, moreover, less one on the opening of the ports per se, than of who would benefit from their new trade. If precedent prevailed, their revenue would go to the shogunate, and with increased revenue the shogunate's policy could be more forceful. Or so the han reasoned, and in 1867 Satow, interpreter to the British legation, knowing the attitude of the han, played on Saigō's fears.[84] In the course of the 1865 negotiations, the British had at one stage pressed for the ports to be opened in 1866, in other words at an earlier date than the agreed deferred date of 1868: at the time that approach endangered the emerging English–Satsuma rapprochement.

All the major han were resentful of the shogun's monopoly of port towns. The trade issue had been a reason for a change in Choshu's stance by 1863.[85] Even Kaga, politically not a confrontational han, shared this concern. At a later date, it opposed the proposed opening of Nanao as a trading port (Niigata, a port to the north of Kaga, designated in the treaties, was a poor one in navigational terms) since if the port were approved for foreign trade, it was likely to be taken into shogunal management.[86] As Satsuma expressed its outlook in Saigō's words in regard to Osaka in 1867, 'we want it to be opened so as to be a benefit to Japan, and not solely for the private advantage of the bakufu'. It should become a national, not a shogunal, concern,

by placing all questions regarding Hiogo in the hands of a committee of 5 or 6 daimios [sic] who would be able to prevent the Bakufu from acting exclusively for its own selfish interests. Hiogo is very important to us. We all owe money to the Osaka merchants, and we have to send the products of our provinces to them every year in payment of our debts. Our affairs will be thrown out of order if the place is opened on the same plan as Yokohama.[87]

The simmering internal crisis came quickly to a head once, in quick succession, a boy shogun was replaced by a forceful figure, and the experienced emperor, Kōmei, alive to the interests of the han, by a boy emperor. As the *tozama* had assumed implicitly that the issues of authority would be resolved before a succession arose and that time was therefore on their side, two deaths shortened the timescale: the spectre of a successful establishment of a more unitary and stronger shogunal government became imminent. The emperor too (whose importance had increased

---

[83] Satow, *A diplomat in Japan*, pp.256, 267.
[84] Satow, *A diplomat in Japan*, p.200.   [85] Satow, *A diplomat in Japan*, p.99.
[86] Satow, *A diplomat in Japan*, pp.236–7.   [87] Satow, *A diplomat in Japan*, pp.183–4.

less because of an 'imperial' philosophy in Japan than because delicate issues of defence and of shifting balance of power made the concept of emperor into a symbol of national unity) would by virtue of Yoshinobu's role become wedded to a shogunate, shortly to be invigorated financially by a trade centred on Osaka/Hyogo from 1 January 1868.

While the idea of a confederacy of han has often been attributed to Ernest Satow (1843–1929), the English diplomat, in negotiations over the opening of the port of Osaka, the concept had originated a few years before among a number of Japanese, both from *tozama* and from within the shogunate itself. Before his assassination, even Ii Naosuke had in mind alliances with daimyo as a means of strengthening the faltering regime. In 1867 there was still no general agreement among *tozama* on how the bakufu (shogunate) should be dealt with, and equally within han boundaries, even in Satsuma, there were shades of opinion. Whether a shogun should remain as a head of a confederated empire, whether he should be reduced in effect to the status of a large daimyo (given the extent of bakufu lands he would of course be the richest, and hence, the leading, daimyo), or whether he should be stripped of power and wealth alike, were all questions on which between and in han there was diversity in opinion.[88] The alliance of Satsuma and Choshu, however, created a political force which, the necessity arising, could move more quickly and decisively than either the loose, incomplete and divided alliance of several large *tozama* which already existed or the bakufu itself in its attempted sponsorship of a shogun-led coalition of han. The combined military resources of the two han also outweighed those of the shogun. The forces for the Choshu expedition had been drawn exclusively from the *fudai*: the build-up was painfully slow, pointing both to bakufu weakness and *fudai* hesitancies alike.

The idea of confederacy, attractive and abroad for several years as an inchoate principle, in 1867 was less a substantive issue than a tactical one. Yoshinobu, having already stolen a march on the *tozama* by securing imperial approval for the opening of Hyogo without deferring to them, saw the proposal as a means of buying time, believing that daimyo when they met in numbers in an assembly at his summons would not only not find common ground but would be outnumbered by the *fudai* supporters of the shogunate. For the two most powerful *tozama*, Choshu and Satsuma, the delays in summoning a daimyo council provided cover for widening their tortuous consultations with the daimyo and high samurai officials of

---

[88] Yamauchi Yōdo, the daimyo of the *tozama* han of Tosa, while favouring change, was less enthusiastic for radical change than Satsuma or Choshu, though one of his principal officials, Itagaki Taisuke, maintained close ties with the southern *tozama* (Shiba, *Le dernier shogun*, p.196).

other han. The secret contacts took shogun and foreign diplomats alike by surprise when events later in the year brought them to light. It was, of course, the comparative ease of co-ordinating Choshu and Satsuma intentions that made speedy action possible. The stakes had been raised by the evidence of a shogunal military build-up (which France was helping to provide and which might come also from the British[89]), and through the fear of shogunal enrichment from the imminent opening of Osaka. The *kuge* or nobles around the emperor were feeble in political perceptions, apart from Iwakura who, long detained because of his radical views, was released after the death of the old emperor, and became a close confidant of the Choshu and Satsuma officials.[90] In the power vacuum, the case for swift action was increasingly strong (Iwakura vacillated as the moment approached, and it was Satsuma and Choshu which gambled on the likely success of action).

On 8 November authority was given in two separate orders to the two han to overthrow the bakufu.[91] What precisely that entailed was itself not clear, and could be interpreted more as a reduction in the status of the shogun than of outright deposition. Before the han could put the decrees into effect, Yoshinobu surrendered his authority as shogun (but neither his lands nor his imperial titles of honour which were the symbol of his 'legitimacy') to the emperor, counting on support from many han and on the prospect of reappointment on new terms. There followed two months of uncertainty as to the implications both of the shogun's resignation of his power, and of the imperial order. The still real role of the shogun is shown in the fact that he continued to handle the foreign relations of Japan. However, surrender of his trust to the emperor put his opponents at a tactical advantage, especially given the fact that a small circle of Choshu and Satsuma men along with Iwakura had a clear idea of their aims.

The future governance of Japan would have been even more complicated if a diminished figure, still rich in acres and in status, was retained in the polity. The end of the year 1867 was one of unfolding drama. Foreign fleets assembled in Osaka bay, with a touch of menace as well as

---

[89] In February 1867 the shogunate also sent two representatives to the United States to purchase warships. Medzini, *French policy in Japan*, p.151.

[90] Satow is misleading in suggesting that radical views were held by 'many of the court nobles' (*A diplomat in Japan*, p.189); it is in reality a reference simply to Iwakura, a courtier of low rank and the only man of vision among them. Members of the imperial court, however, shared the views of other Japanese on defence issues. As emperor Kōmei was a mere boy at his ascent in 1846, the concern in that year was obviously of the court, not of the emperor himself. In later years members of the court displayed both support for and opposition to concession. Donald Keene's *Emperor of Japan* has interesting detail on both Kōmei and his circle of courtiers, though one may disagree with his view of the quality of their views.

[91] Yates, *Saigo Takamori*, p.102.

welcome, for the opening of the port of Hyogo on 1 January 1868; at the same time armies, principally Choshu and Satsuma forces, were advancing on Kyoto. Outright abolition of the shogunate, ignoring both the wide variety of opinion on the subject and the uncertainty about what would replace it, was the simplest option. On 4 January the shogunal palace was occupied and a decree issued unambiguously terminating the shogunate. This was swiftly followed by an order stripping the shogun of all his lands and titles. When Roches and Parkes saw the shogun on 8 January, he said that he had resigned on the basis of deferring matters to a future constitutional meeting of daimyo, and he rejected the order ending the shogunate on the grounds that the emperor did not hold the power to do so.[92] Yoshinobu did not have stomach for a fight, largely because the military options were stacked against him, and it is likely that he might have made peace immediately if he had been allowed to hold on to his lands. Withdrawing from Osaka (its great castle in flames), and defeated at Fushimi on 27 January, he retreated to Edo. Edo castle was surrendered on 3 May. Yoshinobu, living first in Mito and then in Shizuoka, withdrew into private life. In doing so he yielded his position, and in the new regime survived as a prince.[93]

Control of the emperor through the presence of their forces in Kyoto combined with Yoshinobu's serious miscalculation about the likely course of events (he claimed to the diplomats that he had been deceived[94]) meant that the *tozama* forces easily won the first round. Yoshinobu's readiness after his initial defeat to take no further action did, however, save Japan from serious civil war. For that moderation rather than for his actions before and after becoming shogun to strengthen the ailing shogunate, he deserves an honoured place in history. Some supporters of the shogunate were less ready to give up. There were battles in the Ueno district of Edo, later in the northern *fudai* han of Aizu which had loyally supported Edo in the 1860s,[95] and in lingering and feeble fashion a year later in 1869 in Ezo (Hokkaido). The Hokkaido episode had the interesting incidental detail that some of the shogun's French officers chose to fight with the remnants of his forces.[96]

---

[92] Daniels, *Sir Harry Parkes*, p.72. On Roches' later meetings with him, see Medzini, *French policy in Japan*, pp.167–8.

[93] For an interesting account by one of Yoshinobu's granddaughters, see Sakakibara Kisako, *Tokugawa Yoshinobu-ke no kodomo-beya* [The children's quarters in the Tokugawa Yoshinobu household] (Tokyo, 1996). On the historiography of Yoshinobu, see also Totman, *Collapse of the Tokugawa bakufu*, pp.563–4.

[94] Satow, *A diplomat in Japan*, p.301.

[95] On the bitter memories of the defeated Aizu clan, see Mahito Ishimitsu (ed.), *Remembering Aizu: the testament of Shiba Goro*, translated by Teruko Craig (Honolulu, 1999).

[96] Sims, *French policy towards the bakufu*, pp.78–82.

The new men, not being at heart partisans of an open Japan, had no intention of simply endorsing the principles of the treaties. The idea of concessions as a necessary but temporary measure remained alive, even if no longer in the simplistic sense of restoring sakoku (either outright or in the less complete form of a trade conducted in a few remote ports). Nor was restoration of emperor the aim in 1868. Behind the formal concept of restoration, it was the victory of samurai of four han, pre-eminently the two militarily powerful han, Choshu and Satsuma, and secondarily Saga and Tosa, who had spearheaded the onslaught on the shogunate. These han acquired authority rather as the Tokugawa had acquired it in 1600 through a combination of military force, and deployment of the emperor as the fig leaf of legitimacy for a new regime. What emerged was in effect a second bakufu, characterised at one level by an ambiguous legitimacy under the fiction of imperial restoration, and at another level by dominance in government of four han which had acted with more vigour than the others. Beyond the ideas of their surviving in power and of keeping Japan out of the hands of foreigners, the political men of early Meiji times lacked common ground among themselves. Moderation in the style of the Tokugawa shogunate itself would finally save the new Japan from challenge by internal rivals, but it would not of itself create in constitutional terms a modern state. It would take all of twenty-one years for that to come about.

7   Fashioning a state and a foreign policy: Japan 1868–1919

The regime's collapse of the 1860s was set in motion by outside events, and, once the immediate crisis was over, immobilism was in danger of reasserting itself. In 1869 an assembly of representatives of the han, while showing opposition to the shogunate and support for the ideals of Mito and the southern *tozama*, by addressing itself first to peripheral issues proved an ineffective body.[1] Constitutional change was from the outset to test the patience of those outside the circle of early political decision makers. In such a context the burning sense of injustice inherent in the inequality imposed on Japan by the treaties was an essential ingredient for maintaining consensus. Public opinion, increasingly well-defined and shaped by a press, contributed powerfully in the 1880s to defining the moods of a new Japan. The abortive efforts of the 1870s to renegotiate the treaties were followed by overt foot-dragging from the treaty nations in the 1880s. Japanese nationalism in the modern sense of the term, a very vague concept in Tokugawa times, was really born in this period.[2]

Even before the immediate problems of the Restoration had been dealt with, the Iwakura mission, taking with it half of the important political figures of the Restoration including Ōkubo Toshimichi (1830–78), Itō and Kido went abroad for the years 1871–3 (so conscious were they of the risks inherent in so many going that they sought an undertaking from those remaining not to take major decisions).[3] The mission brought with it some fifty young men who were to study abroad. Its purpose was to renegotiate the treaties, as review of the original treaties was possible

---

[1] *PP Japan*, vol. 2, pp.652–8, Summary of events in Japan during the year 1869. For a good account of events in 1869–71, see A. M. Craig, 'The central goverment', in Jansen and Rozman, *Japan in transition*, pp.48–58.
[2] Mitani, *Meiji ishin to nashonarizumu*.
[3] I. Nish, *The Iwakura mission in America and England: a new assessment* (Richmond, Surrey, 1998); Beasley, *Japan encounters the barbarian*, pp.157–77. The report of the secretary of the mission, Kume Kunitake, has been translated recently into English. It makes extensive and fascinating reading. See *The Iwakura embassy, 1871–73: a true account of the ambassador extraordinary and plenipotentiary's journey of observation . . . compiled by Kume Kunitake*, ed. Graham Healey and Chushichi Tsuzuki, 5 vols. (Tokyo, 2002).

from 1872. Though the effort failed, an indirect result was, after years of negotiation, a separate treaty with the United States in 1878, whereby the points in dispute were conceded. However, as the sting in the tail, it was not to enter into force until all the other treaty countries had conceded their old 'treaty' rights. Japanese diplomacy succeeded in bringing together general conferences of its treaty partners in Tokyo in 1882 and again in 1886–7. On both occasions the effort was frustrated by resistance from some countries, in 1882 notably from Harry Parkes, British minister in Tokyo, and the protracted 1886–7 conference was postponed *sine die*. In 1886 an increasingly restive public opinion was coloured also by an incident which seemed to underline inequality in stark terms: a passenger vessel foundered in Japanese waters; all the Japanese passengers drowned, but none of the English crew lost their lives. The English consular court in Kobe later exonerated the crew of charges of criminal negligence.[4] Despairing of general negotiation, Japan reversed policy in 1889 and began a process of negotiating separate treaties with individual countries. The new treaties, however, still specified a separate provision of justice for foreigners. Public opinion, embittered by the events of the 1880s and less conciliatory than its politicians, was more opposed than Japanese negotiators were to paying a relatively high price.[5] The year 1889 has been described 'as a turning point in modern Japanese history'. Ōkuma Shigenobu (1838–1922), the foreign minister, had a leg blown off in an explosion. An attack was made on the czarevitch of Russia on a visit to Japan in 1891. As a result of the unpopularity of the treaties (they were opposed even by Gustave Emile Boissonade de Fontarabie (1829–1910),[6] the French expert who had been retained in 1873 to superintend the modernisation of Japanese law), they were not ratified by the first elected Japanese parliament in 1890.

The 1894 general election was fought on the treaty issue. Public opposition to concession strengthened the hand of the Japanese government. So did the cumulative effect of the changes which had intervened since 1868, and which, in the wake of the Iwakura mission, purposely sought to model Japanese legal structures on a western pattern. One of the conclusions of the mission had been that if Japan were to wring concessions

[4] J.-P. Lehmann, *The roots of modern Japan* (London, 1982), p.293; Sakamoto Takao, *Nihon no kindai* [Modern Japan], vol.2, *Meiji kokka no kensetsu 1871–1890* [The foundation of the Meiji state] (Tokyo, 1999), pp.315–16; S. Hirakawa, 'Japan's turn to the west', *CHJ*, vol. 5 (1989), p.488.

[5] On the wider aspects of popular concern, see chapter 5, 'Treaty revision and self-determination', in K. P. Pyle, *The new generation in Meiji Japan* (Stanford, 1969), pp.99–117.

[6] On the role over twenty-one years of the Frenchman Gustave Emile Boissonade de Fontarabie, see Sims, *French policy towards the bakufu*, pp.261–79.

from the west, it would have to create institutions recognisably like western ones and hence reassuring to outsiders. Codes of criminal law and of practices for criminal courts were adopted in 1882. Progress with criminal law was of course straightforward, as all were in agreement on the protection of the community against crime. Civil law was more difficult as it affected delicate areas of marriage and property. Hence a draft code, ready in 1879, had to be redrafted, and in turn a redraft of 1889 after a tortuous passage was adopted only in 1898. However, procedures for the civil courts had already been implemented by 1890, and finalisation of the law code itself was in sight. From 1894, diplomatic acquiescence from other countries (made possible by these developments) resulted in new treaties radically different from those envisaged in previous negotiations. The old treaty extraterritorial rights were to be ceded within five years. In return foreigners could reside throughout Japan, and enjoy widespread rights: excluded were only the purchase of land and, if agriculture or mining were the object, its leasing. Japanese freedom in settling customs duties would become complete from 1911. The concessions were prompted more by diplomatic considerations than by any corresponding readiness on the part of foreign residents. Their views are neatly illustrated in the irascible comments of the English scholar, Basil Hall Chamberlain (1850–1935):

From the point of view of patriotic Englishmen, the foreign residents in Japan (that is, the class which possess the best knowledge of the state of the case) almost unanimously regard the British Foreign Office with contempt, for having allowed itself to be so grossly misled and roundly beaten.[7]

A consensus in opposition to the unequal treaties, while creating a sense of national unity, was of no help directly in advancing concrete decisions on internal political structures. The new pattern of authority in 1868 rather repeated the pattern of Tokugawa power two centuries before: de facto government by four han within a legally ambiguous framework. The lack of momentum in creating new constitutional structures contrasted with the rapidity of purely administrative changes. A national system of education was quickly created (easily achieved as it harked back to a desire expressed in writings from the time of Nakai Chikuzan in the 1780s); the old han administrations were replaced in 1879–80 by prefectures, and new assemblies in prefectures and townships were, moreover, elective. Samurai in a matter of a few years lost their legal status. This was not of itself difficult, as ideas expressed in late Tokugawa writing and changing

---

[7] B. H. Chamberlain, *Things Japanese, being notes on various subjects connected with Japan for the use of travellers and others* (revised 1905 edn), p.496. In the Tuttle, 1980, reprint edition the title is inverted from the original to '*Japanese things*'.

practices in han as far apart and as conservative as Choshu and Mito had pointed to ways in which samurai status was beginning to lose its exclusive appeal. Japan's first national army emerged: it was national in that all male citizens were, if selected by ballot, obliged to serve. Citizens could, however, buy themselves out, which meant that the army quickly became identified with poor regions, and the balance of its composition shifted from west to east. The first generation of officers, however, came predominantly from Choshu and Satsuma. It was a small army: its effective size was a mere 33,544 men in 1877,[8] a tiny figure for a country of 33 million, facing a hostile outside environment. Meiji Japan was a society of school teachers and postmen rather than soldiers. Either lack of urge or financial inability held back any tendency to militarise Japanese society: the consequence was that early Meiji Japan perpetuated the non-military character of Tokugawa society, virtually the only country in the world to have been at peace for two and a half centuries.

The government, fortunately perhaps, as it proved in the short term incapable of the constitutional change necessary to legitimise sweeping reform, was constricted in its ambitions by acute fiscal constraints. This was despite the fact that it was richer than any Japanese government in history. The old land levy (the so-called 'rice tax') was turned into a real tax payable by all occupiers of land. It was the first national tax. In contrast to the shogunal administration of Tokugawa times, which held only a quarter of the land of Japan even if *tenryō* and lands allocated to its hatamoto lands are combined (and received a share of rice output solely on *tenryō* lands[9]), the new government received an income from all of Japan. In other words, it was from the outset far richer than the shogunate had ever been. However, there were real fiscal constraints. The most immediate was that heavy expenditure was incurred in compensation to daimyo and samurai. Daimyo were dealt with handsomely (essential if acquiescence for a new regime set up on a doubtful legal basis from daimyo lords, most of whom – the powerful southern *tozama* apart – had no say, direct or indirect, in the outcome was to be secured). Not only did they soon become the legal aristocracy of the new Japan (a sharp contrast with the samurai's loss of legal status) but, though free from public demands on their purse, they were given generous pensions amounting to ten per cent of their former gross revenues. Samurai likewise were provided with pensions. In 1874 pensions amounted to forty per cent of public expenditure. Faced with so much of the revenue being swallowed, the new state

---

[8] Tobe Ryōichi, *Nihon no kindai* [Modern Japan], vol. 9, *Gyakusetsu no guntai* [The paradox of the army] (Tokyo, 1998), p.106.

[9] The levy was of the order of forty per cent of the official valuation; but in favoured instances was said to be as little as twenty per cent of actual gross output.

at the outset faced a fiscal crisis. Samurai pensions were replaced from 1876 less generously by their capitalisation in a complex operation in which public liability was reduced in part by cash payments, in part by interest-paying bonds.

The new leaders had inherited no meaningful system of taxation. The effective burden of the new land tax was not much different from the old land 'tax': first pitched at three per cent of the capitalised value of land, it had to be quickly reduced to two and a half per cent.[10] In 1874 the land tax provided eighty-three per cent of revenue; other sources of revenue were few; and widespread innovation by a state with weak legal authority would have encountered resistance (the fact that the *ikki* of late Tokugawa Japan were prompted by resistance to fiscal innovation was painfully fresh in the mind of the first generation of administrators). Next to the land tax, the only source with a large yield proved to be the tax on sake. Foreign trade created a very small income to the state, as the treaties limited customs duties to five per cent. These circumstances acted as a constraint on creating an army, developing Ezo (a region which had defence implications) and supporting infrastructural and industrial development.

The daimyo, as already mentioned, were treated generously in the new Japan. This was not only the case financially but they (along with court nobles) also remained a prominent group in the new, and in other respects, plebeian aristocracy that the new regime created. The samurai fared less well, both economically, and even more in their entire loss of status, legal and social. At the outset, as an ominous sign of the change, the regime opted for a conscript army rather than for a samurai army. Their economic condition, hardly rosy before 1868, worsened; and an existing pattern of engaging in socially lower employments became more marked. If some fared better, it was by the exercise of initiative in striking out in novel directions (a consequence of individual choice, and not of the special motivation often painted for the samurai as a class). Samurai discontent in regions where samurai had been numerous, hence largely in the south, was a factor in the various risings of the 1870s (of which only one, in the most samurai-rich han of all, was militarily serious). This discontent, in its search for a role in the new state, was a factor behind the rise of the political parties; and some samurai, given a tradition of commentary on public affairs, helped to account for the vigour of the new press. Nor was discontent non-productive in a historical sense. Japan's rulers were well aware of it, and this awareness accounted for the fact

---

[10] On the tax, the best introduction in English is Kozo Yamamura, 'The Meiji land tax reform and its effects', in Jansen and Rozman, *Japan in transition*, pp.382–99.

that, even if progress was slow, there was no urge to turn back from the commitment to the creation of a participatory public life. Japan was already highly commercialised in 1868. Entrepreneurs on a substantial scale existed, supplying distant markets within the country (sake, Japan's alcoholic drink, meriting the accolade of early fiscal attention as a revenue earner); a well-developed putting out system in textiles outside the *jōkamachi* (castle towns) had deepening roots in late Tokugawa times; and the great business conglomerates of Meiji Japan, the *zaibatsu*, originated from Tokugawa models. The scale of such houses had been due to the concentrated nature of business through the marketing of rice in Osaka by daimyo and in turn their heavy demand for credit and foreign exchange. In the financial difficulties of Japan in the 1860s some houses failed. Four of the great houses, Kōnoike, Sumitomo and Masuya (all Osaka) and Mitsui (Edo and Kyoto) survived. Iwasaki Yatarō's Mitsubishi can date its origins to the years just before the Restoration. The house of Yasuda followed later. The activities of these ranged – with some difference in pattern from house to house – through trade, banking, manufacturing and shipping. Political contacts helped, as in acquiring early steam ship contracts for instance, but success was due primarily to the possession of capital, and in all cases, old or new, to sheer opportunism. They were also beneficiaries from the forced sale by the government in the 1880s deflation (the so-called Matsukata deflation) of its early industrial enterprises. Japan's rapid and concentrated growth in the 1910s crucially helped their deepening and diversification, especially into manufacturing.

Japan's entrepreneurs at large did not need government incentives or subsidies, and the state in any event was poorly equipped to supply them. They were moreover motivated by an urge for profit, not by a special ethic (of samurai origin) often attributed to them or stressed in their own self-regarding accounts of their careers.[11] Of course, the bigger businesses developed ties with politicians (the *zaibatsu* in particular sided with one or other of the parties) who had contracts to hand out. From the start, political corruption was a problem. Saigō, in every respect the Garibaldi of

---

[11] On Japanese entrepreneurship, see Kozo Yamamura's study of Yasuda, 'A re-examination of entrepreneurship in Meiji Japan 1868–1912', *Economic history review*, 2nd series, vol. 21, no. 1 (April 1968), pp.144–58. See also his comment that 'the end results were often explanations and descriptions which rarely provided anything more useful than the undefined "spirit of samurai" and a tiresome emphasis on Confucian ethics', in 'Entrepreneurship, ownership and management in Japan', in Kozo Yamamura (ed.), *The economic emergence of modern Japan* (Cambridge, 1997), p.295. Some authors have, however, stressed the importance of the state's role (e.g. T. C. Smith, *Political change and industrial development in Japan: government enterprise, 1868–1880* (Stanford, 1955)), though this has been contested, and it was less true of the years from the early 1880s when the early enterprises had been sold.

Japan, when he resigned in 1873 was already concerned at corruption.[12] Edo, with its many daimyo *yashiki* (residences) and temples, had been a city of gardens, and a metropolis of open spaces and beauty.[13] The sale of property, though not unknown, was very restricted in Tokugawa times: in the towns samurai residences, temples and daimyo or shogunal property effectively sterilised huge amounts of land: the absence in the past of a market in sites or land meant that, once total freedom of sale emerged in the Meiji era, social and public restraints such as existed in the west were totally lacking.[14] Unbridled development and speculation followed from 1868, Tokyo becoming a cramped, overbuilt city instead of the garden city it had been. All this change was not divorced from the acquiescence and support of political circles: the first generation of politicians on small salaries seem to have ended their lives as rich men.[15] Ōkuma's name was surrounded in his early political career by scandal, and much later in the inter-war years, the self-seeking repute of politicians was a potent asset to the antidemocratic and militarist attackers of the political system.

Output expanded from early Meiji times. The elasticity of supply of tea and silk is one example of this. Tea output centred on eastern Japan, especially in and around Shizuoka; silk output in more recent times had expanded in the upland region to the north of the Tokyo plain. The progress of tea and silk in the second half of the Tokugawa era had been a result both of refinement of existing skills, and of growing consumer demand. The commercial ability (much of it derived from the business acumen of Tokugawa times) evident in so many activities made it easy also for modern industry to make headway, once an export trade financed imports of cotton or once new technologies were introduced. Moreover, as far as expansion of its cotton textile industry was concerned, the real strength of Japan was not the external market, but the huge internal market. Population, accelerating only slowly before the Meiji Restoration, grew by fifty per cent between 1872 and 1914. Though rapid, this was not in itself an exceptional rise: it compared more or less with trends in western Europe. The real significance of a rise in population was that, taken together with some rise in real incomes, it represented virtually a

---

[12] Yates, *Saigo Takamori*, p.131.

[13] The vice-consul at Yokohama, observing that the daimyo *yashiki* were dilapidated or abandoned, noted that many were in grounds of 20 to 30 acres, and that individual daimyo possessed as many as six properties. *PP Japan*, vol. 5, p.65, Report by vice-consul at Yokohama, pp.51–70.

[14] Kawakatsu Heita, *Fukoku no yūtoku ron* [An essay on civility for a wealthy country] (Tokyo, 2000), pp.52–5.

[15] For an interesting account of the life style of Matsukata, former prime minister and *genrō*, and his family, see Haru Matsukata Reischauer, *Samurai and silk: a Japanese and American heritage* (Tokyo, 1987), pp.101, 104–8, 117–19, 141.

doubling of the effective domestic market. In Meiji Japan, as in the Japan of the 1970s and 1980s, exports hovered around the relatively low rate of ten per cent of national income: the driving force of economic expansion was the home market.[16] One consequence was the renewed growth of Osaka: much business had passed in late Tokugawa times to new intermediaries in its own hinterland, and in early Meiji times to Yokohama which became the main centre of export trade. However, Osaka was able to enlarge its industrial role: always a trade centre, it now became the main location of the factory cotton textile industry. Moreover, while foreign trade was still in the hands of outsiders, the factory textile industry was a native enterprise. It reflected both a maturing of indigenous enterprise, and a new dynamism of the Osaka region. In the 1890s, the trade of Osaka (or more accurately of its outport Kobe, formerly known as Hyogo) came to equal the volume of foreign trade conducted in Yokohama.[17] The rise in incomes in Japan was particularly noticeable in the 1890s, and was evident even in poor rural areas. The perceptive reports from British consuls noted the change, and the quickened pace of industrialisation and its spread from textiles to iron working, engineering and consumer goods at large drew, in the first instance, on the internal market: only later did exports begin to become significant. Some goods such as mechanical toys, paper goods and printed matter such as postcards made a world-wide appearance at an early date, partly because they were cheap but equally because they were not greatly inferior to western goods and sometimes their equal or even superior.

Modern industrialisation depended on imports of raw materials. Imports came largely from Asia, either directly from British India, or from Shanghai as a gathering point for much of the trade of the orient, and in the foreign community (even in the case of the British community, the largest expatriate one in Meiji Japan) Chinese heavily outnumbered other nationalities, thus perpetuating or – more accurately – reconstructing a pattern of Tokugawa times in Nagasaki. The trade imbalances of the 1860s, caused by war within Japan and bad harvests, were quickly righted. Exports then rose more rapidly than imports: given the imperfections of early statistics, the early imbalance may have been overstated. The robustness of the new economy lay in its elastic exports, which were essential to finance imports, and which ensured that reliance on foreign capital was slight except in the very first years or much later in the

---

[16] This is not true of the First World War period when exports soared almost effortlessly, or of the 1930s when a rise in exports (though much less sharp than the earlier one) and depressed rural incomes made exports into a more important determinant of income.

[17] H. D. Smith, 'The Edo-Tokyo transition: in search of common ground', in Jansen and Rozman, *Japan in transition*, p.353.

exceptional circumstances of the Russian war in 1904–5 and its aftermath. The strength of the export trade lay not in new products (cotton yarn began to appear only in the 1880s and cotton cloth in the 1890s and at first in modest quantities), but in traditional products such as tea and silk. As early as 1862 the British consular report from Kanagawa had noted that 'the rapid development in the exportation of this valuable staple [silk] at this port is unprecedented in the east'.[18] The export of silk at the outset was prompted by the crisis in the European silk industry, caused by silkworm disease: in the long term, however, the United States was the main market. The success of silk was also helped by the fact that in the western countries, per capita consumption of silk grew more rapidly than that of any other natural fibre from 1875–7 to 1927–9.[19] Tea was slower at first, but its export then expanded rapidly. Again, and despite rising tea output elsewhere in Asia which was taken by the growing Russian and British markets, it captured the American market.

Thus Japan's ability to fuel its expansion and to pay for the raw materials essential for industrialisation depended on two traditional staple products and on their disposal on what was an entirely new market in the hinterland of what had been the tiny coastal strip of the 'thirteen colonies' of pre-1776 American history. In other words, Japan's export trade depended less on the ending of sakoku itself than on the contemporaneous expansion of the United States. This outcome was in part a consequence of United States trade expansion in the Pacific Ocean once it acquired a Pacific coastline in 1848; headlong population growth and railway building followed to create a huge national market. Had this market not emerged, the effects of the ending by Japan of sakoku would have been modest; the expansion of trade would have been painful, and would have imposed rigid limits on imports and hence on modern industrialisation. Japan has often suffered misfortunes in its history. On this occasion at least the fates were singularly kind. Elastic exports were not foreseen in the 1860s, and the future seemed to lie, in the belief of westerners, in agricultural produce from the relatively underpopulated Tohoku and Hokkaido. In the mid-1870s, Harry Parkes, repeating the error of Honda Toshiaki almost a century previously, saw Japan's future as lying in the creation of agricultural surpluses, rice and in Hokkaido, wheat.[20] Exports soared fourfold up to the early 1890s; tea and raw silk combined accounted for seventy to seventy-five per cent of the

---

[18] *PP Japan*, vol.4, p.45, Report on Kanagawa for 1862. Giovanni Federico noted in *An economic history of the silk industry* that 'Japan began therefore to trade with the west at the best possible time' (p.40).
[19] Federico, *Economic history of the silk industry*, p.43.
[20] *PP Japan*, vol. 5, pp.671–2, 18 July 1876, Report on trade of Japan for 1875.

total.[21] Economic diversification as measured by the importance of non-traditional industry in GDP was therefore slight before the 1890s. Manufactured exports were a mere 8 per cent of the total as late as 1888–93, though a healthier 17.3 per cent in 1898–1902 reflected the stirrings of industrialisation.

If Japan's elastic foreign trade was one factor accounting for Meiji success, an equally important one was self-sufficiency in agriculture. Normally there was a surplus in rice. While the bad harvests of 1865 and 1866 led to novel rice imports, the future pattern was normally of surplus, at times a large one. In Osaka, still behind Yokohama as an export centre (as its new industrial goods did not begin to find foreign markets till after 1890), rice was usually the second largest export. In 1888, because of huge exports of 155,000 tons (c.1 million koku), it was the port's largest export.[22] Thus Japan not only had no need of food imports but in most years had an export income, small or large, from rice. As part of its good fortune, in the quarter century following the Meiji Restoration, weather conditions cannot have fallen far short of the legendary Bunka years (1804–18), and for a population almost twice the size. Some years of course fell below the norm, especially in the Tohoku.[23] But only the protracted monsoon of 1889, with severe flooding in much of Japan, led to widespread and severe shortage.

With harvest failures in 1865–6, coastal shipments to Hyogo had contracted dramatically in 1866 to as little as a quarter of their normal level.[24] More strikingly still, some imports from abroad took place in the ports open for foreign trade. For the first time since the port was fully opened to foreign trade in 1859, a significant quantity of rice was imported to Nagasaki.[25] In 1867 at Kanagawa 500,000 koku were imported.[26] In the

---

[21] The British Parliamentary Papers provide the best evidence of early Japanese trade, both through information collected by the consuls and through the data on exports from Shanghai. Japanese trade statistics did not become regular and reliable until the mid-1870s. For a succinct and readable account of Meiji Japanese trade, see Christopher Howe, *The origins of Japanese trade supremacy: development and technology in Asia from 1540 to the Pacific war* (London, 1996), pp.90–100. On Meiji trade statistics, apart from the many comments in the Parliamentary Papers, see Nishikawa, Odaka and Saitō, *Nihon keizai no 200 nen*, pp.174–6.

[22] *PP Japan*, vol. 8, p.386, Foreign trade of Hyogo and Osaka in 1888.

[23] The heavy monsoon of 1878 is well recorded in Isabella Bird's account of her journey in that year in the Tohoku (*Unbeaten tracks in Japan*): she seems to have been oblivious to the quite singular nature of the weather, a tribute either to her considerable fortitude or to a crashing insensitivity she also displayed.

[24] See chapter 3, p.83.

[25] *PP Japan*, vol. 4, p.226, Consular report on trade of Nagasaki for 1866.

[26] *PP Japan*, vol. 4, p.328, Consul Fletcher to Sir Harry Parkes, Kanagawa, 31 May 1868. Rice was not included in such trade returns as existed in the Japanese ports at this time, and the estimate was based on various figures by the British consuls. The preciseness of the estimate may be suspect. For Hyogo, see *PP Japan*, vol. 4, p.275.

better organised trade of later years, imported quantities could be much higher in the event of domestic shortfall: in the half year to June 1890 in Osaka they exceeded 100,000 tons (700,000 koku).[27] Imports would compensate for only part of a shortfall of twenty per cent or more in the normal harvest in Meiji times of 36 million koku or so. Yet no famine resulted. The countryside itself was changing, partly as a result of further commercialisation, and by the growth of a more differentiated social structure. In particular, the larger farmers were becoming richer and were often involved more directly in marketing. They invested in land, often by foreclosing on mortgages, and also invested in industry.[28] Tenancies had become more common, though the landlords of tenants were usually themselves working farmers, residing in the countryside. The outflow of labour, long a marked feature of advanced regions like the Kinki, became geographically more widespread and in contrast to the migration of Tokugawa times, often followed by return some years later to home districts, it was permanent. Low though wages were in the textile industry and stern the discipline in factory dormitories, they acted like a magnet for many rural girls.[29] The Tohoku still lagged behind other regions, a situation not helped by a rise in its birth rates throughout the Meiji period.

Birth rates generally rose in the Meiji period. While the rise is partly a mere reflection of better statistical information, it was also in part a real rise, promoted by improved economic circumstances and wider outlets offered by migration. However, in the prefectures of the more developed centre and south of Japan, throughout they remained stable and low compared with the Tohoku. In Aomori in the Tohoku the crude birth rate was 43.2 per 1,000 in 1908, while it was a mere 33.4 per 1,000 in Osaka in the same year.[30] The infant mortality rate, a good indicator of living conditions, was possibly in the region of 176 per 1,000 in 1750–1870 and does not seem to have fallen in the Meiji period: the fall began only as late as the 1920s.[31] A sharp deterioration of social conditions in 1931 and 1934 after poor harvests showed that the Tohoku, still poor by national standards, had not shaken off its difficult past. As the national railway system came to be completed, Ueno station on the north side of Tokyo became the point of ingress of migrants from the Tohoku. The district

---

[27] *PP Japan*, vol. 8, p.596, Report on the trade of Hyogo and Osaka in 1890.
[28] G. Rozman, 'Social change' in *CHJ*, vol. 5 (1989), pp.517–20.
[29] M. Hane, 'The textile factory worker', in P. Kornicki, *Meiji Japan: political, economic and social history*, 4 vols. (London, 1998), vol. 2, pp.148–9. On factory labour generally, see Koji Taira, 'Factory labour and the industrial revolution in Japan', in W. J. Macpherson, *The industrialisation of Japan* (Oxford, 1994), pp.258–310.
[30] Nishikawa Shunsaku and Yamamoto Yūzō (eds.), *Nihon keizai-ishi* [Economic history of Japan], vol. 5, *Sangyōka no jidai* [Industrialisation era], pt 2 (Tokyo, 1990), p.230.
[31] O. Saitō, 'Historical demography', p.85; O. Saitō, *Infant mortality in pre-transition Japan: levels and trends*, discussion paper series, no. 273 (Tokyo, 1993), pp.17, 19–20.

around the station remained into modern times visibly poorer and less commercialised than other parts of Tokyo: the station and adjacent Ueno park have become in recent times the point of social contact among illegal or unemployed immigrants from central Asia.

Apart from the 1860s, when exports were in their infancy and the need to import ships and armaments on both shogunal and han account created an adverse balance of payments (worsened by problems in adjusting the currency of a formerly isolated country to the demands of international trade),[32] the export sector did not pose real difficulties for Japan. The idea that the treaties could be renegotiated to end trade concessions or less sweepingly to confine trade to Nagasaki and a few remote centres – much abroad at the end of the 1850s – was no longer seen as realistic. The accompanying idea of the late 1850s that Japan could restore the old status quo by a build-up of military strength – a belief which had been central to securing what was a broad acquiescence in the treaties – evaporated: this was an inevitable consequence of realistic appraisal of the formidable might of western powers and of Japan's own puny fiscal, and hence military, resources.[33] Political calculation rather than the brave and brash assumptions of the bolder spirits of the late 1850s held the upper hand. Defence issues remained sensitive, rapidly shifting, however, from the concept of defending Japan itself from encroachment to protecting or securing a stake in continental bridgeheads in danger of being overrun by westerners.

External issues were at times overshadowed by internal political differences. The messy settlement of 1868 meant on the internal front not only tensions between the great *tozama* and the other han, but the perpetuation of divides which had occurred in the 1850s and 1860s within han themselves (two han had in the early 1860s experienced civil war within their boundaries; Choshu briefly, and in a more debilitating fashion, Mito). In post-1868 times risings occurred in Saga (Hizen) and Tosa in 1874 and in Satsuma in 1877. Only the Satsuma rising – internal strife within Satsuma and revolt against the Meiji government combined – was on a large scale, and its suppression, as in the case of the other and smaller risings, was made easier because some of the han leaders counted among the Meiji politicians who opposed and defeated rebellion. In Satsuma,

---

[32] This took up much space in commentary at the end of the 1850s and the outset of the 1860s. It did not denote corresponding economic difficulties, though the fact that the currency problems were caused in part by what the Japanese officials saw as the bad faith of foreigners added to the unpopularity of the opening of the ports.

[33] The effect of going abroad made Japanese much more aware of the extent of differences and of the need to close the gap. W. G. Beasley, *The Meiji Restoration* (Stanford, 1972), p.209.

Saigō, who had resigned in 1873, was reluctantly drawn into the rebellion. Defeat in 1877 and his own suicide gave Meiji Japan its great tragic victim. The contrasts between Choshu and Satsuma were telling in some respects. The new Choshu leaders, who had changed the policy of their han in the wake of victory in the short-lived civil war at the end of 1864, and who had used an army made up of commoners as well as samurai, had more sweeping views on internal reform than others.[34] In 1868, as a result of the han's own internal political renovation in 1864–5, its leaders already envisaged the pensioning of daimyo, and wider innovation. That contrasted with Satsuma or Tosa where in the 1860s there had been internally a more consistent policy. Above all, Satsuma, with a history of two successive shrewd daimyo, Narioki and Nariakira and later, Hisamitsu (1817–87), regent or de facto daimyo, working closely on a common agenda with their samurai officials, was very different from Choshu. For that reason it had farther to travel in rejection of the old order: having kept its internal good order through the stormy decade of the 1860s, Satsuma, like Mito and Choshu before it, was to succumb to internal tumult in 1877, before supporters of the new order prevailed.

More widespread and lasting than the risings was the emergence of political parties which were intended to harness both support for national constitutional progress and opposition to Choshu and Satsuma dominance. Itagaki Taisuke (1837–1919) of Tosa had admired the views of Saigō on both treaty revision and Korea's relationship with China, but was not prepared to go as far as armed resistance: he founded political parties in 1873 and 1874. His 1873 party was founded in association with Etō Shimpei (1834–74) of Saga (who, however, in the following year led a revolt). Itagaki, his party interest temporarily interrupted by a return to government, resumed his activity from 1878 stressing the principle of consultation with the people:[35] in 1881 he founded the *Jiyūtō* (Liberal Party). The timing was accounted for by the need to bring pressure to bear on the ruling interest in the preparation of the constitution, which growing restiveness over delays had moved to centre stage. Another party was formed in 1882 under the name of *Rikken Kaishinto* (Progressive Constitutional Party) by Ōkuma of Saga, a member of the governing clique squeezed out of government shortly before this. In the main the support base of the *Jiyūtō* was rural, coming from the larger payers of land tax, which ensured that it was geographically widespread. The *Kaishinto* was more urban and intellectual, and consciously modelled on the English party pattern. Ōkuma founded a college, the *Tokyo senmon gakkō* (the future Waseda University), in 1882, which became an

---

[34] Satow, *A diplomat in Japan*, p.326.   [35] Sakamoto, *Nihon no kindai*, vol. 2. pp.232–40.

important centre for training politicians and was very open to outside thought. Fukuzawa Yukichi (1835–1901), writer, journalist and newspaper owner who had already founded a college which later became Keio University, also attached himself to the party, thus further enhancing its urban and intellectual support. He visited the United States three times; he was a strong advocate of modernisation on western lines, and his books sold 250,000 copies.

The absence in Tokugawa times of a state higher education system, of an established state religion and of state-promoted cultural values, far from being a handicap, was a major advantage. The Tokugawa school of 1862 had been turned into the Imperial University in 1877, an official university in effect for training the administrators of the new state. However, the first private universities rivalled it in prestige for other employment, and laid the basis for the powerful private sector in Japanese higher education. They also ensured that much of the educational system remained beyond state control. Thus after Kume Kunitake (1839–1931), formerly secretary to the Iwakura mission and professor at the University of Tokyo, lost his post for an article entitled 'Shinto is ancient custom of heaven worship', which in 1891 questioned in intellectual terms the politically inspired emphasis on Shinto, central to the refurbished divinity of the emperor, he found employment in 1899 at Waseda.[36] The private universities not only brought in outside ideas (as all Japanese universities did), but also deviant forms of thought such as in the early 1920s Marxism or socialism. The universities left, despite official alarm caused by socialism's associations with Russia (the security bugbear of Japan), a powerful imprint on Japanese teaching and intellectual thought.

The most fundamental feature in early government was the dominance of four *tozama* han: Choshu, Satsuma, Tosa and Saga (Hizen). This narrowed down to two from 1881 to 1901. In the first cabinet of 1885, eight of the ten members were from Choshu and Satsuma (four from each). Saigō and Ōkubo of Satsuma and Kido of Choshu had been the three great figures of the Restoration. The former two met a violent end; and frail in health Kido of Choshu died in 1877. The deaths of all three between 1877 and 1878 left the future open to others. In the 1880s and 1890s, Itō, Inoue and Yamagata were the dominant Choshu figures, and Kuroda Kiyotaka (1840–1900) (responsible for the Hokkaido colonisation office), Matsukata Masayoshi (1835–1924) and Saigō Tsugumichi (1840–1902) (brother of Saigō Takamori) were the main Satsuma figures. Itō, who introduced cabinet-style government in 1885, became the first

[36] John S. Brownlee, *Japanese historians and the national myths, 1600–1945: the age of the gods and emperor Jinmu* (Tokyo and Vancouver, 1997), pp.92–102.

prime minister in 1885–8, followed after only a brief interval by Yamagata in 1889–91. Apart from the short-lived Kuroda cabinet of 1888–9, these two men dominated not only the first six years of cabinet government, but the last decade of the century as well. Itō was prime minister in 1892–6, 1898 and 1900–1, and Yamagata in 1898–1900. From 1885 to 1901 the only break with the *Satchō* (i.e. Choshu and Satsuma dominance) pattern was the short-lived Ōkuma (Hizen) cabinet in 1898. Within this sequence of office – setting aside the non-*Satchō*-headed or Ōkuma cabinet – all the prime ministers came from Choshu, except for two cabinets (the Kuroda cabinet in 1888–9 and the Matsukata one in 1896–7), headed by Satsuma politicians.

The interests of Choshu and Satsuma had not coincided either before or after 1881. Choshu's position was helped by the tragic death of the two strong men of early Meiji Japan, both Satsuma men, Saigō the victim of the Satsuma rebellion of 1877, and Okubō, fellow Satsuma man but pillar of the new Tokyo government, assassinated in 1878 in revenge for Saigō's tragic end.[37] Saigō's resignation in 1873 had already made it possible for Choshu to increase its influence over the army: some 2,000 Satsuma men followed his example by resigning. These circumstances provided the opportunity for the rising army prominence of Yamagata of Choshu, who was both chief of staff of the army and a leading politician for much of the Meiji era. The expansion of the army in the 1890s consolidated his position (as well as providing scope for the entry of other Choshu generals into national politics). Katsura Tarō (1847–1913), a prime minister three times within 1901–13, is an outstanding example. A political general of the old school, he was cautious and was prepared to stand up to the armed forces themselves as events in 1912 proved. Tanaka Giichi (1864–1929), a Choshu general who became prime minister in 1927, was of a younger generation, lacked vision, and had a real part in Japan's slide into reckless adventurism at the end of the 1920s. If Satsuma lost out in the army, it preserved its say in the navy, at first a much smaller force. Given the rivalries, as late as 1890 Itō opposed a history of Japan as it might rekindle Choshu and Satsuma conflict in the new parliamentary institutions, and two decades later the twelve-volume official history of Choshu maintained a very neutral tone.[38]

Parties had been opposed by the original clique of ruling politicians of 1868. However, the early story of parties has less to do with official disapproval of them than with the ambitions of their leaders: parties

---

[37] On the character and personality differences between Okubō and Saigō, see Yates, *Saigo Takamori*, pp.183–4.
[38] Craig, *Choshu in the Meiji Restoration*, p.377.

were activated or deactivated in accordance with prospects of office receding or improving. Nevertheless, the political unrest behind the parties together with the active press of the 1880s had made constitutional progress unavoidable.[39] Another factor crucial to its advance was Itō's persistent commitment. He had long studied European constitutions, travelling there in 1882–3 for the purpose of deepening his study, and the constitution was to be his craftsmanship more than that of any other man.[40] Cabinet government was established in 1885; the new constitution was introduced in 1889; the first general election followed in 1890.

A feature of the history of the period is that a strong public opinion existed from the outset. The popular interest in the Perry expeditions can be seen in the rapidity with which woodblock prints in great numbers had been put into circulation in Edo. This opinion variously supported the government or handicapped it (as, for instance, by ruling out the compromises that the government in the late 1880s would have settled for in regard to the unequal treaties). It was also a powerful factor in overcoming caution or foot-dragging in regard to the introduction of the constitution, and gave weight to the discontents voiced by political parties. The activity or inactivity of parties, led by ambitious men, did somewhat less than justice to popular expectations. Awareness of this discontent explains why prefectoral and local government from the outset provided for elections and public participation. Public opinion was supported by a vigorous press (the first modern Japanese-language paper appeared in 1871). It covered a broad range of interests; its appeal was added to by the fiction it published, and the work of the great novelists of the end of the century mostly first featured in instalments in the press. This aspect points to the fact that the rapid development of the press had been helped by the tradition of *kawaraban*, a form of news-sheet published throughout Tokugawa times by booksellers or woodblock printers, originally largely devoted to scandal or colourful stories (and sometimes engaging in political innuendo) and in the final decades of the shogunate featuring real political news. Hence, public opinion was not satisfied with formal changes, and grew restive with the dominance of political life by politicians from Choshu and Satsuma which parliamentary institutions made much more visible. The term *Satchō* (a collective and pejorative word for Satsuma and Choshu) made its appearance in the political vocabulary.

[39] For a summary of the press, see A. A. Altman, 'The press', in Jansen and Rozman, *Japan in transition*, pp.231–47.
[40] See an interesting article by George Akita and Hirose Yoshihiro, 'The British model: Inoue Kowashi and the ideal monarchical system', *Monumenta nipponica*, vol. 49, no. 4 (Winter 1994), pp.413–21.

With restiveness over this dominion and rifts within the *Satchō* alliance itself, the management of political life was bound to prove difficult in the 1890s. Government was now at the mercy of the fickle will of the people and the behaviour of parliamentarians. The lower house in particular had the budgetary powers of modern states, and hence despite some constitutional restraints, had, in theory, the ability to impose its will. To cope with the risks inherent in introducing parliamentary democracy, two steps were taken. The first was to emphasise still further the authority of the emperor (the second, considered later, to protect the continuity of the existing ruling interest). In the constitution, the imperial authority was dealt with in summary fashion, the divine nature of the emperor itself touched on vaguely in an isolated paragraph. However, the imperial rescript on education appeared in 1890.[41] It was not, of course, drafted by the emperor, and a rescript was exhortatory rather than executive. It emphasised the concept of loyalty to a divine emperor in a few words. As Marius Jansen has said, however, the document itself 'seems rather innocuous and platitudinous'.[42] It gained its effectiveness from the general thrust of government policy, marking a further stage in the process, begun in 1868, of manipulating the imperial institution in defence of the legitimacy of power, and its timing was accounted for by the urge to reduce the risks of a leap into the dark with the introduction in 1889 of the novel concept of parliamentary democracy.

Itō had already noted the absence of bonding factors such as national history or religion which western countries enjoyed: the emperor therefore had to fill the void. From the outset of the Meiji regime, in contrast to the older pattern in which the emperor rarely if ever left his *gosho* (or palace) in Kyoto, a sustained programme of visits throughout Japan was planned for the emperor.[43] They were part of the effort to build up the ceremonial functions of the emperor, and in the process to create a public role for the emperor unknown in the past history of the institution.[44] As part of this policy, the emperor also began to participate in the rites at the great shrine in Ise, a step which served both to emphasise his divinity and to strengthen the link with Shinto. The cabinet was far ahead of public opinion. A requirement of registering at Shinto temples proved so unpopular that it had to be abandoned. Policy also represented a break with Japanese intellectual thought. From the seventeenth century into the

---

[41] For a convenient summary and the full text of the rescript, see Gary D. Allinson, *The Columbia guide to modern Japanese history* (New York, 1999), pp.228–32.
[42] Jansen, *The making of modern Japan*, p.410. Its text is reproduced on p.411.
[43] In all, Meiji made 102 tours during his reign. Stephen Large, *Emperors of the rising sun* (Tokyo, 1997), p.23.
[44] T. Fujitani, *Splendid monarchy: power and pageantry in modern Japan* (Berkeley, 1996).

nineteenth century, writers from Razan to Bantō had dealt briefly with the question of imperial origins or even had openly expressed scepticism about the legends. Scepticism was still evident in 1891–2 when doubts cast on Shinto were the occasion of the dismissal of Kunitake. The issue remained a preoccupation of the cabinet. In 1911, in face of school text-books failing for decades to say which of two imperial courts in a quarrel in the fourteenth century had been the legitimate one, the cabinet decreed that the 'southern' court was to be identified as the legitimate one and that this was to be stated in school textbooks. A disenchanted Basil Chamberlain, the great English scholar of Japanese culture, noted sourly the novel and political content introduced into Shinto.[45]

If enhancing the authority of the emperor was one way of preserving Japan from too sweeping changes, the second was to create in the constitution a structure of government which preserved the stake of existing rulers in administration, and also protected the army and navy from political interference.[46] The constitution did not state how ministers were nominated: it specified no role for the houses of parliament or for the emperor. As paragraph forty-five of the constitution stated, however, that ministers gave advice to the emperor, practice was that he nominated them. This was itself a fiction as the emperor acted on the advice of those around him. Early cabinets consisted of nominated office-holders and not of elected members of parliament.[47] In particular, army and naval ministers were drawn from officer ranks (from 1899 appointment, at the insistence of Yamagata Aritomo, in order to eliminate any possibility of political interference, was confined to serving officers). In this way cabinet formation and ministerial appointments were in theory, at least, preserved from interference by the ruling out of politically more amenable (or independent) retired officers. The emperor was also said to have the supreme command of the armed forces. While as a result of this chiefs of staff answered directly to the emperor, it did not give him extra powers. The provision simply reinforced insulation of the administration from parliamentary interference, and, with a real guile, also ensured that at the time the Choshu and Satsuma leaders surrendered little of their power. The older politicians also sought to ensure that their authority lasted beyond retirement. They were known collectively as the *genrō*, a

---

[45] B. H. Chamberlain, 'The invention of a new religion', published in London, 1912. It is reprinted as an appendix to the Tuttle 1980 edition of Chamberlain's *Things Japanese*, pp.531–44.

[46] Allinson, *Columbia guide to modern Japanese history*, pp.228–31, has a succinct summary of the constitution.

[47] The foreign minister, for instance, from 1900 to 1938 was invariably a career diplomat. I. Nish, *Japanese foreign policy 1869–1942* (London, 1977), pp.257–8.

group unprovided for in the constitution, whose advice the emperor took before nominating a prime minister. In turn the new prime minister was expected to consult the *genrō* on any major innovations (a practice which inevitably broke down in time).

The ambition of the Meiji constitution makers, whether in exalting the status of the emperor or in protecting executive office from direct parliamentary or political interference, proved powerless to halt the growth, or more accurately, the revival, of party. The 1890 election itself, with an electorate of nearly half a million, functioned satisfactorily. Ōkuma had already rejoined the *Rikken Kaishinto* in 1889 in anticipation of the election. Other groupings were brought into activity by the prospect of an election, and Itakagi, reappearing in 1889, laid the basis of a revived *Jiyūtō*. Many of those elected to the lower house already had political experience: more than half of them had been elected at one stage in their career to a local assembly. Nearly half of them too were drawn from the class of economically successful figures at local level: well-off peasants of landlord status, or local businessmen.[48] They laid the basis for a more solid political system, and in turn led to the reliance of the parties on strong local figures for their grass-roots support: the strengths and weaknesses of the modern Japanese party system had begun to emerge (and the early *Jiyūtō* well illustrated how parties were factions rather than a monolithic structure). For the men of 1890, taxation had a clear appeal as an issue, and from the outset resistance to increased taxes became a central topic. While the house of representatives appeared to have weaker fiscal powers than its western counterparts (if it rejected a budget, the cabinet could impose a budgetary figure not exceeding the previous year's), the fact that expenditure was rising gave it muscle. As a result, though the old-style politicians did not relish parties, they found they had to deal with them. Itō, the father of the constitution, in the course of his prime ministership of 1892–6 made a deal with Itagaki's Liberals. The support of Ōkuma's party made workable a Matsukata cabinet in 1896–7 (which included Ōkuma from Saga as a minister); and Ōkuma was briefly prime minister in 1898 when he and Itagaki temporarily united their parties. The Matsukata cabinet in 1896–7 and the Ōkuma cabinet in 1898, in breaching, within the first decade of parliament, the *Satchō* monopoly of power, meant that even *Satchō* politicians had to endorse party for the future. Itō became titular chairman of the *Jiyūtō* in 1900: its name now became the *Rikken Seiyūkai* (Constitutional Political Comrades Party). It was a powerful party combining Itō's authority as one of the founding fathers of Meiji Japan and the politically active rural interests: as the

---

[48] R. H. P. Mason, *Japan's first general election 1890* (Cambridge, 1969), p.198.

countryside was more politically aware than the towns, its parliamentary base was large. It dominated Japanese life for a decade or more with two of its senior figures, Saionji Kimmochi (1849–1940) and Katsura, alternating in the prime ministership for eight of the years beween 1901 and 1913.

Revenue issues had already sharply divided Diet and government in the 1890s; the costs of the Russian war strained the relationship further. In 1911–13 budgetary and specifically naval expenditure acquired a key significance. When a Saionji cabinet fell in 1911 in an attempt to cut back expenditure, his successor Katsura (a Choshu general) had to deal with army and navy resistance. Faced with blackmail from the navy, which refused to appoint a minister from its ranks, he appointed by imperial rescript a retired officer. This step, though actually intended to confront the vested interests of the navy, led to a barrage of criticism, prompted by growing resentment of *Satchō* dominance, against Katsura for high-handedness. Ironically Katsura was acting not in defence of *Satchō* interests, but with an aim of freeing government precisely from such pressures: what became in 1913 the *Doshikai*, or Comrades Party, began as an effort by him to find support both among members of the *Seiyūkai* and of the Ōkuma party for a working political majority.[49] This alliance made possible the Ōkuma cabinet in 1914 (Katsura, a broken man as a result of the controversy, had died in 1913), and the emergence of a counterpoise to the well-established, rural and conservative *Seiyūkai*. Whatever can be said about the prime ministerial effectiveness of Ōkuma, now a very old man, his politics represented the urban and constitutional interest. Coming in on a wave of anti-*Satchō* feeling, first the formation of the *Doshikai* party and then the Ōkuma cabinet marked a further stage in Japanese political development. It was also, as the first cabinet favouring popular participation in political life, committed to extending the electoral franchise. Parliamentary politics matured at this time and the 1915 general election was the first general contest on a domestic issue. If the *Seiyūkai* was at first isolated by its outdated conservativism, it soon changed under the organising genius of Hara Kei (1856–1921), who gave it a modern party structure.[50]

Hara, though not a moderniser in any radical sense of the word, was the first politician from the north of Japan to serve as prime minister, and with a preceding career for a time in journalism, was also the first head of a government drawn from outside military and political circles

---

[49] See Tetsuo Najita, *Hara Kei in the politics of compromise 1905–1915* (Cambridge, Mass., 1967), pp.122–41.

[50] On Hara Kei, see E. O. Reischauer and Craig, *Japan: tradition and transformation*, pp.227–9, 233, 234, 238, and Tetsuo Najita, *Hara Kei*.

within the western *tozama*, or, in the case of Saionji Kimmochi, from a princely family.[51] In contrast to past cabinets in which appointed members exceeded elected members, his cabinet of 1918–21 was the first one consisting mainly of parliamentarians,[52] and the first headed by the active president of a party.

He was, of course, already well known for his management of the constituencies by securing support through favours bestowed on them. This showed up early in the matter of railway building. The army wished to opt for the conversion of existing lines to broad gauge, but Hara instead opted to use funds to build more narrow-gauge railways, extending them in constituencies where electoral support was uncertain. Japan entered the 1920s with two well-defined political parties, each committed to moderate political courses: in the fluid nature of Japanese politics, cabinets of either complexion succeeded one another in the 1920s. The *Doshikai* was to rename itself *Minseito*; the *Seiyūkai* brought back the name of *Jiyūtō*.[53] Personalities counted as much or more than policies in their make-up, and in post-1945 Japan, both were to amalgamate as the *Jimintō* (or Liberal Democratic Party), and to dominate Japanese governments to this day apart from the short interlude of the Hosokawa cabinet of 1993 and an even shorter succeeding Hata cabinet.

The founding generation of politicians was fading away. Itō, first resident governor in Korea and strongly opposed to foreign adventures, was later, on a visit to Manchuria in 1909, assassinated by a Korean. Yamagata had retired. Equally tellingly, their role in retirement as *genrō* was also losing effect. In 1914 Yamagata, doyen of the *genrō*, had not been consulted over the declaration of war and neither was he consulted in 1915 when the foreign minister Katō ill-advisedly issued the Twenty-One demands on China. Yamagata's intervention at that stage at least forced the abandonment of the most reckless of the demands. In a crisis in 1928, Saionji, the leading *genrō* of his day (he first came to ministerial office in 1894) – and a much less impressive figure in both character and personal stature – was ignored.

Government was passing from the old guard, realistic in their ambitions for Japan, into newer hands, less experienced especially on the foreign front, less in control of the cabinet, and faced with novel challenges and risks in the Pacific and in China. The army likewise, as it

---

[51] He was himself son of a former *karō*, or chief minister of a han.

[52] Michio Muramatsu, 'Bringing politics back into Japan', in Carol Gluck and S. R. Graubard (eds.), *Showa: the Japan of Hirohito* (New York, 1992), p.143.

[53] For a good account in English of some aspects of Meiji politics, see J. Mark Ramseyer and Frances M. Rosenbluth, *The politics of oligarchy: institutional choice in imperial Japan* (Cambridge, 1995).

grew from a small force into a large army, was headed by a new generation of military officer, with no political background, who, taking for granted the victories in 1895 and 1904–5, saw the army as a source of personal advancement rather than as a political prop to a new state in an uncertain East. In other words the army, like businessmen or *chōnin* in the past, was an interest in the state rather than an institution integrated intimately into society. In this sense it reflected a general characteristic of Japanese society. Social integration across society was weaker than in the west where the presence of sons variously in the army, church, trade and administration (and the corresponding marriage of daughters to holders of these professions) created remarkable homogeneity – what we would call an establishment – in the upper circles of society. The contrast was reinforced by the absence in Japan of a legal profession, a caste of high prestige in western society which recruited across the range of landed and high income families, and a springboard for political advancement. There was also in the western sense no church: the Buddhist religion was divided into many sects, and isolated from dominant intellectual circles (and Shinto priests likewise were even less a powerful interest). In other words, Meiji Japan did not inherit an existing social establishment which by ties of blood, marriage and self-interest held together the dominant institutions of society. It was not that an establishment had been undermined in 1868: the dilemma was that one had not existed in Tokugawa times. Hence the challenge was that of creating, beyond the real consensus of political purpose and culture, a ruling establishment. The difficulty was compounded by strong regional particularisms, and the perpetuation of separate professional divides or interests in army, navy and bureaucracy. Some regions prevailed over others; the army was separate from the navy; the *zaibatsu* stood outside the military and administrative classes, and when they identified with them, they threw in their lot with individual groups (the business house of Mitsubishi identified with the *Rikken Kaishintō*; Mitsui with the *Jiyūtō*), thus not softening but perpetuating the divides. Japan was unusual in displaying at one and the same time the relative weakness of social distinctions between classes,[54] and a marked lack of integration between different professional categories.

When the Meiji Restoration occurred, the new regime inherited the frontier problems of its predecessor Tokugawa regime in the Ryukyus and in Ezo. They were, however, quickly to take second place to Korea. Ezo did so because Russian interest quickly came to focus on the Asian

[54] Basil Chamberlain observed that 'the whole nation is more democratic than ourselves...'. Ota Yuzo, *Basil Hall Chamberlain: portrait of a Japanologist* (Richmond, Surrey, 1998), p.73.

landmass (and on Korea itself) and the Ryukyus because Japan, following the contemporary model of European annexation of Pacific islands (and to forestall any western encroachment), annexed the Ryukyus in 1879. At the outset, however, Ezo and the Ryukyus were important, as while they gradually slipped from centre stage, they were closely related to the Korea question, either by the place of China in the polity of both the Ryukyus and Korea, or by the Russian presence on the perimeter of both Korea and Ezo. In the 1860s, the British had been apprehensive that the Russians would push their frontier forward in Karafuto, that Japan would be unable to resist, and that the advance would have major consequences even for the British. Throughout the 1860s, tensions over issues of trade and defence in Sakhalin gradually grew into clashes in which some Japanese were killed. For the first time in history, two Japanese gunboats were sent to the northern waters in 1874.[55] Because there was little naval and military power, no time was lost at the outset of the Restoration to hire steamers to carry 3,000 samurai families from the defeated han of Aizu northwards. They were settled on the bleak and underpopulated Shimotoka peninsula, facing Ezo, at the northern tip of Aomori.[56] Less disloyal though more miscellaneous and very poor settlers were dispatched directly into Ezo itself. The population of Ezo was a mere 123,668 in 1872, of whom less than half were Japanese (the rest were Ainu).[57] Security reasons (small army and small budget) and a belief in the economic potential of the region led in effect to the immediate activisation of the old ambition of Aizawa and Tokugawa Nariaki of settling the front-line lands. For defence on land the concept adopted was that of farmer-soldiers, settlers who would develop land and provide at little cost a defence force on the spot. The defence of the Ezo region was to remain wholly dependent on the farmer-soldiers.[58] However, in the short term people were moved northwards, pell mell, with no resources and little thought as to how to settle them. Some of the pioneers both in Ezo and in Shimotoka died in the harsh spring of 1870. From Niigata, several trips in 1870 by a large American steamer carried a total of 7,569

---

[55] *PP Japan*, vol. 9, p.252, Report on Hakodate for 1892.

[56] On the resettled Aizu men see Ishimitsu, *Remembering Aizu*. The British reports seem to have been confused by events, very probably by the fact that both Aizu men and others were moved northwards at the same time, and suggested that they had been settled in Ezo. See *PP Japan*, vol. 4, pp.462, where the report for 1869 from Hakodate on 31 January 1870 noted that 800 to 1,000 samurai, principally from Aizu, had been sent northwards by steamer late in 1869.

[57] *PP Japan*, vol. 6, p.754, Report on revenue and expenditure of Japan for 1876–7. Retrospectively 48,867 Japanese were said to be in Hokkaido in 1869. *PP Japan*, vol. 8, p.243, Report on agriculture in Hokkaido for 1887.

[58] *PP Japan*, vol. 10, p.70, Report on Hakodate for the year 1895.

passengers to the north.[59] Many were not even settled as colonists; they were simply employed building roads; by 1872 some were even being shipped back, and few new ones arrived.[60] Much therefore depended on the *Tonden hei* (or farmer-soldiers), introduced in 1873. In 1875 there were 198 families of farmer-soldiers; 509 such families in 1881.[61] The number of soldiers, 1,401 in 1887, was 3,783 by 1896: in the first half of the decade they were rising at a rate of 400 to 500 a year.[62]

The settlement of Hokkaido had proved an uphill task. Only 100,000 settlers were attracted in the first twenty years of the Restoration. Most, moreover, were from the poor Tohoku. Few came from elsewhere, being attracted or dispatched only in exceptional circumstances.[63] Quite un-like other provinces, Ezo was at first run directly from Tokyo, under the administration of a military governor.[64] Its colonisation and the layout of Sapporo were both conducted under the guidance of an American ex-pert, General Caprol from the agricultural college in Washington and his assistants (the parallels with American experience in opening the west had determined the choice of American experts). Direct control proved unsatisfactory; officials usually remained for too short a time; the region, seen more as a possible source of profit for the state than run for the benefit of the settlers, had a negative appeal, and only with the creation of three prefectures for Hokkaido in 1881 (though without elective as-semblies as in Japan proper) did some semblance of civil administration emerge; in 1886 the three prefectures were combined into one. At the end of the 1880s settlement finally began to quicken. The 13,090 migrants of 1889 had become some 60,000 in 1895.[65] Population doubled over the 1890s to 787,880 in 1898.

Hokkaido, following a significant time lag, had become less vulner-able. However, southern Sakhalin and the Kurils, all inhospitable islands, remained lightly settled. If the Russian menace had abated it was only because it was focussed elsewhere. The central concern in the Japanese perspective had gradually became the spectre of vigorous Russian ex-pansion in its own Siberian territories and its growth into an incipient

---

[59] *PP Japan*, vol. 4, p.607, Report on the trade and navigation of Niigata for 1870.
[60] See *PP Japan*, vol. 5, p.112, Report on Hakodate for 1872; p.328, Report on Hakodate for 1873; p.507, Report on Hakodate for 1874.
[61] *PP Japan*, vol. 7, p.295, Report on Hakodate for 1883; *PP Japan*, vol. 8, p.250, Report on Hakodate for 1887.
[62] *PP Japan*, vol. 10, p.70, Report on Hakodate for the year 1895; p.371, Report on Hakodate for 1896.
[63] Thus, 2,400 survivors of the floods in the Nara region were moved in November 1889 to Hokkaido. *PP Japan*, vol. 8, p.421, Report on Hakodate for 1889.
[64] *PP Japan*, vol. 8, p.568, Report on Hakodate for 1890.
[65] *PP Japan*, vol. 10, p.489, Report on Hakodate for 1897; vol. 10, p.615, Report on Hakodate for 1898.

presence in Manchuria and Korea. This fear was heightened by the declining power of China. Japanese concern was in essence an interrelated
one of three regions: Siberia, Korea and China. The agreement in 1875,
whereby the south of Sakhalin was ceded to Russia and Japan was given
the entire string of Kuril islands, reflected less an assured situation acquired by Japan than the shift of Russian interest to the Asian mainland.[66]
That put Korea at the centre of Japanese concerns. Other countries also
had displayed an interest: the French for a time occupied Kangae island,
and in 1871 the Americans, firing on the coast of Korea in revenge for an
attack on a crew, killed 200 Koreans.[67] Korea was to dominate Japanese
thought until the issue was settled by Japanese annexation of the country
in 1910.[68] Foremost in policy was the urge to pre-empt any western territorial interest.[69] Ironically, after the treaty of 1876 between Japan and
Korea, China had at first encouraged Korea to establish relations with
other countries as a counterpoise to Japan's presence.[70]

An expedition to Taiwan in 1873, a minor episode, to punish indigenous people in a Chinese island who had attacked Ryukyu fishermen,
was prompted by an underlying wish not to leave the issue to Chinese
jurisprudence (which saw it as a misdemeanour affecting citizens of two
territories both under Chinese suzerainty). In this case there were precedents, notably the effort by the Japanese to ensure that documents relating
to Ryukyu missions used the Japanese, not the Chinese, language.[71] The
issue of the status of the Ryukyus could not be avoided. With the disap-
pearance of both Satsuma and the shogunate itself, the new Japan had to
assert itself in what seemed to the Japanese (though not to the Chinese) a
constitutional void. The matter had its own urgency, as the risk of preda-
tory occupation of the Ryukyus by one of the western powers had been
evident for a generation. In other words, Japanese actions in defending its
fishermen in 1873 implied Japanese suzerainty over them.[72] In 1879 Meiji
Japan solved the problem by making its claim formal. Done unilaterally,
it was of course opposed by China, though futilely. The peculiar status de
facto of the Ryukyus helped Japan. Ultimately, the fact that the inhabitants were themselves prepared to accept Japanese dominance, more than
China's inability to assert its stake, settled the matter. Satow, dining with
a Ryukyu official in 1881, advised him 'to throw in their lot with Japan

[66] For a comprehensive account of Russian expansion in Asia, see John J. Stephan, *The
Russian Far East: a history* (Stanford, 1994); Sakamoto, *Nihon no Kindai*, vol. 2, *Meiji
kokka no kensetsu*, pp.146–7.
[67] W. LaFeber, *The clash: U.S.–Japanese relations throughout history* (New York, 1997), p.44.
[68] Sakamoto, *Meiji kokka no kensetsu*, p.295.
[69] P. Duus, *The abacus and the sword: the Japanese penetration of Korea 1895–1910* (Berkeley,
1998), p.33.
[70] Duus, *Abacus and the sword*, p.50.
[71] Nakai, *Shogunal politics*, p.334.   [72] Sakamoto, *Nihon no kindai*, vol. 2, p.182.

frankly. He replied that Loocho [Ryukyu] would prefer the old arrangement, but that if China and Japan would be good enough to settle the question of Loocho's status between them, the islanders would willingly accept it.'[73] In 1882 the Ryukyus became the prefecture of Okinawa.

Japan's first diplomatic démarche in 1869 had been to regularise its contacts with Korea. Its urgency can be seen in the fact that for the Japanese who since 1811, the date of the last diplomatic mission from Korea, had let the ties lapse, Korea now became a priority. While the Koreans in the past had responded favourably to Japanese overtures, their response in the 1870s was negative. Ignoring the dilemma for the Japanese that both the shogunate and Tsushima had ceased to exist, they had no wish to depart from the status quo of a small colony of Tsushima men in Pusan, and for the larger issues referred the Japanese to China. The divide in Japan over Korean policy in 1871 was not one between those who favoured invasion and others who did not. Korean policy had simply become a marker of personal rivalries among the new leaders.[74] There was no real divide between them over Korea or even over the use of force. The mission finally sent with general political consent to Korea in 1876 was accompanied by a large naval force (a case of imitating western gunboat diplomacy), and Harry Parkes wryly noted that the ensuing treaty imposed on Korea the sort of unequal treaty loudly complained of at home.[75] The Japanese from the outset of their new regime emphasised the independence in formal terms of Korea. This was a concern which had precedents which were centuries old. The issue had been a subject of differences between Japan and Korea in 1710 when the shogunate, advised by Arai Hakuseki, was concerned with exalting the status of the shogun: if Japan negotiated with Korea on the basis that the shogun's style was *kokuo* (king of a country), it emphasised not simply that the Japanese polity was outside the Chinese system but that relations with Korea likewise were conducted outside it.[76]

For China itself, fear of the Russians (and of the Japanese) accounted for a growing sensitivity to security issues. Moreover, the age-old jurisprudence of China coming, as in the 1590s, to Korea's aid would complicate the tale of the next twenty years.[77] In Korea, a country even more sealed

---

[73] PRO, London, 30/33/15/6, f.61, Satow diary, 12 June 1881.
[74] For a very full account of Japanese policy regarding Taiwan and Korea, see M. J. Mayo, 'The Korean crisis of 1873 and early foreign policy', *Journal of Asian studies*, vol. 31, no. 4 (Aug. 1972), pp.793–819.
[75] *PP Japan*, vol. 3, p.159, Parkes, Tokyo, 27 March 1876.
[76] Nakai, *Shogunal politics*, pp.197, 228–34.
[77] PRO, London, 30/33/15/7, ff.8–9, Satow diary, 16 Sept. 1882, reporting a conversation with an official of the *Gaimushō*, summarising an explanation from the Koreans in 1876 of the relationship between Korea and China.

from the outside world than Japan had been, divides opened up between conservatives who wanted to maintain under a Chinese umbrella its isolation and others ('liberals') who wanted Korea to establish direct contact with the outside world. Ironically, modernising Koreans looked to Japan as a model and as a source of support. Koreans were present unofficially in Tokyo in 1880,[78] and at that time an official mission was shortly expected 'to study recent improvements in Japan on the European model'. Moreover, Koreans were deeply divided on what alliances might best protect the country's interests. In contrast to Japan, there had been neither past study of the west, nor the sophisticated dialogue which had occurred in Japan for almost a century on the growing foreign threat. As Satow – who had close contacts with the Koreans (in part because of his curiosity to learn the language) – observed, 'one cannot help remarking the great disposition the Koreans have to abuse of each other, in that differing from the Japanese, among whom the feeling of comradeship is in most cases so strong'.[79]

On two occasions in the 1880s Chinese forces were sent into Korea, and on both occasions the Japanese were drawn in as well. The Japanese proved cautious: Korean liberals were ultimately disappointed by the fact that Japanese involvement had not been more vigorous.[80] By the end of the 1880s the Russians were invited by conservatives into Korea, a factor which only deepened Japanese apprehensions. The war between Japan and China in 1894 resulted from Chinese slowness in withdrawing from Korea. Over the preceding decade the Chinese had become more assertive in the face of external threats. Further south, in opposition to French encroachment in northern Indochina, Chinese irregulars had intervened in 1883: a possibility of a Franco-Japanese alliance for a time lingered in the air.[81] A decade after Japan's war with China, conflict with Russia was triggered less by Russian expansion at large than by the progressive growth of its influence in Korea. The background over the intervening decade was one of chronic political instability in Korea (twenty-seven prime ministers between 1897 and 1904) and a race by many foreign countries for railway and economic concessions.[82] In November 1896, Satow observed that Ōkuma, the foreign minister,

---

[78] PRO, London, 3/33/15/6, f.21v, f.43v. Satow diary, 15 May, 2 Sept. 1880.
[79] PRO, London, 3/33/15/7, f.10, Satow diary, 22 Sept. 1882. For rather similar comments by Yoshida Shigeru, see J. W. Dower, *Empire and aftermath: Yoshida Shigeru and the Japanese experience, 1878–1954* (Cambridge, Mass., 1979), p.40.
[80] G. A. Lensen, *Korea and Manchuria between Russia and Japan 1895–1904: the observations of Sir Ernest Satow* (Tokyo, 1966), pp.44–5.
[81] Sims, *French policy towards the bakufu*, pp.120–42.
[82] Duus, *Abacus and the sword*, pp.129, 134–68.

'felt rather acutely the difficulties of contending against the preponderance of Russian influence in Korea', something confirmed less than a month later by the words of Chirol, the foreign editor of the London *Times*, back from a visit to Korea, 'where he found Russian influence paramount'.[83] As the sole western country with a land frontier to support their pretensions, railway building in the 1890s (and the prospect of its extension through Manchuria into Korea) gave the Russians a new weight. At the end of the 1890s French influence – with French advisors to the post office, the legal department and the arsenal, and a French company holding a railway-building concession on the Manchurian border – added to Japanese fears, while the Chinese Eastern Railway was a joint Franco-Russian venture.[84] Japan also saw itself deprived of the fruits of victory over China. The Liaotung peninsula had to be relinquished as a result of the Triple Intervention of Russia, Germany and France. This intervention itself might not have caused abiding resentment in Japan, except that in its wake Russia, with its spreading railway interest, negotiated a concession of territory in Liaotung; Germany negotiated one on the Shantung peninsula. Thus, despite its successful war against China, two western concessions now stood like pincers at either side of the Yellow Sea. To counterbalance the Russian and German preponderance in the region, Britain, not to be outdone, wrung a concession from the Chinese at Weihaiwei in the Shantung peninsula. Japan's concerns were relegated to a second place. Of course, to an even greater extent, so were China's.

One of the fruits of defeat by Japan, and of concessions won cynically from an ailing China, was the Boxer rebellion, motivated amid the stirrings of a new nationalism by hatred of foreigners, in the north of China in 1899. The Boxers, on their way murdering missionaries, moved to Peking: there they attacked the foreign compounds. After the rising, in which both Japan and western countries put in military forces to protect foreigners in Peking, the Russians were slow to withdraw their forces, adding to Japanese unease. The Japanese had reluctantly intervened in the first place: there were three western requests to them before they moved. When they did, as the only external power centred on the region, they were able to act swiftly. While the Japanese contingent, largest and best disciplined, was not given the leadership (a reflection on the secondary position in which Japan was cast by western powers), its performance, under an Aizu man, Colonel Shiba, was vital to saving the western community and won great respect for Japan. These circumstances,

[83] Lensen, *Korea and Manchuria*, p.79.
[84] J. A. White, *Transition to global rivalry: alliance diplomacy and the Quadruple Entente, 1895–1907* (Cambridge, 1995), pp.12–13.

together with common Japanese and British fears of Russia, led to the Japanese-British agreement of 1902. Japan was seen as a source of regional stability; western powers welcomed Japanese success in 1904–5 as a victory by the plucky Japanese over the overweening Russians.[85] The Japanese protectorate over Korea in 1905, control of central and local government in 1907 and annexation in 1910, were seen as a welcome response to chronic internal disorder in Korea and as a protection against a recurrence of Russian infiltration. Ominous signs of the depth of Korean feeling showed in the fact that many Koreans emigrated across the borders to Manchuria or to the Russian Far East, and after a rising in 1907 followed by dissolution of the Korean army, further manpower joined the partisan units on the far side of the border. Some 1,400 raids by 70,000 partisans into Korea were said to have occurred in 1908.[86] Militarily Japanese forces were able to contain the challenge. Moreover, the number of Japanese residents, 9,354 in 1904, had jumped to 171,543 by 1910.[87] The Japanese themselves had been deeply divided on the idea of outright annexation of Korea. Itō (assassinated in 1909 by a Korean) and Inoue had opposed it; the army favoured it, the navy opposed.[88] Korea itself did not create a problem with foreign powers. They both accepted the primacy of Japanese interests in Korea, and saw the Japanese presence as a source of regional stability. It was Japan's interest in mainland Asia, first China and then Manchuria, in the 1910s, which imperilled Japanese relationships with other powers.

American and Japanese diplomatic relations were still good in 1905, and it was the American intervention which brought together representatives of the two warring countries at Portsmouth, New Hampshire. American intervention was prompted more by concern that Russia might prevail in the long term than by positive good will. In the background was America's transformation almost overnight into a Pacific colonial power. It had acquired Hawaii in 1898 and in the same year, through its defeat of Spain, had occupied the Philippines. Its commercial stake also expanded in both Manchuria and in China. A large missionary involvement was even more potent in creating a popular American interest: 3,100 American Protestant missionaries entered China in the first decade of the new century.[89] As the late-comer in the race for empire in the east, it

[85] On this war, see Ian Nish, *The origins of the Russo-Japanese war* (London, 1985).
[86] White, *Transition to global rivalry*, p.220; Duus, *Abacus and the sword*, pp.221–4, 229–30.
[87] Duus, *Abacus and the sword*, p.289.   [88] Tetsuo Najita, *Hara Kei*, p.96.
[89] LaFaber, *The clash*, p.66. On missionaries, see an interesting article by Pearl S. Buck, 'Missionaries of empire', in Joseph Barnes (ed.), *Empire in the east* (London, 1934), pp.241–66.

opposed exclusive foreign enclaves, and was an advocate of an Open Doors policy allowing all outside countries to compete on an even basis. As both America and Japan were new and rising powers in the Pacific, tensions were probably inevitable in the long term. The scattered islands in the north Pacific, for long almost ignored by westerners (occasionally visited but rarely a subject of a claim to sovereignty), began finally to fall prey in the second half of the century to acquisition by French, Germans or Americans (a factor central to Japanese apprehension in the 1870s over the Ryukyus). In the case of Japan, the Ryukyus and Taiwan (and in the First World War, seizure of Germany's island possessions in the Pacific), in the case of the United States, Hawaii and the Philippines, gave both countries an involvement in the Pacific. Future mastery of the Pacific was thus added to concern over China and was among the factors which accelerated tensions.

From quite early on, racial prejudice too complicated the story.[90] Japanese emigration goes back no further than 1868. Before arrangements for their new home in the north of Japan had been made, a few Aizu samurai families, probably no more than thirty-five persons, went to America.[91] The first migrants to Hawaii, a handful leaving without permission, were recorded in 1868,[92] and a treaty with Hawaii in 1871, promoted by foreign business interests in Japan, envisaged migrations. Little migration occurred at first, essentially as a result of Meiji government caution. A treaty in 1875–6 between the United States and Hawaii which opened the American market to sugar from Hawaii created scope for labour in the sugar plantations. A total of 945 migrants left for Hawaii in 1884.[93] The British consular report for Kanagawa for that year noted that a special commissioner had acted for the Hawaiian government, and each migrant signed his contract before the prefectural authorities. The migration was not triggered by poverty; the migrants came from a few well-defined regions in the west of Honshu and in Kyushu; they were at a middle level of rural society; in the main they did not envisage permanent settlement; as contract workers it was their intention to return home

[90] An excellent account of the complex currents in American attitudes to Japan and the Japanese is contained in Joseph M. Henning, *Outposts of civilization: race, religion and the formative years of American–Japanese relations* (New York, 2000). See also J. W. Dower, 'Race, language and war in two cultures' and 'Fear and prejudice in US–Japanese relations', in Dower, *Japan in war and peace: essays on history, culture and race* (London, 1993), pp.257–85, 301–35.
[91] John E. Van Sant, *Pacific pioneers: Japanese journeys to America and Hawaii 1850–80* (Urbana, 2000), pp.124–9.
[92] Tadashi Aruga, 'Editor's introduction', *Japanese journal of American studies*, no. 3 (1989), p.4. This issue, the editor's introduction in particular (pp.1–25), is an excellent series of studies on the subject of emigration.
[93] *PP Japan*, vol. 7, pp.451–2, Report on the trade of Kanagawa for 1884.

with their savings. In 1894 a community of 22,000 Japanese, of whom 8,500 were contract workers, existed in Hawaii.[94] Contract workers were recruited through small emigration societies (of which there were about thirty). In 1900 the Japanese government, which had from the very outset sought to satisfy itself that the conditions of employment of migrants were satisfactory, prohibited the migration of contract workers.[95] From this point migrants to Hawaii were free workers (though exit permits were still required, and were given cautiously): about ninety per cent of the migrants were still recruited through emigration societies.[96]

This migration was a very minor one in the huge migratory currents of the late nineteenth century. In the United States, migration from the orient had at first been exclusively Chinese: by 1882 some 300,000 Chinese were living on the west coast, and migrants in the single year 1882 had soared to 38,579. Resistance to movement on this scale led to its termination by the Chinese Exclusion Act of 1882.[97] Resentment of Chinese residents continued, however, and a number were killed on several occasions: twenty in Los Angeles in 1891, and in an attack on a Chinatown in a city in Wyoming, twenty-eight lost their lives.[98] Inevitably this friction set the pattern for opposition to other Asian immigrants as soon as they appeared. In the 1880s, there cannot have been 1,500 Japanese on the west coast. As in Hawaii, the pattern in the new migration was of a large turnover (as many returned). In all, 120,000 actually entered the United States: in 1910, 70,000 Japanese by birth resided there.[99] When Hawaii was taken over by the United States in 1898, Hawaii gained in importance as a transit point. Earnings in America were higher than in Hawaii; using Hawaii as a stepping stone for the journey across the Pacific, over half of the Japanese settling in the United States took this route.

The initial attraction was well-paid work on the rapidly expanding railways of the west coast whose population and economic importance were growing in the 1880s and 1890s. Upwardly mobile, the Japanese

[94] Murayama Yūzo, *Amerika ni ikita nihonjin imin: nikkei issei no hikari to kage* [Japanese immigrants to America: light and shade in the first generation of Japanese-Americans] (Tokyo, 1989). See also his 'Information and emigrants: interprefectural differences of Japanese migration to the Pacific northwest, 1880–1915', *Journal of economic history*, vol. 51, no. 1 (March 1991), pp.125–47.

[95] On Japanese policy, see *PP Japan*, vol. 7, pp.451–2, Report on the trade of Kanagawa for 1884.

[96] Murayama, *America ni ikita nihonjin imin*, p.44.

[97] Bill Ong Hing, *Making and remaking Asian America through immigration policy, 1850–1990* (Stanford, 1993), pp.21, 23.

[98] Murayama, *America ni ikita nihonjin imin*, p.151.

[99] Murayama, *America ni ikita nihonjin imin*, pp.2, 30. If Japanese born in the United States are included, a higher figure results. See Ong Hing, *Making and remaking Asian America*, p.55.

spread into services (especially as owners of hotels, restaurants and laundries) and into market-gardening and agriculture, including quickly the acquisition of land. Newspapers expressed hostility to the migration, and in California in 1905 the state legislature declared unanimously that Japanese immigrants were 'immoral, intemperate, quarrelsome men bound to labour for a pittance'. The state legislature called for a limitation of Japanese immigration. The president, Theodore Roosevelt, ignored the call, but on the west coast the Japanese and Korean Exclusion League was formed. There was a call for the boycott of restaurants owned by Japanese. Two Japanese seismologists who had been dispatched to California to help in the wake of the San Francisco earthquake of 1906 were assaulted. The San Francisco School Board segregated all Japanese, Chinese and Korean students.

From the outset the *Gaimushō* (Foreign Ministry) was very sensitive to hostility abroad. After 1900 refusals of permits increased sharply, and in all subsequent years, permits granted were exceeded by applications turned down.[100] In statistical terms there was a gap between migration from Japan as measured by permits, and American figures for migrants. The difference was to a large extent accounted for by migration from Hawaii, which was not recorded as migration from abroad and which rose in the first decade.[101] Despite the constraints (restrictive issue of permits and American hostility) the total number of immigrants had continued to rise. With west coast alarm becoming a factor of political weight at federal level, in 1907 the immigration of Japanese from Hawaii was prohibited. The following year a major diplomatic confrontation between the two states was defused only by means of an intergovernmental agreement. The Japanese undertook informally to refuse travel documents to the lowest social category, labourers. In exchange for this, wives and children (including spouses to be), could join their families; the American government undertook to bring pressure to bear on the San Francisco School Board to rescind the segregation order.

Furore in 1907–8 occurred on both sides. In May 1907 there was a riot in San Francisco. Some of the Atlantic fleet was sent to augment the Pacific fleet. This gesture of menace was not to be taken seriously, but it does reflect a presidential prudence in not offending the bellicose mood of the hour (including talk of war). In Japan, the press was full of reporting on California; political groups in the Diet protested, and there was a demand for the boycott of American goods. The Aliens Land Acts in California in 1912 were intended to prevent foreign ownership of land (though by leasing, or by corporate ownership loopholes remained)

---

[100] Murayama, *America ni ikita nihonjin imin*, p.35.
[101] Murayama, *America ni ikita nihonjin imin*, p.43.

and a further act in 1920 sought to close existing loopholes including property transfers from alien parents to citizen children.[102] The arrival of brides for Japanese in the United States (the so-called 'picture brides', chosen by their future husbands from photographs supplied by agencies in Japan) was denounced: once again tension was defused by a voluntary prohibition by the Japanese authorities of such brides in 1920. The Philippines did not provide an outlet for Japanese migrants. A combination of Japanese official caution and opposition by the Catholic church, which feared for the dilution of Christianity, ensured that immigration to the islands was negligible, though Japanese were not excluded by law at any time. There were reportedly only nine Japanese residents in 1896.[103] Even later, in the 1930s, despite inter-war Japanese economic penetration of Asia, the Japanese authorities required convincing proof of assured means of livelihood before granting a permit: at that time there were 20,000 Japanese in the Philippines.[104]

The British consul at Kanagawa in his report for 1884 had noted that a scheme had been put forward in the preceding year for migration to British Columbia.[105] In 1893 migration to Canada, Australia, Brazil, Guatemala and Borneo was noted variously as having occurred or as being canvassed.[106] The numbers were not large (in part a consequence of Japanese policy itself), though the interest in emigration also followed from awareness of the outside world created by widening foreign trade. By 1901, Japanese, who even before this could not purchase land in Australia, were effectively excluded.[107] The entry of Japanese who had settled in Canada and Mexico across the common borders of these with the United States was prohibited by 1907 legislation. Eventually the migrations to Mexico and South America, notably Brazil, did acquire some importance: as the sex ratios were better balanced, through natural increase, they were gradually to become significant communities. By the 1930s, there were 128,000 Japanese in Brazil, the record number of immigrants for any single year being 12,000.[108]

---

[102] Ong Hing, *Making and remaking Asian America*, pp.59–60.
[103] J. M. Saniel, *Japan and the Philippines 1868–1898* (New York, 1973), pp.64–5.
[104] W. H. Chamberlin, *Japan over Asia* (London, 1938), p.160.
[105] *PP Japan*, vol. 7, p.452, Report on trade of Kanagawa for 1884.
[106] *PP Japan*, vol. 9, p.594, Report on Osaka and Hyogo for 1884. There were in the 1890s some contract workers on sugar plantations in Queensland, Australia. See H. Frie, 'Japan discovers Australia: the emergence of Australia in the Japanese world view, 1540s–1900', *Monumenta nipponica*, vol. 39, no. 1 (Spring 1984), pp.77–9.
[107] Frie, 'Japan discovers Australia', p.80.
[108] Chamberlin, *Japan over Asia*, pp.22–3. Of the 285,000 immigrants of Japanese descent or *Nikkeijin* counted in 1998 statistics of Japanese population, eighty-two per cent are from Brazil (D. de Carvalho, 'The making of a minority in Japan', *Japan Foundation newsletter*, vol. 27, nos. 3–4 (March 2000), p.21n).

Racial equality was an emotive issue for Japanese public opinion. If Japanese abroad were treated as second-class residents (and put on a par in the United States or Australia with Chinese and Koreans), the issue could not be divorced from the inferior status as a nation from which Japan was rising only as recently as 1902 (with the Anglo-Japanese treaty[109]) or 1905 (victory over Russia). In subtle, or perhaps in unsubtle ways, Japanese victory over a western nation in 1905 added to the problem: for the Japanese, victory over a western power made it all the more intolerable that Japanese citizens should be treated as inferior; for the Americans, a Japanese victory, if welcome in halting Russian pretensions, increased alarms as they might now replace the Russians as a menace to American interests. Rumours circulated that the Japanese in Mexico might form part of a conspiracy to take over the Panama Canal which was under construction. This was an irrational fear, but it does illustrate how racial tensions and the ambitions whetted by an imperial role intertwined. Inevitably, for the Japanese at least, racial equality became an issue in the Versailles treaty negotiations, and perhaps equally inevitably the Americans were insensitive to it. If the modern world in the Atlantic grew out of Versailles, so also did the world of the Pacific.

---

[109] See Yoshitake Oka, 'The first Anglo-Japanese alliance in Japanese public opinion', in Henry and Lehmann, *Themes and theories*, pp.185–93.

8 From peace (Versailles 1919) to war (Pearl Harbor 1941)

In a repetition of a pattern of external forces dictating the pace of internal change, the First World War, a many-sided opportunity rather than a threat, enlarged Japan's external involvement to a scale which could not have been anticipated before 1914, and ultimately, through the complications that followed, led disastrously into what the Japanese were to call the Great Pacific War (1941–5). Once the 1914–18 war began, Britain wished for Japanese support, though hoping to limit Japan's role to action at sea against Germany rather than territorial acquisition. However, Japan went on to occupy the German possessions in Shantung and the German islands in the north Pacific. That far, Japanese involvement, if more than Britain relished, was at least in line with the conventional action of a great power.

While occupation of Shantung was defensible on the principle of realpolitik, the Twenty-One demands made by Japan in 1915 on the Chinese government, whose terms, if conceded, would have involved a measure of political control of China, were a different matter. The demands failed to recognise Chinese nationalism, which, already growing, had become a new force, and represented a potential derailment of Japanese foreign policy. They were denounced by the senior *genrō*, Yamagata, and the objectionable political demands were dropped from the programme (reduced to fifteen demands). On the narrowest criterion, that is, ignoring Chinese rights altogether (the western standard since 1840), the Twenty-One demands were incoherent, at one and the same time an implicit challenge to rival imperial powers and an impulsive formulation of policy by faction rather than by deliberation.

No less seriously, Japan failed to appreciate the geopolitical implications of the pan-Pacific role which the United States had acquired in 1898 (widened by the building between 1903 and 1913 of the Panama Canal). The United States' declaration of its Open Doors policy in Asia in 1899, calling for a level playing-field in access by outsiders to China, marked the public emergence of the United States into the power politics of the region. It foreshadowed the initiative by the American president in setting

239

up the peace conference at Portsmouth, New Hampshire, which brought to an end in 1905 the Russo-Japanese war. Peace in Manchuria did not prove as favourable to the access of American capital as had been hoped, and in 1909 the Americans proposed the internationalisation of the railways in Manchuria, or, failing that, a joint American–British venture to build a new railway in the region.[1]

To the Americans, the Twenty-One demands in 1915 upset entirely the Open Doors concept. The Ishi–Lansing agreement of 1917 traded assurances of American access to Manchuria for American recognition of a special Japanese interest in China. The British and other allied powers had made vague promises of support for Shantung's transfer to Japan. Wishful thinking by the Japanese, resting on such expressions of goodwill, stiffened their resolve: they drew a parallel with the cynical Triple Power intervention of 1895, in which Japanese had to forgo some of the fruits of victory. The Americans, however, whose recognition in 1917 of Japan's special position in China had precluded support for territorial acquisition, were to be forthright from the outset in their wish to restore Shantung to China.

Japan did get the peninsula in 1919 though the fact that it had to relinquish its political rights in 1922 made the price a high one. As always in the case of Japanese delegations, the mission to the peace conference at Versailles had been large, sixty-four members in all. The instructions to the delegation were narrow (some of the Japanese diplomats were demoralised by the low profile maintained by the delegation, and by its isolation in its hotel in the Place Vendôme on which they had descended, even bringing their own cooks with them). The effective leader was Makino Nobuaki (1861–1949) who as a youth had accompanied the Iwakura mission to America in 1871, and remained there for three years as a student (Saionji Kimmochi was the nominal leader, but took little part in the public or private proceedings). The instructions given to the delegation, looking on other issues as inter-western ones, were to confine activity to two topics, recognition of racial equality among nations, and formalising Japanese occupation of Shantung. The two issues were intertwined in a complex fashion. Though they could be seen (once Chinese rights were disregarded) as independent of one another, they were interrelated in the sense that recognition of Japan's political stake in Shantung would not only give Japan a new status in China but by doing so at a full-blown international conference, put Japan on a footing of real equality with the Europeans. China's delegation, though vociferous on the question of Shantung, did not count as one of the five major powers

[1] F. V. Field, 'Battle of the bankers', in Barnes, *Empire in the east*, p.160.

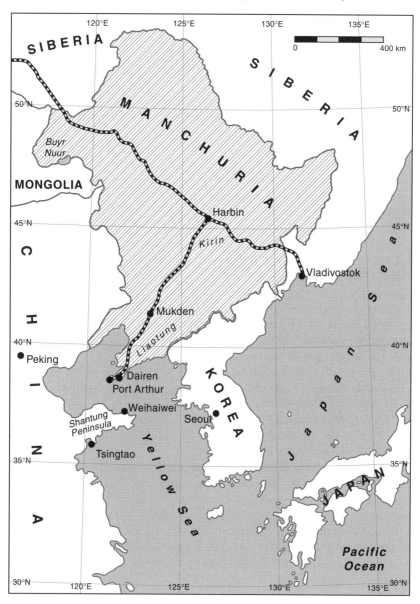

8. Manchuria

at Versailles (the United States, Britain and France, and the two 'new' powers of Italy and Japan).

The inclusion of Japan among the big five quickly revealed how hollow the country's great-power status was. The status was appreciated at the outset as a real prize: a refrain of the time was that Japan had become 'a first-class nation'.[2] On the other hand, the treaty negotiations were conducted in quite a different spirit. The big decisions were taken by Wilson, Lloyd George and Clemenceau at private meetings, and the status of Japan and Italy was maintained rather vestigially in a series of much less important meetings of foreign ministers.

On racial equality, the Japanese encountered dismissive attitudes: in particular the English-speaking countries failed to see the point of the Japanese concern. For the Americans, the issue was on the part of the Japanese a mere bargaining counter, which they intended to trade in, in return for an American climb-down over Shantung.[3] At the first plenary session of the conference, Makino in a powerful and passionate address raised the principle of equality. It encountered resistance also in private negotiations with the Americans and British.[4] A vote in the committee devising the charter of the League of Nations highlighted the humiliation more fully. On their proposal to include a reference to racial equality in the preamble of the charter, the Japanese had a majority on their side: the Americans, the British and Australians were outvoted by the French and other nations (the actual vote was eleven to six). However, President Wilson highhandedly declared that the issue could not be pursued further, as it implied interference in the internal affairs of nations and hence would require unanimity. The proceedings, which received enormous attention in the Japanese press, seemed to confirm that Japan faced a racially motivated external opposition.

All that said, however, neither Japan nor America emerged well from the Shantung episode. Because recognition of its stake in Shantung was a policy which had the backing of the cabinet and of public opinion, Japan's serious misreading of the changed circumstances of China had large (and ultimately disastrous) implications. Subtly it changed Japan's position from one of defending itself against western encroachment into an exploitative role identical to that of other countries. Japan missed a great opportunity as in the case of Korea earlier. China, despite or because of its

---

[2] On early use of the term, see Pyle, *The new generation in Meiji Japan*, pp.198–9.

[3] According to Makino's son-in-law, Makino had genuinely hoped to put the matter to rest at Versailles. Dower, *Empire and aftermath*, p.46.

[4] *Rinen naki gaikō: Pari kōwakaigi* [Foreign policy without ideals: the Paris Peace Conference] (Tokyo, 1996) pp.92–8. The book is based on research for an NHK documentary shown on the British television station, Channel 4, in the late 1980s.

defeat by Japan in 1894–5, had begun to look to Japan as a model for reform and as an example of successful response to external encroachment.
Sun Yat-Sen had lived in Japan, and 1,300 Chinese students entered Japan
in a single year, 1904: in Waseda alone, 651 students had graduated up
to 1910.[5] Hara's welcome of the news of success and even more the
tone of public and press reporting, though comprehensible in the sense
that the Japanese negotiators would not return empty-handed, betrayed
Japanese insensitivity to the underlying implications. However great the
attention the equality issue had received in Japan, the mixed motivations
of the time explain why in the modern historiography, Shantung – Japan's
diplomatic success – rather than equality – Japan's failure – holds as it did
in mid-1919 the central place in the narrative.[6] In other words, Japan had
pushed herself into the club of European powers which, against American
wishes, held extraterritorial interests in China. Interestingly, in 1918 Sir
Ernest Satow, in a letter to another old Tokyo hand in the Foreign Office,
speculated with insight on Japan's place in forthcoming events if she were
cast in the role of defender of China.[7] In their confined role at Versailles
the Japanese gave the impression correctly that material acquisition was a
major part of their agenda, and the equality theme itself (whose adverse
outcome was taken as suggesting a likelihood that Japan would not join
the new League) was dropped only after a meeting between Makino and
the Americans, the precise nature of which is not known but which was
followed by Japanese acceptance of the League of Nations at the final plenary session of the conference. In other words, the equality theme meant
racial equality with westerners rather than equality between the Japanese
and other Asians.

The Japanese were not far wrong in their assumption that the underlying reason for opposition to ceding Shantung to Japan was less the welfare
of China than reluctance to strengthen a new and formidable rival. With
a stake already in the Liaotung peninsula, acquisition of Shantung meant
that Japan, as holder of concessions in the two peninsulas guarding the
approach to the Yellow Sea, held a strategic geopolitical place in north
China. In fourteen years Japan had jumped from a position of inferiority to one which, joined to the advantages of geographical proximity,
made it a regional superpower. Despite American ambitions to expand

---

[5] Kawakatsu Heita, *Kaiyō renpō ron: chikyū o gāden airando ni* [The argument for an oceanic
federation: changing the face of the earth into garden islands] (Tokyo, 2001), p.190.
[6] See e.g. Arima Manabu, *Nihon no kindai* [Modern Japan], vol. 4, *Kokusaika no naka
no teikoku nihon 1905–1924* [Imperial Japan and internationalisation] (Tokyo, 1999),
pp.173–80.
[7] PRO, London, 30/33/11/10, f.47, Satow papers, Satow to Gubbins, 2 June 1918. The
same line of thought as Satow's had already occurred in a letter of the *genrō* Matsukata to
a new prime minister Terauchi in 1916 (H. M. Reischauer, *Samurai and silk*, pp.144–5).

its business interests, Japanese businessmen already outnumbered Americans in Manchuria and China and continued to do so.[8]

If the Japanese emerged badly from the negotiations because of the central role of territorial acquisition in their policy, the Americans did so to no less a degree. Their preparedness, despite objecting to Shantung's transfer to Japan, to defer finally to Japan because of Wilson's fear that Japan might not participate in the planned League of Nations, reflected an ambivalence which was to repeat itself in American policy right up to the outbreak of the Second World War. Opposition to Japan's ambitions, when combined with a readiness to regard Japan's role as an essential element against even greater disorder, meant that through the 1930s acceptance of Japan's stake in Manchuria and in China was seen as less damaging to American business interests than a more principled opposition. In other words, there was more calculation than principle on all sides. China's interests did not enter into the reckoning; provided Japan did not hinder western business access to the region, its role would be regarded, some huffing and puffing apart, as constructive.

The equality and Shantung issues exacerbated public opinion on both sides of the Pacific to the degree that the popular hysteria of 1907–8 was repeated in 1919–20 and more damagingly. As early as 1918, Gubbins, a former Tokyo diplomat, who during the war years was employed in reading the Japanese press for the British Foreign Office, had concluded that 'to my mind difficult days are in store for Japan. New Nations, with China, and Russia where anything can happen, with America, now a great military power, suspicions [sic] ... contain possibilities of great friction, if not worse, in the time to come.'[9] In both Japan and the United States books appeared in 1920–1 talking about a future war. Unease infected even the old Foreign Office hands who, understanding Japan, were in many ways sympathetic to the country. Satow, still retaining warm Japanese recollections, was himself far from being unaffected by the opposition to Japanese claims of racial equality.[10] As early as 1917, he had written that

[8] Howe, *The origins of Japanese trade supremacy*, pp.376–7.

[9] PRO, London, 30/33/11/8, Satow papers, to Satow, 1 Dec. 1918. A useful source on Satow is I. C. Ruxton, *The diaries and letters of Sir Ernest Satow (1843–1929), a scholar-diplomat in east Asia* (Lewiston, N.Y., 1998).

[10] See a passage in a letter of 23 Jan. 1921 to Reay, PRO, London, 30/33/11/18, Satow papers. It is all the more striking because he was capable of very handsome comment on the good faith of Japanese officials (notably, Satow diary, 14 April 1920, PRO, London, 30/33/17/5). His book on Japan was based largely on a manuscript of the 1880s, and publication was prompted solely by suggestions, given the topicality of Japan in 1919, from relatives who had read it. Apart from comments on proofs and on problems with publishers, his diaries have singularly little comment on its genesis, progress or reception and suggest that early Meiji times were occupying little of his thoughts. Though the book contains a sustained critique of Harry Parkes, it cannot be seen as reflecting any views on Japan one way or other in 1919.

I agree that there are no limits to Japanese ambitions, and the worst of it is that they are so remarkably efficient as soldiers and sailors, and in other branches besides diplomatic and consular business. I have been speculating on the possibility of its one day becoming necessary for ourselves and the Americans to put a cut on their ambitions. By the time this war comes to an end the Americans will have become a military power. If it should ever come to a war for this purpose, Hong Kong will be the object of attack for Japan, and next to that the Philippines which the Americans will have some difficulty in defending. They will have to greatly increase their navy . . . [11]

Four years later, he was even more pessimistic, and to a friend observed that 'I cannot help feeling that some day those two countries may have a war.'[12]

The Shantung concession was the factor which led the United States, more for political and economic reasons than principle, to refuse to ratify the treaty. Thus the treaty of Versailles was responsible for the United States' refusal to enter the League of Nations, and ultimately for Japan's subsequent withdrawal when in 1933 it chose to look at the league's role in the Manchurian question as a ganging up against Japan, rather than an issue involving Chinese rights and posing delicate questions about its own foreign relations. Once events were placed in the context of unequal treatment (which since the 1860s had rankled so much in the Japanese mind) and of the self-evident lack of morality in western policy (despite preaching in a lofty tone to others), it was difficult even for moderate Japanese to oppose the outcome of policies, however defective they were. As in the 1860s, despite sharp divides among Japanese, outright opposition was a luxury a vulnerable country could not afford. In the words of a Japanese friend in 1932 to Joseph Grew (1880–1965), the American ambassador, about doubts over the army's Manchurian adventures, 'The people rallied behind the army, like all members of a family will stand behind one member who is being attacked from the outside . . . Any violent move against Japan now will strengthen the family feeling.'[13]

The long-term consequences of Versailles were momentous. The short-term price also was high. Britain, no longer seeing Japan as a shield against Russian encroachment but as a a serious challenger, was alarmed by the changing balance of power. British fears were also worked on by the

---

[11] PRO, London, 30/33/11/10, ff.9–10, Satow papers, 14 Nov. 1917, to Gubbins.
[12] PRO, London, 30/33/11/18, Satow to Reay, 30 Jan. 1921; also 30/33/11/14, John Reay to Satow, 17 Jan. 1921.
[13] Joseph C. Grew, *Ten years in Japan, contemporary record drawn from the diaries and private and official papers of Joseph C. Grew, United States ambassador to Japan 1932–1942* (New York, 1944), pp.67–8. The continuation of the quotation is also interesting, as it reflected the widespread view that moderates would in the end prevail: 'but if everyone stays quiet for a while, there will be a feeling arising against the Army and maybe the Shidehara diplomacy will return'.

Americans: in other words Britain and the United States presented a united face to Japan. The alliance with Britain was not renewed in 1922. Even in 1921 it was seen as already having served its purpose, though failure to renew it, it was quite evident, would be interpreted by Japan as an unfriendly act.[14] A Washington gathering of nine countries took place at the end of 1921 to settle the tensions in the Pacific region (a Pacific counterpart to the Versailles conference of 1919). Among other things, it sought to settle the Shantung issue, while leaving Japanese business interests untouched, by withdrawal of the Japanese military from the concessions. In a naval conference in 1922 (followed up by a further one in 1930) under the aegis of the Washington gathering, for the purpose of limiting a naval race among countries that had been 'allies' as late as 1919, the Americans and English stood together.

The isolation in which Japan had found itself in its pursuit of the equality theme at the Versailles conference was repeated; indeed, in diplomatic terms, Japan was isolated to a degree which it had not been since the beginning of its relationship with the outside world in 1853. Japanese naval strength had become a central concern for the western countries. The Japanese navy had already been a formidable one by 1904. Though its vessels at that time were still built overseas, their technical specifications were ahead of western ones, and the navy's strategy and tactics were more advanced than those of other fleets.[15] Despite the much greater political clout of the army, the gap in expenditure between the two services narrowed over time, and was virtually closed by 1913 (a year in which naval expenditure was the dominant political issue). By the late 1910s an excess of naval over military expenditure bore an ominous message of challenge to western supremacy at sea. Navy expenditure mounted again in the renewed international tensions of the mid-1930s.[16]

The irony of recognition at Versailles was that far from becoming a great power, in the last analysis Japan was still treated simply as top of the second division. The ratio of ships in the naval conferences was 5:5:3. Whatever the relative weight of the three powers, the overall arithmetic meant that the only Asiatic power which had a place in the naval power game in the Pacific was given 3/13 weight.[17] Such a low proportion was hard to defend even in purely naval terms (though the moderate politicians of the 1920s, while hardly comforted by it, chose to live with it)

[14] PRO, London, 30/33/11/18, Satow diary, 27 February 1921.
[15] Howe, *The origins of Japanese trade supremacy*, pp.280–6.
[16] For details of expenditure, see Tobe, *Nihon no kindai*, vol. 9, pp.109, 137, 224.
[17] France and Italy were also covered by the naval conference. The treaty covered Atlantic as well as Pacific, but the post-1919 U.S. navy was effectively a Pacific fleet.

and the agreements both defined and maintained an old-fashioned western dominance. It is perfectly understandable from the Japanese point of
view that the naval treaty was allowed to run out in 1936. Many of the
key administrators and diplomats of the 1930s had been junior members
of the Japanese delegation at Versailles, and bore the marks of the facile
rejection by the allies of the idea of racial equality. Reading back from
later times, the policies of the inter-war period can be seen as combining
a western ambition to preserve the Pacific as a western lake, and by reaction a Japanese resentment, supported by a volatile public opinion, of
the basic unfairness of a western-imposed balance of naval power.

The west was of course now beginning to be challenged even on the
economic front. Japan's economic diversification gathered pace.[18] Urban
population grew rapidly, and its cities acquired a recognisably western-
style infrastructure. Under Hara's guiding hand as the dominant force
behind the *Seiyūkai*, the railway network also filled out rapidly in the first
decade, and the road system began its modernisation. The First World
War accelerated change: Japan was in the fortunate position of being technically a combatant, but out of the war zone. In the absence of competition when the resources of the western countries were being destructively
consumed in war, Japan began to find new niches in outside markets. As
western shipping was equally absent, the Japanese also rapidly expanded
their shipbuilding. The tonnage of construction in 1919 was 600,000
tons, which put its output close to that of Britain and the United States,[19]
at a time when they were feverishly replacing war-time losses; and Japan's
mercantile fleet inevitably emerged also as the third largest in the world.
Japan became in the 1920s the major textile exporter to Asian markets.

Even the Tokyo earthquake of 1923 did not halt things.[20] Recovery
was rapid, and the city's new infrastructure made the city a modern and
largely western-style metropolis. The circular *Yamanote* line, the central
Chūō line and the *Tōyoko* commuter line between Tokyo and Yokohama
were built to provide an efficient overground commuter service; the first
underground line, the *Ginza* line, took shape between 1927 and 1934.
In Osaka the *Hankyū* suburban system linked Osaka, Kobe and Kyoto,
tied to a departmental store to promote custom for store and commuter
line alike. Office workers – forerunners of the modern *salaryman* – were

---

[18] For an effective and economical survey, see W. J. Macpherson, *The economic development
of Japan 1868–1941* (Cambridge, 1987).
[19] Masataka Kosaka, 'The Showa era (1926–89)', in Gluck and Graubard, *Showa: the Japan
of Hirohito*, p.28.
[20] The Tokyo earthquake, along with the Lisbon earthquake of 1755 and the San Francisco
earthquake of 1906, had unique repercussions on world opinion. See Hatano Masaru
and Iimori Akiko, *Kantō daishinsai to nichibei gaikō* [The Kanto earthquake disaster and
Japanese–American diplomatic relations] (Tokyo, 1999).

increasing rapidly in numbers. Women clerical workers were emerging. Most men dressed in western style, and more slowly the same change was followed by women. Land was still cheap, sites in the suburbs costing no more than twice annual clerical salaries. Tokyo became a metropolis of almost 5 million in the 1930s, and was now one of the world's largest cities.[21] Grew, who had visited Japan many years before, in 1932 on his return commented on 'the wide streets and avenues, great modern buildings, luxuriant parks and gardens. The city is going ahead so fast that it is almost impossible for an ancient visitor like myself to catch up with it.'[22] In 1930 motor cars for the first time exceeded rickshaws in number; and the use of taxis became common.[23]

The education system developed apace, not only the secondary schools and pupils, but the university system. From three state universities in 1910 the total number of universities had risen to forty-six in 1930.[24] Up to 1918 the four great private institutions, Waseda, Keio, Meiji and Chuō, did not hold the formal style of university, being rated as *Senmongakkō*. The number and repute of private universities spread rapidly from this point, and by 1930 they held by far the larger part of the expanding student population. Under a common form of university classification the number of students rose threefold in the 1920s: there were over 70,000 in 1930 and about 500 faculty members. The broadening of education led to the diffusion of new ideas, and of specialised journals advocating them. Popular participation in politics was also proposed in ideas such as *minponshugi* (popular sovereignty) and in the societies among University of Tokyo students such as the *Remmeikai* (New Dawn) and *Shinjinki* (New People's Association).[25] Socialist thought and journals advocating it or ideas of social reform had appeared before 1914, and an interest in

[21] The *locus classicus* is, or should be, *Me de miru Tokyo hyaku nen* [A visual view of Tokyo's hundred years], prepared by Tokyo city administration, 1969. Because it identified districts inhabited by *eta* (outcasts) and hence was in conflict with official policy to obliterate the distinction, it was never formally published. See also Kitaoka Shinichi, *Nihon no kindai* [Modern Japan], vol. 5, *Seitō kara gunbu e 1924–1941* [From political parties to militarism] (Tokyo, 1999), pp.121–36, 245–53, 367–9. For a very readable account of Tokyo in the Meiji and Taishō periods, see E. Seidensticker, *Low city, high city, Tokyo from Edo to the earthquake: how the shogun's ancient capital became a great modern city, 1867–1923* (Cambridge, Mass., 1983).

[22] Grew, *Ten years in Japan*, p.26.

[23] D. P. Platt, 'My-car-isma: Motorising the Showa self', in Gluck and Graubard, *Showa: the Japan of Hirohito*, p.233.

[24] For figures see Arima, *Nihon no kindai*, vol. 4, p.161 (on their interpretations, see p.160); and Byron K. Marshall, *Academic freedom and the Japanese imperial university 1868–1939* (Berkeley, 1992), pp.81–3.

[25] J. T. Rimer, *A hidden fire: Russian and Japanese cultural encounters 1868–1926* (Stanford, 1995), p.211. For a very full account of the changes, see Arima, *Nihon no kindai*, vol. 4, pp.272–308.

dealing with social disadvantage, urban and rural alike, grew rapidly.[26] The impact of the Russian Revolution speeded an interest in socialism and communism. Trade unions multiplied. They were already 187 in 1919, and in 1919 at Versailles the Japanese had accepted the principle of participation in the ILO (International Labour Organisation). The number and membership of unions continued to rise through the 1920s, though it did not reach at its peak (1931) more than 7.9 per cent of the labour force.[27] An interest in tenant welfare in rural areas also grew, and tenant organisations had 72,000 members by 1922. The new ideas permeated the universities, and while they were notably strong in the private universities, they were widespread in the state universities. In the University of Tokyo for instance, economics, which became a separate department in 1918, comprised a wide range from pacifists (like Yanaihara Tadao (1893–1961), a Christian pacifist), reformers and socialists to, at the other end of the spectrum, conservatives.[28]

Cinema, radio, theatre, publishing (the Iwanami bunko series – serious books at a cheap price – was launched in 1927) progressed and, as in the west, mass dailies appeared. The teaching of English in schools became widespread, and there was a vogue for western music. Sports flourished, especially baseball, and Japan participated regularly – and with considerable success in 1932 – in the Olympic Games. Tokyo's status as one of the great capitals of the world was further confirmed after the 1936 Berlin Olympic Games in the decision to hold the 1940 Olympiad there. For the upper classes at least a life style which was western and luxurious emerged; and golf had already begun to obsess those who could afford to play it. As in the west, the contrast between luxury and the difficulties of the lower classes could cause indignation. Censure of these adverse trends came from the very different perspectives of both socialist and right-wing (and militaristic) thinkers, all of whom held out wider objectives for society.

If not an egalitarian state, Japan was in some respects traditionally a society in which extremes of wealth were by western standards not pronounced. To understand the concerns of the militarists, one has to appreciate how rapid economic development had adversely affected society, or more accurately how the accumulation of wealth in new activities was accompanied by a fall in the relative incomes of the rural and working

---

[26] For an interesting analytical account, see Peter Duus, 'Liberal intellectuals and social conflict in Taisho Japan', in Tetsuo Najita and Koschmann, *Conflict in modern Japanese history*, pp.412–40. See also P. Duus and I. Scheiner, 'Socialism, liberalism and Marxism, 1901–1931', in *CHJ*, vol. 6, Peter Duus (ed.), *The nineteenth century* (Cambridge, 1988), pp.654–710, and Jansen, *The making of modern Japan*, p.552.

[27] Arima, *Nihon no kindai*, vol. 4, p.268.   [28] Marshall, *Academic freedom*, pp.102–3.

classes. Agricultural incomes fell sharply, and outside agriculture real wages also fell in the early 1930s.[29] While real wages of day labourers in agriculture recovered from their nadir point, they were still in 1938 well below their pre-depression level. On the other hand, in contrast to the static numbers in agriculture, the numbers employed in manufacturing rose from 5.7 million in 1930 to over 7.6 million in 1938, and their real wages rose to a new peak. In other words, the distribution of income (in what had been a relatively egalitarian society, as it has been again in post-1945 times) did shift in a radical fashion, in part because of growth of wealth, but more because of abrupt movements in relative prices in war and post-war boom, and again in the wake of the Great Depression of 1929, which caused a price fall and decimated exports of silk so vital to large regions of central Honshu.

Around 1900 Japan was still underdeveloped in heavy industry and engineering, and (main lines apart) in railway infrastructure. The first steam locomotive was manufactured as late as 1893, the first warship in 1910. Government investment was confined to infrastructure (especially in railways) and heavy industry (iron and engineering). Shipping lines also benefited from subsidies. The Yawata iron works, created in 1895 by a decree of the Diet, was the first step in the development of large-scale heavy industry in Japan, though it took a number of years to become commercially successful.[30] The First World War accelerated industrialisation. In consumer goods, the war-time absence of European competition meant that Japan captured external markets, especially for its textiles. Manufacturing output rose by seventy-two per cent in 1914–19. The rise was especially marked in heavy engineering, Japan now becoming near self-sufficient. It still depended on imported machinery in electrical production. As a consequence of rapid development of electrical infrastructure, consumption of electricity was widespread, and in a technical sense, lines of transition were longer than in most countries, thus permitting the diffusion of the use of electricity afar. By 1913, the capital investment in electricity was already the equivalent of a third of the now huge investment in railways.[31] Even in the Tohoku, the most rural of Japan's major regions, by the early 1930s eighty per cent of households had electric lighting, a high proportion compared with much of western Europe.[32]

---

[29] Macpherson, *The economic development of Japan*, p.43.
[30] Iriye Akira, 'Japan's drive to great-power status', in *CHJ*, vol. 5 (1989), p.771.
[31] E. S. Crawfour, 'Industrialisation and technological change, 1850–1920', in *CHJ*, vol. 6 (1988), p.401.
[32] Kerry Smith, *A time of crisis: Japan, the great depression and rural revitalization* (Cambridge, Mass., 2001), p.23.

The *zaibatsu* did well in the war years, extending their investment in heavy industry. The post-war recession in 1920 which made many firms insolvent benefited them by providing the opportunity of purchasing failing firms cheaply. Financial panic in 1927, caused by the fragility of the many small banks made precarious by loans to ailing firms, added to the banking resources of the *zaibatsu* as an inflow occurred of deposits from smaller and vulnerable banks. Commercial banks, 1,400 in number in 1927, were halved in the four years following the crisis: they were down to 418 in 1936, to be reduced even more dramatically in later years. One of the consequences of the extension of banking under a *zaibatsu* umbrella was a striking change in the method of financing industry. Before 1931 bank loans were much less important than equity in providing the capital of industry. The relationship changed thereafter with bank credit financing expansion: the new characteristic was one which outlived the war and the break-up after 1945 of the *zaibatsu*.[33] A feature of the 1920s was the rise of the so-called new *zaibatsu*, managed less by men with the managerial and conservative outlook of the established conglomerates, and more by men with a technical background, who bought up firms in heavy industry and chemicals in the 1920s, laying the basis for a new layer of conglomerate.

Growth in the inter-war years had been particularly rapid in metals, chemicals and engineering. Between 1930 and 1937 investment goods rose at three times the rate of consumer goods. The share of heavy industry in industrial output rose from twenty-seven per cent in 1920, to forty-seven per cent in 1937 and sixty-eight per cent in 1942. Japan was now also largely self-sufficient in machine tools and precision instruments. Of the eleven major auto manufacturers in post-war Japan, ten are a product of the post-1936 war-related manufactures of trucks, tanks and warships: only Honda is a pure product of the post-surrender period.[34] The country was the dominant supplier of textiles especially in Asian markets. The devaluation of the yen helped. Japan had returned to the gold standard very late in 1930, and had to abandon it at the end of 1931. The yen devalued by approximately forty per cent. The export pattern shifted also to greater dependence on Asian markets especially for textiles: Asian markets rose from 42.6 per cent to 55.9 per cent from 1929 to 1934. However, success rested not only on price competitiveness: it was bolstered by a high degree of specialisation in the types of cloth sent to individual markets, by very efficient marketing (especially close study

[33] For a succinct analysis of the inter-war *zaibatsu*, see Yamamura, 'Entrepreneurship, ownership and management', pp.330–41. See also Kozo Yamamura, 'Japan 1868–1930: a revised view', in Macpherson, *The industrialisation of Japan*, pp.400–43.
[34] J. W. Dower, 'The useful war', in Dower, *Japan in war and peace*, p.14.

of market requirements), and by the fact that Japan's own large imports of raw materials meant that Asian countries did not have an interest in excluding Japanese goods by prohibitive tariffs.[35]

The relative importance of agriculture declined in the war and inter-war years. As a counterpart to this change, urban population grew: from 16.2 per cent in 1903 to 19.4 in 1913, and still more rapidly to 25.2 per cent in 1920.[36] The transition continued thereafter: inheriting sons remained on farms, but other sons, and the wage-paid labour force, continued to drift to the towns.

Agriculture as % of Net Domestic Product (NDP) and of labour force[a]

year	% of NDP	% of labour force
1885	31.8	64.9
1915	25.2	53.4
1940	10.4	41.1

[a] Nishikawa Shunsaku and Abe Takeshi (eds.), *Nihon keizai-shi*, vol. 4, *Sangyōka no jidai*, pt 1 (Tokyo, 1990), p.82.

In 1915, Japan was structurally comparable to Ireland (an agricultural country with an important industrial region in the north-east); in 1940 Japan, at least as far as the proportion of agricultural population was concerned, was comparable to France. The sharper fall in labour's proportion of income compared with its proportion of the labour force reflects the severity of the contraction of farm incomes. The fall in agricultural incomes, and the adverse effects of devaluation and falling real wages (Japan devalued more sharply vis-à-vis the dollar than Britain did in the 1930s[37]) led to major distortion of income distribution in the 1930s.[38] The rural population and workers in export industries suffered acutely. Employers, salaried workers in the growing service sector in the big cities and workers in new industries dependent on the home market fared much better. A wage differential in favour of employees in large firms, which began to emerge around 1920, widened progressively over time.[39] The distortions

[35] Howe, *The origins of Japanese trade supremacy*, pp.216–31.
[36] Nishikawa and Abe, *Nihon keizai-shi*, vol. 4, pt 1, p.59.
[37] See table in Odaka Kōnosuke and Nakamura Takafusa (eds.), *Nihon keizai-shi* [Economic history of Japan], vol. 6, *Nijū kōzō* [Dual structure] (Tokyo, 1989), p.308.
[38] For pertinent comments, see H. Rovosky, 'What are the "lessons" of Japanese economic history?', in Macpherson, *The industrialisation of Japan*, pp.236–7.
[39] M. Morishima, *Why has Japan 'succeeded'?: western technology and the Japanese ethos* (Cambridge, 1996), pp.109–10.

reflected the sharpness and abruptness of changes in the share of exports in GNP. Exports as a percentage of national income soared during the First World War, reaching a huge 27.4 per cent in 1917. This reflected the abnormal circumstances of Japan's war-time situation, in which Japanese exports easily replaced European goods in Asian markets. The proportion inevitably declined quite sharply thereafter. However, it edged above twenty per cent once more from 1933.[40] This high proportion of exports in national income contrasted with a much lower one in the Meiji period (around ten per cent), and in post-Second World War times with a proportion of ten per cent or a little more of income (and also one of the most egalitarian patterns of income distribution in the industrial world). In a very real sense, in the period from 1914 to the 1930s instability in social trends was acute. Inevitably this had both social and political repercussions.

Growth in the twentieth century produced two Japans. The wealth of Tokyo (with its remarkable recovery after the earthquake) and of the expanding conurbation around Osaka contrasted with the difficulties and even decline in the countryside (notably in the silk industry whose American market had collapsed). The life styles and sophisticated consumer outlays of town dwellers, including the new generation of men and women, salaried and wage-paid alike, contrasted with stagnation and even crisis in the rural world. Decline in real incomes caused by inflation in 1917–18 or again in the collapse of prices in 1929 was dramatic. Farm household income was halved between 1929 and 1931. As if that was not bad enough, harvest failure in 1931 and again in 1934 led to acute food shortages, in 1934–5 amounting to near-famine, in the Tohoku.[41] The collapse of the silk industry copper-fastened the poverty of many districts. The indicators of economic activity tell the story: industrial output grew in the 1930s, whereas silk contracted brutally and agricultural prices remained lower than other prices. In other words, the dividend from development centred on those in growth industries and in the new service activities of booming large cities rather than on the countryside. Industrial output by the mid-1930s had fully recovered from the depression, partly through the success of exports from traditional industries to Asian markets benefiting from the depreciated yen and low wages, but more strikingly in a domestic market context through the growth of the heavy

---

[40] See table in Odaka and Nakamura, *Nihon keizai-shi*, vol. 6, p.71. See also Macpherson, *The economic development of Japan*, pp.37–8.

[41] For the 1934–5 near-famine, there is little documentation in western-language sources, but see K. Smith, *A time of crisis*, pp.58–61, 241–68. On the halving of farm household income between 1929 and 1931, see Odaka and Nakamura, *Nihon keizai-shi*, vol. 6, p.52.

chemical industries in the inter-war years from a mere ten per cent of output to forty-five per cent.

Given the plight of rural dwellers, relief for the countryside became an issue by 1932. In the wake of the 15 May incident (the assassination of the prime minister Inukai and attempts on others by a circle of rural activists and officers), representatives from the peasants and from the provinces submitted a stream of petitions to the Diet, and the political parties supported the demands. Rural work programmes were launched to increase the incomes of peasants, and low-interest loans were made available.[42] Problems were highlighted by novel tenancy disputes. Though tenancy had grown in well-off districts long before 1914, its terms became a subject of contention in the inter-war years.[43] The landlords had usually been well-off tenants who themselves farmed and lived in the same village, or in a neighbouring village. As surplus labour left the countryside for the towns, direct management by employing wage-paid labour became less attractive. Many landlords ceased to farm at all, and rented the remainder of their land. In times of economic boom, many of them had already widened their investment outside agriculture. Some became town dwellers and hence in a novel fashion were remote not only from the concerns of their tenants, but from social contact with them.[44] A new class distinction emerged in the countryside. In the Tohoku, tenancy emerged more slowly, and landlord–tenant disputes became numerous only as rural crisis worsened in the early 1930s. The complexity of tenancy is well shown in the case of the village of Sekishiba in Fukushima prefecture. Land-owning families and families which both owned and rented land predominated. In many instances tenants were renting from fellow villagers. Although Sekishiba village itself did not become a centre of public tenancy disputes, the major source of friction in the Tohoku in the 1930s was the attempt by landlord villagers to take land back from tenants either to farm or to sell.[45] The condition of tenants in the 1920s and 1930s both in the Tohoku and elsewhere has been a subject of considerable acrimony, reflecting historiographical or ideological differences among researchers more than disagreement over the basic facts.[46] The

---

[42] T. Nakamura, 'Depression, recovery, and war, 1920–1945', in Yamamura, *The economic emergence of modern Japan*, p.135.

[43] On agrarian conflict and related issues, see Ann Waswo, 'The transformation of rural society, 1900–1950', *CHJ*, vol. 6 (1988), pp.596–603.

[44] Tateshi Mori, 'The history of Japanese agriculture', in *Agriculture and agricultural policy in Japan* (Committee for the Japanese Agriculture Session, XX1 IAAE conference, Tokyo, 1991), p.4.

[45] K. Smith, *A time of crisis*, pp.76–8.

[46] See the exasperated tone of an exchange, going beyond the difference between two scholars as to the facts, in Nishida Yoshiaki, 'Growth of the Meiji landlord system and tenancy

concern of militarists with rural poverty and the luxury of the cities and
of the business classes was far from being with an imaginary problem,
and in a somewhat simplistic way, they – and the militarist idealists were
young rather than old – were engaged in a social critique of a changing
society and were grappling with fundamental problems of equity. In fact,
given a common social concern, the fusion of many socialists with the
militarists, who were anti-capitalist, occurred by 1940.[47]

If growing inequity complicated internal relations, in international relations the issue of race remained uncomfortably present; indeed, it was
aggravated by Japan's attempts to assert itself as a regional power, and
the resentments of Japan by outsiders were further fed by evidence of
successful penetration of markets hitherto dominated by western textile
industries. Allayed momentarily by the diversion of attention for four
years to world war and by Japan's role as an 'ally', the racial issue gained
prominence anew in 1919, and in the United States it turned into objec-
tions to the Japanese 'picture brides'. The contention was regulated in
1920 by another 'gentleman's agreement'. Four years later, the American
immigration law of 1924 excluded Japanese formally, thus heighten-
ing the growing divide.[48] Even Nitobe Inazō, the versatile and partly
American-educated scholar and a pacifist, who had devoted much of his
life to American–Japanese relations, vowed not to visit the United States
again.[49] General Ishiwara Kanji (1889–1949) of the War College fore-
saw a growing struggle culminating in a contest with the aid of air power
for world leadership between the United States, which he perceived as
the leader of western civilisation, and Japan, the leader of Asia. Japan
should begin to strengthen itself by taking over control of north-east Asia
(including Manchuria). He was later, as staff officer of the Kwantung
army in 1931, one of the officers who helped to stage the Manchurian
incident. Neither Ishiwara nor Nitobe is representative of Japanese thinking at large in the 1920s, but from their very different backgrounds, one
pacifist and pro-western, the other militarist and xenophobic, they both
point to shifts in thought.

disputes after World War 1: a critique of Richard Smethurst', *Agricultural development
and tenancy disputes in Japan, 1870–1940'*, *Journal of Japanese studies*, vol. 15, no. 2
(Summer 1989), pp.389–415 and R. J. Smethurst, 'A challenge to orthodoxy and its
orthodox critics: a reply to Nishida Yoshiaki', *Journal of Japanese studies*, vol. 15, no. 2
(Summer 1989), pp.417–37, and especially the comments by Smethurst on pp.434–5.

[47] R. P. G. Steven, 'Hybrid constitutionalism in prewar Japan', *Journal of Japanese studies*,
vol. 3, no. 1 (Winter 1977), p.133.

[48] See Carol Gluck, 'Introduction', in Gluck and Graubard, *Showa: the Japan of Hirohito*,
p.xlviii.

[49] For some observations at the time on the depth of feeling in Japan on the subject, see
G. C. Allen, *Appointment in Japan: memories of sixty years* (London, 1983), pp.54–6, 128.

One issue – Korea – festered in Japan's own backyard, though it received little attention in the inter-war years, and proved in the long term part of the high price Japan paid for its colonial expansion. After 1918, faced with deepening opposition (encouraged by the endorsement of the rights of small nations at Versailles), the well-intentioned paternalism of a new governor-general, despite his highly critical attitude to Japanese contempt for Koreans, would quickly founder.[50] Stern repression and loss of life occurred in putting down resistance in 1919. Harsh policy over the next two decades was accompanied not only by compulsory learning of the Japanese language, but by the requirement of assuming Japanese family names in place of Korean ones.[51] Total alienation of the population and a deepening of Korean dislike of the Japanese followed. Politically self-defeating though the Japanese role proved in both Korea and Taiwan, reappraisal of it has suggested its significance in modernising the two countries. The Japanese who visited Korea in 1876 with the first mission were greatly shocked at the poor and primitive conditions.[52] Under Japanese occupation, infrastructure and commercialisation advanced apace, but as in all cases of resistance to colonial rule, such aspects inevitably take second place in the story of the relations between the coloniser and colonised.[53]

Leaving aside the dark stain of Korea (both events in that country and the massacre of Koreans in Tokyo in 1923), the 1920s overall represented a picture of balanced political development. The country had matured politically in the preceding years; the 1915 election was fought on well-defined lines; and Hara, who was to be prime minister in 1918–21, gave the *Seiyūkai* itself, which at first lagged behind the *Doshikai*, a modern party structure and outlook. The two big parties succeeded one another regularly in government between 1924 and 1932.

Adult male suffrage was introduced in 1925. The electorate, 1/2 million in 1889, had become 1 million in 1900, 3 million in 1919 and jumped to 12 million in 1925. The lower house had become more important, and the press was more influential. Internal calm had its counterpart in a cautious foreign policy, intent on minimising conflicts of interest.

---

[50] R. Devine, 'Japanese rule in Korea after the March First uprising: Governor-general Hasegawa's recommendations', *Monumenta nipponica*, vol. 52, no. 4 (Winter 1997), pp.523–7.

[51] For an interesting account see Richard E. Kim, *Lost names: scenes from a Korean boyhood* (Berkeley, paperback edn 1998).

[52] See *PP Japan*, vol. 3, pp.155–8 [translation of report by a member of the 1876 Kuroda mission to Korea].

[53] For an interesting survey of the literature, see Andre Schmid, 'Colonialism and the "Korea problem" in the historiography of modern Japan', *Journal of Asian studies*, vol. 59, no. 4 (Nov. 2000), pp.951–76.

Hara agreed in 1920 that the scope of the Quadruple Loan consortium of Britain, the United States, France and Japan, to regulate lending to China, would include Manchuria in its terms of reference, thus giving the United States some say in the South Manchurian Railway. Shidehara Kijūrō (1872–1951), the foreign minister, though pressed by England, refused in 1924 to get involved in China when civil war led to attacks by nationalists on extraterritorial possessions.[54] Again, Japan declined to join Britain and the United States at the time of the Nankin incident in 1927 when a wave of attacks had occurred on foreign residents.[55] This has been criticised as a display of 'indifference' to western interests, which had the consequence of reducing, by the lack of readiness to cooperate with western powers, the likelihood of their later support for Japan's position in Manchuria.[56] On the other hand, in the light of the past delicateness of China, it was in fact sensitive and realistic, and if it had become a basis of future Japanese policy might have made it easier for Japan to steer a middle course through the political storms to confront it. Japanese forces were drawn into Shantung in 1927 and 1930 for several months to protect Japan's interests there from attack. This did not lead to either domestic or foreign controversy but ominously it illustrated how Japan could easily, and to a degree defensibly, be drawn into military intervention. The China problem was accompanied by the Pacific (and American) problem. When the naval interest made an enormous fuss over the naval treaty of 1930, the prime minister Hamaguchi Osachi (1870–1931) stood up to the naval interest (and, attacked by an assassin, died months later).

Changes in social thought and intellectual life in the 1910s and 1920s both in their direction and issues brought Japan close to western countries. At the same time, if new opinion came into existence, it led also to vigorous reactions from conservative interests. These reactions were all the more vigorous, because they fed directly on existing, long-standing fears. The spread of trade unions and the strong intellectual vogue of socialist thought raised the spectre of an underground Russian threat, always close to the fore in Japanese concerns. That worry was all the more potent because of the instability of China and unease about the future in Manchuria (the reason for the reluctance of the army to withdraw from Siberia in 1918–22), and the fact that the Soviet regime, no less than its czarist predecessor, maintained an emphasis on strengthening of its eastern empire. While other countries wound down military outlays, Japan's rose to record levels in 1919–22. In the case of the army, Japan's expensive

---

[54] Kosaka, 'The Showa era', p.34.
[55] Ikuhiko Hata, 'Continental expansion, 1905–1946', in *CHJ*, vol. 6 (1988), pp.286–7.
[56] S. Kitaoka, 'Diplomacy and the military in Showa Japan', in Gluck and Graubard, *Showa: the Japan of Hirohito*, p.161.

and ultimately fruitless involvement in Siberia accounted for it. But even more striking was the rise in naval expenditure, in 1921 twice the level of the inflated army expenditure.[57] It added to the alarm so evident in both British and American opinion.

The expenditure on the armed forces was potentially destabilising. The outcome depended on two factors, the first the structure of the army, the second, a rise of militarism. As for the first factor, there was lack of clarity about the army's political place in the nation. It was an artificial construct, lacking entirely, in contrast to western models, in inherited traditions from past military service, and the armed forces were in their origins a contribution by Satsuma and Choshu to the new nation. The army itself was modelled on what, after 1868, the Japanese took to be best western practice (German and French). It was also a small army, and in its dramatic growth in the 1890s and 1900s its officer cadres expanded at a rapid rate which diluted what was at best simply an incipient tradition. With growth from a force of 40,000 in the early 1880s to almost 200,000 men by 1903, the military codes were redrafted. The military code of 1882, modelled on French and German patterns, was also replaced within two decades by new instructions, and changed again in a wholesale fashion and by a new generation of officers between 1908 and 1913: emphasis was placed on fighting spirits and victory at any cost, devotion to the emperor and blind obedience to officers as a son shows to a father.[58] Created on few and fragile traditions, the army was in the long term to reveal contradictory traits. On the one hand, it acquired from its post-1900 remodelling an autocratic and harsh chain of command in which on occasion officers struck with blows officers of low grade, and they, commissioned and non-commissioned officers alike in turn, struck the rank and file. On the other hand, senior officers showed – as early as the Siberian campaign in 1918–22 – a preparedness to take decisions which were in direct conflict with cabinet policy, and simultaneously, in sharp contrast to the harsh disciplinary code, a readiness to gloss over politically motivated insubordination by their juniors. Such a situation represented a serious structural weakness: the absence of coherent tradition left little inbuilt obstacle to independent army behaviour, and also, as a direct consequence, to erratic action and internal rivalries. The dangers had become very evident in 1918–22 when, in line with the policy of the western powers to support the white opposition to the Soviet regime, the army sent more men and kept them longer in the Siberian campaigns than the cabinet had approved. The expensive campaign had no material

[57] Tobe, *Nihon no kindai*, vol. 9, pp.109, 137, 224.
[58] Yuki Tanaka, *Hidden horrors: Japanese war crimes in World War II* (Boulder, Colo., 1998), pp.207–9.

benefit for Japan, and served only to add to burgeoning distrust in the west.

Problems recurred in June 1928 when army officers assassinated Chang Tso-lin, the warlord head of a Manchurian political faction backed by the Japanese as a political protection of their burgeoning business interests, with the blame being put on Chinese terrorists. The *Seiyūkai* prime minister Tanaka tried a cover up: confronted by the new emperor, he eventually resigned. With the deadly attack by a rural fanatic on Hamaguchi in the commotion in 1930 over naval limitations, a cycle of killings and attempted killings followed in 1932 and 1936. Apart from Hara's killing by an 'idealist' in 1921, assassination had not occurred since 1889. The prime minister, Inukai, was killed in 1932 (two years after the attempt on Hamaguchi – who died months later from his wounds – and thus the third killing of a prime minister in eleven years). A large number of political figures, including the prime minister, were envisaged as targets in 1936. The assassinations in 1921 and 1930 were conducted by isolated individuals. The 1930 assassin himself, however, was a young peasant from a background of ties between army radicals and Tohoku peasantry. Assassins in 1932 were drawn from a circle of rural activists and army and naval officers;[59] in 1936 from a large group of young officers – some 1,500 in all – imbued with strong sentiments of rescuing Japan from effete business and political domination. They took the *shishi* of the 1860s as their role model. Many higher officers shared both the contempt of their juniors for the political system and the urge to refocus Japanese life on higher ideals and on popular welfare. Hence they were reluctant to disavow the idealists. The military arrested the mutineers in 1936 only when the emperor said he was ready to give orders for the Imperial Guard Division to do so.

Tensions between the navy and army in 1936 had their origins in existing rivalries (and naval resentment that some of the victims and intended victims of 1936 had been naval officers). Naval expenditure was at the heart of the constitutional crisis in 1912–13, and opposition to restrictions on the scale of the navy was the motivating force in opposition to the Hamaguchi cabinet of 1930. The Russo-Japanese conflict of 1904–5 led to naval expenditure maintaining the momentum gained on the eve of war: Admiral Tōgō also emerged as the war's major hero. The rise of the United States as a Pacific power, the symbolic move of its Atlantic fleet into the Pacific in 1907, and Japanese action at sea in the First World War, all underlined the role of sea power. In unprecedented fashion, in every year from 1916 to the end of 1930, naval expenditure exceeded

---

[59] For detail of the rural involvement, see K. Smith, *A time of crisis*, pp.80–3, 86.

army expenditure. The rivalry was a bitter one; only Manchuria in 1931 closed the expenditure gap, making navy and army expenditure equal; the rivalry, and the squandering of resources it led to, was to endure even in the darkest days of the Second World War.

In the first forty years of the Restoration the naval and army leaders were men with a broad view of political realities. Yamagata Aritomo of Choshu, for a long period leader of the army and a major politician (prime minister in 1889–91 and 1898–1900), reinforced the links between army and politics. Katsura, another Choshu general, followed as a prime minister in nine of the years between 1901 and 1913, and a further seven prime ministers were admirals or generals. This was not in itself a danger in the case of military men with a political background, and who were aware of the costs of war if detached from well-defined political aims (shades of Eisenhower's role as president of the United States in the 1950s). The real problem lay in the emergence of a new generation of officer in a force which expanded very rapidly in the 1890s and whose ethos as a fighting force and role within the state were still only being fashioned. With the expansion of the army, its officers were increasingly dawn from rural northern Japan (a dramatic break with past *Satchō* domination), and from poorer backgrounds generally. They were trained from the time they finished schooling in military academies formed at the time of the great expansion of the army. Unlike the older generation, who were aware of western models, and had often visited or even trained in the west (Katsura visited the west four times), the graduates of these academies were little touched by traditions, Japanese or foreign: the break with the past is reflected in the wholesale creation of new manuals for the army in the first decade of the twentieth century. Thus, background, education, isolation from wider society, and sympathies for the lot of rural society, which they contrasted with corruption and the luxurious life styles of politicians and businessmen, resulted in a change from an army integrated into the political society of its day, into a separate and isolated caste, with many of its members actively hostile to the conventional political world.

Japanese politicians were already trapped by their unstable cabinet system of government. With the decline or fading away of the old guard, they lacked, or appeared to lack, stature. Hara was the last politician who controlled events (and even then only to a limited extent in the case of Siberia[60]). A member of the metropolitan Police Board of Tokyo in 1932 could see in the cabinets only 'the same old politicians, working for themselves and for the good of their parties . . . The politicians talk about saving

---

[60] Siberia has been said to have been his most serious international problem. Arima, *Nihon no kindai*, vol. 4, p.185.

money for the government . . . at the same time they have appointed various friends to positions that are quite unnecessary.'[61] Baron Makino, who
had been the effective head of the Japanese delegation to the Versailles
peace conference, in 1932 – in Grew's recording – summarised the situation accurately but complacently:

> The elder statesmen who had carefully controlled the policy of the country had
> now mostly gone and . . . a sort of interim was taking place before the younger
> generation had developed its own statesmen, but . . . this would come about in
> time. He said he was an optimist as to the future.[62]

The dangers would then lie in the risks that arose when the military
men increasingly shared no common ground with politicians. As cabinets would be brought down by defection, the mere threat of resignation
by the military or naval ministers was sufficient to force civilian politicians
to compromise. There were also factions within each of the services (traditionalist officers (of Satchō background), new men, militarist idealists).
The second factor, reinforcing a changing army and rising expenditure, and made the more serious by the comparatively isolated place of
the armed forces in the new society, was the rise of militarism, itself linked
to an outlook which identified the army with the welfare of the rural population and which saw politicians and businessmen as having a vested
interest between nation and emperor. The motivating force (careerism
apart) of militarism was the fear of socialism and of its potential grip
on society. The kernel of the outlook can be traced back as far as 1910
when Tanaka Giichi, a Choshu general, formed the Imperial Military
Reserve Association.[63] He represented the transition from the old view
of the army as a tool of society into a new perception of the army as the
protective force of the fabric of a society menaced from abroad and by
real or imagined internal subversion: the association evolved to become
a declared bastion, especially in the 1930s, against subversive ideas. In
March 1928, when a proposal for amendments to the Public Order law
imposing penalties for advocating changes in national policy or abolition
of private property were rejected by the Diet, Tanaka had them enacted
as an emergency imperial decree after the Diet had adjourned. Under its
terms thousands of Marxists were rounded up. In the 1930s, the association was to acquire a hold especially in the poor rural areas, notably

---

[61] Grew, Ten years in Japan, pp.27–8.
[62] Grew, Ten years in Japan, p.32. There is a more staggering summary of Makino's complacency in an account of a later conversation (Grew, p.156). On Makino's influence on
Grew, see also Dower, Empire and aftermath, pp.109–12, and on his outlook generally,
pp.224, 248–9.
[63] R. Storry, Japan and the decline of the west in Asia (London, 1979), p.131.

in the Tohoku where the army provided a regular outlet for unemployed sons. Military sympathies with the region became closer in the wake of the food crises of 1931 and 1934, both because so many army officers had come from there, and because there was a sense of urgency concerning the creation of welfare for the peasants as a security against the political contagion of communism. The sympathies are the more understandable as these two failures were exceptional for the twentieth century. To put them in perspective, since the short harvest of 1903, only two harvests, 1906 and 1928 (and in later times 1945 and 1993) fell far short of the norm.[64] Poverty in the Tohoku was made more severe by the low prices of the early 1930s. The poor health of many conscripts from the region underlined the army interest further. Symbolically, in 1932 the army was appointing the sons of farmers to plum duties such as the Imperial Guard, and the sons of wealthy families no longer received the preference they had in the past.[65] Militarists linked military adventurism in Manchuria with the prospect of outlets for a settler population and hence with the rural welfare of the Tohoku, as well as with the creation of a barrier against the expansion of the Soviet Union. The Japanese expansion there was, however, largely in the towns; ironically, Manchuria held out little appeal for an unskilled population, and offered little opportunity for the poor of the Tohoku. Despite Japan's long involvement in Manchuria, in 1930 there were only 250,000 Japanese resident there,[66] a figure much smaller than the 750,000 in Taiwan and Korea.

In 1932, the prime minister Inukai Tsuyoshi (1855-1932) was opposed to what had happened in Manchuria. According to his son's later account, on the eve of his assassination in 1932 he was intending to force the army to withdraw from Manchuria. For the extremists, moderate politicians and also businessmen were the enemies. In 1932 not only was the prime minister assassinated, but a Mitsui executive was killed, and attacks were made on the offices of political parties and on police headquarters. The pattern was similar in 1936.[67] The active fanatics of that year, members of a widespread network of young officers, favoured a 'Shōwa Restoration', i.e. rule by the army in the emperor's name. Worship of the emperor was

---

[64] The rice riots of 1918 did not reflect a matching failure of the rice crop (it was favourable in the Tohoku). The doubling of rice prices between 1917 and 1918 reflected in part war-time inflation, and the outbreak of the riots, urban rather than rural (significantly starting with the womenfolk of the fishing community in a town in Fukuyama), in late 1918, approximated to the nadir point in the course of the war-time halving of real wages.

[65] Grew, *Ten years in Japan*, p.19.

[66] Barnes, *Empire in the east*, p.56; I. Nish, *Japan's struggle with internationalism: Japan, China and the League of Nations, 1931-3* (London, 1993), p.246.

[67] Close to many of the senior politicians, Grew in *Ten years in Japan* provides a fascinating account.

heavily emphasised and any criticism of his role was attacked. These men were opposed to the urban and constitutional values of existing political society. They denounced political corruption, and saw themselves as purifying the state by the armed forces acting in the name of the emperor and reconstituting its institutions.

Interest in Manchuria was less in its wealth than in its value as a security shield against Russia. Russian forces in east Asia were larger than Japanese forces there. Nor was the Japanese fear in itself irrational. For an American author in the 1930s – the secretary of the Council of the Institute of Pacific Relations – Russian activities in Siberia (including new railway lines in Siberia, and double-tracking of much of the Trans-Siberian railway) brought with them 'the promise of the threat of sudden and violent change in the human geography of the whole Pacific basin'.[68] Fear of the Soviet Union – and fear of Soviet communism as a threat to internal security – was somewhat akin to earlier fears that either Christian Russians or convert Ainu would seduce people from their allegiance. Interestingly – and a proof of the topicality of their message for the times – Aizawa's *Shinron* was published in a new edition by the commercially astute publishing house of Iwanami in 1931, and Golownin's account appeared in a fresh translation in 1942.[69] The vivid memory of the rice riots in Tokyo in 1918 (in some ways a repetition of the traumatic *uchi kowashi* of 1787 or 1837) and the interest in socialism among intellectuals helped to fuel this fear. In the relatively relaxed 1920s this fear had produced the Peace Preservation law of 1925.

The freeing of the emperor from the influence of corrupt politicians and a revived code of bushido were for right-wing interests two vehicles for protecting the nation. This meant carrying to new heights the concept of the divinity of the emperor and exalting his status. It brought to an end the period following the 1891–2 and 1911 controversies, when in distinctive Japanese fashion a line was drawn between scholarship, which remained free to criticise texts, and popular education, for which approval of school textbooks by the ministry of education, hitherto a routine step, became a highly sensitive requirement.[70] In the 1930s respect for the emperor was carried to absurd heights by militarists and by their supporters in the ministry of education, and was used as a device to intimidate, for either ideological or career reasons, those with whom they differed.

The more exalted claims for the opaque institution of emperor rested on the authority of myths committed to writing in the ninth century. For

---

[68] Joseph Barnes, 'Soviet Siberia', in Barnes, *Empire in the east*, p.87.
[69] Wakabayashi, *Anti-foreignism*, p.xii; Tokuriki Shintarō, *Nihon furyo jikki: Gorōunin* [True account of a Japanese prisoner: Golownin], 2 vols. (Tokyo, 1984), vol. 1.
[70] Brownlee, *Japanese historians and the national myths*, pp.96–106, 118–25, 141, 144–5.

political reasons the issue acquired a weight which no Japanese writers had bothered giving it for the preceding 300 years. The central historical issue was whether the first fourteen emperors, starting with Jimmu, were historical figures, and whether in chronological terms the imperial line had begun in 660 BC or 40 BC. To some extent the historical problem could be solved by redating Jimmu to 40 BC and in private in 1940 no serious historian believed in foundation in 600 BC. However, if that would have solved the historical problem, it would have worsened the political one. The earlier date had its attractions less because of intellectual commitment to the historical authenticity of the myths than because, if Japan had its own imperial line long before Chinese culture entered Japan, Japan was culturally the equal of China. In Japan's new confrontation with China in the 1930s, the antiquity of its imperial house would add to Japan's stature. In 1935, Minobe Tatsukichi (1873–1948), a member of the upper house of parliament, a retired professor of law in Tokyo and who had often lectured in the imperial palace by invitation, was attacked for his public view, consonant with the constitution but far removed from the pretensions of ultra-loyalists, that the emperor was an organ of government. The grounds for attack were that in declaring the emperor to be subordinate to the constitution he had insulted the emperor and he had to resign his parliamentary position.

Though most scholars regarded the imperial origins as mythical, they participated in the politically inspired celebrations in 1940 of the 2,600th anniversary of the inauguration of the emperor Jimmu. A politically motivated hysteria led to some causes célèbres, and it was helped by the highly factionalised state of academic departments within the state universities.[71] Five years after the Minobe affair, controversy affected another professor, the Waseda historian Tsuda Sōkichi (1873–1961), against whom and his publisher, Iwanami (who published literature from both the far right and the left), legal proceedings were taken. Tsuda, who both wrote and taught that the accounts of imperial origins were myths of the distant past filtered by the vested interests of the bureaucrats of earlier times and were difficult to believe, had encountered no problems as a professor in a private university. However, when he lectured by invitation at the University of Tokyo in 1939, his views were challenged by conservatives there. The only court case in which a professor from a private university was prosecuted for insulting the emperor followed in 1940. Some fifty to sixty scholars supported Tsuda's right to express his views, one of these being the young Maruyama Masao (1914–96) who, in the

---

[71] Byron K. Marshall, 'Professors and politics: the Meiji academic elite', in Kornicki, *Meiji Japan*, vol. 4, p. 313.

University of Tokyo, collected eighty-nine signatures to a petition. Tsuda and his publisher Iwanami were sentenced to three and two months in jail which in the end they did not serve.[72]

The Tsuda case underlines the complexity of the situation. In the private institutions there was an assured freedom of views. Even in the state universities, many did not agree with the official view, and public controversy grew out of factionalism in which conservative faculty members turned on their more radical colleagues and enlisted the support of the authorities against them (the case is not wholly different from the personal and factional rivalries among men of diverse backgrounds, Watanabe Kazan, Takano Chōei and others, over defence planning in Edo bay in 1839 in which one faction enlisted shogunal support against the others). In the economics department in the University of Tokyo, where nine professors either were removed or resigned in 1937–9, there was a wide spread of opinion from pacifists such as Yanaihara at one end of the spectrum to outright militarists at the other end. The president removed the right-wing figure who had brought on the trouble in the department as well as the other eight.[73] Many teachers retained their independence of outlook, and it has been suggested that as a means of expressing dissent in covert fashion, historians turned to the study of economic history and class conflict. Maruyama Masao noted that 'in the second half of the twenties came Marxism, sweeping through the Japanese intelligentsia like a whirlwind and drawing the academic world too into its turbulence'. Maruyama published his first work in 1940, 'reverently' correcting an unintended slighting reference to an early emperor because a senior professor had hinted at its indelicacy, and he was still writing in 1944 when he was called up for his military service.[74] This material was later republished as part of his famous *Studies in the intellectual history of Tokugawa Japan*. Viewed in this light, the re-echoes of the politics of his own days as a junior lecturer are more central to his book than the actual study of the past itself. As a historical study it is flawed by its search for evidence in historical times of dissent defined in western terms.

A distinctive emphasis on the emperor in the new militaristic approach had a counterpart in an emphasis on bushido, the moral code of the warrior. Bushido, as it is known in the west, is a romantic construct by

---

[72] Brownlee, *Japanese historians and the national myths*, pp.134–5, 193–8.
[73] Marshall, *Academic freedom*, pp.159–67.
[74] Some of Maruyama's introduction to the English translation of his *Studies in the intellectual history of Tokugawa Japan*, especially pp.xv–xxxiii, is particularly illuminating. The book, which first appeared in 1952, was based on work originally published in 1940–4. For a very perceptive critique of Maruyama, see Takeshi Sasaki, 'Maruyama and the spirit of politics', *Japan quarterly* (Jan.–March 1997), pp.59–63.

the politically moderate and highly westernised Nitobe Inazō in a book published in Philadelphia in 1899 (revised in 1905) and translated into Japanese only in 1909.[75] To Satow, well acquainted and sometimes boisterously so in carousings in the 1860s with many of the founders of Meiji Japan, so outmoded a word was bushido that when Nitobe's book appeared, he expressed surprise at evidence that the term had a historical existence at all.[76] Nitobe's enthusiasm to explain Japan to the west drew heavily on western concepts of chivalry, and he went on to say that bushido 'in a large measure explains why the Red Cross movement, considered so peculiarly Christian, so readily found a firm footing among us'.[77] In contrast to the many ethical and philosophical codes which swamped Japanese thought in Tokugawa times, it had no literature.[78] The sole written record was the very disjointed and varied recollections by a retired retainer of the sayings of a Saga daimyo (who had died in 1700) and his circle, and which in turn were committed to paper by a third party before 1716. They were, moreover, unknown outside Saga until a woodblock edition in 1834 made Mito scholars aware of them. Their limited impact even then can be seen in the fact that over seventy-three years only an edition in 1887 and an abridged one in 1907 followed.[79] Even c.1716 the recollections had been put on paper in a manuscript collection known as the *Hagakure* precisely because the way of the warrior – *bushi no michi* or, using the Chinese readings of the kanji, *bushidō* – had disappeared: 'During the last thirty years customs have changed: now when young samurai get together, if there is not just talk about money matters, loss and gain, secrets, clothing styles or matters of sex, there is

[75] For a history of editions, see a new Japanese translation of Nitobe by Naramoto Tatsuya, *Nitobe Inazō: bushidō* (Tokyo, 1997), p.214. The book was quickly translated into many other western languages, and the original English edition, somewhat revised, ran into many printings.

[76] To the scholarly Aston, Satow wrote that 'the use of the term *bushido* as early as the eighteenth century is noteworthy, as most people, among them myself, have thought it was quite a modern neologism' (PRO, London, 30/33/11/3, Satow papers, 11 Aug. 1908). Satow seems to be referring specifically to the word bushido, following the *on* or Chinese pronunciation, as opposed to the term *bushi no michi*, which employs the identical kanji but renders them in *kun* or Japanese pronunciation.

[77] Inazō NITOBE, *Bushido, the soul of Japan: an exposé of Japanese thought* (New York, 1905, reprint 1993), p.46. The 1905 edition was itself not the first one. First reprinted by Tuttle in 1969, it was in its twenty-eighth printing in 1993. The 1905 introduction to the book by William Elliott Griffis had added to the strangeness of the whole enterprise.

[78] Nitobe had to admit that 'It is not a written code; at best it consists of a few maxims handed down from mouth to mouth or coming from the pen of some well-known warrior or savant. More frequently it is a code unuttered and unwritten, possessing all the more the powerful sanction of veritable deed, and of a law written on the fleshy tablets of the heart' (Nitobe, *Bushidō* (1993), p.5).

[79] Koike Yoshiaki, *Hagakure: bushi to hōkō* [Hagakure: the warrior's voice] (Tokyo, 1999), pp.38, 42–3.

no reason to gather together at all.'[80] Ogyū Sorai, alive to some debate on the matter, dismissed the way of the warrior with words of scorn.[81] Whatever prompted the halting revival of interest in the concept, it was finally to prove not the humane and idealistic code set out by Nitobe but a crude effort by militarists to find, in defiance of the long *Pax Tokugawa*, martial valour at the centre of Japanese virtue. Hiraizumi Kiyoshi, the senior professor of history in the University of Tokyo, closely linked to the plotters of 26 February 1936, wrote *Bushidō no fukkatsu* (The revival of bushido) in 1933: Japaneseness must be emphasised and to do this 'we must pay no heed to considerations of life or death, gain or loss, and with united hearts we must awaken the spirit of *Bushidō* that has slumbered so long in our breasts'.[82] Apart from the 1887 edition and an abbreviated edition of the *Hagakure* published in 1907, the only editions were in the significant years 1935 and 1941; it was they which were to make the concept widely known.[83]

The weakness of Japanese cabinets showed when they became prey to interrelated worries about political instability in China, and about Russian strength in the east, made more ominous by fear of communistic subversion. Advocacy by militarists of action carried weight in weak cabinets. After Hara, who presided over the first new-style cabinet, no politician really stands out. Saionji, the *genrō* of the inter-war years, and Konoe Fuminaro (1891–1945), several times a prime minister and a politician who survived through the years 1937–45, over-rated by moderate contemporaries, were very poor stuff indeed. The civilians in cabinets were

---

[80] Tsunetomo Yamamoto, *Hagakure*, translated by W. S. Wilson (Tokyo, 1983), p.34. The original does not survive. In all, nineteen manuscript copies are known to exist (*Mikawa monogatari: Hagakure* [A tale of Mikawa: Hagakure] (*Nihon shisō taikei*, no. 26, Iwanami, Tokyo, 1974), pp.685–7). It achieved celebrity in modern times by being taken up in Mishima Yukio's *Hagakure nyūmon*, 1972 (translated by K. Sparling under the title *The samurai ethic and modern Japan: Yukio Mishima on Hagakure* (Tokyo, 1978, 5th printing 1993). However, even Mishima recognised the ambiguity of bushido as a motive force in admitting, while writing, that 'the spirit of those young men [kamikaze pilots] who for the sake of their country hurled themselves to certain death is closest in the long history of Japan to the clear ideal of action and death offered in *Hagakure*', and that 'even if they went of their own free will, they were rounded up into attack forces by coercion and sent to certain death' (Mishima, *The samurai ethic*, p.101).

[81] Sorai, making comments on Buddhism and Shinto, went on to dismiss bushido, which he saw as useful only for war: 'It is the height of folly to neglect to rule the country by means of the arts of peace, and to imagine that good government can be achieved by sticking out one's elbows and assuming a fearful countenance, terrifying the people with the threat of punishment and attempting to belabour the country into obedience' (McEwan, *Ogyū Sorai*, p.133). Many of the archaic passages of the *Hagakure* would have amply merited such strictures.

[82] Brownlee, *Japanese historians and the national myths*, p.178. On Hiraizumi, see also Jansen, *The making of modern Japan*, pp.603–4.

[83] Koike, *Hagakure: bushi to hōkō*, p.43.

more concerned with short-term political management than with coherent development. The cabinet had been divided on Manchurian intervention in 1931. Had Saionji been a strong personality, he could as *genrō* have spoken out in 1931–2 against the army in the name of the emperor, and a coalition might have rallied around him. However, his overriding and shortsighted concern was to protect the emperor from involvement in controversy.

A party of national unity in 1932–4 was an effort to create a consensus. Frictions between ministries and armed forces, divides within the armed forces, and weak politicians, gave an impression that no one was in charge. A large segment of public opinion did not approve of the military; on the other hand, expansion itself was very popular because its economic benefits (real or spuriously lauded) were appreciated. Moreover, an assertion of Japan's rights against what was seen as a hostile and selfish western opposition understandably rang a chord of assent among most Japanese. It was possible in the 1930s to combine unease about military adventures with some enthusiasm for the broad thrust of policies in Manchuria and even China.

The electoral politics of 1936–7 and the general election results point to the complexity of Japanese outlook at the time. In the general election in February 1936 the seats in the lower house held by the *Seiyūkai* fell from 301 to 146; the *Minseito*'s seats, after a campaign in which it had electioneered on the slogan 'parliamentary government or fascism', rose from 146 to 205. The timing of the attempted coup d'état by the young officers in favour of a 'Shōwa Restoration' may even have been determined by an urge to upstage the impact of the election result. Another general election in 1937 resulted in the faction at the centre of the government party, the *Shōwa-kai*, getting only nineteen seats. Moderate socialists did well across the decade: five seats in 1932, eighteen in 1936 and thirty-seven in 1937 (getting nine per cent of the vote). The press too, as the Tokyo correspondent of the *Christian Science Monitor* reported, was 'distinguished by a happy irresponsibility in reporting and commenting on news. The Japanese press on the whole is inclined toward liberalism rather than toward ultra-nationalism.'[84] External observers drew too much comfort from these circumstances. They assumed that politicians might in the end be able to assert control of political life: they advised caution, as firm steps would strengthen the military faction. Grew, the American ambassador, who was under no illusion about their strength and who believed that they would not be displaced, could argue as late as December 1939 that 'Shidehara diplomacy has existed; it can exist again.

---

[84] Chamberlin, *Japan over Asia*, pp.231–2.

There will be time enough to speak of sanctions when the resources of diplomacy have been exhausted . . . I believe that these resources may yet win the day.'[85]

Yet another party of national government was formed in 1937 under Konoe. The object of cabinets was to try and control the army, by means either of a unity coalition or a non-party coalition. However, the failed plot of 1936 which damaged the prestige of the army in the view of the electorate ended in paradoxically strengthening its hand in politics. The old rule that only serving generals and admirals might be appointed as service ministers (abandoned in 1912) was restored under the Hirota cabinet. While the object was to prevent the entry of military figures disgraced in 1936 into politics, it simply strengthened the role of the armed forces in determining the composition and policy of cabinets.[86] Cabinets from the 1910s were drawn from the lower house, from bureaucrats and from the armed forces. The armed forces in the 1930s refused to serve under party prime ministers. In turn, the lower house opposed the armed forces: the only two cabinets headed by military men with durations of four and four and a half months respectively were among the shortest-lived of Japanese cabinets.[87] A consequence of the obduracy of the army forces was that political parties were more and more frozen out of cabinets. However, given the rivalry between the different interests, that did not create strong cabinets: between 1937 and late 1941 there was on average a new cabinet every six months. Behind such a passing parade of cabinet members, army and navy dominance of the cabinets increased, and finally members of the armed forces were appointed to posts usually held in the past by civilians: generals as ambassadors to Germany and the Soviet Union, and an admiral to the United States. Finally, in October 1941, Tōjō Hideki (1884–1948), the chief of staff, became prime minister: as the war progressed he took over responsibility as well for military procurement and even resumed office as chief of staff.

In 1937, the massive intervention in China did not occur out of an agreed strategy. At the time of the Marco Polo Bridge incident, generals on the ground, anxious to avoid escalation, favoured settlement. The cabinet disregarded their views. Unfortunately, in 1937 a divide on general strategy and on China's place within it was developing in Tokyo. Within the higher reaches of the defence establishment, one school of thought, the Imperial Faction – of whom Ishiwara, now attached to the ministry of

[85] Grew, *Ten years in Japan*, p.305. On Yoshida's influence on Grew, see Dower, *Empire and aftermath*, pp.212–16.
[86] See the insightful comments in E. O. Reischauer and Craig, *Japan: tradition and transformation*, p.253.
[87] Steven, 'Hybrid constitutionalism in prewar Japan', pp.124–5.

war in Tokyo, was an exponent – favoured concentration on Manchuria (reflecting a perception of Russia as the main threat), confining action further afield to the areas of north China adjacent to Manchuria; the other school of thought, *Tōseiha* (Unified control), attached less importance to the Russian threat and favoured a takeover of China at large.[88] This group included Tōjō. The army rebels in 1936 had belonged to the Imperial Faction; this gave Tōjō and the *Tōseiha* faction the excuse for purging their rivals.[89] In consequence in 1937 the thinking of the war ministry, shifting from concern with Russia to a bolder strategy embracing China, favoured decisive action, whereas the army general staff, more cognisant of the challenge of combining cover against a Soviet threat and the heavy demands of war in China, were more cautious. Armistices were made on the spot by officers, and cancelled on orders from Tokyo. A pun at the time was that there was not a *Nihon-gun* (Japanese army) but a *ni-hon-gun* (two armies).[90]

The navy favoured the *Tōseiha* as the policy provided wider scope for a naval role. There were other divides. The army favoured German alliance; the navy and the foreign office opposed it. The navy was unhappy about the prospect of war in 1941, and felt that Japan would not win a conflict with the United States, after the initial successes. At the same time, for its own tactical reasons, it did not wish to seem defeatist, and drew up its own daring plans, predictably and accurately enough on the argument that the only hope lay in knocking out the American navy at the outset. Underlying the whole conflict was an overambitious defence policy, attempting to provide Japan with sufficient force to deal simultaneously with the world's largest land forces (those of China and the Soviet Union) and its largest navies (British and American fleets).[91] The roots of these divides went back to the aftermath of the 1904–5 war,[92] and to the navy's success in discarding its Cinderella role.

Invasion of China, after the incident on 7 July 1937 at the Marco Polo Bridge, 20 kilometres to the south-east of Peking, drew Japan for the first time into general and undeclared war. This was fundamentally detrimental to Japan's interest. For one thing, victory outside the immediate hinterlands of the great cities of eastern China was beyond Japanese resources. For another thing, it would make war with the west more likely. Conflict had quickly widened into taking over Peking and other

---

[88] This debate existed as early as 1921–2. See Grew, *Ten years in Japan*, p.184.
[89] Kase Toshikazu, *Eclipse of the sun* (London, 1951), p.35.
[90] Quoted in Storry, *Japan and the decline of the west in Asia*, p.153.
[91] G. M. Berger, 'Politics and mobilisation in Japan 1931–1945', in *CHJ*, vol. 6 (1988), pp.112–13.
[92] Ikuhiko Hata, 'Continental expansion, 1905–1941', pp.275–6.

cities in the north. On 23 August sea-borne troops were landed near Shanghai and captured that city after bitter fighting. These troops, reinforced by fresh troops, landed at Hangzhou bay to the south of Shanghai on 9 November, then struck out for Nankin, 300 kilometres inland, centre of the Chinese nationalist government, which finally fell on 13 December. The fall of Nankin is seen as the prelude to the massacres since known as the Rape of Nankin. At one level, the excesses stemmed from the now well-established limitations of Japanese command structures. Though the leader of the invading force, Matsui Iwane, had given orders that prisoners were not to be killed, the orders were disregarded on the spot. The army had a good record in the Chinese and Russian wars. The attitudes of senior military officers in the Chinese war of 1894–5 were very positively chivalrous, and despite a massacre in Port Arthur in 1894, the record was unblemished enough for Nitobe Inazō in 1899 to laud the Japanese sense of chivalry. In the war with Russia, prisoners of war had been well treated. In 1937 on the other hand, a conscious contempt for the norms of warfare was displayed in the field.

Army behaviour also reflected contempt for the Chinese, and possibly the consequences of the explicit rejection of the Chinese value system in favour of western values after 1868, of which Fukuzawa was the great advocate. In 1885, noting China's inability to stand on its own feet in defence of its interests, he abandoned the idea of common interest among Asian countries: 'Japan should part with Asia.'[93] The crude behaviour of western troops in China in the nineteenth century, and which the Japanese had observed at close hand at the time of the Boxer rising, can itself have hardly served as a good model. Whatever their good record at that time or the lauding in 1899 by Nitobe Inazō of Japanese chivalry, the massacre of Chinese civilians, mostly males, but including women and children, in three days of looting on the occupation of Port Arthur in late 1894, if seemingly at the time an isolated event, may have been a portent of the future.[94] Japanese who had served in Korea and Manchuria during the Russo-Japanese war of 1904–5 are said to have returned home with undisguised scorn for the barbarity, poverty, filth and servile nature of the inhabitants they had encountered.[95] In 1917, Gubbins, in reading the Japanese press for the Foreign Office, reported that the Japanese were aware of Chinese ill-will occasioned by the contempt with which they were

---

[93] Jansen, *China in the Tokugawa world*, p.106.
[94] For accounts of the massacre in English, see S. Lone, *Japan's first modern war: army and society in the conflict with China, 1894–95* (London, 1994), pp.143, 154–63, and Keene, *Emperor of Japan*, pp.492–5.
[95] Daikichi Irokawa, *The culture of the Meiji period* (Princeton, paperback edn 1988), p.298.

treated by the Japanese in both China and Japan.[96] Blamed by rumour for poisoning wells in the wake of the earthquake in 1923, over 1,000 Koreans and some Chinese were killed in Tokyo.[97] The number of Koreans may even have been as high as 6,000.[98] It did not augur well for the future, and suggests behavioural reasons, which were non-military, as well as militarily operational ones for the conduct of Japanese soldiers.[99]

Leaving aside wider cultural considerations, and for the moment ignoring debate about its scale, what more immediate circumstances account for the massacre? At one level, as the Japanese force landed at Hangzhou bay was not provided with food and non-military supplies, from the outset the requisitioning of supplies was a built-in part of the operation. Inevitably that meant looting, which of course easily became a cover for murder and rape. At another level, defeated Chinese, adopting civilian attire, mingled with the population: the sense that civilians included large numbers of combatants may have provided justification of a sort for cold-blooded killings. However, while the first invaders had encountered heavy losses as a result of determined Chinese resistance, the troops landed at Hangzhou bay were fresh troops, and met only light resistance. Yet the massacres began shortly after they landed and not, as usually suggested, solely after the battle for Nankin itself, when through hotheadedness it would be more understandable though scarcely excusable. Hence the massacres raise issues, which are in many ways more disturbing than the statistical one of how many were actually massacred. Propaganda and denial, double counting of deaths, later manipulation of evidence (including even of photographic evidence) only add to the complexity and controversy.

Reports, whether well-founded or ill-founded, about the behaviour of Chinese soldiers earlier in the 1937 campaign may have spread alarm among fresh and untried Japanese soldiers. But if the higher figures suggested for killings prove correct, it rules out psychological factors as a sufficient explanation.[100] Debate has been polemical rather than scientific,

[96] PRO, London, 30/33/11/8, Satow papers, Gubbins, 22 Jan. 1917.
[97] Kitaoka, *Nihon no kindai*, vol. 5, pp.25–6.
[98] Arima, *Nihon no kindai*, vol. 4, p.264.
[99] In a decision on a case brought by three Chinese for compensation on 28 June 2002, the Tokyo District Court recognised as fact that a massacre by members of the Japanese army occurred in Liaoning province in China in 1932 when 3,000 local residents were rounded up on the ground that they were collaborating with Chinese guerrillas (*Japan times*, 29 June 2002 under heading 'Court recognises massacre, rejects redress'). The court accepted the government's claim that the state was not obligated to assume responsibility for damages for the actions of its imperial predecesssor.
[100] Analysis of Japanese behaviour on the lines of that of the German atrocities in Belgium and north-east France in the first three months of the First World War may provide some insight into the behaviour of troops. J. Horne and A. Kramer, *German atrocities, 1914: a history of denial* (New Haven, 2001).

especially in the matter of the number of victims. Reflecting differing political views, they have varied from totals of 300,000 or more to a denial
of any massacres. Contrary to the external suggestions of silence on the
issue, there is a huge Japanese literature, cumulatively larger than that
written abroad. What is striking is the polarisation within Japanese views
themselves between the two extremes. As for the scale of massacre, John
Rabe, the German head of the International Committee for the Nankin
Safety Zone, had reckoned losses at 50,000 to 60,000, and the historian,
Hata Ikuhiko, has estimated executions of prisoners at 30,000, and the
civilian toll at 40,000 to 60,000.[101] Figures in this range are probably the
most credible. Honda Katsuichi, the *Asahi Shinbun* journalist who used
both official evidence and the testimony of surviving Chinese witnesses
and who emphasised that killing preceded the surrender of Nankin,
claimed that 'the victims of the massacre numbered in the hundreds of
thousands'.[102] However, he admitted that he had not made his own 'estimates or investigations of these figures', and his more recent figure seems
to be more cautiously a figure in excess of 100,000. It is of course still
a large figure, even if well below the figures popularised afresh in recent
and renewed controversy.[103]

The issue had become controversial from the mid-1950s when Ien-
aga Saburo, the author of a school history textbook, at the time several
years in use, was asked by the ministry of education to delete passages
relating to the Nankin massacres: he pursued the government over two
decades through the law courts in what became a famous case.[104] The
ministry of education did not prescribe the actual textbooks used in class-
rooms in middle high schools: however, choice was confined to selecting
a textbook from those which had received official approval. In 1982 the
ministry of education recommended to authors of textbooks submitted
for approval to describe the events in China as an 'advance' rather than
an 'invasion'. There was uproar in Japan itself, and international protests
from China and Korea.[105] While the order of 1982 was misrepresented

[101] Ikuhiko HATA, 'The Nankin atrocities: fact and fable', *Japan echo*, vol. 28, no. 4 (Aug. 1998), p.51.
[102] Katsuichi Honda, *The Nankin massacres: a Japanese journalist confronts Japan's national shame*, ed. Frank Gibney (New York, 1999), p.285. His views on the figures in 1997 as reported by the editor are said to be 'a bit over 100,000 but not approaching 200,000' (Introduction, p.xiii).
[103] For example, see Iris Chang, *The rape of Nankin: the forgotten holocaust of World War II* (New York, 1997). For a critique, see Ikuhiko HATA, 'The Nankin atrocities', pp.47–57, and in the same issue pp.58–60, two short appendices entitled 'The Nankin massacre in print: a recent bibliography', and 'Japanese textbook treatment of the Nankin massacre', *Japan echo*, vol. 28, no. 4 (Aug. 1998).
[104] For an accessible summary of this case, see Ian Buruma, *The wages of guilt: memories of war in Germany and Japan* (New York, 1994), p.188–201.
[105] Yoshimasa Irie, 'The history of the textbook controversy', *Japan echo*, vol. 24, no. 3 (Aug. 1997), pp.34–8. References to the 'comfort women' (women, mainly Korean,

in the press as the imposition of a requirement on the authors of text-books rather than, as it was, a suggestion, the fact that the ministry – widely regarded in Japan, and with reason, as conservative and narrow – made it at all is more significant than the language in which the ministry's communication was couched. The result was the very opposite of what the ministry intended: it became easier for authors to face the issue, and for publishers to expect approval for the wording of texts they submitted. As a result, given the difficult circumstances – on the one hand an urge to deny the events and on the other an urge, especially among left-wing teachers, even to exaggerate them – the issue was subsequently covered in the school textbooks on the whole, in the controversial circumstances, in a fair manner.[106]

However, controversy erupted anew in 2001 around the approval, with 137 revisions sought and made, of a new textbook prepared by the highly nationalistic Society to Make New History Textbooks. The question re-mains whether the Monbusho (ministry of education) remains at heart re-actionary, or whether in giving approval for this textbook it simply lacked the courage to directly confront an aggressive group spoiling for a fight and who, at the end of several years of agitation, had finally launched their own textbook. The text itself – an effective one in presentation – is open to question. Its markedly nationalistic tone and penchant for military de-tail are more notable than the omissions and commissions highlighted in debate over it. The now obligatory reference to the Nankin massacres is arguably in the strict sense formally correct even if the tone of both the original and revised wording is evasive.[107] In the case of the absence

compelled to serve in brothels for the Japanese forces) brought into textbooks led to protest from a group calling itself the *Atarashii rekishi kyōkasho o tsukuru kai* (Society to Make New History Textbooks). It is somewhat over the top, and its leading figure, Nishio Kanji, is professor of German literature, not of history. His own writing, while correct in saying that the account of Tokugawa history has been too dark and needs to be fundamentally reappraised, is quite strident, and lacking in credibility. For an example of his views in English, see 'Rewriting Japanese and world history', *Japan echo*, vol. 24, no. 3 (Aug. 1997), pp.39–44. For a particularly strident expression of them see his article 'Acknowledge U.S. war crimes' in *Japan times*, 26 Aug. 1997. His views are set out at some length in Nishio Kanji, *Rekishi o sabaku orokasa: atarashi rekishi kyōkasho no tame ni* [It is unwise to behave as a judge of history: the case for new historical textbooks] (Tokyo, 1997). The history textbooks are, it should be noted, very summary accounts of Japanese history: the presence or absence of a few phrases has a disproportionate effect in interpreting the presentation, and explains why controversy has hinged so heavily on the wording of single phrases.

106 Ikuhiko HATA, 'The Nankin massacre in print' and 'Japanese textbook treatment of the Nankin massacre'.

107 For interesting comments on the controversy, see a review of another book by Donald Richie under the title 'A bird's eye view of history' in *Japan times*, 22 April 2001. See also Hiroaki Sato, 'Conflcting views of Japanese history', *Japan times*, 24 Sept. 2001, as to how the issues are dealt with in other textbooks.

of reference to 'comfort women' (women either freely recruited for or forced into army brothels), it may be asked whether the issue, which is covered in other modern textbooks, is itself de rigueur for an elementary textbook, as left-wing Japanese opinion and Chinese and Korean governments demand?[108] Perhaps it is not, but doubts about the sense of proportion of the editors of the textbook arise when on the other hand something as relatively minor in the scale of great events as the controversial loss of Japanese lives in the English passenger ship in 1886 is prominently highlighted in the text and supported by the reproduction of a contemporary newspaper cartoon. Reference to the Nankin massacre is introduced not in the description of the *événements* of 1937 (debate in the textbook controversy has been longstanding as to whether they should be described as an 'invasion' or merely as an 'advance') but within the account of the Tokyo trial, where its impact is further blunted by reference to issues, in themselves quite legitimate, about the legal validity of the tribunal and its operation.

If Nankin has taken pride of place in modern controversy, it was of course at the time only a stage within a protracted campaign which quickly widened further afield. Japanese forces entered French Indochina in 1940 and with their movement into the south of the territory in September 1941, invasion became an ominous reality. At the same time peremptory demands were made on foreign countries such as the Netherlands for resources from their colonies. The export of oil from the United States to Japan was finally banned in 1941. This in effect made conflict with the United States inevitable. In any event, quite apart from its relations with the United States (there is debate, though without compelling evidence, as to whether a more moderate opposition in the United States' diplomatic notes to Japan's involvement in China might have made it easier to reach accommodation), Japan was already launched on extension of its conquests from China into south-east Asia.

The attack on Pearl Harbor occurred on 7 December 1941 (8 December, Japanese time). Many debates still revolve around the attack. On the Japanese side, the central debate is whether the failure to deliver the declaration of war before the bombers struck Pearl Harbor was caused by the material problems in decoding messages garbled in the transmission of a long text in a protracted sequence of relays, and of which the crucial

---

[108] On 'comfort women', see Yoshiaki Yoshimi, *Comfort women: sexual slavery in the Japanese military during World War II* (New York, 2000). For the attitudes of the Japanese Society to Make New History Textbooks to comfort women, see Yoshimi, pp.15–17. The amount of attention the issue has engendered in Japan over the 1990s would, however, arguably warrant inclusion of reference, if only because it has assumed a central place in the whole dialogue of apology.

and final one was sent at a late hour from Tokyo to Washington, or by mere gross incompetence within the embassy (the balance of truth leans toward the former).[109] When the declaration of war was finally delivered, the State Department was already aware both of its content and of the actual occurrence of the attack. On the American side, the justice or otherwise of the demotions of some of the Pacific naval commanders has long been a subject of discussion. A debate – going back to the 1940s – suggesting that there was a Roosevelt conspiracy to allow the attack to take place as an excuse to enter the war has been recently and stridently revived.[110] However, claims, intended to strengthen this case, that the American penetration of the Japanese codes was more extensive than assumed (it has been long known that the diplomatic codes had been cracked) had not been established: the naval code JN25 does not seem to have been effectively penetrated at the end of 1941.[111] The claim of a conspiracy at the time to withhold from the American command at Pearl Harbor knowledge of an intended attack lacks compelling evidence.[112] The suggestion that the Japanese strike fleet broke radio silence even to the point of sending messages *en clair* also seems to be unfounded. In

[109] See Seishiro Sugihara, *Between incompetence and culpability: assessing the diplomacy of Japan's foreign ministry from Pearl Harbor to Potsdam* (Lanham, Md., 1997) for a very strident critique of the foreign ministry. The failure to deliver the completed document in time (forty-five minutes later than the instructed time) seems, however, more a consequence of the constraints on the embassy: garbling of the message in the course of radio transmission, and exiguous typing resources (as the embassy had already been instructed to discharge its local staff). The longwinded document (communicated in fourteen transmissions over a day) may also not have been seen, either by the embassy staff or by the Americans, as an actual declaration of war. The Americans in fact took what they were decoding to be an intimation of a future declaration rather than a declaration in itself, and were more impressed by a message from Tokyo, also decoded by the Americans, to destroy the codes. See unpublished paper by Takeo Iguchi, 'Enigma of the memorandum of the Japanese government submitted to the United States government at the time of Japan's attack on Pearl Harbor – historic error or design revisited'. On the evidence that an explicit declaration of war may have been suppressed by the war ministries and by the foreign ministry and its terms kept from the Washington embassy, see Dick Wilson, 'Did Japan declare war?', *Asian affairs*, vol. 31, pt 1 (Feb. 2000), pp.37–40, and Tai Kawabata, 'What was fair in war not a question of timing: documents suggest memo meant to deceive U.S., keep Pearl Harbor attack secret', *Japan times*, 7 Dec. 1999; Takeo Iguchi, 'True scenario of surprise attack on Pearl Harbor', *Asahi evening news*, 4 June 2000.

[110] Robert B. Stinnett, *Day of deceit: the truth about FDR and Pearl Harbor* (New York, 2000).

[111] Michael Smith, *The emperor's codes: Bletchley Park and the breaking of Japan's secret ciphers* (London, 2000), p.100.

[112] Stinnett's book, rather like Sugihara's, overargues its case. The only positive element in the argument is the hostility to Japan of Arthur H. McCollum, head of the Far East desk of the Office of Naval Intelligence, and a memorandum written by him in October 1940, which advocated bringing a conflict to a head quickly. That does not, however, prove that those above him were party to a conspiracy to ignore intelligence.

December events were influenced more by uncertainty about the objectives of the Japanese naval forces, the sheer wealth of radio traffic at large and inability to decode naval signals, complacency at a top level over the imminence of a threat (the apprehensions of the naval commanders on the spot were more realistic than views in Washington), widespread western underestimation of Japanese naval capacity and, even more incredibly, an essentially relaxed and peace-time chain of communication between outposts and Washington.

Whatever the circumstances, the attack itself launched a war on a scale which neither Japanese nor Americans had quite anticipated. The attack and conduct of the war is identified with the Tōjō cabinet of 1941–4 in which Tōjō carried many responsibilities beside that of prime minister. The mobilisation of economic resources was very imperfect until 1943.[113] Japan never became fascist; governments remained coalitions; repression was a feature of public life only in a qualified and limited sense (opposition even within the cabinet was never completely extinguished). In Japan, in contrast to Italy or Germany, the antidemocratic forces were not a dynamic, purposeful, united group.[114] The strange antimodernism of the militarist element showed in public orders which reached absurdity, as in decreeing in 1940 that 'concubines may no longer have telephones... Golf is to be played hereafter only for the purpose of building up physical stamina.'[115] Tōjō was not a dictator but a politician presiding over a coalition, and like his predecessors depended on the acquiescence of a cabinet for his own survival. In 1944 some in the cabinet refused to continue to serve, and other politicians refused to join.

The conflict between navy and army came very much into the open in 1942. The army wanted to put more emphasis on the land war in China and Burma; the navy (highly critical of, as its naval critics put it, the army's 'walks' in and beyond China) on the campaigns in the Solomons, New Guinea and the Midway (an island in the Central Pacific). Aircraft and most other weapons were divided 50:50 between the two forces in recognition of the stalemate. In 1944 when the Marshall Islands were attacked,

---

[113] R. Rich, 'Economic mobilization in wartime Japan: business, bureaucracy and military in conflict', *Journal of Asian studies*, vol. 38, no. 4 (Aug. 1979), p.691. Japan never became anti-Semitic, something which would not have made sense in any event, as there were few if any Jews in Japan. While a few writers, who closely followed Nazi themes, repeated German anti-Jewish views, they were not of consequence (an important point to mention as the charge of anti-Semitism has been levelled against the Japanese government). The spectacular instance of the Japanese consul in Lithuania, Sugihara Chiune, issuing some 10,000 visas to Jews who with their help escaped through Japan, should be noted (see H. Levine, *In search of Sugihara: the elusive Japanese diplomat who risked his life to rescue 10,000 Jews from the Holocaust* (New York, 1996)).

[114] E. O. Reischauer and Craig, *Japan: tradition and transformation*, p.265.

[115] Grew, *Ten years in Japan*, pp.327–8.

the army's priority was its own campaign to reduce Imphal in Manipur, and resources continued to be squandered on these campaigns which were not central to Japan's survival. The building of the famous – or notorious – Burma railway over 415 kilometres of rugged terrain in dense jungle and under some of the world's highest rainfall between June 1942 and August 1943 raises many of these questions.[116] The railway is best known in the west, more especially in Britain, for its prisoner-of-war camps, and for the harshness of their regimes and appalling death rate. Asians – forced labour more than prisoners of war – were much more numerous in the workforce and their losses correspondingly greater.[117] While the Burma railway raised both moral issues and issues of international law, its mere building represented a misdirection of resources – already overstretched and inadequate – in support of an unrealistic ambition of making Burma a springboard for an invasion of the Imphal area of northwest India: the strategic objectives were not well-defined (and were political rather than military). As it happened, the completion of the railway did not solve existing supply problems in long lines of communication, and the 1944 campaign was to become a dismal failure on all fronts.

Two cabinets in 1944–5 divided into a war party and a peace party. The military faction was also at odds with itself: in the second or Koiso cabinet, the chiefs of staff favoured continuation of war; the ministers of war and navy favoured its termination. After the dropping of the atomic bombs, the cabinet divided more or less equally on the question of surrender. Only the emperor's proposal and his adherence to it made a decision possible, thus bringing to an end the saga of early Shōwa Japan. In retrospect, the outbreak of war in 1941 can be seen as marking the death throes of the imperial Japan 'restored' in 1868. Neither the United States nor Japan had been a world power in 1853. However, the growth of strength of the United States, its aggressively imperial stance in the Pacific, its racial prejudices, its unilaterally defined Open Doors policy, made it a highly menacing force, just as Japan's actions, however defensive in motivation, turned Japan into an overt threat to United States hegemony. Repeating the pattern of 1600 and of 1868, external events, in this instance surrender in 1945, were once more the catalyst of change. Japan was occupied for the first time in its history.

What lessons does Japan's history, as outlined in this book, offer that may be relevant to the country's future? The question arises readily at the stage of looking at Japan's total defeat and American Occupation.

---

[116] In a huge literature, Eric Lomax's *The railway employee* (London, 1995) is particularly interesting as it is, as the title suggests, by a railway employee.

[117] Michiko Nakahara, 'Asian labourers along the Burma–Thailand railroad', *Waseda journal of Asian studies*, vol. 15 (1993), pp.88–107.

The first is that, when under pressure, Japan performed very well. Thus sakoku realistically mirrored the circumstances of east Asia in the early 1630s: incomplete subjugation of Kyushu, external threat at several levels, and the fact that in a region in which general foreign trade was suspect, Japan's own needs were limited and well defined. Likewise, two centuries later the response to the foreign crisis looming from the 1840s was a considered one, and the diplomacy of the 1850s and 1860s amid very real difficulties was a success. Moreover, realisation came quickly that the treaties, wrung from a weak Japan in 1854–5 and more particularly in 1858, could not be readily undone, and that reform or change on many fronts, offering reassurance to westerners, offered the most effective way of advancing their undoing. This arresting combination of modernisation and conservatism was repeated anew under the post-1945 Occupation, when Japan after its crushing defeat adapted itself to novel circumstances with great success. The second lesson is, however, that outside such periods of crisis, Japan's responses have been distinctly less successful: in the post-1868 decades, despite and indeed because of English and American welcome of Japan's interest in Korea as a stabilising factor, Japan entirely missed the opportunity to take the moral leadership of east Asia (with all the dramatic consequences that that would have entailed). It would have been difficult in any event to assume that mantle in the key region of Korea, if only because of divides among Koreans and outside interference by Chinese and Russians in Korea's affairs. The point, however, is that the constraints such a role would impose were never seriously recognised. Emerging in 1905 as a regional superpower, Japan's own sense of inferiority dictated a policy of opportunism and narrow considerations, and its 'profitable' First World War on the side of the allies led in the following peace to rapid deterioration in the relationship. Japan was by no means solely at fault. Its success, far too rapid for Japan's leaders to digest, was matched by a western determination that such success should not threaten its stake in Asia: in turn, knowledge of western jealousies was itself decisive in ensuring that Japan saw politics in terms of a very simplistic them-or-us equation.

In some respects, up to 1945 Japan had remained the bakufu that it had still been under Meiji: a wide range of groups existed whose interests never fully converged; cabinets remained unstable and even more short-lived; and Japan drifted into war under a series of unstable and short-lived coalitions. The consequence of Allied Occupation was at first swift change: a new constitution (renouncing the use of war and the concept of imperial divinity), a peace treaty, a defence pact with the United States. Occupation also imposed rapid change in other directions. Land reform (meaning the ending of farm tenancy) had been an aim of bureaucracy between the wars, but except for some token measures, it could not be achieved because weak governments depended on local support from landlords – successful farmers and usually not large landowners in the European sense – and precisely for that reason an electoral force to be politically placated.[118] Land reform came swiftly under the Occupation.[119] Other reforms followed as well: new and liberal labour laws, the grant of the electoral franchise to women, the dissolution of the *zaibatsu*, the restructuring on American lines of the educational system. In no period of Japanese history was change so rapid and sweeping. For those reasons General Douglas MacArthur (1880–1964), the greatest proconsul of modern times, dominates the story of the early post-war years even more than Yoshida Shigeru (1876–1967), the other major figure of early post-war Japan, whose dominance of the political landscape in heading five of the six cabinets between 1946 and 1954 compensated for the all too familiar and persistent pattern of short-lived administrations.

Ironically, if the Occupation solved some problems, it also revealed that political change, even imposed from the outside, was itself powerless to overcome stubborn continuities. Prime ministers remained prisoners of circumstances and of the fact that the ruling party itself was a coalition of diverse interests. Even if the Liberal Democratic Party (the outcome of the *Jiyūtō* and *Minseito* combining) dominated politics, its freedom of action was constrained by a powerful socialist party and by widespread opposition in towns, especially among school teachers, university professors[120] and left-wing labour unions, to any return to the policies of the past, to changing the constitution to legitimise the armed forces, and to collective defence commitments between Japan and the United States. When politicians by clumsiness or design strayed – or stray – into such sensitive issues, controversy was and remains strong. Japan continues to present an image of a society, economically and intellectually rich and vibrant, in which the political system is incapable of making rapid change. Having renounced

[118] Matsuo Tarō, 'Airurando tōchi rippō to Ishiguro Nōsei' [Agricultural policy in Ireland and Ishiguro Nōsei], *Keizai shirin* (*The Hosei University economic review*), vol. 45, no. 3 (Oct. 1997), pp.81–136. In a shortened version this appeared in English in vol. 46, no. 2/3 (Oct. 1978), pp.1–51 as 'Researches on Irish land laws undertaken by Japanese bureaucrats facing the tenancy question in the 1920s'.

[119] Land reform is misunderstood if a close analogy is made with the land systems of Ireland or Britain or latifundia of southern Europe or Latin America (for a useful short account of Japanese landlords, see Ann Waswo, *Japanese landlords: the decline of a rural elite* (Berkeley, 1977)). Landowners were numerous in rural communities often themselves holding some land on tenancy and tenancy was a feature within rural society rather than its basis.

[120] Albert Craig, whose book *Choshu in the Meiji Restoration* was published in 1961, observed that 'when in Japan in 1956–7 I was immersed in a sea of marxist historiography' (p.377).

war in the Occupation-imposed constitution, and a large segment of the population remaining resolutely opposed to any hint of possible military adventure, the second largest economic power in the world plays a barely perceptive role in international assemblies (its delegations, if anything, are more self-effacing than the often silent but shrewd Japanese negotiators at Versailles). The defence pact with the United States and the continued presence of American bases, the largest in Asia, in Okinawa, are a reminder of Japan's uncommon position. The defence forces, designated in 1954 as *Jieitai*, or self-defence force, under the *Bōeichō* (or defence agency), directly answerable to the prime minister (as the constitution rules out maintenance of armed forces recognised as such), are kept discreetly out of the picture; control of the police is highly decentralised;[121] and in major emergencies the responses of defence forces and police alike, intentionally made dependent on formal political decisions at the highest level, cannot be swift (with the consequence, for instance, of abject failure in the first few days following the Kobe earthquake in 1995). Abroad Japan depends on the United States defence shield. This dependence prompted the Americans well into the 1990s into frequent arrogant demands on Japan and at a more popular level into wild bouts of Japan bashing (with some United States bashing as response). However, Japan cannot contemplate giving up its American associations. It cannot do so less because its constitution renounces war than because it cannot afford to infuriate the Americans, and would also face internal political storms.

Moreover, Japan's relatively successful relationship with the world beyond east Asia is a consequence precisely of its failure to play an international role. Had Japan sought a forceful role consistent with its wealth, success and dynamism, its exercise by a new player to the scene would have been resented. In the economic field, it has over the years met a more sympathetic, or at least tactful, response from the European Union than from the United States. In the political arena, Japan's position has been complicated by a recent shift in the approach of the United States, which would now like Japan to carry a higher responsibility for, or more accurately, under American direction, a higher share of the costs of regional defence. That, however, adds to complications with Japan's immediate neighbours. As the history textbook debate of modern times or the hostility in east Asia to occasional visits by prime ministers to the Yasukuni shrine (the shrine for Japan's war dead) shows, the issue is very much alive. It is not simply one of resentment of Japanese official insensitivity, real though that often is. Neighbour countries of east Asia equally

---

[121] Even under revised arrangements in 1951–4, police administration remained decentralised to the prefectural and city level. Before then, every community of 5,000 was entitled to an autonomous police force. Dower, *Empire and aftermath*, pp.347–8.

display an urge, helped by a strong feeling in Japan against military commitments, for keeping alive memory of Japan's past with the intention of casting Japan in the role of pariah state and thus depriving it of a role at all.

China's growing strength militarily and economically and the uncertainties about the constancy of the United States as an ally in future keeps preoccupation in Japan about external security alive. An independent development of Japan's foreign policy is virtually impossible. First, internal divides pose almost unique restraints on a rich country. Second, Japan's multiple relationships with the United States – and security dependence – are a severe constraint on its freedom of action. Third, its urge to establish good relations with its Asian neighbours has to take account, above all, of suspicion in Korea (in which Japanese occupation after 1910 simply reinforced the never-forgotten memory of the invasion by Hideyoshi – for Korea, Japan's Cromwell – in the 1590s) and in China, and of the fact that other countries in south-east Asia have not entirely discarded wartime memories. The ongoing history textbook controversy, in which both Korean and Chinese governments have on occasion expressed views, is a reminder of the sensitivities.

In a sense, Japan's place in the world has never been settled since 1868. Even the literature on Japan at home and abroad has been a debate, shifting in emphasis but never ending. It may take the form of the literature around 1900 idealising Japan by fantasists, Japanese like Nitobe, foreign like Lafcadio Hearn (1850–1904).[122] Half a century later, after 1945, study abroad of Japan was carried out by a generation of scholars, American mostly, who learned or perfected their Japanese to cope with the challenge of war, and later became scholars of Japan.[123] The scholars

---

[122] On Nitobe, see text above, p.266. On Hearn, in a large growing literature, see Paul Murray, *A fantastic journey: the life and literature of Lafcadio Hearn* (London, 1993); Hirakawa Sukehiro, *Orientaru-na yume: Koizumi Yakumo to rei no sekai* [An orientalist dream: Koizumi Yakumo and the world of spirits] (Tokyo, 1996); S. Hirakawa (ed.), *Rediscovering Lafcadio Hearn: Japanese legends, life and culture* (Folkestone, Kent, 1997).

[123] The outstanding case is Donald Keene, who has written a very interesting autobiographical account (*On familiar terms: a journey across cultures* (New York, 1994)). Ronald Dore and Louis Allen provided instances of language learning for war-time tasks serving as a preliminary task for later scholarly careers, as did Richard Storry (see Sir William Deakin, 'In memory of Richard Storry', in Henry and Lehmann, *Themes and theories*, pp.xi–xv). E. O. Reischauer was part of the war-time group in Washington: however, he had been born in Japan and was already conversant with the language. The account of Carmen Blacker's career in P. F. Kornicki and J. McMullen, *Religion in Japan: arrows to heaven and earth* (Cambridge, 1996), is an interesting one of war-time language learning put to rather routine tasks but blossoming later into high scholarship. Hugh Cortazzi's *Japan and back and places elsewhere* (London, 1998), pp.18–46, has an account of war-time and early post-war Japanese language learning and service. For brief biographies,

of that generation stand out as the high-water mark of foreign and especially American study of Japan.[124] What made post-war American scholarship so much a product of its time was the urge to find evidence of a
tradition of dissent in Japanese history, which would provide underpin-
ning for a reshaped – and in part American-imposed – democracy. This
approach itself drew on the Japanese historiography of the 1930s: that
had stressed *ikki*, or unrest, as a central feature of Tokugawa times, and
also revived obscure writing such as Honda Toshiaki's, edited in 1936 by
Honjō Eijirō.[125]

Two American professors, Hugh Borton and Tsunoda Ryūsaku, both
at Columbia, played a prominent role in the early development of what
was at the time the minuscule field of Japanese studies in the United
States. Borton especially was influenced by Japanese work on *ikki*; Tsunoda Ryūsaku, in search of 'independent Japanese thinkers',[126] found to
his satisfaction one in Honda Toshiaki. Donald Keene, who had studied
under Tsunoda, acknowledged in 1952 his indebtedness, just as Lensen
in 1959 dedicated *The Russian push towards Japan* to Borton. In 1940
the foreword to *Japan's emergence as a modern state* by E. H. Norman
(1909–57), the first analytical text in English on Japanese history, published by an American think-tank in New York, the Institute of Pacific
Relations, for the purpose of 'relating unofficial scholarship to the problems rising from the present situation in the Far East',[127] expressed indebtedness to both Tsunoda and Borton. Norman's work has if anything

Saeki Shōichi and Haga Tōru, *Gaikokujin ni yoru Nihon ron no meichō: Goncharofu kara Pange made* [The main foreign writings on Japanology: from Goncharofu to Pange] (Tokyo, 1987), is useful.

[124] For this opinion, see Niji Kenji, 'Japanese studies in the US: historical development and present state', in *Kyoto conference on Japanese studies*, vol. 4 (International Research Center for Japanese Studies, Kyoto, 1994), pp.123–31.

[125] *Honda Toshiaki shū*, with a long introduction by Honjō Eijirō (1888–1973). Honjō, professor in Kyoto University, was not a Marxist. Now a much neglected figure in Japan as abroad, he had, as an obituary in 1974 noted, an influence on western views of Japanese economic history by the publication in English of his *The social and economic history of Japan* in 1935 and of *Economic theory and history of Japan in the Tokugawa period* in 1943 (Horie Yasuzō, 'Honjō Eijirō sensei o omou', *Shakai-keizai shigaku* [Social and economic history], vol. 39, no. 4 (1974), pp.111–13). See also Imatani Akira, 'Honjō Eijiro 1888–1973', in *20 seiki no rekishika-tachi* [Historians of the twentieth century], vol. 1, *Nihon*, pt 1 (Tokyo, 1997), 133–42. In historiographical terms he merits more attention than he has received.

[126] This concern evident in his teaching, according to Keene, 'probably stemmed from the need he felt to believe that the traditional intellectual life of the Japanese was not monolithic but allowed the possibility of dissent' (Keene, *On familiar terms*, p.12).

[127] Foreword by the Secretary-general of the Institute of Pacific Relations, which was the publisher of the book. The importance of Tsunoda is brought out in Niji Kenji, 'Japanese studies in the US', pp.126–7. Tsunoda spent much of his life in the United States, returning to Japan for his final years. On his life, see Masano KANO, 'Tsunoda Ryūsaku: his achievements and thoughts', *Transactions of editorial department of the*

been overpraised: it reflects the drift of Japanese writing in the 1930s, and its political preoccupations all too often overwhelm it. As a protégé of Borton he was later drawn into the Allied Occupation administration: he then had close ties with Maruyama Masao, the Japanese political philosopher, who, like Norman, wanted to find the roots of political failures of the 1930s in institutional defects inherited from Tokugawa history, and who wholeheartedly adopted Norman's stressing of the obscure figure of Andō Shōeki.[128]

When Grew (who, as ambassador in Tokyo in the 1930s, had held out the prospect of Japanese politicians asserting themselves against militarists) became head after 1942 of the far eastern section of the State Department, Borton, Edwin Reischauer and other scholars were drafted into its service.[129] Reischauer was later, as head of academic Japanese history in Harvard, to become the leading figure, as John Dower put it, in 'a generation of specialists originally trained for wartime intelligence or for the occupation of Japan... their influence has dominated the field ever since'.[130] They have been criticised for taking an unduly optimistic view of the strength of pre-war democratic forces, of being obsessed with economic growth, and of not looking at society as a whole. Such criticism in part echoed academic infighting between members of a younger generation and a powerful academic establishment at Harvard, Princeton,

---

university history [Waseda], vol. 29 (Sept. 1997), pp.163–96; 'Tsunoda Ryūsaku: sono ayumi to omoi' [Tsunoda Ryūsaku: his life and thought], *Newsletter from Asakawa research committee: Asakawa kanichi kenkyūkai nyūsu*, no. 28 (April 1997); Nakamura Naomi, 'Tsunoda Ryūsaku sensei ni tsuite' [Concerning Tsunoda Ryūsaku], *Newsletter from Asakawa research committee*, no. 18 (Aug. 1994).

[128] E. H. Norman, 'Andō Shōeki and the anatomy of Japanese feudalism', *Transactions of the Asiatic Society of Japan*, 3rd series, vol. 2 (Dec. 1949); Maruyama, *Intellectual history of Tokugawa Japan*, p.xxix. See also Yasunaga, *Andō Shōeki*, pp.6, 301–2. Dower stressed 'Norman's intent, particularly in the case of Andō, which was written at white heat at the Canadian Embassy in Tokyo in the summer of 1949, in collaboration with Okubo Genji, and simultaneously prepared in Japanese and English editions. Norman confided privately at the time that one of his objectives was to turn Japanese intellectuals away from their fixation upon the importation of American-style democracy and remind them that their own tradition provided a basis for populism, iconoclasm and liberalism' (John Dower, 'E. H. Norman, Japan and the uses of history', in John Dower (ed.), *Origins of the modern Japanese state: selected writings of E. H. Norman* (New York, 1975), p.68).

[129] There is a re-echo of Grew's views in the optimistic appraisal of political opposition in 1936–7 in E. O Reischauer and Craig, *Japan: tradition and transformation*, pp.253–5, which concluded that the Japanese people had maintained 'a moderate, anti-military position'. Dower has shrewdly identified the weakness in the facile division between military and civilians (Dower, 'E. H. Norman', p.51). The place of Hugh Borton, both in Japanese studies – pre- and post-war – and in war-time and post-war public service, has become much clearer through the recent appearance of his *Spanning Japan's modern century: the memoirs of Hugh Borton* (Lanham, Md., 2002).

[130] Dower, 'E. H. Norman', p.31.

Yale and Michigan.[131] It was also criticism, variously left-wing or simply anti-establishment, directed in the post-Vietnam war era against a generation of scholars identified with advice given to government and open to the criticism of viewing the world in terms of American values.[132] From a wider perspective than the ingrown world of Japanese studies, criticism is somewhat less than fair. Like Grew, patron to many of them, they played a role in mitigating before and after 1945 the demonisation of Japan or its people in American high policy. In 2002, thirty years after the storm in American Japanology, their work seems part of a distinctive phase in American intellectual thought, engaged seriously with the outside world, informed by enlightened self-interest, and even generosity of spirit.[133]

The intellectual essence of criticism was that study had concentrated on men rather than systems and on directing a generation of new students into studies of 'nationalism, personal crises of identification and alienation, the transvaluation of values and the like'.[134] As another critic put it, 'broad studies of socio-economic change still represented a minor rivulet in the history field at large through the mid-1960s. The young historian eager to rise in the profession was better advised, therefore to write an intellectual biography or an in-depth political study, and most of them did.'[135] The belief that characters in historical situations could have changed things in real life, or at least that traditions existed to strengthen the support for future change in society, was certainly present from the outset in this work.[136] In the earliest wide-ranging study of Tokugawa Japan, in 1955 J. W. Hall, the father-figure of the active researchers of

---

[131] See Dower, 'E. H. Norman'; also R. W. Bowen (ed.), *E. H. Norman: his life and scholarship* (Toronto, 1984). For a very strong criticism of Norman's scholarship, see George Akita, 'An examination of E. H. Norman's scholarship', *Journal of Japanese studies*, vol. 3, no. 2 (Summer 1977), pp.375–419. For a more sympathetic view, see several contributions in L. T. Woods (ed.), *Japan's emergence as a modern state: political and economic problems of the Meiji period* (Vancouver, 2000).

[132] For an interesting account of his doubts about the 'modernisation' theory which informed his work when published in 1957, see introduction to the 1985 edition of Robert Bellah, *Tokugawa religion: the cultural roots of modern Japan* (New York, 1985). In Jansen's words, 'Generational conflict was at work on both sides of the Pacific' (*CHJ*, vol. 5 (1989), p.45).

[133] Of Reischauer, sometimes strongly criticised, see the warm comment by Donald Keene in *On familiar terms*, pp.90–5.

[134] Dower, 'E. H. Norman', p.76.

[135] Gary D. Allinson, 'E. H. Norman on modern Japan: towards a constructive assessment', in Bowen, *E. H. Norman: his life and scholarship*, p.113.

[136] The theme runs through the final chapter, 'The legacy', of Dore's *Education in Tokugawa Japan*, first published in 1965. The chapter ends with a sentence stating that 'perhaps the best that can be said of the legacy which Tokugawa educators bequeathed to the modern period is that ... there was still a sufficient glimmer of inspiration to make rebels of the *best* of their pupils' (London, 1984 edn, p.316 (italics mine)).

the 1950s, presented Tanuma as a moderniser in intent (even in the area of foreign trade), who had been made a scapegoat then and later for the failings of Japanese society.[137] In 1970 a volume of studies was given the significant title of *Personality in Japanese history.*[138]

Yet the critics and those they criticised were not poles apart. With the exception of writers like Thomas Smith and Kozo Yamamura (different in their approach but wide-ranging in their interests), a remarkably high proportion of the writing of the new generation of historians remained fixated on personality and motivation: revealingly one of the early collective works by the younger historians was itself entitled *Conflict in modern Japanese history: the neglected tradition.*[139] The exploitative background and social conflict, itself present in older writing, was simply enhanced. For older historians, the system despite its defects had a potential for improvement. It was modernising individuals who were required: the system itself could admit of their proving successful. For others, the system, both the earlier one in Tanuma times (for some an era of dawning hopes), and the later or post-Tanuma one, was exploitative, and change could be wrought not by individual action but by a sweeping change of social structure. This interpretation shaded into the arguments which occurred in the violent left-wing-driven controversy in Japan after 1945 over the 'emperor system' or imperial institution.[140] This controversy,

---

[137] For a summary of his views, see Hall, *Tanuma Okitsugu*, pp.141–2. He concluded that 'In retrospect one cannot help feeling a certain pity for a man whom fate has treated so badly ... In the period which bears his name are discernible many of the movements which in later years were to make possible Japan's spectacular adjustment to the modern world. It is gratifying, therefore, to find that, in the remaining years of the Tokugawa period, there were those who realized that not all of what Tanuma had stood for had been evil and who had the courage to break the pattern of condemnation to express their approval of his policies.'

[138] Berkeley, 1970, ed. A. M. Craig and D. H. Shively.

[139] Tetsuo Najita and J. V. Koschmann (eds.). Princeton, 1982. In the introduction Tetsuo Najita wrote that 'in workshops over the past several years, it became apparent to us that the developmental scheme widely applied to the study of modern Japan neglects large portions of that history' (p.9). Revealingly the title of a later book by one of the participants, G. M. Wilson, was *Patriots and redeemers in Japan* (Chicago, 1992). This approach was influenced also by what in Japan was called *minshū shi* (people's history) in the 1960s and 1970s. On this, see Carol Gluck, 'The people in history: recent trends in Japanese historiography', *Journal of Asian studies*, vol. 38, no. 1 (Nov. 1978), pp.25–50.

[140] Herbert P. Bix, the author of a left-wing interpretation of rural unrest, has recently written a book attacking strongly Hirohito (*Hirohito and the making of modern Japan* (New York, 2000)). There is no doubt that the Occupation authorities wished to exonerate Hirohito from all responsibility; Bix's book, while a useful antidote to the improbable idea of an emperor who did not know what was going on around him and who was immune to the feelings of many, if not most, Japanese, goes beyond that position to cast him in the role of a leader of the war party. That is much more doubtful. On the origins of the concept of 'emperor system' in 1932, see Jansen, 'Introduction', in *CHJ*, vol. 5 (1989), p.42; Kenneth J. Ruoff, *The people's emperor: democracy and the Japanese monarchy*

which painted a lurid picture of the past as part of an argument against continuation of any of its political institutions, provided encouragement for work by a number of American historians of a younger generation either on social unrest or on conflict. The difference between generations lay less in description of actual conditions than in the assessment of capacity for change: for the older generation society was capable of reform by individuals; for others, it was so fundamentally flawed that it required total institutional change. Capacity for change apart, descriptions of actual conditions did not differ greatly on either side of the divide. Hall, in many ways the most influential of the early historians, wrote in 1955 of 'an obscure and decaying feudal society...harsh inflexible regime,... vulnerable to the softening process of internal decay...[of which] collapse was imminent'.[141] As late as 2000, Marius Jansen, war-time student of Japanese, later Harvard graduate, and a close collaborator of Hall, could state that from 1790, 'in retrospect it can be seen that the regime had become more rigid, less resilient, and less adventurous'.[142] Ironically, some left-wing historians, suspicious of capitalism, capitalist classes and the ties between capitalists and politicians, have been much more sensitive to Japan's external dilemmas, and to the difficulties of apportioning responsibilities for a deteriorating political situation in pre-war east Asia. It is a theme which Dower claimed can be found in E. H. Norman, and which comes out strongly both in his book defending Norman against criticism and in Dower's other writings.

In some ways all historical scholarship of Japan is isolated, cut off from historical studies at large, its isolation imperfectly concealed by fashionable concepts and language borrowed from other historiographies or from the social sciences. This has influenced the way in which the *rangakusha* are cast as heroic and tragic figures rather than as difficult and opinionated men in a story of bureaucratic infighting in an administratively poorly structured system. Moreover, given the fundamental importance attached to foreign trade in western intellectual thought, sakoku is seen as an intrinsically damaging and perverse policy. Few, if any, historians outside Japan (and not many within it) have mounted a defence of sakoku as coherent, and rational in the context of trade, indigenous and western alike, in east Asia in the seventeenth century, or in later times, as long as external military considerations did not change, a defensible or realistic policy. When sakoku has been reinterpreted, it has been by seeing a full-blown sakoku as a policy emerging only in 1804. In this way it fits

(Cambridge, Mass., 2001), pp.32–3. On post-1954 argument about the system, see Ruoff, pp.5, 45, 133, 159–83, 200, 202, 229–35, 245–6.
[141] Hall, *Tanuma Okitsugu*, pp.1, 2.   [142] Jansen, *The making of modern Japan*, p.244.

into the framework of a society seen as falling after Tanuma's time into progressive decay. The real-world sequence of decrees defining or modifying the *uchi harai* policy, a sophisticated internal debate by an isolated people, is simplified. Western historiography remains prisoner of the attitudes which drove western policy in the 1850s towards seeking to prise Japan open, and, a century later, of assumptions which underlay the new history writing of the 1950s. Ironically, Matsudaira Sadanobu, Tanuma's successor and arguably the most enlightened of Japanese prime ministers, was now cast by Hall and others as a villain halting a process of change and dooming Japan to a reinforced sakoku and a reinforced despotism.[143]

Entirely outside the scholarly context, in the 1980s and 1990s there has been a huge literature, both Japanese and foreign, variously praising or criticising Japan, sometimes finding in Japanese business a wonder management to be learned by others, and sometimes, and more recently, in a dramatic reversal of subject matter, highlighting the weakness of Japanese business and administrative society, either writing Japan off for the new century or, less frequently, seeing Japan as capable of recovery and finding its place in the world again. This writing from the 1980s or in the new version from the late 1990s repeats a well-established pattern of debates occurring in rather well-defined periods as happened around 1905 (in the wake of victory over Russia[144]), or again in 1920–1 when, however overblown the writing in Japan or the United States, it accurately mirrored a build-up of tensions which came to a head a decade later. If one judges by the tone of modern writing, Japan remains a special case, its place in the world economy still not settled.

In the economic field globalisation does not of itself pose a greater threat than it does to other economic powers. Arguably the shift by Japanese companies of some manufacturing to centres with lower labour costs leaves them well-placed in a more competitive international trade. The stagnant economy of the 1990s and the weaknesses of the banking system followed the sharp fall in value of assets in balance sheets inflated in the boom. The concept of structural reform as a solution to slow growth is in any event a simplistic approach of the 1990s, evident more than a decade or more ago in the facile advice proffered to the Soviet Union and more consistently in the now increasingly criticised approach of the IMF

---

[143] The most up-to-date account of Matsudaira, seeing a continuity in political policy from Tanuma's time, is Fujita Satoru's *Matsudaira Sadanobu*. Oom's *Charismatic bureaucrat* is a sympathetic account of the man in English.

[144] I. Nish, 'The growth of Japanese studies in Britain', in *Occasional papers, no. 6: current issues in social science research* (Hosei University, Tokyo, 1989). This has some interesting comments on early twentieth-century British interest in Japan, suggesting its official inspiration.

to its borrowers. Globalisation of course can threaten stable business relations, as in the abrupt change in Nissan, the car manufacturing company
(now under the control of a French company, Renault), in buying com-
petitively its steel from Japanese manufacturers rather than on the basis of
fixed proportions from its regular suppliers. However, structural reform is
all too often presented as a mantra addressing all problems, stretched beyond the narrow confines of changes in industry and in relations between
industry and the state, into a case for wholesale privatisation and a general
rolling back of the role of the state. Too often presented in a purely domestic context, it should also not be divorced from an inherently unstable
international relationship: of the world's two major economies, one saves
too much (Japan) and the other spends too much (the United States), on
a vastly larger scale reminiscent of the destabilising relationship between
the United States (then the lender) and Germany (the borrower) in the
1920s. Japan's huge savings are invested abroad in search of a higher return than the near nominal one at home; American household saving is
often negative, and the consequent deficit in the balance of payments has
to be financed by a massive capital inflow. Faced with consumers who,
anticipating crisis, even increased savings rather than expenditure, the
Japanese government has resorted to deficit financing based on the sale
of government bonds, to reflate the economy. Such a financial nexus is
inherently unhealthy for the Japanese saver (who has low rewards) and
for the Americans (whose consumer profligacy is unsustainable).

Japan's problems do not arise from a general need, vaguely or sweepingly defined, for structural reform, but are due to two circumstances.
First, chronic oversaving (a classic case of what is in the interest of the
individual not necessarily serving equally the interest of the community,
hence wasteful because the costs of capital are too low or, if invested
in other countries, give a modest return) has many distorting effects.
Secondly, if the financial costs of reflating should be shifted from fiscal
deficit to extra taxes, a fiscal system notably less flexible than those of
other industrial countries (a legacy of its underdeveloped taxation system of Tokugawa and Meiji times), characterised by direct taxation more
than indirect taxation, deprives it of manoeuvre. To these factors should
be added an agriculture heavily supported both because of the political
overrepresentation of rural constituencies and ecological and historical
circumstances.

The key structural weakness in Japan remains a political one. At one
level, that is reflected in chronic cabinet instability which has persisted
from the outset of a parliamentary system in the 1890s, and remained
in evidence during the Second World War or in the later 'Yoshida years'
when Yoshida Shigeru enjoyed a unique ascendancy. The succession of

war-time management of output (belated and not always skilful) and prolonged, and at times painful, post-war reconstruction (skilfully managed)
created close ties between business, bureaucracy and politicians. These
ties have outlived their usefulness, and in the normal course of events
would have eroded. That they have not done so is due to the vested interest of politicians across the system in opposing any loss of patronage,
and the consequent difficulty of reform-minded politicians in prevailing against such a conspiracy. Inevitably the costs, not only political but
financial, of such failure increase with time: they have become particularly evident in recent years when public works (with some justification)
were expanded as a measure to promote economic recovery. The consequence has been a multiplication of dams, highways and the extension
of *shinkansen* lines, either on an economically unjustifiable scale, or in a
diffuse pattern which is particularly insidious because the focus primarily
rests on regional interactions of vested interests. The pattern is in a sense
a peculiar repeat of the story of the later stages of railway building in the
early twentieth century, though much more expensive and in the absence
of the sound public finances of the earlier years.

It is not in Japan's interest to restructure on a simplistic model, based
on facile or superficial assumptions often from outside, and which all
deflect attention, sometimes intentionally, from the root domestic problem. Like European societies (which do not follow the American model,
itself increasingly discredited by the rampant scandals of recent times,
and cosy relationships not unlike those in Japan), Japan has an interest
in preserving its admirable health insurance system, and its remarkably
egalitarian distribution of income (if it departs from that radically, it will,
on precedent, build up serious social unrest in the future). It also has in
the long term an interest in enhancing social welfare, very uneven outside the areas of health and old age (and which, if we disregard the deficit
in the public finances, would ease the pressures to save), and in making
more equitable the social costs of the restructuring of industry, required
in Japan (as elsewhere) at the end of a period of easy growth. These problems are to some degree those of other industrial countries. It has too a
problem – not a unique one – of an ageing population: in the background
lies the question of whether immigration, to a society which before the
1980s had no tradition of immigration, will be at least a partial solution
to future labour supply. In contrast to other advanced countries, Japan
has never recognised refugee status as a basis for admission. The refugee
issue is not in itself an immigration problem; it is, however, in terms of international jurisprudence, an issue that raises one of the dilemmas which
Japan will face if it were to assume the wider role in the world that some
of its administrators and politicians envisage or hope for.

Japan is a country with a wide debate on policy. The history textbook case carries the weight it does precisely because there has been vigorous debate within Japan. There are arguably, as there were in Tokugawa and Meiji times, too many opinions (and, as in those days, not always well-grounded). Public opinion is strong, volatile and, for understandable historical reasons, often oversensitive on issues of relations with other countries, especially the United States, or any suggestion of *gaiatsu* (foreign pressure). If in crisis the strength of Japan has been its sense of unity (a characteristic noted by that shrewd observer of Meiji times, Sir Ernest Satow), in other times it is rather like a convoy (or a Japanese committee): it proceeds at the pace of the slowest vessel (or member). The fact that the LDP (Liberal Democratic Party) of post-1945 times (successor to the ruling political parties of the past, and in every respect a mirror image of the now dead Christian Democratic Party of post-1945 Italy) is increasingly discredited in public opinion, makes it less able to deliver change, and coalition itself, already for a decade a prop to its waning ascendancy, is no easy solution. Japanese senior politicians spend far more time, as even the most casual listening to television news bulletins shows, in conclave with party members than do their colleagues in other industrial counties (and under such pressures some politicians, recklessly for a domestic audience, make facile comments without thought to their effect abroad). Ministries too, even at bureaucratic level, are much more independent fiefdoms than in the west. In these areas structural reform is certainly necessary, but outside them, the case for reform is not compelling and is even ideologically motivated. The case is made more often outside Japan, and the superficiality or simplification of internal comment sometimes smacks of the more enthusiastic Meiji advocacy of westernisation. The irony of Japanese society is that its central reform problem lies not in business or in economic or social structures, but in the dimension of modern Japan which since 1890 has most successfully resisted all change, the political system itself. It would seem as if only general crisis could impel change. In other words, only a sense of threat, wider than the real but diffuse public unease of the present days, could harness Japanese energies, and entail reform. The general fear of western dominance in Asia brought about the Meiji Restoration and propelled the sweeping changes of subsequent decades. Again, the Occupation from 1945, a political challenge both to change and to conserve, made possible a remarkable Japanese adaptation to its new circumstances, as well as accounting for the unique durability of Yoshida in a weak and unstable parliamentary system. In a world where there are no heroes and where political survival itself is not an issue, the catalyst is harder to see.

The long recession of the 1990s has at least led to a pause in the hostility of comments on Japan so evident in the 1980s, or somewhat later in the aggressive effort by the United States to put the onus on others in addressing its own adverse trade imbalance. On the economic front at least, on the balance of probabilities Japan will sooner or later reacquire its momentum. On the political front, however, if it should seek to strike out on its own in its external relations, it will encounter internal divides on what policy should be (if Japan remains true to the form of the last 400 years, internal circumstances will not be the factor generating political innovation). If it should get its permanent seat on the Security Council of the United Nations, for instance, the country's external complications and divided domestic public opinion will not leave its diplomats free to play a large role. Moreover, if it should attempt to play a role weighted in proportion to its economic importance, it will certainly encounter resentment in the outside world. In some respects, a seat is important for its own esteem as a 'first-class nation', a status which remains in doubt through Japan's discreet place in the world, variously imposed on it from outside or self-imposed. Japan's hollow first-class status in 1919 at Versailles is repeated in its role as an economic superpower without the corresponding political status. Internal restraints on its role are compounded by external ones: its delicate relationships with the United States, and with its two closest Asian neighbours (indeed with all of those parts of Asia which it overran in the early 1940s). In the many ironies of history, its closest neighbour of all is a western power, Russia, which in 1945 occupied the south of Sakhalin, Kunashiri and Etorofu, and with whom a peace treaty still has not been signed. The concluding irony is that the country which for 250 years successfully avoided foreign complications (and in the process enjoyed internal harmony, economic development and external peace) faces many challenges, known ones in the present, unknown ones in the future. The uncertainties of its future relations with Russia, China, and the United States are all the greater because Japan's relations with these countries depend not only on it cultivating its own ties with each of them, but on interactions between them prompted by other interests and conflicts, and which are beyond Japan's influence or control.

Tokugawa shoguns[1]

	years of rule	date of death[2]
Ieyasu	*1603–1605*	*1616*
Hidetada	*1605–1623*	*1632*
Iemitsu	*1623–1651*	
Ietsuna	1651–1680	
Tsunayoshi	*1680–1709*	
Ienobu	*1709–1712*	
Ietsugu	*1713–1716*	
Yoshimune	*1716–1745*	*1751*
Ieshige	1745–1760	1761
Ieharu	1760–1786	
Ienari	*1787–1837*	*1841*
Ieyoshi	1837–1853	
Iesada	*1853–1858*	
Iemochi	*1858–1866*	
Yoshinobu ('Keiki')	*1866–1867*[3]	1913

Notes
1. Italicised shoguns are mentioned in the text of the book.
2. Date of death, if different from end of period of rule.
3. Or, depending on definition, early January 1868.

Main regnal periods[1]

Keichō	1596–1615
Kan'ei	1624–1644
Kanbun	1661–1673
Genroku	1688–1704
Shōtoku	1711–1716
Kyōhō	1716–1736
Hōreki	1751–1764
Meiwa	1764–1772
An'ei	1772–1781
Tenmei	1781–1789
Kansei	1789–1801
Bunka	1804–1818
Bunsei	1818–1830
Tempō	1830–1844
Kōka	1844–1848
Kaei	1848–1854
Ansei	1854–1860
Keiō	1865–1868
Meiji	1868–1912
Taishō	1912–1926
Shōwa	1926–1989

Note

1. Regnal periods were declared once or more often during the life of individual emperors, and provided the formal basis for calendar dating. The list is confined to the names most widely used to denote their periods. Some are obscure, and little used outside specialised texts. Some are widely known, and have a personality all their own: for instance, Genroku conveys a significance somewhat akin to the use of *siècle de Louis Quatorze* in French history.

Glossary

bakufu	Literally tent or campaign administration, and as such appropriate to the original role of shogun as a military commander. In Tokugawa times the term reappeared, employed as a slighting usage to belittle the shogun's administration, by its opponents in the 1860s.
bakuhan taisei	Modern term combining in abbreviated form the terms *bakufu* and *han*, and adding the term *taisei* (or structure). A system in which power was shared between the governments of daimyo and shogunate.
bakumatsu	A somewhat elastic term referring to the closing decades of the Tokugawa dynasty.
bansho-shirabeshō	Reorganised banshowagegoyō of 1856 with a wider role in research and teaching.
banshowagegoyō	Office for translating foreign books, established in 1811.
bugyō	Senior hatamoto officers of shogunate, responsible notably as machi bugyō for the administration of cities. Recruited from the kanjō bugyō grade.
buke shohatto	Law regulating relations between shogunate and han.
bushidō	The way of the warrior, or ethical code of warriors. Little written about apart from the obscure *Hagakure* in Saga han in the early eighteenth century until a revival of interest at the end of the nineteenth century.
chōnin	Townsmen, town inhabitants, or merchants.
Daigaku no kami	Head of the academy, term applied to the head of the Hayashi academy.

daikan	Administrator of middle rank, of hatamoto status, responsible for administration of directly held territories and collection of revenue.
daimyō	Literally, controllers of large land areas, territorial rulers in Japan, variously fudai and tozama.
Ezo	The islands to the north of Honshu. The largest island (the future Hokkaido) was distinguished by the name Ezo-ga-shima.
fudai	Daimyo followers of the shogun, either already Tokugawa vassals before the battle of Sekigahara (1600), or receiving the status as a reward after the battle or in later times. From the larger fudai were recruited the rōjū or ministers of the shogunate.
fukoku kyōhei	Rich country, strong defence. Slogan emerged in Tokugawa period, but popularised in early Meiji period as a summary of policy.
fūsetsugaki	Reports of external news made in Nagasaki on arrival by captains of Chinese or Dutch vessels to the shogunate.
gaiatsu	Foreign pressure, not a term contemporaneous with the Tokugawa period.
gaikoku bugyō	Five officers of bugyo rank created in 1858 to take charge of foreign relations.
genrō	Elder statesmen, meaning politicians retired from office and consulted by the emperor on forming a new cabinet, or by the prime minister in times of crisis.
gokenin	Lower ranks of directly retained samurai of the shogunal administration. Some were employed by hatamoto, but tendency was for them to be employed by the shogun rather than hatamoto.
gōshi	A term originally applied widely to samurai but restricted in later times to samurai residing in the countryside and supporting themselves from and personally overviewing their land. As the rank was also conceded for services to commoners, gōshi could reflect diverse social origins. Gōshi were some or many in about twelve han. They were most numerous in Satsuma, where they constituted the main body of samurai, both socially and administratively.

goyōkin	From 1761 forced loans from merchants in Osaka.
han	Term denotes territorial unit held by a daimyō. The term itself is a later usage. The older usage was ryōgoku.
Hankachō	Registers of decisions in criminal cases.
hansatsu	Promissory notes or paper money issued by han administrations. Shogunate itself did not issue paper money.
Haruma	From Halma, the name of the author of a Dutch–French dictionary taken as model for the two great dictionaries of Dutch and Japanese compiled on either side of 1800, and japanised as *Haruma*.
hatamoto	Directly retained samurai of shogun. While the upper limit to hatamoto incomes was 10,000 koku, most had small incomes measured in hundreds of koku. From them were recruited the senior administrators of the shogunate.
hofreis	Dutch term for visit (prior to 1791, annual) to Edo by members of the Dutch factory in Deshima. In Japanese, sanpu.
honbyakushō	Farmers or peasants whose land holdings were recorded in Hideyoshi valuation of property.
hyōjōsho	Judicial offices of shogunate.
ikki	Communal action or protest.
itowappu	Monopsonistic regulation of silk purchases in Nagasaki.
jiken	Modern term denoting an incident or event of some consequence or notoriety.
jōkamachi	Castle town.
juku	School, as in shijuku (private school/academy).
jusha	Confucian scholar.
kaibō gakari (kakari)	Officials in charge of maritime defence, loosely applied to duties defined in Matsudaira's time, but officials formally designated as such appeared only from 1845.

kan   Unit of weight of 1,000 momme or 6 kin (8.27 lb or 3.75 kg). Silver coinage passed by weight, in other words in kan of silver, or a fraction thereof.

kana   The Japanese syllabaries of forty-eight syllables, hiragana and katakana, which were used in place of kanji, indicated inflections in words, or served as a furigana (how to read a kanji) on the margins of kanji. In modern practice, hiragana variously replaces individual kanji or for clarity indicates word endings and universally it indicates inflections: katakana is used to indicate foreign words (not of Chinese classical origin).

kanji   Chinese character or ideogram representing a word or a syllable in a compound.

kanjō bugyō   Senior officers of the Kanjōsho. As such they also acceded to demanding administrative functions outside the Kanjōsho.

Kanjōsho   Finance office, office for supervising receipt and expenditure of income from tenryō.

Kansai   Literally region to west of Hakone barrier. Includes Osaka and Kyoto (located in Kinki), but otherwise in contrast to Kantō lacking a precise geographical definition.

Kantō   Literally region to east of Hakone barrier. Region around Edo, well-defined in geographical sense.

kiheitai   Mixed armed bands of commoners and samurai, established in Choshu in 1863.

kin   Unit of weight, 160 momme (.6 kg), approximately six to the kan (see kan above).

kinsei   Early modern, as opposed to kindai (modern).

kōbugattai   Union of emperor and shogun, slogan of 1860s.

kogaku   Ancient learning, or study involving study of the ancient classics themselves rather than reliance on later commentators on them.

koku   Equivalent of 5 bushels of rice, the amount of rice to feed one person for a year. Used as a measure of han wealth and of income of individuals. Koku also used to denote displacement of ships.

kokudaka   Valuation of lands expressed in koku.

kokugaku   National learning, or learning with an emphasis on Japanese-language texts as opposed to Chinese-language texts.

kokutai   Literally, 'national essence'. Term used by Aizawa Seishisai in *Shinron* of 1825, denoting sense of national

	solidarity, and given an exalted significance by militarists of the 1930s.
kuni	Province. The provinces had long lost administrative significance. However, as the han varied in extent or even in their survival, the term had a precise geographical meaning, and for that reason was widely used (and employed in Tokugawa population statistics).
kura	Literally, warehouse. The term designated the rice sent to Osaka on han account as opposed to rice marketed on merchant account.
metsuke	The lower of two grades of senior officials, metsuke and ō-metsuke, originally with a primarily judicial or police role, but also playing a role parallel to that of kanjō bugyō and as the real working horses of senior administration were often entrusted with major adminstrative or political responsibilities.
momme	One-thousandth part of a kan weight, 3.75 grams (see kan and kin above).
nengō	Emperors designated a name for the period of their rule; on some occasions an emperor changed the name during his lifetime.
ō-metsuke	See metsuke.
opperhoofd	Head of the Dutch factory on the island of Deshima in Nagasaki. From the Portuguese word for captain, known as Oranda kapitan (Dutch kapitan).
picul	Measure of weight, 133 lb.
rangaku	Dutch studies, and by extension all western studies.
rōjū	Senior councillor, the equivalent of cabinet minister in western countries.
rōnin	Samurai either deprived of his stipend, or having given one up, and hence masterless or a free agent.
ryō	Unit of account for gold currency in the Edo region.
ryōgae	Exchange of silver currency for gold currency.
samurai	Originally a warrior class, increasingly simply bureaucratic class which executed the duties, lowly and high, of daimyo administration. In shogunate the terms were hatamoto and gokenin.

sanke (go-sanke)	The three families. Term designates the three collateral families created by awards of land to three sons of Tokugawa Ieyasu, constituting the han of Kii, Owari and Mito.
sankin kōtai	Term for visit in every second year by daimyo and attendants to Edo. His wife and children remained permanently in Edo.
Satchō	Somewhat pejorative term for Satsuma-Choshu dominance of post-1868 politics.
Sengoku	'Warring states', term denoting long period in sixteenth century of civil war.
shinpan	Families related to the Tokugawa, either directly or merely honorifically, of fudai status.
Shinron	'New Theses', text of 1825 by Aizawa Seishisai.
Shintō	Animistic beliefs, oldest religion of Japan.
shishi	Men of high purpose, who had given up their stipend from a daimyo and as rōnin pursued political activism in the 1860s.
shōgun	Commander for quelling barbarians. Head from earlier times of the administration and forces of Japan. In the Sengoku period a figurehead, with power left in the hands of a sort of regent. Re-established as effective ruler of Japan by Tokugawa Ieyasu.
shōheikō	Term introduced in the 1790s to denote the Hayashi academy on the Shōheizaka, also designated, in a new role as official academy to the shogunate, as Shōheizakagakumonjo in 1797.
shūmon aratame chō	Registers of religious affiliation held in temples, compiled in or after the 1620s.
tairō	Term assumed on occasion by the leading rōjū in time of crisis.
tennō	Emperor. In most of Japanese history, a figurehead, with a legitimising role. Post-1868 constitutional innovation gave the office a new significance.
tenryō	Directly managed lands of the shogun, i.e. lands not ceded to fudai daimyo or to hatamoto. Districts within the tenryō were administered by daikan.

Tohoku	The north-east of Japan, a region with a cooler summer, harsh winter, and poorer and less populous than elsewhere.
tōjin	Chinese.
tōsen	Chinese vessel, meaning vessel manned by Chinese, rather than one necessarily arriving from China.
tozama	Literally, distant or more precisely 'outside' daimyo, whose han existed in 1600 and were not part of the band of warriors and leaders around Tokugawa Ieyasu, prior to his ascent. As outsiders they did not participate in Tokugawa government.
tsūji	Interpreters of either Dutch or Chinese at Nagasaki.
Tsūkō ichiran	Survey of external relations. Study by Hayashi family of the foreign relations of Japan, of which the first part was executed in 1849–53.
uchi harai	Policy of firing on and driving off foreign vessels. Best known in 1825 decree.
uchi kowashi	Riot involving destruction of property, most common in, but not confined to, cities.
Wajin	Japanese as opposed to people of other races. Mainly used to distinguish in Ezo Japanese from Ainu (but also distinguishing Japanese from Ryukyu islanders).
zaibatsu	Clique or group with wealth. In singular denotes a business conglomerate, in plural the conglomerates collectively. Term came into use c.1910. Some originated in Tokugawa times, diversifying originally from commerce or metal working into banking and other activities. Others originated in early Meiji times. Diversification of activities grew apace with the modernisation of the economy. The term new zaibatsu is sometimes applied to post-1930s firms heavily concentrated on manufacturing, and not originating from more diverse activities.
zeni	Copper coin or coinage.

Introduction to bibliography

Japanese history has an impressively large literature in English. Scarcely existent at the end of the 1930s, it is now huge. It is difficult to survey it briefly without the likelihood, indeed the certainty, of serious omission and the risk of unfairness in generalisation. This survey is intended to survey the broad trends in the historiography, and hence it necessarily omits referring to a number of works of real consequence. For full surveys of Japanese history, though now somewhat dated, volumes 3 to 6 of the *Cambridge History of Japan*, published between 1988 and 1991, make a good starting point to more advanced reading. The *Kodansha Encyclopedia of Japan* (9 vols., Tokyo, 1983) is a user-friendly and remarkably readable reference source for both history and institutions.

While Japanese history textbooks in English are moderately numerous, comparatively few of them integrate a broad spread of themes. This is especially the case for works on the post-1868 period which tend to concentrate on Japan's economic success. Works surveying earlier periods take a much broader view of Japan's history. In addition, western preoccupations or perceptions, inevitable in works for a western audience, sometimes have a patronising air. This characteristic is itself contributed to, however, by the fact that western themes and scholarly approaches were and are applied in much work in Japanese itself. This is especially so in the case of philosophical and political thought, where Germanic influence was strong up to the Second World War. The political philosopher, Maruyama Masao, in his immensely influential *Studies in the intellectual history of Tokugawa Japan* (1952, English translation, Princeton, 1974), started with Hegel in his very first line.[1] While much Japanese history of the 1930s and of the post-war years was in a loose sense Marxist (as was Maruyama's approach despite his denials), it would be far more accurate to say that a theoretical approach more than Marxism as such was dominant, and that it was as much evident in non-Marxist as in Marxist work.

[1] See the amusing account by the young G. C. Allen on board ship on his way out to Japan in 1922 of his introduction to a Japanese professor who declaimed that 'I am a Hegelian philosopher.' *Appointment in Japan*, p.3.

The American historian, John Dower, has warned against too readily dismissing much Japanese writing on account of its Marxism: to do so, he argued, entails an injustice to its historical achievements. Despite a common western influence on all Japanese historians whether studying Japanese history or the history of western countries, there was and still is a dichotomy between those who study and teach western history and those who pursue Japanese history. There are exceptions of course: an obvious one is Ōtsuka Hisao of the University of Tokyo, who studied western history closely and transferred his western model into his work on Japanese history. His approach was a conscious adaptation of Weberian thought; his interest in Japanese history was prompted by the need to find a basis for Japanese economic recovery.[2] The divide may be disappearing in recent years, at any rate in economic history and more certainly so in demographic history. The cost of intercontinental travel, limiting contact, helped to shape the structure of history until recent decades. Japanese historians rarely went abroad, or, as in the case of Ōtsuka Hisao, once and late in a lifetime.[3] Only in the 1980s did the real cost of travel begin to become low, doubly so because of the concurrent rise in real incomes.[4]

The intersection of Marxist thought and the concerns of the Allied Occupation authorities to restructure Japan come out strikingly in the friendship between Maruyama and E. H. Norman. Norman's work, Marxist in its orientation, was at the time acclaimed. The earlier and prolific work by Honjō Eijirō (1888–1973) (two of whose works had appeared in English, *The social and economic history of Japan* (Kyoto, 1935) and, several years later, *Economic theory and history of Japan in the Tokugawa period* (Tokyo, 1943; New York, 1965), received little attention.[5] The trajectory of Honjō's reputation is remarkably similar to that of Henry Sée in France in the same period: both were attuned to the world-wide rise of economic history, both were prolific and source-driven historians; but, devoid of intellectual preconceptions, they were later rejected

---

[2] On Ōtsuka Hisao, see the important article by Kazuhiko Kondō, 'The modernist inheritance in Japanese historical studies: Fukuzawa, Marxists and Ōtsuka', in G. Daniels and Chushichi Tsuzuki (eds.), *History of Anglo-Japanese relations 1600–2000*, 5 vols. (Basingstoke, 2001), vol. 5, pp.173–88.

[3] Ōtsuka Hisao, *The spirit of capitalism: the Max Weber thesis in an economic historical perspective* (Tokyo, 1982).

[4] On the overlooked travel factor, see the interesting lines by S. Hirakawa, *Lafcadio Hearn in international perspectives* (Comparative literature and culture program, University of Tokyo, September 2001), p.38. See also L. M. Cullen, 'Professor Matsuo Taro, 1933–1997', *Keizai shirin*, Hosei University, vol. 66, no. 2 (Oct. 1998), p.54.

[5] See obituary by Horie Yasuzō, 'Honjō Eijirō sensei o omou', *Shakai-keizai shigaku*, vol. 39, no. 4 (1974). The Shakai kezaishi gakkai [Social and economic history society] was founded in Tokyo in 1931, and its journal began to appear in the same year. The timing is thus very close to similar events in British and French economic history.

or more accurately ignored in writing on the history of their respective countries. Honjō's two books in English, or the book in English of 1937 by his University of Tokyo counterpart Tsuchiya Takeo (with Honjō the founder of economic history in Japan), are not mentioned, for instance, in John Dower's excellent *Japanese history and culture from ancient to modern times: seven basic biographies* (Manchester, 1986), and are absent also from other recent bibliographies.[6] Recent renewed interest in Norman contrasts with the obscurity in which Honjō still languishes.

The post-war western historiography of Japan can be broadly regarded as starting with John W. Hall's *Tanuma Okitsugu 1719–1788: forerunner of modern Japan* in 1955, which presented Tanuma as a precursor of modernisation whose legacy was aborted by subsequent reaction. Hall himself played a large role in encouraging students into Japanese history, and his accounts of sources are still useful.[7] Robert N. Bellah's *Tokugawa religion: the values of pre-industrial Japan* (Glencoe, Ill., 1957), hailed at the time and influenced by the urge to find an explanation of Japan's economic resilience, followed close on the heels of Hall's book.[8] Two authors stand out for their durability and influence: Marius B. Jansen, whose first book was published in 1954 and his final one in 2000, the year of his death, and Donald Keene, whose first book in 1952, one of the earliest post-war studies, *The Japanese discovery of Europe* (reprint Stanford, 1969), is still widely influential, and whose study of emperor Meiji has appeared in 2002. A work edited by him and Tsunoda Ryūsaku, one of the fathers of Japanese studies in the United States, along with W. Theodore de Bary, *Sources of Japanese tradition* (New York, 1958), remains an invaluable reference source for a wide variety of material, both cultural and historical.

At the outset a clear pattern existed of topics being determined either by directly contemporary concerns of the early 1950s, or, if not, by interest in the post-1868 history that may have shaped the conflict in 1941–5. Thus, Marius B. Jansen started from a subject which pointed to a promise, ultimately blighted, of a benign profile in Japanese–Chinese relations, in *The Japanese and Sun Yat-Sen* (Cambridge, Mass., 1954).

---

[6] Tsuchiya, *An economic history of Japan*. It first appeared in the *Transactions of the Asiatic society of Japan*, vol. 15 (Dec. 1937). In contrast to Honjō, Tsuchiya was a 'Marxist', though not an ideologically prominent one.

[7] J. W. Hall, *Japanese history: a guide to Japanese reference and research materials* (Ann Arbor, Center for Japanese Studies, bibliographical series, no. 4, 1954); 'Materials for the study of local history in Japan: pre-Meiji daimyo records', *Harvard journal of Asiatic studies*, vol. 20, nos. 1 and 2 (June 1957), reprinted in J. W. Hall and Marius B. Jansen (eds.), *Studies in the institutional history of early modern Japan* (Princeton, 1968), pp.143–68.

[8] However, his attention to Shinto, which he treats seriously, does redeem it. In other words, its generalisations apart, there is a solid core of real value.

The first book of Ronald Dore, a young British official in the post-war Allied Occupation, was *Land reform in Japan* (Oxford, 1959); Thomas C. Smith in his early career examined the role of the state in early Meiji development in *Political change and industrial development in Japan: government enterprise, 1868–1880* (Stanford, 1955); and, in a slightly younger generation, Kozo Yamamura cut his teeth on *Economic policy in post-war Japan: growth versus economic democracy* (Berkeley, 1967). Even general books were directed to making Japan's post-war or earlier background understandable. The pattern was foreshadowed in the 1940s by George Sansom, who had already written *Japan: a short cultural history* in 1931, publishing his first work on a wider theme in 1940, and in E. H. Norman's writing from 1940 to 1949.[9] Ruth Benedict's *The chrysanthemum and the sword: patterns of Japanese culture* (Boston, 1946) was another influential work, though one which in Jansen's words 'called forth an old-fashioned, nineteenth-century ideal type'.[10]

Historians moved on from their early Occupation-oriented books to more purely scholarly work. One of them, in doing so, wrote the most enduring interpretation to appear from these years, Thomas Smith's *The agrarian origins of modern Japan* (Stanford, 1959). This book broke with the 'modernisation' concern of other historians, and looked at the past for its own sake. It modestly played down its claim to originality and acknowledged its indebtedness to the work of Japanese scholars. A number of his articles over later years, gathered together in *Native sources of Japanese industrialization 1750–1920* (Berkeley, 1988), also serve as a stimulating introduction for students. Of a younger generation of historians, the three who come closest to rivalling his sustained writing are Kozo Yamamura, whose career began a decade later than Smith's, Conrad Totman and Tetsuo Najita. Yamamura set out challengingly his wider views on Japanese history in 1973,[11] with much writing to follow. Totman, as well as publishing the massive *The collapse of the Tokugawa bakufu, 1862–1868* (Honolulu, 1980) and works on woodland management, wrote a biography of Tokugawa Ieyasu and several general works. Tetsuo Najita, starting in 1967 from a biography of Hara Kei (the prime minister assassinated in 1921), widened out into political and intellectual thought.

Work in the 1960s and 1970s tended to concentrate on biography (Jansen's *Sakamoto Ryōma and the Meiji Restoration* setting the trend in

---

[9] James Murdoch had published *A history of Japan*, 3 vols. (London, 1925–6). However, it is more commentary on events and their antecedents than history.
[10] Jansen, *The making of modern Japan*, p.770.
[11] Kozo Yamamura, 'Towards a reexamination of the economic history of Tokugawa Japan 1600–1867', *Journal of economic history*, vol. 33, no. 3 (Sept. 1973), pp.509–41.

1961), personality, and the evolution of political thought. A substantial number of studies devoted attention to dissidents and to social conflict generally, and writing in later years sometimes represented a subtle dissent from the academic establishment created by the capable and strong-willed individuals who launched the early post-war historiography. Some even adopted a Marxist orientation. Their writing added to the emphasis on *ikki* already present in earlier writing, viewing them as proof of an inherently unjust society and of crisis which could be ended only by radical reform. As radical social reform did not take place under the Meiji regime, the approach was itself a critique of Japanese society, following the trajectory of Maruyama's interpretation. More recently, James White in *Ikki: social conflict and political protest in early modern Japan* (Ithaca and London, 1995) has sought to combine study of *ikki* with acceptance of the picture now emerging in the writing of Japanese economic historians of improvements in the first half of the nineteenth century.[12] For him the later *ikki* reflected the imminent political collapse of Tokugawa Japan; peasants who were already better off were emboldened to rise and demand more.

As a means of understanding Japan or – reflecting the 1950s preoccupations which coloured western study – of accounting for the political path Japan took from 1868 or perhaps more pertinently from 1890, Japanese political thought is less fruitful than it appears at first sight. Thought in Tokugawa times had been highly eclectic (the prevalence of eclecticism was dismissed by Maruyama,[13] who wanted to find a well-defined theme in Japanese thought leading ultimately to the dominance of the militarist faction of the 1930s). The significance attributed to earlier thought can all too easily be read back from later concerns rather than rest on its own intrinsic content. Antecedents in earlier history for the role assumed by the emperor (or which he was required to play) are doubtful. The approach involves underestimating the extent of the politically interested manipulation of the imperial office after 1868. If there is a role for the emperor in pre-Meiji history it is more in the form explored by Fujita Satoru.[14] There is no clear progression in earlier thought, and the emperor's place in the polity emerged when, as crisis unfolded, consensus in society in face of novel challenges seemed to be necessary. Sharp divides on the momentous issues of the day among Japanese themselves in the 1860s had already given importance to the need for a symbol of unity.

---

[12] For a review of it see L. M. Cullen in *Japan Foundation newsletter*, vol. 14, no. 4 (Nov. 1996), pp.20–1.

[13] Maruyama, *Intellectual history of Tokugawa Japan*, pp.140–3.

[14] Fujita, *Kinsei seiji-shi to tennō*.

The emphasis the emperor has acquired in modern study was enlarged by the belief in singular samurai values (usually associated also
with Confucianism). Samurai values through the han schools had been
given wide significance confidently by Ronald P. Dore in *Education in
Tokugawa Japan* (London, 1965). As for the wider import of a samurai ethic as a basis for either westernisation or economic success, Kozo
Yamamura pointed to the weakness of the case for the ethical sense of
samurai serving as a basis for entrepreneurial activity.[15] Scholarly though
the work on political thought may be, it often seems to be flawed by
easy assumptions about persistent economic or political crisis in the
background. Thus, Ooms's *Tokugawa ideology: early constructs 1570–1680*
(Princeton, 1985, paperback Ann Arbor, 1998) considered the possibility
that the emperor–shogun relationship reflected a delegation of authority,
but opted finally for the belief that the relationship was determined by
the exercise of naked power by the Tokugawa family. H. D. Harootunian's *Towards Restoration: the growth of political consciousness in Tokugawa
Japan* (Berkeley, 1970, paperback 1980), while primarily a useful exploration of themes in a number of writings by pre-Restoration activists, is
coloured by the sweeping statement that the *uchi harai* order of 1825
was 'little more than a tired restatement of Tokugawa isolationism, which
revealed the incapacity of the bakufu to see beyond the immediate implications of events'. However, if such claims are discounted, much of
this writing is invaluable on aspects of Japan, as is Harootunian's account
of the decade of the 1860s. Moreover, H. Ooms's *Charismatic bureaucrat: a political biography of Matsudaira Sadanobu 1758–1829* (Chicago,
1975) put Matsudaira in a far better context than that posited for him
in Hall's study of Tanuma, and his more recent *Tokugawa village practice:
class, status, power, law* (Berkeley, 1996), on an altogether different plane,
opens up study from concrete evidence of the experience, in some regards
benign, of individuals under Tokugawa civil law. J. Victor Koschmann's
The Mito ideology: discourse, reform, and insurrection in Tokugawa Japan
(Berkeley, 1987), as an account of Mito han and its most famous ruler
Tokugawa Nariaki, is almost alone in English (and there are not too many
in Japanese). In Tetsuo Najita's prolific work, his *Visions of virtue in Tokugawa Japan: the Kaitokudō merchant academy of Osaka* (Chicago, 1987) is
an essential reference on the school and its intellectual ramifications (even
if Nakai Rikken's ties to the rebel Ōshio Heihachirō seem overstressed).
P. Nosco, as editor of *Confucianism and Tokugawa culture* (Princeton,
1984), has made a signal contribution in underlining the enduring strength of Confucian thought. It has over the decades too easily been put into

---

[15] Yamamura, 'A re-examination of entrepreneurship in Meiji Japan'.

facile parallels of reactionary Confucian thought running counter to new awareness of wider values, and of a conflict between those who wanted to keep Japan closed and those who argued the case for its opening. In more recent decades, as Ph.D. programmes have become better established, the profile of scholarship has changed; there is less virtuoso work, and subjects tend to be well-defined and confined (the basis already of the controversial charge against the historiography made by Dower and Allinson two decades ago[16]). Hall, in his *Government and local power in Japan, 500 to 1700: a study based on Bizen province* (Princeton, 1966), provided a model of future work, and Craig even more so with his wide-ranging and bold study of *Choshu in the Meiji Restoration* (Cambridge, Mass., 1961). Much work has been executed in studies of individual han. An outstanding example of the new generation of work is James L. McClain's study in *Kanazawa: a seventeenth-century Japanese castle town* (New Haven, 1982), of the castle town of Kaga han. A number of other works reflect the han focus in research, notably for Kaga han Philip C. Brown in *Central authority and local autonomy in the formation of early modern Japan: the case of Kaga han* (Stanford, 1993), for Yonezawa, Hirosaki and Tokushima by Mark Ravina in *Land and lordship in early modern Japan* (Stanford, 1999), and for Tosa by Luke S. Roberts in *The merchant origins of economic nationalism in 18th century Tosa* (Cambridge, 1998). Other studies with a strong local focus include a study of the silk industry in the province of Shinano (Karen Wigen, *The making of a Japanese periphery 1750–1920* (Berkeley, 1995)) and of fisheries in Ezo (David L. Howell, *Capitalism from within: economy, society and the state in a Japanese fishery* (Berkeley, 1995). Less centred on han or regions, there is a significant number of other studies as well. Most of the work has been in the United States, though studies in Germany (encouraged also by the establishment in 1988 of the splendid Deutsches Institut fur Japanstudien in Tokyo), France and Italy represent a small but growing corpus and, in the wake of the tradition established earlier by Nish, Beasley, Dore and Storry, and more recently by Blacker, McMullen and Kornicki, there has been a steady output of invaluable studies in Britain.[17] An example of a wide range of international interest is a collection of studies relating to the translation of a botanical work in Japan (*Dodonaeus in Japan: translation and the scientific mind in the Tokugawa period*, ed. W. F. Van de Welle and Kazuhiko Kasaya (Leuven, 2001)).

---

[16] Dower, 'E. H. Norman', pp.3–101; Allinson, 'E. H. Norman on modern Japan', pp.99–120.

[17] On these studies, see Harumi Befu, 'Japan as other: merits and demerits of overseas Japanese studies', in J. Kreiner (ed.), *Japan in global context: papers presented on the occasion of the fifth anniversary of the German Institute for Japanese Studies* (Tokyo, 1994), pp.33–45.

On international political relationships, Beasley, Nish and Storry have over long years made a prolific contribution, and more recently Peter Duus covers the Korea involvement in great but readable detail. If the western literature has been patronising in some regards, the literature on the diplomatic front, in contrast to much of the older literature, Marxist or left-wing, in Japanese itself, has been understanding of Japan's international dilemmas, and often critical of the stance assumed by western powers. Dower, dissenting from the easy consensus in early western writing on Japan, has written a number of powerful books, quite apart from his biography of Yoshida Shigeru, the post-war prime minister, *Empire and aftermath: Yoshida Shigeru and the Japanese experience, 1878–1954* (Cambridge, Mass., 1979). In particular, a collection of his essays, *War without mercy: race and power in the Pacific war* (New York, 1986), is a thought-provoking volume, and it has had a sequel in a less uni-dimensional outlook in a growing number of modern studies.

Surprisingly little has been written in English on sakoku itself, trade, bureaucracy, the huge Nagasaki office and its *modus operandi*, and on policy generally under the Tokugawa. R. Toby's *State and diplomacy in early modern Japan: Asia in the development of the Tokugawa bakufu* (Princeton, 1984; paperback Stanford, 1991) is from a formidable knowledge of the sources a powerful argument, centred mainly on the seventeenth century, that though a closed country Japan had a rational foreign policy. But Toby apart, sakoku itself is not well served in English. Grant Goodman's *The Dutch impact on Japan (1600–1853)* (Leiden, 1967) and Keene's *The Japanese discovery of Europe: Honda Toshiaki and other discoverers*, which in 1952 was a remarkably early text in the post-war historiography (translated into Japanese and still much quoted in Japan), are, even in later revised form, out of date. Yoneo Ishii's *The junk trade from southeast Asia: translations from the tōsen fūsetsugaki 1674–1723* (Institute of southeast Studies, Singapore, 1998) is a rare item which makes accessible in English some of the *fūsetsugaki* or reports submitted at Nagasaki by Chinese vessels. For the reader in English, sakoku is best captured in the contemporary writing of four Europeans who visited Japan. Kaempfer, medical doctor in the Dutch factory in 1690 and 1691, is the most famous (now available in a splendid edition by B. Bodart-Bailey, though lacking some of the appendices, from the University of Honolulu Press, 1999). Thunberg's account of his sojourn in Deshima in 1775 (English edition published only in 1795, French in 1796) remains a vivid glimpse of Japan by an outsider. Isaac Titsingh, *opperhoofd* in Nagasaki, whose writings appearing posthumously in 1819–22 and 1834 in French and English were the outcome of a fascination which long outlived his stays there in 1779–84, had an easy rapport with Japanese in Nagasaki, which he continued in correspondence after he left Japan.[18] C. R. Boxer many years ago wrote a very good account of Titsingh in his *Jan Compagnie in Japan 1600–1817* (The Hague, 1936 and 1950). Very recently Titsingh's correspondence has been edited in two volumes (Frank Lequin, *The private correspondence of Isaac Titsingh 1785–1811* (Amsterdam, 1990)), and Titsingh's life and work are likely to merit more attention in the future. Lequin's *Isaac Titsingh (1745–1811) een passie voor Japan: leven en werk van de grondlegger van de Europese Japanologie* (Alphan an de Rijn, 2002) – with a very warm dedication to the memory of C. R. Boxer – is a first step in that direction. The fourth figure is the Russian naval officer, Wasely M. Golownin (Vasilii M. Golovnin), whose accounts appeared in Russian; one, a *Narrative of my captivity in Japan during the years 1811, 1812 and 1813*, was translated into English in 1818, and the other, *Recollections of Japan*, was translated the following year. His *Narrative* (reprinted in 1975 and, more recently, by the Japan Library in 2000) is, as Sir Ernest Satow expressed it, 'the entrancing narrative of Golownin... perhaps the most lifelike picture of Japanese official manners that is anywhere to be met with'.[19]

Uchi harai, in some respects the other side of the sakoku coin, has a small literature; it badly needs a close survey not only in English but in Japanese. Wakabayashi, in his translation of Aizawa Seishisai's *Shinron* of 1825 (all too often dismissed as a piece of xenophobia) in *Antiforeignism and western learning in early modern Japan: the New Theses of 1825* (Cambridge, Mass., 1986), prefaced the text with a substantial introduction, covering the immediate historical background. The actual unfolding of *uchi harai* policy, though much mentioned, is obscure, and in Japanese and in English alike, the pattern of its evolution and its rationale (an intelligent one, once isolation is accepted as a legitimate policy) is underestimated. For earlier times, the Christian presence in Japan has been overemphasised in English (one of Boxer's books is even entitled *The Christian century in Japan*). C. R. Boxer's numerous writings, some

---

[18] Titsingh's account, written in the hope of making known a country which he said was all too unknown, likewise was published only after his death (*Cérémonies usitées au Japon pour les mariages et les funérailles* (Paris, 1819), and *Mémoires et anecdotes sur la dynastie des Djogouns, souverains du Japon* (Paris, 1820)). The English edition appeared as *Illustrations of Japan; consisting of private memoirs and anecdotes of the reigning djogouns, or sovereigns of Japan* (London, 1822). These works were substantially ready for publication at the time of his death in 1812. His remaining work on Japanese annals appeared in much altered form a decade later (*Nihon o dai etsi ran, ou annales des empereurs du Japon* (Paris, 1834)).

[19] Satow, *A diplomat in Japan*, p.41. A new Japanese translation appeared however in 1984, made by Tokuriki Shintaro in two volumes under the title, *Nihon furyo jikki: Gorounin* [True account of a Japanese prisoner: Golownin].

of them almost seventy years old, and ahead of their time and on a varied canvas, explored many aspects. Stress on anti-Christian feeling, often taken as the driving force behind sakoku, rather than on fear of the outsider, has led to underestimation of the political and military motivation behind sakoku.

Michael Cooper's *They came to Japan: an anthology of European reports on Japan 1543–1640* (London, 1965) is important, for its extracts from the Jesuits, keen observers, indeed the last westerners to travel freely in Japan for almost 300 years, and largely devoid of the patronising tone uppermost in the writing of many who made the acquaintance of Japan in the 1860s and later. The four lay writers of sakoku times from the west, Kaempfer, Thunberg, Titsingh and Golownin (Golovnin), all wrote of Japan as an advanced country. The views of these men were to be discounted in later commentary. The introduction by the English editor to Golownin's *Recollections* reads as if he had not read Golownin's own sensitive text.[20] The earliest work, Kaempfer's *The history of Japan*, first published in 1727, was still regarded as late as the 1850s as the authoritative introduction to Japan, and favourable views in the other writings were dismissed not as corroboration of good things but mere uncritical repetition.

Biography is a fruitful source of information. Starting from excellent short biographies by Berry and Totman on Toyotomi Hideyoshi (1982, 1989) and Tokugawa Ieyasu (1983) respectively, biographies exist on Tanuma (Hall, 1955), Sakamoto Ryōma (Jansen, 1961), Ōkubo (Masakazu Iwata, 1964) Hara Kei (Tetsuo Najita, 1967), Yoshida Shigeru (Dower, 1979), Sadanobu (Ooms, 1975) and Saigō Takamori (Yates, 1995), and in a somewhat different category Kate Wildman Nakai's study of Arai Hakuseki is an excellent one of the man and his times (Cambridge, Mass., 1988).[21] Mizuno Tadakuni needs a biography (especially as in Japanese Fujita has put him and his times in a new context). Yoshimune, the greatest of all the shoguns, and the two capable daimyo of Satsuma, Shimazu Shigehide and Shimazu Nariakira, while they have biographies in Japan, lack accounts in English. Tokugawa Nariaki, Mito's most celebrated daimyo, languishes in Japanese as well as in English. The work by the historical novelist Ryōtarō Shiba on Tokugawa Yoshinobu, fifteenth and last shogun, *Saigō no shōgun* (Tokyo, 1967), though presenting a somewhat dated background, is also useful.

---

[20] Golownin, *Recollections*, pp.i–lxxxix.
[21] Nakai, *Shogunal politics*. On Arai Hakuseki, see also Ackroyd, *Autobiography of Arai Hakuseki*.

A major contribution lies in a number of collective works which bring a wide range of authors and topics together. The most useful, in chronological order, are:

John W. Hall and M. Jansen (eds.), *Studies in the institutional history of early modern Japan* (Princeton, 1968)

A. M. Craig and D. H. Shively (eds.), *Personality in Japanese history* (Berkeley, 1970)

Tetsuo Najita and I. Scheiner (eds.), *Japanese thought in the Tokugawa period 1600–1868* (Chicago, 1978)

J. W. Hall, Nagahara Keiji and Kozo Yamamura (eds.), *Japan before Tokugawa: political consolidation and economic growth 1500 to 1650* (Princeton, 1981)

Tetsuo Najita and J. Victor Koschmann (eds.), *Conflict in modern Japanese history: the neglected tradition* (Princeton, 1982)

Michio Nagai and Miguel Urrutia (eds.), *Meiji ishin: restoration and revolution* (Tokyo, 1985)

Marius B. Jansen and G. Rozman (eds.), *Japan in transition, from Tokugawa to Meiji* (Princeton, 1986)

Carol Gluck and S. R. Graubard (eds.), *Showa: the Japan of Hirohito* (New York, 1992)

Jansen and Rozman's volume is particularly important as a study of a number of broad aspects of the economic and social background, and hence makes a good introductory read. Michio Nagai and Miguel Urrutia's volume is an excellent collection of studies of Japan in the era of restoration. Craig and Shively's volume, while it might be criticised for its emphasis on personality, provides a series of very good short biographies of major figures.

If the economic history of pre-Meiji times in English is slight, this is not true of the post-1868 literature. It is large, and especially for the twentieth century the reader is very well served. It was foreshadowed in the history by G. C. Allen's *A short economic history of Japan* in 1946, and by W. W. Lockwood's *The economic development of Japan: growth and structural change 1868–1938* in 1965. The expanding literature of the 1950s is open to the criticism that it reflected the belief that Japan would serve as a model for less developed countries (which involved assuming that Japan was backward in 1868) and also that there were special reasons for Japan's success. Some of the literature, pursuing the holy grail of Japanese success, is now dated, as the lustre of Japanese achievements is somewhat tarnished by a decade of stagnation. W. J. Macpherson's *The economic development of Japan 1868–1941* (Cambridge, 1987) is the best introduction to this large subject, and it is supported by an excellent bibliography. Macpherson's *The industrial-isation of Japan* (Oxford, 1994) brings together twenty-one articles from many sources on Japan's economic development. A very wide-ranging work worth singling out is Christopher Howe's *The origins of Japanese trade supremacy: development and technology in Asia from 1540 to the Pacific war* (London, 1996).

Japan is rich in illustrative material, partly because the structure of houses did not lend itself to a display of oil painting, and other – and cheaper – forms of artistic depiction suited domestic arrangements better. When Perry's fleet arrived in 1853 it was soon surrounded by small boats bobbing up and down in the water while enterprising artists made sketches for prints which were rushed out. For a guide to pictorial evidence from Tokugawa times, as opposed to artistic study of the huge mass of material, the NHK series *Edo jihō* (Life in Edo times) in six volumes (Tokyo, 1991–3) is best. Because it was abundant and cheap, pictorial representation covers domestic and working conditions far more intimately and frequently than does the canon of illustration in the west. Even famine, precisely because it was rare, caught the attention of the tireless artists. The most dramatic instance is the powerful scroll of famine in Kyoto in 1837, the *Tenpō hachinen kimin kyūjutsu zukan* in the Chester Beatty Library in Dublin.[22] But there are other instances also. Exhibition catalogues are good. Especially important is the magnificent catalogue of the *Via orientalis: porutogaru to nanban bunka ten: mesase tōhō no kuniguni* (Via orientalis: Portugal and Nanban culture exhibition: voyages to eastern countries), for the 450th anniversary of the coming of the Portuguese, in Seson bijutsukan, Tokyo, 1993; and the catalogue of the dazzling Yoshimune exhibition of 1995 in the Suntory Gallery, Tokyo, *Shogun Yoshimune to sono jidai ten*. Also rich in illustration is the catalogue of the *Kinsei Nagasaki no akebono* (The dawn of modern Nagasaki), Kenritsu bijutsukan hakubutsukan exhibition 1993. Shigeo Sorimachi, *Japanese illustrated books and manuscripts in the Chester Beatty Library* (Kobunso, Tokyo, 1979) and *Nihon no monogatari e* (Oriental treasures from the Chester Beatty Collections, Suntory Gallery, Tokyo, 1989) are a source of a rich variety of material. *Nanban shorai kara genbaku made* (From the arrival of European culture to the atomic bomb, Culture Department, Education Board, Nagasaki city, 1980), reproduces many of the best known illustrations of the western presence in Nagasaki. Three recent books by T. Screech, while some of their observations on politics

[22] Another scroll in the Chester Beatty Library, also by the same artist, Tanaka Yubi, depicts the harvest festival in Osaka after the good harvest of 1839, *Tenpō jūnen honen odori zukan*.

or economics are open to question, are of considerable interest, combining knowledge of the painting with a formidable grasp of documentary sources. As for the historiography in Japanese, it is vast, comparable to that of the major western countries. The range of printed material drawn on for this study is comparatively limited, and is open to the criticism that it only partly covers the field, or is highly selective. Japan has almost as high a participation in higher education as the United States, which means many textbooks for an undergraduate readership and for educated adults and a large number of monographs by a huge faculty. Inevitably there is much repetition of the same ground in texts, and their quality is uneven. Only a few scholars have spread their attention across a wide number of themes. The outstanding example is probably the indefatigable Ōishi Shinzaburō, who has written a large number of readable monographs, including a biography of Tanuma, and with Ichimura Yūichi probably the best succinct account of sakoku under the title *Sakoku: yuruyaka-na jōhō kakumei* (Tokyo, 1995). On political history perhaps the most interesting new work is associated with Fujita Satoru, Mitani Hiroshi and, on twentieth-century history, with Kitaoka Shinichi; on demography very positively so with Hayami Akira, Saitō Osamu and others; and on trade, much studied in a magisterial range of work in the past, new approaches are being explored by a younger generation including Kawakatsu Heita and others.[23] In such a vast literature the best introduction for those who read the language is probably the various series of multi-author volumes, or the series of single-author volumes. The number of these series is large, and their quality high. Two series are particularly important. In political history, the 16-volume *Nihon no kindai* published by Chuokoron-sha, only recently completed, is the most up to date. In economic history *Nihon keizai-shi*, published by Iwanami shoten in the years around 1990, still holds the field: it is thorough, and shows no sign of soon being replaced.

The journal literature is huge. The best guide to work is the annual bibliography in *Shigaku zasshi*. Its *2000 nen no rekishi gakai*, its bibliography for 2000, runs to 452 pages. Much writing of real value is buried in little-known journals published by universities and featuring research by their own teachers and graduates, and not always accessible even in the big Tokyo libraries. For English-speaking readers, *Acta asiatica* is particularly invaluable: it contains in its earlier years a number of articles in English by leading Japanese historians on important themes. One has to

---

[23] In English the best illustration of this work is perhaps A. J. Latham and Kawakatsu, *Japanese industrialization*.

be singled out, the article by Itō Tasaburō on 'The book banning policy of the Tokugawa shogunate' (no. 22, 1972, pp.36–61), a subject of misunderstanding not only in most western books but in many Japanese ones.

Overall, Japanese historiography has painted a pessimistic picture of trends. This is not in itself unusual for a national historiography. One has to refer only to Ireland or to India for parallels,[24] though in both cases a colonial context gave writers an urge to assume a pessimistic posture for the sake of the political dividend it yielded. However, Japan had no colonial past, though the Meiji revolution of 1868 did lead its leaders and their intellectual supporters to dismiss the Tokugawa antecedents. This is reflected in the entry of the term of derision, bakufu, which in the 1860s opponents of the shogunate used, into the language as the habitual term to denote the administration of all fifteen shoguns. The eclecticism of Japanese thought which from the 1920s made it easy to take up Marxism as a philosophic model, as knowledge of it spread through the world in the wake of the Russian Revolution, copper-fastened an oppressive picture of the past. While Marxism is absent from much modern work, it is also true that young Japanese scholars are still prone to pick on new and fashionable theories from outside Japan. In contrast to past neglect, in recent decades the Edo period has begun to become fashionable. This can be seen in the opening in 1993 of the magnificent Edo-Tokyo Museum, the success of the Yoshimune exhibition in the Suntory Gallery in 1995, the interest aroused by the entertaining but highly fictional NHK TV drama series on Yoshimune and more recently, in the wake of yet another NHK costume-drama series, a plethora of books on Tokugawa Yoshinobu ('Keiki'). Biographies have multiplied on Yoshimune, and on the formerly obscure Yoshinobu. Ryōtarō Shiba, with his study of Yoshinobu (translated into French, English, Spanish and German) in 1967, was well ahead of the posse.

Non-Marxists as well as Marxists, in other words writers such as Honjō and Otsuka, accepted a gloomy view of the past. So did the American historian Hugh Borton from Columbia in 1937 who distilled the detail of Japanese work into an unqualifiedly depressing account of *ikki* in more than 200 pages in the *Transactions of the Asiatic society of Japan* (2nd series, vol. 16 (May 1938), pp.1–219). In one of his later works, *Japan's modern century* (New York, 1955), one chapter was even entitled 'The dictatorship collapses 1857–1867'. Hall in his 1955 study of Tanuma reflected an emphasis which was already universal: the

[24] See Morris D. Morris, 'Towards a reinterpretation of nineteenth century Indian economic history', *Journal of economic history*, vol. 23, no. 4 (Dec. 1963), pp.606–18.

difference was simply that he raised Tanuma above these gloomy horizons. T. C. Smith's work was a contrast with this narrow perspective: his *Agrarian origins* gave credit to a robust strength in Japanese agriculture, just as in his famous later article on castle towns, 'Pre-modern economic growth: Japan and the west' (*Past and present*, no. 60 (Aug. 1973)),[25] he saw the decline of population in the east-coast towns as reflecting the spread of industry to the countryside, not a decline of the economy at large. Yamamura in 1973 took an even bolder stand and has written on a wide range of themes, and uniquely his interests have ranged from the pre-Tokugawa period right up to the 1950s. His major work with Susan Hanley, *Economic and demographic change in preindustrial Japan 1600–1868* (Princeton, 1977) presented an optimistic account of economic change in Tokugawa times; Susan Hanley has developed this more explicitly in regard to income and living standards.[26]

These revisionist conclusions depended in part on examination of demographic evidence. Demographic history in recent decades increasingly has taken centre stage in economic history, especially in the reconstitution of family history from temple records pioneered by Hayami Akira and his successor Saitō Osamu and others. An English-language text by Hayami, *The historical demography of pre-modern Japan* (Tokyo, 2001), makes some of his conclusions more accessible.[27] The question of living standards is a large and complex field, and there is no easy way of establishing consensus (it is somewhat akin to the debate on the standard of living during the Industrial Revolution which for decades kept controversy alive in English historiography). The fact that the population grew slowly from mid-Tokugawa times and family size was small prompted much comment. Twenty-five years ago, T. C. Smith in his *Nagahara: family planning and population in a Japanese village 1717–1830* (Stanford, 1977) argued that evidence existed of family planning, by way of abortion or infanticide. However, subsequent work in other small communities has not provided supporting evidence. Moreover, the studies by Hayami have brought out contrasts in demographic growth between regions and, within regions, differing patterns between old-settled lands on valley floors and more recently settled land on neighbouring upland slopes. The trend in current work in economic history is to see economic

[25] Reprinted in T. C. Smith, *Native sources of Japanese industrialization*, pp.15–49.
[26] Susan Hanley, 'A high standard of living in nineteenth-century Japan: fact or fantasy?', *Journal of economic history*, vol. 43, no. 1 (March 1983), pp.183–92; 'Standard of living in nineteenth-century Japan: reply to Yasuba', *Journal of economic history*, vol. 46, no. 1 (March 1986), pp.225–6; *Everyday things in pre-modern Japan: the hidden legacy of material culture* (Berkeley, 1997).
[27] See also an article by him on 'Population changes', in Macpherson, *The industrialisation of Japan*, pp.88–125.

growth as taking place, despite the setback of the 1830s, in the first half of
the nineteenth century. This is parallel to a more sympathetic view taken
of Mizuno Tadakuni's role in Fujita Satoru's work.[28]

One of the strengths of Japanese history has been highly detailed work,
often rather technical in approach, having an appeal to specialists and, in
terms of pages or even volumes, on a grand scale. In the case of knowledge of the west and mastery of Dutch, there has been an impressive
succession of works, all too often even in Japan ignored except by specialists: Kure Shūzō's vast study, *Shiiboruto sensei: sono shōgai oyobi kogyō*
(Tokyo, 1926), now available in a German translation as *Philipp Franz
Von Siebold: leben und werk* (2 vols., Deutsches Institut fur Japanstudien,
Tokyo, 1996); Uehara Hisashi's exhaustive study, *Takahashi Kageyasu no
kenkyū* (Tokyo, 1977); Katagiri Kazuo's many works on the Nagasaki
interpreters; and Sugimoto Tsutomu's magisterial five-volume study of
Japanese knowledge of Dutch, *Edo jidai ran-gogaku no seiritsu to sono tenkai*
(Tokyo, 1976–82). Trade was studied in the works of Yamawaki Teijirō,
Katō Eiichi, Nagazumi Yōko, Yanai Kenji and others. Publication of
materials on the surveying work in Ezo, as important politically as geographically, has been greatly added to in recent years. The strength of
Japanese scholarship (justifiably defended with vigour by Dower) is well
represented in han and city history; while they vary in depth from han to
han (reflecting the richness of the sources), they represent a formidable
contribution by groups of historians. Hokkaido, Mito, Osaka and
Nagasaki, all with major political and economic significance in Tokugawa
history, have been served by magisterial series. For sakoku, despite a host
of lesser works, the *Taigai kōshō* volume of the *Nagasaki ken-shi* (Tokyo,
1985) is still the best modern overview.

A problem for the study of Japanese history is that administration was
not centralised. Below the senior officials at the level of *kanjō bugyō* and
metsuke, what might be described as clerks exercising a permanent role
were, outside the accounting and justice departments, remarkably few,
and no well-defined administrative structures existed for the regular execution of tasks and the management of records pertaining to them. A consequence was that while accounting, taxing and legal documents tended
to be preserved (and a large number of lesser officials spent their lives
in handling this paper), other documents served only an immediate purpose. If not either transcribed into compilations or summarised in *nikki* or
diaries, they have disappeared, and what statistical evidence has survived
is either to be found in han records or elsewhere, if existing at all, mostly

---

[28] Fujita, *Tenpō no kaikaku*; *Bakuhansei kokka no seiji shi-teki kenkyū: tenpō-ki no chitsujo,
gunji, gaikō*.

originating from the Nagasaki bugyo office. In the han themselves, the actual demographic returns from village headmen to the han authorities do not survive in han records: where they do, it is in copies retained by village headmen. The *Tsūkō ichiran*, a compendium of documents on foreign relations, was compiled from many sources in 1849–53 by a team of twelve men working for the Hayashi family. The published compilation of historical records dating from 1846 by the Shiryō hensanjo in Tokyo, known as the *Dai nihon ishin shiryō*, is based not on office files of Tokugawa times, but on correspondence drawn in modern times from many sources, even on occasion from American records. A parallel series beginning from a later date (1853), *Dai nihon bakumatsu gaikoku kankei monjo* rests on compact collections which reveal the progressive emergence of systematic office routines and record-keeping for the now-permanent negotiations with the foreign powers. The records of the *Banshowagegoyō* (Translations Bureau) have not survived, and records of the Osaka bugyo office are few. A large number of Nagasaki records have survived, not only the *Hankachō*, or books of criminal judicial decisions, but an extensive though miscellaneous range of documents on trade and diplomacy. Their survival is partly a function of luck, as the post-1868 neglect of them could easily have led to their destruction. However, it was helped by the fact that the Nagasaki bugyo office was the largest administrative office of Tokugawa Japan. In other words their bulk served as a factor in survival as much as good luck itself. However, despite these survivals, the huge administrative correspondence of the office is missing almost in its entirety, a reflection more on what was retained at the time than on losses in Meiji times. As a result the *dagregisters* of the Dutch factory (formerly held in Deshima, now in The Hague) are vital to piecing together some of the story. They were essential to Katagiri Kazuo in putting together even the story of the corps of 150 or so interpreters who were at the centre of the administrative and statistical functioning of the huge office.

The Hayashi family, compilers of the *Tsūkō ichiran*, are also the source of the main surviving records of the Edo administration, now in the National Diet Archives. Some of their books and manuscripts are to be found in the *Kenritsu chūō toshokan* in Shizuoka. As for its character, Japanese administration was less secretive than obscure or rudimentary: the *fūsetsugaki*, supplied by the Dutch, and supposedly highly confidential, survive in many locations, and in some instances in more than one centre. It is difficult to describe such a porous administration as oppressive. It was, however, arbitrary: if few officials were involved and lines of command were unclear, internal and at times deadly personal rivalries arose which were not easily mediated. While work has been done on the arcane processes of communication in Chinese with Korea (Nakao

Hiroshi, *Chōsen tsūshin shi to Tokugawa bakufu* [History of diplomatic ties with Korea under the Edo bakufu] (Meiseki shoten, Tokyo, 1997), the regular administrative functioning of Tokugawa Japan still needs to be studied on a documentary basis. A cabinet of four to six *rōjū* or ministers, helped by *kanjō bugyō*, was overwhelmed. Matsudaira Sadanobu, prime minister 1787–93, gave some impetus to change; in the absence of an administrative staff under the *rōjū* and *kanjō bugyō*, the Hayashi family were given some overview in new and critical tasks such as the surveying of Ezo and foreign affairs. Policy responsibilities devolved on the *kanjō bugyō* and *metsuke*, but they in turn were officers deputed for specific tasks as need or crisis dictated: they had no permanent corps of clerks below them, and had to work in tandem with the Hayashi family, with Takahashi Kageyasu, and, if the problem lay outside Edo, with han authorities. With a real challenge to sakoku in prospect, the Hayashi were ordered in 1849 to compile the *Tsūkō ichiran*, and the head of the family was chief negotiator with the Americans in 1854. Real administrative change began from 1845, and finally the Hayashi themselves were effectively replaced from 1858 (Hayashi Akira, the negotiator of the treaty in 1854, himself died in 1859). Their work before 1858 is concealed by many of their surviving papers being taken over in the 1860s by others, and when the papers were finally deposited in the archives (*Naikaku bunko*), they were deposited by the later custodians. The descriptions of the documents in the modern calendars reflect their final administrative home but from internal evidence their earlier history was sometimes more varied than the summary details suggest.

While there is no work on administration viewed as a bureaucratic machine, two books are useful for the reader who wants to get a picture of the governmental structures of the shogunate. The first is Kozo Yamamura's *A study of samurai income and entrepreneurship* (Cambridge, Mass., 1974), of much wider import than its title suggests; the second is Conrad Totman's *Politics in the Tokugawa bakufu 1600–1843* (Cambridge, Mass., 1967; paperback edition, Berkeley, 1988), which is in substance a survey of shogunal political and administrative structures.

Foreign archives have been much used in works in recent decades on relations with Japan by both Japanese and foreign historians. A particularly rich source for Japanese history is provided by the reports and papers in the British parliamentary papers. In the early years they contain even diplomatic reports and internal memoranda between consuls and the minister in Edo; they also have intermittently very substantial reports on special subjects, and on an annual basis reports on trade from various ports. For the first decade or more of foreign trade, they provide the only true figures of Japanese foreign trade. The papers relating to Japan up to

1899 have been brought together in ten volumes in the Irish University Press edition of the parliamentary papers.[29] An important supplementary source to the political papers in the Public Record Office in London is found in the papers and diaries of Sir Ernest Satow. They contain much more information and over a wider period than his *Diplomat in Japan*, which consists essentially of extracts from his diaries drawn up in the 1880s and finally published at the prompting of family members in the wake of the Versailles treaty of 1919 (the 1921 book has been reprinted by ICG Mus, Inc., New York and Tokyo, 2000).[30] His papers include also the letters he received from two old Tokyo hands, W. G. Aston (1841–1911) and J. H. Gubbins (1852–1929).[31] On their deaths, his own letters to Aston were returned to him: as a result both sides of the correspondence often survive. As a whole the Satow papers are not only a fascinating commentary on Japan but a unique one sustained over sixty years.

[29] See *Sekai o utsusu daieiteikoku: eikoku gikai shiryō o yomu* [The world seen from imperial Britain: reading the British parliamentary papers], *Chiiki kenkyū ronshū* [Regional studies], *tokushū* [special issue], vol. 3, no. 1 (March 2000). On the parliamentary papers as a source for Japanese history, see L. M. Cullen, 'Eikoku gikai shiryō to Nihon' [British parliamentary papers and Japan], *Chiiki kenkyū ronshū*, vol. 3, no. 1 (March 2000), pp.17–24.

[30] See also *Collected works of Ernest Mason Satow*, 12 vols. (Bristol and Tokyo, 1998), and on Satow himself the 'Introduction' by N. Brailey in vol. 1, pp.i–xx.

[31] See *Collected works of William George Aston*, and 'Introduction' by P. F. Kornicki in vol. 1, pp.xii–xxv; and Ian Nish, 'John Harrington Gubbins 1852–1929', in I. Nish and J. E. Hoare (eds.), *Britain and Japan: biographical portraits*, 3 vols. (Richmond, Surrey, 1994–9), vol. 2, pp.107–36.

Bibliography

1. MANUSCRIPT

KENRITSU CHŪŌ TOSHOKAN, SHIZUOKA

Copies of Edo and Nagasaki *Haruma*
Japanese translation of Golownin's *Narrative* (Ms AJ 12). (The published text
as edited by Wada Toshiaki from the Hakodate copy of the manuscript as
Soyaku nihon kiji: Gorounin [Diary of my tribulations in Japan: Golownin]
is in vol. 6 of *Hoppō mikōkai komonjo shūsei* [Collection of unpublished or
inaccessible private documents for the northern region] (Tokyo, 1980)).

NAIKAKU BUNKO

Various documents in early *bunka* period relating to Ezo, especially years *bunka*
5, 207/472; *bunka* 7, 185/283; *bunka* 9, 185/192; *bunka* 10, 185/281

KENRITSU CHŪŌ TOSHOKAN, NAGASAKI

Bugyōsho records, 13/4 (Seiyama collection), letter written in 1807 by a bugyo
official describing events in Ezo in 1806 and 1807

SHIIBORUTO KINENKAN, NAGASAKI (VON SIEBOLD MEMORIAL
BUILDING)

Copy of Nagasaki *Haruma*
Nakamura collection (contemporary translations in Dutch and Japanese of correspondence between the Nagasaki bugyo and the *Oranda kapitan* and other
contemporary documents, including Chinese *fūsetsugaki*)

UNIVERSITY OF NAGASAKI, KEIZAIGAKUBU TOSHOKAN

511 M186 French text of Russian message, Japanese translation and correspondence (contemporary copies) regarding the message left at Soya in 1807 in
a small volume from the *bugyōsho*

PUBLIC RECORD OFFICE, LONDON

Private deposits, 30/33 diaries, and correspondence of Sir Ernest Satow

CHESTER BEATTY LIBRARY, DUBLIN

Picture scrolls by Tanaka Yubi of famine in Kyoto 1837 (*Tenpō hachinen kimin kyūjutsu zukan*), and harvest festival in Osaka 1839 (*Tenpō jūnen hōnen odori zukan*)

2. PRINTED

SHIRYŌ HENSANJO, TOKYO

Dai nihon, ishin shiryō [Japan, sources for the Restoration], 1st series (7 vols.), 2nd series (5 vols.), 3rd series (7 vols.) (Tokyo, 1938–43, reprinted 1984–5)
Dai nihon, kinsei shiryō, Kondō Jūzō ezo-chi kankei shiryō [Japan, sources for early modern history, Kondo Juzo sources for relations with Ezo territories], 3 vols. (Tokyo, 1984–9), plus supplementary box with maps and pamphlet (Tokyo, 1993)
Dai nihon komonjo, bakumatsu gaikoku kankei monjo [Public records of Japan, records of Bakumatsu foreign relations], vols. 1–33 (Tokyo, 1910–61, reprinted 1984–6)
Historical documents relating to Japan in foreign countries: an inventory of microfilm acquisitions in the library of the University of Tokyo Historiographical Institute, 5 vols. (Tokyo, 1963–6)
Tokyo daigaku Shiryō hensanjo ho [Reports of the University of Tokyo Historiographical Institute], vol. 3 (Tokyo, 1968), pp.24–63; vol. 5 (Tokyo, 1970), pp.76–9; vol. 6 (Tokyo, 1971), pp.58–79

KENRITSU TOSHOKAN, NAGASAKI

Hankachō: Nagasaki bugyōsho hanketsu kiroku 1666–1867 [Nagasaki bugyo office: register of Nagasaki bugyo decisions in criminal matters], 11 vols. (Nagasaki, 1959–61)
Yorozu ticho (containing details of the staff of the Nagasaki *bugyōsho* 1855 (Nagasaki, 2001)

KENRITSU CHŪŌ TOSHOKAN, SHIZUOKA

Edo bakufu kyūzō yōsho mokuroku [Catalogue of the former Edo bakufu collection of western books] (Shizuoka, 1971)
Onko-chishin: Shizuoka kenritsu chūō toshokanzō no kichōsho shōkai [Drawing lessons from the study of the past: introduction to rare books in the Shizuoka prefectural central library collection] (Shizuoka, 1997)

PUBLISHED UNDER OTHER AUSPICES

Hoppō mikōkai komonjo shūsei [Collection of unpublished or inaccessible private documents for the northern region, 10 vols. (Tokyo, 1959–90), ed. Wada Toshiaki, Kurata Hidetoshi and Terazawa Hajime

Nagasaki bugyōsho kankei monjo chōsa hōkoku sho, Nagasaki ken bunkazai hōkoku, dai 131 shū [Reports of investigations into the Nagasaki bugyo office, Nagasaki-ken, cultural reports, collection number 131] (Nagasaki-ken kyoiku iinkai, 1998)

Tsūkō ichiran, 8 vols. (Tokyo, 1913)

Tsūkō ichiran zokushū [*Tsūkō ichiran,* continuation], 5 vols. (Osaka, 1968–73)

PREFECTURAL AND CITY HISTORIES

Hirosaki shi-shi [History of Hirosaki city], 2 vols. (Tokyo, 1963–4, reprint Tokyo, 1973)

Hokkaidō-shi [History of Hokkaido], 7 vols. (Tokyo, 1936–7, reprint Osaka, 1989–90), vol. 2 (Tokyo, 1937, reprint Osaka, 1990)

Mito shi-shi [History of Mito city], 9 vols. (1963–98), middle series, vol. 3 (Mito, 1976)

Nagasaki ken-shi [History of Nagasaki prefecture] (Tokyo, 1973–85), *Taigai kōshō* vol. [External relations] (Tokyo, 1985)

Osaka fu-shi [History of Osaka administrative district], 7 vols. plus supplementary vol. (Osaka, 1978–91) *kinsei* [Early modern period], pt 1, vol. 5 (Osaka, 1985); *kinsei,* pt 2, vol. 6 (Osaka, 1987); *kinsei,* pt 3, vol. 7 (Osaka, 1989)

Osaka shi-shi [History of Osaka city], 10 vols. (Osaka, 1988–96), vol. 4 (Osaka, 1990)

BOOKS AND ARTICLES, CONTEMPORARY AND LATER

Abiko, Bonnie, 'Persecuted patriot: Watanabe Kazan and the Tokugawa Bakufu', *Monumenta nipponica,* vol. 44, no. 2 (Summer 1989), pp.199–219

Ackroyd, Joyce, *Told around a brushwood fire: the autobiography of Arai Hakuseki* (Tokyo, 1979)

Akita, George, 'An examination of E. H. Norman's scholarship', *Journal of Japanese studies,* vol. 3, no. 2 (Summer 1977), pp.375–419

Akita, George and Yoshihiro Hirose, 'The British model: Inoue Kowashi and the ideal monarchical system', *Monumenta nipponica,* vol. 49, no. 4 (Winter, 1994), pp.413–21

Akizuki Toshiyuki, *Nichirō kankei to saharin-tō: bakumatsu meiji shonen no ryōdo mondai* (Tokyo, 1994)

Nihon hokuhen no tanken to chizu no rekishi (Sapporo, 1999)

Alcock, Sir Rutherford, *The capital of the tycoon: a narrative of three years residence in Japan,* 2 vols. (London, 1863)

Allen, G. C., *A short economic history of Japan* (London, 1946)

Appointment in Japan: memories of sixty years (London, 1983)

Allinson, G. D., 'E. H. Norman on modern Japan: towards a constructive assessment', in R. W. Bowen (ed.), *E. H. Norman: his life and scholarship* (Toronto, 1984), pp.99–120

The Columbia guide to modern Japanese history (New York, 1999)

Altman, A. A., 'The press', in M. B. Jansen and G. Rozman (eds.), *Japan in transition: from Tokugawa to Meiji* (Princeton, 1986), pp.231–47

Alvares, Manuela and Alvares, Jose, *Porutogaru nihon kōryū shi* (Tokyo, 1992)

Aoki Koji, *Hyakushō-ikki sogo nenpyō* (Tokyo, 1971)

Aoki Michio, 'Bakuhansei-shi kenkyū to hyakushō ikki kenkyū', in Minegishi Sumio, Fukaya Katsumi, Satō Kazuhitō, Aoki Michio (eds.), *Ikki-shi nyūmon*, 5 vols. (Tokyo, 1981), vol. 1, pp.219–86

Aoki Toshiuki, *Zaison rangaku no kenkyū* (Kyoto, 1998)

Arakawa Hidetoshi, *Kikin no rekishi* (Tokyo, 1967)

Arima Manabu, *Nihon no kindai*, vol. 4, *Kokusaika no naka no teikoku nihon 1905–1924* (Tokyo, 1999)

Aruga Tadashi, 'Editor's introduction', *Japanese journal of American studies*, no. 3 (1989), pp.1–25

Ashton, T. S., *An economic history of England in the eighteenth century* (London, 1954)

Aston, W. G., 'Russian descents in Saghalin and Itorup in the years 1806 and 1807', *Transactions of the Asiatic Society of Japan*, vol. 1 (1874), pp.86–95

Collected works of William George Aston, 6 vols. (Bristol and Tokyo, 1997)

'H. M. Phaeton at Nagasaki in 1808', in *Collected works of William George Aston*, 6 vols. (Bristol and Tokyo, 1997), vol. 1, pp.107–20

Atwell, W. S., 'International bullion flows and the Chinese economy, circa 1530–1650', *Past and present*, no. 95 (May 1982), pp.68–90

Barnes, Joseph, 'Soviet Siberia', in Joseph Barnes (ed.), *Empire in the east* (London, 1934), pp.87–116

Barnes, Joseph (ed.), *Empire in the east* (London, 1934)

Beasley, W. G., *The Meiji Restoration* (Stanford, 1972)

'The foreign threat and the opening of the ports', in *CHJ*, vol. 5 (1989), pp.259–307

'Japanese castaways and British interpreters', *Monumenta nipponica*, vol. 46, no. 1 (Spring 1991), pp.92–4

Great Britain and the opening of Japan 1834–1858 (1951, paperback edn, Folkestone, Kent, 1995)

Japan encounters the barbarian: Japanese travellers in America and Europe (Newhaven, 1995)

Befu Harumi, 'Japan as other: merits and demerits of overseas Japanese studies', in J. Kreiner (ed.), *Japan in global context: papers presented on the occasion of the fifth anniversary of the German Institute for Japanese Studies* (Tokyo, 1994), pp.33–45

Bellah, Robert, *Tokugawa religion: the cultural roots of modern Japan* (New York, 1985)

Benedict, Ruth, *The chrysanthemum and the sword: patterns of Japanese culture* (Boston, 1946)

Benyowsky, Mauritius Augustus Comte de, *Memoirs and travels of Mauritius Augustus Comte de Benyowsky* (London, 1790; Glasgow, 1904)

Berger, G. M., 'Politics and mobilisation in Japan 1931–1945', in *CHJ*, vol. 6 (1988), pp.97–153

Berry, M. E., *Hideyoshi* (Cambridge, Mass., 1989)

Bicker, Robert A. (ed.), *Ritual and diplomacy: the Macartney mission to China 1792–4* (London, 1993)

Bird, Isabella, *Unbeaten tracks in Japan* (London, 1880, reprint Tokyo, 1984).

Bix, H. P., *Peasant protest in Japan 1590–1884* (Newhaven, 1986)

Hirohito and the making of modern Japan (New York, 2000)

Bodart-Bailey, B. M. (ed.), *Kaempfer's Japan: Tokugawa culture observed* (Honolulu, 1999)

Bodart-Bailey, B. M. and Massarella, D. M. (eds.), *The furthest goal: Engelbert Kaempfer's encounter with Tokugawa Japan* (Folkestone, 1995)

Bolitho, H., *Treasures among men: the fudai daimyo in Tokugawa Japan* (New Haven, 1974)

'Travellers' tales: three eighteenth-century travel journals', *Harvard journal of Asiatic studies*, vol. 50, no. 2 (Dec. 1990), pp.485–504

Borton, Hugh, 'Peasant uprisings in Japan of the Tokugawa era', *Transactions of the Asiatic society of Japan*, 2nd series, vol. 16 (May 1938), pp.1–219

Japan's modern century (New York, 1955)

Spanning Japan's modern century: the memoirs of Hugh Borton (Lanham, Md., 2002)

Bowen, R. W. (ed.), *E. H. Norman: his life and scholarship* (Toronto, 1984)

Boxer, C. R., *A true description of the mighty kingdoms of Japan and Siam by Francis Caron and Joost Schouten: reprinted from the English edition of 1663* (London, 1935)

Jan Compagnie in Japan 1600–1817 (The Hague, 1936)

'Isaac Titsingh 1745–1811', in C. R. Boxer, *Jan Compagnie in Japan 1600–1817* (The Hague, 1936), pp.134–81

The Christian century in Japan 1549–1650 (Manchester, 1951)

Portuguese merchants and missionaries in feudal Japan 1540–1640 (London, 1986)

Brailey, N. 'Introduction', in *Collected works of Ernest Mason Satow*, 12 vols. (Bristol and Tokyo, 1998), vol. 1, pp.i–xx

Broughton, W. R., *A voyage of discovery to the north Pacific Ocean*, 2 vols. in 1 (London, 1804)

Brown, P. C., 'The mismeasure of land: land surveying in the Tokugawa period', *Monumenta nipponica*, vol. 42, no. 2 (Summer 1987), pp.115–55

Central authority and local autonomy in the formation of early modern Japan: the case of Kaga han (Stanford, 1993)

Brownlee, John S., *Japanese historians and the national myths, 1600–1945: the age of the gods and emperor Jinmu* (Tokyo and Vancouver, 1997)

Buck, Pearl S., 'Missionaries of empire', in Joseph Barnes (ed.), *Empire in the east* (London, 1934), pp.241–66

Buruma, Ian, *The wages of guilt: memories of war in Germany and Japan* (New York, 1994)

Cambridge history of Japan, vol. 3, Yamamura, Kozo (ed.), *Medieval Japan* (Cambridge, 1990)

Cambridge history of Japan, vol. 4, Hall, J. W. and McClain, J. L. (eds.), *Early modern Japan* (Cambridge, 1991)

Cambridge history of Japan, vol. 5, Jansen, M. B. (ed.), *The nineteenth century* (Cambridge, 1989)

Cambridge history of Japan, vol. 6, Duus, Peter (ed.), *The twentieth century* (Cambridge, 1988)

Carput, J. C. Van der and Wilson, R. A. (eds.), *Henry Heusken: Japan journal 1855–61* (Rutgers, 1964)

Carvalho, D. de, 'The making of a minority in Japan', *Japan Foundation newsletter*, vol. 27, nos. 3–4 (March 2000), 19–21

Chamberlain, B. H., *Things Japanese, being notes on various subjects connected with Japan for the use of travellers and others* (revised 1905 edn, reprinted Tokyo, 1980)

'The invention of a new religion' (1912, reprinted as an appendix to the 1980 edition of Chamberlain, title restyled as *Japanese things*), pp.531–44.

Chamberlin, W. H., *Japan over Asia* (London, 1938)

Chambliss, W. J. *Chiraijima village, land tenure, taxation and local trade 1818–1884* (Tucson, 1965)

Chang, Iris, *The rape of Nankin: the forgotten holocaust of World War II* (New York, 1997)

Collcutt, Martin, 'Zen and the Gozan', in *CHJ*, vol. 3 (1990), pp.583–652

Cooper, M., *They came to Japan: an anthology of European reports on Japan 1543–1640* (London, 1965, new edn 1981)

A copy of the Japan diary received on a Danish ship 18 July 1674 and given to Sir Robert Southwell by Sir Nathaniel Hearne (in *Kaempfer*, 1728 edn, vol. 2, as a second appendix, separately paginated)

Cortazzi, H., 'The pestilentially active minister: Dr Willis's comments on Sir Harry Parkes', *Monumenta nipponica*, vol. 39, no. 2 (Summer 1984), pp.147–61

Japan and back and places elsewhere (London, 1998)

Craig, A. M., *Choshu in the Meiji Restoration* (Cambridge, Mass., 1961)

'The central goverment', in M. B. Jansen and G. Rozman (eds.), *Japan in transition: from Tokugawa to Meiji* (Princeton, 1986), pp.48–58

Craig, A. M. and Shively, D. H. (eds.), *Personality in Japanese history* (Berkeley, 1970)

Crawfour, E. S., 'Industrialisation and technological change, 1885–1920', in *CHJ*, vol. 6 (1988), pp.385–450

'Economic change in the nineteenth century', in *CHJ*, vol. 5 (1989), pp.569–617

Cullen, L. M., review in *Japan Foundation newsletter*, vol. 14, no. 4 (Nov. 1996), pp.20–1

'Professor Matsuo Taro, 1933–1997', *Keizai shirin* (Hosei University), vol. 66, no. 2 (Oct. 1998), pp.47–70.

'Eikoku gikai shiryō to Nihon', *Chiiki kenkyū ronshū*, vol. 3, no. 1 (March 2000), pp.17–24

Daniels, G., *Sir Harry Parkes: British representative in Japan 1865–83* (Richmond, Surrey, 1996)

Daniels, G. and Tsuzuki Chushichi (eds.) *History of Anglo-Japanese relations 1600–2000*, 5 vols. (Basingstoke, 2001)

Deakin, Sir William, 'In memory of Richard Storry', in S. Henry and J.-P. Lehmann (eds.), *Themes and theories in modern Japanese history: essays in memory of Richard Storry* (London, 1988), pp.xi–xv

Dermigny, L., *La Chine et l'occident, le commerce a Canton au xviii^e siecle*, 4 vols. (Paris, 1964)

Devine, R. 'Japanese rule in Korea after the March First uprising: Governor-general Hasegawa's recommendations', *Monumenta nipponica*, vol. 52, no. 4 (Winter 1997), pp.523–7

Doeff, H., *Herinneringen uit Japan* (Harlem, 1833)

Doi Ryōzō, *Bakumatsu gonin no gaikoku bugyō: kaikoku o jitsugen saseta bushi* (Tokyo, 1997)

Dore, R. P., *Land reform in Japan* (Oxford, 1959)

Education in Tokugawa Japan (London, 1984)

Dower, J. W., 'E. H. Norman, Japan and the uses of history', in J. W. Dower (ed.), *Origins of the modern Japanese state: selected writings of E. H. Norman* (New York, 1975), pp.3–101

Empire and aftermath: Yoshida Shigeru and the Japanese experience, 1878–1954 (Cambridge, Mass., 1979)

Japanese history and culture from ancient to modern times: seven basic biographies (Manchester, 1986)

War without mercy: race and power in the Pacific war (New York, 1986)

Japan in war and peace: essays on history, culture and race (London, 1993)

'The useful war', in J. W. Dower, *Japan in war and peace: essays on history, culture and race* (London, 1993), pp.9–32

'Race, language and war in two cultures' and 'Fear and prejudice in US–Japanese relations', in J. W. Dower, *Japan in war and peace: essays on history, culture and race* (London, 1993), pp.257–85, 301–35

Dower, J. W. (ed.), *Origins of the modern Japanese state: selected writings of E. H. Norman* (New York, 1975)

Dunn, Charles J., *Everyday life in traditional Japan* (London, 1969, reprint Tokyo, 1972)

Duus, Peter, 'Liberal intellectuals and social conflict in Taisho Japan', in Tetsuo Najita and J. V. Koschmann (eds.), *Conflict in modern Japanese history: the neglected tradition* (Princeton, 1982), pp.412–40

The abacus and the sword: the Japanese penetration of Korea 1895–1910 (Berkeley, 1998)

Duus, Peter and Scheiner, I., 'Socialism, liberalism and Marxism, 1901–1931', in *CHJ*, vol. 6 (1988), pp.654–710

Dyson, T. and Grada, C. O. (eds.), *The demography of famines: perspectives from the past and the present* (Oxford, 2002)

Earns, L. R. and Burke-Gaffney, B., *Across the gulf of time: the international cemeteries of Nagasaki* (Nagasaki, 1991)

Eberspacher, Cord, 'Johan Georg Keyserling (1696–1736): a German horseman at Nagasaki and Edo', *Crossroads: a journal of Nagasaki history and culture*, no. 2 (Summer 1994), pp.9–25

Edo jihō, 6 vols. (Tokyo, 1991–3)

Elliott, Mark C., 'The limits of Tartary: Manchuria in imperial and national geographies', *Journal of Asian studies*, vol. 59, no. 3 (Aug. 2000), pp.603–46

Federico, G., *An economic history of the silk industry 1830–1930* (Cambridge, 1997)

Feenstra Kuiper, J., *Japan in de buitenvereld in de achtiende eeuw* (The Hague, 1921)

Field, F. V., 'Battle of the bankers', in Joseph Barnes (ed.), *Empire in the east* (London, 1934), pp.149–81

Fisher, G. M., 'Kumazawa Banzan, his life and ideas', *Transactions of the Asiatic Society of Japan*, 2nd series, vol. 16 (1938), pp.223–356

Frie, H., 'Japan discovers Australia: the emergence of Australia in the Japanese world view, 1540s–1900', *Monumenta nipponica*, vol. 39, no. 1 (Spring 1984), pp.55–81

Frois, Luis, *Traité de Luis Frois, S. J. (1585) sur les contradictions des moeurs entre Européens et Japanais*, translated from the Portuguese by Xavier de Castro (Paris, 1993)

Fujiki Hisashi and G. Elison, 'The political position of Oda Nobunaga', in J. W. Hall, K. Nagahara and K. Yamamura (eds.), *Japan before Tokugawa: political consolidation and economic growth 1500 to 1650* (Princeton, 1981), pp.149–93

Fujino Tamotsu, *Kyūshū to tenryō* (Tokyo, 1984)

Tokugawa seiken ron (Tokyo, 1991)

Fujita Satoru, *Bakuhansei kokka no seiji shi-teki kenkyū: tenpō-ki no chitsujo, gunji, gaikō* (Tokyo, 1984)

Tenpō no kaikaku (Tokyo, 1989)

Matsudaira Sadanobu (Tokyo, 1993)

'Jūkyū seiki zenhan no nihon: kokumin kokka keisei no zentei', *Nihon tsū-shi*, vol. 15 (Tokyo, 1995), pp.3–67

Kinsei seiji-shi to tennō (Tokyo, 1999)

'Taigai Kankei no dentōka to sakoku sohō kan no kakuritsu', in Fujita Satoru (ed.), *Jūnana seiki no nihon to higashi ajia* (Tokyo, 2000), pp.187–218

'Mondai teiki', in Fujita Satoru (ed.), *Jūnana seiki no nihon to higashi ajia* (Tokyo, 2000), pp.3–10

'Kinsei seiji shi to san dai kaikaku ron: Kenkyū shi no seiri to tenbō', in Fujita Satoru (ed.), *Bakuhansei kaikaku no tenkai* (Tokyo, 2001), pp.3–14

'Kansei kaikaku to ezo-chi seisaku', in Fujita Satoru (ed.), *Bakuhansei kaikaku no tenkai* (Tokyo, 2000), pp.113–39

Kinsei no san daikaikaku (Tokyo, 2002)

Fujita Satoru (ed.), *Jūnana seiki no nihon to higashi ajia* (Tokyo, 2000)

Bakuhansei kaikaku no tenkai (Tokyo, 2001)

Fujitani, T., *Splendid monarchy: power and pageantry in modern Japan* (Berkeley, 1996)

Fukuzawa Yukichi, *The autobiography of Fukuzawa Yukichi*, translated by KIYOOKA Eiichi (Tokyo, 1948)

Gluck, Carol, 'The people in history: recent trends in Japanese historiography', *Journal of Asian studies*, vol. 38, no. 1 (Nov. 1978), pp.25–50

Gluck, Carol and Graubard, S. R. (eds.), *Showa: the Japan of Hirohito* (New York, 1992)

Golownin, W. M., *Narrative of my captivity in Japan in the years 1811, 1812 and 1813*, 2 vols. (London, 1818)

Recollections of Japan (London, 1819)

Nihon furyo jikki: Gorounin, translated by Tokuriki Shintaro, 2 vols. (Tokyo, 1984)

Goodman, G. K., *The Dutch impact on Japan (1600–1853)* (Leiden, 1967)

Grew, Joseph C., *Ten years in Japan, contemporary record drawn from the diaries and private and official papers of Joseph C. Grew, United States ambassador to Japan 1932–1942* (New York, 1944)

Haberland, Detlef, Michel, Wolfgang and Gossmann, Elizabeth (eds.), *Heutiges Japan. Engelbert Kaempfer, werke, kritische ausgabe in einzelbanden*, 2 vols. (Munich, 2001)

Hall, J. W., *Japanese history: a guide to Japanese reference and research materials* (Ann Arbor, Center for Japanese Studies, bibliographical series, no. 4, 1954)

Tanuma Okitsugu 1719–1788: forerunner of modern Japan (Cambridge, Mass., 1955; reprint 1982)

'Materials for the study of local history in Japan: pre-Meiji daimyo records', *Harvard journal of Asiatic studies*, vol. 20, nos. 1 and 2 (June 1957), reprinted in J. W. Hall and M. B. Jansen (eds.), *Studies in the institutional history of early modern Japan* (Princeton, 1968), pp.143–68

Government and local power in Japan, 500 to 1700: a study based on Bizen province (Princeton, 1966)

Hall, J. W. and Jansen, M. B. (eds.), *Studies in the institutional history of early modern Japan* (Princeton, 1968)

Hall, J. W., Nagahara, K. and Yamamura, K. (eds.), *Japan before Tokugawa: political consolidation and economic growth 1500 to 1650* (Princeton, 1981)

Hamashita Takeshi, 'The tribute trade system and modern Asia', in A. J. H. Latham and H. Kawakatsu (eds.), *Japanese industrialization and the Asian economy* (London, 1994), pp.91–107

Hamashita Takeshi and Kawakatsu Heita, *Ajia kōeki ken to Nihon kōgyōka 1500–1900* (Tokyo, 1991)

Hane, M., 'The textile factory worker', in P. Kornicki, *Meiji Japan: political, economic and social history 1868–1912*, 4 vols. (London, 1998), vol. 2, pp.142–72

Hanley, Susan, 'A high standard of living in nineteenth-century Japan: fact or fantasy?', *Journal of economic history*, vol. 43, no. 1 (March 1983), pp.183–92

'Standard of living in nineteenth-century Japan: reply to Yasuba', *Journal of economic history*, vol. 46, no. 1 (March 1986), pp.225–6

Everyday things in pre-modern Japan: the hidden legacy of material culture (Berkeley, 1997)

Hanley, Susan, and Yamamura, Kozo, *Economic and demographic change in pre-industrial Japan 1600–1868* (Princeton, 1977)

Harootunian, H. D., *Towards Restoration: the growth of political consciousness in Tokugawa Japan* (Berkeley, 1970, paperback edn 1984)

'Late Tokugawa culture and thought', in *CHJ*, vol. 5 (1989), pp.168–258

Harris, Townsend, *The complete journal of Townsend Harris* (Tokyo, 2nd edn 1959)

Hata Ikuhiko, 'Continental expansion, 1905–1941', in *CHJ*, vol. 6 (1988), pp.271–314

'The Nankin atrocities: fact and fable', *Japan echo*, vol. 28, no. 4 (Aug. 1998), pp.47–57

'The Nankin massacre in print: a recent bibliography', and 'Japanese textbook treatment of the Nankin massacre', *Japan echo*, vol. 28, no. 4 (Aug. 1998), pp.58–60

Hatano Masaru and Iimori Akiko, *Kantō daishinsai to nichibei gaikō* (Tokyo, 1999)
Hayami Akira, *Kinsei nōson no rekishi jinkōgaku-teki kenkyū: shinshū suwa chihō no shūmon aratame-chō bunseki* (Tokyo, 1973)
'Population changes', in M. B. Jansen and G. Rozman (eds.), *Japan in transition* (Princeton, 1986), pp.280–317
Kinsei nōbi chihō no jinkō, keizai, shakai (Tokyo, 1992)
'Population changes', in W. J. Macpherson, *The industrialisation of Japan* (Oxford, 1994), pp.88–125
The historical demography of pre-modern Japan (Tokyo, 2001)
Hayami Akira and Kurosu Satomi, 'Regional diversity in demographic and family patterns in pre-industrial Japan', *Journal of Japanese studies*, vol. 27, no. 2 (Summer 2001), pp.290–321.
Hayami Akira and Miyamoto Matao (eds.), *Nihon keizai-shi, vol. 1, keizai shakai no seiritsu: 17–18 seiki* (Tokyo, 1988)
Hayashi Rokurō, *Nagasaki tōtsūji: dai tsūji Hayashi Dōei to sono shūhen* (Tokyo, 2000)
Healey, Graham and Tsuzuki Chushichi (eds.), *The Iwakura embassy, 1871–73: a true account of the ambassador extraordinary and plenipotentiary's journey of observation . . . compiled by Kume Kunitake*, 5 vols. (Tokyo, 2002)
Henning, Joseph M., *Outposts of civilization: race, religion and the formative years of American–Japanese relations* (New York, 2000)
Henry, S. and Lehmann, J.-P. (eds.), *Themes and theories in modern Japanese history: essays in memory of Richard Storry* (London, 1988)
Hesselink, R. H., 'A Dutch New Year at the Shirandō Academy: 1 January 1795', *Monumenta nipponica*, vol. 50, no. 2 (Summer 1995), pp.205–23
Prisoners from Nambu: reality and make-believe in seventeenth-century Japanese diplomacy (Honolulu, 2002)
Hing, Bill Ong, *Making and remaking Asian America through immigration policy, 1850–1990* (Stanford, 1993)
Hirakawa Sukehiro, 'Japan's turn to the west', *CHJ*, vol. 5 (1989), pp.432–98
Orientaru-na yume: Koizumi Yakumo to rei no sekai (Tokyo, 1996)
Lafcadio Hearn in international perspective (Comparative literature and culture program, University of Tokyo, Sept. 2001)
Hirakawa Sukehiro (ed.), *Rediscovering Lafcadio Hearn: Japanese legends, life and culture* (Folkestone, 1997)
Hiraoka Masahide, *Nichiro kōshō-shi-wa: ishin zengo no nihon to roshia* (Tokyo, 1982)
Honda Katsuichi, *The Nankin massacres: a Japanese journalist confronts Japan's national shame*, ed. Frank Gibney (New York, 1999)
Honjō Eijirō, *The social and economic history of Japan* (Kyoto, 1935)
Economic theory and history of Japan in the Tokugawa period (Tokyo, 1943; New York, 1965)
Honjō Eijirō (ed.), *Honda Toshiaki shū* (Tokyo, 1936)
Hora Tomio, *Mamiya Rinzō* (Tokyo, 1960)
Horie Yasuzō, 'Honjō Eijirō sensei o omou', *Shakai-keizai shigaku*, vol. 39, no. 4 (1974), pp.111–13
Horne, J. and Kramer, A., *German atrocities, 1914: a history of denial* (New Haven, 2001)

Howe, Christopher, *The origins of Japanese trade supremacy: development and technology in Asia from 1540 to the Pacific war* (London, 1996)
Howell, David L., *Capitalism from within: economy, society and the state in a Japanese fishery* (Berkeley, 1995)
Ichimura Yūichi and Ōishi Shinzaburō, *Sakoku: yuruyaka-na jōhō kakumei* (Tokyo, 1995)
Iguchi Takeo, 'True scenario of surprise attack on Pearl Harbor', *Asahi evening news*, 4 June 2000
'Enigma of the memorandum of the Japanese government submitted to the United States government at the time of Japan's attack on Pearl Harbor – historic error or design revisited' (unpublished paper)
Iida Kanae, *Eikoku gaikōkan no mita bakumatsu nihon* (Tokyo, 1995)
Ikeda Kiyoshi, 'The Douglas mission and British influence on the Japanese navy', in S. Henry and J.-P. Lehman (eds.), *Themes and theories in modern Japanese history* (London, 1988), pp.171–84
Imatani Akira, 'Honjō Eijiro 1888–1973', in *20 seiki no rekishika-tachi*, vol 1., *Nihon* pt 1 (Tokyo, 1997), pp.133–42
Irie Yoshimasa, 'The history of the textbook controversy', *Japan echo*, vol. 24, no. 3 (Aug. 1997), pp.34–8
Iriye Akira, 'Japan's drive to great-power status', in *CHJ*, vol. 5 (1989), pp.721–82
Irokawa Daikichi, *The culture of the Meiji period* (Princeton, paperback edn 1988)
Ishida Sumio, *Edo no oranda i* (Tokyo, 1988)
Ishii Yoneo, *The junk trade from southeast Asia: translations from the tōsen fūsetsugaki 1674–1723* (Singapore, 1998)
Ishikawa, Shigeru, *Economic development in Asian perspective* (Tokyo, 1967)
Ishimitsu Mahito (ed.), *Remembering Aizu: the testament of Shiba Goro*, translated, with introduction and notes, by Teruko Craig (Honolulu, 1999)
Itazawa Takeo, *Oranda fūsetsu-sho no kenkyū* (Tokyo, 1938)
Itō Tasaburō, 'The book banning policy of the Tokugawa shogunate', *Acta asiatica*, no. 22 (1972), pp.36–61
Iwao Seiichi, 'Reopening of the diplomatic and commercial relations between Japan and Siam during the Tokugawa period', *Acta asiatica*, no. 4 (1963), pp.1–31
'Japanese foreign trade in the 16th and 17th centuries', *Acta asiatica*, no. 30 (1976), pp.1–18
Oranda fūsetsugaki shūsei: a collection of the 'world news' presented annually by the Dutch factory, 2 vols. (Tokyo, 1979)
'The development of the study and compilation of *Oranda fūsetsugaki shūsei*', in Iwao Seiichi, *Oranda fūsetsugaki shūsei . . .* (Tokyo, 1979), vol. 2, pp.1–27
Iwata Masakazu, *Ōkubo Toshimichi, the Bismarck of Japan* (Berkeley, 1964)
Jannetta, Ann Bowman, *Epidemic and mortality in early modern Japan* (Princeton, 1987)
Jansen, M. B. *The Japanese and Sun Yat-Sen* (Cambridge, Mass., 1954)
Sakamoto Ryōma and the Meiji Restoration (Princeton, 1961)
'Introduction', in *CHJ*, vol. 5 (1989), pp.1–49
China in the Tokugawa world (Cambridge, Mass., 1992)
The making of modern Japan (Cambridge, Mass., 2000)

Jansen, M. B. and G. Rozman (eds.), *Japan in transition, from Tokugawa to Meiji* (Princeton, 1986)

Jinnai Hidenobu, 'The spacial structure of Edo', in Nakane Chie and Ōishi Shinzaburō (eds.), *Tokugawa Japan: the social and economic antecedents of modern Japan* (Tokyo, 1991), pp.124–46

Kaempfer, Engelbert, *The history of Japan, giving an account of the ancient and present state and government of that empire...*, 2 vols. (London, 1727)

The history of Japan, giving an account of the ancient and present state of that empire... to which is added, part of the journal of a voyage to Japan, made by the English in the year 1673 (London, 1728)

see also Bodart-Bailey; and Haberland, Michel and Gossmann (eds.)

Kanbashi Norimasa, *Shimazu Nariakira* (Tokyo, 1993)

Kano Masanao, 'Tsunoda Ryūsaku: sono ayumi to omoi', *Newsletter from Asakawa research committee: Asakawa kanichi kenkyūkai nyūsu*, no. 28 (April 1997)

'Tsunoda Ryūsaku: his achievements and thoughts', *Transactions of editorial department of the university history* [Waseda], vol. 29 (Sept. 1997), pp.163–96

Kase Toshikazu, *Eclipse of the sun* (London, 1951)

Kassel, Marleen, *Tokugawa Confucian education: the Kangien academy of Hirose Tanso (1892–1856)* (Albany, N.Y., 1996)

Katagiri Kazuo, 'Bakumatsu ni okeru ikokusen ōsetsu to oranda-tsūji Baba Sajūrō', *Kaiji-shi kenkyū*, no. 10 (April 1968), pp.1–36

Oranda tsūji no kenkyū (Tokyo, 1985)

Mikan rangaku shiryō no shoshi-teki kenkyū (Tokyo, 1997)

Oranda yado Ebiya no kenkyū, 2 vols. (Kyoto, 1998)

Edo no orandajin: kapitan no edo sanpu (Tokyo, 2000)

Katō Eiichi, 'Development of Japanese studies on sakoku (closing the country): a survey', *Acta asiatica*, no. 22 (1972), pp.84–103

'The Japanese–Dutch trade in the formative period of the seclusion policy: particularly on the raw silk trade by the Dutch factory at Hirado, 1620–40', *Acta asiatica*, no. 30 (1976), pp.34–84

Kawabata Tai, 'What was fair in war not a question of timing: documents suggest memo meant to deceive U.S., keep Pearl Harbor attack secret', *Japan times*, 7 Dec. 1999

Kawakatsu Heita, *Atarashii ajia no dorama* (Tokyo, 1994)

Fukoku no yūtoku ron (Tokyo, 2000)

Kaiyō renpō ron: chikyū o gâden airando ni (Tokyo, 2001)

Kawauchi Hachirō, *Tokugawa Nariaki Date Munenari ōfuku shokanshū* (Tokyo, 1993)

Keene, Donald, *The Japanese discovery of Europe: Honda Toshiaki and other discoverers* (Stanford, 1969)

On familiar terms: a journey across cultures (New York, 1994)

Emperor of Japan: Meiji and his world, 1852–1912 (New York, 2002)

Kenji Niji, 'Japanese studies in the US: historical development and present state', in *Kyoto conference on Japanese studies*, vol. 4 (International Research Center for Japanese Studies, Kyoto, 1994), pp.123–31

Kikakuten-kikin-shokuryō kiki o norikoeru (Nagoya City Museum, 1999)

Kikuchi Isao, *Kikin no shakai-shi* (Tokyo, 1994)

Kinsei no kikin (Tokyo, 1997)

'Kyōhō Tenmei no kikin to seiji kaikaku: chūō to chihō, kenryoku to shijō keizai', in Fujita Satoru (ed.), *Bakuhansei kaikaku no tenkai* (Tokyo, 2001), pp.56–85

Kim, Richard E., *Lost names: scenes from a Korean boyhood* (Berkeley, paperback edn 1998)

Kinsei Nagasaki no akebono (Kenritsu bijutsukan hakubutsukan (Nagasaki, 1993)

Kitajima Manji, *Toyotomi Hideyoshi no chōsen shinryaku* (Tokyo, 1995)

Kitaoka Shinichi, 'Diplomacy and the military in Showa Japan', in Carol Gluck and S. R. Graubard (eds.), *Showa: the Japan of Hirohito* (New York, 1992), pp.155–76

Nihon no kindai, vol. 5, *Seitō kara gunbu e 1924–1941* (Tokyo, 1999)

Kizaki Hiromi, 'Tsūkō ichiran no hensan to denrai ni kansuru kōsatsu', *Kaiji-shi kenkyū*, no. 47 (March 1990), pp.54–70

'Tsūkō ichiran no shoshigaku-teki kōsatsu', *Kaiji-shi kenkyū*, no. 49 (April 1992), pp.66–77

'Shozōshō yori mitaru shōheizaka gakumonjo no tokushitsu – ikokusen uchi hari rei to taigai jōhō', *Tochigi-shigaku*, no. 8 (March 1994), pp.109–42

Kobata A., 'The production and uses of gold and silver in sixteenth- and seventeenth-century Japan', *Economic history review*, vol. 18, no. 2 (1965), pp.245–66

Kodansha encyclopedia of Japan, 9 vols. (Tokyo, 1983)

Koike Yoshiaki, *Hagakure: bushi to hōkō* (Tokyo, 1999)

Kondō Kazuhiko, 'European Japanology at the end of the seventeenth century', *Bulletin of the School of African and Oriental Studies*, vol. 56, pt 3 (1993), pp.502–24

'The modernist inheritance in Japanese historical studies: Fukuzawa, Marxists and Ōtsuka', in G. Daniels and Chushichi Tsuzuki (eds.), *History of Anglo-Japanese relations 1600–2000*, 5 vols. (Basingstoke, 2001), vol. 5, pp.173–88

Kornicki, P. F. 'Japanese medical and other books at the Wellcome Institute', *Bulletin of the School of Oriental and African Studies*, vol. 60, pt 3 (1997), pp.489–510

'Introduction', in *Collected works of William George Aston*, 6 vols. (Bristol and Tokyo, 1997), vol. 1, pp.xii–xxv

Meiji Japan: political, economic and social history, 4 vols. (London, 1998)

Kornicki, P. F. and McMullen, J., *Religion in Japan: arrows to heaven and earth* (Cambridge, 1996)

Kosaka Masataka, 'The Showa era (1926–89)', in Carol Gluck and S. R. Graubard (eds.), *Showa: the Japan of Hirohito* (New York, 1992), pp.27–47

Koschmann, J. V., *The Mito ideology: discourse, reform, and insurrection in Tokugawa Japan* (Berkeley, 1987)

Kreiner, J. (ed.), *Japan in global context: papers presented on the occasion of the fifth anniversary of the German Institute for Japanese Studies* (Tokyo, 1994)

Krusenstern, I. F., *Voyage round the world in the years 1803, 1804, 1805 and 1806*, 2 vols. (London, 1813)

Memoir of . . . Admiral Ivan de Krusenstern (London, 1856)

Kumazawa Tōru, 'Bakumatsu no sakō mondai to eikoku no gunji senryaku: 1864 nen no tai-nichi sensō keikaku ni tsuite', *Rekishigaku kenkyū*, no. 700 (1997, pt. 8), pp.13–27

Kure Shūzō, *Shiiboruto sensei: sono shōgai oyobi kogyō* (Tokyo, 1926)

Philipp Franz Von Siebold: leben und werk, 2 vols. (Tokyo, 1996)

LaFeber, W., *The clash: U.S.–Japanese relations throughout history* (New York, 1997)

Langsdorff, G. H. Von, *Voyages and travels in various parts of the world during the years 1803, 1804, 1805, 1806, and 1807*, 2 vols. (London, 1813)

Large, Stephen, *Emperors of the rising sun* (Tokyo, 1997)

Latham, A. J. H., 'The dynamics of intra-Asian trade: the great entrepots of Singapore and Hong Kong', in A. J. Latham and H. Kawakatsu (eds.) *Japanese industrialization and the Asian economy* (London, 1994), pp.145–93

Latham, A. J. and Kawakatsu Heita (eds.), *Japanese industrialization and the Asian economy* (London, 1994)

Lehmann, J.-P., *France and Japan 1850–1885* (Oxford, 1975)

The roots of modern Japan (London, 1982)

Lensen, G. A., *Korea and Manchuria between Russia and Japan 1895–1904: the observations of Sir Ernest Satow* (Tokyo, 1966)

The Russian push towards Japan: Russian-Japanese relations 1697–1875 (New York, 1971)

Lequin, F., *The private correspondence of Isaac Titsingh 1785–1811*, 2 vols. (Amsterdam, 1990)

Isaac Titsingh (1745–1811) een passie voor Japan: leven en werk van de grondlegger van de Europese Japanologie (Alphan an de Rijn, 2002)

Levine, H., *In search of Sugihara: the elusive Japanese diplomat who risked his life to rescue 10,000 Jews from the Holocaust* (New York, 1996)

Lidin, O. G., *The life of Ogyū Sorai: a Tokugawa Confucian philosopher* (Lund, 1973)

Ogyū Sorai's journey to Kai in 1706, with a translation of the Kyochukiko (London and Malmo, 1983)

Lockwood, W. W., *The economic development of Japan: growth and structural change 1868–1938* (Princeton, 1965)

Lomax, Eric, *The railway man* (London, 1995)

Lone, S., *Japan's first modern war: army and society in the conflict with China, 1894–95* (London, 1994)

McClain, J. L., *Kanazawa: a seventeenth-century Japanese castle town* (New Haven, 1982)

'Space, power, wealth and status in seventeenth-century Osaka', in J. L. McClain and Wakita Osamu (eds.), *Osaka: the merchants' capital of early modern Japan* (Ithaca, 1999), pp.44–79

A modern history of Japan (New York, 2002)

McClain, J. L. and Wakita Osamu (eds.), *Osaka: the merchants' capital of early modern Japan* (Ithaca, 1999)

McClain, J. L., Merriman, J. M. and Kaoru Ugawa (eds.), *Edo and Paris: Urban life and the state in the early modern era* (Ithaca, 1994)

McEwan, J. R., *The political writings of Ogyū Sorai* (Cambridge, 1962)

Macpherson, W. J., *The economic development of Japan 1868–1941* (Cambridge, 1987)

Macpherson, W. J. (ed.), *The industrialisation of Japan* (Oxford, 1994)

Marshall, Byron K., *Academic freedom and the Japanese imperial university 1868–1939* (Berkeley, 1992)

'Professors and politics: the Meiji academic elite', in P. Kornicki (ed.), *Meiji Japan, political, economic and social history*, 4 vols. (London, 1998), vol. 4, pp.296–318

Maruyama Masao, *Studies in the intellectual history of Tokugawa Japan* (Princeton, 1974; reprint 1989)

Mason, R. H. P., *Japan's first general election 1890* (Cambridge, 1969)

Massarella, Derek, *A world elsewhere: Europe's encounter with Japan in the sixteenth and seventeenth centuries* (New Haven, 1990)

Matsui Masato, 'Shimazu Shigehide 1745–1833: a case study of daimyo leadership' (Ph.D. thesis, University of Hawaii, 1975)

Matsumoto Kenichi, *Nihon no kindai*, vol. 1, *Kaikoku-ishin 1853–1871* (Tokyo, 1998)

Matsumoto Shigeru, *Motoori Norinaga 1730–1801* (Cambridge, Mass., 1970)

Matsuo Tarō, 'Airurando tōchi rippō to Ishiguro Nōsei', *Keizai shirin* (Hosei University), vol. 45, no. 3 (Oct. 1977), pp.81–136.

'Researches on Irish land laws undertaken by Japanese bureaucrats facing the tenancy question in the 1920s', *Keizai shirin* (Hosei University), vol. 46, no. 2/3 (Oct. 1978) pp.1–51

Matsuura Rei, *Tokugawa Yoshinobu: shōgun-ke no meiji ishin* (Tokyo, 1975; 2nd and enlarged edn 1997)

Mayo, M. J., 'The Korean crisis of 1873 and early foreign policy', *Journal of Asian studies*, vol. 31, no. 4 (Aug. 1972), pp.793–819

Me de miru Tokyo hyaku nen (Tokyo city administration, 1969)

Medzini, M., *French policy in Japan during the closing years of the Tokugawa regime* (Cambridge, Mass., 1971)

Mikawa monogatari: Hagakure, ed. Saiki Kazuma, Okayama Taishi and Sagara Tōru (*Nihon no shiso* series, no. 26, Iwanami, Tokyo, 1974)

Minami Kazuo, *Bakumatsu edo shakai no kenkyū* (Tokyo, 1978)

Minchinton, Walter, 'The Canaries in the British trade world of the eighteenth century', in Francisco Morales Padron (ed.), *IX Coloquio de historia Canario-Americana* (Las Palmas, 1990)

Minegishi Sumio, Fukaya Katsumi, Satō Kazuhitō and Aoki Michio (eds.), *Ikki-shi nyūmon*, 5 vols. (Tokyo, 1981)

Mishima Yukio, *The samurai ethic and modern Japan: Yukio Mishima on Hagakure* (Tokyo, 1978; 5th printing, 1993) (translation by K. Sparling of *Hagakure nyūmon*, 1972)

Mitani Hiroshi, 'Tai-ro kinchō no kōchō to shikan', in *Nihon rekishi taikei*, vol. 3, *kinsei* (Tokyo, 1988), pp.903–14

'Tenpō-ka'ei no taigai mondai', in *Nihon rekishi taikei*, vol. 3, *kinsei* (Tokyo, 1988), pp.1127–51

'Kaikoku, kaikō o meguru shodaimyō no taigai iken', in *Jukyū seiki no Yokahama* (Yokohama kinsei-shi kenkyū-kai and Yokohama kaiko-shiryokan, Yokohama, 1993), pp.3–24

Meiji ishin to nashonarizumu: bakumatsu no qaikō to seiji (Tokyo, 1997)

Miyamoto Matao, 'Bukka to maguro Keizai no dōkō', in Shinbo Hiroshi and Saitō Osamu (eds.), *Nihon keizai-shi*, vol. 2, *Kindai seichō no taido* (Tokyo, 1989), pp.68–126.

Miyashita Saburō, *Nagasaki bōeki to Osaka yunyū kara sōyaku e* (Osaka, 1997)

Waran isho no kenkyū to shoshi (Tokyo, 1997)

Miyazaki Kentarō, *Kakure Kirishitan no shinkō sekai* (Tokyo, 1996)

Miyoshi Masao, *As we saw them: the first embassy to the United States* (New York, 1994)

Moeshart, H. J., 'The Shimonoseki affair, 1863–64', in Ian Nish (ed.), *Contemporary European writing on Japan* (Ashford, 1988), pp.44–50

Mori Tateshi, 'The history of Japanese agriculture', in *Agriculture and agricultural policy in Japan* (Committee for the Japanese Agriculture Session, XX1 IAAE conference, Tokyo, 1991)

Morishima, M., *Why has Japan 'succeeded'?: western technology and the Japanese ethos* (Cambridge, 1996)

Morland, M. C., 'Watanabe Kazan 1793–1841: tradition and innovation in Japanese painting' (Ph.D., University of Michigan, 1989)

Morris, Morris D., 'Towards a reinterpretation of nineteenth century Indian economic history', *Journal of economic history*, vol. 23, no. 4 (Dec. 1963), pp.606–18

Morris-Suzuki, T., *A history of Japanese economic thought* (London, 1989)

Muramatsu Michio, 'Bringing politics back into Japan', in Carol Gluck and S. R. Graubard (eds.), *Showa: the Japan of Hirohito* (New York, 1992), pp.141–54

Murayama Yūzo, *Amerika ni ikita nihonjin imin: nikkei issei no hikari to kage* (Tokyo, 1989)

'Information and emigrants: interprefectural differences of Japanese migration to the Pacific northwest, 1880–1915', *Journal of economic history*, vol. 51, no. 1 (March 1991), pp.125–47

Murdoch, James, *A history of Japan*, 3 vols. (London, 1925–6)

Murray, Paul, *A fantastic journey: the life and literature of Lafcadio Hearn* (London, 1993)

Nagahara Keiji and Yamamura, Kozo, 'Shaping the process of unification: technological progress in sixteenth- and seventeenth-century Japan', *Journal of Japanese studies*, vol. 14, no. 1 (Winter 1988), pp.77–109

Nagai, Michio and Urrutia, Miguel (eds.), *Meiji ishin: restoration and revolution* (Tokyo, 1985)

Nagazumi Yōko, 'Japan's isolationist policy as seen through Dutch source materials', *Acta asiatica*, no. 22 (1972), pp.18–35

Tōsen yūshutsu-yūnyu-hin sūryō ichiran 1637–1833 nen: fukugen, tōsen-kamotsu aratame-chō, kinan-nimotsu, kaiwatashi-chō (Tokyo, 1987)

Kinsei shoki no gaikō (Tokyo, 1990)

Najita, Tetsuo, *Hara Kei in the politics of compromise 1905–1915* (Cambridge, Mass., 1967)

'Ōshio Heihachirō (1793–1837)', in A. M. Craig and D. H. Shively (eds.), *Personality in Japanese history* (Berkeley, 1970), pp.155–79

Visions of virtue in Tokugawa Japan: the Kaitokudō merchant academy of Osaka (Chicago, 1987)

Tokugawa political writings (Cambridge, 1998)

'Ambiguous encounters: Ogata Kōan and international studies in late Tokugawa Osaka', in James L. McClain and O. Wakita (eds.), *Osaka: the merchants' capital of early modern Japan* (Ithaca, 1999), pp.213–42

Najita, Tetsuo and Koschmann, J. Victor (eds.), *Conflict in modern Japanese history: the neglected tradition* (Princeton, 1982)

Najita, Tetsuo and Scheiner, I., *Japanese thought in the Tokugawa period 1600–1868* (Chicago, 1978)

Nakahara Michiko, 'Asian labourers along the Burma–Thailand railroad', *Waseda journal of Asian studies*, vol. 15 (1993), pp.88–107

Nakai, Kate Wildman, *Shogunal politics: Arai Hakuseki and the premises of Tokugawa rule* (Cambridge, Mass., 1988)

Nakamura Naomi, 'Tsunoda Ryūsaku sensei ni tsuite', *Newsletter from Asakawa research committee* [Asakawa kanichi kenkyūkai nyūsu], no. 18 (Aug. 1994)

Nakamura Tadashi, *Kinsei Nagasaki bōeki-shi no kenkyū* (Tokyo, 1988)

'Nagasaki bugyōsho kankei monjo ni tsuite', in *Nagasaki bugyosho kankei manjo chōsa hōkoku sho, Nagasaki ken bunkazai hōkoku, dai 131 shū* (Nagasaki, 1998), pp.1–21

Kinsei taigai kōshō shi ron (Tokyo, 2000)

Nakamura Takafusa, 'Depression, recovery, and war, 1920–1945', in Kozo Yamamura (ed.), *The economic emergence of modern Japan* (Cambridge, 1997), pp.116–58

Nakane Chie and Ōishi Shinzaburō, *Tokugawa Japan: the social and economic antecedents of modern Japan* (Tokyo, 1991)

Nakanishi Akira, Tsuchiya Ryōichi, Miyasaka Masahide and Itō Toshiya, *The history of surgery in Nagasaki* (Nagasaki, 1999)

Nakao Hiroshi, *Chōsen tsūshin shi to Tokugawa bakufu* (Tokyo, 1997)

Nanban shorai kara genbaku made (Culture Department, Education Board, Nagasaki, 1980)

Naramoto Tatsuya, *Nitobe Inazō: bushidō* (Tokyo, 1997)

Narazaki Muneshige, *Hiroshige: the 53 stations of the Tokaido* (1969, 8th printing: Tokyo, 1982)

Naruiwa Sōzō, *Bakumatsu nihon to furansu gaikō: reon rosshu no sentaki* (Tokyo, 1997)

Nihon no monogatari e (Suntory Gallery, Tokyo, 1989)

Nish, I., *Japanese foreign policy 1869–1942* (London, 1977)

The origins of the Russo-Japanese war (London, 1985)

'The growth of Japanese studies in Britain', in *Occasional papers, no. 6: current issues in social science research* (Hosei University, Tokyo, 1989)

Japan's struggle with internationalism: Japan, China and the League of Nations, 1931–3 (London, 1993)

'John Harrington Gubbins 1852–1929', in I. Nish and J. E. Hoare (eds.), *Britain and Japan: biographical portraits*, 3 vols. (Richmond, Surrey, 1994–9), vol. 2, pp.107–36

The Iwakura mission in America and England: a new assessment (Richmond, Surrey, 1998)

Nish, I. (ed.), *Contemporary European writing on Japan* (Ashford, Kent, 1988)

Nish, I. and Hoare, J. E. (eds.), *Britain and Japan: biographical portraits*, 3 vols. (Richmond, Surrey, 1994–9)

Nishida Yoshiaki, 'Growth of the Meiji landlord system and tenancy disputes after World War 1: a critique of Richard Smethurst, *Agricultural development and tenancy disputes in Japan, 1870–1940*', *Journal of Japanese studies*, vol. 15, no. 2 (Summer 1989), pp.389–415

Nishikawa Shunsaku, *Fukuzawa Yukichi to sannin no kōshin tachi* (Tokyo, 1985)

Nishikawa Shunsaku and Abe Takeshi (eds.), *Nihon keizai-ishi*, vol. 4, *Sangyōka no jidai*, pt 1 (Tokyo, 1990)

Nishikawa Shunsaku and Saitō Osamu, 'The economic history of the restoration period', in Michio Nagai and Miguel Urrutia (eds.), *Meiji ishin: restoration and revolution* (Tokyo, 1985), pp.175–91

Nishikawa Shunsaku and Yamamoto Yūzō (eds.), *Nihon keizai-ishi*, vol. 5, *Sangyōka no jidai*, pt 2 (Tokyo, 1990)

Nishikawa Shunsaku, Odaka Kōnosuke and Saitō Osamu (eds.), *Nihon keizai no 200 nen* (Tokyo, 1996)

Nishio Kanji, *Rekishi o sabaku orokasa: atarashi rekishi kyōkasho no tame ni* (Tokyo, 1997)

'Rewriting Japanese and world history', *Japan echo*, vol. 24, no. 3 (Aug. 1997), pp.39–44

'Acknowledge U.S. war crimes', *Japan times*, 26 Aug. 1997

Nitobe Inazō, *Bushido, the soul of Japan: an exposé of Japanese thought* (New York, 1905, reprint, 1993)

Norman, E. H., 'Andō Shōeki and the anatomy of Japanese feudalism', *Transactions of the Asiatic Society of Japan*, 3rd series, vol. 2 (Dec. 1949)

Nosco, P., 'Introduction: Neo-Confucianism and Tokugawa discourse', in *Confucianism and Tokugawa culture* (Princeton, 1984), pp.3–26

Nosco, P. (ed.), *Confucianism and Tokugawa culture* (Princeton, 1984)

Numata Jirō, 'Dutch learning (Rangaku) in Japan: a response pattern to the foreign impact', *Acta asiatica*, no. 22 (1972), pp.62–72

Numata Jirō and Mizuguchi Shigeo, *Benyofusuki kōkai-ki* (Tokyo, 1971)

Ōba Osamu (ed.), *Tōsen shinkō kaitō roku, Shimabara bon tōjin fūsetsugaki, Wappu tomechō* (Kyoto, 1974)

Odaka Kōnosuke and Nakamura Takafusa (eds.), *Nihon keizai-shi*, vol. 6, *Nijū kōzō* (Tokyo, 1989)

Ogata Tomio (ed.), *Edo jidai no yōgakusha-tachi* (Tokyo, 1972)

Ohashi Yukihiro, 'Kirishitan kinsei to shūmon aratame seido', in Fujita Satoru (ed.), *Jūnana seiki no nihon to higashi ajia* (Tokyo, 2000), pp.69–99

Ohkura Takehiko and Shinbō Hiroshi, 'The Tokugawa monetary policy in the eighteenth and nineteenth centuries', *Explorations in economic history*, vol. 15 (1978), pp.101–24

Ōishi Shinzaburō, *Tanuma Okitsugu no jidai* (Tokyo, 1991, reprint, 1997)

Shōgun to sobayōnin no seiji (Tokyo, 1995)

Oka Yoshitake, 'The first Anglo-Japanese alliance in Japanese public opinion', in S. Henry and J.-P. Lehmann (eds.), *Themes and theories in modern Japanese history*, pp.185–93 (London, 1988)

Ogata Tomio (ed.), *Edo jidai no yōgakusha-tachi* (Tokyo, 1972)

Ooms, H., *Charismatic bureaucrat: a political biography of Matsudaira Sadanobu 1758–1829* (Chicago, 1975)

Tokugawa ideology: early constructs 1570–1680 (1985; reprint Ann Arbor, 1998)

Tokugawa village practice: class, status, power, law (Berkeley, 1996)

Ōtani Tsunehiko, 'Shiiboruto jiken no haikei to Mamiya Rinzō: shiron "Rinzō wa mikoku shiteinai" ', *Shiiboruto kinenkan Narutaki kiyō*, no. 5 (Shiiboruto kinenkan, Nagasaki, 1995), pp.37–72

Ōtsuka Hisao, *The spirit of capitalism: the Max Weber thesis in an economic historical perspective* (Tokyo, 1982)

Pacheco, Diego, 'The founding of the port of Nagasaki and its cession to the Society of Jesus', *Monumenta nipponica*, vol. 25, nos. 3–4 (1970), pp.303–23

Padron, Francisco Morales (ed.), *IX Coloquio de historia Canario-Americana* (Las Palmas, 1990)

Parmentier, Jan and Laarhoven, Ruurdje (eds.), *De avonturen van een VOC-soldaat: het dagboek van Carolus Van der Haeghe 1699–1705* (Zutphen, 1994)

Paske-Smith, M. (ed.), *Report on Japan to the secret committee of the English East India Company by Sir Stamford Raffles*, with a preface by M. Paske-Smith (London, 1971)

Pérouse, Jean-Francois de Galaup de la, *The journal of Jean-Francois de Galaup de la Pérouse*, translated by John Dunmore, 2 vols. (London, 1994)

Perrin, Noel, *Giving up the gun: Japan's reversion to the sword, 1543–1879* (Boulder, Colo., 1979)

Platt, D. P., 'My-car-isma: Motorising the Showa self', in Carol Gluck and S. R. Graubard (eds.,), *Showa: the Japan of Hirohito* (New York, 1992), pp.229–44

Plummer, Katherine, *The shogun's reluctant ambassadors: Japanese sea drifters in the north Pacific*, 3rd edn (Portland, Oreg., 1991)

Proust, Jacques, *Europe au prisme du Japon: xvi*^{e}*–xviii*^{e} *siècle* (Paris, 1997)

Pyle, K. P., *The new generation in Meiji Japan* (Stanford, 1969)

Ramseyer, J. Mark and Rosenbluth, Frances M., *The politics of oligarchy: institutional choice in imperial Japan* (Cambridge, 1995)

Ravina, M., *Land and lordship in early modern Japan* (Stanford, 1999)

Reischauer, E. O. and Craig, A. M., *Japan: tradition and transformation* (Tokyo, 1978)

Reischauer, Haru Matsukata, *Samurai and silk: a Japanese and American heritage* (Tokyo, 1987)

Rich, R., 'Economic mobilization in wartime Japan: business, bureaucracy and military in conflict', *Journal of Asian studies*, vol. 38, no. 4 (Aug. 1979), pp.689–706

Richie, Donald, 'A bird's eye view of history', *Japan times*, 22 April 2001

Rimer, J. T., *A hidden fire: Russian and Japanese cultural encounters 1868–1926* (Stanford, 1995)

Rinen naki gaikō: Pari kōwakaigi (Tokyo, 1996)

Roberts, L. S., *Mercantilism in a Japanese domain: the mercantile origins of nationalism in 18th-century Tosa* (Cambridge, 1988)

Rostow, Walt, *Stages of economic growth: a non-communist manifesto* (Cambridge, 1960)

Rovosky, H., 'What are the "lessons" of Japanese economic history?', in W. J. Macpherson, *The industrialisation of Japan* (Oxford, 1994), pp.215–39

Rozman, G., 'Social change', in *CHJ*, vol. 5 (1989), pp.499–568

Rubinger, R., *Shijuku: private academies of the Tokugawa period* (Princeton, 1979, 1982)

Ruoff, Kenneth J., *The people's emperor: democracy and the Japanese monarchy* (Cambridge, Mass., 2001)

Ruxton, I. C., *The diaries and letters of Sir Ernest Satow (1843–1929), a scholar-diplomat in east Asia* (Lewiston, N.Y., 1998)

Saeki Shōichi and Haga Tōru, *Gaikokujin ni yoru Nihon ron no meicho: Goncharofu kara Pange made* (Tokyo, 1987)

Saitō Osamu, *Shōka no sekai, uradana no sekai: Edo to Ōsaka no hikaku tōshi shi* (Tokyo, 1987)

Gender, workload and agricultural progress: Japan's historical experience in perspective, discussion paper series A, no. 268 (Hitotsubashi University, Tokyo, 1993)

Infant mortality in pre-transition Japan: levels and trends, discussion paper series, no. 273 (Institute of economic research, Hitotsubashi University, Tokyo, 1993)

'Historical demography: methodology and interpretations', in *Historical studies in Japan (VIII) 1988–1992* (National committeee of Japanese historians, Tokyo, 1995), pp.77–89

'Jinkō', in Nishikawa Shunsaku, Odaka Kōnusuke and Saitō Osamu (eds.), *Nihon keizai no 200 nen* (Tokyo, 1996), pp.37–54

Chingin to rōdō to seikatsu suijun: Nihon keizai-shi ni okeru 18–20 seiki (Tokyo, 1998)

'The frequency of famines: demographic correctives in the Japanese past', in T. Dyson and C. O. Grada (eds.), *The demography of famines: perspectives from the past and the present* (Oxford, 2002), pp.218–39

Sakai, R. K., 'Shimazu Nariakira and the emergence of national leadership in Satsuma', in A. M. Craig and D. H. Shively (eds.), *Personality in Japanese history* (Berkeley, 1970), pp.209–33

Sakakibara Kisako, *Tokugawa Yoshinobu-ke no kodomo-beya* (Tokyo, 1996)

Sakamoto Takao, *Nihon no kindai*, vol. 2, *Meiji kokka no kensetsu 1871–1890* (Tokyo, 1999)

Saniel, J. M., *Japan and the Philippines 1868–1898* (New York, 1973)

Sansom, George, *Japan: a short cultural history* (London, 1931)

Sasaki Takeshi, 'Maruyama and the spirit of politics', *Japan quarterly*, (Jan.–March 1997), pp.59–63

Sato Hiroaki, 'Conflicting views of Japanese history', *Japan times*, 24 Sept. 2001

Satō Shōsuke, *Takano Chōei* (Tokyo, 1997)

Satō Tsuneo and Ōishi Shinzaburō, *Hin no shikan o minaosu* (Tokyo, 1995)

Satow, Ernest Mason, *Collected works of Ernest Mason Satow*, 12 vols. (Bristol and Tokyo, 1998)

A diplomat in Japan (London, 1921; reprint New York and Tokyo, 2000)

Scheiner, Irwin, 'The mindful peasant: sketches for a study of rebellion', *Journal of Asian studies*, vol. 32, no. 4 (Aug. 1973), pp.579–91

Schmid, Andre, 'Colonialism and the "Korea problem" in the historiography of modern Japan', *Journal of Asian studies*, vol. 59, no. 4 (Nov. 2000), pp.951–76

Screech, T., *The western scientific gaze and popular imagery in later Edo Japan: the lens with the heart* (Cambridge, 1996)

Sex and the floating world: erotic images in Japan 1700–1820 (London, 1999)

The shogun's painted culture: fear and creativity in the Japanese states 1760–1829 (London, 2000)

Seidensticker, E., *Low city, high city, Tokyo from Edo to the earthquake: how the shogun's ancient capital became a great modern city, 1867–1923* (Cambridge, Mass., 1983)

Sekai o utsusu daieiteikoku: eikoku gikai shiryō o yomu, Chiiki kenkyū ronshū, tokushū [special issue], vol. 3, no. 1 (March 2000)

Shiba Ryōtarō, *Saigō no shōgun* (Tokyo, 1967)

Le dernier shogun, translated by Corinne Atlan (Arles, 1992)

Shiiboruto no edo sanpu ten (Shiiboruto kinenkan, Nagasaki, 2000)

Shimomura Fujio, 'Disintegration of the political principles of the Edo regime and the formation of the han clique', *Acta asiatica*, no. 9 (1965), pp.1–30

Shinbō Hiroshi and Saitō Osamu, 'The economy on the eve of industrialisation', chapter 10 in a revised and expanded chapter to appear in an English-language edition of Hayami Akira and Miyamoto Matao (eds.), *Nihon keizai-shi*, vol. 1, to be published by Oxford University Press

Shinbō Hiroshi and Saitō Osamu (eds.), *Nihon keizai-shi*, vol. 2, *Kindai seichō no taidō* (Tokyo, 1989)

Shirai Tetsuya, 'Chiri -tadashi to Kansei kaikaku: kanjōshō no katsudō o chūshin ni', in Fujita Satoru (ed.), *Bakuhansei kaikaku no tenkai* (Tokyo, 2001), pp.87–112

Shogun Yoshimune to sono jidai ten (Suntory Gallery, Tokyo, 1995)

Siebold, P. F. Von, *Nippon: archiv zur beschreibung von Japan*, 2 vols. (Tokyo, 1965)

Sims, R., *French policy towards the bakufu and Meiji Japan* (London, 1998)

Smethurst, R. J., 'A challenge to orthodoxy and its orthodox critics: a reply to Nishida Yoshiaki', *Journal of Japanese studies*, vol. 15, no. 2 (Summer 1989), pp.417–37

Smith, H. D., 'The Edo-Tokyo transition: in search of common ground', in M. B. Jansen and G. Rozman (eds.), *Japan in transition: from Tokugawa to Meiji* (Princeton, 1986), pp.347–74

Smith, Kerry, *A time of crisis: Japan, the great depression and rural revitalization* (Cambridge, Mass., 2001)

Smith, Michael, *The emperor's codes: Bletchley Park and the breaking of Japan's secret ciphers* (London, 2000)

Smith, T. C., *Political change and industrial development in Japan: government enterprise, 1868–1880* (Stanford, 1955)

The agrarian origins of modern Japan (Stanford, 1959)

'Pre-modern economic growth: Japan and the west', in T. C. Smith, *Native sources of Japanese industrialization 1750–1920* (Berkeley, 1988), pp.15–49; first published in *Past and present*, no. 60 (Aug. 1973)

Nagahara: family planning and population in a Japanese village 1717–1830 (Stanford, 1977)

Native sources of Japanese industrialization, 1750–1920 (Berkeley, 1988)

'The land tax in the Tokugawa period', in T. C. Smith, *Native sources of Japanese industrialization 1750–1920* (Berkeley, 1988), pp.50–70

Sorimachi Shigeo, *Japanese illustrated books and manuscripts in the Chester Beatty library* (Tokyo, 1979)

Souza, G. B., *The survival of empire: Portuguese trade and society in China and the South China Sea, 1630–1754* (Cambridge, 1986)

Stephan, John J., *Sakhalin: a history* (Oxford, 1971)

The Kuril Islands: Russian-Japanese frontier in the Pacific (Oxford, 1974)

The Russian Far East: a history (Stanford, 1994)

Steven, R. P. G., 'Hybrid constitutionalism in prewar Japan', *Journal of Japanese studies*, vol. 3, no. 1 (Winter 1977), pp.99–133

Stinnett, Robert B., *Day of deceit: the truth about FDR and Pearl Harbor* (New York, 2000)

Storry, R., *Japan and the decline of the west in Asia* (London, 1979)

Sugihara, Seishiro, *Between incompetence and culpability: assessing the diplomacy of Japan's foreign ministry from Pearl Harbor to Potsdam* (Lanham, Md., 1997)

Sugimoto Tsutomu, *Edo jidai ran-gogaku no seiritsu to sono tenkai*, 5 vols. (Tokyo, 1976–82)

Edo yōgaku jijō (Tokyo, 1990)

Edo no oranda ryū i shi (Tokyo, 2002)

Suzuki Kōzō, *Edo no keizai seisaku to gendai: Edo ga wakareba ima ga mieru* (Tokyo, 1993)

Taguchi Eiji, *Saigo no Hakodate bugyō no nikki* (Tokyo, 1995)

Taira Koji, 'Factory labour and the industrial revolution in Japan', in W. J. Macpherson (ed.), *The industrialisation of Japan* (Oxford, 1994), pp.258–310

Takase Tamotsu, 'Kaga han no kaiun seisaku to fukushiki no fune donya: shuto shite tsuru tonya-kabu no hōkai', *Kaiji-shi kenkyū*, no. 7 (Oct. 1966), pp.58–74.

'Kaga han no Kyōhō-ki no Tsugaru, Nanbu, Matsumae bōeki', *Kaiji-shi kenkyū*, no. 17 (Oct. 1991), pp.1–12.

Takizawa Takeo, *Nihon no kahei no rekishi* (Tokyo, 1996)

Tames, R., *Servant of the shogun* (Tenterden, 1981)

Tanaka Yuki, *Hidden horrors: Japanese war crimes in World War II* (Boulder, Colo., 1998)

Tanji Kenzō, 'Ka'ei-ki ni okeru Edo-wan bōbi mondai to ikokusen taisaku: Uraga bugyō mochiba o chūshin to shite', *Kaiji-shi kenkyū*, no. 20 (April 1973), pp.98–112

Tashiro Kazui, 'Tsushima han's Korean trade, 1684–1710', *Acta asiatica*, no. 30 (1976), pp.85–105

Thunberg, C. P., *Voyages de C. P. Thunberg au Japon*, 2 vols. (Paris, 1796; English version, London 1795)

Titsingh, Isaac, *Cérémonies usitées au Japon pour les mariages et les funérailles* (Paris, 1819)

Mémoires et anecdotes sur la dynastie des Djogouns, souverains du Japon (Paris, 1820)

Illustrations of Japan; consisting of private memoirs and anecdotes of the reigning djogouns, or sovereigns of Japan (London, 1822)

Nihon o dai etsi ran, ou annales des empereurs du Japon (Paris, 1834)

Tobe Ryōichi, *Nihon no kindai*, vol. 9, *Gyakusetsu no guntai* (Tokyo, 1998)

Toby, R. P., *State and diplomacy in early modern Japan: Asia in the development of the Tokugawa bakufu* (Stanford, 1991)

'Both a borrower and a lender be: from village moneylender to rural banker in the Tempō era', *Monumenta nipponica*, vol. 46, no. 4 (Winter 1991), pp.483–512

Tomioka Gihachi, *Shio no michi o saguru* (Tokyo, 1983)

Totman, Conrad, 'Political reconciliation in the Tokugawa Bakufu: Abe Masahiro and Tokugawa Nariaki', in A. M. Craig and D. Shively, (eds.), *Personality in Japanese history* (Berkeley, 1970), pp.180–208

The collapse of the Tokugawa bakufu, 1862–1868 (Honolulu, 1980)

Tokugawa Ieyasu (San Francisco, 1983)

Politics in the Tokugawa bakufu 1600–1843 (Berkeley, 1988)

The green archipelago: forestry in preindustrial Japan (Berkeley, 1989)

Early modern Japan (Berkeley, 1993)

The lumber industry in early modern Japan (Honolulu, 1995)

A history of Japan (Malden, Mass., and Oxford, 2000)

Toyama Mikio, *Nagasaki bugyō: Edo bakufu no mimi to me* (Tokyo, 1988)

Tsuchiya Takao, 'An economic history of Japan', in *Transactions of the Asiatic society of Japan*, 2nd series, vol. 15 (Dec. 1937), pp.iii–xviii, 1–269.

Tsunoda, R., de Bary, W. Theodore and Keene, Donald, *Sources of Japanese tradition* (New York, 1958)

Turnbull, Stephen, *The Kakure Kirishitan of Japan: a study of their development, beliefs and rituals to the present day* (Japan Library, Richmond, Surrey, 1998)

Uehara Hisashi, *Takahashi Kageyasu no kenkyū* (Tokyo, 1977)

Van Sant, John E., *Pacific pioneers: Japanese journeys to America and Hawaii 1850–80* (Urbana, 2000)

Vaporis, C. N., *Breaking barriers: travel and the state in early modern Japan* (Cambridge, Mass., 1994)

Velde, P. Van der, 'The Dutch language as a medium of western science', in P. Van der Velde and Cynthia Viallé, *The Deshima dagregisters: their original tables of contents*, 10 vols. (Leiden, 1986–97) vol. 8 (1760–80) (Leiden, 1994)

Vermeulen, Ton, Velde, Paul Van der, Viallé, Cynthia and Blussé, Leonard (eds.), *The Deshima dagregisters: their original tables of contents*, 10 vols. (Leiden, 1986–97)

Verwayen, F. B., 'Tokugawa translations of Dutch legal texts', *Monumenta nipponica*, vol. 53, no. 3 (1998), pp.335–57

Via orientalis: porutogaru to nanban bunka ten: mesase tōhō no kuniguni (Tokyo, 1993) (English translation of text on pp.225–48)

Vlastos, S., *Peasant risings in Tokugawa Japan* (Berkeley, 1990)

Wakabayashi, B. T., *Anti-foreignism and western learning in early modern Japan: the New Theses of 1825* (Cambridge, Mass., 1986)

Japanese loyalism reconstructed: Yamagata Daini's Ryushu Shinron of 1759 (Honolulu, 1995)

Wakita Osamu, *Kinsei Osaka no keizai to bunka* (Kyoto, 1994)

Walker, Brett L., *The conquest of Ainu lands: ecology and culture in Japanese expansion, 1590–1800* (Berkeley, 2001)

Walthall, Anne (ed.), *Social protest and popular culture in eighteenth-century Japan* (Tucson, 1986)

Peasant uprisings in Japan (Chicago, 1991)

Waswo, Ann, *Japanese landlords: the decline of a rural elite* (Berkeley, 1977)
'The transformation of rural society, 1900–1950', in *CHJ*, vol. 6 (1988), pp.541–605
Welle, W. F. Van de and Kazuhiko Kasaya (eds.), *Dodonaeus in Japan: translation and the scientific mind in the Tokugawa period* (Leuven, 2001)
White, J. A., *Transition to global rivalry: alliance diplomacy and the Quadruple Entente, 1895–1907* (Cambridge, 1995)
White, James W., *Ikki: social conflict and political protest in early modern Japan* (Ithaca and London, 1995)
Wigen, K., *The making of a Japanese periphery 1750–1820* (Berkeley, 1995)
Wilson, Dick, 'Did Japan declare war?', *Asian affairs*, vol. 31, pt. 1 (Feb. 2000), pp.37–40
Wilson, G. M., 'The Bakumatsu intellectual in action: Hashimoto Sanai in the political crisis of 1858', in A. M. Craig and D. Shively (eds.), *Personality in Japanese history* (Berkeley, 1970), pp.234–63
Patriots and redeemers in Japan (Chicago, 1992)
Wong, J. Y. *Deadly dreams: opium and the Arrow War (1856–1860) in China* (Cambridge, 1998)
Woods, L. T. (ed.), *Japan's emergence as a modern state: political and economic problems of the Meiji period* (Vancouver, 2000)
Wray, W. D., 'Shipping: from sail to steam', in M. B. Jansen and G. Rozman (eds.), *Japan in transition: from Tokugawa to Meiji* (Princeton, 1986), pp.248–70
Yamakawa Kikue, *Women of the Mito domain: recollections of samurai family life*, translated by Kate Wildman Nakai (Tokyo, 1992)
Yamamoto Hirofumi, *Kanei jidai* (Tokyo, 1989)
Sakoku to kaikin no jidai (Tokyo, 1995)
Yamamoto Tsunetomo, *Hagakure*, translated by W. S. Wilson (Tokyo, 1983)
Yamamoto Yuzō and Umemura Mataji (eds.), *Nihon keizai-shi*, vol. 3, *Kaikō to ishin* (Tokyo, 1989)
Yamamura, Kozo, 'A re-examination of entrepreneurship in Meiji Japan 1868–1912', *Economic history review*, 2nd series, vol. 21, no. 1 (April 1968), pp.144–58; reprinted in W. J. Macpherson (ed.), *The industrialisation of Japan* (Oxford, 1994), pp.326–40
'Towards a reexamination of the economic history of Tokugawa Japan 1600–1867', *Journal of economic history*, vol. 33, no. 3 (Sept. 1973), pp.509–41
A study of samurai income and entrepreneurship: quantitative analyses of economic and social aspects of the samurai in Tokugawa and Meiji Japan (Cambridge, Mass., 1974)
'Returns on unification: economic growth in Japan, 1550–1650', in J. W. Hall, Kenji Nagahara and Kozo Yamamura (eds.), *Japan before Tokugawa: political consolidation and economic growth 1500 to 1650* (Princeton, 1981), pp.327–72
'The Meiji land tax reform and its effects', in M. B. Jansen and G. Rozman (eds.), *Japan in transition: from Tokugawa to Meiji* (Princeton, 1986), pp.382–99
'From coins to rice: hypotheses on the *kandaka* and *kokudaka* systems', *Journal of Japanese studies*, vol. 14, no. 2 (Summer 1988), pp.341–67

'Japan 1868–1930: a revised view', in W. J. Macpherson (ed.), *The industrialisation of Japan* (Oxford, 1994), pp.400–43

'Entrepreneurship, ownership and management in Japan', in Kozo Yamamura (ed.), *The economic emergence of modern Japan* (Cambridge, 1997), pp.294–352

Yamamura, Kozo (ed.), *The economic emergence of modern Japan* (Cambridge, 1997)

Yamashita Takashi, *Sakoku to kaikoku* (Tokyo, 1996)

Yamawaki Teijirō, *Kinsei nichū bōeki-shi no kenkyū* (Tokyo, 1961)

Nagasaki no tōjin bōeki (Tokyo, 1964)

Nukeni: sakoku jidai no mitsu bōeki (Tokyo, 1965)

'The great trading merchants, Cocksinja and his son', *Acta asiatica*, no. 30 (1976), pp.106–16

Nagasaki no oranda shōkan sekai no naka no sakoku nihon (Tokyo, 1980)

Yanai Kenji, *Sakoku nihon to kokusai kōryū*, 2 vols. (Tokyo, 1988)

Kokusai shakai no keisai to kinsei nihon (Tokyo, 1998)

Yao Keisuke, *Kinsei oranda bōeki to sakoku* (Tokyo, 1998)

Yasunaga Toshinobu, *Andō Shōeki: social and ecological philosopher in eighteenth-century Japan* (New York, 1992)

Yates, Charles L., *Saigo Takamori: the man behind the myth* (London, 1995)

Yonemoto, Marcia, 'The spacial "vernacular" in Tokugawa maps', *Journal of Asian studies*, vol. 59, no. 3 (Aug. 2000), pp.647–66

Yoshiaki Yoshimi, *Comfort women: sexual slavery in the Japanese military during World War II* (New York, 2000)

Yoshida Tsunekichi, *Ansei no taigoku* (Tokyo, 1991)

Yotarō Sakudō, 'The management practices of family business', in Nakane Chie and Ōishi Shinzaburō, *Tokugawa Japan: the social and economic antecedents of modern Japan* (Tokyo, 1991), pp.147–66

Yuzo, Ota, *Basil Hall Chamberlain: portrait of a Japanologist* (Richmond, Surrey, 1998)

Zoku shintō taikei: hachishū bunsō Tokugawa Nariaki (Tokyo, 1999)

Index